NATIONAL PARK
FOUNDATION

P9-DNZ-992

The Official Guide to

America's
National Parks

FOURTEENTH EDITION

Fodor's Travel Publications, Inc.
New York • Toronto • London • Sydney • Auckland
www.fodors.com/

The Official Guide to America's National Parks

Writers: John Blodgett, Martha Connors, Tom Griffith
Editors: Linda Cabasin, Mark Sullivan
Production Editor: Evangelos Vasilakis
Research Assistance: Research assistance provided by the National Park Service: Office of Communications; Division of Park Planning and Protection; Harpers Ferry Center Publications Division
Cover photo: Jeff Vanuga, (Deer doe, Grand Teton National Park)
Color Insert Design: Tina Malaney
Manufacturing Production: Angela L. McLean

Copyright

Fourteenth Edition
ISBN: 978-0-87637-127-5
ISSN 1930-6245

Special Sales

Fodor's Travel Publications are available at special discounts for bulk purchases for sales promotions or premiums. Special editions, including personalized covers, excerpts of existing guides, and corporate imprints, can be created in large quantities for special needs. For more information, write to Special Markets/Premium Sales, Fodor's Travel Publications, 1745 Broadway, MD 3-1, New York, NY 10019, or e-mail specialmarkets@randomhouse.com.

PRINTED IN THE UNITED STATES OF AMERICA

10 9 8 7 6 5 4 3 2 1

CONTENTS

The National Park Foundation   vi

How to Use This Book   viii

About Your Visit   xii

Maps   xvii

Map 1: Connecticut, Maine, Massachusetts,
New Hampshire, New York, Rhode Island, Vermont . . . xviii

Map 2: Maryland, New Jersey, Pennsylvania, Virginia,
West Virginia xx

Map 3: Alabama, Florida, Georgia, North Carolina,
South Carolina. xxii

Map 4: Arkansas, Kentucky, Louisiana, Mississippi,
Tennessee xxiv

Map 5: Illinois, Indiana, Michigan, Minnesota, Ohio,
Wisconsin. xxvi

Map 6: Iowa, Kansas, Missouri, Nebraska,
North Dakota, Oklahoma, South Dakota. xxviii

Map 7: Arizona, Nevada, New Mexico, Texas, Utah xxx

Map 8: Colorado, Idaho, Montana, Wyoming xxxii

Map 9: California, Oregon, Washington xxxiv

Map 10: Alaska and Hawaii xxxvi

Map 11: American Samoa, North Mariana Islands,
Puerto Rico, Virgin Islands, Washington, DC xxxviii

America's National Parks   1

Alabama. 3
Alaska. 8
Arizona. 27
Arkansas. 50
California. 59
Colorado 89
Connecticut. 103
District of Columbia 105
Florida. 120
Georgia 133
Hawaii 143
Idaho 151
Illinois 157
Indiana. 158
Iowa. 162
Kansas 165
Kentucky 171
Louisiana 175

Maine 180
Maryland 183
Massachusetts 196
Michigan 211
Minnesota 219
Mississippi 225
Missouri 232
Montana 239
Nebraska 246
Nevada 253
New Hampshire 256
New Jersey 258
New Mexico 262
New York 277
North Carolina 297
North Dakota 307
Ohio 311
Oklahoma 318
Oregon 321
Pennsylvania 326
Rhode Island 342
South Carolina 343
South Dakota 350
Tennessee 356
Texas 365
Utah 379
Vermont 390
Virginia 392
Washington 409
West Virginia 422
Wisconsin 429
Wyoming 432
American Samoa 441
Guam 443
Puerto Rico 445
Virgin Islands 447

Other National Parklands   **453**

Special-Interest Parks 454
Affiliated Areas 460
National Heritage Areas 468
National Trails System 474
Wild & Scenic Rivers System 480

Lodging Contact Information   **488**

Index   **491**

THE NATIONAL PARK FOUNDATION

Every year millions of visitors travel to America's iconic national parks, which include some of the most stunning places on Earth. From Yosemite to Yellowstone, the National Park Service preserves and protects more than 84 million acres of awe-inspiring landscapes, treasured historical sites, and rich cultural treasures.

The National Park Foundation, the official charity of America's national parks, raises private funds that directly aid, support, and enrich America's nearly 400 national parks and their programs. Chartered by Congress as the nonprofit partner of the National Park Service, the National Park Foundation plays a critical role in conservation and preservation efforts, establishing national parks as powerful learning environments and giving all audiences an equal and abundant opportunity to experience, enjoy, and support America's treasured places.

This book, as the official guide, helps support the work of the National Park Foundation. So when you take it home, you'll be helping to preserve and protect America's best idea-the national parks.

For more information on how you can support the national parks, visit www.nationalparks.org.

Officers

Chair
The Honorable Ken Salazar
Secretary, United States Department of the Interior

Vice Chair
John Nau III
President and CEO, Silver Eagle Distributors, L.P.

Secretary
Jon Jarvis
Director, National Park Service

President and CEO
Neil Mulholland

Treasurer
John Seiter
Capitol Group (Retired)

Directors

HOW TO USE THIS BOOK

The national parks are the focus of this guide, and you'll find a thumbnail sketch of each along with information about what you'll see and do there. It should help you immeasurably as you plan your travels.

In these pages the alphabet rules. Parks are grouped by states, and both the states and the parks they contain are arranged in alphabetical order. Some parks straddle state lines or have units in more than one state; you'll find the text for these in the chapter devoted to the state in which the headquarters are found. Affiliated areas, which are not federally owned or administered by the National Park Service but that draw on technical or financial aid from the Park Service, are listed in the Other National Parklands section at the end of the book, along with the couple of dozen national trails, national heritage areas, and national rivers that are not administered by the Park Service. At the end of each chapter are cross-references to all affiliated areas and multistate parks found within the boundaries of the state covered by the chapter. Regional maps at the front of the book pinpoint locations of the parks (or, in the case of multistate entities, of their headquarters).

What to See & Do

The activities and pastimes offered by the park begin this section, followed by a list of park **Facilities,** such as visitor centers, contact and ranger stations, museums, hiking trails, book and gift stores, and so on. Often the best place to start your visit is at the visitor center, where you can pick up maps of the park, view interpretive exhibits, and obtain in-depth information about attractions.

In addition to opportunities for outdoor or cultural pastimes, many parks also sponsor special programs, which operate either year-round or seasonally. In the **Programs & Events** section we've spelled out those you'll find year in and year out and noted when others are available. These are orchestrated when demand warrants and when staff and funding permit.

Sometimes programs are cut and hours scaled back at short notice. Although you can rest assured that all information in this book was checked thoroughly by the park rangers themselves at press time, it's always a good idea to confirm information when it matters—especially if you're making a detour to visit a specific place.

The **Tips & Hints** section helps you plan a safe and enjoyable visit. If a park is very remote, you'll want to prepare in advance by packing food or supplies. Of course, you'll need to check for park-specific rules, regulations, and advisories before you go and once you're there.

Food, Lodging & Supplies

The **Camping** section lets you know where to put up a tent or park your RV in or near the park. We provide you with information on the number of sites at a campground, the price range for one night, and the facilities you can expect to find—flush, vault, or pit toilets; hot or cold showers; and RV hookups. Most drive-in campsites in the national parks are run on a first-come, first-served basis. If you're traveling during peak summer months, arrive as early as possible or have standby reservations at a nearby public or private campground. You can make reservations in advance through the National Recreation Reservation Service (tel. 877/444–6777 or www.recreation.gov). Reservations are available up to six months in advance; not all campgrounds may be available.

Most national park campgrounds can accommodate RVs, although you will usually find only basic facilities. Electrical hookups, water pumps, and disposal stations are available only at a handful of locations.

In the **Hotels** and **Restaurants** sections, we list lodging and dining establishments in the park or near it. Accommodations in and near national parks range from chain hotels and motels with modern appliances to rough and rugged wilderness camps with kerosene lamps instead of electricity. Cabins with housekeeping facilities are popular, as are small, family-owned bed-and-breakfasts and the occasional grand old hotel. If you're traveling in high season—roughly between Memorial Day and Labor Day—make reservations three or four months in advance or more, if you can. At some of the most famous lodgings, some people reserve for the next summer as they check out. Hotel prices listed in this book are for two people in a standard room in high season. Prices drop as much as 25% in low season.

Restaurants were chosen for proximity to the parks and convenience for the traveler, with lunch service the priority; prices reflect the range in cost for main courses at lunch. Remember, prices are likely to be higher for dinner.

Fees, Hours & Regulations

This section includes the entry fee to the park, if any, and the cost of special services, such as tours, the hours of operation for the park and all its visitor centers, and information about permits and park regulations. For example, in many parks where backcountry camping is allowed, you are required to register at the visitor center and obtain a permit before embarking, and sometimes a fee is charged.

Types of Parks

There are a variety of parks, and each type is indicated by an icon, as follows:

 National Parks contain a variety of resources protected by large areas of land or water. **National Preserves** also protect specific resources but allow activities not permissible in national parks, such as hunting, fishing, and the extraction of minerals and fuels, so long as they do not jeopardize natural values. **National Reserves** are like National Preserves, but are managed not by the Park Service proper but instead by local or state authorities.

National Memorials are primarily commemorative of a historical subject or person.

National Monuments, usually smaller than national parks and lacking their diversity, preserve at least one nationally significant resource.

Parks designated as **National Historic Sites** preserve places and commemorate people, events, and activities important in the nation's history. **National Historical Parks** are similar but are larger and more complex.

National Military Parks, National Battlefield Parks, National Battlefield Sites, and **National Battlefields** are all associated with American military history.

National Recreation Areas are set aside purely for recreational use. **National Lakeshores and National Seashores** preserve shorelines and islands while providing water-oriented recreation. **National Rivers and Wild and Scenic Riverways** protect ribbons of land bordering streams that have not been dammed, channelized, or otherwise altered. Besides preserving rivers in their natural state, these areas provide opportunities for outdoor activities. **National Scenic Trails** are long-distance footpaths that wind through areas of natural beauty. **National Parkways** include roadways and the ribbons of land flanking them, offering leisurely drives through areas of scenic interest.

OTHER TERMS USED IN THIS BOOK

The section of the guide titled "Other National Parklands" also discusses Affiliated Areas and National Heritage Areas. An **Affiliated Area** is a significant property preserved in the United States or Canada that has not been designated by Congress as one of the 397 units of the National Park System but that draws on the financial or technical expertise of the National Park Service. Some of these sites have been recognized by Acts of Congress; others have been designated National Historic Sites by the secretary of the interior. (Some National Historic Sites are part of the park system proper, whereas some are Affiliated Areas.) There are also a number of **National Heritage Areas** around the country, which conserve the nation's natural and cultural heritage and make it accessible to visitors. These regions, mainly private property, are managed by partnerships among federal, state, and local governments and private nonprofit organizations.

National park areas may also have additional designations assigned by the United Nations Educational, Scientific, and Cultural Organization (UNESCO) in accordance with the World Heritage Convention. **World Heritage Sites** are irreplaceable properties of outstanding international significance; **Biosphere Reserves,** exemplifying some of the world's varied ecosystems, provide a field for research and education, serve as repositories of genetic diversity, and provide baseline data for monitoring global environmental change.

ABOUT YOUR VISIT

More than ever, our national parks are being discovered and rediscovered by travelers who want to spend their vacations appreciating nature, watching wildlife, and taking adventure trips. But as the number of visitors to the parks increases, so does stress on wildlife and plant life. Tourism can drum up concern for the environment, but it can also cause great physical damage to parks. As you visit the parks, please keep in mind that these lands will not thrive without your care, nor will they last without your support. And use common sense to keep your visit as safe as it will be enjoyable.

Entrance Fees

The entrance fees charged by many national park areas are noted in the text. If your travels will take you to many national parks, consider purchasing the **America the Beautiful National Parks and Federal Recreation Lands Pass** ($80), which admits you and up to three other adults 16 and over to all parks that charge entrance fees. (Camping and parking cost extra.) A percentage of the proceeds from sales of the pass helps to fund important projects in the park. You can purchase the pass by phone at 888/275–8747 Ext. 1, online at www.store.usgs.gov/pass, or at any participating federal recreation site.

The **Senior Pass** ($10), for those 62 and older, and the **Access Pass** (free), for travelers with disabilities, both entitle holders to entry to all national parks, plus 50% off fees for the use of many park facilities and services. You must show proof of age and of U.S. citizenship or permanent residency (such as a U.S. passport, driver's license, or birth certificate) and, if requesting the Access Pass, proof of your disability. You can obtain your Access or Senior Pass in person at participating federal recreation sites or through the mail with an application form available online. A **Military Pass** (free) for active service members and their families is available at most parks that charge an entrance fee.

Staying Safe

Motor-vehicle accidents, drownings, and falls are among the leading causes of death in the national parks. These are accidents that common sense can help you avoid. If you find yourself in an emergency situation, call 911 and the park rangers; there are telephone booths at the visitor centers and other locations throughout the parks. Some parks have their own emergency numbers as well.

Before you go, be sure to pack a first-aid kit, including a first-aid manual. Keep in mind that even in summer, the weather can change unexpectedly—especially in mountainous parks. Temperatures can rise into the 90s during the day and drop into the teens or lower at night. Always have warm clothing and rain gear handy, no matter how promising the day.

WILD ANIMAL ENCOUNTERS

As human development shrinks wildlife habitats, animal encounters are increasingly common in national parks. To avoid attracting bears, raccoons, and other scavengers, be sure to animal-proof your food supplies. At many developed campsites, animal-proof containers are available; in the backcountry, hang food in a bag or container at least 15 feet above ground and as far away from the trunk of the tree as possible. Stay away from bears and their cubs, and try not to hike at dawn or dusk, when encounters with mountain lions are most common. If you do see one, inch away steadily without turning your back or bending down.

Staying Healthy

ALTITUDE SICKNESS

One of the most common problems for hikers is altitude sickness, which results when you ascend above 8,500 feet without proper acclimatization. To help prevent altitude sickness, spend a night or two at a higher elevation before attempting any strenuous physical activity. If you have a history of heart or circulatory problems, talk to your doctor before planning a visit to areas at high altitudes.

Symptoms of altitude sickness include headache, nausea, vomiting, shortness of breath, weakness, and sleep disturbance. If any of these occur, retreat to a lower altitude. Altitude sickness can develop into high-altitude pulmonary edema and high-altitude cerebral edema, both of which can be permanently debilitating or fatal.

ANIMAL & SNAKE BITES

Some animals, especially rodents, carry dangerous diseases. If you are bitten by a wild animal, see a doctor as soon as possible. Many animal bites require a tetanus shot and, if the animal could be rabid, a rabies shot.

Snakes do everything to avoid you, but in the event that you have a run-in and are bitten, act quickly. If it's a harmless snake, treat as you would any other puncture wound. If it's poisonous, have the victim lie down and remain as still as possible to minimize the spread of venom through the body. Keep the wound below the rest of the body, and have another person seek medical help immediately.

GIARDIA

You can't see giardia, but these tiny waterborne organisms can turn your stomach inside out. Carry bottled water for day trips; drinking water is available at many campgrounds. If you're hiking into the backcountry and can't carry enough water, you must purify all spring or stream water, no matter how clear. The easiest way to purify water is to drop in a water-purification tablet, or 8 drops of chlorine bleach or 20 drops of iodine per gallon of water. You can also filter it through a water-purification pump, available at camping equipment stores. Boiling water, another method, takes time and uses fuel. But if it is the only method available, allow the water to boil for at least 10 minutes, longer at high altitudes.

HAZARDS OF HIKING, PRECAUTIONS TO TAKE

Always choose hiking trails suitable to your physical condition and the amount of weight you plan to carry. Consider the length of the trail, its steepness, and how acclimated you are to the altitude at the start and finish. Always be aware of the possibility of altitude sickness. Every hiker planning multiday backcountry trips, particularly those traveling solo, should leave their intended route, planned length of trip, and return date with a park ranger before setting out.

Proper clothing is essential, especially on more rigorous hikes. Hiking boots should be well broken in and sturdy, with good traction and ankle support. On less demanding trails, athletic shoes are fine. Wear thick wool socks, and always bring a second pair in case one gets wet. Rain gear is a good idea, since the weather in most of the national parks can change drastically within moments. Always carry at least 2 quarts of water per person per day, even more if you are staying overnight or are hiking in hot weather.

HYPOTHERMIA & FROSTBITE

It does not have to be below freezing for hypothermia to strike: this potentially fatal decrease in body temperature occurs even in relatively mild weather. Symptoms are chilliness and fatigue, followed by shivering and mental confusion. The minute you spot these signs, seek shelter, remove wet clothing, and wrap the victim in warm blankets or a sleeping bag—if possible get into the sleeping bag with him or her. High-energy food and hot drinks also aid recovery.

Frostbite is caused by exposure to extreme cold for a prolonged period of time. Symptoms include the numbing of ears, nose, fingers, or toes; white or grayish-yellow skin is a sure sign. Take frostbite victims into a warm place as soon as possible, and remove wet clothing. Then immerse the affected area in water that's warm—not hot—or wrap the area in a warm blanket. Do not rub, as this may permanently damage tissues. When thawing begins, have the victim exercise the area to stimulate blood circulation. If bleeding or other complications develop, get to a doctor as soon as possible.

LYME DISEASE

This potentially debilitating illness is caused by a virus carried by deer ticks, which thrive in dry, brush-covered areas. Before walking in woods, brush, or through fields in areas where Lyme disease has been found, spray yourself thoroughly with tick repellent and wear pants tucked into socks, and long sleeves. When you undress, search your body for ticks and remove them with rubbing alcohol and tweezers. Watch the area for several weeks. Some people develop a rash or flu-like symptoms; if this happens, see your physician immediately. Lyme disease is treated with antibiotics.

PLANT POISONS

Learn to recognize poison ivy, poison oak, and poison sumac, and avoid them. If you accidentally step into a patch, wash exposed skin immediately with soap and water, and do not touch clothing that has been in contact with the plants. If a rash and blisters develop, use calamine lotion or cortisone cream to relieve itching.

SUNBURN & HEATSTROKE

Always protect yourself from the sun. At higher altitudes, where the air is thinner, the ultraviolet rays are stronger. Sun reflected off snow, sand, or water can do special damage, even on overcast days. Liberally apply a sunscreen of SPF 15 or higher before you go out, and wear a wide-brimmed hat and sunglasses.

If you are exposed to extreme heat for a prolonged period, you run the risk of heatstroke (also known as sunstroke), a serious medical condition. It begins quite suddenly with a headache, dizziness, and fatigue but can quickly lead to convulsions and unconsciousness or even death. If someone in your party develops any of the symptoms, have one person go for help, move the victim to a shady place, wrap him or her in wet clothing or bedding, and try to cool him or her down with water or ice.

Leave No Trace

FIRE PRECAUTIONS

When it comes to fires, never take a chance. Always build them in a safe place (away from tinder of any kind) and use a fireplace or fire grate if one is available. Clear the ground in the immediate area so wind cannot blow sparks into dry leaves or grass, keep your fire small, and never leave it unattended. Throw used matches into the fire, and always have a pot of water or sand next to your campfire or stove. Don't build fires when you're alone. When you are finished with your fire, be sure it is out cold—you should be able to touch it with your bare hands. Never cook in your tent or a poorly ventilated space.

MINIMUM-IMPACT CAMPING & HIKING

The little extra effort it takes to use the parks responsibly goes a long way toward ensuring the future of North America's natural beauty. Do not leave garbage on trails or in campgrounds. If you hike in the backcountry, carry out what you've carried in, including all your trash. Bury human waste at least 100 feet from any trail, campsite, or water source in a hole at least 8 inches deep; some parks and many environmental organizations advocate packing out even human waste. Do not wash dishes or clothing in lakes and streams. If you must use soap, make sure it is biodegradable, and carry water in clean containers 100 feet away from its source before using it for cleaning.

In national parks that include dunes and barrier islands, walk only on marked pedestrian paths. Over time, climbing on the dunes causes erosion and weakens the primary dune system. Never pick dune grasses, which also help ensure the preservation of the dunes.

PETS IN THE PARKS

Generally, pets are allowed only in parks' developed areas, including drive-in campgrounds and picnic areas, but they must be kept on a leash at all times. With the exception of guide or service dogs, pets are not allowed inside buildings, on most trails, on beaches, or in the back-country. They also may be prohibited in areas controlled by concessionaires. Some parks have kennels, which charge a small daily fee. Be sure to inquire about restrictions on pets before leaving home.

RESPECTING WILDLIFE

Have respect for the creatures you encounter: never sneak up on them, don't disturb nests and other habitats, and don't touch animals or try to remove them from their habitat, even for the sake of a photograph. Never stand between animal parents and their young, and never surround an animal or group of animals. To help protect endangered species, report any sightings.

VOLUNTEERING

Air pollution, acid rain, wildlife poaching, and encroaching development are among the threats to America's national parks. These problems are being addressed by the National Park Service, but you can help by donating time or money. The National Park Service's Volunteers in the Parks program welcomes volunteers to do anything from paperwork to lecturing on environmental issues. To participate, you must apply to the park where you would like to work, or visit the website at www.nps.gov/volunteer. To make a donation, contact the National Park Foundation, the official charitable partner of the National Park Service (1201 I St. NW, Suite 550B, Washington, DC, 20005, tel. 202/354–6460, fax 202/371–2066, www.nationalparks.org).

On the Web

The website of the National Park Service, **www.nps.gov,** has complete information about each park. The National Park Foundation's site, **www.nationalparks.org,** can also greatly enhance your experience. You can learn about National Park Foundation programs, find out how you can give something back to the parks, and buy an annual parks pass.

America's National Parks

When you think of exploring the country's nearly 400 national parks, you might imagine endless vistas like those in Utah's Bryce Canyon. But beyond spectacular landscapes, you can also discover important memorials and battlefields, scenic trails, wild rivers, unspoiled coastlines, and even homes or neighborhoods where history was made. In short, these parks tell the story of America.

San Juan National Historical Site | Puerto Rico

Built by the Spanish in the 16th century, massive El Morro is one of three forts guarding Old San Juan.

Valley Forge National Historical Park | Pennsylvania

During the Revolutionary War, General George Washington's troops camped here through the brutal winter of 1777–78.

Badlands National Park | South Dakota

Steep canyons, sharp ridges, and sawtooth spires mark the landscape of the 244,000-acre Badlands National Park, home to intriguing fossils of mammals from the Oligocene era.

A total of 28 blocks of white marble from the hills of Georgia were transformed into the iconic statue of Abraham Lincoln that gazes down over the National Mall.

Martin Luther King, Jr. Memorial
District of Columbia

One of the nation's newest memorials commemorates the slain civil rights leader's legacy and his stirring speeches.

Muir Woods National Monument | California

A grove of majestic coastal redwoods, delicate ferns, and abundant wildflowers pay homage to naturalist John Muir.

Mesa Verde National Park | Colorado

The ancestors of today's Puebloan peoples, including the Zuni and Hopi tribes, constructed the impressive cliff dwellings in Mesa Verde and nearby archaeological sites.

Grand Canyon National Park | Arizona

Take your pick of the North Rim or South Rim: both vantage points offer spectacular views of the Colorado River as it meanders through this 6,000-feet-deep gorge.

Boston National Historical Park | Massachusetts

The Freedom Trail passes places where America's revolutionary spirit was forged, including the Old South Meeting House.

Hawaii Volcanoes National Park | Hawaii

Mauna Loa, the world's most massive volcano, and Kilauea, the world's most active, give this park its name.

Point Reyes National Seashore | California

Perched on a cliff, the 19th-century Point Reyes Lighthouse is a good spot to watch for migrating whales. Beachgoers can explore miles of sandy shores.

Carlsbad Caverns National Park | New Mexico

Seemingly endless subterranean chambers, clusters of stalactites and stalagmites, and delicately wrought rock formations distinguish Carlsbad Caverns.

Death Valley National Park
California

"Sailing stones" that seem to race across the bone-dry landscape are among the unforgettable sights in this massive park.

Gettysburg National Military Park | Pennsylvania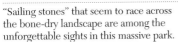

A Civil War–era cannon and a statue stand as moving memorials on the battlefield's Cemetery Ridge.

Mount Rainier National Park | Washington

Crowned by the glacier-covered mountain that gives the park its name, this unspoiled preserve includes waterfalls, rain forests, and subalpine flowering meadows.

Yellowstone National Park | Wyoming

Although Old Faithful and other geysers draw crowds to this 2.2-million-acre national park, one of its most eye-catching features is the brilliantly colored Morning Glory Pool.

Mount Rushmore National Memorial | South Dakota

The carved faces of George Washington, Thomas Jefferson, Theodore Roosevelt, and Abraham Lincoln look out from Mount Rushmore, a huge slab of granite in the Black Hills.

Canyon de Chelly National Monument | Arizona

Native American guides lead visitors past Spider Rock and other gravity-defying rock formations in Canyon de Chelly.

Cape Hatteras National Seashore | North Carolina

Cape Hatteras Light, the country's tallest brick lighthouse, towers over the beautiful coastline and barrier islands.

Colonial National Historical Park | Virginia

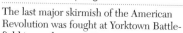

The last major skirmish of the American Revolution was fought at Yorktown Battlefield in southeastern Virginia.

Petrified Forest National Park | Arizona

In eye-popping shades of pink, yellow, orange, and crimson, logs of petrified wood contrast with the stark desert landscape.

Blue Ridge Parkway | North Carolina

Connecting the Shenandoah Valley and Great Smoky Mountains, the 469-mile-long parkway is popular in autumn, when leaf-peepers turn out for the spectacular foliage.

Glacier National Park | Montana

The rugged mountain scenery, crystal-clear lakes, and 25 glaciers of this 1-million-acre park make it a favorite destination of hikers, bikers, horseback riders, and seekers of solitude.

Denali National Park & Preserve | Alaska

Anchored by Mount McKinley, this 6.1-million-acre park has majestic snow-covered peaks and sprawling glaciers.

Navajo National Monument | Arizona

Cliff dwellings, abandoned seven centuries ago, provide a glimpse into the lives of ancient Pueblo peoples.

New Bedford Whaling National Historical Park | Massachusetts

The 1894 schooner *Ernestina* is a highlight of a historic district that brings to life the area's seafaring traditions.

Rocky Mountain National Park | Colorado

Herds of elk are a common sight in the park, especially in autumn when they descend from the high country.

Yosemite National Park | California

From the heights of Glacier Point you can spot many of Yosemite's most popular attractions, including 2,425-foot Yosemite Falls and the peaks of El Capitan and Half Dome.

Panoramic views of the heavily forested Blue Ridge Mountains are around every bend of the 105-mile-long Skyline Drive, which winds its way through this 197,411-acre park.

Great Smoky Mountains National Park | Tennessee

The country's most visited national park is known for its old-growth forests, carpets of wildflowers, and animal life ranging from spotted salamanders to black bears.

Acadia National Park | Maine

With its rugged coastline, massive granite peaks, and historic carriage roads cutting through the evergreens, Acadia has become a Maine icon.

Independence National Historical Park | Pennsylvania

The famous Liberty Bell is one of more than a dozen historic attractions in Philadelphia that recall the country's early days.

Natchez Trace Parkway Mississippi

Running from Mississippi to Tennessee, this scenic drive includes outdoor opportunities such as horseback riding.

Zion National Park | Utah

One of the country's most thrilling hikes, the trail to Angels Landing runs along the top of a steep ridge, with views of spectacular cliffs and deep chasms in every direction.

Statue of Liberty National Monument | New York

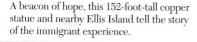

A beacon of hope, this 152-foot-tall copper statue and nearby Ellis Island tell the story of the immigrant experience.

Harpers Ferry National Historical Park | West Virginia

Museums and trails in this historic riverfront town explore topics from John Brown and the Civil War to the environment.

Arches National Park | Utah

Spires, pinnacles, pedestals, and balanced rocks, as well as a huge concentration of natural sandstone arches, make Arches unlike anything else in the Southwest.

Maps

Mont

Ottawa ⭐

Massena

Plat
Potsdam

Saranac Lake

Lake
Placid

11

Watertown

ADIRONDACK
FOREST
PRESERVE

Toronto   Lake Ontario

NEW YORK

Oswego

81

Glens

Niagara
Falls

Rochester

38 Rome

Oneida   Utica

Sarat
Spri

Tonawanda

90

39 Auburn   Syracuse

90

Schenectady

40   Buffalo   Batavia

Geneva

Lake Erie

Five Fingers Lakes   Cortland

Albar

Dunkirk

90

Hornell

Ithaca

81

Oneonta

CATSKILL
FOREST
PRESERVE

17   Jamestown

17

Elmira

Binghamton

88

Olean   Wellsville

17

35 36   King

Monticello   Poughk
Middletown

34

Scranton

PENNSYLVANIA

West
NEW   Point
JERSEY   Yo

New York

24 – 32

2

Newa

0 _____ 100 miles

0 _____ 150 km

Connecticut
Weir Farm NHS........................**20**

Maine
Acadia NP.............................**2**
Saint Croix Island
International Historic Site...............**1**

Massachusetts
Adams NHP..........................**15**
Boston African American NHS...........**9**
Boston Harbor Islands NRA.............**14**
Boston NHP..........................**10**
Cape Cod NS.........................**17**
Frederick Law Olmsted NHS............**11**
John Fitzgerald Kennedy NHS...........**12**
Longfellow House–Washington's
Headquarters NHS **13**
Lowell NHP..........................**6**

Minute Man NHP **16**
New Bedford Whaling NHP.............**18**
Salem Maritime NHS **7**
Saugus Iron Works NHS................**8**
Springfield Armory NHS................**5**

New Hampshire
Saint-Gaudens NHS....................**3**

New York
African Burial Ground NM **32**
Castle Clinton NM....................**24**
Eleanor Roosevelt NHS................**34**
Federal Hall N MEM..................**25**
Fire Island NS **21**
Fort Stanwix NM.....................**38**
Gateway NRA........................**26**
General Grant N MEM................**27**

Governors Island NM **31**
Hamilton Grange N MEM **28**
Home of Franklin D. Roosevelt NHS **35**
Martin Van Buren NHS **33**
Sagamore Hill NHS **22**
Saint Paul's Church NHS **23**
Saratoga NHP **37**
Statue of Liberty NM **29**
Theodore Roosevelt Birthplace NHS **30**
Theodore Roosevelt Inaugural NHS **40**
Vanderbilt Mansion NHS **36**
Women's Rights NHP **39**

Rhode Island
Roger Williams N MEM **19**

Vermont
Marsh-Billings-Rockefeller NHP **4**

Maryland

Antietam NB......................**28**
Assateague Island NS..............**36**
Catoctin Mountain Park............**26**
Chesapeake & Ohio Canal NHP........**42**
Clara Barton NHS **31**
Fort McHenry NM & Historic Shrine **30**
Fort Washington Park **32**
Greenbelt Park...................**35**
Hampton NHS....................**29**
Monocacy NB....................**27**
Piscataway Park **33**
Thomas Stone NHS **34**

New Jersey

Great Egg Harbor NSRR.............**13**
Morristown NHP **3**
Paterson Great Falls NHP............**1**
Thomas Edison NHP................**2**

Pennsylvania

Allegheny Portage Railroad NHS **16**
Delaware Water Gap NRA **6**
Edgar Allan Poe NHS **10**
Eisenhower NHS **14**
Flight 93 N MEM **17**
Fort Necessity NB **20**
Friendship Hill NHS **19**
Gettysburg NMP **15**
Hopewell Furnace NHS **8**
Indepedence NHP.................**11**
Johnstown Flood N MEM............**18**
Middle Delaware NSR..............**5**
Steamtown NHS...................**7**
Thaddeus Kosciuszko N MEM **12**
Upper Delaware SRR **4**
Valley Forge NHP **9**

Virginia

Appomattox Courthouse NHP **52**
Arlington House, the
Robert E. Lee Memorial **37**
Booker T. Washington NM **53**
Cedar Creek & Belle Grove NHP.......**43**
Colonial NHP....................**49**
Fort Monroe NM **50**
Fredericksburg & Spotsylvania
County Battlefields Memorial NMP......**45**
George Washington Birthplace NM **38**
George Washington Memorial Parkway **40**
Maggie L. Walker NHS **47**
Manassas NBP **46**
Petersburg NB **51**
Prince William Forest Park **39**
Richmond NBP **48**
Shenandoah NP **44**
Wolf Trap NP
for the Performing Arts **41**

West Virginia

Appalachian NST **25**
Bluestone NSR...................**22**
Gauley River NRA **23**
Harpers Ferry NHP................**24**
New River Gorge NR...............**21**

MAP 2: MARYLAND, NEW JERSEY,

NEW YORK

ford

Mansfield

Sayre

81

NEW YORK

6

Carbondale

Honesdale

4

Scranton

84

New York City

Williamsport

Wilkes Barre

East Stroudsburg

5

Paterson

1

Lock Haven

80

Milton

Stroudsburg

80

3

Newark

2

State College

Lewisburg

Selinsgrove

6

Morristown

Easton

Jersey City

PENNSYLVANIA

Lewistown

Bethlehem

78

7

New Brunswick

Altoona

81

Allentown

New Hope

Princeton

Raystown Lake

76

Harrisburg

Reading

Delaware River

Trenton

wn

15

Lebanon

76

Valley Forge

Norristown

Lakewood

Bedford

83

8

Lancaster

9

Camden

Asbury Park

Chambersburg

14

15

York

Philadelphia

10 – 12

NEW JERSEY

70

Gettysburg

Hanover

Newark

Wilmington

erland

26

Reisterstown

Aberdeen

New Castle

Vineland

Atlantic City

insburg

24

25

Frederick

30

Chestertown

Millville

arpers Ferry

28

27

29

Essex

Dover

Delaware Bay

13

ester

Brunswick

Baltimore

Dundalk

Cape May

Middleburg

Silver Spring

35

MARYLAND

DELAWARE

Lewes

Culpeper

40

31

Annapolis

Milford

Rehoboth Beach

66

46

37

42

Washington, D.C.

St. Michaels

Easton

13

Georgetown

41

32

Dale City

38

Alexandria

Cambridge

Seaford

Ocean City

29

34

33

50

Solomons

Salisbury

39

St. Charles

45

Fredericksburg

17

36

Chincoteague

Charlottesville

64

Chesapeake Bay

ATLANTIC OCEAN

mattox River

48

47

Richmond

60

13

RGINIA

360

Hopewell

85

Petersburg

Williamsburg

49

Newport News

64

Hampton

51

50

Virginia Beach

95

Portsmouth

58

Emporia

Suffolk

Norfolk

N

0

100 miles

0

150 km

xxi

Alabama

Horseshoe Bend NMP. **37**
Little River Canyon N PRES. **38**
Russell Cave NM **39**
Tuskegee Airmen NHS /
Tuskegee Institute NHS **36**

Florida

Big Cypress N PRES **33**
Biscayne NP **30**
Canaveral NS **29**
Castillo de San Marcos NM. **27**
De Soto N MEM **34**
Dry Tortugas NP **32**
Everglades NP **31**
Fort Caroline N MEM. **25**
Fort Matanzas NM. **28**
Gulf Islands NS **35**
Timucuan Ecological &
Historic Preserve **26**

Georgia

Andersonville NHS **21**
Chattahoochee River NRA **18**
Chickamauga &
Chattanooga NMP **20**
Cumberland Island NS **24**
Fort Frederica NM **23**
Fort Pulaski NM. **15**
Jimmy Carter NHS **22**
Kennesaw Mountain NBP. **19**
Martin Luther King Jr. NHS **17**
Ocmulgee NM **16**

North Carolina

Blue Ridge Parkway. **7**
Cape Hatteras NS **3**
Cape Lookout NS. **4**
Carl Sandburg Home NHS **8**
Fort Raleigh NHS **2**
Guilford Courthouse NMP **6**
Moores Creek NB **5**
Wright Brothers N MEM **1**

South Carolina

Charles Pinckney NHS **13**
Congaree Swamp NM **12**
Cowpens NB. **9**
Fort Sumter NM **14**
Kings Mountain NMP **10**
Ninety Six NHS **11**

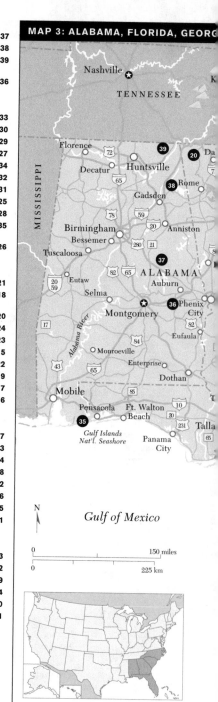

MAP 3: ALABAMA, FLORIDA, GEORG

Arkansas

Arkansas Post N MEM **20**
Buffalo NR **24**
Fort Smith NHS **22**
Hot Springs NP **21**
Little Rock Central High School NHS **25**
Pea Ridge NMP **23**
President William Jefferson Clinton
Birthplace NHS **26**

Kentucky

Abraham Lincoln Birthplace NSP **1**
Cumberland Gap NHP **3**
Mammoth Cave NP **2**

Louisiana

Cane River Creole NHP **18**
Jean Lafitte NHP **17**
New Orleans Jazz NHP & PRES **16**
Poverty Point NM **19**

Mississippi

Brices Cross Roads NBS **11**
Natchez NHP **15**
Natchez Trace NST **13**
Natchez Trace Parkway **13**
Tupelo NB **12**
Vicksburg NMP **14**

Tennessee

Andrew Johnson NHS **4**
Big South Fork NR and
Recreation Area **5**
Fort Donelson NB **9**
Great Smoky Mountains NP **7**
Obed Wild & Scenic River **6**
Shiloh NMP **10**
Stones River NB **8**

MAP 4: ARKANSAS, KENTUCKY,

LOUISIANA, MISSISSIPPI, TENNESSEE

OHIO

Cincinnati
Newport
Covington

INDIANA

71 75 27

Ashland
64 23
Frankfort
Morehead

Louisville
64
Bardstown
Pleasant
Hill
Lexington
Danville
Prestonsburg

Henderson
Owensboro
Elizabethtown ❶
Madisonville
127
15
Berea

KENTUCKY
❷ 65 68
London
Hazard

24

Cumberland River
Cumberland 23

Paducah 24 68
Bowling
Green
Middlesboro ❸
Kingsport

Hopkinsville
Middlesboro
75
Johnson
City

Mayfield
❺ 27
Morristown
Greeneville

Paris ❾ Clarksville
Nashville
40 ❻
Oak
Ridge
Knoxville

79
70
Murfreesboro
Maryville ❼
Gatlinburg ❹

40 13 ❽
TENNESSEE
24
Athens
NORTH
CAROLINA

Jackson
Columbia
Selmer
❿ Lawrenceburg
65
Fayetteville
Cleveland

phis
Chattanooga
SOUTH
CAROLINA

Holly
Springs
Corinth
45

xford ⓫

Tupelo ⓬

Columbus

Atlanta

Birmingham

GEORGIA

ISSISSIPPI

Meridian
20
59

ALABAMA

Montgomery

Laurel

Hattiesburg

galusa

Biloxi 10
Mobile
Pensacola
FLORIDA

Gulfport Pascagoula
Ocean
Springs

ns

N

0   150 miles

0   225 km

Mississippi
Delta

XXV

Illinois
Lincoln Home NHS **22**

Indiana
George Rogers Clark NHP **20**
Indiana Dunes NL **21**
Lincoln Boyhood N MEM **19**

Michigan
Isle Royale NP **7**
Keweenaw NHP **8**
Pictured Rocks NL **9**
River Raisin NBP **11**
Sleeping Bear Dunes NL **10**

Minnesota
Grand Portage NM **1**
Mississippi NR & RA **4**
Pipestone NM **3**
Voyageurs NP **2**

Ohio
Cuyahoga Valley NP **14**
Dayton Aviation Heritage NHP **18**
First Ladies NHS **15**
Hopewell Culture NHP **16**
James A. Garfield NHS **13**
Perry's Victory &
International Peace Memorial **12**
William Howard Taft NHS **17**

Wisconsin
Apostle Islands NL **6**
St. Croix
NSR **5**

Iowa

Effigy Mounds NM **13**
Herbert Hoover NHS **14**

Kansas

Brown v. Board of Education NHS. **21**
Fort Larned NHS. **24**
Fort Scott NHS **28**
Nicodemus NHS **23**
Tallgrass Prairie N PRES. **25**

Missouri

George Washington Carver NM **19**
Harry S Truman NHS **20**
Jefferson National Expansion
Memorial **15**
Ozark NSR **17**
Ulysses S. Grant NHS **16**
Wilson's Creek NB **18**

Nebraska

Agate Fossil Beds NM **8**
Homestead NM of America. **22**
Missouri NRR. **12**
Niobrara NSR. **11**
Scotts Bluff NM **9**

North Dakota

Fort Union Trading Post NHS **1**
Knife River Indian Villages NHS **3**
Theodore Roosevelt NP. **2**

Oklahoma

Chickasaw NRA **27**
Washita Battlefield NHS **26**

South Dakota

Badlands NP. **7**
Jewel Cave NM **5**
Minuteman Missile NHS. **10**
Mount Rushmore N MEM **4**
Wind Cave NP **6**

MAP 6: IOWA, KANSAS, MISSOURI,

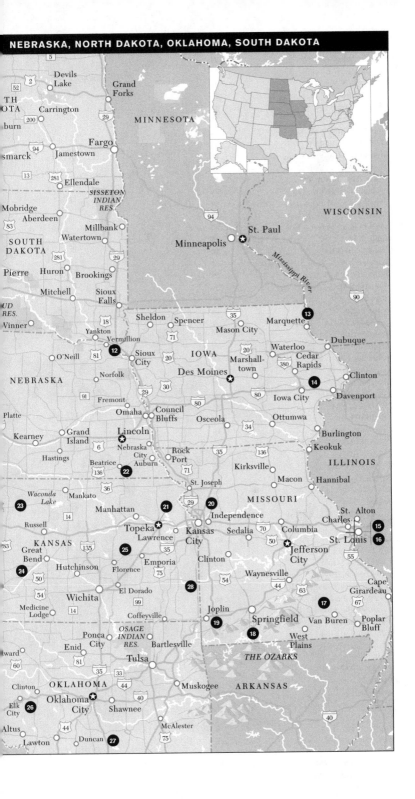

Arizona

Canyon de Chelly NM **33**
Casa Grande Ruins NM **23**
Chiricahua NM **20**
Coronado N MEM **19**
Fort Bowie NHS **21**
Glen Canyon NRA **13**
Grand Canyon NP **15**
Hohokam Pima NM **24**
Hubbell Trading Post NHS **32**
Montezuma Castle NM **26**
Navajo NM **16**
Organ Pipe Cactus NM **17**
Petrified Forest NP **29**
Pipe Spring NM **14**
Saguaro NP **22**
Sunset Crater Volcano NM **30**
Tonto NM **25**
Tumacácori NHP **18**
Tuzigoot NM **27**
Walnut Canyon NM **28**
Wupatki NM **31**

Nevada

Great Basin NP **2**
Lake Mead NRA **1**

New Mexico

Aztec Ruins NM **35**
Bandelier NM **44**
Capulin Volcano NM **34**
Carlsbad Caverns NP **41**
Chaco Culture NHP **36**
El Malpais NM **38**
El Morro NM **37**
Fort Union NM **46**
Gila Cliff Dwellings NM **39**
Pecos NHP **45**
Petroglyph NM **43**
Salinas Pueblo Missions NM **42**
White Sands NM **40**

Texas

Alibates Flint Quarries NM **49**
Amistad NRA **54**
Big Bend NP **52**
Big Thicket N PRES **59**
Chamizal N MEM **50**
Fort Davis NHS **51**
Guadalupe Mountains NP **47**
Lake Meredith NRA **48**
Lyndon B. Johnson NHP **58**
Padre Island NS **56**
Palo Alto Battlefield NHP **55**
Rio Grande Wild &
Scenic River **53**
San Antonio Missions NHP **57**

Utah

Arches NP **5**
Bryce Canyon NP **7**
Canyonlands NP **10**
Capitol Reef NP **6**
Cedar Breaks NM **8**
Golden Spike NHS **3**
Natural Bridges NM **11**
Rainbow Bridge NM **12**
Timpanogos Cave NM **4**
Zion NP **9**

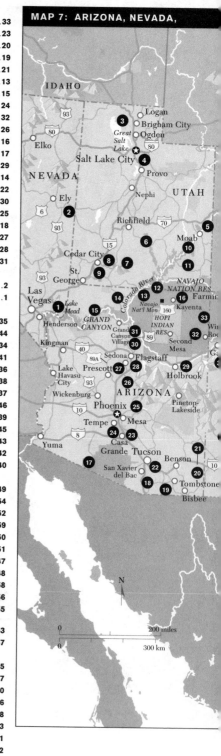

MAP 7: ARIZONA, NEVADA,

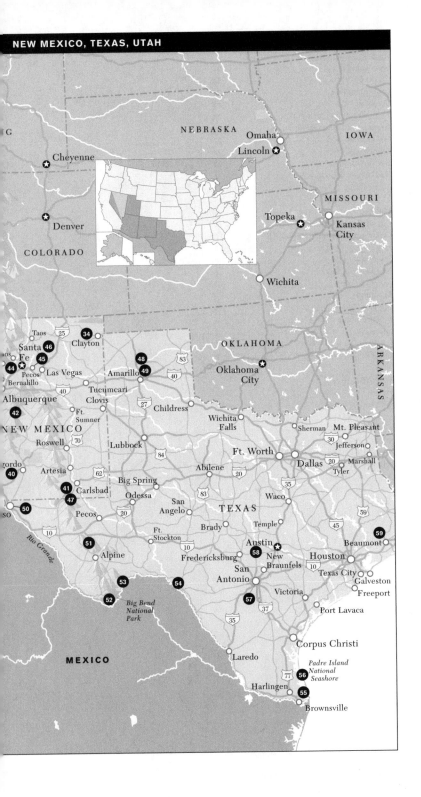

Colorado

Bent's Old Fort NHS **27**
Black Canyon of the
Gunnison NP **20**
Colorado NM **19**
Curecanti NRA. **21**
Dinosaur NM **18**
Florissant Fossil Beds NM. **26**
Great Sand Dunes NP & PRES **25**
Hovenweep NM. **22**
Mesa Verde NP **24**
Rocky Mountain NP. **17**
Sand Creek Massacre NHS **28**
Yucca House NM **23**

Idaho

City of Rocks NRES. **10**
Craters of the Moon NM & PRES **7**
Hagerman Fossil Beds NM **9**
Minidoka NHS **8**
Nez Perce NHP **6**

Montana

Big Hole NB. **5**
Bighorn Canyon NRA **3**
Glacier NP **1**
Grant-Kohrs Ranch NHS **4**
Little Bighorn Battlefield NM. **2**

Wyoming

Devils Tower NM. **15**
Fort Laramie NHS. **16**
Fossil Butte NM. **14**
Grand Teton NP. **13**
John D. Rockefeller Jr.
Memorial Parkway **12**
Yellowstone NP **11**

MAP 8: COLORADO, IDAHO,

California

Cabrillo NM	39
Channel Islands NP	35
Death Valley NP	34
Devils Postpile NM	26
Eugene O'Neill NHS	22
Fort Point NHS	23
Golden Gate NRA	24
John Muir NHS	21
Joshua Tree NP	38
Kings Canyon NP	31
Lassen Volcanic NP	18
Lava Beds NM	15
Manzanar NHS	32
Mojave N PRES	37
Muir Woods NM	20
Pinnacles NM	30
Point Reyes NS	19
Port Chicago Naval Magazine NM	28
Redwood NP	16
Rosie the Riveter / World War II Home Front NHP	27
San Francisco Maritime NHP	25
Santa Monica Mountains NRA	36
Sequoia & Kings Canyon NPs	33
Whiskeytown-Shasta-Trinity NRA	17
Yosemite NP	29

Oregon

Crater Lake NP	13
Lewis & Clark NHP	11
John Day Fossil Beds NM	12
Oregon Caves NM	14

Washington

Ebey's Landing NHRES	2
Fort Vancouver NHS	10
Lake Chelan NRA	7
Lake Roosevelt NRA	6
Mount Rainier NP	8
North Cascades NP	4
Olympic NP	3
Ross Lake NRA	5
San Juan Island NHP	1
Whitman Mission NHS	9

MAP 9: CALIFORNIA, OREGON

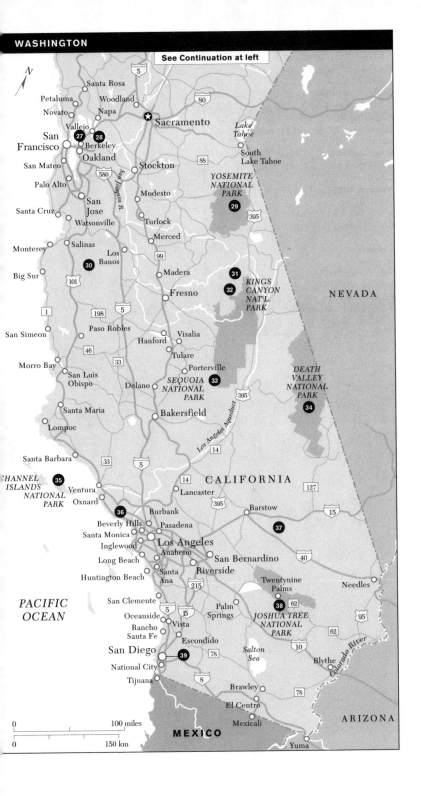

See Continuation at left

Santa Rosa

Petaluma
Woodland
Novato Napa

Vallejo

San
Francisco
27 28 Berkeley
Oakland

San Mateo

Palo Alto

Santa Cruz

San
Jose

Watsonville

Monterey Salinas

Los
Banos

Big Sur

30

San Simeon

Paso Robles

Morro Bay

San Luis
Obispo

Santa Maria

Lompoc

Santa Barbara

CHANNEL
ISLANDS
NATIONAL
PARK

35

Ventura
Oxnard

Sacramento

Modesto

Turlock

Merced

Madera

Fresno

Hanford

Delano

Visalia

Tulare

Porterville

SEQUOIA
NATIONAL
PARK

Bakersfield

Lake
Tahoe

South
Lake Tahoe

YOSEMITE
NATIONAL
PARK

29

Stockton

31

32

KINGS
CANYON
NAT'L.
PARK

NEVADA

33

DEATH
VALLEY
NATIONAL
PARK

34

CALIFORNIA

Lancaster

Burbank

Beverly Hills
Santa Monica

Inglewood

Long Beach

Pasadena

Los Angeles
Anaheim

Santa
Ana

Huntington Beach

36

San Clemente

Oceanside

Rancho
Santa Fe

San Diego

National City

Tijuana

PACIFIC
OCEAN

Riverside

San Bernardino

Barstow

37

Twentynine
Palms

Needles

38

62

JOSHUA TREE
NATIONAL
PARK

62

Palm
Springs

Vista

Escondido

39

Salton
Sea

Blythe

Brawley

El Centro

Mexicali

MEXICO

Yuma

ARIZONA

0   100 miles

0   150 km

Monterey Salinas

Alaska

Alagnak Wild River. **14**
Aniakchak NM & PRES. **13**
Bering Land Bridge N PRES **12**
Cape Krusenstern NM. **11**
Denali NP & PRES **17**
Gates of the Arctic NP & PRES **8**
Glacier Bay NP & PRES **22**
Katmai NP & PRES. **15**
Kenai Fjords NP. **19**
Klondike Gold Rush NHP. **21**
Kobuk Valley NP **9**
Lake Clark NP & PRES. **16**
Noatak N PRES **10**
Sitka NHP. **23**
Wrangell-St. Elias NP & PRES **20**
Yukon-Charley Rivers N PRES **18**

Hawaii

Haleakala NP **3**
Hawaii Volcanoes NP. **7**
Kalaupapa NHP **2**
Kaloko-Honokohau NHP. **5**
Pu'uhonua o Honaunau NHP **6**
Pu'ukohola Heiau NHS **4**
World War II Valor in the Pacific NM **1**

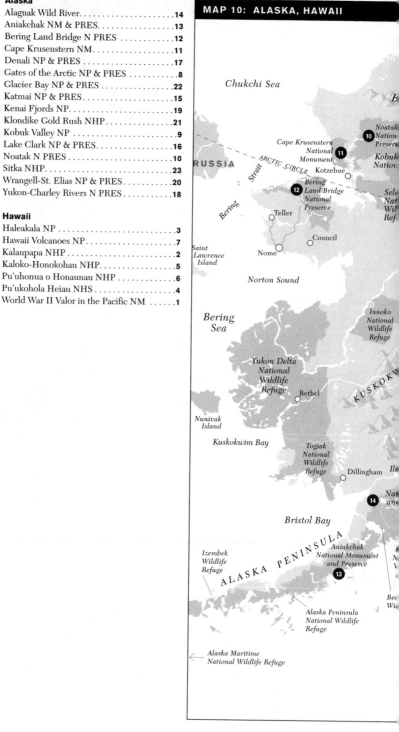

KAUAI

Wailua

Lihue

Waimea Poipu

NIIHAU

Kauai Channel

OAHU ❶☆ Waikiki

Honolulu

Kaiwi

Channel

HAWAII

❷ **MOLOKAI**

MAUI

Lahaina

Lanai City Kahului

Kihei Hana

LANAI Wailea

Wailea ❸

Alenuihaha Channel

PACIFIC OCEAN

Volcanoes ❹
National Park

Waimea

*Mauna
▲Kea* Hilo

Kailua-Kona ❺

*Mauna
▲Loa*

❻ ❼ *Kilauea
Crater*

HAWAII
(The Big Island) Naalehu

0 ——— 50 miles

0 ——— 50 km

N

---

*f the Arctic
tional Park
nd Preserve*

❽

*Kanuti Flats
National
Wildlife
Refuge*

River

Baker Livengood Chena
Hot Springs

*tional
efuge*

Fairbanks

Yukon

Yukon-
❶❽ Charley Rivers
National
Preserve

R.

Dawson
City

CANADA

Delta Jct. Boundary

NTAINS *Denali
National Park
and Preserve*

❶❼ Cantwell

Mt. McKinley

GEORGE PARKS
HWY.

RANGE Paxson

Tok

Slano *Tetlin
National
Wildlife
Refuge*

Willow Palmer

Glennallen

*Wrangell-
St. Elias*

❷⓿
*National Park
and Preserve*

Whitehorse ☆

SKA

❶❻

*lark
Park
serve* Tyonek
Kenai

Anchorage

Whittier

Valdez

*Chugach
National Forest*

*Prince
William
Sound*

Cordova

Mt. St. Elias

YUKON TERR.

BRITISH COLUMBIA

Skagway

Seward ❶❾

*Kenai
Fjords
National
Park*

Homer

Cook *Inlet*

*Kenai National
Wildlife Refuge*

ak

*Chugach
National
Forest*

*Glacier Bay
National Park
and Preserve*

❷❷

Haines ❷❶

Juneau ☆

Hoonah

PACIFIC OCEAN

Gulf of Alaska

❷❸

Sitka

*Tongass
National
Forest*

N

0 ——— 100 miles

0 ——— 150 km

American Samoa
National Park of American Samoa. **7**

Guam
War in the Pacific NHP **6**

Puerto Rico
San Juan NHS **8**

Virgin Islands
Buck Island Reef NM **3**
Christiansted NHS. **4**
Salt River Bay NHP &
Ecological Preserve **5**
Virgin Islands Coral Reef NM. **2**
Virgin Islands NP **1**

Washington, D.C.
Garter G. Woodson Home NHS **24**
Constitution Gardens. **28**
Ford's Theatre NHS. **20**
Franklin Delano Roosevelt
Memorial **11**
Frederick Douglass NHS **9**
Korean War Veterans Memorial **16**
Lincoln Memorial. **14**
Lyndon Baines Johnson
Memorial Grove on the Potomac **12**
Martin Luther King, Jr. Memorial. **19**
Mary McLeod Bethune
Council House NHS **21**
National Capital Parks **25**
National Mall **23**
Pennsylvania Avenue NHS **22**
Potomac Heritage NST **27**
Rock Creek Park **26**
Theodore Roosevelt Island **13**
Thomas Jefferson Memorial **10**
Vietnam Veterans Memorial **15**
Washington Monument **17**
White House. **18**

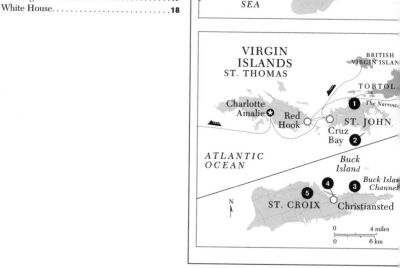

MAP 11: AMERICAN SAMOA, NORTH

PACIFIC
OCEAN
OFU
TAU

AMERICAN
SAMOA

N

Pago
Pago

TUTUILA

PACIFIC
OCEAN

NORTH
MARIANA
ISLANDS

Tanapag

SAIPAN

TINIAN

PACIFIC
OCEAN

Agana

PACIFIC
OCEAN

GUAM

PHILIPPINE
SEA

VIRGIN
ISLANDS
ST. THOMAS

BRITISH
VIRGIN ISLAN

TORTOL

The Narrow

Charlotte
Amalie

Red
Hook

ST. JOHN

Cruz
Bay

ATLANTIC
OCEAN

Buck
Island

Buck Isla
Channel

ST. CROIX

Christiansted

0   4 miles

0   6 km

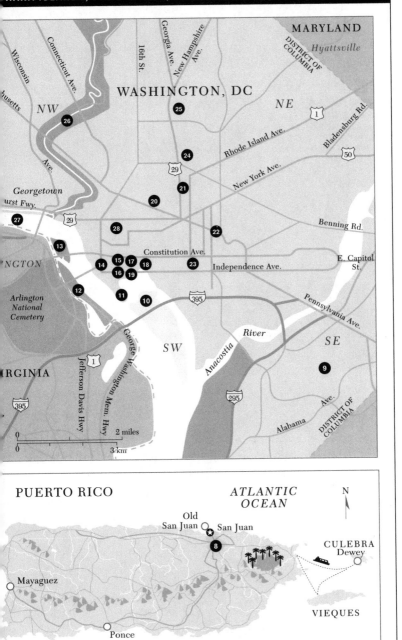

America's National Parks

ALABAMA

Horseshoe Bend
National Military Park

In east-central Alabama, near Dadeville

On March 27, 1814, General Andrew Jackson's Tennessee Army of 3,300 regulars, militia, and allied warriors defeated 1,000 Red Stick Creek warriors led by Chief Menawa. The bloody battle ended the Creek War, broke the tribe's power in the Southeast, and added Creek lands comprising three-fifths of present-day Alabama and one-fifth of Georgia to the United States. The park was established in 1959.

WHAT TO SEE & DO

Bicycling, canoeing, fishing, hiking, picnicking, touring museum and battlefield, watching video program and electric map presentations. **Facilities:** Visitor center, auditorium, 3-mile nature trail, 3-mile tour road, 10-mile unpaved access roads (hiking only), boat ramp. Bookstore, picnic area with grills, tables and pavilions. **Programs & Events:** Living-history programs (Feb.–Aug.), including firing demonstrations, evening campfire and lantern programs, musket drill. Battle anniversary encampment (last weekend, Mar.). **Tips & Hints:** Go Mar.–June or Sept.–Nov. for better weather. Busiest May and June, least crowded Dec. and Jan.

FOOD, LODGING & SUPPLIES

Camping: None in park. In Wind Creek State Park: Wind Creek Campground (4325 Rte. 128, 7 miles southeast of Alexander City, tel. 256/329–0845, www.alapark.com; 642 sites; $19–$22; flush toilets, hookups). **Hotels:** None in park. In Alexander City: Hampton Inn (1551 Elkahatchee Rd., tel. 256/234–2244, www.hamptoninn.hilton. com; 61 rooms; $109), Jameson Inn (4335 U.S. 280, tel. 256/234–7099 or 800/526–3766, www.jamesoninns.com; 60 rooms; $70). **Restaurants:** None in park. In Alexander City: Zaxby's (4497 U.S. 280, tel. 256/234–2181, www.zaxbys.com; $6–$9). **Groceries & Gear:** None in park. In Wind Creek State Park: The Country Store (4325 Rte. 128, Alexander City, tel. 256/329–0845).

FEES, HOURS & REGULATIONS

Free. No hunting or firearms. Leashed pets only. Pedestrian traffic only on nature trails. Park open daily 8–5. Visitor center open daily 9–4:30. Fishing permit required and available at the Country Store in Wind Creek State Park.

HOW TO GET THERE

12 miles north of Dadeville on Rte. 49. Closest airport: Birmingham (80 miles).

CONTACTS

Horseshoe Bend National Military Park (11288 Horseshoe Bend Rd., Daviston, AL 36256, tel. 256/234–7111, www.nps.gov/hobe). Dadeville Chamber of Commerce (185 S. Tallassee St., Dadeville, AL 36853, tel. 256/825–4019, www.dadeville.com). Wind Creek State Park (4325 Rte. 128, Alexander City, AL 35010, tel. 256/329–0845, www.alapark.com).

Little River Canyon National Preserve

In northeastern Alabama, near Fort Payne

The nation's longest mountaintop river and one of the Southeast's deepest canyons create an awe-inspiring backdrop for the preserve. Formed by river waters that are among the nation's purest, the canyon's cliffs tower more than 300 feet and enclose vast biodiversity, including more than 100 rare and endangered species. Recreational opportunities abound, including hiking, biking, rock climbing, hunting, and fishing. The preserve was authorized on October 24, 1992.

WHAT TO SEE & DO

Canoeing, fishing, hiking, horseback riding, hunting, kayaking, mountain biking, picnicking, rock climbing, wading, walking. **Facilities:** Little River Canyon Center, Canyon Rim Drive, overlooks. Gift shop, grills, pavilion, and picnic tables. **Tips & Hints:** Be prepared for challenging rapids and rock climbing. Watch footing on scenic bluffs and cliffs. Go late Oct.–early Nov. for fall colors, Mar.–June for wildflowers.

FOOD, LODGING & SUPPLIES

🏕 **Camping:** In the park: Backcountry area (4322 Little River Tr. NE, tel. 256/845–9605; 3 sites; free; pit toilets, grills, picnic tables). 🏨 **Hotels:** In the park: DeSoto State Park Lodge (265 Rte. 951, off Rte. 35; tel. 256/845–5380 or 800/568–8840; 25 rooms; $75). In Fort Payne: Hampton Inn (1201 Jordan Rd. SW, tel. 256/304–2600, www.hamptoninn.hilton.com; 56 rooms; $129). ✗ **Restaurants:** In the park: DeSoto State Park Lodge (265 Rte. 951, Fort Payne, off U.S. 35, tel. 256/845–5380; $5–$6), Little River Café (4608 DeSoto Pkwy., tel. 256/845–2225; $5–$8). ⛏ **Gear:** In the park: DeSoto State Park Country Store & Information Center (13883 County Rd. 89, Fort Payne, tel. 256/845–5075).

FEES, HOURS & REGULATIONS

Entrance fee: $3 per vehicle at Canyon Mouth Day Use Area. Alabama state fishing and hunting licenses required. Leashed pets only. Hunting restricted to wildlife management area in season only. No vehicles off roads. Limited bicycling in DeSoto State Park. No collecting rocks or plants. No weapons, alcohol, or fireworks. Park open daily. Canyon Mouth Park open daily 8–8.

HOW TO GET THERE

From Chattanooga, TN, take I–24 west to I–59 south to Fort Payne Exit 222 and follow signs to the preserve. From Birmingham, AL, take I–59 north to Fort Payne Exit 218 (Rte. 35). Take Rte. 35 to the preserve. Closest airports: Chattanooga (45 miles), Birmingham (100 miles), Atlanta (100 miles).

CONTACTS

Little River Canyon National Preserve (4322 Little River Tr. NE, Fort Payne, AL 35967, tel. 256/845–9605, fax 256/997–9129, www.nps. gov/liri). DeKalb County Tourist Association (1503 Glenn Blvd. SW, Fort Payne, AL 35968, tel. 256/845–3957, fax 256/845–3946, www. visitatlantasdekalbcounty.com). DeSoto State Park Camping Reservations & Information Center (13883 Rte. 89, Fort Payne, AL 35967, tel. 256/845–5075). Fort Payne Chamber of Commerce (300 Gault Ave. N., Fort Payne, AL 35967, tel. 256/845–2741, www.fortpaynechamber.com).

Russell Cave National Monument

In northeastern Alabama, near Bridgeport

Russell Cave was inhabited for almost 10,000 years, from at least 7000 BC to AD 1650. Virtually no other place in the region offers so many clues to how the "First Americans" fed, clothed, and protected themselves. The monument was proclaimed on May 11, 1961.

WHAT TO SEE & DO

Living-history demonstration, touring cave. **Facilities:** Information center, museum, trail. Bookstore. **Programs & Events:** Daily interpretive programs at 11 including guided cave walks. **Tips & Hints:** Plan to spend at least one hour in the museum area and cave mouth. Add one hour for conducted programs. Busiest July and Oct., least crowded Dec. and Jan.

FOOD, LODGING & SUPPLIES

Camping: None at monument. Near Scottsboro: Jackson County Park (2302 County Park Rd., tel. 256/574–4719; 144 sites; $10–$18; flush toilets, showers, hookups). **Hotels:** None at monument. In Scottsboro: Comfort Inn and Suites (25775 John T. Reid Pkwy., tel. 256/259–8700, www.comfortinn.com; 77 rooms; $89). **Restaurants:** None at monument. In Scottsboro: The Blue Willow Bistro & Antiques (303 E. Willow St., tel. 256/259–3462; $5–$10). **Groceries & Gear:** None at monument. In Bridgeport: Big Daddy's Outdoors (52680 U.S. 72, tel. 256/495–9225; closed Sun.).

FEES & HOURS

Free. Monument open daily 8–4:30.

HOW TO GET THERE

7 miles northwest of Bridgeport via Rtes. 75 and 98. Closest airport: Chattanooga, TN (45 miles).

CONTACTS

Russell Cave National Monument (3729 County Rd. 98, Bridgeport, AL 35740, tel. 256/495–2672, www.nps.gov/ruca). Greater Jackson County Chamber of Commerce (407 E. Willow St., Scotsboro, AL 35768, tel. 256/259–5500 or 800/259–5508, www.jacksoncountychamber.com). Jackson County Park (2302 County Park, Scottsboro, AL 35769, tel. 256/574–4719).

Tuskegee Airmen National Historic Site

In east-central Alabama, in Tuskegee

This site commemorates and interprets the actions of the Tuskegee Airmen during World War II. The Airmen included African American pilots, navigators, mechanics, and others trained by the Army Air Corps program to fly and maintain combat aircraft. The Tuskegee Airmen overcame segregation and prejudice to become one of the most highly respected fighter groups during the war. Their achievements, together with those of the men and women who supported them, paved the way for full integration of the U.S. military. The site was authorized on November 6, 1998.

WHAT TO SEE & DO

Touring historic site. **Facilities:** Visitor center, museum. Bookstore. **Tips & Hints:** Plan to spend at least one hour. Busiest Feb.–May, least crowded Sept.–Dec.

FEES & HOURS

Free. Site open daily 9–4:30.

HOW TO GET THERE

From I–85, take Exit 38 and follow signs to site. Closest airport: Montgomery (50 miles).

CONTACTS

Tuskegee Airmen National Historic Site (1616 Chappie James Ave., Tuskegee, AL 36083, tel. 334/724–0922, www.nps.gov/tuai). Chewacla State Park (124 Shell Toomer Pkwy., Auburn, AL 36830, tel. 334/887–5621). Tuskegee Area Chamber of Commerce (121 S. Main St., Tuskegee, AL 36083, tel. 334/727–6619, www.tuskegeeareachamber.org). Tuskegee National Forest (125 National Forest Rd. 949, Tuskegee, AL 36083, tel. 334/727–2652).

Tuskegee Institute National Historic Site

In east-central Alabama, in Tuskegee

In 1881, at the age of 26, Booker T. Washington became the first principal of the newly formed Normal School for Colored Teachers in Tuskegee. George Washington Carver joined the faculty in 1896 and revolutionized agricultural development in the South in the early 20th century. Preserved here are the brick buildings the students constructed, Washington's home, and the George Washington Carver Museum. The site was authorized on October 26, 1974.

WHAT TO SEE & DO

Touring the Historic Campus District, visiting Carver Museum and The Oaks. **Facilities:** Carver Museum; The Oaks, home of Booker T. Washington; walking tour through Historic Campus District. Bookstore. **Programs & Events:** Ranger-led tours of The Oaks. **Tips & Hints:** Plan to spend at least two hours at the Carver Museum and The Oaks. Busiest Feb.–May, least crowded Sept.–Dec.

FEES & HOURS

Free. Site and George Washington Carver Museum open daily 9–4:30. The Oaks open by reservation only.

HOW TO GET THERE

The site is on the campus of Tuskegee University in Tuskegee. The university is on Old Montgomery Rd., 1½ miles northwest of downtown Tuskegee, 35 miles east of Montgomery, and 20 miles west of Auburn. From I–85, take Exit 38 and travel north on Rte. 81 for 6 miles to Tuskegee. Closest airport: Montgomery (50 miles).

CONTACTS

Tuskegee Institute National Historic Site (1212 W. Montgomery Rd., Tuskegee Institute, Tuskegee, AL 36088, tel. 334/727–3200, www.nps.gov/tuin). Chewacla State Park (124 Shell Toomer Pkwy., Auburn, AL 36830, tel. 334/887–5621). Tuskegee Area Chamber of Commerce (121 S. Main St., Tuskegee, AL 36083, tel. 334/727–6619, www.tuskegeeareachamber.org). Tuskegee National Forest (125 National Forest Rd. 949, Tuskegee, AL 36083, tel. 334/727–2652).

See Also

Natchez Trace Parkway, Mississippi. *Natchez Trace National Scenic Trail,* Mississippi. *Selma to Montgomery National Historic Trail, and Trail of Tears National Historic Trail,* in Other National Parklands.

ALASKA

Alagnak Wild River

On Aleutian Range, near King Salmon

The 69 miles of federally designated Alagnak Wild River runs out of Kukaklek Lake in the Katmai National Preserve. It offers outstanding white-water floating, as well as abundant wildlife and sportfishing for rainbow trout, char, grayling, and salmon. The wild river was established on December 2, 1980.

WHAT TO SEE & DO

Fishing, float trips, hunting, wildlife watching. **Facilities:** King Salmon Visitor Center. **Tips & Hints:** Bring rain gear, waterproof footgear, and wool clothing. Busiest July and Aug., least crowded Dec. and Jan.

FOOD, LODGING & SUPPLIES

Camping: In the park: Backcountry camping allowed. Outside the park: Brooks Camp (Brooks River area, tel. 877/444–6777; 18 sites; $12 per person; vault toilets, showers [fee], no hookups). **Hotels:** None in park. In Anchorage: Merrill Field Inn (420 Sitka St., tel. 907/276–4547 or 800/898–4547, www.merrillfieldinn.com; 39 rooms; $72–$90). **Restaurants:** None in park. In Anchorage: Gwennie's Old Alaskan Restaurant (4333 Spenard Rd., tel. 907/243–2090, www.gwenniesrestaurant.com; $10–$26). In King Salmon: Eddie's Fireplace Inn (1 Main St., tel. 907/246–3435; $8–$10). **Groceries:** None in park. In King Salmon: Alaska Commercial Co. (100 Southside Eskimo Creek, tel. 907/246–6109).

FEES, HOURS & REGULATIONS

Free. Permits (free) recommended for all primitive camping. Alaska state fishing license required. Park open daily.

HOW TO GET THERE

Via boat from King Salmon. Charter flights are available from Anchorage, King Salmon, Kodiak, and other nearby towns on the mainland.

CONTACTS

Alagnak Wild River (Box 245, King Salmon, AK 99613, tel. 907/246–3305, www.nps.gov/alag). Alaska Public Lands Information Centers (605 W. 4th Ave., Suite 105, Anchorage, AK 99501, tel. 907/271–2737, www.alaskacenters.gov).

Aniakchak National Monument & Preserve

On Alaska Peninsula, near Port Heiden

The Aniakchak Caldera covers 10 square miles and is one of the great dry calderas in the world. Located in the volcanically active Aleutian Mountains, the Aniakchak last erupted in 1931. Inside the crater are lava flows, cinder cones, and explosion pits, as well as Surprise Lake, the source of the Aniakchak River, which cascades through a 1,500-foot gash in the crater wall. The site also contains the Aniakchak Wild River. The site was proclaimed a national monument in 1978 and established as a national monument and preserve in 1980.

WHAT TO SEE & DO

Fishing, float trips, wildlife watching. **Tips & Hints:** Bring wool clothing, rubber boots, and good rain gear. Bring all food if camping, and be sure tents can withstand bad weather: the caldera is subject to violent windstorms. Busiest Aug. and Sept., least crowded Jan. and Feb.

LODGING & SUPPLIES

⚑ **Camping:** Backcountry camping only. ⊞ **Hotels:** None in park. In King Salmon: King Salmon Inn (Mile 13 Alaska Peninsula Hwy., tel. 907/246–3444 or 888/224–7648; kingsalmoninn.com; 23 rooms, 1 suite, $240–$330). ⚑ **Groceries:** None in park. In Port Heiden: Jack's Store (New Meshik Mall, tel. 907/837–2217).

FEES, HOURS & REGULATIONS

Free. Backcountry permits available from Aniakchak office in King Salmon. Alaska state fishing license required. Park open daily.

HOW TO GET THERE

Regular flights are available from Anchorage to King Salmon. Regular and charter flights are available from King Salmon to Port Heiden, a 10-mile hike over open tundra from the monument. Closest airport: Port Heiden.

CONTACTS

Aniakchak National Monument & Preserve (Box 245, King Salmon, AK 99613, tel. 907/246–3305, www.nps.gov/ania). Alaska Public Lands Information Centers (605 W. 4th Ave., Suite 105, Anchorage, AK 99501, tel. 907/644–3661, www.alaskacenters.gov).

Bering Land Bridge National Preserve

In the west, on Seward Peninsula, near Nome

The preserve is a remnant of the land bridge that connected Asia to North America more than 13,000 years ago. The land bridge is now beneath the Chukchi Sea and the Bering Sea. During the glacial epoch, whenever ocean levels fell enough to expose the land bridge, people and animals migrated into the area. Archaeologists agree that it was across this Bering Land Bridge, also called Beringia, that early humans passed between Asia and northwestern Alaska. The preserve is home to paleontological and archaeological resources, large populations of migratory birds, wildlife (including brown bear, moose, caribou, musk oxen, and reindeer), and ash explosion craters and lava flows. The park was proclaimed a national monument in 1978 and a preserve in 1980.

WHAT TO SEE & DO

Backpacking, bird and wildlife viewing, canoeing, coastal boating, cross-country skiing, dogsledding, fishing, hiking, hunting, observing Eskimo reindeer herding, river floating, snowmobiling. **Facilities:** Visitor center (214 Front St., Nome 99762). **Programs & Events:** Interpretive talks, demonstrations, Junior Ranger Program (all May–Aug.). **Tips & Hints:** Be prepared to be self-sufficient. Exposure and hypothermia are threats throughout the year. Temperatures in summer are usually around 50°F on the coast and 65°F–75°F inland. Snow, freezing temperatures, and long periods of clouds, rain, and wind are possible year-round. Summer days are long, almost without darkness. Average Jan. lows are -15°F on the coast and -50°F in the interior. Winds average 8–12 mph but can reach 70 mph in storms. Winter days are short, with only a few hours of light. Go May–June for rare migratory bird viewing. Busiest June–Aug., least crowded Jan. and Feb.

FOOD, LODGING & SUPPLIES

⚠ **Camping:** In the park: Serpentine Hot Springs (south-central area of preserve near Taylor; primitive cabin with 16 bunk beds; free). 6 primitive cabins scattered elsewhere in park. Backcountry camping allowed. Nearby: Salmon Lake Campground (north end of Salmon Lake, 38 miles north of Nome, tel. 907/443–2177; 6 sites; free). 🏨 **Hotels:** None in park. In Nome: Nome Nugget Inn (315 W. Front St., tel. 907/443–4189, www.nomenuggetinnhotel.com; 47 rooms; $90–$110), Aurora Inn (302 E. Front St., tel. 907/443–3838, www.aurorainnome. com; 54 rooms; $155–$260). ✗ **Restaurants:** None in park. In Nome: Airport Pizza (406 Bering St., tel. 907/443–7992; $15–$25), Polar Café (224 Front St., tel. 907/443–5191; $10–$15).

FEES, HOURS & REGULATIONS

Free. Alaska hunting and fishing licenses required. No helicopters or all-terrain vehicles. Preserve open daily. Nome Visitor Center open weekdays, 8–5.

HOW TO GET THERE

Accessible only by foot travel, small aircraft, and boats in summer and fall, by snowmobile, dogsled, cross-country skis, or small plane on skis in winter and spring. Closest airports: Kotzebue (40 miles), Nome (70 miles).

CONTACTS

Bering Land Bridge National Preserve (Box 220, Nome, AK 99762, tel. 907/443–2522 or 800/471–2352, www.nps.gov/bela). Nome Convention

& Visitors Bureau (301 Front St., Box 240, Nome, AK 99762, tel. 907/443–6555, fax 907/443–5832, www.visitnomealaska.com).

Cape Krusenstern National Monument

In northwestern Alaska, near Kotzebue

Archaeological sites along a succession of 114 lateral beach ridges illustrate every known Eskimo cultural period in Alaska over 4,000 years. Older sites are located inland along the foothills. The monument includes a representative example of the Arctic coastline along the Chukchi Sea. The monument was proclaimed on December 1, 1978.

WHAT TO SEE & DO

Backpacking, boating, canoeing, hiking, kayaking, wildlife watching. **Facilities:** Information center and park headquarters in Kotzebue. No facilities in park. **Programs & Events:** Interpretive talks and demonstrations (Kotzebue; June–Aug.). Junior Ranger Program (June–Aug.). **Tips & Hints:** Prepare to be self-sufficient. Wear sturdy hiking boots and rubber boots for wet terrain. Expect high winds throughout the year; short, mild, cool, and sunny summers with 24 hours of daylight for one month; and long, severe, harsh, extremely cold winters with one hour of daylight by Dec. 1. Guard against hypothermia, giardia lamblia, wild animals, mosquitoes, and biting flies. Don't interfere with subsistence camps, fishnets, or other equipment. Respect property and privacy. Busiest July and Aug., least crowded Nov.–Jan.

FOOD, LODGING & SUPPLIES

Camping: Backcountry camping only. **Hotels:** None in park. In Kotzebue: Nullagvik Hotel (308 Shore Ave., tel. 907/442–3331, www.nullagvikhotel.com; 78 rooms; $259–$299). **Restaurants:** None in park. In Kotzebue: Nullagvik Restaurant (308 Shore Ave., tel. 907/442–3331, www.nullagvikhotel.com; $12–$27). **Groceries & Gear:** None in park. In Kotzebue: Alaska Commercial Co. (395 Bison St., tel. 907/442–3285).

FEES, HOURS & REGULATIONS

Free. Reservations recommended for most visitor services from commercial vendors. Open daily. Park Headquarters (Kotzebue) open weekdays 8–5. Northwest Arctic Heritage Center hours mid-May–mid-Sept., daily 8–6.

HOW TO GET THERE

Accessible by plane from Fairbanks or Anchorage to Kotzebue; scheduled flights available from Kotzebue to the villages of Noatak, Kivalina, Shungnak, Ambler, Kobuk, Kiana, and Noorvik; summer access to and through the monument via nonmotorized watercraft and aircraft; air taxis are available year-round.

CONTACTS

Western Arctic National Parklands (Box 1029, Kotzebue, AK 99752, tel. 907/442–3890, www.nps.gov/cakr).

Denali National Park & Preserve

In south-central Alaska

Denali, the "High One," is the name the Athabascan people gave to Mt. McKinley (20,320 feet), the massive peak that crowns the 600-mile Alaska Range. The park's 6.1 million acres include countless other spectacular mountains and large glaciers. Denali encompasses a complete subarctic ecosystem, which is populated with grizzly bears, wolves, Dall sheep, caribou, and moose. Mt. McKinley National Park was established in 1917 and designated an international biosphere reserve in 1976. The park's name was changed to Denali, and it was tripled in size with the addition of new park and preserve lands in 1980.

WHAT TO SEE & DO

Backpacking, bicycling, bus touring, cross-country skiing, dog mushing, hiking, mountaineering (permit required on Mt. McKinley and Mt. Foraker), snowshoeing, stargazing, wildlife viewing. **Facilities:** 2 visitor centers: Denali (mile 1.2, Denali Park Rd.), Eielson (mile 66, Denali Park Rd.); Talkeetna Mountaineering Center ranger station. Bookstores. **Programs & Events:** Ranger and naturalist programs (late May–mid-Sept.). **Tips & Hints:** Best weather late May–early Sept. Plan to spend at least one day to tour the park road by shuttle or tour bus, several days for hiking. Reserve ahead for camping and shuttle to avoid a possible one- to two-day wait for bus availability during peak season. Bring rain gear and hiking boots in summer when weather is cool and damp. Bring specialized cold-weather gear for winter visits, when temperatures drop to -40°F or lower. Read *Mountaineering: Denali National Park and Preserve* to begin planning mountain climbs in the park. Busiest July and Aug., least crowded Jan. and Feb.

FOOD, LODGING & SUPPLIES

⚠ **Camping:** 6 campgrounds in the park: Igloo Creek (mile 34, Park Rd.; 7 sites; $9; vault toilets), Riley Creek (park entrance; 146 sites; $14–$28; flush toilets), Sanctuary River (mile 23, Park Rd.; 7 sites; $9; vault toilets), Savage River (mile 13, Park Rd.; 33 sites; $22–$28; flush and vault toilets), Teklanika River (mile 29, Park Rd.; 53 sites; $16; vault toilets), Wonder Lake (mile 85, Park Rd.; 28 sites; $16; flush toilets). Backcountry camping available (permit required). In Healy: McKinley RV Park & Campground (mile 248.5, George Parks Hwy., tel. 907/683–1418, www.mckinleyrv.com; 62 sites; $10–$38; flush toilets, showers, hookups). 🏨 **Hotels:** In the park: Camp Denali (mile 89, Park Rd., tel. 907/683–2290; 17 cabins; $1,200–$1,400 for 3 days, including meals, transportation, and guided outings; closed mid-Sept.–June), Denali Backcountry Lodge (mile 89, Park Rd., tel. 907/783–1342 or 800/841–0692; 30 cabins; $390–$450, including meals and transportation; closed mid-Sept.–early June), North Face Lodge (mile 89, Park Rd., tel. 907/683–2290; 15 rooms; $1,400 for 3 days, including meals, transportation, and guided outings; closed mid-Sept.–June). In Healy: Motel Nord Haven (mile 249.5, George Parks Hwy., tel. 907/683–4500 or 800/683–4501, www.motelnordhaven.com; 28 rooms; $140–$180). ✕ **Restaurants:** In the park: Morino Grill in Denali Visitor Center campus (tel. 907/683–9225; $7–$15). Nearby: Perch Restaurant (mile 224 on George Parks Hwy., tel. 907/683–2523, www.denaliperchresort. com; $10–$31), McKinley-Denali Salmon Bake (1 mile north of park entrance, tel. 907/683–2733, www.denaliparksalmonbake.com; $8–$17; closed Oct.–Apr.). In Healy: Totem Inn (mile 248.7, George Parks Hwy., tel. 907/683–2420, www.thetoteminn.com; $9–$13). ♿ **Groceries & Gear:** In the park: Riley Creek Mercantile (park entrance, tel. 907/683–9246). Near Healy: Lynx Creek General Store (mile 238, George Parks Hwy., tel. 907/683–2548).

FEES, HOURS & REGULATIONS

Entrance fee: $10 per person. Fees vary for shuttle and tour bus (reservations available, tel. 907/272–7275 or 800/622–7275, fax 907/264–4684). Backcountry permits required for overnight camping (free). Camper bus pass ($34) needed to reach most backcountry sites. Mountaineering permits ($350) must be applied for 60 days in advance. No snowmobiling in wilderness area. Park open daily. Denali Visitor Center open mid-May–mid-Sept., daily 8–6. Murie Science and Learning Center open mid-Sept.–mid-May, daily 9–4, and mid-May–mid-Sept., daily 9:30–5. Eielson Visitor Center open June–mid-Sept., daily 9–7.

HOW TO GET THERE

Denali is accessible by car or the Alaska Railroad (tel. 907/265–2494 or 800/544–0552, www.alaskarailroad.com) from Anchorage and Fairbanks. In summer, a variety of private bus and van services operate daily from Anchorage and Fairbanks. The park and preserve is on Rte. 3 (George Parks Hwy.), 240 miles north of Anchorage, 125 miles south of Fairbanks, and 12 miles south of Healy. The Denali Park Rd. is accessible by private vehicle for 15 miles to the Savage River Bridge. Shuttles and tour buses travel farther into the park. Mountaineering headquarters is in Talkeetna, 100 miles north of Anchorage. Closest airport: Fairbanks.

CONTACTS

Denali National Park & Preserve (Box 9, Denali Park, AK 99755, tel. 907/683–9532, www.nps.gov/dena). Alaska Mountaineering School (Box 566, Talkeetna, AK 99676, tel. 907/733–1016, www.climbalaska. org). Denali Chamber of Commerce (Box 437, Healy, AK 99743, tel. 907/683–4636, www.denalichamber.com).

Gates of the Arctic
National Park & Preserve

In central Brooks Range, near Bettles, in the north

This park and preserve may be Alaska's ultimate wilderness park. The National Park Service manages the 8.4-million-acre park and preserve and maintains the land's wild and undeveloped character. There are no roads, trails, or visitor services here. In this, the park system's northernmost park, visitors experience the natural world much as it was when wilderness advocate Robert Marshall visited it more than 70 years ago. The area was proclaimed a national monument in 1978 and established as a park and preserve in 1980.

WHAT TO SEE & DO

Dogsledding, fishing, hiking, kayaking, mountain climbing, rafting, snowshoeing. **Facilities:** Ranger station at Anaktuvuk Pass (not always staffed, so call ahead). Bettles ranger station (open year-round); Coldfoot visitor center (June–Sept.). Book sales outlet (Bettles, Coldfoot). **Programs & Events:** Backcountry orientation and limited interpretive programs available at a park ranger station in Bettles (by request). Interpretive programs at Coldfoot (June–Sept., daily). **Tips & Hints:** Plan to be self-sufficient in the park, where contact with other visitors is rare. Be knowledgeable about camping and hiking in bear country. Contact park staff in Anaktuvuk Pass, Bettles, or Coldfoot for updated information before going into the park. Bring plenty of insect repellent and head nets. Biting mosquitoes and gnats in summer can make a stay unbearable. Insect numbers decline by late Aug. Go May–Sept. to avoid snow. Winter temperatures (Oct.–Mar.) usually are subzero and can drop to as low as -60°F. Busiest July and Aug., least crowded Oct.–Jan.

FOOD, LODGING & SUPPLIES

⛺ **Camping:** Backcountry camping only. 🏨 **Hotels:** None in park. In Bettles: Bettles Lodge (100 Bettlesfield, tel. 907/692–5111, www.bettleslodge.com; 14 rooms; $175–$195). ✖ **Restaurants:** None in park. In Bettles: Bettles Lodge (100 Bettlesfield, tel. 907/692–5111, www.bettleslodge.com; $12–$20).

FEES, HOURS & REGULATIONS

Free. Alaska state fishing, hunting, or trapping licenses required. Commercial guide required for nonresidents hunting in preserves for certain species. Hunting in preserve areas only. No motorized vehicles. Pets must be under control at all times. No restrooms. Park and preserve open daily. Visitor center in Bettles open daily 8–5; in Anaktuvuk Pass, May–Sept., daily 8–5; in Coldfoot, May–Sept., daily 8–5.

HOW TO GET THERE

The park and preserve are accessible on foot, by small aircraft, or by boat. Bettles and Anaktuvuk Pass, 160 miles and 240 miles north of Fairbanks, are nearest to the center of the park. Neither has road access. Scheduled air service from Fairbanks is available daily. Coldfoot, which provides access to the east section of the park and preserve, is 250 miles north of Fairbanks via the Elliot and Dalton highways.

CONTACTS

Gates of the Arctic National Park & Preserve (Box 26030, Bettles, AK 99726, tel. 907/692–5494, www.nps.gov/gaar). Anaktuvuk Pass Ranger Station (tel. 907/661–3520). City of Bettles (Box 26023, Bettles Field, AK 99726, tel. 907/692–5191).

Glacier Bay National Park & Preserve

In southeastern Alaska, near Gustavus

Glacier Bay is a 3.2-million-acre wilderness park accessible only by boat or plane. Just 200 years ago a solid sheet of ice covered what is now the bay. In two centuries, the glacial ice has retreated 65 miles and left a newly barren landscape to be recolonized by plant and animal life. You can travel by boat from a lush green rain forest up to the impressive tidewater glaciers and, perhaps, see wildlife along the way, including bears, mountain goats, whales, seals, eagles, and puffins. The site was created as a national monument in 1925 and designated a national park in 1980. The park was designated a Biosphere Reserve in 1986 and a World Heritage Site in 1992.

WHAT TO SEE & DO

Fishing, hiking, kayaking, viewing glaciers by boat. **Facilities:** Glacier Bay Visitor Center (Bartlett Cove). Book and map sale area. **Programs & Events:** Ranger-guided hikes, walks, evening programs (mid-May–mid-Sept.). **Tips & Hints:** Bring rain gear: Glacier Bay gets more than 75 inches per year. Busiest June and July, least crowded Nov. and Dec.

FOOD, LODGING & SUPPLIES

Camping: In the park: Bartlett Cove (¼ mile south of the Bartlett Cove dock; walk-in tent camping; free; permit required). **Hotels:** In the park: Glacier Bay Lodge (Bartlett Cove, tel. 907/264–4600 or 888/229–8687; 56 rooms; $174–$245; closed mid-Sept.–mid-May). In Gustavus: Gustavus Inn (mile 1, Gustavus Rd., tel. 907/697–2254 or 800/649–5220, www.gustavusinn.com; 13 rooms; $190). **Restaurants:** In the park: Glacier Bay Lodge (179 Bartlett Cove, tel. 888/229–8687; $5–$13). In Gustavus: Bear Track Inn (Rink Creek Rd., Gustavus, tel. 907/697–3017 or 888/697–2284, www.beartrackinn.com; $10–$28; closed Oct.–Apr.). **Groceries & Gear:** None in park. In Gustavus: Bear Track Mercantile (Dock Rd., tel. 907/697–2358), Gusto Building Supply (25 Dock Rd., tel. 907/697–2297).

FEES, HOURS & REGULATIONS

Free. Glacier Bay Lodge offers daily boat trips to the glaciers ($185). Backcountry permits (free) and camper orientation required. Permit required for pleasure-boat operators to enter Glacier Bay or dock at

Bartlett Cove (June–Aug.). Because the number of permits is limited, planning ahead is strongly advised. Permits can be issued for up to seven days. Alaska state fishing and hunting license required. Hunting in preserve only. No pets onshore except in Bartlett Cove, where they must be leashed and are restricted to certain areas. Park open daily. Visitor center open May, daily 8–5; June–Aug., daily 7–9; Sept.–Apr., daily 8–5.

HOW TO GET THERE

60 miles northwest of Juneau. Flights are available from Juneau, Skagway, or Haines to Gustavus, which is 10 miles by road from Bartlett Cove, the park headquarters. Ferries also run from Juneau to Gustavus.

CONTACTS

Glacier Bay National Park & Preserve (Box 140, Gustavus, AK 99826, tel. 907/697–2230, fax 907/697–2654, www.nps.gov/glba). Gustavus Visitor Association (Box 167, Gustavus, AK 99826, tel. 907/697–2454, www.gustavusak.com).

Katmai National Park & Preserve

In southeastern Alaska, near King Salmon

Variety marks this vast land, where lakes, forests, mountains, and marshlands abound in wildlife. The Alaska brown bear—the world's largest carnivore—thrives here, feeding on red salmon that spawn in the many lakes and streams. Wild rivers and renowned sportfishing add to the attractions of this subarctic environment. In 1912 Novarupta Volcano erupted violently here, forming the ash-filled Valley of Ten Thousand Smokes, where steam rose from countless fumaroles. Today only a few active vents remain. The park also contains part of the Alagnak Wild River. The site was proclaimed as Katmai National Monument in 1918 and established as a national park and preserve in 1980.

WHAT TO SEE & DO

Backcountry camping, bear viewing, boat touring, bus touring, fishing, hiking. **Facilities:** 2 visitor centers: King Salmon (next to the airport terminal), Brooks Camp (open June–mid-Sept.). Bear-viewing platforms. Bookstore. **Programs & Events:** Ranger-led cultural walks, interpretive programs, evening multimedia programs (June–mid-Sept., Brooks Camp). **Tips & Hints:** Be prepared for cold, windy, rainy weather as well as some warm, sunny days in summer. Temperatures usually hover around 60°F. Winter days receive six hours of sunlight. Get bear-resistant canisters at visitor centers. Be prepared for bears in vicinity of Brooks Camp. Very close encounters with bears are common and require visitors to move briskly. Go in July and Sept. for best bear viewing. Expect waits and time limits on bear-viewing platforms in July. Busiest July, least crowded Jan. and Feb.

FOOD, LODGING & SUPPLIES

Camping: In the park: Brooks Camp (On the Brooks River, 30 miles from King Salmon; 17 sites; $8 per person; vault toilets, showers). Backcountry camping allowed. **Hotels:** In the park: Brooks Lodge (tel. 907/243–5448 or 800/544–0551; 16 rooms; $174–$615; closed Oct.–May), Grosvenor Lodge (tel. 907/243–5448 or 800/544–0551; 3 cabins; $2,500 for 3 days, including meals, lodging, guided outings, and gear; closed Oct.–May), Kulik Lodge (tel. 907/243–5448 or 800/544–0551; 12 cabins; $2,600 for 3 days, including meals, lodging, guided outings, and gear; closed Oct.–May). ✕ **Restaurants:** In the park: Brooks Lodge (tel. 907/243–5448; $15–$32). **Groceries & Gear:** In the park: Brooks Lodge Trading Post (tel. 907/243–5448).

FEES, HOURS & REGULATIONS

Free. Reservations recommended for daily bus tour ($88) from Brooks Lodge (tel. 907/243–5448 or 800/544–0551) to the Valley of Ten Thousand Smokes and Ukak Falls. Backcountry permits are recommended and are available at Brooks Camp and King Salmon. No capsicum bear spray allowed on commercial flights. Park open daily. Park Service and concession services offered at Brooks Camp early June–mid-Sept.

HOW TO GET THERE

290 miles southwest of Anchorage on the Alaska Peninsula, just west of King Salmon; no road access. Daily commercial flights run between Anchorage and King Salmon. Charters, air taxis, and boat tours available from King Salmon, Anchorage, Homer, and Kodiak. Scheduled service into Brooks Camp available from King Salmon by floatplane and boat. Many area lodges provide their own transportation to the park.

CONTACTS

Katmai National Park & Preserve (Box 7, King Salmon, AK 99613, tel. 907/246–3305, www.nps.gov/katm). Alaska Public Lands Information Center (605 W. 4th Ave., Suite 105, Anchorage, AK 99501, tel. 907/644–3661, www.alaskacenters.gov). Katmailand (concessionnaire, www.katmailand.com).

Kenai Fjords National Park

In south-central Alaska, near Seward

Harding Icefield—300 square miles in size and one of four major ice caps in the United States—is one of the attractions in this coastal mountain park. Tens of thousands of birds breed in the park's rich, varied rain forest, and sea lions, otters, and seals inhabit the park's waters. The 600,000-acre site was proclaimed a national monument in 1978 and established as a national park in 1980.

WHAT TO SEE & DO

Bird and wildlife viewing, boat touring, fishing, hiking, kayaking. **Facilities:** Information center (Memorial Day–Labor Day), trails. Bookstore. **Programs & Events:** Ranger-led walks (Memorial Day–Labor Day). **Tips & Hints:** Weather is usually overcast and cool in this maritime climate, and it rains often. May is the driest month, following months see increasing precipitation, and the wet, stormy fall begins in Sept. Expect summer daytime temperatures between 45°F and 70°F. Bring wool or synthetic clothing and sturdy rain gear, including pants, coat, and a hat. Stay on the glacier trail and off the ice. Commercial guides provide camping, fishing, and kayaking services. Get bear-resistant canisters at visitor center. Air charters provide flightseeing and fjord access. Boat tours and charters are available in Seward. In summer, boat tours ply the coast, observing calving glaciers, seabirds, and marine mammals. Boat charters offer overnight fjord trips and fishing trips to the fjords and Resurrection Bay. Busiest July and Aug., least crowded Nov.–Jan.

FOOD, LODGING & SUPPLIES

🏕 **Camping:** In the park: Exit Glacier (Exit Glacier Rd., 3 miles out of Seward; 12 sites; free), 3 backcountry coastline cabins ($50) in the fjords of Holgate Arm, Aialik Bay, and North Arm, accessible by boat, kayak, or small plane. 🏨 **Hotels:** None in park. In Seward: Hotel Seward (221 5th Ave., tel. 907/224–8001 or 800/440–2444, www.hotelsewardalaska. com; 61 rooms; $109–$279). ✕ **Restaurants:** None in park. In Seward: Ray's Waterfront (1316 4th Ave. on the harbor, tel. 907/224-5606, www. rayswaterfrontak.com; $9–$21). ⛄ **Groceries & Gear:** None in park. In Seward: Safeway (1907 Seward Hwy., tel. 907/224–6900).

FEES & HOURS

Free. Park open daily. Kenai Fjords Information Center open Memorial Day–Labor Day, daily 8:30–7. Park headquarters open weekdays 8–5.

HOW TO GET THERE

The park is 126 miles south of Anchorage on Seward Hwy. The park's headquarters and visitor center are in Seward's small harbor. Bus and commuter flight service link Seward and Anchorage. Ferries connect Seward with Homer and Seldovia via Kodiak and provide service to Valdez and Cordova. The Alaska Railroad serves Seward from Anchorage mid-May–mid-Sept. Exit Glacier can be reached in summer by car on an 8.6-mile paved road and a short trail. The Harding Icefield is accessible by air or trail. Air and boat charters provide access to the fjords.

CONTACTS

Kenai Fjords National Park (Box 1727, Seward, AK 99664, tel. 907/422–0500, fax 907/422–0571, www.nps.gov/kefj). Seward Chamber of Commerce (2001 Seward Hwy., Seward, AK 99664, tel. 907/224–8051, www.sewardchamber.org).

Klondike Gold Rush National Historical Park

In Skagway and in Seattle, WA

There are two separate parks under this name: one in Skagway, Alaska, and the other in Seattle, Washington. The park includes 15 restored historic buildings in Skagway, plus the Chilkoot and White Pass trails. Miners used the trails in 1897 and 1898 to reach the rich Yukon gold fields. Hikers can retrace the miners' footsteps on the Chilkoot Trail. The White Pass and Yukon Route Railway, constructed between 1898 and 1900, runs a train through the pass to Fraser, British Columbia, each summer. News of the gold strike in Canada's Yukon Territory spread from Seattle across the country, and most prospectors left for the northern gold fields from Seattle. Today, the Seattle park has a visitor center in the Pioneer Square Historic District, the center of gold-rush activity. The park was established on June 30, 1976.

WHAT TO SEE & DO

In Skagway: Hiking, ranger-led walks, sightseeing, touring the historic district. In Seattle: Gold-panning demonstration, ranger-led walks, touring Pioneer Square. **Facilities:** In Skagway: Visitor center and hiker information center (2nd Ave. and Broadway), exhibit area in the old Railroad Bldg. (2nd Ave.), Mascot Saloon (Broadway and 3rd Ave.), Moore House (5th Ave. and Spring St.), interpretive displays (town of Dyea), wayside exhibits (Alaska Marine Highway Ferry Terminal, Broadway). In Seattle: Visitor center, historic district. Bookstores at both units. **Programs & Events:** In Skagway: film (May–Sept., hourly), guided walking tours of historic district (May–Sept., five times daily), ranger-led tours of Dyea (June–Aug.), tours of Moore House (May–Sept). In Seattle: gold-panning demonstration (summer), movie, walking tour of Pioneer Square. **Tips & Hints:** In Skagway: Tours and buses pick up and drop off hikers at both ends of Chilkoot Trail. Go May and June for best weather, mid-July for blooms, Aug. for salmon run. In Seattle: Allow 2½ hours for exhibits, movies, and gold-panning demonstration in summer. Busiest June and July, least crowded Dec. and Jan.

FOOD, LODGING & SUPPLIES

🏕 **Camping:** In the park: Dyea Campground (10 miles north of Skagway, tel. 907/983–9200; 22 sites; pit toilets; $10). 🏨 **Hotels:** None in park. In Skagway: Sgt. Preston's Lodge (Broadway and 6th Ave., tel. 866/983–2521, sgtprestons.eskagway.com; 40 rooms; $90–$125). ✕ **Restaurants:** None in park. In Skagway: Skagway Fish Co. (on the waterfront, tel. 907/983–3474; $15–$20). ⛏ **Groceries & Gear:** None in park. In Skagway: Skagway True Value Hardware (400 Broadway, tel. 907/983–2233), Mountain Shop (355 4th St., tel. 907/983–2544).

FEES, HOURS & REGULATIONS

Skagway: Free. Moore House tour free. Backcountry permits required to hike the Chilkoot Trail (available from Trail Center, June–Aug.; call 800/661–0486). Alaska state fishing license required. No hunting on Chilkoot Trail. No motorized or mechanized equipment on trail. Pets must be on leash. Visitor center open May–Sept., daily 8–6. Trail Center open daily 8–5. Moore House open May–Sept., daily 10–5. Mascot Saloon exhibit open May–Sept., daily 8–6. Seattle: Free. Visitor center open daily 9–5.

HOW TO GET THERE

Skagway: 80 miles north of Juneau by air or water and 110 miles south of Whitehorse, Yukon (Canada), by road. Closest airport: Skagway. Seattle: From I–5 or I–90, exit on 4th Ave., make a left on Main St. Closest airport: SeaTac (10 miles).

CONTACTS

Skagway: Klondike Gold Rush National Historical Park (Box 517, Skagway, AK 99840, tel. 907/983–2921, fax 907/983–9249, www.nps.gov/klgo). Skagway Convention & Visitors Bureau (Box 1029, Skagway, AK 99840, tel. 907/983–2854, fax 907/983–3854, skagway.com). Seattle: Klondike Gold Rush National Historical Park (117 S. Main St., Seattle, WA 98104, tel. 206/553–7220, www.nps.gov/klse).

Kobuk Valley National Park

In northwestern Alaska, near Kotzebue

Located above the Arctic Circle, this 1.8-million-acre park preserves the central Kobuk River valley, the Great Kobuk Sand Dunes, and the Little Kobuk and Hunt River Dunes. Here are the northernmost limits of the boreal forest, as well as caribou, wolf, fox, and grizzly and black bear. The site was proclaimed a national monument in 1978 and redesignated in 1980.

WHAT TO SEE & DO

Backpacking, boating, canoeing, hiking, kayaking, rafting, wildlife watching. **Facilities:** Information center and park headquarters in Kotzebue. No facilities in park. Sales area. **Programs & Events:** Interpretive talks and demonstrations at information center (June–Aug.). Junior Ranger Program (June–Aug.). **Tips & Hints:** Prepare to be self-sufficient. Wear sturdy hiking boots and rubber boots for wet terrain. Expect occasional high winds throughout the year and short, cool, and sunny summers with 24 hours of daylight in June. Winters are long, dark, and extremely cold. Guard against hypothermia, giardiasis, wild animals, mosquitoes, and biting flies. Don't interfere with subsistence camps, fishnets, or other equipment. Respect property and privacy. Busiest July and Aug., least crowded Nov.–Jan.

FOOD, LODGING & SUPPLIES

None in park. See Cape Krusenstern National Monument.

FEES & HOURS

Free. Park open daily. Information center open mid-May–mid-Sept., daily 8–6.

HOW TO GET THERE

Kotzebue is 26 miles north of the Arctic Circle in northwest Alaska. Access to Kotzebue is by Alaska Airlines. To reach the park, air taxis and scheduled and charter flights are available. In summer, access is by nonmotorized watercraft and aircraft. In winter, access is by aircraft.

CONTACTS

Western Arctic National Parklands (Box 1029, Kotzebue, AK 99752, tel. 907/442–3890, www.nps.gov/kova).

Lake Clark National Park & Preserve

In southwestern Alaska, near Port Alsworth

Covering 4 million acres, this spectacular park and preserve stretches from the shores of Cook Inlet across the Chigmit Mountains to the tundra-covered hills of the western interior. The Chigmits, the junction of the Alaska and Aleutian ranges, are an awe-inspiring array of jagged mountains and glaciers that include Mt. Redoubt and Mt. Iliamna, two active volcanoes. The 50-mile-long Lake Clark and other waters in the park are vital salmon habitats for the Bristol Bay salmon fishery, one of the world's largest sockeye salmon-fishing grounds. Anglers find trophy fish; hikers explore high tundra slopes; river runners thrill to the Tlikakila, Mulchatna, or Chilikadrotna wild rivers; and campers find lakeshore sites inspirational. The site was proclaimed a national monument in 1978 and established as a national park and preserve in 1980.

WHAT TO SEE & DO

Backpacking, bird and wildlife viewing, fishing, flightseeing (charters, Port Alsworth, Kenai, Anchorage), hiking, hunting, kayaking, mountaineering, river running (rentals, Anchorage, Kenai, Port Alsworth). **Facilities:** Visitor center (Port Alsworth), backcountry patrol cabins (Telaquana Lake, Twin Lakes, Crescent Lake, and Chinitna Bay), trails. Book sales area, post office. **Programs & Events:** Multimedia shows and presentations (as staffing permits). **Tips & Hints:** Go in summer for best fishing, Sept. for fall colors. Prepare to be self-sufficient for backcountry travel. Stay away from game trails and fresh signs of bears. Bring extra food and cooking fuel. Expect 50–65°F temperatures June–Aug., with considerable precipitation. Plan for frost and snow as early as Aug. Plan for strong winds any time and winter temperatures to -40°F. Respect private property within park boundaries. Weather changes can delay scheduled pickup by aircraft by several days. Busiest June–Sept., least crowded Jan. and Feb.

FOOD, LODGING & SUPPLIES

🏕 **Camping:** Backcountry camping only. 🏨 **Hotels:** None in park. In Port Alsworth: The Farm Lodge (on the lake, tel. 907/781–2208 or 888/440–2281, www.thefarmlodge.com; 5 cabins; $290), Alaska's Back Country Inn (77 Paradise Pl., tel. 907/781–2239, www.alaskasbackcountryinn.com; 1 condo; $150 first person, $75 each additional). ✗ **Restaurants:** None in park. ⛄ **Groceries & Gear:** None in park.

FEES, HOURS & REGULATIONS

Free. No access via car. Alaska state fish and hunting licenses required. Hunting and trapping in preserve only. No gathering of plants or live

ALASKA

trees. Leashed pets only. Park and preserve open daily. Visitor center open June–Aug., Mon.–Sat., 8–5; Sept.–May, weekdays, 8–5.

HOW TO GET THERE

150 miles southwest of Anchorage on the west side of Cook Inlet and the north end of the Alaska Peninsula. Access to the Lake Clark region is by air only. A one- to two-hour flight from Anchorage, Kenai, or Homer provides access to most points within the park and preserve. Scheduled commercial flights between Anchorage and Iliamna, 30 miles outside the boundary, also provide access. Floatplanes may land on lakes. Wheeled planes land on open beaches, gravel bars, or private airstrips in or near the park.

CONTACT

Lake Clark National Park & Preserve (1 Park Pl., Port Alsworth, AK 99653, tel. 907/781–2218, www.nps.gov/lacl).

Noatak National Preserve

In northwestern Alaska, near Kotzebue

One of North America's largest mountain-ringed river basins with an unaltered ecosystem, the 5.8-million-acre Noatak is home to many Arctic plants and animals and offers superlative wilderness float-trip opportunities. The Noatak was proclaimed a national monument in 1978, established as a national preserve in 1980, and designated a Biosphere Reserve in 1976.

WHAT TO SEE & DO

Backpacking, boating, canoeing, hiking, hunting, rafting, wildlife watching. **Facilities:** Information center and park headquarters in Kotzebue. No facilities in park. **Programs & Events:** Interpretive talks and demonstrations at ranger station (June–Aug.). Junior Ranger Program (June–Aug.). **Tips & Hints:** Prepare to be self-sufficient. Wear sturdy hiking boots and rubber boots for wet terrain. Expect occasional high winds throughout the year; short, mild, cool, and sunny summers with 24 hours of daylight for one month; and long, severe, harsh, extremely cold winters with one hour of daylight by Dec. 1. Guard against hypothermia, giardia lamblia, wild animals, mosquitoes, and biting flies. Don't interfere with subsistence camps, fishnets, or other equipment. Respect property and privacy. Busiest July and Aug., least crowded Nov.–Jan.

FOOD, LODGING & SUPPLIES

None in park. See Cape Krusenstern National Monument.

FEES & HOURS

Park open daily. Northwest Arctic Heritage Center in Kotzebue open June–Sept., weekdays 8:30–6:30; Sat. 10:30–6:30; Oct.–May, Tues.–Fri., 9–noon and 1–6; Sat. noon–4.

HOW TO GET THERE

Kotzebue is 26 miles north of the Arctic Circle in northwest Alaska. Access to Kotzebue is by Alaska Airlines. To reach the park, air taxis and scheduled and charter flights are available. In summer, access is by motorized and nonmotorized watercraft, aircraft, and foot. In winter, access is by snowmobiles and aircraft.

CONTACTS

Western Arctic National Parklands (Box 1029, Kotzebue, AK 99752, tel. 907/442–3890, www.nps.gov/noat). Kotzebue Public Lands Information Center (Box 1029, Kotzebue, AK 99752, tel. 907/442–3760).

Sitka National Historical Park

In southeastern Alaska, near Sitka

Sitka was the cultural and political hub of Russian America in the early 19th century. In 1867, Russia ended its 126-year New World enterprise with the sale of Alaska to the United States for $7.2 million. The park was designated a national monument in 1910, making it the oldest and smallest federal park in Alaska. The temperate rain-forest park consists of the site of a fort that stood here in 1804, a sizable totem-pole collection, the cultural center, and the restored Russian Bishop's House, which was built in 1843. The 113-acre site was proclaimed in 1910 and designated a national historical park in 1972.

WHAT TO SEE & DO

Bird and wildlife viewing, picnicking, touring the restored Russian Bishop's House, viewing exhibits and salmon-spawning stream, walking, watching film and local artisans at work in the cultural center. **Facilities:** Visitor center, Russian Bishop's House, cultural center, trails, interpretive signs. Bookstore, picnic area. **Programs & Events:** Russian Bishop's House tours (May–Sept., daily; rest of year, by appointment), film (by request). Guided walks (June–Sept., depending on staff availability). **Tips & Hints:** Bring rain gear and rubber boots. Visit June–Aug. Busiest July and Aug., least crowded Dec. and Jan.

FOOD, LODGING & SUPPLIES

Camping: None in park. In Sitka: Starrigavan Recreation Area Campground (Halibut Point Rd., tel. 877/444–6777; 31 sites; $12–$30; pit toilets. **Hotels:** None in park. In Sitka: Westmark Sitka (330 Seward St., tel. 907/747–6241 or 800/544–0970, www.westmarkhotels.com; 105 rooms; $179–$199). **Restaurants:** None in park. In Sitka: Agave (236 Lincoln St., tel. 907/966–0702, www.agavesitka.com; $9–$12). **Gear:** None in park. In Sitka: The Work & Rugged Gear Store (407 Lincoln St., tel. 907/747–6238).

FEES, HOURS & REGULATIONS

Entrance fee: $4 for Russian Bishop's House. Free Oct.–Apr. Alaska state fishing license required. Leashed pets only. No bike riding. No camping. No fires. No motorized vehicles on trails. Park grounds open summer, daily 6 AM–10 PM; fall–spring, daily 7 AM–8 PM. Visitor center open May–Sept., daily 8–5; Oct.–Apr., Mon.–Sat. 8–5. Russian Bishop's House open May–Sept., daily 9–5; rest of year, by appointment.

HOW TO GET THERE

A 10- to 15-minute walk from downtown Sitka. The Bishop's House is downtown. Closest airport: Sitka (1½ miles).

CONTACTS

Sitka National Historical Park (103 Monastery St., Sitka, AK 99835, tel. 907/747–0110, fax 907/747–5938, www.nps.gov/sitk). Sitka Convention & Visitors Bureau (303 Lincoln St., Box 1226, Sitka, AK 99835, tel. 907/747–5940, fax 907/747–3739, www.sitka.org).

Wrangell–St. Elias National Park & Preserve

In southeastern Alaska

This 13.2-million-acre park and preserve, the largest in the United States and one of the largest protected roadless wilderness areas in the world, encompasses towering mountains, glaciers, meandering rivers, and volcanoes. Here the Chugach, Wrangell, St. Elias, and Alaska mountain ranges converge to form what is considered the "mountain kingdom of North America." The park and preserve contains the continent's largest assemblage of glaciers and greatest collection of peaks above 16,000 feet. Mt. St. Elias (18,008 feet) is the second-highest peak in the United States. The site was proclaimed a national monument in 1978, a World Heritage Site in 1979, and a park and preserve in 1980.

WHAT TO SEE & DO

Backpacking, fishing, flightseeing, hiking, hunting, kayaking, mountain biking, mountaineering, river floating, wildlife viewing. **Facilities:** Visitor centers (Copper Center, Kennicott); ranger stations at Yakutat, Slana, and Chitina; trails. Bookstore. **Programs & Events:** Multimedia program. Interpretive talks and hikes (June–Aug.). **Tips & Hints:** Thoroughly research your visit to the Wrangells. This is a vast expanse of rugged wilderness with few services. Develop map- and compass-reading skills for backcountry travel. Be prepared for unpredictable weather, potentially dangerous stream crossings, and grizzly and black bear encounters. Road access to park is via Nabesna and McCarthy roads, both gravel-surfaced. Take an air taxi to view the park's mountain wilderness. Visit mid-May–Sept. for best weather. Busiest July and Aug., least crowded Dec. and Jan.

FOOD, LODGING & SUPPLIES

⚠ **Camping:** Primitive campgrounds along McCarthy and Nabesna roads. Backcountry camping, including cabins, available elsewhere in the park. 🏨 **Hotels:** In the park: Kennicott Glacier Lodge (tel. 907/

258–2350; 35 rooms; $175–$269; closed mid-Sept.–mid-May), Mc-Carthy Lodge & Ma Johnson's Hotel (tel. 907/554–4402; 20 rooms; $149–$185; closed mid-Sept.–mid-May). ✗ **Restaurants:** In the park: Kennicott Glacier Lodge (tel. 907/554–4477; $8–$12; closed mid-Sept.–mid-May), Golden Saloon (tel. 907/554–4402; $12–$29; closed mid-Sept.–mid-May). ⛺ **Groceries & Gear:** In park: McCarthy Mercantile (no phone). In Glennallen: Sparks General Store (mile 189, Glenn Hwy., tel. 907/822–5990), Omni Parks Place (mile 187.5, Glenn Hwy., tel. 907/822–3334).

FEES, HOURS & REGULATIONS

Free. Alaska state fishing and hunting license required. ATVs in designated areas only, permit required. Park open daily. Visitor center open Labor Day–Memorial Day, weekdays 8–4:30; Memorial Day–Labor Day, daily 9–6. Ranger stations open Memorial Day–Labor Day, daily hours vary.

HOW TO GET THERE

The park visitor center is 199 miles east of Anchorage via Rte. 1, about 260 miles southeast of Fairbanks via Rtes. 2 and 4, and 105 miles north of Valdez via Rte. 4. Air service between Glennallen and Anchorage.

CONTACTS

Wrangell–St. Elias National Park & Preserve (Box 439, Copper Center, AK 99573, tel. 907/822–5234, fax 907/822–7216, www.nps.gov/wrst). Copper Valley Chamber of Commerce (Box 469, Glennallen, AK 99588, tel. 907/822–5555, www.coppervalleychamber.com).

Yukon-Charley Rivers National Preserve

In east-central Alaska, near Eagle

On the Canadian border in central Alaska, the 2.5-million-acre preserve protects 115 miles of the 1,800-mile Yukon River and the entire Charley River basin. Numerous rustic cabins and historic sites are reminders of the importance of the Yukon River during the 1898 gold rush. Peregrine falcons nest in bluffs overlooking the river, and the preserve's rolling hills are home to an array of wildlife. The Charley, a 106-mile-long wild river, is considered to be the most spectacular river in Alaska. The site was proclaimed a national monument in 1978 and established as a national preserve in 1980.

WHAT TO SEE & DO

Bird and wildlife viewing, exploring historic trapping, mining, and woodcutter sites, fishing, hunting, river running. **Facilities:** Eagle Visitor Center. Book and map sale area. **Programs & Events:** Video presentations. Yukon Quest dogsled race (Feb.). **Tips & Hints:** Be prepared to be self-sufficient. Winter temperatures are as low as -60°F, and summer highs can reach 90°F. Busiest June and Aug., least crowded Nov. and Dec.

FOOD, LODGING & SUPPLIES

🏕 **Camping:** In the park: 6 cabins along the Yukon River corridor at Nation Bluff, Glenn Creek, Coal Creek, Smith Creek, Washington Creek, and the Kandik River mouth, plus historic Slaven's Roadhouse at the mouth of Coal Creek. Backcountry camping allowed. 🏨 **Hotels:** None in park. In Eagle City: Falcon Inn Bed & Breakfast (220 Front St., tel. 907/547–2254, falconinn.mystarband.net; 5 rooms; $125–$145). ✖ **Restaurants:** None in park or nearby. 🛒 **Groceries & Gear:** None in park. In Eagle City: Eagle Trading Co. (36 Front St., tel. 907/547–2220).

FEES, HOURS & REGULATIONS

Free. Alaska state hunting and fishing license required. No artifact collecting. Preserve open daily. Eagle field office open weekdays 8–4:30. Visitor center open mid-May–mid-Sept., daily 8–4:30; mid-Sept.–mid-May, weekdays 8–4:30.

HOW TO GET THERE

The preserve is in east interior Alaska, 150 miles east of Fairbanks. Air taxis serve Eagle, located upriver, and Circle, downriver of the preserve. Eagle is at the end of Taylor Hwy., and Circle is on Steese Hwy. The preserve is reached by either river or air travel along the Yukon or by flying in to upper Charley River.

CONTACTS

Yukon-Charley Rivers National Preserve Headquarters (4175 Geist Rd., Fairbanks, AK 99709, tel. 907/457–5752, www.nps.gov/yuch). Yukon-Charley Rivers National Preserve Field Office (Box 167, Eagle, AK 99738-0167, tel. 907/547–2233).

See Also

Alatna Wild River, Aleutian World War II National Historic Area, Aniachak Wild River, Charley Wild River, Chilikadrotna Wild River, Iditarod National Historic Trail, John Wild River, Kobuk Wild River, Mulchatna Wild River, Noatak Wild River, North Fork of the Koyukuk Wild River, Salmon Wild River, Tinayguk Wild River, and Tlikakila Wild River, in Other National Parklands.

ARIZONA

Canyon de Chelly National Monument

In northeastern Arizona, near Chinle

At the base of sheer red cliffs and in caves inside canyon walls are ruins of Native American villages built between AD 350 and 1300. The monument presents southwestern Native American history from the earliest Pueblos to the Navajo who currently live and farm here. The monument was designated on April 1, 1931.

WHAT TO SEE & DO

Hiking, horseback riding, Jeep touring (rentals, Chinle), picnicking, pictograph viewing. **Facilities:** Visitor center, car and hiking trails. **Programs & Events:** Guided tours of canyon available year-round; ranger-led hikes and programs available Memorial Day–Labor Day. **Tips & Hints:** Beware of quicksand, deep dry sand, cliffs, loose rocks, and flash floods. Inner canyons impassable in winter and during and after heavy rains. Busiest May and Aug., least crowded Dec. and Jan.

FOOD, LODGING & SUPPLIES

Camping: In the park: Cottonwood Campground (near visitor center, tel. 928/674–2106; 93 sites; $10; flush toilets). **Hotels:** In the park: Thunderbird Lodge (Rte. 7, 3 miles east of U.S. 191, tel. 928/674–5841 or 928/674–5842; 73 rooms; $97–$114). In Chinle: Holiday Inn (Rte. 7, tel. 928/674–5000, www.holidayinn.com; 108 rooms; $105–$119). **Restaurants:** In the park: Thunderbird Lodge (Rte. 7, 3 miles east of U.S. 191, tel. 928/674–5841 or 800/679–2473; $15–$25). **Groceries:** None in park. In Chinle: Bashas' Market (U.S. 191 and Rte. 7, tel. 928/674–3465).

FEES, HOURS & REGULATIONS

Free. Driving along the canyon bottom and hiking within the canyon both require a Park Service permit (free) and an authorized Navajo guide ($15–$20 per hour), except for hikes along the 2½-mile White House Ruins Trail. Drive on paved roads only. No vehicles over 40 feet at park campground. Visitor center open daily 8–5.

HOW TO GET THERE

3 miles east of U.S. 191, near Chinle, via Exit 333 off I–40. Closest airports: Gallup, NM (98 miles), Albuquerque, NM (180 miles).

CONTACT

Canyon de Chelly National Monument (Box 588, Chinle, AZ 86503, tel. 928/674–5500, www.nps.gov/cach).

Casa Grande Ruins National Monument

In south-central Arizona, in Coolidge

Among the 60 prehistoric Native American sites preserved at Casa Grande Ruins National Monument, Casa Grande, the four-story caliche building built 650 years ago, is the most prominent. Its purpose in the Hohokam culture, which flourished for 1,000 years in the Sonoran Desert, has never been determined. The site was established as a federal reservation in 1892 and a national monument in 1918.

WHAT TO SEE & DO

Picnicking, touring archaeological sites. **Facilities:** Visitor center, museum, 80-person theater, observation platform, self-guided trail. Bookstore, covered picnic tables. **Programs & Events:** Slide presentations, interpretive programs (Nov.–Apr.). Archaeology tours for Arizona State Archaeology month (Mar.), American Indian Music and Arts Fest (Feb.), other special events scheduled Dec.–Apr. **Tips & Hints:** Summer temperatures can reach 115°F, and there's little shade. Go from mid-Oct.–early May for mild weather. Busiest Jan.–Mar., least crowded July and Aug.

FOOD, LODGING & SUPPLIES

⚠ **Camping:** None in park. Nearby: Picacho Peak State Park (Exit 219 off I–10, tel. 520/466–3183; 85 sites; $25; flush toilets, showers, hookups). 🏨 **Hotels:** None in park. In Florence: Holiday Inn Express (240 W. Hwy 287., tel. 520/868–9900, www.hiexpress.com; 90 rooms; $110–$160). ✕ **Restaurants:** None in park. In Florence: Old Pueblo Restaurant (505 S. Main St., tel. 520/868–4784; $7–$15). ⌂ **Groceries & Gear:** None in park. In Coolidge: Walmart (1695 N. Arizona Blvd., tel. 520/723–0945).

FEES, HOURS & REGULATIONS

Entrance fee: $5. Monument and visitor center open daily 9–5.

HOW TO GET THERE

On the north edge of the city of Coolidge, 60 miles southeast of Phoenix and 70 miles northwest of Tucson. Closest airport: Phoenix (50 miles).

CONTACTS

Casa Grande Ruins National Monument (1100 Ruins Dr., Coolidge, AZ 85228, tel. 520/723–3172, fax 520/723–7209, www.nps.gov/cagr). Coolidge Chamber of Commerce (320 W. Central Ave., Coolidge, AZ 85228, tel. 520/723–3009, www.coolidgechamber.org).

Chiricahua National Monument

In southeastern Arizona, near Willcox

A volcanic eruption 27 million years ago, 1,000 times greater than the eruption at Mt. St. Helens, laid down 2,000 feet of ash and pumice that fused into rock and later eroded into the huge balanced rocks, towering spires, and massive stone columns present in the monument today. Now the intersection of two deserts and two mountain ranges, Chiricahua's 12,000 acres represent one of the premier areas of biological diversity in the Northern Hemisphere. Also on-site is the Faraway Ranch, originally the homestead of Swedish immigrants and later a working cattle and guest ranch. The monument was proclaimed in 1924 and transferred to the Park Service in 1933.

WHAT TO SEE & DO

Auto touring, bird and wildlife viewing, hiking, picnicking, touring historic ranch. **Facilities:** Visitor center, hiking trails. **Programs & Events:** Interpretive walks, talks, evening programs, tours of Faraway Ranch house (Jan.–May, Sept.–Dec., times vary). **Tips & Hints:** Get food and gas in Willcox. Watch for rattlesnakes. Drive carefully on winding scenic road. Avoid rainy season (July–Sept.). Bring light clothing that you can layer in summer, when temperatures range from 50°F to 95°F each day, and warm clothing in winter, when temperatures range from 10°F to 60°F each day, with wind chills possibly below zero. Busiest Mar. and Apr., least crowded June and July.

FOOD, LODGING & SUPPLIES

Camping: In the park: Bonita Canyon (½ mile north of visitor center; 25 sites; $12; flush toilets). **Hotels:** None in park. In Pearce: Sunglow Ranch (14066 S. Sunglow Rd., tel. 520/824–3334 or 866/786–4569, www.sunglowranch.com; 11 rooms; $259–$395, including meals). **Restaurants:** None in park. In Willcox: Big Tex BBQ (130 E. Maley St., tel. 520/384–4423; $6–$10). **Groceries & Gear:** None in park. In Willcox: Safeway (650 N. Bisbee Ave., tel. 520/384–3952), Hometown IGA (510 N. Bisbee Ave., tel. 520/384–0159).

FEES & HOURS

Entrance fee: $5. Visitor center open daily 8–4:30.

HOW TO GET THERE

120 miles east of Tucson via Exit 340 (Willcox) off I–10, Rtes. 186 and 181. Closest airports: Tucson (120 miles), Phoenix (235 miles).

CONTACTS

Chiricahua National Monument (12856 E. Rhyolite Creek Rd., Willcox, AZ 85643, tel. 520/824–3560 Ext. 302, www.nps.gov/chir). Willcox Chamber of Commerce & Agriculture (1500 N. Circle I Rd., Willcox, AZ 85643, tel. 520/384–2995, www.willcoxchamber.com).

Coronado National Memorial

On United States–Mexico border, east of Nogales

The 4,750-acre memorial commemorates the first major exploration of the American Southwest by Europeans. The scenic overlook at Montezuma Pass offers sweeping views of the San Pedro River Valley, which is believed to have been the expedition route of Vasquez de Coronado in 1540. The natural environment typifies the "sky island" mountains of southeast Arizona, with desert grasslands and oak woodlands. Near the visitor center is a large limestone cave with stalactites, stalagmites, and flowstones; this is open to the public. The site was authorized as an International Memorial on August 18, 1941, and redesignated on November 5, 1952.

WHAT TO SEE & DO

Biking, bird-watching, caving, hiking, picnicking. **Facilities:** Visitor center, outdoor interpretive exhibits, hiking trails. Book and map sales, picnic tables. **Tips & Hints:** Go between spring and fall for best hiking. Busiest Feb. and Mar., least crowded July and Aug.

FOOD, LODGING & SUPPLIES

Camping: None in park. In Huachuca City: Tombstone Territories RV Resort (2111 E. Hwy. 82, tel. 877/316–6714, www.tombstoneterritories.com; 102 sites; $34–$38; hookups). **Hotels:** None in park. In Sierra Vista: Windemere Hotel & Conference Center (2047 S. Rte. 92, tel. 520/459–5900 or 800/825–4656, www.windemerehotel.com; 149 rooms; $60–$108). **Restaurants:** None in park. In Sierra Vista: Mesquite Tree Restaurant (S. Rte. 92 at Carr Canyon Rd., tel. 520/378–2758, www.mesquitetreesierravista.com; $10–$25). **Groceries & Gear:** None in park. In Sierra Vista: Big 5 Sporting Goods (135 S. Rte. 92, tel. 520/459–1801). In Hereford: Canyon General Minimart (S. Rte. 92, tel. 520/378–0223).

FEES, HOURS & REGULATIONS

Free. Flashlights (one per person, two if traveling alone) are required to visit Coronado Cave. No hunting. Pets on Crest Trail only. No bikes or motorized vehicles on trails. Memorial open daily dawn–dusk. Visitor center open daily 8–4.

HOW TO GET THERE

50 miles south of I–10 off Rte. 92. The turnoff from Rte. 92 onto Coronado Memorial Rd., which leads to E. Montezuma Canyon Rd., is 16 miles south of Sierra Vista and 21 miles west of Bisbee. Closest airports: Sierra Vista (20 miles), Tucson (95 miles), Phoenix (210 miles).

CONTACTS

Coronado National Memorial (4101 E. Montezuma Canyon Rd., Hereford, AZ 85615, tel. 520/366–5515 Ext. 2300, fax 520/366–5705, www.nps.gov/coro). Sierra Vista Convention & Visitors Bureau (3020 E. Tacoma St., Sierra Vista, AZ 85635, tel. 520/417–6960 or 800/288–3861, fax 520/417–4890, www.visitsierravista.com).

Fort Bowie
National Historic Site

In southeastern Arizona, near Bowie and Willcox

Fort Bowie commemorates the bitter conflict between the Chiricahua Apaches and the U.S. government. For more than 30 years Fort Bowie and Apache Pass were the focal points of military operations that culminated in the surrender of Geronimo in 1886 and the banishment of the Chiricahuas to Florida and Alabama. It was the site of the Bascom Affair, a wagon train massacre; and the Battle of Apache Pass, where a large force of Chiricahua Apaches under Mangus Coloradas and Cochise fought the California Volunteers. The remains of Fort Bowie, the adobe walls of post buildings, and the ruins of a Butterfield Stage Station are carefully preserved. The site was authorized in 1964 and established in 1972.

WHAT TO SEE & DO

Bird-watching, hiking, picnicking, touring fort ruins. **Facilities:** Visitor center, hiking trails. Bookstore, picnic tables. **Tips & Hints:** Plan at least a two-hour hike to fort and back. Busiest Mar. and Apr., least crowded June–Aug.

FOOD, LODGING & SUPPLIES

🏕 **Camping:** None in park. In Bowie: Mountain View RV Park (off Exit 362 at I–10, tel. 520/847–2510; 34 sites; $12–$28; flush toilets, showers, hookups). 🏨 **Hotels:** None in park. In Willcox: Muleshoe Ranch (6502 N. Muleshoe Ranch Rd., R.R. 1, Box 1542, tel. 520/212–4295; 5 units; $180–$195; closed June–late Sept.), Days Inn (724 N. Bisbee Ave., tel. 520/384–4222, www.daysinn.com; 73 rooms; $50). ✗ **Restaurants:** None in park. In Willcox: Big Tex BBQ (130 E. Maley St., tel. 520/384–4423; $6–$10). ⛏ **Gear:** None in park. In Willcox: Ace Hardware (914 W. Rex Allen Dr., tel. 520/384–4446).

FEES & HOURS

Free. Visitor center open daily 8–4:30. Ruins Trail open daily sunrise–sunset.

HOW TO GET THERE

116 miles east of Tucson and 227 miles southeast of Phoenix via I–10. From Willcox, off I–10, take Rte. 186 to the Fort Bowie turnoff, then drive 8 miles on unpaved road to Fort Bowie Trailhead. Closest airports: Tucson (116 miles), Phoenix (227 miles).

CONTACTS

Fort Bowie National Historic Site (3203 S. Old Fort Bowie Rd., Bowie, AZ 85605, tel. 520/847–2500, www.nps.gov/fobo).

Glen Canyon National Recreation Area

In northern Arizona, near Page, and southern Utah

The 1.2-million-acre recreation area lies in the midst of the country's most rugged canyon country and some of the most scenic backpacking country on the Colorado Plateau. Lake Powell, the second-largest man-made lake in the United States, stretches for 186 miles along the old Colorado River channel with a shoreline of 1,960 miles. The construction of the Glen Canyon Dam and the creation of Lake Powell were flashpoints for environmental preservation groups. The park is now a major draw for water sports and camping. It includes the world's largest natural bridge (Rainbow Bridge National Monument, in Utah); Lees Ferry, which contains two historic district properties; and the Orange Cliffs unit next to Canyonlands National Park in Utah. The recreation area is administered by the National Park Service, and was established on October 27, 1972.

WHAT TO SEE & DO

Backpacking, boating (rentals at park marinas, Page, AZ; Big Water and Ticaboo, UT), fishing, four-wheel driving, hiking, hunting, mountain biking, picnicking, swimming, waterskiing. **Facilities:** 3 visitor centers: Carl Hayden (Glen Canyon Dam on U.S. 89), Bullfrog (Rte. 276), and Navajo Bridge Interpretive Center (U.S. 89A, near Lees Ferry); beaches, outdoor interpretive exhibits, hiking trails, marinas. Book and map sales, gift shops, picnic tables. **Programs & Events:** Ranger programs (Memorial Day–Labor Day). **Tips & Hints:** Know and follow all boating-safety and water-quality regulations. Boats must be certified free of zebra mussels. Use of portable toilets is a must. Bring a hat and be prepared for little, if any, shade. Call or check park website to find out about the lake's water level. Busiest July and Aug., least crowded Jan. and Feb.

FOOD, LODGING & SUPPLIES

Camping: 4 campgrounds in the park: Bullfrog (78 sites; $43; flush toilets, hookups), Halls Crossing (64 sites; $43; flush toilets, hookups), Lees Ferry (54 sites; $12; pit toilets), Wahweap (250 sites; $13–$58; flush toilets, hookups). 2 primitive camping areas ($10; pit toilets; permit required for some sites), Lake Powell shoreline camping (free). **Hotels:** In the park: Lake Powell Resort (100 Lake Shore Dr., Page, tel. 888/896–3829; 350 rooms; $101–$159. Near the park: Debbie's Hideaway (119 8th Ave., Page, tel. 928/645–1224, www.debbieshideaway.com; 6 suites, 3 apartments; $99–$149). **Restaurants:** In the park: Rainbow Room (100 Lake Shore Dr., Page, tel. 888/896–3829). Near the park: Dam Bar & Grille (644 N. Navajo, Page, tel. 928/645–2161; $7–$25). **Groceries & Gear:** None in park. In Page: Lake Powell Waterworld (920 Hemlock, tel. 928/645–8845), Safeway (Lake Powell Blvd., tel. 928/645–2064), Stix Bait & Tackle (5 S. Lake Powell Blvd., tel. 928/645–2891).

FEES, HOURS & REGULATIONS

Entrance fee: $7 per person on foot, bicycle, or motorcycle; $15 per vehicle. Boat launch fee: $16 for first vessel, $8 for each additional vessel. Mountain bikes on established roads only. Backcountry camping permit required for Orange Cliffs district (available from Canyonlands National Park in Utah), and for Escalante district (available from Escalante Interagency Visitor Center). Arizona or Utah state fishing or hunting license required. Hunting allowed in restricted areas in season, license required. Leashed pets permitted in most areas. No pets at Rainbow Bridge. Park and roads open daily, except the Chains and Wahweap overlooks, which are open daylight hours only. Carl Hayden Visitor Center open daily 8–5. Bullfrog Visitor Center open intermittently May–Sept. Navajo Bridge Interpretive Center open mid-Apr.–Oct., daily 9–5, Nov.–early Apr., weekends 10–4.

HOW TO GET THERE

Glen Canyon Dam and the Wahweap Marina are near Page, AZ, on U.S. 89. North sections of the area, Bullfrog, Halls Crossing, and Hite and the Orange Cliffs may be reached from U.S. 95 and Rte. 276. Lees Ferry and the Navajo Bridge Interpretive Center are off U.S. 89A near Marble Canyon. Closest airports: Page (3 miles), Phoenix (275 miles).

CONTACTS

Glen Canyon National Recreation Area (Box 1507, Page, AZ 86040, tel. 928/608–6404, www.nps.gov/glca). Escalante Interagency Visitor Center (755 W. Main St., Escalante, UT 84726, tel. 435/826–5499, www.blm.gov).

Grand Canyon National Park

In northern Arizona, north of Flagstaff

One of the most spectacular examples of erosion anywhere in the world is the Grand Canyon, where the incomparable vistas have dazzled visitors for centuries. As it carves through the earth, the Colorado River opens an incomparable geologic record, from the 270-million-year-old limestone on the canyon rims to the metamorphic rock at the bottom of the gorge, estimated at 1.8 billion years old. The striated rock and towering buttes and mesas become saturated with color at sunrise and sunset. The canyon reaches a depth of nearly 6,000 feet, and the distance from the North Rim to the South Rim averages about a mile. Among the best hiking trails are Bright Angel, the Rim trail, and the North and South Kaibab trails. In addition to the awesome canyon and rock formations, the park encompasses ancient Native American ruins, a vintage railway between the town of Williams and the South Rim, photography studios, old copper mines, and plenty of designated lookout points. Grand Canyon Village, on the South Rim, has the fullest concentration of facilities, with a bank and ATM, post office, groceries, and supplies. The Grand Canyon was proclaimed as a forest preserve in 1893 and a game preserve in 1906, a national monument in 1908, transferred to the National Park Service and established as a national park in 1919, and declared a World Heritage Site in 1979.

WHAT TO SEE & DO

Air, bus, and car touring; biking (rentals); fishing; hiking; horseback riding; mule riding; rafting. **Facilities:** Grand Canyon Visitor Center (South Rim, west of Mather Point), Yavapai Geology Museum (5 miles north of South Rim park entrance), Desert View Visitor Center (eastern park entrance at South Rim), and North Rim Visitor Center (Bright Angel Peninsula, North Rim). North Rim Backcountry Information Center (in Administration Building) and South Rim Backcountry Information Center (near Parking Lot D). Tusayan Museum and Ruin (west of Desert View), guided tours, hiking trails, IMAX movie theater (Tusayan). Bookstores, gift shops, photo shop. **Programs & Events:** Ranger-led walks, talks, and evening programs; air tours; mule trips; horse rides; Kolb Studio art exhibits. Grand Canyon Field Institute seminars, backpacking trips, and river trips (Mar.–Nov.). Grand Canyon Music Festival (Aug.–Sept.). Check the *Guide* on arrival for schedule of additional activities and events. **Tips & Hints:** Plan several months ahead for lodging, backcountry permits, rafting trips, and mule trips. Download the Trip Planner at http://go.nps.gov/15gd82. Bring an extra set of car keys. Always carry water in your car. Keep your gas tank full. Use shuttle transportation within the park. Never feed animals. Don't hike alone, and avoid hiking during the hottest part of summer days. When hiking, pack light and always stay on the trail. Remember that hiking at high altitudes is exceptionally tiring. Do not try to hike down to the bottom of the canyon and back in one day. Do not attempt to swim in the Colorado River. Drink and eat frequently during outdoor activities. If you are going into the backcountry, you must follow the "leave no trace" principles. For the best photos, take pictures in the morning or late afternoon. Watch carefully for changing weather conditions. Be prepared for a variety of climates. Expect snow in winter and cool nights in summer at the South Rim (elevation approximately 7,000 feet) and snow almost any time of year at North Rim (elevation approximately 8,000 feet). In summer, inner canyon temperatures can reach 120°F on canyon floor. Avoid crowds by making a very early start. Expect crowds during winter holiday weekends, spring break, and all summer. Busiest June and July, least crowded Jan. and Feb.

FOOD, LODGING & SUPPLIES

🏕 **Camping:** 4 campgrounds in the park: Desert View (South Rim; 50 sites; $12; flush toilets; closed mid-Oct.–mid-May), Mather (South Rim; 313 sites; $18–$50; flush toilets, showers), North Rim (72 sites; $18–$25; flush toilets, showers; closed mid-Oct.–mid-May), Trailer Village (South Rim, tel. 303/297–2757 or 888/297–2757; 80 sites; $34.50; flush toilets, showers, hookups). Backcountry camping allowed (permit required). 🏨 **Hotels:** On the South Rim: Bright Angel Lodge (Grand Canyon Village, tel. 303/297–2757 or 888/297–2757; 30 rooms, 42 cabins; $49–$67, $84–$127 cabins), El Tovar Hotel (Grand Canyon Village, tel. 928/638–2631; 78 rooms; $123–$286), Kachina Lodge (Grand Canyon Village, tel. 303/297–2757 or 888/297–2757; 49 rooms; $173–$184), Maswik Lodge (Grand Canyon Village, tel. 303/297–2757 or 888/297–2757; 250 rooms, 28 cabins; $77–$119, $64 cabins), Phantom Ranch (Canyon floor, tel. 303/297–2757 or 888/297–2757; 4 dorms, 2 cabins; $45, $145 cabins), Thunderbird Lodge (Grand Canyon Village, tel. 303/297–2757 or 888/297–2757; 55 rooms; $173–$184), Yavapai Lodge (Grand Canyon Village, tel. 303/297–2757 or 888/297–2757; 358 rooms; $114–$163). On the North Rim: Grand Canyon Lodge (tel. 928/638–2611 or 877/386–4383; 44 rooms, 157 cabins; $116–$192; closed mid-Oct.–mid-May). ✕ **Restaurants:** On the South Rim: Arizona Room (Grand Canyon Village, tel. 928/638–2631; $12–$22), Bright Angel Restaurant (Grand Canyon Village, tel. 928/638–2631; $6–$14), El Tovar Dining Room (Grand Canyon Village, tel. 928/638–2631; $17–$25). On the North Rim: Grand Canyon Lodge (tel. 928/638–2611; $15–$24; closed mid-Oct.–mid-May). ⛟ **Groceries & Gear:** On the South Rim: Canyon Village Marketplace. On the North Rim: Camper store near campground.

FEES, HOURS & REGULATIONS

Entrance fee: $12 per person on foot, bicycle, or motorcycle; $25 per vehicle. Free shuttle service in Grand Canyon Village. Mule trips to Abyss Overlook: $122.81 (tel. 303/297–2757, 888/297–2757 reservations). Permit required for all backcountry camping ($10 for permit plus $5 per person per day, available from Backcountry Information Center, tel. 928/638–7875). No bikes on trails except for Greenway system on the South Rim. Arizona state fishing license required (Canyon Village Marketplace, South Rim). Pets must be leashed at all times and are not allowed below the canyon rim, in park lodgings, or on park buses. South Rim open year-round, daily. North Rim Rd. open mid-May–mid-Oct., daily. Grand Canyon Visitor Center and Yavapai Geology Museum open daily 8–5. Desert View Visitor Center open daily 9–5. North Rim Visitor Center open mid-May–mid-Oct., daily 8–6. North Rim Backcountry Information Center open mid-May–mid-Oct., 8–noon and 1–5. South Rim Backcountry Information Center open daily 8–noon and 1–5.

HOW TO GET THERE

Grand Canyon Village on the South Rim is 60 miles north of I–40 at Williams via U.S. 64 and 80 miles northwest of Flagstaff via U.S. 180. The North Rim is 44 miles south of Jacob Lake via Rte. 67. Train service (tel. 800/843–8724) is available from Williams. Free shuttles run from Tusayan to Grand Canyon Village in the summer. Taxis are available from Grand Canyon National Park Lodges, tel. 928/638–2822. Closest airports: Tusayan (8 miles), Flagstaff (80 miles), Phoenix (220 miles), Las Vegas, NV (291 miles).

CONTACTS

Grand Canyon National Park (Box 129, Grand Canyon, AZ 86023, tel. 928/638–7888, 877/444–6777 campground reservations, www.nps.gov/grca). Arizona Office of Tourism (2702 N. 3rd St., Suite 4015, Phoenix, AZ 85004, tel. 800/842–8257, www.arizonaguide.com). Flagstaff Convention & Visitors Bureau (211 W. Aspen Ave., Flagstaff, AZ 86001, tel. 928/774–9541, www.flagstaffarizona.org). Flagstaff Visitor Center (1 E. Rte. 66, Flagstaff, AZ 86001, tel. 928/774–9541 or 800/379–0065.

Grand Canyon Chamber of Commerce & Visitor's Bureau (Box 3007, Grand Canyon, AZ 86023, tel. 928/638–2901, grandcanyoncvb.org). Page–Lake Powell Chamber of Commerce (608 Elm St., Suite C, Box 727, Page, AZ 86040, tel. 928/645–2741, www.pagechamber.com). Williams Chamber of Commerce (200 W. Railroad Ave., Williams, AZ 86046, tel. 800/863–0546, www.williamschamber.com). Xanterra Parks & Resorts (6312 S. Fiddlers Green Cir., Suite 600 N, Greenwood Village, CO 80011, tel. 303/600–3400 or 888/297–2757, fax 303/600–3600, www.xanterra.com).

Hohokam Pima National Monument

In south-central Arizona, south of Phoenix

Preserved here are the archaeological remains of a Hohokam village that was occupied between AD 300 and AD 1100. Hohokam is a Pima Indian word meaning "those who have gone."

WHAT TO SEE & DO

The site is closed to the public.

CONTACT

Hohokam Pima National Monument (c/o Casa Grande Ruins National Monument, 1100 Ruins Dr., Coolidge, AZ 85228, tel. 520/723–3172, www.nps.gov/pima).

Hubbell Trading Post National Historic Site

In northeastern Arizona, near Ganado

This site within the Navajo Nation commemorates the distinctive role of the Native American trader in the American Southwest. The post has a preeminent place in the history and ethnography of the Navajo people. It still functions much the way Juan Lorenzo Hubbell operated it in the late 1800s and early 1900s and is internationally renowned for authentic and high-quality Native American arts. The site was designated a National Historic Site in 1965, and stewardship was transferred to the National Park Service in 1967.

WHAT TO SEE & DO

Buying arts and crafts, jewelry, and rugs; picnicking; touring the post and Hubbell homestead; watching Navajo weavers. **Facilities:** Visitor center, trading post, Hubbell homestead, Navajo-churro sheep. Bookstore, picnic tables. **Programs & Events:** Navajo culture talks, tours of the Hubbell family home. Native American Arts Auction (Apr. and Oct.), Luminaria Night (Dec.). **Tips & Hints:** Navajo Nation time is one hour later than time in the State of Arizona Apr.–Oct., because the Navajo Nation observes daylight saving time but the State of Arizona does not. Busiest June and July, least crowded Nov.–Feb.

FOOD, LODGING & SUPPLIES

Camping: None in park. Available in Canyon de Chelly National Monument. **Hotels:** None in park. In Chinle: Best Western Canyon de Chelly Inn (100 Main St., tel. 928/674–5874 or 800/327–0354, www.bestwestern.com; 104 rooms; $108–$120). **Restaurants:** None in park. In Ganado: Ramon's (Rte. 264, tel. 928/755–3404; $6–$13). **Groceries & Gear:** In the park: Hubbell Trading Post. In Ganado: Mustang Convenience Store (Hwy. 191, tel. 928/755–3261).

FEES & HOURS

Free. Visitor center open Oct.–Apr., daily 8–5; May–Sept., daily 8–6. Historic home tours $2.

HOW TO GET THERE

On Rte. 264, ½ mile west of Ganado. Closest airports: Gallup, NM (60 miles), Albuquerque, NM (180 miles), Phoenix (320 miles).

CONTACTS

Hubbell Trading Post National Historic Site (Box 150, Ganado, AZ 86505, tel. 928/755–3475, fax 928/755–3405, www.nps.gov/hutr). Gallup-McKinley County Visitor Information and Chamber of Commerce (103 W. U.S. 66, Gallup, NM 87301, tel. 505/722–2228, www.thegallupchamber.com).

Montezuma Castle National Monument

In central Arizona, near Camp Verde

Montezuma Castle is one of the best-preserved prehistoric structures in the Southwest. Despite the romantic name, it has no actual connection to Montezuma; it was dubbed this by early Western settlers who thought that the building was associated with the Aztec emperor. In fact, Sinagua farmers began building the five-story, 20-room dwelling in the 12th century. A detached unit of the monument, known as Montezuma Well, is a blue-green pool, a limestone sink that measures more than 350 feet across and supplied irrigation water to the prehistoric people. The monument was proclaimed in 1906.

WHAT TO SEE & DO

Hiking, picnicking, viewing the ancient dwelling and well. **Facilities:** Visitor center, interpretive trails. Book and map sales, picnic tables. **Programs & Events:** Ranger talks. **Tips & Hints:** Avoid summer heat. Go in spring or fall. Busiest Mar. and Apr., least crowded Dec. and Jan.

FOOD, LODGING & SUPPLIES

Camping: None at site. Near Cottonwood: Dead Horse Ranch State Park (off Rte. 89A, tel. 928/634–5283; azstateparks.com; 123

sites; $15–$25; flush toilets, showers, hookups). ☷ **Hotels:** None in park. In Camp Verde: Hotel at Cliff Castle (555 Middle Verde Rd., tel. 800/524–6343, www.cliffcastlecasinohotel.com; 82 rooms; $84–$104). ✕ **Restaurants:** None in park. In Camp Verde: The Gathering (Hotel at Cliff Castle, 555 Middle Verde Rd., tel. 800/524–6343; $6–$10). ⚑ **Groceries & Gear:** None in park. In Camp Verde: Bashas' Supermarket (650 W. Finnie Flat Rd., tel. 928/567–4585).

FEES, HOURS & REGULATIONS

Entrance fee: $5. Leashed pets only. Monument and visitor center open daily 8–5.

HOW TO GET THERE

3 miles north of Camp Verde on Montezuma Castle Hwy., off I–17. Closest airports: Flagstaff (50 miles), Phoenix (95 miles).

CONTACTS

Montezuma Castle National Monument (Box 219, Camp Verde, AZ 86322, tel. 928/567–3322, www.nps.gov/moca). Camp Verde Chamber of Commerce and Visitors Center (385 S. Main St., Camp Verde, AZ 86322, tel. 928/567–9294, www.visitcampverde.com).

Navajo National Monument

In northeastern Arizona, near Kayenta

Well-preserved cliff dwellings abandoned around AD 1300 by Pueblo peoples are the attractions in this park. Built and occupied for only 50 years, the cliff dwellings represent one of the final settlements of farmers who adapted to the area's scarce rainfall to grow crops, build houses, and raise families. Betatakin/Talastima and Keet Seel/Kawestima are among the cliff dwellings at the site. A designated overlook at the ruddy sandstone dwellings of Betatakin offers a terrific view. There are limited hiking opportunities to see Betatakin and Keet Seel close up. You can watch Navajo artisans at work in the visitor center. The monument was proclaimed on March 20, 1909.

WHAT TO SEE & DO

Hiking, picnicking, viewing ruins. **Facilities:** Visitor center, guided and self-guided tours, hiking trails. Arts and crafts store, bookstore, picnic tables. **Programs & Events:** Ranger-led tours (Memorial Day–Labor Day). **Tips & Hints:** Bring plenty of water. Get gas and food in Black Mesa. Busiest July and Aug., least crowded Jan. and Feb.

FOOD & LODGING

⚠ **Camping:** In the park: Sunset View Campground (near visitor center; 48 sites; free; flush toilets), Canyon View Campground (near visitor center; 14 sites; free). Backcountry camping available at Keet Seel (free permit required). ☷ **Hotels:** None in park. In Kayenta: Hampton Inn (U.S. 160, tel. 928/697–3170, www.hamptoninn.hilton.com; 73 rooms; $189). In Tuba City: Quality Inn (10 N. Main St., tel. 928/283–4545 or 800/644–8383, www.qualityinn.com; 80 rooms; $113–

$158). ✗ **Restaurants:** None in park. In Page: DC's Backyard BBQ (693 N. Navajo Dr., tel. 928/645–0075, www.dcsbackyardbbq.com; $9–$17), Slackers Quality Grub (635 Elm St., tel. 928/645-5267, www. slackersqualitygrub.com; $5–$10).

FEES, HOURS & REGULATIONS

Free. Access to Betatakin ruins by ranger-guided tour only. Back-country permits (free) required for hike to Keet Seel; permit covers overnight stay. Advance reservations required for Keet Seel (tel. 928/672–2700). Surrounding backcountry land is Navajo property and off limits to visitors. No collecting. No wood or charcoal fires. Camp stoves only. Visitor center open late May–mid-Sept., daily 8–6; mid-Sept.–late May., daily 9–5.

HOW TO GET THERE

The visitor center turnoff at Black Mesa on Rte. 564 is 50 miles north-east of Tuba City and 19 miles southwest of Kayenta off U.S. 160. Turn north on Rte. 564 and travel 9 miles to the visitor center. Closest air-ports: Page (88 miles), Phoenix (250 miles).

CONTACT

Navajo National Monument (Box 7717, Shonto, AZ 86054, tel. 928/672–2700, fax 928/672–2703, www.nps.gov/nava).

Organ Pipe Cactus National Monument

In southwestern Arizona, near Ajo

This monument gives you a rare chance to see the extraordinary plants and animals that can survive the extreme climate of the Sonoran Desert—including the namesake organ pipe cactus, a large cactus rarely found in the United States. These multi-armed cacti tend to grow on south-facing slopes, and you can see them from the scenic road that loops through the park. Gila monsters, rattlesnakes, and scorpions are among the creatures that have adapted to the region's extreme temperatures, intense sunlight, and infrequent rainfall. The monument was proclaimed in 1937 and designated a Biosphere Reserve in 1976.

WHAT TO SEE & DO

Backpacking, bird and wildlife viewing, car touring, hiking, mountain biking, picnicking. **Facilities:** Visitor center, self-guided nature trail. Bookstore, picnic tables. **Programs & Events:** Guided hikes, interpretive talks and evening programs. **Tips & Hints:** Beware of the cactus and six varieties of rattlesnakes, as well as Gila monsters and scorpions. Be prepared for desert walking. Carry a minimum of 1 gallon of drinking water per person per day. Best time to camp and hike is mid-Nov.–mid-Mar. Go mid-Mar.–mid-Apr. for flowers and Apr.–Sept. for migrating birds. Busiest Jan.–Mar., least crowded July and Aug.

FOOD, LODGING & SUPPLIES

Camping: 2 campgrounds in the park: Alamo (15 miles from visitor center; 4 sites; $8; pit toilets), Twin Peaks (2 miles from visitor center; 208 sites; $12; flush toilets). **Hotels:** None in park. In Ajo: Guest House Inn Bed & Breakfast (700 W. Guest House Rd., tel. 520/387-6133, www.guesthouseinn.biz; 4 rooms; $89), Marine Motel (1966 N. Ajo Gila Bend Hwy., tel. 520/387-7626, www.marinemotel.com; 21 rooms; $44–$61). **Restaurants:** None in park. In Ajo: Marcella's Restaurant (1117 W. Dorsey St., tel. 520/387–4139; $5–$10). **Groceries:** None in park. In Ajo: Olsen's Market (601 N. 2nd Ave., tel. 520/387–5641).

FEES, HOURS & REGULATIONS

Entrance fee: $4 per person on foot, bicycle, or motorcycle; $8 per vehicle. No collecting. No hunting. No off-road vehicles. No pets in backcountry; leashed pets elsewhere. Special trails marked for pet use. Mountain bikes on maintained roads only. Monument open daily. Visitor center open Jan.–Mar., daily 8–5; Apr.–Dec., daily 8:30–4:30; call to verify times.

HOW TO GET THERE

Monument headquarters is 22 miles south of Why via Rte. 85. Closest airports: Phoenix (115 miles), Tucson (150 miles).

CONTACTS

Organ Pipe Cactus National Monument (10 Organ Pipe Dr., Ajo, AZ 85321, tel. 520/387–6849, www.nps.gov/orpi). Ajo Chamber of Commerce (400 E. Taladro St., Ajo, AZ 85321, tel. 520/387–7742, www.ajochamber.com).

Petrified Forest National Park

In eastern Arizona, near Holbrook

Petrified Forest has one of the world's largest and most colorful concentrations of petrified wood. The wood was fossilized by mineral deposits, some now brightly colored: pink, deep red, yellow, orange, and white. It's scattered in logs and chunks, and the Agate House is built with petrified wood pieces. The park's approximately 134,000 acres include part of the multihued badlands of the Painted Desert, archaeological sites, and displays of fossils that are more than 200 million years old. Also here is a recovering remnant of "shortgrass prairie" and its inhabitants. The park was designated a national monument in 1906 and a national park in 1962.

WHAT TO SEE & DO

Backpacking, hiking, walking, wildlife viewing, scenic drives. **Facilities:** Painted Desert Visitor Center (Exit 311, off I–40), Painted Desert Inn National Historic Landmark, Rainbow Forest Museum, walking trails, interpretive signs. Gift shops, covered picnic tables. **Programs & Events:**

Ranger-led interpretive talks, walks, and hikes. Summer Solstice at Puerco Pueblo, a prehistoric solar calendar at work. **Tips & Hints:** Watch out for rattlesnakes and king snakes. Prepare for summer temperatures near 90°F, high elevation (5,000–6,234 feet), low humidity, and high winds, particularly in spring. The rainy season, mid-July–early Sept., is a dramatic time to visit, but beware of lightning storms. Visit in spring and fall. Busiest July and Aug., least crowded Dec. and Jan.

FOOD, LODGING & SUPPLIES

Camping: Backcountry camping only (permit required). **Hotels:** None in park. In Holbrook: Best Western Adobe Inn (615 W. Hopi Dr., tel. 928/524–3948 or 877/524–3948, www.bestwestern.com; 54 rooms; $72–$100). **Restaurants:** In the park: Painted Desert Oasis (North Entrance, tel. 928/524-3756; $6–$10). In Holbrook: El Rancho (867 Navajo Blvd., tel. 928/524–3332; $5–$10). **Groceries:** In the park: Painted Desert Oasis (North Entrance, tel. 928/524–3756).

FEES, HOURS & REGULATIONS

Entrance fee: $5 per person on foot, bicycle, or motorcycle, $10 per private vehicle. Backcountry permits required for overnight trips. Collecting strictly forbidden. Gift shops sell petrified wood that has been legally obtained from private land outside the park. Motorized vehicles and bicycles on paved roads only. No four-wheel-drive vehicles or mountain biking. No pets in buildings or in backcountry. Leashed pets permitted elsewhere in park, service animals allowed in buildings. Park, visitor center, and museum open mid-May–early Sept., daily 7–7; Sept.–May, daily 8–5. Park gates are locked at night.

HOW TO GET THERE

The park stretches between I–40 and U.S. 180 (Exit 285 at Holbrook). From the west, enter the south end of the park off U.S. 180. Travel through the park and exit at I–40 E. From the east, enter at Exit 311 off I–40. Travel through the park to U.S 180 on to Holbrook and I–40 W. The north entrance is 25 miles east of Holbrook on I–40. The south entrance is 19 miles east of Holbrook on U.S. 180. Closest airports: Holbrook (25 miles), Gallup, NM (72 miles), Flagstaff (119 miles), Albuquerque, NM (208 miles).

CONTACTS

Petrified Forest National Park (Box 2217, Petrified Forest, AZ 86028, tel. 928/524–6228, www.nps.gov/pefo). Holbrook Chamber of Commerce (100 E. Arizona St., Holbrook, AZ 86025, tel. 928/524–6558 or 800/524–2459, www.ci.holbrook.az.us).

Pipe Spring National Monument

In northern Arizona, near Fredonia

Pipe Spring's waters allow plant and animal life to thrive in this desert region north of the Grand Canyon. Beginning at least 1,000 years ago, ancestral Puebloans and later Paiutes hunted, gathered, and raised crops in the area. In 1871, Mormon pioneers built a fort, called Winsor Castle, over the main spring and established a cattle-ranching operation. The monument commemorates Western pioneer settlement and Native American–pioneer interactions on the frontier. Its museum includes exhibits on the history of the Kaibab Paiutes and Mormon pioneers. The monument was proclaimed on May 31, 1923.

WHAT TO SEE & DO

Hiking, touring fort and grounds. **Facilities:** Visitor center and museum, audio stations on grounds, ½-mile hiking trail. Bookstore and gift shop. **Programs & Events:** Ranger-guided tours of fort. Ranger talks (June–Sept., 2–3 times a day), cultural demonstrations (June–Sept., 3–6 times a week). **Tips & Hints:** Services in the area are scarce, so fill your gas tank as often as possible and carry water in your car. Go Mar. and Apr. or Sept. and Oct. for bird migrations, May and Sept. for flower blooms. Busiest July and Aug., least crowded Dec. and Jan.

FOOD, LODGING & SUPPLIES

Camping: None at site. Nearby: Kaibab Band of Paiute Indians Campground (off Rte. 389, tel. 928/643–7245; 40 sites; $5–$10; flush toilets, showers, hookups). **Hotels:** None in park. In Kanab, UT: Shilo Inn (296 W. 100 N on U.S. 89, tel. 435/644–2562 or 800/222–2244, www.shiloinns.com; 117 rooms; $69–$89). **Restaurants:** None in park. In Kanab, UT: Rocking V Café (97 Center St., tel. 435/644–8001, www.rockingvcafe.com; $9–$13). **Groceries & Gear:** None in park. In Kanab, UT: Glaziers Family Market (264 S. 100 E, tel. 435/644–5029), Willow Canyon Outdoor Company (263 S. 100 E, tel. 435/644–8884).

FEES, HOURS & REGULATIONS

Entrance fee: $5. No bikes or motorized vehicles. No pets in historic buildings. Leashed pets only on sidewalks. Monument and visitor center open June–Sept., daily 7–5; Sept.–May, daily 8–5.

HOW TO GET THERE

15 miles west of Fredonia, AZ, via Rte. 389; 60 miles east of Hurricane, UT, via Rte. 59 and Rte. 389. Closest airports: St. George, UT (65 miles), Las Vegas, NV (189 miles), Phoenix (357 miles).

CONTACTS

Pipe Spring National Monument (HC 65, Box 5, Fredonia, AZ 86022, tel. 928/643–7105, fax 928/643–7583, www.nps.gov/pisp). Kane County Travel Council (78 S. 100 E, Kanab, UT 84741, tel. 435/644–5033, www.kaneutah.com).

Saguaro National Park

In south-central Arizona, near Tucson

The saguaro cactus, which can grow 50 feet tall in a 200-year life span, was the primary reason for creating the park, which has districts on the west and east sides of Tucson. (The west side is smaller but more heavily visited.) But the park is home to many other wonders as well. More than 1,000 species of plant life dot the lower elevations of the 91,453-acre park. Douglas fir and Ponderosa pine are common in forests at 8,000 feet. Nearly 200 miles of hiking trails challenge visitors; you can also visit cactus gardens and drive or cycle along scenic loop routes. Numerous historic structures blend into the vistas, and ancient Hohokam petroglyphs abound in this predominantly wilderness park. The site was proclaimed a national monument in 1933 and redesignated a national park in 1994.

WHAT TO SEE & DO

Bicycling, hiking, scenic drives. **Facilities:** 2 visitor centers: East District (Old Spanish Trail at Freeman Rd., east of Tucson), Red Hills West District (Kinney Rd., west of Tucson); hiking trails. Bookstore, covered picnic tables. **Programs & Events:** Interpretive walks and talks. **Tips & Hints:** Bring plenty of water and sunscreen. Go late Mar.–early Apr. (usually) for desert plant blooms, Mar.–May for saguaro blooms. Busiest Nov.–Mar., least crowded June and July.

FOOD, LODGING & SUPPLIES

Camping: Backcountry camping area in Rincon Mountain District. Nearby: Colossal Cave Mountain Park (16721 E. Old Spanish Trail, tel. 520/647–7275, www.colossalcave.com; 57 sites; $3–$5; pit toilets), Tucson Mountain Park (Kinney Loop Rd., between Gate Pass Rd. and Arizona Sonora Desert Museum, tel. 520/877–6000, www.pima.gov; 135 sites; $10–$20; flush toilets, hookups). **Hotels:** None in park. In Tucson: White Stallion Ranch (9251 W. Twin Peaks Rd., tel. 520/297–0252 or 888/977–2624, www.whitestallion.com; 41 rooms; $143–$318). **Restaurants:** None in park. In Tucson: Wildflower Grill (7037 N. Oracle Rd., tel. 520/219–4230, www.foxrc.com/wildflower.html; $15–$23), Vivace (4310 N. Campbell Ave., tel. 520/795–7221, www.vivacetucson.com; $10–$33). **Gear:** None in park. In Tucson: REI (160 W. Wetmore Rd., tel. 520/887–1938).

FEES, HOURS & REGULATIONS

Entrance fee: $5 per person on foot or bicycle, $10 per vehicle. Backcountry permit ($6) required and available at East District Visitor Center. No pets on trails; leashed pets on roads. Both district roads open daily 7 AM–sunset. Visitor centers open daily 9–5.

HOW TO GET THERE

Reach East District and park headquarters from Tucson by driving east on Speedway, Broadway, or Old Spanish Trail; reach West District via Speedway Blvd. W. Closest airports: Tucson, Phoenix (115 miles).

CONTACTS

Saguaro National Park (3693 S. Old Spanish Trail, Tucson, AZ 85710, tel. 520/733–5153, fax 520/733–5183, www.nps.gov/sagu). Tucson Chamber of Commerce (465 W. St. Mary's Rd., Tucson, AZ 85701, tel. 520/792–1212, www.tucsonchamber.org).

Sunset Crater Volcano National Monument

In north-central Arizona, near Flagstaff

A volcano that erupted—between 1040 and 1100—when molten rock sprayed high into the air out of a crack in the ground, is protected here. Periodic eruptions formed a cinder cone 1,000 feet high, a dramatic black shape with a reddish rim. Lava that flowed from the base of the volcano appears now as a stark, jagged landscape. You can't hike into the crater, but you can follow a trail around the base, take a scenic loop drive, or climb another, smaller volcano nearby. The site was proclaimed a national monument in 1930 and transferred from the Forest Service in 1933.

WHAT TO SEE & DO

Hiking, picnicking, scenic drives, walking. **Facilities:** Visitor center and movie (2 miles east of U.S. 89 on Forest Rd. 545), interpretive exhibits, hiking trails, self-guided walks. Book and map sales area, picnic tables. **Programs & Events:** Ranger-guided walks, evening programs (Fri., Sat., and some weekdays, June–Aug.). **Tips & Hints:** Watch for razor-sharp lava when hiking. Wear closed, sturdy shoes. Drink water and reduce activity at high elevation (7,000 feet). Use caution on unpaved roads because vehicles can become stuck in soft cinders (in dry weather) or mud (during flash floods). Come June–Oct. for best weather. Busiest June and July, least crowded Jan. and Feb.

FOOD, LODGING & SUPPLIES

Camping: None at site. In Coconino National Forest: Bonito Campground (Rte. 545, off U.S. 89, 12 miles north of Flagstaff, tel. 928/526–0866; 43 sites; $18; flush toilets, pit toilets; closed mid-Oct.–Apr.). **Hotels:** None in park. In Flagstaff: Radisson Woodlands Plaza Hotel (1175 W. Rte. 66, tel. 928/773–8888 or 800/333–3333, www.radisson.com; 183 rooms; $189). **Restaurants:** None in park. In Flagstaff: Buster's Restaurant & Bar (1800 S. Milton Rd., tel. 928/774–5155, www.busters-restaurant.com; $7–$13), Café Express (16 N. San Francisco St., tel. 928/774–0541; $5–$9), Cottage Place (126 W. Cottage Ave., tel. 928/774–8431; $25–$30). **Groceries & Gear:** None in park. In Flagstaff: Fry's Food & Drug Store (201 N. Switzer Dr., tel. 928/774–2719), Peace Surplus (14 W. Rte. 66, tel. 928/779–4521).

FEES, HOURS & REGULATIONS

Entrance fee: $5 adults, free ages 15 and under. Sunset Crater Volcano closed to hiking but other nearby volcanoes can be climbed. No pets on trails; leashed pets only in parking lots and picnic areas. No bicycles or motorized equipment on hiking trails. No hunting. Park open daily sunrise–sunset. Visitor center open May–Oct., daily 8–5; Nov.–Apr., daily 9–5.

HOW TO GET THERE

Reach park from Flagstaff via U.S. 89 for 13 miles and Forest Rd. 545 for 2 miles. Closest airports: Flagstaff (15 miles), Phoenix (155 miles).

Sunset Crater Volcano National Monument (6400 N. Hwy. 89, Flagstaff, AZ 86004, tel. 928/526–0502, fax 928/714–0565, www.nps.gov/sucr). Flagstaff Convention & Visitors Bureau (1 E. Rte. 66, Flagstaff, AZ 86001, tel. 928/774–9541, www.flagstaffarizona.org). Flagstaff Visitor Center (1 E. Rte. 66, Flagstaff, AZ 86001, tel. 928/774–9541 or 800/842–7293).

Tonto National Monument

In south-central Arizona, near Globe

Well-preserved cliff dwellings here were occupied during the 13th and 14th centuries by the Salado culture, which farmed the Tonto Basin Valley. It's the only Salado site in the park system. The monument was proclaimed in 1907.

WHAT TO SEE & DO

Hiking to cliff dwellings, picnicking, touring museum. **Facilities:** Visitor center (1 mile off Rte. 188), hiking trails. Bookstore, covered picnic tables. **Programs & Events:** Upper Cliff Dwelling tours and guided hikes (Nov.–Apr.); Lower Cliff Dwelling interpretive talks, self-guided tours. Open House to Upper Cliff Dwelling (mid-Mar.). **Tips & Hints:** Make reservations in advance for Upper Cliff Dwelling tour. Watch out for snakes and cactus. Stay on trail. Visit Nov.–Apr. Busiest Jan.–Mar., least crowded June–Aug.

FOOD, LODGING & SUPPLIES

Camping: None at site. Schoolhouse Campground (Rte. 188, 24 miles from Globe, tel. 928/467–3200; 211 sites; $6; vault toilets). **Hotels:** None at site. In Globe: El Rey Motel (1201 E. Ash St., tel. 928/425-4427; 23 rooms; $36). **Restaurants:** None at monument. In Globe: Chalo's (902 E. Ash St., tel. 928/425–0515, www.chalosglobe.com; $5–$9). **Groceries & Gear:** None at site. In Payson: Bashas' Supermarket (142 E. U.S. 260, tel. 928/474–4495).

FEES, HOURS & REGULATIONS

Entrance fee: $3 per person. Reservations required for hiking to Upper Cliff Dwellings. No pets on Upper Cliff Dwelling trail. Leashed pets only at visitor center and Lower Cliff Dwelling trail. No hunting. No resource gathering. No fires. Park and visitor center open daily 8–5, Lower Cliff Dwelling trail open daily 8–4.

HOW TO GET THERE

30 miles northwest of Globe via Rte. 188; 55 miles south of Payson via Rte. 188; 83 miles northeast of Phoenix via U.S. 60 and Rte. 188. Closest airport: Phoenix (77 miles).

CONTACTS

Tonto National Monument (26260 N. Arizona Hwy. 188 #2, Roosevelt, AZ 85545, tel. 928/467–2241, fax 928/467–2225, www.nps.gov/tont). Globe-Miami Regional Chamber of Commerce (1360 N. Broad St.,

Globe, AZ 85501, tel. 928/425–4495, www.globemiamichamber.com).
Rim Country Regional Chamber of Commerce (100 W. Main St., Payson, AZ 85547, tel. 928/474–4515, www.rimcountrychamber.com).

Tumacácori National Historical Park

In southern Arizona, near Nogales

Tumacácori was first visited by a missionary, Father Eusebio Francisco Kino, in 1691; in 1751 Jesuit Catholic priests built a church here. At that time, Tumacácori was near the northern frontier of the Spanish colonial empire. The Jesuits, and later the Franciscans, attempted to convert the native population to Christianity and incorporate them into Spanish society. The conversion of these native people, known as the Pima, was only partly successful. The settlement was abandoned in 1848; now you will find the stabilized ruins of the Franciscan church, a garden, a cemetery, and other outbuildings. Tumacácori is also one of the ends of a 4.5-mile section of the Juan Bautista de Anza National Historic Trail, which links with Tubac Presidio State Historic Park on the route taken by Captain Juan Bautista de Anza on his founding expedition to San Francisco in 1775–76. The park was proclaimed a national monument in 1908 and redesignated a national historical park in 1990.

WHAT TO SEE & DO

Picnicking, self-guided and ranger-led tours of the church and other historic structures. **Facilities:** Visitor center, museum, hiking trail, outdoor interpretive signs. Bookstore, picnic tables. **Programs & Events:** Ranger-led tours, tours to missions San Cayetano de Calabazas and Los Santos Ángeles de Guevavi (Jan.–Mar.), crafts demonstrations such as tortilla, paper-flower, and pottery making (Oct.–Apr.). Fiesta (1st weekend, Dec.); Anza Day Reenactment Mass (Oct.). **Tips & Hints:** Allow two hours to see the park. Prepare for 100°F temperatures in summer and below-freezing temperatures on winter nights. Bring rain gear if visiting June–Sept. Busiest Jan.–Mar., least crowded June–Sept.

FOOD, LODGING & SUPPLIES

Hotels: None in park. In Amado: Amado Territory Inn (3001 E. Frontage Rd., tel. 520/398–8684, amadoinn.com; 9 rooms; $129–$139). **Restaurants:** None in park. In Tumacácori: Wisdom's Café (1931 E. Frontage Rd., tel. 520/398-2397, www.wisdomscafe.com; $6–$17; closed Sun.). In Rio Rico: San Cayetano Restaurant (Resort at Rio Rico, 1069 Camino Caralampi, tel. 520/281–1901, www.esplendor-resort.com; $20–$30). **Groceries & Gear:** None in park. In Carmen: The Carmen Store (2035 E. Frontage Rd., tel. 520/398–2760).

FEES, HOURS & REGULATIONS

Entrance fee: $3 adults, free ages 15 and under. No hunting, bicycling, or collecting historic or natural artifacts. Park open daily 9–5.

HOW TO GET THERE

Tumacácori is 45 miles south of Tucson and 18 miles north of the Mexican border in Nogales via Exit 29 or 34 off I–19. Closest airport: Tucson (45 miles).

CONTACT

Tumacácori National Historical Park (Box 8067, Tumacácori, AZ 85640, tel. 520/398–2341, www.nps.gov/tuma).

Tuzigoot National Monument

In central Arizona, near Cottonwood

Tuzigoot, an Apache word meaning "crooked water," is the remnant of a Sinagua village built between AD 1100 and AD 1400. The original pueblo was two stories high in places and had 77 ground-floor rooms. Although this site is not as well preserved as the dwellings at Montezuma Castle (see separate listing), it's larger in scope. Exhibits in the visitor center tell the story of Sinagua culture through artifacts excavated on site. Designated hiking trails take you into and atop the pueblo. The monument was proclaimed on July 25, 1939.

WHAT TO SEE & DO

Bird-watching, hiking, viewing pueblo. **Facilities:** Visitor center, hiking trails. Book sale area. **Programs & Events:** Interpretive programs. **Tips & Hints:** Visit in spring and fall. Busiest Mar. and Apr., least crowded Dec. and Jan.

FOOD, LODGING & SUPPLIES

Camping: None at site. See Montezuma Castle National Monument. **Hotels:** None at monument. In Cottonwood: Pines Motel (920 S. Camino Real, tel. 928/634–9975, www.azpinesmotel.com; 14 rooms; $60–$80). **Restaurants:** None at monument. In Cottonwood: Nic's Italian Steak & Crab House (925 N. Main St., tel. 928/634–9626, nicsaz.com; $8–$27). **Groceries:** None at monument. In Cottonwood: Safeway (1635 E. Cottonwood La., tel. 928/634–3711).

FEES, HOURS & REGULATIONS

Entrance fee: $5. Leashed pets only. Visitor center and monument open daily 8–5.

HOW TO GET THERE

2 miles east of Clarkdale along Historic Rte. 89A and 50 miles south of Flagstaff via Rte. 89A. Closest airports: Flagstaff (50 miles), Phoenix (110 miles).

CONTACTS

Tuzigoot National Monument (Box 219, Camp Verde, AZ 86322, tel. 928/634–5564, www.nps.gov/tuzi). Cottonwood Chamber of Commerce (1010 S. Main St., Cottonwood, AZ 86326, tel. 928/634–7593, www.cottonwoodchamberaz.org).

Walnut Canyon National Monument

In north-central Arizona, near Flagstaff

Cliff dwellings built by the Sinagua people between 1100 and 1250 are preserved in this monument. Using existing limestone alcoves, the Native Americans built side and front walls, and nature provided the roof overhang. At this site, you can enter some of the ruins, getting an incomparable feel for life centuries ago. The presence of water at the time the Sinagua lived in the canyon probably made this a very desirable place to live. The Sinagua (Spanish for "without water") were dryland farmers who grew crops on the canyon rims and supplemented their diet by hunting and gathering. Their departure around 1250 is a subject of speculation, but archaeologists think that Hopi people who live on mesas in northern Arizona today are probably the descendants of the Sinagua. The park was proclaimed on November 30, 1915.

WHAT TO SEE & DO

Hiking, picnicking, touring cliff dwellings. **Facilities:** Visitor center, self-guided interpretive trails, interpretive exhibits. Bookstore, picnic tables. **Programs & Events:** Ranger-guided hikes, interpretive talks (June–Sept.). **Tips & Hints:** The Island Trail may be strenuous: it descends 240 steps at an elevation of 6,800 feet. Strollers aren't allowed on Island Trail. Limited parking space for large vehicles. Busiest June and July, least crowded Dec. and Jan.

FOOD, LODGING & SUPPLIES

None at monument. See Sunset Crater Volcano National Monument for Flagstaff listings.

FEES, HOURS & REGULATIONS

Entrance fee: $5, free ages 16 and under. No pets on trails or in visitor center. Reservations required for ranger-guided tours. No hunting or firearms. No open fires. Gas stoves only. No collecting potsherds, rocks, pinecones, flowers. Park and visitor center open May–Oct., daily 8–5; Nov.–Apr., daily 9–5.

HOW TO GET THERE

10 miles east of Flagstaff, off I–40 via Exit 204. Closest airports: Flagstaff (10 miles), Phoenix (155 miles).

CONTACTS

Walnut Canyon National Monument (6400 N. Hwy. 89, Flagstaff, AZ 86004, tel. 928/526–3367, fax 928/527–0246, www.nps.gov/waca). Flagstaff Convention & Visitors Bureau (211 W. Aspen Ave., Flagstaff, AZ 86001, tel. 928/774–9541, www.flagstaffarizona.org). Flagstaff Visitor Center (1 E. Rte. 66, Flagstaff, AZ 86001, tel. 928/774–9541 or 800/379–0065).

Wupatki National Monument

In north-central Arizona, near Flagstaff

The monument preserves the ruins of red sandstone pueblos built about 1100 by Ancestral Puebloans—including Wupatki, the largest and most influential pueblo in the region at the time. Wupatki had nearly 100 rooms and was originally three stories tall. Next to this main pueblo is a blowhole, a fissure where air is forced in or out according to atmospheric pressure; this may have had spiritual significance for the early inhabitants. Near Wupatki are a few smaller pueblos: Lomaki, Wukoki, and Citadel, easily reached by walking. Made from slabs of sandstone, limestone, and basalt and held together with clay-based mortar, the dwellings were inhabited until about 1250. The modern Hopi are believed to be partly descended from these people. The monument was proclaimed on December 9, 1924.

WHAT TO SEE & DO

Picnicking, self-guided walking to four sites. **Facilities:** Visitor center, interpretive exhibits. Book and map sale area, picnic tables. **Programs & Events:** Discovery hikes (Nov.–Mar., Sat. for 3–4 hours). **Tips & Hints:** Busiest Apr. and May, least crowded Dec.–Feb.

FOOD, LODGING & SUPPLIES

None at site. See Sunset Crater Volcano National Monument for Flagstaff listings.

FEES, HOURS & REGULATIONS

Entrance fee: $5 adults, free ages 15 and under. No pets or bikes on trails. No off-trail hiking. Monument open daily sunrise–sunset. Visitor center open daily 9–5.

HOW TO GET THERE

40 miles north of Flagstaff via U.S. 89 and Forest Rd. 545, a 35-mile loop road that connects Wupatki with Sunset Crater Volcano National Monument. Closest airports: Flagstaff (46 miles), Phoenix (190 miles).

CONTACTS

Wupatki National Monument (6400 N. Hwy. 89, Flagstaff, AZ 86004, tel. 928/679–2365, fax 928/679–2349, www.nps.gov/wupa). Flagstaff Convention & Visitors Bureau (211 W. Aspen Ave., Flagstaff, AZ 86001, tel. 928/774–9541, www.flagstaffarizona.org). Flagstaff Visitor Center (1 E. Rte. 66, Flagstaff, AZ 86001, tel. 928/774–9541 or 800/379–0065).

See Also

Lake Mead National Recreation Area, Nevada. *Juan Bautista de Anza National Historic Trail,* in Other National Parklands.

ARKANSAS

Arkansas Post National Memorial

In southeastern Arkansas, near Gillett

This memorial on the banks of the Arkansas River commemorates the site's complex history as the earliest semi-permanent French settlement in the Lower Mississippi River valley, which began when Henri de Tonti established the "Poste de Arkansea" in 1686 at a Quapaw village near the confluence of the Mississippi and Arkansas Rivers. After a century of struggle among the French, Spanish, and English for control of interior North America, the United States bought the area in 1803 from the French as part of the Louisiana Purchase. The post thrived in the first half of the 19th century, serving as territorial capital of Arkansas from 1819 to 1821. After the relocation of the capital to Little Rock in 1821, the post community fell into decline. Many of the remaining structures were destroyed by the U.S. Army and Navy attack on the Confederate fort on January 11, 1863. Activities include fishing, watching wildlife, and exploring remnants of the town site and Civil War earthworks. The memorial was authorized on July 6, 1960.

WHAT TO SEE & DO

Bird and wildlife viewing, fishing, hiking, picnicking, touring museum. **Facilities:** Visitor center, orientation film, hiking trails, outdoor interpretive exhibits. Bookstore, picnic tables with fire grills. **Programs & Events:** Self-guided tours of town site and nature trails. Special events, living-history programs and demonstrations. **Tips & Hints:** Watch for alligators. The park is extremely hot and humid in summer; drink plenty of water and wear insect repellent. Busiest May and June, least crowded Nov. and Dec.

FOOD, LODGING & SUPPLIES

⛺ **Camping:** None at memorial. In Dumas: Pendleton Bend Campground (426 Rte. 212, tel. 877/444–6777, www.recreation.gov; 31 sites; $16–$19; flush toilets, showers, hookups), Wilber D. Mills Campground (599 Rte. 212, tel. 877/444–6777, www.reserveamerica.com; 21 sites; $16; flush toilets, showers, hookups). In Tichnor: Merrisach Lake Campground (148 Merrisach La., tel. 877/444–6777, www.recreation. gov; 67 sites; $11–$19; flush toilets, showers, hookups). 🏨 **Hotels:** None at memorial. In Dumas: Days Inn (501 U.S. 65 S, tel. 870/382–4449, www.daysinn.com; 53 rooms; $61). ✗ **Restaurants:** None at memorial. In Gillett: Rice Paddy (4379 U.S. 165 S, tel. 870/548–2223; $7). ⛁ **Groceries & Gear:** None at memorial. In Dewitt: Marty Mart (207 S. Whitehead Dr., tel. 870/946–2936).

FEES, HOURS & REGULATIONS

Free. Arkansas state fishing license required. No hunting. Fires in grills only. Leashed pets only. Park open daily 8–dark. Visitor center open daily 8–5.

HOW TO GET THERE

On Rte. 169, 9 miles south of Gillett via U.S. 165 (Great River Rd.); 17 miles northeast of Dumas via U.S. 165. Closest airport: Little Rock (100 miles).

CONTACT

Arkansas Post National Memorial (1741 Old Post Rd., Gillett, AR 72055, tel. 870/548–2207, fax 870/548–2431, www.nps.gov/arpo).

Buffalo National River

In north-central Arkansas, near Harrison

Totaling about 95,700 acres, this area encompasses 135 miles of the 150-mile-long Buffalo River, which begins as a trickle in the Boston Mountains, 15 miles above the park boundary. Following what is likely an ancient riverbed, the Buffalo cuts its way through massive limestone and sandstone bluffs and travels east through the Ozarks and into the White River. It's a terrific place to go canoeing and kayaking. The national river has three designated wilderness areas totaling 36,000 acres within its boundaries. It was authorized on March 1, 1972.

WHAT TO SEE & DO

Canoeing (rentals), fishing, hiking, horseback riding, picnicking, swimming. **Facilities:** Tyler Bend Visitor Center (Middle District, 11 miles north of Marshall on U.S. 65); 2 ranger stations: Pruitt Upper District Ranger Station (5 miles north of Jasper on Rte. 7) and Buffalo Point Ranger Station (17 miles south of Yellville on Rtes. 14 and 268); more than 100 miles of trails. Bookstores, picnic tables. **Programs & Events:** Ranger-led hikes, canoe trips, and evening programs (Memorial Day–Labor Day). **Tips & Hints:** Allow an hour for visitor center. Bring a wet suit if you plan to canoe Dec.–Feb., rain gear Mar.–May, shorts and T-shirts June–Aug. For best floating, go to Upper District Mar.–May, to Middle District May and June, and to Lower District June–Aug. Water levels vary greatly with the weather. Check river conditions with visitor center before canoeing. Park busiest June and July, least crowded Jan. and Feb.

FOOD, LODGING & SUPPLIES

Camping: 15 campgrounds in the park (280 sites; $10–$30; some flush toilets, some vault toilets, some showers, some hookups). **Hotels:** In the park: Buffalo Point Cabins (tel. 870/439–2812; 12 cabins; $75–$100). In Harrison: Quality Inn (1210 U.S. 62/65 N, tel. 870/ 741–7676, www.qualityinn.com; 93 rooms; $80–$105). In Jasper: Cliff House Inn & Restaurant (Scenic 7 Byway, tel. 870/446–2292, www. cliffhouseinnar.com; 5 rooms; $80–$98). In Yellville: Eagle's Nest

Lodge (Rte. 235, tel. 870/449–5050, www.eaglesnestlodgeyellville.com; 20 rooms; $59–$105). ✗ **Restaurants:** None in park. In Jasper: Cliff House Inn & Restaurant (Scenic 7 Byway, tel. 870/446–2292, www. cliffhouseinnar.com; $8–$27; no dinner). ⌁ **Groceries & Gear:** None in park. In Jasper: Bob's Supermarket (Rte. 7 S, tel. 870/446–2381).

FEES, HOURS & REGULATIONS

Free. Park open daily. Tyler Bend Visitor Center open daily 8–5. Park headquarters open weekdays 8–4:30. Pruitt Upper Station open Feb.– Sept., hours vary. Buffalo Point Ranger Station open daily 8:30–4:30.

HOW TO GET THERE

Middle District: U.S. 65 south from Harrison for 31 miles; Upper District: Rte. 7 or 43 from Harrison; Lower District: U.S. 65 south out of Harrison 5 miles, then U.S. 62/412 east and Rte. 14 south. Closest airports: Harrison (31 miles), Fayetteville (80 miles), Springfield, MO (80 miles), Little Rock (150 miles).

CONTACTS

Buffalo National River Headquarters (402 N. Walnut St., Suite 136, Harrison, AR 72601, tel. 870/365–2700, www.nps.gov/buff). Tyler Bend Visitor Center (2322 Tyler Bend Rd., St. Joe, AR 72675, tel. 870/ 439–2502). Harrison Chamber of Commerce (621 E. Rush, Harrison, AR 72601, tel. 870/741–2659, www.harrison-chamber.com). Jasper/ Newton County Chamber of Commerce (204 N. Spring St., Jasper, AR 72641, tel. 870/446–2455, www.theozarkmountains.com). Yellville Chamber of Commerce (Box 369, Yellville, AR 72687, tel. 870/449– 4676, www.yellville.com).

Fort Smith National Historic Site

In downtown Fort Smith, in western Arkansas, on the Oklahoma border

The site commemorates a significant phase of America's westward expansion and stands as a reminder of 80 turbulent years in the history of federal Indian policy. It includes the remains of two frontier forts and the 19th-century federal court of the Western District of Arkansas and the Indian Territory. Its visitor center is in a former barracks, courthouse, and jail. The first Fort Smith was established on December 25, 1817, by the U.S. Rifle Regiment to maintain peace between local Osage Indians and emigrating Cherokees. The second version, which stood from 1838 to 1871, was a focal point of regional Civil War operations; afterward, it became the seat of a federal court. Judge Isaac Parker, known as the "Hanging Judge," served here; he was given the moniker for putting 79 men to death during his tenure. You can see the restored courtroom, jail cells, and gallows, as well as a commissary storehouse. Fort Smith is also tied to the Trail of Tears, as countless Native Americans passed through here after being forced from their ancestral lands in the east. The site was authorized on September 13, 1961.

WHAT TO SEE & DO

Bird-watching, touring historic buildings, walking river trail with wayside exhibits. **Facilities:** Visitor center, walking trails, indoor and outdoor interpretive exhibits. Bookstore. **Programs & Events:** Daily interpretive talks at 11 and 2, guided tours of courtroom, jail, and gallows (by reservation), children's programs, living-history programs, artillery and musket demonstrations. **Tips & Hints:** Nooses are hung on the gallows on the anniversaries of executions conducted here 1873–1896. Busiest June and July, least crowded Dec. and Jan.

FOOD, LODGING & SUPPLIES

Hotels: None at site. In Fort Smith: Holiday Inn (700 Rogers Ave., tel. 479/783–1000, www.holidayinn.com; 255 rooms; $144–$169). **Restaurants:** None at site. In Fort Smith: Hamburger Barn (317 Garrison Ave., tel. 479/782–0233, www.thehamburgerbarn.com; $7–$15), Varsity Grill Restaurant (318 Garrison Ave., tel. 479/494–7173; $7–$20). **Groceries & Gear:** None at site. In Fort Smith: Point Liquor & Convenience Store (1116 Grand Ave., tel. 479/783–1600), Harps Marketplace (3100 Grand Ave., tel. 479/783–3690).

FEES & HOURS

Entrance fee: $4, free ages 15 and under. Visitor center open daily 9–5.

HOW TO GET THERE

On Rogers or Garrison Ave., turn south at 4th St. Turn right onto Garland Ave. On the next block is the main parking lot. Closest airport: Fort Smith (8 miles).

CONTACTS

Fort Smith National Historic Site (301 Parker Ave., Fort Smith, AR 72901, tel. 479/783–3961, fax 479/783–5307, www.nps.gov/fosm). Fort Smith Convention & Visitors Bureau (2 N. B St., Fort Smith, AR 72901, tel. 800/637–1477, www.fortsmith.org).

Hot Springs National Park

In west-central Arkansas, in Hot Springs

The park's 47 hot springs, which lack the sulfur odor and taste of many hot springs, are at the heart of a great social and medical resort. In its heyday, between 1890 and 1950, the park's eight monumental bathhouses catered to crowds of health seekers. Today the park preserves the finest collection of historic bathhouses in the United States. Approximately 700,000 gallons of natural thermal water still flow out of the mountainside and into the beautifully landscaped Bathhouse Row area each day. Much of the water is still supplied to traditional bathhouses, jug fountains, hotels, and the Levi Hospital. Hot Springs Reservation was set aside on April 20, 1832; dedicated to public use as a park on June 16, 1880; and redesignated a national park on March 4, 1921.

WHAT TO SEE & DO

Bicycling (rentals in Hot Springs), climbing observation tower, hiking, fishing, picnicking, scenic drives, taking thermal baths, touring historic Fordyce Bathhouse. **Facilities:** Visitor center (Fordyce Bathhouse, 369 Central Ave.), hiking trails, interpretive signs. Book-and-gift shop, picnic tables with fire grills. **Programs & Events:** Guided tours of Fordyce Bathhouse. Thermal springs tours (May–Sept.), special programs and hikes. Constitution Week (Sept. 17–23). **Tips & Hints:** Go in Apr. for dogwood blooms and spring warbler migration, May–July for magnolias, Oct. and Nov. for fall colors. Busiest June and July, least crowded Jan. and Feb.

FOOD, LODGING & SUPPLIES

Camping: In the park: Gulpha Gorge (off U.S. Hwy. 70B; 40 sites; $10–$24; hookups, flush toilets). **Hotels:** None in park. In Hot Springs: Arlington Hotel (239 Central St., tel. 501/623–7771, www.arlingtonhotel.com; 460 rooms; $75–$90), Austin Hotel (305 Malvern Ave., tel. 501/623–6600, www.theaustinhotel.com; 200 rooms; $90–$230). **Groceries & Gear:** Walmart (4019 Central Ave., tel. 501/525–3457).

FEES, HOURS & REGULATIONS

Free. Thermal water bathing $30–$76 at Buckstaff Bathhouse (509 Central Ave., tel. 501/623-2308, www.buckstaffbaths.com) and $18–$45 at Quapaw Baths and Spa (413 Central Ave., tel. 501/609–9822, www.quapawbaths.com). Physical therapy using thermal water available outside park at Levi Hospital (300 Prospect Ave., Hot Springs, tel. 501/624–1281). Hot Springs Mountain Tower, $8. Arkansas state fishing license required (available at local Walmarts). No vehicles or bicycles on sidewalks and trails. No vehicles over 30 feet on Hot Springs Mountain Dr. No hunting. Do not remove or disturb any plant, animal, rock, or other object. Leashed pets only. Service animals only in visitor center. Park open daily. Visitor center open daily 9–5.

HOW TO GET THERE

From I–30, take U.S. 70 or U.S. 270 to the city of Hot Springs, which adjoins the park. Park visitor center is on Central Ave., along Bathhouse Row. Closest airports: Hot Springs (4 miles), Little Rock (55 miles).

CONTACTS

Hot Springs National Park (101 Reserve St., Hot Springs, AR 71901, tel. 501/620–6715, fax 501/624–3458, www.nps.gov/hosp). Hot Springs Convention & Visitors Bureau (134 Convention Blvd., Hot Springs, AR 79101, tel. 800/543–2284, www.hotsprings.org).

Little Rock Central High School National Historic Site

In central Arkansas, in Little Rock

Little Rock Central High School, now a National Historic Site, is an emblem of the often-violent struggle over school desegregation and represents the federal government's commitment to eliminating separate systems of education for blacks and whites. The site honors nine black students, known as the Little Rock Nine, who were the first African Americans to attend this high school, initiating public school desegregation in 1957. The governor of Arkansas tried to stymie integration; federal troops had to be posted at the school to enforce the law and protect the Nine, who endured continual harassment. Central is the only operating high school in the nation to be designated a national historic site; it has a commemorative garden. The site was designated on November 6, 1998.

WHAT TO SEE & DO

Touring the school, viewing exhibits. **Facilities:** Central High National Historic Site Visitor Center, audiovisual presentations. Book-and-gift shop. **Programs & Events:** Guided tours of visitor center and high school (reservations required).

FOOD, LODGING & SUPPLIES

Hotels: None at site. In Little Rock: Doubletree Hotel (424 W. Markham, tel. 501/372–4371 or 800/222–8733, www.doubletree.hilton. com; 288 rooms; $109–$169), Peabody Hotel (200 W. Markham, tel. 800/732–2639, www.peabodylittlerock.com; 396 rooms; $169–$229). ✗ **Restaurants:** None at site. In Little Rock: Sonny Williams' Steak Room (500 President Clinton Ave., Suite 100, tel. 501/324–2999, www. sonnywilliamssteakroom.com; $16–$50; closed Sun.).

FEES, HOURS & REGULATIONS

Free. No pets. Site open daily, 9–4:30.

HOW TO GET THERE

Take I–630 to Martin Luther King Dr. exit, go left on Martin Luther King Dr., then right on Daisy L. Gatson Bates Dr. Site is at the intersection of Park St. Closest airport: Little Rock (7 miles).

CONTACTS

Central High School National Historic Site (2120 Daisy L. Gatson Bates Dr., Little Rock, AR 72205, tel. 501/374–1957, www.nps.gov/ chsc). Little Rock Convention & Visitors Bureau (426 W. Markham, Little Rock, AR 72201, tel. 501/376–4781, www.littlerock.com).

Pea Ridge National Military Park

In northwestern Arkansas, near Rogers

The 4,300-acre park represents one of the best-preserved Civil War battlefields in the country. The March 7–8, 1862, battle, which pitted Major General Earl Van Dorn's 13,000 Confederates against 10,250 Union soldiers under Brigadier General Samuel Curtis, saved Missouri for the Union. The Confederate force included 800 Cherokees, and one-third of the Union army was made up of German immigrants recruited near St. Louis. The park includes a reconstruction of Elkhorn Tavern, site of bitter fighting on both days. The park also includes a 2½-mile segment of the Trail of Tears, the route used by the Cherokees between 1838 and 1839 when they were forcibly moved from their homeland to the Indian Territories of Oklahoma and Arkansas. The site was authorized on July 20, 1956.

WHAT TO SEE & DO

Hiking, horseback riding, picnicking, scenic drive, touring museum, wildlife viewing. **Facilities:** Visitor center, 7-mile tour road, 11-mile horse trail, 10-mile hiking trail. Bookstore, picnic tables. **Programs & Events:** Living-history demonstrations and education programs (summer weekends as staffing permits), tours of Elkhorn Tavern (Memorial Day–Labor Day as staffing permits). Battle anniversary (weekend nearest Mar. 7–8). **Tips & Hints:** Busiest May–July, least crowded Jan. and Feb.

FOOD, LODGING & SUPPLIES

Camping: None at site. In Rogers: Beaver Lake Hide-A-Way Campground (8369 Campground Circle, tel. 479/925–1333, www.beaverlakehideaway.com; 89 sites; $14–$22; flush toilets, showers, hookups). **Hotels:** None in park. In Eureka Springs: Best Western (101 E. Van Buren, tel. 479/253–9551 or 800/221–3344, www.bestwestern.com; 85 rooms; $90–$117). In Rogers: Beaver Lake Lodge (14733 Dutchman Dr., tel. 479/925–2313, www.beaverlake.com/beaverlakelodge; 26 rooms; $79). **Restaurants:** None in park. In Eureka Springs: Bubba's Barbecue (166 W. Van Buren, tel. 479/253–7706, www.bubbasbarbecueeurekasprings.com; $5–$23; closed Sun.), Forest Hill Restaurant (3016 E. Van Buren St., tel. 479/253–2422, www.foresthillrestaurant.com; $7–$16). Near Rogers: Bean Palace (11045 War Eagle Rd., tel. 479/789–5343 Ext. 307, www.wareaglemill.com; $4–$7; no dinner, closed Mon.–Thurs. in Jan. and Feb.). **Groceries & Gear:** Walmart (406 S. Walton Blvd., tel. 479/273–0060).

FEES, HOURS & REGULATIONS

Entrance fee: $10 per vehicle; $5 per person ages 15 and older. No recreational sports. No hunting or trapping. Park and visitor center open daily 8–5, 9–4 in winter. Road open daily 8–5.

HOW TO GET THERE

80 miles southwest of Springfield, MO, via U.S. 60, Rte. 37, and U.S. 62; 90 miles northeast of Fort Smith, AR, via I–44, I–540, U.S. 71, and U.S. 62 east; and 120 miles east of Tulsa, OK, via the Cherokee Turnpike and U.S. 412, U.S. 71, and U.S. 62 east. Closest airports: Bentonville, AR (25 miles), Springfield, MO (82 miles).

CONTACTS

Pea Ridge National Military Park (15930 Hwy. 62, Garfield, AR 72732, tel. 479/451–8122, fax 479/451–0219, www.nps.gov/peri). Greater Eureka Springs Chamber of Commerce & Visitor Information Center (516 Village Circle Dr., Eureka Springs, AR 72632, tel. 479/253–8737, www.eurekaspringschamber.com). Rogers–Lowell Area Chamber of Commerce (317 W. Walnut St., Rogers, AR 72756, tel. 479/636–1240, www.rogerslowell.com).

See Also

Trail of Tears National Historic Trail, in Other National Parklands.

President William Jefferson Clinton Birthplace National Historic Site

In southwest Arkansas, northeast of Texarkana

William Jefferson Clinton, the 42nd president of the United States, was born to Virginia Blythe on August 19, 1946, and named after his father, who died before his birth. Today his modest Hope, Arkansas, boyhood home, where he learned many of the early lessons that defined his life and presidency, is preserved. Former President Clinton spoke during the dedication ceremonies on April 16, 2011.

WHAT TO SEE & DO

Biking with rangers through historic sites in Hope, touring the boyhood home and grounds, viewing exhibits in the visitor center. **Facilities:** Visitor center, boyhood home. Bookstore. **Programs & Events:** Guided tours every 30 minutes. Park rangers lead 4-mile bicycle tour of Clinton-related sites in Hope (late May-June, weekends 10–noon; tel. 870/777-4455; participants must supply their own bikes and helmets). **Tips & Hints:** Begin your visit at the park visitor center, where you can view exhibits and learn more about President Clinton's early life in Hope. Go July–Aug. for the best weather; visit Dec. and Jan. to avoid crowds.

FOOD, LODGING & SUPPLIES

⚠ **Camping:** None at site. In Hope: Hope Village Inn & RV Park (2611 N. Hazel St., tel. 870/777–4665; 32 sites, $15–$20; flush toilets, showers, hookups). ⛺ **Hotels:** None in park. In Hope: Holiday Inn Express (2600 N. Hervey St., tel. 870/722-6262, www.hiexpress.com; 61 rooms; $105–$115). ✗ **Restaurants:** None in park. In Hope: Dos Loco Gringos (2406 N. Hervey St., tel. 870/777-3377; $5–$22). ⛳ **Groceries & Gear:** None in park. In Hope: Super 1 Foods (909 N. Hervey St., tel. 870/777-5001).

FEES, HOURS, & REGULATIONS

Free. No unleashed pets. Park and visitor center open daily 9–4:30.

HOW TO GET THERE

President Clinton's Birthplace Home is in Hope, 30 miles northeast of Texarkana off I-30, and 110 miles southwest of Little Rock. Take I–30 Exit 30 and travel south on State Hwy. 278 for about 2 miles. The park is at 2nd and S. Hervey Sts. Closest airport: Texarkana (30 miles)

CONTACTS

President William Jefferson Clinton Birthplace Home (117 S. Hervey St., Hope, AR 71801, tel. 870/777-4455, www.nps.gov/wicl). Hope-Hempstead County Chamber of Commerce (204 S. Main St., Hope, AR 71801, tel. 870/777-3640, fax 870/722-6154, www. hopechamberofcommerce.com).

CALIFORNIA

Cabrillo National Monument

In southwestern California, in San Diego

The site commemorates Juan Rodríguez Cabrillo's 1542–43 expedition, the first European exploration of the West Coast of the United States. The park is home to the Old Point Loma Lighthouse, one of the first lighthouses built on the West Coast, and remnants of coastal defense structures from World War II. It also preserves a beautiful landscape of tide pools and coastal sage scrub (among the most endangered in the world). The view of San Diego from the site is said to be the finest harbor view in the nation. It's a great place to whale-watch, too. There are several permanent exhibits, including the reconstructed interior of the 1880s lighthouse, photos and film footage shot during World War II displayed in a former army radio building, and films on Cabrillo, the tide pools, and the Pacific gray whale in the visitor center. The site was established on October 14, 1913.

WHAT TO SEE & DO

Bird and wildlife viewing, exploring tide pools, hiking, whale-watching. **Facilities:** Visitor center with outdoor interpretive exhibits, movies, hiking trail. Bookstore. **Programs & Events:** Ranger-guided tours, lighthouse programs, and frequent costumed interpretive programs available year-round. Gray whale talks and watching (Dec.–Feb.), wildflower walks (Feb.–Apr.), tide pool walks (Nov.–May). Whale Watch Weekend with speakers, films, whale programs, children's programs (Jan.). **Tips & Hints:** Go in winter for clearest weather, Dec.–Feb. for whale migration. Bring binoculars for whale-watching. For the best look at tide pools, go on winter afternoons during full and new moon periods for extreme low tides. Wear shoes with good traction, particularly on the tide pools. Stay on hiking trails and beware of rattlesnakes. Keep away from the cliff edges, as they are very unstable. Busiest Mar.–Aug., least crowded Oct.–Jan.

FEES, HOURS & REGULATIONS

Entrance fee: $3 per person on foot, bicycle, or motorcycle; $5 per vehicle; free ages 15 and under. Pets may be taken to tide pools when leashed. No bikes on trails or sidewalks. No swimming, surfing, or diving. Park and visitor center open daily 9–5.

HOW TO GET THERE

10 miles from downtown San Diego; from I–8 or I–5, take the Rosecrans Ave. exit. Drive south on Rosecrans, head west on Cañon St., then south to end of Catalina Blvd. Closest airport: San Diego (8 miles).

CONTACTS

Cabrillo National Monument (1800 Cabrillo Memorial Dr., San Diego, CA 92106, tel. 619/557–5450, fax 619/226–6311, www.nps.gov/cabr). San Diego Convention & Visitors Bureau (750B St., Suite 1500, San Diego, CA 92101, tel. 619/236–1212, www.sandiego.org).

Channel Islands National Park

Off the southern coast, in the Santa Barbara Channel

In this park are five islands (Anacapa, Santa Barbara, Santa Cruz, Santa Rosa, and San Miguel) and 125,000 acres of submerged lands that provide habitat for marine life, from microscopic plankton to Earth's largest creature—the blue whale. Like the Galapagos Islands, the Channel Islands have nurtured unique plant and animal species. It's an exceptional place for kayaking, bird-watching, and diving; you can also see the remnants of Chumash life and visit one of the largest known sea caves, named the Painted Cave for its colorful lichen and algae. You can get a taste of the islands without even leaving the mainland by stopping by the visitor center in Ventura, which has a film, marine life exhibits, an observation tower, and a tide pool. In addition, Channel Islands Live lets visitors to the center interact with rangers on virtual dives and hikes; the programs are also available on the Internet. The park was proclaimed a national monument April 26, 1938, and designated a Biosphere Reserve in 1976 and a national park on March 5, 1980.

WHAT TO SEE & DO

Bird-watching, boating, camping, diving, fishing (license required), hiking, kayaking, picnicking, snorkeling, swimming, whale-watching. **Facilities:** Mainland visitor center at Ventura (1901 Spinnaker Dr.), 3 others on Anacapa, Santa Barbara, and Santa Cruz islands, hiking trails. Book and map sales (Ventura), picnic tables. **Programs & Events:** Ranger programs (weekends 11 and 3), guided walks (daily, times vary), interactive programs (Memorial Day–Labor Day, Wed. and Sat. at 2). **Tips & Hints:** Be prepared for high winds; wear shoes with sturdy, nonslip soles. Bring binoculars for whale- or bird-watching. Visit Jan.–Mar. to see migrating gray whales, in spring to see wildflowers. Busiest July and Aug., least crowded Oct.–Dec.

FOOD, LODGING & SUPPLIES

△ **Camping:** 6 campgrounds in the park: Anacapa Island (7 sites; $15; pit toilets), Del Norte (Santa Cruz Island; 4 sites; $15; pit toilets), San Miguel Island (9 sites; $15; pit toilets), Santa Barbara Island (10 sites; $15; pit toilets), Santa Rosa Island (15 sites; $15; pit toilets), Scorpion Valley (Santa Cruz Island; 25 sites, $15; 6 group sites, $40; pit toilets). ⊡ **Hotels:** None in park. In Ventura: Clocktower Inn (181 E. Santa Clara St., tel. 805/652–0141, www.clocktowerinn.com; 49 rooms; $89–$99). ✕ **Restaurants:** None in park. In Ventura: Anacapa Brewing Co. (472 E. Main St., tel. 805/643–2337, anacapabrewing.com; $7–$15).

⚖ **Groceries:** None in park. In Ventura: Vons Market (2433 Harbor Blvd., tel. 805/642–6761), Village Market at the Marina (1559 Spinnaker Dr., tel. 805/644–2970).

FEES, HOURS & REGULATIONS

Free. Boat landing permits, required for private land on Santa Cruz Island, available from the Nature Conservancy (tel. 805/898–1642). No pets. No mountain bikes. Park open daily. Visitor centers open daily 8:30–5.

HOW TO GET THERE

The park is off the Santa Barbara/Ventura coastline. Closest park island is 11 miles and farthest is 55 miles from visitor center at Ventura. Transportation available through boat and airplane concessionaires. Private boats permitted. Closest airports: Oxnard (5 miles), Santa Barbara (30 miles), Los Angeles (70 miles).

CONTACTS

Channel Islands National Park (1901 Spinnaker Dr., Ventura, CA 93001, tel. 805/658–5730, fax 805/658–5799, www.nps.gov/chis). Ventura Visitors & Convention Bureau (101 S. California St., Ventura, CA 93001, tel. 805/648–2075, www.ventura-usa.com).

Death Valley National Park

In eastern California, in Death Valley

Despite the severity of Death Valley's geology and desert climate, more than 1,000 species of plants and 98 species of animals live within the park's boundaries. Also in the park, which experiences hotter temperatures than any other place in the world, are snow-covered peaks, rugged canyons, and beautiful sand dunes. In extremely wet years, perhaps once a decade, wildflowers come into bloom, a striking sight in such a landscape. This is the country's largest national park outside Alaska; you can reach some of the most spectacular areas only by taking a four-wheel-drive vehicle. Badwater Basin is the lowest point in North America, at 282 feet below sea level. In addition to the incredible natural sights—the volcanic deposits of Artists Palette, the salt flats and giant sand dunes, Ubehebe Crater, the salt pinnacles of the Devil's Golf Course—there are some man-made sights, such as the Harmony Borax Works and the 1920s Moorish mansion called Scotty's Castle. The center of activity in the park is Furnace Creek Village, where you'll find the visitor center; the other accommodations within the park are at Stovepipe Wells Village. Despite the punishing temperatures, the park draws a wave of mostly European travelers in July and August. The park was proclaimed a national monument in 1933 and redesignated a national park in 1994. It was designated a part of the Colorado and Mojave Desert Biosphere Reserve in 1984.

WHAT TO SEE & DO

Bicycling, bird-watching, hiking, horseback riding, picnicking, scenic drives. **Facilities:** Furance Creek Visitor Center (Rte. 190), ranger station (Stovepipe Wells), Borax Museum (Furnace Creek Ranch), hiking trails, wayside exhibits. Book and map sales area, gift shop, picnic tables. **Programs & Events:** Guided tours of Scotty's Castle (year-round). Ranger-guided talks, evening slide programs (Nov.–Apr.). 49ers Encampment (2nd week, Nov.). **Tips & Hints:** Always check on weather conditions before hiking or driving. Be prepared for extremely hot temperatures Apr.–Oct. Flash floods are a risk; watch for water running in washes and across road dips. Do not hike in lower elevations in hot weather. Always carry plenty of water in the car and on hikes. When no trail is available, hike on the hardest, most durable surfaces. Beware of rattlesnakes, scorpions, and black widow spiders. Do not enter any mines. Note that cell phones do not work in all areas of the park. Dress warmly when visiting the mountains in winter. Best time to visit: Oct.–Apr. Visit Mar. and Apr. for wildflowers, May–Oct. to hike Telescope Peak. Busiest Feb.–mid-Apr. and Nov., least crowded Dec. and Jan.

FOOD, LODGING & SUPPLIES

⚠ **Camping:** 9 campgrounds in the park: Emigrant (8 miles south of Stovepipe Wells Village; 10 sites; free; flush toilets), Furnace Creek (near Furnace Creek Visitor Center; 136 sites; $12–$18; flush toilets), Mahogany Flat (Emigrant Canyon Rd.; 10 sites; free; pit toilets; closed Dec.–Feb.), Mesquite Spring (near Grapevine Ranger Station; 30 sites; $12; flush toilets), Stovepipe Wells (near Stovepipe Wells Village; 190 sites; $12; flush toilets; closed late Apr.–mid-Oct.), Sunset (Rte. 190, near Airport Rd.; 290 sites; $12; flush toilets; closed late Apr.–mid-Oct.), Texas Spring (near Furnace Creek Visitor Center; 92 sites; $14; flush toilets; closed late Apr.–mid-Oct.), Thorndike (Emigrant Canyon Rd.; 6 sites; free; pit toilets; closed Dec.–Feb.), Wildrose (Emigrant Canyon Rd.; 23 sites; free; flush toilets). Backcountry camping (permit required). 🏨 **Hotels:** In the park: Inn at Furnace Creek (Rte. 190, tel. 760/786–2345; 66 rooms; $340–$470; closed mid-May–mid-Oct.), Ranch at Furnace Creek (Rte. 190, tel. 760/786–2345; 224 rooms; $134–$219), Panamint Springs Resort (Rte. 190, tel. 775/482–7680; 15 rooms; $79–$149), Stovepipe Wells Village (Rte. 190, tel. 760/786–2387; 83 rooms; $98–$160). ✗ **Restaurants:** In the park: Inn at Furnace Creek Dining Room (tel. 760/786–3385; $6–$12; closed mid-May–mid-Oct.), 49er Cafe (tel. 760/786–2345; $7–$10; closed mid-May–mid-Oct.), Panamint Springs Restaurant (tel. 775/482–7680; $8.50–$25), Stovepipe Wells Toll Road Restaurant (tel. 760/786–2387; $10–$20). ᗡ **Groceries & Gear:** In the park: Furnace Creek Ranch General Store (Rte. 190, tel. 760/786–2381).

FEES, HOURS & REGULATIONS

Entrance fee: $10 per person on foot, bicycle, or motorcycle; $20 per vehicle. Guided tours of Scotty's Castle $15. Permits required for backcountry camping (free). No collecting or disturbing natural, historical, or archaeological features. Don't feed or disturb wildlife. All vehicles, including motorcycles, trail bikes, bicycles, and four-wheel drives, must remain on established roads. No hunting or firearm use. Leashed pets only. No pets on trails or in wilderness. Park open daily. Visitor center open daily 8–5.

HOW TO GET THERE

From U.S. 395, take Rte. 190, 136, or 178. From U.S. 95, take Rte. 267, 373, or 374. From I–15, take Rte. 127 at Baker to Rte. 178 or 190. Closest airport: Las Vegas, NV (120 miles).

CONTACTS

Death Valley National Park (Box 579, Death Valley, CA 92328–0579, tel. 760/786–3200, fax 760/786–3246, www.nps.gov/deva). Stovepipe Wells Ranger Station (tel. 760/786–2342).

Devils Postpile National Monument

In east-central California, near Mammoth Lakes

Hot lava cooled and cracked to form fractured basalt columns 40 to 60 feet high that resemble a giant rock pipe organ. The 798-acre monument high in the Sierra Nevada also protects the 101-foot Rainbow Falls and Soda Springs, carbonated mineralized springs. It's accessible in summer only by shuttle bus, which begins operation when the roads are cleared of snow, usually June or early July, and runs through the Wednesday after Labor Day. The John Muir and Pacific Coast trails cross the monument. It was proclaimed in 1911 and transferred to the Park Service in 1933.

WHAT TO SEE & DO

Fishing, hiking to springs and falls. **Facilities:** Ranger station, trails. **Programs & Events:** Ranger-led interpretive programs, campfire programs (July–Labor Day). **Tips & Hints:** Stay back from cliff edges. Store food properly to avoid bears. Busiest July and Aug., least crowded Oct.–June.

FOOD, LODGING & SUPPLIES

Camping: In the park: Devils Postpile (near ranger station; 21 sites; $14; flush toilets). **Hotels:** None in park. In Mammoth Lakes: Tamarack Lodge & Resort (take Lake Mary Rd. off Rte. 203, tel. 760/934–2442 or 800/626–6684, www.tamaracklodge.com; 10 rooms, 38 cabins; $119–$449). **Restaurants:** None in park. Near Mammoth Lakes: CJ's Grill (343 Old Mammoth Rd., tel. 760/934–3077; $7–$14). **Groceries & Gear:** None in park. In Mammoth Lakes: General Store (Reds Meadow Resort, end of Rte. 203, tel. 800/292–7758; closed Oct.–May).

FEES, HOURS & REGULATIONS

Shuttle fee: $7. Between June and Labor Day, day-use visitors must use shuttle bus, which runs from Mammoth Mountain Inn 7–7. $10 per vehicle rest of the year. California fishing license required. No hunting. Leashed pets only. No bikes off road. Monument open mid-June–Oct.

HOW TO GET THERE

10 miles west from U.S. 395 on Rte. 203 to Minaret Summit, then 7 miles on a paved narrow mountain road. Closest airports: Mammoth (22 miles), Reno, NV (181 miles).

CONTACT

Devils Postpile National Monument (Box 3999, Mammoth Lakes, CA 93546, tel. 760/934–2289, www.nps.gov/depo).

Eugene O'Neill National Historic Site

Near San Francisco, in Danville

Eugene O'Neill, the architect of modern American theater and the only Nobel Prize–winning playwright from the United States, lived at Tao House from 1937 to 1944. Here he wrote his final and most successful plays: *The Iceman Cometh, Long Day's Journey Into Night,* and *A Moon for the Misbegotten.* Since 1980, the National Park Service has been restoring Tao House and its courtyard and orchards. Reservations are required for park visits, including free transportation to the park and a free guided tour of the home and courtyard. The site was authorized on October 12, 1976.

WHAT TO SEE & DO

Facilities: Visitor center, bookstore. **Programs & Events:** On-site plays in May and Sept. **Tips & Hints:** Best time to visit is Mar.–May and Sept. and Oct. Busiest Apr.–June, least crowded Dec. Stairs only to second floor.

FOOD, LODGING & SUPPLIES

Camping: None at site. In Mount Diablo State Park: Junction (intersection of Southgate and Northgate Rds., tel. 800/444–7275, www. parks.ca.gov; 6 sites; $30; flush toilets, showers), Juniper (2 miles below the summit on Summit Rd., tel. 800/444–7275, www.parks.ca.gov; 36 sites; $30; flush toilets, showers), Live Oak (1 mile above Southgate entrance station, off Southgate Rd., tel. 800/444–7275, www.parks.ca.gov; 22 sites; $30; flush toilets, showers). **Hotels:** None at site. In Walnut Creek: Marriott Hotel (2355 N. Main St., tel. 925/934–2000 or 800/828–5613, www.marriott.com; 338 rooms; $129–$169). **Restaurants:** None at site. In Danville: Basil Leaf Café (501 Hartz Ave., tel. 925/831–2828, www.thebasilleafcafe.com; $8–$15). **Groceries & Gear:** None at site. In Danville: Longs (650 San Ramon Valley Blvd., tel. 925/820–1446), Lunardi's (345 Railroad Ave., tel. 925/855–8920).

FEES, HOURS & REGULATIONS

Free. Reservations required to visit the park (tel. 925/838–0249). Guided tours of Tao House available Wed., Thurs., Fri., and Sun. at 10 and 2. Allow 2½ hours, which includes transportation to and from the park. Self-guided tours are available Sat. on a first-come, first-served basis; shuttles leave downtown Danville at 10, noon, and 2.

HOW TO GET THERE

Danville is 26 miles east of San Francisco off I–680 in San Ramon Valley. Closest airports: Oakland (30 miles), San Francisco (43 miles).

CONTACTS

Eugene O'Neill National Historic Site (Box 280, Danville, CA 94526-0280, tel. 925/838–0249, fax 925/838–9471, www.nps.gov/euon). Danville Area Chamber of Commerce (117 E. Town and Country Dr., Danville, CA 94526, tel. 925/837–4400, www.danvilleareachamber.com). Mount Diablo State Park (Clayton; take I–680 to Danville, Diablo Rd. exit, then 3 miles east to Mt. Diablo Scenic Blvd., tel. 925/837–2525, www.mdia.org).

Fort Point National Historic Site

In the Presidio, San Francisco

Situated beneath the Golden Gate Bridge, Fort Point is a classic example of the coastal fortifications constructed by the U.S. Army Corps of Engineers during the mid-19th century. Built before the beginning of the Civil War, the brick-and-granite fort embodies the commercial and strategic military importance of San Francisco. Between 1933 and 1937 the fort was used as a base of operations for the construction of the Golden Gate Bridge. During World War II, Fort Point was occupied by 100 soldiers with searchlights and rapid-fire cannon as part of the protection of a submarine net strung across the bay entrance. The site was established on October 16, 1970.

WHAT TO SEE & DO

Touring fort, viewing photography and history exhibits. **Facilities:** Ranger station, museum. Bookstore. **Programs & Events:** Ranger-guided tours (daily), cannon drill demonstrations (daily), education programs. Crabbing program (Mar.–Oct.), candlelight tours (Oct.–Feb.). **Tips & Hints:** Allow at least one hour for your visit. Watch your step while visiting the fort as the surfaces are uneven. Weather at Fort Point is cool and windy. Summer months can be cold, with fog rolling into San Francisco Bay. Winters are generally cold with variable precipitation. Go in spring and fall for best weather. Busiest June–Aug., least crowded Dec. and Jan.

FEES, HOURS & REGULATIONS

Free. Fort open Oct.–May, Fri.–Sun. 10–5, June–Sept., daily 10–5. Confirm times with website.

HOW TO GET THERE

Beneath the south end of the Golden Gate Bridge. Turn off U.S. 101 at the bridge and turn left on Lincoln Blvd. Closest airport: San Francisco (15 miles).

CONTACTS

Fort Point National Historic Site (Fort Mason, Bldg. 201, San Francisco, CA 94123, tel. 415/556–1693, www.nps.gov/fopo). San Francisco Travel (201 3rd St., Suite 900, San Francisco, CA 94103, tel. 415/974–6900, www.sanfrancisco.travel).

Golden Gate National Recreation Area

In San Francisco area

This recreation area is the second-largest national park adjacent to an urban area in the world. Comprising more than 80,000 acres, the park encompasses 28 miles of shoreline in San Francisco, Marin, and San Mateo counties, including ocean beaches, redwood forest, lagoons, marshes, former military properties, and Alcatraz Island. The area also includes Fort Point National Historic Site and Muir Woods National Monument (see separate entries for each). The park was established in 1972 and designated a U.N. World Biosphere Reserve in 1988.

WHAT TO SEE & DO

Bicycling, bird-watching, board sailing, golfing, hiking, picnicking, sailing, swimming, walking. **Facilities:** 7 visitor centers: Alcatraz, Fort Mason, Fort Point (see separate listing), Golden Gate Pavilion, Lands End, Marin Headlands, Muir Woods (see separate listing); museum, hiking trails. Picnic tables. **Programs & Events:** Year-round programs available. **Tips & Hints:** Allow two or three days to see all sections of the recreation area. Expect windy, cool temperatures, fog in summer, and best weather in spring and fall. Busiest July and Aug., least crowded Dec.–Feb.

LODGING

⚠ **Camping:** 4 campgrounds in the park: Bicentennial (Battery Wallace; 3 walk-in tent sites; free; no pets), Hawkcamp (Bobcat Trail, 4 miles from Marin Headlands Visitor Center; 3 hike-to tent sites; free; pit toilets; no pets), Haypress (¾ mile from Tennessee Valley parking lot; 5 walk-in tent sites; free; no pets), Kirby Cove (near Golden Gate Bridge; 4 walk-in tent sites; $25; pit toilets; closed Nov.–Mar.).

FEES, HOURS & REGULATIONS

Entrance fee: Prices vary for Alcatraz Island and include ferry transportation and audio tour. Reservation required for Alcatraz (tel. 415/981–7625, www.alcatrazcruises.com). Ferry transportation fee: $28 round-trip. Permit required for backcountry camping at Marin Headlands. Alcatraz open daily 9:30–5. Fort Mason Visitor Center open weekdays 8:30–4:30. Golden Gate Bridge Pavilion open daily 9–6. Lands End Visitor Center open daily 9–5. Marin Headlands Visitor Center open daily 9:30–4:30. Fort Mason Visitor Center open weekdays 8:30–4:30. Nike Missile Site open at Marin Headlands Wed.–Fri. and 1st Sun. of the month 12:30–3:30.

HOW TO GET THERE

Much of the recreation area is within walking distance of San Francisco, with other areas up to an hour's drive away. The recreation area follows the city's north and west shoreline, extending down the peninsula. Across Golden Gate Bridge in Marin County, follow access roads off U.S. 101, including Alexander Ave., Shoreline Rte., and Sir Francis Drake Blvd., to the recreation area. Recreation area lands in San Mateo County are accessible via Skyline Blvd. Because traffic is sometimes heavy and parking is limited, public transportation is recommended. San Francisco's Municipal Railway (MUNI) system provides frequent service from downtown to shoreline destinations, including Fort Mason and Lands End. MUNI also connects to other Bay Area transit systems: Golden Gate Transit (GGT) in Marin County, Bay Area Rapid Transit (BART) and Alameda–Contra Costa Transit (AC TRANSIT) in the East Bay, and San Mateo Transit (SAM TRANS) in the peninsula area. Hornblower Cruises & Events provides transportation to Alcatraz. Closest airports: San Francisco (16 miles) and Oakland (21 miles).

CONTACTS

Golden Gate National Recreation Area Headquarters (Fort Mason, Bldg. 201, San Francisco, CA 94123, tel. 415/561–4700, www.nps.gov/goga). Other visitor information centers: Lands End (2-22 Merrie Way, San Francisco, CA 94121, tel. 415/561–4323); Marin Headlands (Bldg. 948, Fort Barry, Sausalito, CA 94965, tel. 415/331–1540. San Francisco Travel (201 3rd St., Suite 900, San Francisco, CA 94103, tel. 415/974–6900, www.sanfrancisco.travel). See also Fort Point National Historic Site and Muir Woods National Monument.

John Muir National Historic Site

In San Francisco Bay area, in Martinez

Naturalist John Muir lived in this 14-room Victorian home from 1890 until his death in 1914. Also preserved are 326 acres of open space and 8½ acres of his fruit ranch. Muir served as first president of the Sierra Club and advocated for the creation of Yosemite, Sequoia, Mount Rainier, and Grand Canyon national parks. He popularized the idea of preserving wild lands not for their commodities (timber, grazing, and water resources) but for their wildness, openness, and natural splendor. The site was authorized on August 31, 1964.

WHAT TO SEE & DO

Hiking, picnicking, touring the house and grounds. **Facilities:** Visitor center, hiking trail. Bookstore, picnic tables. **Programs & Events:** Guided tours, bird-watching excursions, wildflower walks. Full-moon walks (June–Aug.). Muir's Birthday (3rd Sat. in Apr.). **Tips & Hints:** Busiest Apr.–June, least crowded Sept. and Jan.

FOOD, LODGING & SUPPLIES

Camping: None at site. See Eugene O'Neill National Historic Site. **Hotels:** None at site. In Martinez: Best Western John Muir Inn (445 Muir Station Rd., tel. 925/229–1010, www.bestwestern.com; 115 rooms; $96.50–$130). **Restaurants:** None at site. In Martinez: Carrows (500 Center Ave., tel. 925/228–0600; $7–$10). **Groceries & Gear:** None at site. In Martinez: Safeway (6688 Alhambra Ave., tel. 925/933–0540), Rite Aid Pharmacy (1165 Arnold Dr., tel. 925/372–0945).

FEES, HOURS & REGULATIONS

Free. Leashed pets only. No smoking. No food in house. No mountain bikes on nature trail. Park and visitor center open daily 10–5.

HOW TO GET THERE

In the San Francisco metro area, on the East Bay in Martinez. Take Alhambra Ave. exit off Rte. 4 between I–80 and I–680. Closest airport: Oakland (30 miles).

CONTACTS

John Muir National Historic Site (4202 Alhambra Ave., Martinez, CA 94553, tel. 925/228–8860, fax 925/228–8192, www.nps.gov/jomu). Martinez Chamber of Commerce & Visitors Information Center (603 Marina Vista, Martinez, CA 94553, tel. 925/228–2345, www.martinezchamber.com).

Joshua Tree National Park

In southeastern California, near Twentynine Palms

A beautiful and strange Joshua Tree forest, rugged geological formations, a handful of palm oases, mining history, homesteading history, and peace and quiet are the attractions at this 792,750-acre park. It's a prime spot for rock climbing and hiking. Two different deserts meet at Joshua Tree: in the north and west you'll find the Mojave Desert; and in the south and east it's the Colorado Desert, a subsystem of the Sonoran Desert. The site was designated a national monument in 1936, redesignated a national park in 1994, and designated a Biosphere Reserve in 1984.

WHAT TO SEE & DO

Backpacking, boulder hopping, hiking, mountain biking, picnicking rock climbing (rentals, town of Joshua Tree). **Facilities:** 4 visitor centers: Joshua Tree Visitor Center (Rte. 62), Cottonwood (off I–10), Black Rock Nature Center (Yucca Valley), Oasis (Joshua Tree), hiking trails. Bookstore and sales areas, picnic tables. **Programs & Events:** Ranger-led hikes, interpretive talks, and campfire programs (mid-Oct.–May). **Tips & Hints:** Be prepared for all types of weather. Temperatures can reach 110°F June–Sept. Bring plenty of water, at least 1 gallon per person per day. Go Feb.–mid-May for flowers, Feb.–Apr. and in fall for bird migrations; and in spring, fall, and winter for best weather. Busiest Mar. and Apr., least crowded July and Aug.

FOOD, LODGING & SUPPLIES

 Camping: 9 campgrounds in the park: Belle (Pinto Basin Rd.; 18 sites; $10), Black Rock (Joshua Ln.; 100 sites; $15; flush toilets), Cottonwood (near Cottonwood visitor center; 62 sites; $15; flush toilets), Hidden Valley (near Barker Dam; 39 sites; $10), Indian Cove (near ranger station; 101 sites; $15), Jumbo Rocks (Park Blvd.; 125 sites; $10), Ryan (California Riding and Hiking Tr.; 31 sites; $10), Sheep Pass (Park Blvd.; tel. 800/365–2267; 6 sites; $25–$40), White Tank (Pinto Basin Rd.; 15 sites; $10). **Hotels:** None in park. In Twentynine Palms: 29 Palms Inn (73950 Inn Ave., tel. 760/367–3505, www.29palmsinn.com; 24 units; $70–$336), Roughley Manor (74744 Joe Davis Rd., tel. 760/367–3238, www.roughleymanor.com; 12 units; $135–$160). **Restaurants:** None in park. In Yucca Valley: The Rib Co. (56193 Twentynine Palms Hwy., tel. 760/365–1663, www.theribco. com; $8.50–$22). **Groceries & Gear:** None in park. In Twentynine Palms: Circle K (5681 Adobe Rd., tel. 760/367–2672).

FEES, HOURS & REGULATIONS

Entrance fee: $5 per person on foot, bicycle, or motorcycle; $15 per vehicle. No hunting. Leashed pets only. Pets may not be left alone and are restricted to campgrounds and dirt road areas. Mountain bikes only on roads open to motorized vehicles. Park open daily. Joshua Tree and Oasis visitor centers open daily 8–5. Cottonwood Visitor Center open daily 8–4. Black Rock Nature Center open Oct.–May, Mon.–Thurs. 8–4, Fri. noon–8.

HOW TO GET THERE

50 miles north of Palm Springs. From I–10, take Rte. 62 north to the town of Joshua Tree and turn south on Park Blvd. to reach west entrance. Park entrances also at Twentynine Palms (15 miles east of Joshua Tree) and off I–10 (47 miles east of Palm Springs). Closest airport: Palm Springs.

CONTACTS

Joshua Tree National Park (74485 National Park Dr., Twentynine Palms, CA 92277, tel. 760/367–5500, 877/444–6777 campground reservations, fax 760/367–6392, www.nps.gov/jotr). Joshua Tree Chamber of Commerce (6448 Hallee Rd., Suite 9, Joshua Tree, CA 92252, tel. 760/366–3723, www.joshuatreechamber.org). Twentynine Palms Chamber of Commerce (73484 Twentynine Palms Hwy., Twentynine Palms, CA 92277, tel. 760/367–3445, www.29chamber.org). Yucca Valley Chamber of Commerce (56711 Twentynine Palms Hwy., Yucca Valley, CA 92284, tel. 760/365–6323, www.yuccavalley.org).

Kings Canyon National Park

See Sequoia and Kings Canyon National Parks.

Lassen Volcanic National Park

In northeastern California, near Mineral

All four types of volcanoes in the world are found in Lassen Volcanic National Park. Lassen Peak, possibly the world's largest plug dome volcano, erupted in May 1914 and was active through 1921. Today the park has bubbling mudpots and steaming fumaroles, great lava pinnacles, lava flows, and jagged craters. Two great mountain ranges, the Sierra Nevada and Cascades, intersect with the Modoc Plateau of the Great Basin, where flora and fauna from these three geological provinces intermingle. Much of the park is accessible only by cross-country skiing and snowshoeing from late fall to mid-spring because of heavy snow. The park was established on August 9, 1916.

WHAT TO SEE & DO

Cross-country skiing, snowshoeing, fishing, hiking, horseback riding, picnicking, scenic drives, viewing volcanic landscape and hydrothermal features. **Facilities:** Kohm Yah-mah-nee Visitor Center, Loomis Museum (near Manzanita Lake), wayside interpretive signs, hiking trails. Book and map sale areas, gift shop, café, picnic tables. **Programs & Events:** Talks, walks, and evening programs (late June–Labor Day, daily), snowshoe walks (Jan.–Mar.). **Tips & Hints:** Buy park road guide. Ground around hydrothermal areas is dangerously thin; stay on boardwalks and supervise children closely when near hydrothermal areas. Watch for lightning. Wear layers of clothing. Temperatures may vary from freezing to 90°F. Go late July–mid-Aug. for flowers, and Aug. and Sept. for best hiking and car touring. Busiest July and Aug., least crowded Dec. and Jan.

FOOD, LODGING & SUPPLIES

⚑ **Camping:** In the park: Butte Lake (end of Butte Lake Rd.; 101 sites; $16–$50; flush toilets), Crags (5 miles south of Manzanita Lake; 45 sites; $12; vault toilets), Juniper Lake (east shore of Juniper Lake; 18 sites; $10–$30; vault toilets), Lost Creek (5 miles south of Manzanita Lake; 8 group sites; $50; vault toilets), Manzanita Lake (near Manzanita Lake entrance; 179 sites; $18; flush toilets, pay showers), Southwest (near Kohm Yah-mah-nee Visitor Center; 20 walk-in sites; $14; flush toilets), Summit Lake North (12 miles south of Manzanita Lake; 46 sites; $18; flush toilets), Summit Lake South (12 miles south of Manzanita Lake; 48 sites; $16; vault toilets), Warner Valley (near ranger station on Hot Springs Creek; 18 sites; $14; vault toilets). Backcountry camping allowed (free permit required). 🏨 **Hotels:** In the park: Drakesbad Guest Ranch (tel. 866/999–0914; 19 rooms; $140–$169, including three meals per day; closed Oct.–May). ✗ **Restaurants:** In the park: Drakesbad Guest Ranch (tel. 530/529–1512; reservations essential; closed Oct.–May). Near Chester: St. Bernard Lodge (44801 Rte. 36, 10 miles west of Chester, tel. 530/258–3382, www.stbernardlodge.com; $5–$10). ⚘ **Groceries:** In park: Manzanita Lake Camper Store (Mazanita Lake Campground, northwest edge of the park). In Mineral: Lassen Mineral Lodge General Store (Rte. 36, tel. 530/595–4422).

FEES, HOURS & REGULATIONS

Entrance fee: $5 per person on foot, bicycle, or horse; $10 per vehicle or motorcycle. Permits (free) required for backcountry camping. California state fishing license required. No hunting. Bikes on paved roads and campgrounds only. No motorized or mechanized equipment on trails. No pets beyond roads or campgrounds. Leashed pets only. Park open daily. Park road usually closes between late Oct. and mid-June because of snow. Kohm Yah-mah-nee Visitor Center open May–Nov., daily 9–5. Dec.-Apr., daily 9–4. Loomis Museum open June–Oct., daily 9–5.

HOW TO GET THERE

52 miles east of Red Bluff via Rte. 36, and 48 miles east of Redding via Rte. 44. Closest airport: Redding (48 miles).

CONTACTS

Lassen Volcanic National Park (Box 100, Mineral, CA 96063-0100, tel. 530/595–4480, fax 530/595–3262, www.nps.gov/lavo). Lake Almanor Area Chamber of Commerce & Visitors Bureau (162 Main St., Box 1198, Chester, CA 96020, tel. 530/258–2426, fax 530/258–2760, www. chester-lakealmanor.com). Shasta Cascade Wonderland Association (1699 Rte. 273, Anderson, CA 96007, tel. 530/365–7500, fax 530/365–1258, shastacascade.com).

Lava Beds National Monument

In northern California, near Tulelake

Lava Beds National Monument is on the north face of the Medicine Lake shield volcano, the largest of its kind in the Cascade Range. Numerous cinder cones, spatter cones, and lava flows cover the landscape, as well as more than 700 lava-tube caves. The monument also contains sites associated with the Modoc War of 1872–73, including Captain Jack's Stronghold, a natural fortress used by Modoc Indians for four months to withstand a siege by the U.S. Army. A separate site—Petroglyph Point—contains an outstanding collection of Native American rock art. The site was proclaimed in 1925 and transferred from the Forest Service in 1933.

WHAT TO SEE & DO

Bird-watching, cave exploration, picnicking, walking. **Facilities:** Visitor center (Indian Well), Mushpot Cave interpretive trail. Book sale area, picnic tables. **Programs & Events:** Fern Cave tour (May–Oct., Sat. only; reservations required), Crystal Cave tours (Dec.–Mar., Sat. only; reservations required). Guided walks, evening programs, living-history programs (Memorial Day–Labor Day). **Tips & Hints:** Watch for low ceilings, steep trails and stairways, and uneven footing in lava-tube caves. Carry more than one light source (free at visitor center). Wear hard-sole shoes and protective headgear (nominal charge at visitor center). Notify ranger if exploring caves not listed in park brochure or if using own lighting equipment. Watch for rattlesnakes. Busiest July and Aug., least crowded Jan. and Feb.

FOOD, LODGING & SUPPLIES

Camping: In the park: Indian Wells (near visitor center, south end of park; 42 sites; $10; flush toilets). Backcountry camping allowed. **Hotels:** None in park. In Tulelake: Fe's Bed & Breakfast (660 Main St., tel. 877/478–0184, www.fesbandb.com; 4 rooms; $60–$70). **X Restaurants:** None in park. In Tulelake: Mike & Wanda's (423 Modoc Ave., tel. 530/667–3226; $8–$17). **Groceries & Gear:** None in park. In Tulelake: Jock's Supermarket (395 Modoc Ave., tel. 530/667–2612).

FEES, HOURS & REGULATIONS

Entrance fee: $5 per person on foot, bicycle, or motorcycle; $10 per vehicle. No hunting, gathering of specimens, or collecting souvenirs. No pets in caves or on trails. No trail bikes or motorized vehicles on trails. No backcountry fires. Park grounds open year-round. Visitor center open Memorial Day–Labor Day, daily 8:30–6; Labor Day–Memorial Day, daily 8:30–5.

HOW TO GET THERE

24 miles from Tulelake and 58 miles from Klamath Falls, OR, off Rte. 161 and Rte. 139. Closest airport: Klamath Falls.

CONTACT

Lava Beds National Monument (1 Indian Wells Headquarters, Tulelake, CA 96134, tel. 530/667–8113, fax 530/667–2737, www.nps.gov/labe).

Manzanar National Historic Site

In eastern California, near Independence

A reminder of a sad episode in U.S. history, the residential portion of the Manzanar War Relocation Center has been designated a National Historic Site. Manzanar was one of 10 camps at which Japanese American citizens and resident aliens were forcibly confined after the attack on Pearl Harbor, most for the duration of World War II. In the process, many lost their homes and businesses. Located at the foot of the imposing Sierra Nevada in eastern California's Owens Valley, Manzanar is one of the best-preserved of these camps. The restored camp auditorium serves as an interpretive center with exhibits, two movie theaters, and a bookstore. Historic orchards, rock gardens, foundations, and other evidence of the camp remain. A guard tower has been reconstructed, and a historic World War II–era mess hall restored. Two replica barracks have been built in Block 14; there are plans to rebuild the communal latrines and laundry room. Manzanar was authorized as a National Historic Site on March 3, 1992.

WHAT TO SEE & DO

Car touring, guided tours. **Facilities:** Interpretive center with exhibits and audiovisual programs. Bookstore. Eastern California Museum, 6 miles north in Independence, exhibits Manzanar artifacts. **Programs & Events:** Ranger-led programs. Annual Manzanar Pilgrimage (last Sat. in Apr.), when former internees, their families, friends, and others gather at the Manzanar cemetery for a program and interfaith religious service. **Tips & Hints:** Plan at least one hour for the interpretive center, and another hour to explore the site by car or on foot. Self-guided tour brochures available. Be prepared for extreme temperatures, strong winds, and blowing dust at any time of year. Bring water and sunscreen, and wear a hat and sturdy walking shoes. Busiest Apr.–Sept., least crowded Nov.–Feb.

FOOD, LODGING & SUPPLIES

Camping: None in park. In Independence: Grays Meadow Campground (Onion Valley Rd., tel. 877/444–6777; 31 sites; $14–$16; flush toilets). **Hotels:** None at site. In Independence: Independence Inn (440 S. Edwards St., tel. 530/945–0103, www.independenceinn.net; 7 rooms; $65–$85), Mt. Williamson Hotel (515 S. Edwards St., tel. 760/878–2121; 8 cabins; $65–$95). **Restaurants:** None at site. In Lone Pine: Seasons Restaurant (206 S. Main St., tel. 760/876–8927; $10–$23). **Groceries & Gear:** None in park. In Independence: Independence Shell and Mini-Market (350 S. Edwards St., tel. 760/878–2172).

FEES & HOURS

Free. Site open daily, dawn–dusk. Interpretive center open Nov.–Mar., daily 9–4:30; Apr.–Oct., daily 9–5:30.

HOW TO GET THERE

9 miles north of Lone Pine, off U.S. 395, and 6 miles south of Independence. Closest airport: Independence (6 miles), Lone Pine (9 miles), Bishop (40 miles).

CONTACT

Manzanar National Historic Site (5001 Hwy. 395, Box 426, Independence, CA 93526-0426, tel. 760/878–2194 Ext. 3310, fax 760/878–2949, www.nps.gov/manz).

Mojave National Preserve

In southeastern California, near Baker

Largely untouched by modern development, this 1.6-million-acre preserve is the meeting place of the Mojave, Great Basin, and Sonoran deserts, and it has a remarkable scenic diversity. In the western section of the preserve are Joshua trees, cinder cones, and the huge, shimmering Kelso Dunes. Hole-in-the-Wall, meanwhile, is an aptly named geologic formation that offers a challenging climb down a vertical chute (with metal handholds) into the pockmarked Banshee Canyon. The preserve was established on October 31, 1994.

WHAT TO SEE & DO

Car and four-wheel-drive touring (rentals, Barstow, CA, and Las Vegas, NV), hiking, hunting. **Facilities:** 2 information centers: Kelso Depot Visitor Center (2701 Barstow Rd.), Hole-in-the-Wall (Black Canyon Rd., 10 miles north of Essex Rd.). Zzyzx Desert Studies Center, a California State University field center within the park. Book and map sales areas, picnic tables. **Programs & Events:** Interpretive talks (on request). Campfire programs (Oct.–Apr.). **Tips & Hints:** Carry and drink plenty of water, at least 1 gallon per person per day. Fill gas tank and check fluids and tires before entering preserve. Respect privately owned lands within the preserve. Be cautious of cattle in the road because of open-range grazing: approach slowly and pass quietly. Watch out for snakes, including rattlesnakes, and tarantulas (most commonly seen in fall mating season). Be prepared for strong winds in fall and late winter–early spring. Best times to visit are fall and spring, when temperatures are moderate. Go Mar.–May for wildflower blooms. Busiest Mar. and Apr., least crowded Sept., June, and July.

FOOD, LODGING & SUPPLIES

Camping: In the park: Black Canyon (across from Hole-in-the-Wall Information Center; equestrian/group site; $25; pit toilets), Hole-in-the-Wall (35 sites; $12; pit toilets), Mid Hills (26 sites; $12; pit toilets). Backcountry camping allowed. **Hotels:** None in park. In Baker: Wills Fargo Motel (72252 Baker Blvd., tel. 760/733–4477; 31 rooms; $65–$75). **Restaurants:** In the park: The Beanery (Kelso Depot Visitor Center, tel. 760/252-6165; $6–$10). In Baker: The Mad Greek (72112 Baker Blvd. at I–15, tel. 760/733–4354; $7–$15). **Groceries & Gear:** None in park. In Nipton: Nipton Trading Post (107355 Nipton Rd., tel. 760/856–2335).

FEES, HOURS & REGULATIONS

Free. California state hunting license required. No target shooting. Confined or leashed pets only. Don't leave pets unattended or in closed vehicles or trailers in extreme heat. No bicycles or motorized vehicles allowed in wilderness areas. No collecting firewood. Preserve open daily. Kelso Depot Visitor Center open daily 9–5. Hole-in-the-Wall Information Center weekends 9–4, as staffing permits.

HOW TO GET THERE

60 miles southwest of Las Vegas, NV, and 60 miles northeast of Barstow, CA, between I–15 and I–40. Closest airports: Las Vegas, NV, and Ontario, CA (150 miles).

CONTACTS

Mojave National Preserve (2701 Barstow Rd., Barstow, CA 92311, tel. 760/252–6100, fax 760/252–6174, www.nps.gov/moja). Baker Area Chamber of Commerce (Box 131, Baker, CA 92309, tel. 760/733–4469, bakerchamber.org). Barstow Area Chamber of Commerce (681 N. First Ave., Suite 698, Barstow, CA 92312, tel. 760/256–8617, www.

barstowchamber.com). Needles Area Chamber of Commerce (Box 705, Needles, CA 92363, tel. 760/326–2050, www.needleschamber.com).

Muir Woods National Monument

Near San Francisco

"This is the best tree-lovers monument that could possibly be found in all the forests of the world," declared conservationist John Muir when describing this grove of majestic coastal redwoods. The forest of towering trees and canyon ferns is a wonderfully tranquil place. Other park attractions are Redwood Creek, wildflowers, forest wildlife, and nearby Muir Beach. The site was proclaimed on January 9, 1908.

WHAT TO SEE & DO

Hiking, wildflower viewing, wildlife viewing, walking. **Facilities:** Visitor center, trails. **Programs & Events:** Ranger talks, seasonal activities. Earth Day (Jan.), Summer Solstice Celebration (June), Winter Solstice Celebration (Dec.). **Tips & Hints:** Park is cool, shaded, and moist year-round. Visit mid-week early or late in the day to avoid peak crowd times. Busiest Apr.–Oct., least crowded Dec. and Jan.

FOOD, LODGING & SUPPLIES

Camping: None in park. In Mount Tamalpais State Park: Pantoll Campground (801 Panoramic Hwy., tel. 415/388–2070; 16 sites; $25; flush toilets). **Hotels:** None in park. In Muir Beach: Pelican Inn (10 Pacific Way, at Rte. 1, tel. 415/383–6000; 7 rooms; $190–$275). **Restaurants:** In the park: Muir Woods Trading Company (tel. 415/388–7059; $5–$10). **Groceries & Gear:** None in park. In Mill Valley: Mill Valley Market (12 Corte Madera Ave., tel. 415/388–3222).

FEES, HOURS & REGULATIONS

Entrance fee: $7 adults, free ages 15 and under. No pets on trails. No bikes. No picnicking. No portable radios. No RV parking. No vehicles over 35 feet long on steep, winding road leading to monument. Park open daily 8–sunset.

HOW TO GET THERE

12 miles north of the Golden Gate Bridge via U.S. 101 and Rte. 1. Closest airport: San Francisco (29 miles).

CONTACTS

Muir Woods National Monument (Mill Valley, CA 94941, tel. 415/388–2596, fax 415/389–6957, www.nps.gov/muwo). See also Golden Gate National Recreation Area.

Pinnacles National Monument

In central California, entrances near Soledad and Hollister

The monument preserves the rock formations known as "The Pinnacles," talus caves, and wilderness areas. The spires and crags that inspired the park's name are remnants of ancient volcanic activity that is part of the long geologic history of the San Andreas Rift Zone. Pinnacles is on the Pacific Plate. Its sister rock, the other part of the same volcanic activity, is on the North American Plate. Pinnacles has moved almost 200 miles northwest as the plates have shifted over millions of years. The monument was established on January 16, 1908.

WHAT TO SEE & DO

Bird-watching, caving, hiking, rock climbing, wildflower viewing. **Facilities:** Pinnacles Visitor Center (east entrance on Rte. 146), West Pinnacles Visitor Contact Station (west entrance on Rte. 146), indoor and outdoor interpretive exhibits, hiking trails. Book and map sale areas, picnic tables. **Programs & Events:** Guided hikes and interpretive talks (Mar.–Nov.). Night hikes (spring, summer, and fall). **Tips & Hints:** Prepare for temperatures of 110°F in summer. Carry plenty of water. Wear sturdy footwear. Trail elevations range from 800 feet to 3,300 feet. Bring flashlights to visit the caves, accessed by the Balconies Cave trail on the west side of the park. Go between Feb. and May for wildflowers. Go during the week in spring to avoid crowds (and limited parking). Busiest Mar.–May, least crowded July and Aug.

FOOD, LODGING & SUPPLIES

🏕 **Camping:** In park: Pinnacles (Rte. 146, tel. 831/389–4538; 134 sites; $23–$36; flush toilets, showers, hookups). 🏨 **Hotels:** None in park. In Hollister: Best Western San Benito Inn (660 San Felipe Rd., tel. 831/637–9248, www.bestwestern.com; 42 rooms; $108–$140). ✗ **Restaurants:** None in park. In King City: Wildhorse Café (50630 Mesa Verde Rd., tel. 831/385–4312; $6–$15). ⛏ **Groceries & Gear:** None in park. In Paicines: General Store (12261 Airline Rte., tel. 831/628–3293).

FEES, HOURS & REGULATIONS

Entrance fee: $3 per person on foot or bicycle; $5 per motorized vehicle. No pets, bikes, or strollers on trails. No pets beyond parking and picnic areas. Leashed pets only. Charcoal fires only. No firewood gathering. No hunting. Watch out for tarantulas (especially in autumn, the mating season), black widow spiders, and rattlesnakes. Be wary of poison oak in shaded areas of woodlands. Park open daily 7:30–8. Pinnacles Visitor Center open daily 9:30–5. West Pinnacles Visitor Contact Station open daily 9–4.

HOW TO GET THERE

The monument's east entrance is 33 miles south of Hollister via Rte. 25 and Rte. 146. The west entrance is 13 miles east of Soledad via Rte.

146. No connecting road through the monument. Closest airport: San Jose (75 miles).

CONTACTS

Pinnacles National Monument (5000 Rte. 146, Paicines, CA 95043, tel. 831/389–4485, www.nps.gov/pinn). King City Chamber of Commerce (200 Broadway St., Suite 40, King City, CA 93930, tel. 831/385–3814, www.kingcitychamber.com). San Benito County Chamber of Commerce (650 San Benito St., Suite 130, Hollister, CA 95023, tel. 831/637–5315, www.sanbenitocountychamber.com).

Point Reyes National Seashore

On the northern coast, near Point Reyes Station

This peninsula north of San Francisco is noted for long beaches backed by tall cliffs and lagoons, forested ridges, and offshore bird and sea lion colonies. Highlights include the short Earthquake Trail, which passes by what was likely the epicenter of the devastating 1906 quake, and the late-19th-century Point Reyes Lighthouse, a good spot to watch for whales. There's also a bird observatory (most easily reached via Bolinas). The small towns of Olema, Point Reyes Station, and Inverness are in or border on the park. The seashore was authorized in 1962, established in 1972, and designated a Biosphere Reserve in 1988.

WHAT TO SEE & DO

Beachcombing, bicycling (rentals, Olema), bird-watching, fishing, hiking, horseback riding (rentals, Fivebrooks, tel. 415/663–1570), kayaking, whale-watching. **Facilities:** 3 visitor centers: Bear Valley (Bear Valley Rd., Olema), Lighthouse (Sir Francis Drake Blvd., 23 miles from Bear Valley), and Ken Patrick (Drakes Beach, off Sir Francis Drake Blvd.); 140 miles of hiking trails, outdoor exhibit panels. **Programs & Events:** Programs on lighthouses and lifeboat stations, gray whales, seals and sea lions, wildflowers, birds, geology, Native Americans, tide pools (throughout the year). Native American Big Time Festival (4th Sat., July), Sand Sculpture Contest (Sun. of Labor Day weekend). **Tips & Hints:** The lighthouse can be reached only by descending 300 stairs. It's occasionally closed because of high winds. Check tide tables before walking on the beaches; high tides can trap you. Not all beaches have lifeguards on duty. Stay away from the cliff edges and do not walk below the cliffs, as there may be falling rocks. After hiking, carefully check your body for ticks, as ticks carrying Lyme disease have been found in the area. Go Feb.–May for flowers, Dec.–Apr. for migrating gray whales, Nov.–Apr. for breeding elephant seals, Aug.–Feb. for migrating birds. Busiest Aug. and Dec., least crowded Feb. and Apr.

FOOD, LODGING & SUPPLIES

Camping: 5 campgrounds in the park: Tomales Bay (north of Indian Beach; boat-in beach camping area; $20–$50; pit toilets), Coast Camp

(2 miles from Laguna Trailhead; $20–$50; pit toilets), Glen Camp (6 miles from Five Brooks Trailhead; $20–$50; pit toilets), Sky Camp (western side of Mt. Wittenberg; $20–$50; pit toilets), Wildcat Camp (6 miles from Bear Valley; $20–$50; pit toilets). **⊞ Hotels:** In the park: Point Reyes Hostel (1390 Limantour Spit Rd., tel. 415/663–8811; 45 beds; $24). In Inverness: Ten Inverness Way (10 Inverness Way, tel. 415/669–1648, www.teninvernessway.com; 5 rooms; $145–$170). **✗ Restaurants:** In the park: Drakes Beach Café (tel. 415/669–1297; $4–$12). In Inverness: Priscilla's (12781 Sir Francis Drake Blvd., tel. 415/669–1244, www.priscillasinverness.com; $9–$16; closed Tues.).

FEES, HOURS & REGULATIONS

Free. Shuttle fee for whale viewing $5. Camping permits required (available at Bear Valley Visitor Center). California fishing license required. No hunting. No pets or bikes in wilderness. No car camping. Seashore open daily sunrise–sunset. Bear Valley Visitor Center weekdays 9–5, weekends 8–5. Lighthouse Visitor Center Thurs.–Mon. 10–4:30. Ken Patrick Visitor Center weekends and holidays 10–5.

HOW TO GET THERE

45 miles north of San Francisco via U.S. 101 and Sir Francis Drake Blvd. or via Rte. 1. Closest airport: San Francisco.

CONTACTS

Point Reyes National Seashore (Bear Valley Visitor Center, Point Reyes, CA 94956, tel. 415/464–5100, www.nps.gov/pore).

Port Chicago Naval Magazine National Memorial

In the north-central part of the state, northeast of San Francisco

In the darkness of July 17, 1944, San Francisco residents were jolted awake by a massive explosion that cracked windows and brightened the night sky. At Port Chicago Naval Magazine, 320 men were instantly killed in World War II's worst homeland disaster when two ships being loaded with ammunition for the Pacific theater troops blew up. Five thousand tons of TNT destroyed the deepwater harbor and piers. Amazingly, the harbor and pier were back up and running in a month. Port Chicago Naval Magazine was dedicated as a national memorial in 1994.

WHAT TO SEE & DO

Touring the site. **Facilities:** The memorial is within an active military installation. **Programs & Events:** Ranger-guided tour by appointment only. **Tips & Hints:** Call several weeks in advance to ensure a reservation.

FOOD & LODGING

⛺ Camping: None in park. **⊞ Hotels:** None in park. In Martinez: Americas Best Value (3999 Alhambra Ave., tel. 925/228-7471, www.

abvimartinez.com; 60 rooms; $55–$60). ✗ **Restaurants:** None in park. In Martinez: Mangia Bene Restaurant (1170 Arnold Dr., tel. 925/228-9123, www.mangiabenerestaurant.com; $11–$19.

FEES, HOURS & REGULATIONS

Free. Visitor access to the memorial is by two-week advance reservation only. Tours are conducted Thurs.–Sat. at 1:30. Allow 90 minutes. All visitors are shuttled to the memorial by park service vehicles from the Concord Naval Weapons Station. Reservations: 952/228–8860.

HOW TO GET THERE

Take I–680 to Hwy. 242, exit at Port Chicago Hwy. N, make right into visitor parking lot of Military Ocean Terminal Concord. Closest airport: Oakland (45 miles).

CONTACTS

Port Chicago Naval Magazine National Memorial (4202 Alhambra Ave., Martinez, CA 94520, tel. 925/228-8860, www.nps.gov/poch). Martinez Chamber of Commerce (603 Marina Vista Ave., Martinez, CA 94553, www.martinezchamber.com).

Redwood National & State Parks

In northwestern California, near Orick

Running for 40 miles along the Pacific Coast, this park is best known for its magnificent old-growth redwoods, some of the world's tallest trees. Redwoods can live more than 2,000 years and grow to over 300 feet tall. Less well known are the park's prairies, oak woodlands, and coastal and marine ecosystems. Besides the national park, the area encompasses three state parks: Prairie Creek Redwoods, Del Norte Coast Redwoods, and Jedediah Smith Redwoods. The park was established in 1968 and designated a World Heritage Site in 1980 and an International Biosphere Reserve in 1983.

WHAT TO SEE & DO

Backpacking, bicycling, bird-, elk-, and whale-watching, hiking, horseback riding and tours, picnicking, scenic drives. **Facilities:** 5 visitor centers: Crescent City (1111 2nd St.), Hiouchi (Rte. 199), Jedediah Smith (U.S. 101, Hiouchi), Prairie Creek (Newton Drury Scenic Pkwy., off U.S. 101), Thomas H. Kuchel (U.S. 101, Orick); hiking trails, outdoor interpretive exhibits. Bookstores, picnic tables. **Programs & Events:** Ranger-led programs and children's programs (Memorial Day–Labor Day), environmental education programs (by reservation only). **Tips & Hints:** Wear layers of clothing to handle varying temperatures between coastal and inland sections. Bring rain gear and good walking shoes. After hiking, carefully check your body for ticks, as ticks carrying Lyme disease have been found in the area. Do not hike alone. Both mountain lions and bears inhabit the parklands. If you see one, do not run away; wave your arms to scare it off. Backpackers can borrow animal-proof food canisters at the Thomas H. Kuchel Visitor Center. Busiest July and Aug., least crowded Dec. and Jan.

FOOD, LODGING & SUPPLIES

🔥 **Camping:** In the parks: Mill Creek (Del Norte Coast Redwoods State Park; 88 sites; $35; flush toilets, showers; closed Oct.–Apr.), Jedediah Smith Redwoods State Park (106 sites; $35; flush toilets, showers), Elk Prairie (Prairie Creek Redwoods State Park; 75 sites; $35; flush toilets, showers), Gold Bluffs Beach (Prairie Creek Redwoods State Park; 29 sites; $35; flush toilets, showers). Backcountry camping allowed. 🏨 **Hotels:** None in park. In Crescent City: Oceanfront Lodge (100 A St., tel. 707/465–5400, www.oceanfrontlodge1.com; 53 rooms; $179–$229). ✖ **Restaurants:** None in parks. In Crescent City: Harbor View Grotto (150 Starfish Way, tel. 707/464–3815; $5–$15). 🍴 **Groceries & Gear:** None in park. In Klamath: Woodland Villa Grocery Store (15870 U.S. 101, tel. 707/482–2081).

FEES, HOURS & REGULATIONS

Free. Permit required for backcountry camping (tel. 707/464–6101). Redwood Creek Trail is impassable during high water. California state fishing license required. No pets on any trails. Leashed pets allowed only in campgrounds, on park roads, and on beaches. Park open daily. Crescent City, Jedediah Smith, Prairie Creek, and Thomas H. Kuchel visitor center hours daily Mar.–Oct., 9–5; Nov.–Feb. 9–4. Hiouchi Information Center May–mid-Nov., daily 9–5.

HOW TO GET THERE

The park runs along U.S. 101 from Hiouchi (Rte. 199) to Crescent City and down to Orick. Park headquarters and information center is in Crescent City. Thomas H. Kuchel Visitor Center is 335 miles north of San Francisco on U.S. 101 about 2 miles west of Orick. Closest airports: Crescent City (11 miles), Arcata/Eureka (26 miles).

CONTACTS

Redwood National Park (1111 2nd St., Crescent City, CA 95531, tel. 707/464–6101, www.nps.gov/redw). Crescent City–Del Norte County Chamber of Commerce (1001 Front St., Crescent City, CA 95531, tel. 800/343–8300, exploredelnorte.com). Orick Chamber of Commerce (Box 234, Orick, CA 95555, tel. 707/488–2885, www.orick.net).

Rosie the Riveter/ World War II Home Front National Historical Park

Near San Francisco Bay, in Richmond

Several historic sites, including a waterfront shipyard, a hospital, child-development centers, and fire stations, make up this park, which commemorates the home-front workforce and its contributions during World War II. The shipyards, one of 56 war industries in Richmond, were the most productive in the country in the early 1940s. The park especially honors the women, called "Rosies," who joined the wartime effort in great numbers. Minorities and other groups are also recognized. The park was established on October 24, 2000.

WHAT TO SEE & DO

Touring World War II cargo ship, viewing exhibits in visitor center. **Facilities:** Visitor center at Historic Ford Building Complex, Rosie the Riveter Memorial in Marina Bay Park, S.S. *Red Oak Victory,* observation point. **Tips & Hints:** This park is under development. Some sites are not open to the public. The visitor center has exhibits and driving maps.

FEES, HOURS & REGULATIONS

Free. S.S. *Red Oak Victory* suggested donation $5; tours Tues., Thurs., Sat., and occasionally Sun., 10–3. Visitor center open daily 10–5. Rosie the Riveter Memorial open dawn–dusk.

GETTING THERE

To get to the Rosie the Riveter Memorial from I–80, take I–580 toward Richmond/San Rafael, then the Marina Bay/S. 23rd St. exit. Turn left onto Marina Bay Pkwy., right onto Regatta Blvd., and left at Melville Sq. to Marina Bay Park.

To get to Visitor Education Center (1414 Harbour Way S.) from I–580, take the Harbour Way South exit. Follow road to the end, where the center is in a small building on east side of large Ford assembly building. Closest airports: Oakland (12 miles), San Francisco (17 miles).

CONTACTS

Rosie the Riveter/World War II Home Front National Historical Park (2566 Macdonald Ave., Richmond, CA 94804, tel. 510/232–5050, www.nps.gov/rori). S.S. *Red Oak Victory* (Richmond Museum of History, Box 1267, Richmond, CA 94802, tel. 510/235–7387, www.ssredoakvictory.com).

San Francisco Maritime National Historical Park

In San Francisco

Included in this park are a fleet of historic ships, a maritime museum, and a maritime library. The fleet includes the 1886 square-rigger *Balclutha,* the 1895 schooner *C.A. Thayer,* the 1891 scow schooner *Alma,* the 1890 ferryboat *Eureka,* the 1914 paddlewheel tug *Eppleton Hall,* and the 1907 steam tugboat *Hercules.* The visitor center includes a walk-through exhibit of San Francisco maritime history, and the library offers an extensive collection of photographs and other historic documents. The park was established in 1988.

WHAT TO SEE & DO

Attending boatbuilding classes, library research, picnicking, touring historic vessels, viewing exhibits, visiting museum. **Facilities:** Visitor center, museum, library. Bookstore and gift shop. **Programs & Events:** Steam-engine and living-history demonstrations; educational talks and walks; sea chantey singing. Ranger-led bay sails aboard *Alma* (summer, fee applies), Sea Music Concert Series (fall), Christmas at Sea (winter). **Tips & Hints:** Use public transportation to get to the park. The best time to visit is in fall. Busiest July and Aug., least crowded Dec. and Jan.

FEES & HOURS

Entrance fee: free to museum, visitor center, aquatic park, library (by appointment only). Boarding pass for historic vessels: $5 adults, free ages 15 and under. Visitor center open Memorial Day-Sept. 15, daily 9:30–5:30; Sept. 16–Memorial Day, daily 9:30–5. Hyde Street Pier open Memorial Day-Sept. 15, daily 9:30–5:30; Sept. 16–Memorial Day, 9:30–5.

HOW TO GET THERE

West end of Fisherman's Wharf, at the intersection of Hyde and Jefferson streets. The Hyde Street cable-car terminates in the park, the F-Line Streetcar terminates two blocks from park entrance. Closest airport: San Francisco (15 miles).

CONTACTS

San Francisco Maritime National Historical Park Visitor Center (499 Jefferson St., San Francisco, CA 94109, tel. 415/447–5000, www.nps.gov/safr). San Francisco Travel (201 3rd St., Suite 900, San Francisco, CA 94103, tel. 415/974–6900, www.sanfrancisco.travel).

Santa Monica Mountains National Recreation Area

Near Los Angeles

The Santa Monica Mountains rise above Los Angeles, widen to meet the curve of Santa Monica Bay, and reach their greatest height facing the ocean, forming a beautiful and multifaceted landscape. Residents use "L.A.'s backyard" for mountain biking and hiking. For sensational views, drive along Mulholland Highway, which cuts through the park. The recreation area is a cooperative effort that joins federal, state, and local park agencies with private preserves and landowners to protect the natural and cultural resources of this transverse mountain range and seashore. Within this recreation area are Topanga, Leo Carillo, Point Mugu, and Malibu Creek state parks. The area was established on November 10, 1978.

WHAT TO SEE & DO

Attending festivals and cultural workshops and events, bird- and whale-watching, hiking, horseback riding (rentals), mountain biking, picnicking, surfing, swimming, walking. **Facilities:** Beilensen Interagency Visitor Center (26876 Mulholland Hwy., Calabasas); Satwiwa Native American Indian Culture Center (Lynn Rd., Newbury Park), Sooky Goldman Nature Center (2600 Franklin Canyon Dr., Beverly Hills), over 500 miles of trails. Bookstore. **Programs & Events:** Rangerled walking tours, cultural programs, nature walks. Seasonal activities and special events include guided tours of historic Paramount Ranch western movie set, Silent Films under the Stars. Contact park for copy of "Outdoors" calendar of events. **Tips & Hints:** Expect hot, dry summers (80°F–100°F) and relatively cool, wet winters (40°F–70°F). Plan for coastal side of the mountains to be 10–15 degrees cooler than inland side during summer (in winter this pattern is reversed). Bikers must yield to hikers; hikers must yield to equestrians. Watch out for poison oak and rattlesnakes. Bring plenty of water. Busiest May and June, least crowded Dec. and Jan.

FEES, HOURS & REGULATIONS

Free. Parking fee at most state parks and some local parks within recreation area. Fee for some special events. Park open daily 8–sunset. Visitor center open daily 9–5.

HOW TO GET THERE

West of Griffith Park in Los Angeles County and east of Oxnard Plain in Ventura County. U.S. 101 (Ventura Freeway) borders the mountains on the north, and Rte. 1 (Pacific Coast Hwy.) and the Pacific Ocean form the southern boundary. Access is via many roads that cross the mountains between these two highways. Part of the park stretches into the Simi Hills north of U.S. 101. To reach the visitor center from U.S. 101, take Las Virgenes Rd., travel south on Las Virgenes Rd., turn east (left) on Mulholland Hwy. The driveway to the visitor center will be on the right-hand side. Closest airports: Los Angeles (15 miles), Burbank (20 miles).

CONTACTS

Santa Monica Mountains National Recreation Area (26876 Mulholland Hwy., Calabasas, CA 91302, tel. 805/370–2301, www.nps.gov/samo). Santa Monica Convention & Visitors Bureau (1920 Main St., Suite B, Santa Monica, CA 90401, tel. 310/393–7593 or 800/544–5319, www. santamonica.com).

Sequoia & Kings Canyon National Parks

In east-central California, near Three Rivers

Sequoia, the second-oldest national park in the United States, was established in 1890 to protect the towering sequoias in Giant Forest, including the General Sherman Tree, the world's largest living tree. The excellent Giant Forest Museum traces the ecology of sequoias (open summer only). Sequoia also contains Crystal Cave, filled with marble stalactites and stalagmites, and Mt. Whitney, the highest mountain in the lower 48 states. General Grant Grove, in Kings Canyon, is home to the General Grant Tree, the second largest on earth. Together, Sequoia and Kings Canyon cover more than 865,000 acres. A small portion of what is now Kings Canyon was set aside in 1890 as General Grant National Park. In 1940, General Grant was absorbed into the new and larger Kings Canyon National Park, which eventually grew to include the South Fork of the Kings River and 456,552 acres of backcountry wilderness. Sequoia National Park was established on September 25, 1890, and Kings Canyon National Park was established on March 4, 1940.

WHAT TO SEE & DO

Backpacking, cross-country skiing, fishing, hiking, horseback riding, scenic drives, snowshoeing, visiting museum and cave. **Facilities:** 4 visitor centers: Cedar Grove (end of Rte. 180, Kings Canyon National Park), Foothills (Generals Rte., Sequoia National Park), Grant Grove (Rte. 180, Kings Canyon National Park), Lodgepole (Lodgepole Rd., just off Generals Hwy., Sequoia National Park); museum, outdoor interpretive exhibits and signs, 140 miles of scenic roads, 800 miles of hiking trails. Book and map sales. **Programs & Events:** Ranger-led walks, talks, and evening programs; field seminars; horseback rides (June–Sept.); Crystal Cave tours (May–Oct.); snowshoe walks (Dec.–Feb., depending on snowfall). Nation's Christmas Tree Ceremony (2nd Sun. of Dec., General Grant Tree in Kings Canyon). **Tips & Hints:** Plan on a two-hour drive from the entrance on the Generals Hwy. to the Rte. 180 entrance. Add two to three hours for a side trip to Cedar Grove in Kings Canyon. Bring rain gear and layered clothing for hiking. Use extra caution when driving, as many park roads are steep and narrow. Black bears inhabit the parks. Do not feed the bears or any wild animals. Follow food-storage regulations whether you are day hiking, camping, or backpacking. Parks busiest June–Aug., least crowded Jan. and Feb.

FOOD, LODGING & SUPPLIES

⚑ **Camping:** 14 campgrounds in park (1,295 sites; $12–$20; some flush toilets, some pit toilets, some showers). Backcountry camping allowed. ⊞ **Hotels:** In the parks: John Muir Lodge (Grant Grove Village, tel. 866/522–6966; 36 rooms; $69–$186), Wuksachi Lodge (Generals Hwy., tel. 559/565–4070 or 888/252–5757, www.visitsequoia.com; 102 rooms; $160–$375). In Three Rivers: Lazy J Ranch Motel (39625 Sierra Dr., tel. 559/561–4449 or 888/315–2378, www.americasbestvalueinn.com; 18 rooms; $115–$145). ✕ **Restaurants:** In the parks: Grant Grove Village Restaurant (tel. 866/522–6966; $7–$15). In Three Rivers: Gateway Restaurant & Lodge (45978 Sierra Dr., tel. 559/561–4133, www.gateway-sequoia.com; $10–$20). ⬧ **Groceries & Gear:** In the parks: Grant Grove Village General Market (tel. 866/522–6966).

FEES, HOURS & REGULATIONS

Entrance fee: $10 per person on foot, bicycle, or motorcycle; $20 per vehicle. Backcountry permit ($15) required for all backcountry camping. California state fishing license required. No bikes on trails. Bear-proof storage required for food, trash, toiletries, baby wipes, and any other such scented items. Road to Mineral King in Sequoia National Park open Memorial Day–Oct., weather permitting. Vehicles longer than 22 feet not allowed on Generals Hwy. between Hospital Rock Picnic Area and Giant Forest in Sequoia. Rte. 180 to Cedar Grove in Kings Canyon open May–Oct. Parks open daily. Call individual visitor centers for hours of operation.

HOW TO GET THERE

There are no roads into the parks from the east. From the west, take Rte. 180 from Fresno to enter Kings Canyon and Rte. 198 from Visalia to enter Sequoia. Generals Hwy. connects the two roads, making loop trips possible. In winter, the Generals Hwy. between Lodgepole and Grant Grove may be closed by snow. Closest airport: Fresno (55 miles).

CONTACTS

Sequoia & Kings Canyon National Parks (47050 Generals Hwy., Three Rivers, CA 93271, tel. 559/565–3341, www.nps.gov/seki).

Whiskeytown-Shasta-Trinity National Recreation Area

In northern California, near Redding

Nestled in the rugged Klamath Mountains watershed, Whiskeytown preserves much of the colorful history of the California gold rush and has a wealth of water-oriented and backcountry opportunities. Although Whiskeytown Lake is smaller than Shasta or Trinity Lakes, its clear, blue water attracts many recreationists to its shores. The park contains four impressive waterfalls that can be seen all year. The recreation area was authorized in 1965 and established in 1972.

WHAT TO SEE & DO

Backpacking, boating (rentals, Oak Bottom Marina and in Redding), canoeing, fishing, gold-panning, hiking, horseback riding, hunting, kayaking, mountain biking, picnicking, sailing, scuba diving, swimming, waterskiing. **Facilities:** Visitor information center (junction of Rte. 299 and Kennedy Memorial Dr., 8 miles west of Redding); 90 miles of backcountry roads and trails, outdoor interpretive exhibits and signs. Book and map sales. **Programs & Events:** Guided walks, evening programs, demonstrations and talks pertaining to natural and cultural resources of the area, tours of Tower House Historic District. National Park Week Celebration (Apr.). **Tips & Hints:** Bears and mountain lions inhabit the park. If you see one, do not run; make noise and wave your arms to scare it off. Keep all scented items (food, toiletries, and other such items) in airtight, bear-proof containers. Dispose of all trash in bear-proof garbage cans. Watch out for rattlesnakes. Beware of abandoned mine shafts. Go in spring for wildflowers and hiking, although trails may be too wet for mountain biking and horseback riding. Go in summer for water activities, camping, and fishing, and in fall for foliage, hiking, mountain biking, and horseback riding before beginning of rainy season. Busiest June and July, least crowded Dec. and Jan.

FOOD, LODGING & SUPPLIES

⚠ **Camping:** 3 campgrounds in park: Brandy Creek (near Brandy Creek Marina; tel. 530/246–1225; 36 sites; $14), Dry Creek (near Brandy Creek Beach; tel. 877/444–6777; 2 group sites; $75; pit toilets), Oak Bottom (Oak Bottom Beach on Whiskeytown Lake; tel. 530/359–2269; 120 sites; $18–$22; flush toilets, showers). Backcountry camping available. 🏨 **Hotels:** None in park. In Redding: Red Lion Inn (1830 Hilltop Dr., tel. 530/221–8700, redlion.rdln.com; 192 rooms; $113–$124). ✗ **Restaurants:** None in park. In Redding: Black Bear Diner (2605 Hilltop Dr., tel. 530/221–7600, $8–$20). ⛽ **Groceries & Gear:** In the park: limited supplies and groceries at Oak Bottom Marina.

FEES, HOURS & REGULATIONS

Entrance fee: $5 per vehicle. Fee charged for Whiskey Creek Group Picnic Area (reservations required, tel. 877/444–6777). Permits required (free) for backpacking and backcountry camping. Permits for gold-panning ($1) required. California hunting and fishing license required. No motorized vehicles on trails. Horses and mountain bikes restricted to certain trails. No dogs on designated beaches. Leashed dogs elsewhere. Recreation area open daily. Certain areas (some restrooms and several backcountry roads) closed in winter. Visitor center open Memorial Day–Labor Day, daily 9–5; Labor Day–Memorial Day, daily 10–4.

HOW TO GET THERE

8 miles west of Redding on Rte. 299. Closest airports: Redding (16 miles), Sacramento (165 miles).

CONTACTS

Whiskeytown National Recreation Area (Box 188, Whiskeytown, CA 96095-0188, tel. 530/246–1225, fax 530/246–5154, www.nps.gov/whis). Greater Redding Chamber of Commerce (747 Auditorium Dr., Redding CA 96001, tel. 530/225–4433, www.reddingchamber.com). Redding Convention & Visitors Bureau (777 Auditorium Dr., Redding, CA 96001, tel. 530/225–4100 or 800/874–7562, fax 530/225–4354, www.visitredding.com).

Yosemite National Park

In east-central California, surrounding Yosemite Village

Yosemite Valley is the heart of the magnificent 1,200-square-mile park that spurred conservationist John Muir and photographer Ansel Adams to some of their best achievements. The park is so large that it can be grouped into several different areas. Yosemite Valley is famed for its waterfalls, such as the 2,425-foot Yosemite Falls, highest in North America, and the granite monoliths of El Capitan and Half Dome.

Some of the best views of this valley can be seen from Glacier Point. The Wawona area, near the south entrance, has a cluster of historic buildings and the Mariposa Grove of giant sequoias. Both Wawona and Yosemite Valley are open year-round. The Hetch Hetchy area is also open year-round. However, the high-elevation areas of Tuolumne Meadows and Glacier Point are inaccessible by car in winter. There are a few developed areas within the park, including Wawona and Yosemite Village in Yosemite Valley, which has lodges, restaurants, a photography gallery, a medical center, and other services. Yosemite Valley and Mariposa Big Tree Grove were granted to the State of California in 1864. The national park was established in 1890. The federal government accepted lands returned by the state in 1906. The El Portal site was authorized in 1958. The park was designated a World Heritage Site in 1984.

WHAT TO SEE & DO

Backpacking, bicycling (rentals), bird and wildlife viewing, cross-country skiing, fishing, golf, hiking, horseback riding, ice skating, rafting, rock climbing, scenic drives, skiing, swimming, viewing geological features and waterfalls. **Facilities:** 4 visitor centers: Valley (Yosemite Valley), Big Oak Flat (Rte. 120), Wawona (Wawona Rd.), and Tuolumne (Tuolumne Meadows); museum; 196 miles of scenic roads; 800 miles of hiking trails. Bookstores. **Programs & Events:** Ranger-led walks, talks, and evening programs; bus and tram tours; horseback rides; theatrical events. **Tips & Hints:** Plan to spend at least four hours touring Yosemite Valley and two days to visit entire park. Drive slowly and keep an eye out for wildlife on the roads. Use turnouts to pull completely off the road to look at views or take photographs. Do not enter the water near the brim of a waterfall. Check water conditions with park staff, and swim only when the water is low. Dress in layers and bring rain gear to accommodate weather changes. Expect warm, dry summers; most moisture falls Jan.–Mar. Busiest July and Aug., least crowded Nov. and Jan.

FOOD, LODGING & SUPPLIES

Camping: 13 campgrounds in park (1,410 sites; $5–$20; some flush toilets, some vault toilets). Backcountry camping allowed. **Hotels:** In the park: Ahwahnee Hotel (99 rooms, 24 cottages; $357), Curry Village (18 rooms, 71 cabins, 414 tent cabins; $95–$339), Redwoods Guest Cottages (tel. 209/375–6666; 120 units; $88–$500), Wawona Hotel (104 rooms; $143–$234), White Wolf Lodge (4 cabins, 24 tent cabins; $124–$157), Yosemite Lodge (245 rooms; $152–$227). **Restaurants:** In the park: Ahwahnee Dining Room (tel. 209/372–1489; $11–$15), Mountain Room Restaurant (tel. 209/372–1281; $16–$27). **Groceries & Gear:** In the park: The Village Store (9012 Village Dr., tel. 209/372–1253).

FEES, HOURS & REGULATIONS

Entrance fee: $10 per person on foot, bicycle, or bus; $20 per vehicle. Free shuttle bus in east end of Yosemite Valley (year-round) and between Wawona and the Mariposa Grove of Giant Sequoias and from Tuolumne Meadows to Tenaya Lake (June–Sept.). California fishing license required. Wilderness permit ($5) required for any backcountry camping (tel. 209/372–0740). No pets on trails or beaches or in backcountry or public buildings. Leashed pets restricted to specific campgrounds. No hunting. No discharging weapons. Don't deface or remove natural historic features. Tioga Pass entrance is closed Nov.–early June. Park open daily. Yosemite Valley Visitor Center open mid-June–mid-Sept, daily 9–6; mid-Sept.–mid-June, daily 9–5. Tuolumne Meadows Visitor Center open June–Sept., daily 9–5. Wawona Visitor Center open May–Sept., daily 8:30–5. Big Oak Flat Visitor Center open May–Sept., daily 8–5.

HOW TO GET THERE

There are four entrances to the park: the south entrance on Rte. 41 north from Fresno, the Arch Rock entrance on Rte. 140 east from Merced, the Big Oak Flat entrance on Rte. 120 east from Modesto and Manteca, and the Tioga Pass entrance on Rte. 120 west from Lee Vining and U.S. 395. Closest airports: Merced (80 miles), Fresno (94 miles), San Francisco (200 miles).

CONTACTS

Yosemite National Park (Box 577, Yosemite, CA 95389, tel. 209/372–0200, www.nps.gov/yose). Lee Vining Chamber of Commerce (Box 130, Lee Vining, CA 93541, tel. 760/647–6629, www.leevining.com). Mariposa County Visitors Center (5158 Hwy. 140, Mariposa, CA 95338, tel. 209/966–7081 or 866/425–3366, www.yosemiteexperience. com). Yosemite Sierra Visitors Bureau (41969 Rte. 41, Oakhurst, CA 93644, tel. 559/683–4636, www.yosemitethisyear.com).

See Also

AIDS Memorial Grove National Memorial, California National Historic Trail, Port Chicago Naval Magazine National Memorial, Juan Bautista de Anza National Historic Trail, Kern River, Kings River, Klamath River, Merced River, Pacific Crest National Scenic Trail, Pony Express National Historic Trail, and Tuolumne River, in Other National Parklands.

COLORADO

Bent's Old Fort National Historic Site

In southeastern Colorado, between La Junta and Las Animas

Preserved here is a reconstructed adobe trading post on the old Santa Fe Trail. In its heyday (1833–49), the fort was the largest American-owned commercial center in the 700 miles between Independence, Missouri, and Santa Fe, New Mexico. The park was established on June 3, 1960.

WHAT TO SEE & DO

Hiking; touring the fort; visiting the sales area, trade room, and bookstore. **Facilities:** Fort and fort furnishings, nature trail, audiovisual program. Bookstore, sales area and trade room, picnic area. **Programs & Events:** Daily one-hour ranger-guided tours; historic-lifestyle demonstrations (June–Aug.). Kids' Quarters (July), Living History Encampment (1st weekend in June), Holiday Celebration (Dec.). **Tips & Hints:** Busiest Apr.–Aug., least crowded Jan. and Feb.

FOOD, LODGING & SUPPLIES

Camping: None in park. In John Martin Reservoir State Park (30703 County Rd. 24, south of U.S. 50, tel. 719/829–1801, www.parks. state.co.us): Lake Hasty Campground (109 sites; $16–$24; flush toilets, showers, hookups). **Hotels:** None in park. In La Junta: Holiday Inn Express (27994 Frontage Rd., tel. 719/384–2900, www.hiexpress.com; 59 rooms; $108). **Restaurants:** None in park. In La Junta: Village Inn (5 Walmart Wy., tel. 719/384–1084; $7–$12). In Las Animas: Bent's Fort Inn (U.S. 50, ¼ mile east of Las Animas, tel. 719/456–0011, www. bentsfortinn.com; $5–$7). **Groceries & Gear:** None in park. In La Junta: Loaf & Jug Store (101 N. Main St., tel. 719/384–8360).

FEES, HOURS & REGULATIONS

Tour fee: $3 adults, $2 ages 6–12, free ages 5 and under. Permits required in advance for commercial filming. No pets allowed in fort rooms. Park open June–Aug., daily 8–5:30; Sept.–May, daily 9–4.

HOW TO GET THERE

6 miles east of La Junta and 13 miles west of Las Animas on Rte. 194; 75 miles east of Pueblo and 140 miles west of Garden City, KS, via U.S. 50. Closest airport: Pueblo (75 miles).

CONTACTS

Bent's Old Fort National Historic Site (35110 Rte. 194 E, La Junta, CO 81050-9523, tel. 719/383–5010, fax 719/383–2129, www.nps.gov/beol). John Martin Reservoir State Park (30703 Rte. 24, Hasty, CO 81044, tel.

719/829–1801, 800/678–2267 campground reservations, www.parks. state.co.us). La Junta Chamber of Commerce (110 Santa Fe Ave., La Junta, CO 81050, tel. 719/384–7411, www.lajuntachamber.com).

Black Canyon of the Gunnison National Park

In southwestern Colorado, east of Montrose

Carved by the Gunnison River, the walls of schist and gneiss in Black Canyon are some of the most imposing in North America. The canyon and its rims are home to black bears, mule deer, golden eagles, and peregrine falcons. The site was proclaimed a monument on March 2, 1933, and was redesignated a national park on October 21, 1999.

WHAT TO SEE & DO

Cross-country skiing, fishing, hiking, picnicking, rock climbing, snow-shoeing, wildlife viewing. **Facilities:** Visitor center (Gunnison Point, South Rim), amphitheater, auditorium, interpretive signs, trails. Book sale area. **Programs & Events:** Ranger-guided and evening programs (Memorial Day–Labor Day), ranger-guided snowshoe walks (Jan.–Mar., snowshoes provided), full-moon ranger-guided cross-country ski programs along the rim (weekends only, mid-Jan.–early Mar., reservations required, tel. 970/249–1914 Ext 423). **Tips & Hints:** Hiking in the canyon is strenuous, and a permit is required. Go mid-May–mid-June for wildflowers, late Sept. for fall foliage. Busiest July and Aug., least crowded Dec. and Jan.

FOOD, LODGING & SUPPLIES

Camping: In the park: North Rim (13 sites; $12; pit toilets), South Rim (88 sites; $12–$18; pit toilets). Backcountry camping allowed. In Montrose: Cedar Creek RV Park (126 Rose La., tel. 970/249–3884 or 877/425–3884, www.cedarcreekrv.com; 43 sites; $22.50–$35.50; flush toilets, showers, hookups), Montrose Black Canyon National Park KOA (200 N. Cedar Ave., tel. 970/249-9177 or 800/562–9114, www.montrosekoa.com; 79 sites, 4 cabins; $15–$39.50; flush toilets, showers, hookups). **Hotels:** None in park. In Montrose: Best Western Red Arrow Motor Inn (1702 E. Main St., tel. 970/249–9641, www.bestwestern.com; 57 rooms; $117–$130). In Crawford: Hitching Post Hotel & Feed Store (313 Rte. 92, tel. 970/921–5040, www. hitchingposthotel.com; 10 rooms; $60–$90). **Restaurants:** None in park. In Montrose: Red Barn Restaurant & Lounge (1413 E. Main St., tel. 970/249–9202; redbarnmontrose.com; $6–$25). **Groceries & Gear:** None in park. In Montrose: Safeway (1329 S. Townsend Ave., tel. 970/249–8822).

FEES, HOURS & REGULATIONS

Entrance fee: $15 per vehicle. Wilderness permits (free) required for inner canyon. Colorado state fishing license required. No vehicles or bicycles off roads. No pets in wilderness, leashed pets elsewhere. Fires only in campground grates. South Rim open year-round, North Rim closed in winter when snowfall is over 4 inches. South Rim Visitor Center open June–Sept., daily 8–6; Oct.–May, daily 8:30–4.

HOW TO GET THERE

South Rim is 15 miles east of Montrose via U.S. 50 and Rte. 347, North Rim is 11 miles south of Crawford, off Rte. 92 (6 miles unpaved). There is no bridge between the rims. Closest airport: Montrose (15 miles).

CONTACTS

Black Canyon of the Gunnison National Park (102 Elk Creek, Gunnison, CO 81230, tel. 970/641–2337, fax 970/249–3127, www.nps.gov/blca). Montrose Association of Commerce & Tourism (1519 E. Main St., Montrose, CO 81401, tel. 970/249–5000, fax 970/249–2907, www.montroseact.com).

Colorado National Monument

In west-central Colorado, near Grand Junction

The towering red sheer-walled canyons and monoliths here reflect the environment and history of this colorful sandstone country. Residents include bighorn sheep, golden eagles, mountain lions, and lizards. The monument was proclaimed on May 24, 1911.

WHAT TO SEE & DO

Bicycling, bird-watching, hiking, picnicking, rock climbing, scenic drives. **Facilities:** Visitor center, overlooks, trails. Bookstore, picnic area. **Programs & Events:** Audiovisual programs; summer ranger and Junior Ranger programs. **Tips & Hints:** Plan to spend two to five hours at the monument. Busiest June and July, least crowded Dec. and Jan.

FOOD, LODGING & SUPPLIES

Camping: In the park: Saddlehorn (80 sites; $20; flush toilets). Backcountry camping allowed. **Hotels:** None in park. In Grand Junction: Doubletree (743 Horizon Dr., tel. 970/241–8888, doubletree.hilton.com; 273 rooms; $154–$184). **Restaurants:** None in park. In Grand Junction: Dolce Vita (336 Main St., tel. 970/242–8482, www.dolcevitagrandjunction.com; $8–$14).

FEES, HOURS & REGULATIONS

Entrance fee: $10 per vehicle; $5 per person. Permit required (free) for backcountry camping. No pets on trails; leashed pets on paved surfaces. Park open daily. Visitor center open Memorial Day–Sept., daily 8–6; Oct.–Memorial Day, daily 9–5.

HOW TO GET THERE

From the east, exit I–70 at Horizon Dr. for east entrance. From the west, take Exit 19 to west entrance. Closest airport: Grand Junction (15 miles).

CONTACT

Colorado National Monument (Fruita, CO 81521, tel. 970/858–3617, fax 970/858–0372, www.nps.gov/colm).

Curecanti National Recreation Area

In southwestern Colorado, west of Gunnison

Three reservoirs, extending for almost 40 miles between the towns of Gunnison and Montrose, form the heart of Curecanti. Blue Mesa Reservoir, stocked with trout and salmon, is a mecca for anglers and water-sports enthusiasts. Bald eagles and both sandhill and whooping cranes migrate through the area in spring and fall. The area is named after Curecanti, a subchief of the Ute Indians, who lived here when European settlers arrived in the 1800s. The park is administered under a February 11, 1965, cooperative agreement with the Bureau of Reclamation.

WHAT TO SEE & DO

Boating (rentals, Elk Creek and Lake Fork marinas), cross-country skiing, fishing (rentals, Elk Creek and Lake Fork marinas), hiking, ice fishing, picnicking, snowshoeing, swimming, waterskiing, windsurfing. **Facilities:** 2 visitor centers: Elk Creek and Cimarron. Bookstores, fire grates, picnic tables. **Programs & Events:** Ranger-led evening programs and boat tours (Memorial Day–Labor Day). **Tips & Hints:** You have to hike down 232 steps to get to the boat dock. Bring water and a jacket. Go May–Aug. for wildflowers, May and Sept. for bird migrations, all year for fishing. Busiest July and Aug., least crowded Dec. and Mar.

FOOD, LODGING & SUPPLIES

Camping: 10 campgrounds in the park: Cimarron (U.S. 50, 20 miles east of Montrose, tel. 970/249–4074; 22 sites; $12; flush toilets; closed Oct.–mid-May), Dry Gulch (U.S. 50, 17 miles west of Gunnison, tel. 970/641–2337; 10 sites; $12; vault toilets; closed Oct.–mid-May), East Elk Creek (U.S. 50, 16 miles west of Gunnison, tel. 970/641–2337; group site; $50; vault toilets; closed Oct.–mid-May), East Portal (East Portal Rd., below Crystal Dam at bottom of canyon, tel. 970/641–2337; 15 tent sites; $12; vault toilets; closed Oct.–mid-May), Elk Creek (U.S. 50, 16 miles west of Gunnison, tel. 970/641–2337 Ext. 205; 179 sites; $12; flush toilets, electricity, showers), Gateview (off unpaved road off Rte. 149, at extreme southern end of Lake Fork Arm, tel. 970/641–2337; 7 sites; free; vault toilets; closed Oct.–mid-May), Lake Fork (U.S. 50, 27 miles west of Gunnison, tel. 970/641–2337; 87 sites; $12; flush toilets, showers; closed Oct.–mid-May), Ponderosa (Soap Creek Rd., tel. 970/641–2337; 29 sites; $12; vault toilets; closed Oct.–mid-May), Red Creek (off U.S. 50, 19 miles west of Gunnison, tel. 970/641–2337; 2 sites, group site; $12, $25 group site; vault toilets; closed Oct.–mid-May), Stevens Creek (U.S. 50, 12 miles west of Gunnison, tel. 970/641–2337; 54 sites; $12; vault toilets; closed Oct.–mid-May).

Backcountry camping allowed. 🏨 **Hotels:** None in park. In Gunnison: Seasons Inn (412 E. Tomichi Ave., tel. 970/641–0700; 24 rooms; $68–$95). ✕ **Restaurants:** In the park: Pappy's Restaurant (24830 U.S. Hwy. 50, tel. 970/641–0403; $7–$13; closed Oct.–mid-May). ⛽ **Groceries & Gear:** In the park: Elk Creek Marina Store (at Elk Creek Marina, tel. 970/641–0707). In Gunnison: Gunnison Lakeside Resort Store (28357 W. U.S. 50, tel. 970/641–0477, closed mid-Nov.–Apr.).

FEES, HOURS & REGULATIONS

Free. Boat permit required ($4 for 2 days, $10 for 14 days, $30 per year) on Blue Mesa Reservoir. Boat tours Memorial Day–Labor Day, daily at 10 and 12:30 ($16, $8 ages 12 and under). Colorado fishing license required. Leashed pets only. No bikes or motorized vehicles on trails. Park open daily. Elk Creek Visitor Center open Memorial Day–Sept., daily 8–6; Oct.–Apr., hours vary. Cimarron visitor center open mid-May–late Sept., hours vary.

HOW TO GET THERE

Park headquarters is 15 miles west of Gunnison on U.S. 50. Closest airport: Gunnison.

CONTACTS

Curecanti National Recreation Area (102 Elk Creek, Gunnison, CO 81230, tel. 970/641–2337, fax 970/641–3127, www.nps.gov/cure). Gunnison Country Chamber of Commerce (500 E. Tomichi Ave., Gunnison, CO 81230, tel. 970/641–1501, www.gunnison-co.com). Montrose Association of Commerce & Tourism (1519 E. Main St., Montrose, CO 81401, tel. 970/249–5000, fax 970/249–2907, www.montroseact.com).

Dinosaur National Monument

In northwestern Colorado and northeastern Utah

The monument is the only national park that protects a dinosaur quarry: the Carnegie Quarry, where you can see 1,500 dinosaur fossils encased in a rocky cliff. The fossil site represents one of the best windows scientists have into the world of late Jurassic (149-million-year-old) dinosaurs. Archaeological sites reveal that people have lived in this region for more than 10,000 years. The site's Green and Yampa river canyons are of great ecological, scenic, and recreational value. The park was established on October 4, 1915.

WHAT TO SEE & DO

Fishing, hiking, rafting, scenic drives, white-water boating. **Facilities:** 2 visitor centers: Quarry Visitor Center (7 miles north of Jensen, UT) and Canyon Visitor Center (2 miles east of Dinosaur, CO). Bookstores, picnic areas. **Programs & Events:** Dinosaur and nature talks, guided walks, evening campground talks, self-guided driving tours, self-guided nature trails. **Tips & Hints:** Visit in fall for smallest crowds and nicest weather. Busiest June and July, least crowded Dec. and Jan.

FOOD, LODGING & SUPPLIES

Camping: 6 campgrounds in the park: Deerlodge Park (off U.S. 40, 53 miles northeast of headquarters; 8 tent sites; $8 when water is available, otherwise free; vault toilets), Echo Park (Harpers Corner Dr., 38 miles north of headquarters; 22 tent sites; $8; vault toilets), Gates of Lodore (off 318, far north corner of park; 17 sites; $8; vault toilets), Green River (Cub Creek Rd., 5 miles east of Dinosaur Quarry; 88 sites; $12; flush toilets; closed Nov.–mid-Apr.), Rainbow Park (Island Park Rd.; 2 tent sites; free; vault toilet), Split Mountain (Cub Creek Rd., 4 miles east of Dinosaur Quarry; 4 group sites; $35; flush toilets). Backcountry camping allowed. **Hotels:** None in park. In Craig: Holiday Inn (300 S. Hwy. 13, tel. 970/824–4000, www.holidayinn.com; 152 rooms, 19 suites; $89). In Vernal, UT: Landmark Inn Bed & Breakfast (301 E. 100 S, tel. 435/781–1800 or 888/738–1800, www.landmark-inn.com; 7 rooms, 3 suites; $84–$159), Best Western Antlers (423 W. Main St., tel. 435/789–1202, www.bestwestern.com; 44 rooms; $120). **Restaurants:** None in park. In Craig: Gino's Neighborhood Pizzeria & Grill (572 Breeze St., tel. 970/824–6323; $10–$20). In Vernal, UT: Bar-B-Qued (1525 W. U.S. 40, tel. 435/781–2273, www.barbquedvernal.com; $7.50–$26). **Groceries & Gear:** None in park. In Vernal, UT: Davis Jubilee (575 W. Main St., tel. 435/789–2001), True Value Hardware (280 W. Main St., tel. 435/781–1556).

FEES, HOURS & REGULATIONS

Entrance fee: $5 per person on foot, bicycle, or motorcycle; $10 per vehicle. Utah or Colorado state fishing license required. White-water boating permit required (tel. 970/374–2468), backcountry camping permit required (free). Park open daily. Quarry Visitor Center open Sept.–mid-June, daily 9–5, mid-June–Aug., daily 8:30–5:30; Canyon Visitor Center open mid-May–late Sept., daily 9–5.

HOW TO GET THERE

The main access points to the park are Dinosaur Quarry, 7 miles north of Jensen, UT, on Rte. 149, and Monument Headquarters, 2 miles east of Dinosaur, CO, on U.S. 40.

CONTACT

Dinosaur National Monument (4545 E. U.S. 40, Dinosaur, CO 81610-9724, tel. 435/781–7700, fax 435/781–7735, www.nps.gov/dino). Vernal Area Chamber of Commerce (134 W. Main St., Vernal, UT 84078, tel. 435/789–1352, www.dinoland.com).

Florissant Fossil Beds National Monument

In central Colorado, 40 miles west of Colorado Springs

The 6,000-acre monument preserves one of the world's most comprehensive fossil sites of late Eocene life. Some 34 million years ago, a volcanic field erupted and buried a redwood forest at the site in volcanic mud. The ash and mudflows sealed Lake Florissant's bottom sediments. Trapped within these sediment layers are thousands of insect species and 140 different plants, along with fish, birds, and mammals. The monument was established on August 25, 1969.

WHAT TO SEE & DO

Hiking, picnicking, taking interpretive walks, touring 1878 homestead and petrified redwood forest. **Facilities:** Visitor center, Hornbek Homestead, amphitheather, outdoor exhibits, 13 miles of trails. Book and map sales area, picnic areas. **Programs & Events:** Ranger-led interpretive programs (mid-June–Sept., daily 10–4 on the hour), guided walks (June–Sept.), special programs on fossils, elk watches (mid-June–Oct., weekends). Hornbek Homestead Open House (last weekend in July, 2nd weekend in Dec.). **Tips & Hints:** Be prepared for high-altitude (8,400 feet) conditions, rapidly changing weather, and moderate physical activity. Go June and July for wildflowers; Sept. and Oct. for fall colors, fewer people, and elk activity. Busiest July and Aug., least crowded Dec. and Jan.

FOOD, LODGING & SUPPLIES

Camping: None in park. Near Divide: Mueller State Park (Rte. 67 off U.S. 24, tel. 719/687–2366 or 800/678–2267, www.parks.state. co.us; $16–$20; 132 sites; flush toilets, showers, hookups). **Hotels:** None in park. In Victor: Victor Hotel (4th St. and Victor Ave., tel. 719/ 689–3553, www.victorhotelcolorado.com; 20 rooms; $79). In Woodland Park: Country Lodge (723 W. U.S. 24, tel. 719/687–6277, www. woodlandcountrylodge.com; 60 rooms; $119–$139). **X Restaurants:** None in park. In Woodland Park: Mangia Mangia! (407 E. Grace Ave., tel. 719/687–3400, www.mangiamangiawp.com; $7–$19). **Groceries & Gear:** In Florissant: Sinclair (2839 W. U.S. 24, tel. 719/748–8080). In Woodland Park: City Market (777 Gold Hill Pl. N, tel. 719/687–3592).

FEES, HOURS & REGULATIONS

Entrance fee: $3 adults, free ages 16 and under. Reservations required (tel. 719/748–3253) for four-hour summer programs on wildlife, ecology, and history. No fossil collecting, hunting, off-road vehicle travel. No firearms. No pets in backcountry. No pets, horses, bicycles, or motorized vehicles on trails. Park and visitor center open June–Aug., daily 8–7; Sept.–May, daily 8–4:30.

HOW TO GET THERE

Teller County Rd. 1½ miles south of Florissant, 35 miles west of Colorado Springs on U.S. 24. Closest airport: Colorado Springs.

CONTACTS

Florissant Fossil Beds National Monument (Box 185, Florissant, CO 80816, tel. 719/748–3253, fax 719/748–3164, www.nps.gov/ flfo). Greater Woodland Park Chamber of Commerce (210 E. Midland Ave., Woodland Park, CO 80863, tel. 719/687–9885, www. woodlandparkchamber.com).

Great Sand Dunes National Park & Preserve

In south-central Colorado, near Alamosa

In a corner of the remote San Luis Valley in the Colorado Rockies, the Great Sand Dunes rise to heights of nearly 750 feet, forming the tallest sand dunes in North America. Covering 30 square miles, the park provides opportunities for hiking, wilderness camping, and exploring. The monument was proclaimed in 1932 and became a national park and preserve in 2004.

WHAT TO SEE & DO

Photography, dune climbing, hiking, picnicking, snowshoeing, walking, cross-country skiing. **Facilities:** Visitor center, outdoor amphitheater. Grills, picnic tables. **Programs & Events:** Self-guided trails, ranger programs, evening slide programs, night sky programs (May–Sept.). **Tips & Hints:** Hike dunes with closed-toe shoes on early or late on summer days. Typical summer temperatures of 80°F cause sand temperature to rise to 140°F. Go in spring or early summer to visit Medano Creek, which flows until mid-June at the base of the dunes. Go in July for wildflowers, Aug. for prairie sunflowers, late Sept. for fall foliage. Busiest June and July, least crowded Dec. and Jan.

FOOD, LODGING & SUPPLIES

Camping: In the park: Piñon Flats (88 sites; $20; flush toilets). Backcountry camping allowed (with free permit). In Mosca: Great Sand Dunes Oasis (5400 Rte. 150 N, tel. 719/378–2222, www.greatdunes.com; 90 sites, 4 cabins; $23–$36, $48 cabins; flush toilets, showers, hookups; closed Nov.–Mar.). **Hotels:** None in park. Nearby: Great Sand Dunes Lodge (7900 Rte. 150 N, tel. 719/378–2900, www.gsdlodge.com; 12 rooms; $89–$130; closed late Oct.–mid-Mar.). In Alamosa: Best Western Alamosa Inn (2005 Main St., tel. 719/589–2567 or 800/459–5123, www.bestwestern.com; 53 rooms; $90–$117). **Restaurants:** None in park. Nearby: Great Sand Dunes Oasis (5400 Rte. 150 N, tel. 719/378–2222, www.greatdunes.com; $7–$15; no dinner Mon.–Thurs. except in summer; closed Nov.–Apr.). **Groceries & Gear:** None in park. Nearby: Great Sand Dunes Oasis (5400 Rte. 150 N, tel. 719/378–2222; closed Nov.–Mar.).

FEES, HOURS & REGULATIONS

Entrance fee: $3 adults, free ages 15 and under. Backpacking permits required (free). Colorado state fishing license required. Leashed pets only. Pets permitted in day use areas and high mountain trails. Protect pets from hot sand in summer. Mountain bikes, motor vehicles on established roads only. No mechanized vehicles on dunes. No all-terrain vehicles, hunting, firewood gathering. Park open daily. Visitor center open June–Aug., daily 8:30–6; Nov.–Feb., daily 9–4:30; Mar.–May, Sept. and Oct., daily 9–5:30.

HOW TO GET THERE

38 miles northeast of Alamosa on Rte. 150. Closest airport: Alamosa.

CONTACTS

Great Sand Dunes National Park & Preserve (11999 Rte. 150, Mosca, CO 81146, tel. 719/378–6399, fax 719/378–6310, www.nps.gov/grsa). Alamosa Convention & Visitors Bureau (601 State Ave., Alamosa, CO 81101, tel. 800/258–7597, www.alamosa.org).

Hovenweep National Monument

In southwestern Colorado, near Cortez, and in southeast Utah, near Blanding

Hovenweep protects some of the finest examples of Ancestral Puebloan stone architecture. The inhabitants of Hovenweep were part of the large farming culture that lived in the area from 500 BC until AD 1300, and their well-preserved stone towers and pueblo-style buildings perch on large boulders and slickrock canyon rims. The monument—noted for its solitude, clear skies, and undeveloped natural character—was proclaimed on March 2, 1923.

WHAT TO SEE & DO

Guided and self-guided tours of cliff dwellings, towers, and pueblos; picnicking. **Facilities:** Ranger station, trails. Bookstore, picnic tables. **Programs & Events:** Ranger-led and self-guided tours. Evening programs (late May–late Sept.). **Tips & Hints:** Plan to spend one to two hours visiting ranger station, 2-mile Square Tower Group area trail, and archaeological sites. Go in spring or fall for best hiking. Bring insect repellent in late May and early June when biting gnats are out. Go before noon in summer to avoid heat. Avoid late-afternoon winter visits because of remote location and possible storms. Dirt roads may become impassable during and after storms. Busiest May and Sept., least crowded Jan. and Feb.

FOOD, LODGING & SUPPLIES

Camping: In the park: Hovenweep Campground (near visitor center; 31 sites; $10; flush toilets). No backcountry camping. **Hotels:** None in park. In Cortez: Best Western Turquoise Inn & Suites (535 E. Main St., tel. 970/565–3778 or 800/547–3376, www.bestwestern. com; 77 rooms; $120–$130). **Restaurants:** None in park. In Cortez: J. Fargo's Family Dining and Micro Brewery (1209 E. Main St., tel. 970/564–0242, www.jfargos.com; $9–$11). **Groceries:** None in park. In Blanding: Clark's Market (820 S. Main St., tel. 435/678–2721).

FEES, HOURS & REGULATIONS

$6 per vehicle. No climbing on ancient walls or collecting artifacts. Hiking on established trails only. Mountain bikes on roadways only. Ranger station open Oct. and Apr., daily 8–5; May–Sept., daily 8–6; Nov.–Mar., daily 8–4:30. Trails open sunrise–sunset.

HOW TO GET THERE

From Cortez, CO, the monument can be reached via U.S. 491/160 south and McElmo Canyon Rd. west. Follow Hovenweep signs. From Blanding or Bluff, UT, turn east off U.S. 191 on Rte. 262. Follow Hovenweep signs. From Pleasant View, CO, turn west off U.S 491. Follow Hovenweep signs. Closest airports: Cortez (40 miles), Durango (95 miles).

CONTACTS

Hovenweep National Monument (McElmo Rte., Cortez, CO 81321, tel. 970/562–4282, fax 970/562–4283, www.nps.gov/hove).

Mesa Verde National Park

In southwestern Colorado, near Cortez

Covered mostly by piñon and juniper forest, this 52,485-acre park preserves the cliff dwellings and surface sites of the Ancestral Pueblo people, or Anasazi, who lived in the area between 550 and 1300. Elevations range from about 6,000 feet in the canyon bottoms to 8,427 feet at Park Point. The park was established in 1906 and designated a World Heritage Site in 1978.

WHAT TO SEE & DO

Hiking, touring cliff dwellings, visiting museum. **Facilities:** Visitor and Research Center with ticket sales desk and interpretive exhibits, Chapin Mesa Museum, Morefield Ranger Station (May–mid-Aug.), amphitheaters, kiosk. Gas station, gift shops (Morefield, Fair View, Chapin Mesa), laundry, picnic areas with grates, post office. **Programs & Events:** Tours of Balcony House, Cliff Palace, Long House; Spruce Tree House tours (self-guided early Mar.–early Nov., ranger-led rest of the year), evening campfire programs at Morefield Campground (May–Sept.), Junior Ranger Program. Holiday Open House (Christmas). **Tips & Hints:** Plan ahead for guided tours, which require tickets from the Visitor and Research Center. Take it slow at 7,000 feet elevation. The park's best weather is in May, Sept., and Oct. Go in late May for flowers and late Sept. for fall colors. Busiest June–Aug., least crowded Jan. and Feb.

FOOD, LODGING & SUPPLIES

Camping: In the park: Morefield (tel. 970/533–7731 or 800/449–2288; 267 sites; $27; flush toilets, showers, hookups; closed mid-Oct.–mid-May). No backcountry camping. Group campsites available (reservations required, tel. 970/533–7731). **Hotels:** In the park: Far View Lodge (tel. 970/533–7731 or 800/449–2288; 150 rooms; $130–$160; closed mid-Oct.–mid-Mar.). **Restaurants:** In the park: Far View Terrace (tel. 970/529–4444; $8–$12; closed mid-Oct.–early May), Metate Room (tel. 970/529–4422; $9–$28; closed late Oct.–mid-Apr.), Spruce Tree Terrace (tel. 970/529–4521; $3–$8). **Groceries & Gear:** In the park: Spruce Tree Terrace Shop (tel. 970/529–4521). In Cortez: Safeway (1580 E. Main St., tel. 970/564–9590). In Mancos: P & D Grocery (280 E. Frontage Rd., tel. 970/533–7932).

FEES, HOURS & REGULATIONS

Entrance fee: $5 per person, $15 per private noncommercial vehicle ($10 Labor Day–Memorial Day). Balcony House, Cliff Palace, and Long House are accessible only by ranger-led tour; fees apply. No hunting. No pets in cliff dwellings, park buildings, or on trails. Leashed pets elsewhere. No mountain biking or trails for bicycles. Bicycling discouraged because of narrow roads. No motorized vehicles on trails. Entrance road open daily. Mesa Top Loop Drive open daily 8–sunset, weather permitting. Wetherill Mesa Road open Memorial Day–Labor Day, daily 9–4:15. Cliff Palace and Balcony House loop open only for cross-country skiing or walking in winter. Cliff Palace generally open Apr.–Oct., daily. Balcony House open mid-May–mid-Oct., daily. Visitor center open Apr.–Oct., daily 8–5. Chapin Mesa Museum open mid-Apr.–mid-Oct., daily 8–6:30; mid-Oct.–mid-Apr., daily 8–5.

HOW TO GET THERE

36 miles west of Durango and 9 miles east of Cortez via U.S. 160. Closest airports: Cortez (12 miles), Durango (52 miles).

CONTACTS

National Park Service (Box 8, Mesa Verde, CO 81330, tel. 970/529–4465, fax 970/529–4637, www.nps.gov/meve). Cortez Chamber of Commerce (928 E. Main, Cortez, CO 81321, tel. 970/565–3414, fax 970/565–8373, www.cortezchamber.com). Durango Chamber of Commerce (111 S. Camino del Rio, Box 2587, Durango, CO 81302, tel. 970/247–0312, fax 970/385–7884, www.durangobusiness.org).

Rocky Mountain National Park

In north-central Colorado, near Estes Park

Spectacular snow-mantled peaks overlooking verdant subalpine valleys and glistening lakes are draws at this park. Tundra predominates, as one-third of the park is above tree line and is a major reason these peaks and valleys have been protected. More than one-quarter of the plants found here are also native to the Arctic. At lower elevations, ponderosa pine and juniper, Douglas fir, blue spruce, lodgepole pine, and aspen can be found. Wildflowers dot meadows and glades. As the elevation rises, Engelmann spruce and subalpine fir take over in the subalpine ecosystem. Openings in these cool, dark forests produce wildflower gardens where the blue Colorado columbine reigns. At the upper edges of this zone, twisted, gnarled timberline trees hug the ground. Then the trees give way to fragile alpine tundra. The park was established in 1915 and designated an International Biosphere Reserve in 1977.

WHAT TO SEE & DO

Backpacking, cross-country skiing, fishing, hiking, horseback riding, picnicking, snowshoeing, wildlife watching. **Facilities:** 5 visitor centers:

Beaver Meadows–park headquarters (2½ miles west of Estes Park on U.S. 36), Kawuneeche (1½ miles north of Grand Lake on U.S. 34), Alpine (23 miles west of Beaver Meadows and Fall River entrances), Fall River (4½ miles west of Estes Park on U.S. 34), Moraine Park Visitor Center (on Bear Lake Rd., 1½ miles from Beaver Meadows entrance on U.S. 36). Sheep Lake information station (2 miles west of Fall River entrance), Holzwarth Historic Site (8 miles north of Kawuneeche visitor center on U.S. 34); amphitheaters, auditoriums, roadside pullouts with wayside interpretive exhibits, trails. Book and map sales areas, picnic areas. **Programs & Events:** Junior Ranger program; ranger-led walks, talks, and hikes. **Tips & Hints:** Watch for signs of altitude sickness (nausea, dizziness, headache, insomnia, rapid heartbeat, and shortness of breath); make sure to acclimatize and hydrate often. Park roads are 7,500–12,183 feet above sea level. Get below tree line by early afternoon to avoid lightning. Go June and July to see bighorn sheep, late June and July for wildflowers, mid-July–early Sept. for nontechnical climb up Longs Peak, and Sept.–early Oct. for elk mating season. Busiest July and Aug., least crowded Jan. and Feb.

FOOD, LODGING & SUPPLIES

Camping: 5 campgrounds in the park. First-come, first-served campgrounds: Longs Peak (off Hwy. 7; 26 sites; $20; flush toilets [summer]; vault toilets [winter]; open year-round), Timber Creek (off Trail Ridge Rd., 8.2 miles north of Kawuneeche Visitor Center; 98 sites; $20; flush toilets [summer]; vault toilets [winter]; open year-round), Aspenglen (off U.S. 34, ½ mile south of Fall River entrance; 54 sites; $20; flush toilets; open late-May–mid-Sept.), Glacier Basin (off Bear Lake Rd.; 150 sites; $20; flush toilets; open late May–late Sept.), Moraine Park (off Bear Lake Rd.; 245 sites; $20; flush toilets; open year-round). Backcountry camping allowed. **Hotels:** None in park. In Estes Park: Appenzell Inn (1100 Big Thompson Ave., tel. 970/586–2023 or 800/475–1125, estesparklodging.com; 34 suites; $85–$265), Econo Lodge (1650 Big Thompson Ave., tel. 970/586–3386, www.econolodge.com; 47 rooms, 4 suites; $139). In Grand Lake: Gateway Inn (200 W. Portal Rd., tel. 970/627–2400 or 877/627–1352, gatewayinn.com; 31 rooms; $120–$170), Mountain Lake Lodge (10480 U.S. 34, tel. 970/627–8448, www.grandlakelodging.net; 11 cabins; $119). **Restaurants:** In the park: Trail Ridge Store snack bar, next to Alpine Visitor Center. In Estes Park: Nicky's Cattleman Steakhouse (1350 U.S. 34, tel. 970/586–5376, www.nickysestespark.com). In Grand Lake: The Historic Rapids Lodge & Restaurant (209 Rapids La., tel. 970/627–3707, rapidslodge.com; $10–$38). **Groceries & Gear:** None in park. In Estes Park: B&B Food Mart (1110 Woodstock Dr., tel. 970/586–5749), Rocky Mountain Gateway (3450 Fall River Rd., tel. 970/577–0043).

FEES, HOURS & REGULATIONS

Entrance fee: $10 per person on foot, bicycle, or motorcycle; $20 per private vehicle; free ages 15 and under. Colorado state fishing license required. Advance camping reservations for summer season (tel. 877/444–6777, www.recreation.gov). Backcountry permits required (tel. 970/586–1242 or write Backcountry Office, Rocky Mountain National

Park, Estes Park, CO 80517, no telephone reservations May 16–Sept. 30. $20 fee May–Oct. for each backcountry permit issued). No hunting. Pets allowed only in picnic areas, campgrounds, and along roadsides. Pets must be on leashes no longer than 6 feet. They must be attended at all times and never left alone in vehicles or at campsites. Bicycles on roads only. No motorized vehicles permitted off-road. Park open daily. Trail Ridge Rd. (U.S. 34) usually closed mid-Oct.–Memorial Day weekend. Beaver Meadows and Kawuneeche visitor centers open year-round; call for hours. Alpine Visitor Center, Fall River Visitor Center, Moraine Park Visitor Center, Sheep Lakes information station, and Holzwarth Historic Site open seasonally; call for hours.

HOW TO GET THERE

From the east via U.S. 34, U.S. 36, and Hwy. 7; from the west via U.S. 40 and U.S. 34. Closest airports: Denver (70 miles), Cheyenne, WY (91 miles).

CONTACTS

Rocky Mountain National Park (Estes Park, CO 80517, tel. 970/586–1206, www.nps.gov/romo). Estes Park Visitor Center (500 Big Thompson Ave., Estes Park, CO 80517, tel. 800/443–7837 or 970/577–9900, www.visitestespark.com). Grand Lake Chamber of Commerce (West Portal Rd. and U.S. 34, Box 429, Grand Lake, CO 80447, tel. 800/531–1019 or 970/627–3402, www.grandlakechamber.com).

Sand Creek Massacre National Historic Site

In Eads, 1 hr and 45 mins southeast of Colorado Springs

The site honors the victims of one of the bloodiest moments in Colorado history, the Sand Creek Massacre in 1864. Soldiers and volunteers commanded by Col. John Chivington attacked a peaceful Indian encampment that the U.S. government had promised to protect. Nearly 200 Cheyenne and Arapaho, mostly women, children, and elderly, were slaughtered and their bodies mutilated. The site was authorized in November 2000.

WHAT TO SEE & DO

Hiking. **Facilities:** Bookstore, picnic tables. **Programs & Events:** Cheyenne and Arapaho tribes hold the annual Spiritual Healing Run, a relay that starts at the Sand Creek Massacre National Historic Site and ends in Denver the next day (Nov.). For more information, call 406/592–3599. **Tips & Hints:** Spring and fall are the most pleasant times to visit, June–Aug. is hot, and Dec.–Feb. can be too cold.

FOOD & LODGING

Camping: None in park. Nearby: In John Martin Reservoir State Park: Lake Hasty Campground (30703 County Rd. 24, south of U.S.

50, tel. 719/829–1801, www.parks.state.co.us; 109 sites; $16–$24; flush toilets, showers, hookups). ▥ **Hotels:** None in park. In Rocky Ford: Lady Bohannon Guest House (1401 Swink Ave., tel. 866/782–5239, www.ladybohannon.com; 2 rooms; $95). In Lamar: Rodeway Inn Cow Palace (1301 N. Main St., tel. 719/336–7753, www.rodewayinn.com; 101 rooms; $89. ✕ **Restaurants:** None in park. In La Junta: Village Inn (5 Walmart Wy., tel. 719/384–1084; $7–$12), Mexico City Café (1617 Raton Ave., tel. 719/384–9818; $4–$7). ♨ **Groceries & Gear:** None in park. In Eads: Stop & Shop (1111 Main St., tel. 719/438–5881).

FEES, HOURS & REGULATIONS
Free. Open daily 9–4.

HOW TO GET THERE
Hwy. 194 E, 18 miles northeast of Eads, CO. Closest airport: Colorado Springs (135 miles).

CONTACTS
Sand Creek Massacre National Historic Site (910 Wansted St., Eads, CO 81036, tel. 719/438–5916, www.nps.gov/sand).

Yucca House
National Monument

In southwestern Colorado, near Cortez

This large prehistoric Indian pueblo site west of Mesa Verde is as yet unexcavated. There are no public facilities or services. The monument was proclaimed on December 19, 1919.

CONTACT
Yucca House National Monument (c/o Box 8, Mesa Verde National Park, CO 81330, tel. 970/529–4465, fax 970/529–4637, www.nps.gov/yuho).

See Also

Cache la Poudre River, Continental Divide National Scenic Trail, Pony Express National Historic Trail, and Santa Fe National Historic Trail, in Other National Parklands.

CONNECTICUT

Weir Farm National Historic Site

In southwestern Connecticut, in Wilton and Ridgefield

Weir Farm National Historic Site preserves and interprets the farm, summer home, and studio of J. Alden Weir (1852–1919), one of the founders of the Impressionist tradition in American art. The 60-acre site also includes the studio of the sculptor Mahonri Young (1877–1957). The site was authorized on October 31, 1990.

WHAT TO SEE & DO

Touring historic home, stone walls, and gardens; walking trails. **Facilities:** Visitor center, historic home, artist studios, gardens and trails. Gift shop. **Programs & Events:** Guided tours, art history and stone wall programs, self-guided walking tours, Junior Ranger program, "Take Part in Art" plein-air painting. **Tips & Hints:** Expect to see structures and landscapes that inspired artists to paint rather than an art gallery. Wear comfortable walking shoes for hikes. Visit in spring and fall. Busiest July–Oct., least crowded Jan. and Feb.

FOOD, LODGING & SUPPLIES

Camping: None in park. In Southbury: Kettletown State Park (1400 George's Hill Rd., tel. 203/264–5678; 68 sites; $17–$27; flush toilets; closed Oct.–mid-May). **Hotels:** None in park. In Danbury: Residence Inn Danbury (22 Segar St., tel. 203/797–1256, www.marriott. com; 78 rooms; $129–$189). **Restaurants:** None in park. In West Redding: LumberYard Pub (2 Main St., tel. 203/544–7287, www.lumberyardpub.com; $8–$18). **Groceries:** None in park. In Ridgefield: Ancona's Market (720 Branchville Rd., tel. 203/544–8436).

FEES, HOURS & REGULATIONS

Free. Grounds open daily dawn–dusk. Visitor center open Apr.–Nov., Thurs.–Sun. 10–4; Dec.–Mar., weekends 10–4. No buses, RVs, or large vehicles in parking lot. Dogs on leashes permitted. No hunting. No mountain or trail bikes, motorized or mechanized equipment on trails. Connecticut state fishing license required.

HOW TO GET THERE

From I–95 or I–84 take U.S. 7 to Rte. 102 west, left at Old Branchville Rd., left at Nod Hill Rd.; 1 mile to parking lot. Closest airports: LaGuardia in New York City (55 miles), Westchester County in White Plains, NY (30 miles).

CONTACTS

Weir Farm National Historic Site (735 Nod Hill Rd., Wilton, CT 06897, tel. 203/834–1896, fax 203/834–2421, www.nps.gov/wefa).

Western Connecticut Convention & Visitors Bureau (Box 968, Litchfield, CT 06759, tel. 860/567–4506, www.visitfairfieldcountyct.com).

See Also

Appalachian National Scenic Trail, West Virginia. *Farmington River (West Branch) and Quinebaug & Shetucket Rivers Valley National Heritage Corridor,* in Other National Parklands.

DISTRICT OF COLUMBIA

Carter G. Woodson Home

U Street Historic District, northwest D.C.

The Carter G. Woodson Home was where African American scholar and activist Dr. Carter Woodson lived from 1922 to 1950. Woodson dedicated his life to studying and bringing to light African American history, and was the second black man to graduate from Harvard. He created publishing outlets for black scholars and African American history, and was instrumental in founding Negro History Week, which turned into Black History Month. The home was acquired by the National Park Service in 2005. The Mary McLeod Bethune Council House, within walking distance to the west, temporarily holds the Woodson exhibits. The Bethune House was a famous gathering spot for African American leaders: it's where Martin Luther King Jr. and other black leaders organized during the 1963 March on Washington. Mary McLeod Bethune grew up during the Southern reconstruction, a child of slaves. She rose to prominence as an activist, educator, and presidential adviser to four presidents. She founded Bethune Cookman University, and the National Council of Negro Women in 1935.

WHAT TO SEE & DO

The Woodson Home will be closed until further notice. Mary McLeod Bethune Council House will temporarily host exhibits, including photographs and a 20-minute movie about Carter Woodson. **Facilities:** Visitor center. **Programs & Events:** Lesson plans and material for teachers, twice-a-year Junior Ranger program for students interested in genealogy, research access to the National Archives for Black Women's History.

FEES, HOURS & REGULATIONS

Free. Bethune House visitor center open Mon.–Sat. 9–5, except holidays. Groups need to make reservations in advance (tel. 202/673–2402).

HOW TO GET THERE

The Woodson Home is at 1538 9th St., NW, a five-minute walk from the Shaw–Howard University Metro station on the Green Line. For Bethune House, take the Metro to McPherson Square on the Orange and Blue lines.

CONTACTS

Woodson Home (1538 9th St., NW, Washington, DC 20001, 202/673–2402, www.nps.gov/cawo). Mary McLeod Bethune Council House

(1318 Vermont Ave., NW, Washington, DC 20005, tel. 202/673–2402, www.nps.gov/mamc).

Constitution Gardens

On the National Mall

The 50-acre garden, built during the U.S. Bicentennial in 1976, is a tribute to the founding of the nation with a memorial to the 56 signers of the Declaration of Independence. Included in the gardens are a 6½-acre lake and a 1-acre island. The site was authorized in 1974 and dedicated in 1978.

WHAT TO SEE & DO

Touring garden. **Facilities:** Memorial, trails, benches. Bookstores at nearby Lincoln Memorial, Washington Monument, and Jefferson Memorial. **Programs & Events:** Ranger-led interpretive programs and talks, walking tours (various sites around the Mall). Constitution Day Naturalization Ceremony (Sept. 17). Special events available. **Tips & Hints:** Plan to spend a day or more visiting the Mall. Busiest Apr. and May, least crowded Jan. and Feb.

FEES & HOURS

Free. Gardens open daily.

HOW TO GET THERE

Between the Washington Monument and the Lincoln Memorial, bordered by Constitution Ave., 17th St., and the Reflecting Pool; nearest Metro subway stations: Foggy Bottom or Farragut West on the Blue and Orange lines. Closest airport: Reagan Washington National.

CONTACTS

National Capital Parks–Central (The National Mall, 900 Ohio Dr. SW, Washington, DC 20242, tel. 202/426–6841, www.nps.gov/coga).

Ford's Theatre National Historic Site

In Washington, D.C.

On the night of April 14, 1865, President Abraham Lincoln was shot in Ford's Theatre by John Wilkes Booth. The president died in the early hours of April 15 in the small back bedroom of a boardinghouse across the street. An act of April 7, 1866, provided for purchase of Ford's Theatre by the federal government. It was redesignated as Lincoln Museum in 1932 and Ford's Theatre (Lincoln Museum) in 1965. The house where Lincoln died was authorized in 1896. Both were transferred to the Park Service in 1933 and combined as a historic site in 1970.

WHAT TO SEE & DO

Touring theater, museum, and boardinghouse. **Facilities:** Theater, museum, House Where Lincoln Died (Petersen's House), Center for Education and Leadership. Bookstore. **Programs & Events:** 15-minute narratives (daily at 9:45, 10:45, 11:45, 2:45, and 3:45). **Tips & Hints:** Busiest Apr. and May, least crowded Jan. and Feb. There is a timed-ticket system for entry, with limited tickets available on day of entry; order through Ticketmaster (tel. 800/982–2787).

FEES & HOURS

Free. Site open daily 9–5. Theater and museum close during matinee performances.

HOW TO GET THERE

In downtown Washington, DC, at 511 10th St. NW, between E and F Sts. Nearest Metro subway station is Metro Center at 11th and G Sts.

CONTACT

Ford's Theatre National Historic Site (511 10th St. NW, Washington, DC 20004, tel. 202/426–6924, www.nps.gov/foth).

Franklin Delano Roosevelt Memorial

Along the Potomac River

The outdoor memorial to the nation's 32nd president is divided into four outdoor galleries, or rooms, one for each of FDR's terms in office. The granite memorial includes sculptures that depict the launching of the New Deal, a fireside chat, an urban breadline, FDR and his dog Fala, and Eleanor Roosevelt's role as First Lady and human-rights advocate. An FDR Memorial Commission was established in 1955, and the memorial was dedicated in 1997.

WHAT TO SEE & DO

Touring memorial. **Facilities:** Memorial, ranger office with interpretive panels. Bookstore. **Programs & Events:** Ranger-led interpretive programs. **Tips & Hints:** Take Metrorail to avoid street parking. Go in early spring or fall for best weather, early to mid-Apr. for cherry blossoms.

FEES, HOURS & REGULATIONS

Free. Leashed pets only. No food or drink. No smoking, bicycling, skating, jogging, picnicking, or sports activity. Rangers on duty daily 9:30 AM–11:30 PM. Bookstore open daily 8 AM–10 PM.

HOW TO GET THERE

At the junction of Ohio and W. Basin Drs., in W. Potomac Park, midway between the Lincoln and Jefferson memorials. Nearest Metro subway stations: Smithsonian Institution, Arlington National Cemetery, Foggy Bottom. Closest airport: Reagan Washington National.

CONTACTS

National Mall and Memorial Parks (The National Mall, 900 Ohio Dr. SW, Washington, DC 20242, tel. 202/426–6841, www.nps.gov/frde). Destination DC (901 7th St. NW, 4th fl., Washington, DC 20005, tel. 202/789–7000, www.washington.org).

Frederick Douglass National Historic Site

In the southeast part of the city

Frederick Douglass, the nation's leading 19th-century African American spokesman, made his home here from 1877 until his death in 1895. The site explores Douglass's efforts to abolish slavery and his struggle for human rights, equal rights, and civil rights for all people. Among his achievements, Douglass was U.S. minister to Haiti in 1889. Cedar Hill, his 21-room mansion on 8½ acres, has been preserved with more than 75% of its original furnishings. The site was authorized as the Frederick Douglass Home in 1962 and redesignated in 1988.

WHAT TO SEE & DO

Touring house, watching film. **Facilities:** Visitor center, house. Bookstore. **Programs & Events:** Film (every ½ hour), interpretive talks, guided house tours (throughout day, reservations available, tel. 877/444–6777). **Tips & Hints:** Busiest Jan.–June, least crowded July–Sept.

FEES & HOURS

Free. Reservations are required for group tours of 11 or more and cost $1.50 per person. (Call 877/559–6777 at least one week in advance.) Site open Nov.–Mar., daily 9–4:30; Apr.–Oct., daily 9–5.

HOW TO GET THERE

Take the 11th St. Bridge (toward Anacostia) to Martin Luther King Jr. Ave. Go 3 blocks, turn left on W St. Follow W St. for 4 blocks to the visitor center parking lot on right.

CONTACT

Frederick Douglass National Historic Site (1411 W St. SE, Washington, DC 20020-4813, tel. 202/426–5961, www.nps.gov/frdo).

Korean War Veterans Memorial

On the National Mall

The garden memorial to the veterans of the Korean War (1950–54) includes a black granite wall with murals by Louis Nelson of New York City, a reflecting pool, and 19 statues of infantrymen by sculptor Frank C. Gaylord. The memorial was authorized in 1986 and dedicated in 1995.

WHAT TO SEE & DO

Viewing memorial. **Facilities:** Information kiosk with computer to look up and print out information on soldiers killed or missing in action during Korean War. Bookstore in Lincoln Memorial. **Programs & Events:** Ranger-led interpretive talks and programs. **Tips & Hints:** Plan to spend a day or more touring the National Mall.

FEES, HOURS & REGULATIONS

Free. No biking or in-line skating at memorial. Memorial open daily. Park rangers on duty 9:30 AM–11:30 PM. Bookstore at the Lincoln Memorial open daily 8:30 AM–10 PM.

HOW TO GET THERE

Off Independence Ave. and Daniel French Dr., across from the Lincoln Memorial. Nearest Metro subway station: Foggy Bottom, at 23rd and I Sts. NW, on the Blue and Orange lines. Limited parking available on Ohio Dr. SW, off Independence Ave.

CONTACTS

National Mall and Memorial Parks (The National Mall, 900 Ohio Dr. SW, Washington, DC 20242, tel. 202/426–6841, www.nps.gov/kowa).

Lincoln Memorial

On the National Mall

Constructed as a tribute to the president who led the country through its greatest trial—the Civil War—the Lincoln Memorial houses the famous statue that is 19 feet tall, 19 feet wide, and carved from 28 blocks of white Georgia marble. The memorial was authorized in 1911, dedicated in 1922, and transferred to the Park Service in 1933.

WHAT TO SEE & DO

Viewing memorial. **Facilities:** Memorial. Bookstore. **Programs & Events:** Ranger-led talks and interpretive programs. Ranger-led walking tours (June–Aug.). **Tips & Hints:** Plan to spend a day or more visiting the Mall. Busiest Apr. and May, least crowded Jan. and Feb.

FEES, HOURS & REGULATIONS

Free. No biking or in-line skating in memorial. Memorial open daily. Rangers on duty 9:30 AM–11:30 PM. Bookstore hours daily 8:30 AM–10 PM.

HOW TO GET THERE

Off Constitution Ave. and 23rd St. NW. Nearest Metro subway station: Foggy Bottom, 23rd St., and I St. NW, on the Blue and Orange lines.

CONTACTS

National Mall and Memorial Parks (The National Mall, 900 Ohio Dr. SW, Washington, DC 20242, tel. 202/426–6841, www.nps.gov/linc).

Lyndon Baines Johnson Memorial Grove on the Potomac

Along the Potomac River

This memorial to the nation's 36th president, in Lady Bird Johnson Park, consists of a serpentine pattern of walks and trails leading to a granite monolith. The trails are shaded by hundreds of white pine and dogwood trees and framed by azalea and rhododendron bushes. Thousands of yellow daffodils bloom in season. The focal point of the grove is a tall, rugged monolith of sunset-red granite that stands 19 feet high and weighs 43 tons. Spaced along the walkway surrounding the stone, four granite markers bear quotations from Lyndon B. Johnson's speeches. The site was authorized in 1973 and dedicated in 1976.

WHAT TO SEE & DO

Fishing, picnicking, strolling. **Facilities:** Grove, granite memorial. Picnic tables. **Programs & Events:** Ranger-led talks and guided tours. **Tips & Hints:** Busiest May–July, least crowded Nov.–Jan.

FEES, HOURS & REGULATIONS

Free. Washington, DC, fishing license required. Grove open daily during daylight hours.

HOW TO GET THERE

In Lady Bird Johnson Park, on the George Washington Memorial Pkwy. west of I–95 and the 14th St. Bridge. Parking at nearby Columbia Island Marina. Closest airport: Reagan Washington National.

CONTACT

Lyndon Baines Johnson Memorial Grove on the Potomac (c/o George Washington Memorial Pkwy., Turkey Run Park, McLean, VA 22101, tel. 703/289–2500, www.nps.gov/gwmp).

Martin Luther King, Jr. Memorial

On the National Mall in Washington, DC

Commemorating a legacy of leadership in the civil rights movement, the Martin Luther King, Jr. Memorial is the newest and among the most powerful monuments in the nation's capital. Rising from the banks of the Tidal Basin, the solid granite memorial includes 17 quotes that bring to life the spirit of equal rights, freedom, and tolerance espoused by Dr. King. The memorial was dedicated October 16, 2011.

WHAT TO SEE & DO

Reading interpretive panels, touring memorial. **Facilities:** Memorial, interpretive panels. **Programs & Events:** Ranger-led interpretive programs. **Tips & Hints:** Visit in the morning for best light and smallest crowds. Take Metrorail to avoid street parking. Go in early spring or fall for best weather, late Mar.–mid-Apr. for cherry blossoms.

FEES, HOURS & REGULATIONS

Free. The memorial is open 24 hours a day. Rangers are on duty to answer questions daily 9:30 AM–11:30 PM and to provide interpretive programs daily 10 AM–11 PM. Leashed pets only. No food or drink. No smoking, bicycling, skating, jogging, picnicking, or sports activity.

HOW TO GET THERE

I–395 provides access to the National Mall from the south, and I–495, New York Ave., Rock Creek and Potomac Parkway, George Washington Memorial Parkway, and the Cabin John Parkway provide access from the north. Metro train and bus routes extend throughout the district to the suburbs, and nearly all will bring you to the Mall. Closest airport: Reagan (6 miles).

CONTACTS

National Mall and Memorial Parks (The National Mall, 900 Ohio Dr. SW, Washington, DC 20242, tel. 202/426–6841, www.nps.gov/mlkm). Destination DC (901 7th St. NW, 4th fl., Washington, DC 20005, tel. 202/789–7000, www.washington.org).

Mary McLeod Bethune Council House National Historic Site

In Washington, DC

Commemorated here are the life of Mary McLeod Bethune (1875–1955) and the organization she founded, the National Council of Negro Women. The site includes her three-story Victorian home, which housed the council, and a two-story carriage house in which the National Archives for Black Women's History is located. Bethune founded Bethune-Cookman College in Daytona Beach, Florida, and served as an adviser on African American affairs to four presidents. The site was authorized in 1991.

WHAT TO SEE & DO

Touring home. **Facilities:** Visitor center, home, carriage house (by appointment only). Bookstore, research facility (by appointment only). **Programs & Events:** Ranger-guided tours. Black History Month (Feb.), Women's History Month (Mar.), Annual Open House for Dupont-Kalorama Museum Walk Weekend (1st full weekend, June). Martin Luther King Jr. Birthday Commemoration (Jan. 19), Bethune Birthday Celebration (July 10). Other special programs. **Tips & Hints:** Busiest June and July, least crowded Oct. and Nov.

FEES & HOURS

Free. Site and visitor center open daily, 9–5. Last tour starts at 4.

HOW TO GET THERE

In northwest Washington, DC, on Vermont Ave. Nearest metro stations: McPherson Sq. on the Blue and Orange lines; U St. Cardozo on the Green line.

CONTACT

Mary McLeod Bethune Council House National Historic Site (1318 Vermont Ave. NW, Washington, DC 20005, tel. 202/673–2402, fax 202/673–2414, www.nps.gov/mamc).

National Mall

In Washington, DC

This tree-lined, 146-acre park stretches from the Capitol to the Lincoln Memorial and is a principal axis in the plan developed by French engineer Pierre L'Enfant in 1790. The Mall was authorized in 1790 and transferred to the Park Service in 1933.

WHAT TO SEE & DO

Attending outdoor events, jogging, picnicking, playing sports, strolling. **Facilities:** Mall. Bookstores. **Programs & Events:** Ranger-led interpretive programs, walks, talks at surrounding monuments and memorials. **Tips & Hints:** Plan to spend a day or more to visit the Mall, monuments, memorials, and museums. Busiest Apr. through July, least crowded Jan. and Feb.

FEES & HOURS

Free. Mall open daily. Memorials and monuments on Mall open daily.

HOW TO GET THERE

The Mall is in downtown Washington, DC, between Constitution and Independence Aves. The Smithsonian Metro stop comes out on the National Mall.

CONTACTS

National Mall and Memorial Parks (The National Mall, 900 Ohio Dr. SW, Washington, DC 20024, tel. 202/426–6841, www.nps.gov/nama).

National Mall and Memorial Parks

In Washington, DC

The District of Columbia has more than 300 parks, parkways, and reservations, including Battleground National Cemetery, the President's Park (Lafayette Park north of the White House and the Ellipse south of the White House), and a variety of military fortifications and green areas. The park was authorized in 1790 and transferred to the Park Service in 1933.

WHAT TO SEE & DO

Bicycling, fishing, golfing, ice skating, jogging, paddleboating, picnicking, playing team sports, sightseeing, swimming. **Facilities:** More than 300 parks, parkways, and reserved lands around the capital. **Programs & Events:** Outdoor ice skating at National Gallery of Art Sculpture Garden Ice Rink (7th St. and Constitution Ave., tel. 202/289–3360) and Pershing Park Ice Rink (14th St. and Pennsylvania Ave., tel. 202/737–6938). Hispanic Heritage Month (Sept.–Oct.), Annual Civil Rights Film Festival (Jan.). **Tips & Hints:** Busiest July and Oct., least crowded Jan. and Feb.

FEES, HOURS & REGULATIONS

National Gallery of Art Sculpture Garden Ice Rink: $7 adults, $6 ages 12 and under, $3 for skate rentals; open Mon.–Thurs. 10–9, Fri. and Sat. 10 AM–11 PM, Sun. 11–9. Pershing Park Ice Rink: $6.50 adults, $5.50 ages 12 and under, $2.50 for skate rentals; open Mon.–Thurs. 11–9, Fri. 11–11, Sat. 10 AM–11 PM, Sun. 11–7.

HOW TO GET THERE

The 300 parks are located throughout the District of Columbia. Closest airport: Reagan Washington National.

CONTACTS

National Mall and Memorial Parks (900 Ohio Dr. SW, Washington, DC 20024, tel. 202/426–6841, www.nps.gov/nacc or www.nps.gov/nace). Destination DC (901 7th St. NW, 4th fl., Washington, DC 20005, tel. 202/789–7000, www.washington.org).

Pennsylvania Avenue National Historic Site

Between the White House and U.S. Capitol

The nation celebrates the election of a president every four years with a parade on the world-famous 1¼-mile stretch of Pennsylvania Avenue. Other national heroes and foreign leaders have been honored with parades and motorcades here as well. Known as "America's Main Street," the site also encompasses Ford's Theatre National Historic Site, several blocks of the Washington commercial district—including the Old Post Office—and a number of federal structures. The site was authorized on September 30, 1965.

WHAT TO SEE & DO

Attending theatrical performances; ice skating; shopping; sightseeing; touring National Archives, FBI, National Museum of American Art, and National Gallery. **Facilities:** Museums, theaters, and stores. **Programs & Events:** Ranger-led tours of the Old Post Office Tower. **Tips & Hints:** Busiest July and Aug., least crowded Jan. and Feb.

FEES & HOURS

Free. Site open daily.

HOW TO GET THERE

The site is in downtown Washington, between the Capitol and the White House, and includes the architecturally and historically significant areas in the Pennsylvania Ave. area. There are Metro stations at Federal Triangle and Metro Center.

CONTACTS

Pennsylvania Avenue National Historic Site (National Mall and Memorial Parks, 900 Ohio Dr. SW, Washington, DC 20024, tel. 202/606–9686, www.nps.gov/paav).

Potomac Heritage National Scenic Trail

Along the Potomac River between Virginia and Maryland; in Washington, DC; and in western Pennsylvania.

Linking the Potomac and upper Ohio river basins, the Potomac Heritage National Scenic Trail network follows the paths explored by George Washington. You can follow the same routes today on foot, bicycle, horse, and by boat to discover contrasting landscapes between the Chesapeake Bay and the Allegheny Highlands. With the C&O Canal Towpath as the spine, the trail network includes the Allegheny Passage, the Laurel Highlands Hiking Trail, various Potomac Heritage Trail sections in Northern Virginia, the Civil War Defenses of Washington Trail, the Northern Neck Heritage Trail, and a southern Maryland bicycling route. The trail system was established on March 28, 1983.

WHAT TO SEE & DO

Biking, boating, cross-country skiing, hiking, horseback riding, visiting historic sites and natural areas. **Facilities:** Visitor Information Center (Harpers Ferry). **Programs & Events:** Guided hikes, bicycle tours. **Tips & Hints:** Occasional trail flooding–check local weather conditions.

CONTACTS

Potomac Heritage National Scenic Trail Office, National Park Service, Box B, Harpers Ferry, WV 25425, tel. 304/535–4014, www.nps.gov/pohe).

Rock Creek Park

In the northwest and northeast parts of the city

One of the nation's oldest national parks, Rock Creek is home to more than 3,000 acres of hardwood forest, meadows, and streams that form ribbons of green through the nation's capital. The park offers hiking, bicycling, horseback riding, picnicking, and boating. A nature center and planetarium, historic Peirce Mill, 18th-century Old Stone House, and the remains of Civil War forts round out the area's natural and cultural attractions. The park was authorized in 1890 and transferred to the Park Service in 1933.

WHAT TO SEE & DO

Attending concerts at Carter Barron Amphitheatre; bicycling (rentals, Thompson's Boat House); bird-watching; boating (rentals, Thompson's Boat House); exercising on exercise trails and recreational fields; fishing (license required); golfing (rentals, Rock Creek Golf Course); hiking; horseback riding (rentals, Rock Creek Horse Center); jogging; kite flying; painting and sketching; picnicking; playing tennis; touring the forts, Old Stone House, Peirce Mill (Wed.–Sun. 10–4), and Peirce Barn (Wed.–Sun. 10–5). **Facilities:** Nature Center and Planetarium with exhibits, children's nature discovery room, and auditorium (5200 Glover Rd. NW), Peirce Mill (Tilden St. and Beach Dr. NW), Old Stone House (3051 M St. NW, Georgetown), forts, golf course, recreation fields, amphitheater, tennis courts, trails. Book sales areas, picnic pavilions, tables, grills. **Programs & Events:** Ranger-guided nature walks and planetarium shows (Nature Center); ranger-guided tours (Peirce Mill, Old Stone House, Dumbarton Oaks, Meridian Hill Park, and other sites). **Tips & Hints:** The best seasons to visit are spring and fall. Busiest July and Aug., least crowded Dec. and Jan.

FEES, HOURS & REGULATIONS

Free. Washington, DC, fishing license required. Leashed pets only. Bikes on paved bike trails and roads only. No collecting rocks, firewood, animals, plants, natural or cultural objects. Park open daily during daylight hours. Beach Dr. between Military and Broad Branch roads closed to cars from Sat. 7 AM–Sun. 7 PM and on holidays. No trucks or buses. Nature Center open Wed.–Sun. 9–5.

HOW TO GET THERE

In Washington, DC, at Military Rd. NW and Glover Rd. NW, about 1 mile east of Connecticut Ave. NW and ½ mile west of 16th St. NW. The Friendship Heights Metro station is nearest the Nature Center, the Van Ness Metro station is nearest the Peirce Mill, and the Foggy Bottom Metro station is nearest the Old Stone House.

CONTACTS

Rock Creek Park (3545 Williamsburg La. NW, Washington, DC 20008, tel. 202/895–6000, 202/895–6070 [Nature Center]; fax 202/895–6015, www.nps.gov/rocr).

Theodore Roosevelt Island

On the Potomac River

This 89-acre wooded island is a memorial to the outdoorsman, naturalist, and visionary who was the 26th president. The outdoor memorial captures the spirit of this energetic president. Trails lead through the marsh, swamp, and forest on the island. The site was authorized in 1932 and transferred to the Park Service in 1933. The memorial was dedicated on October 27, 1967.

WHAT TO SEE & DO

Bird-watching, fishing, hiking, jogging, touring memorial, walking. **Facilities:** Kiosk, memorial, wayside exhibits, trails, 2,800-foot boardwalk through swamp. **Programs & Events:** Guided tours (reservations required). Ranger-led programs and tours. Roosevelt Birthday Celebration (Oct.). **Tips & Hints:** Busiest May–July, least crowded Nov.–Jan.

FEES, HOURS & REGULATIONS

Free. Washington, DC, fishing permit required. Island open daily during daylight hours. Bicycles not allowed. Pets on leash only.

HOW TO GET THERE

The parking area is reached via the northbound lane of the George Washington Memorial Pkwy. on the Virginia side of the Potomac River in Rosslyn. A footbridge connects the island to the Virginia shore. Visitors may also exit the Metro at Rosslyn, take a 20-minute walk to the Key Bridge, and join the Mount Vernon Trail to the island. Closest airport: Reagan Washington National.

CONTACT

Theodore Roosevelt Island (c/o George Washington Memorial Pkwy., Turkey Run Park, McLean, VA 22101, tel. 703/289–2500, www.nps.gov/this).

Thomas Jefferson Memorial

Near the Potomac River

Thomas Jefferson, author of the Declaration of Independence and third U.S. president, is memorialized here. The interior walls present inscriptions from his writings. Rudolph Evans sculpted the statue. John Russell Pope and his associates Otto Eggers and Daniel Higgins designed the memorial. The memorial was authorized in 1934 and dedicated in 1943.

WHAT TO SEE & DO

Attending ranger interpretive programs and talks, viewing memorial. **Facilities:** Bookstore. **Programs & Events:** Ranger-led interpretive talks (daily). Ranger-led walking tours of National Mall (Memorial Day–Labor Day). Cherry Blossom Festival (early Apr.). **Tips & Hints:** Busiest Apr.–July, least crowded Jan. and Feb.

FEES, HOURS & REGULATIONS

Free. No in-line skating or bicycling in memorial. Memorial open daily. Rangers on duty 9:30 AM–11:30 PM.

HOW TO GET THERE

The memorial is on the south bank of the Tidal Basin south of the National Mall. A parking lot at the memorial provides two-hour parking. The Smithsonian Metro stop comes out on the National Mall.

CONTACTS

National Mall and Memorial Parks (The National Mall, 900 Ohio Dr. SW, Washington, DC 20024, tel. 202/426–6841, www.nps.gov/thje).

Vietnam Veterans Memorial

On the National Mall

The names of more than 58,000 soldiers who were killed in the Vietnam War or are missing are engraved in the black granite walls of the memorial. The memorial's mirrorlike surface reflects the surrounding trees, lawns, monuments, and people, creating a quiet place to remember and honor all Vietnam veterans. The memorial also includes the Statue of Three Servicemen and the Vietnam Women's Memorial. The memorial was authorized in 1980 and dedicated in 1982.

WHAT TO SEE & DO

Viewing and finding names on memorial. **Facilities:** Memorials, statue. Bookstore in Lincoln Memorial. **Programs & Events:** Ranger-led talks and programs. **Tips & Hints:** Plan to spend a day or more visiting all the sites on the National Mall. Busiest Apr. and May, least crowded Jan. and Feb.

FEES, HOURS & REGULATIONS

Free. No bicycling or in-line skating at memorial. Memorial open daily. Rangers available 9:30 AM–11:30 PM.

HOW TO GET THERE

Off Constitution Ave. and 23rd St. NW. Nearest metro subway station: Foggy Bottom, 23rd and I St. NW, on the Blue and Orange lines.

CONTACTS

National Mall and Memorial Parks (The National Mall, 900 Ohio Dr. SW, Washington, DC 20024, tel. 202/426–6841, www.nps.gov/vive).

Washington Monument

On the National Mall

The graceful obelisk rises 555 feet to dominate the capital skyline and serves as a memorial to the nation's first president and leader of the American Revolution, George Washington. The monument was authorized in 1848, dedicated in 1885, and transferred to the Park Service in 1933. Note: at this writing, the Washington Monument was closed for repairs after an earthquake that occurred on August 23, 2011. A reopening date had not been announced.

WHAT TO SEE & DO

Taking elevator to top of monument. **Facilities:** Monument and grounds. Bookstore. **Programs & Events:** Elevator rides to top of monument, ranger-led interpretive programs and talks (daily). **Tips & Hints:** Plan to spend a day or more visiting sites on the Mall. Busiest June and July, least crowded Jan.–Mar.

FEES & HOURS

Free. Advance reservations for elevator ride available (tel. 877/444–6777 or pick up at ticket kiosk on 15th St., at base of monument). Monument open daily 9–5 (last trip up 4:45).

HOW TO GET THERE

In downtown Washington, DC, on the National Mall, midway between the U.S. Capitol and the Lincoln Memorial. The Metro stops at the Smithsonian on the Mall, and there's a parking lot at the monument.

CONTACTS

National Mall and Memorial Parks (The National Mall, 900 Ohio Dr. SW, Washington, DC 20024, tel. 202/426–6841, www.nps.gov/wamo).

White House

North of the Washington Monument

Every president except George Washington has lived, entertained, and conducted the nation's business at the White House. The White House was transferred to the National Park Service on August 10, 1933.

WHAT TO SEE & DO

Touring White House. **Facilities:** Visitor center, White House. **Programs & Events:** Limited self-guided tours. **Tips & Hints:** Call in advance to find out updated tour information. Busiest Apr.–Aug., least crowded Jan. and Feb.

FEES, HOURS & REGULATIONS

Free. Tour requests must be submitted through your U.S. senator or representative and are accepted up to six months in advance. Call 202/456–7041 for tour information. Self-guided tours are available Tues.–Thurs. 7:30–11, Fri. 7:30–noon, Sat. 7:30–1 (excluding federal holidays). No photos or videotaping. No strollers (strollers stored at visitor center). No animals, oversize backpacks, balloons, food or beverages, chewing gum, electric stun guns, fireworks or firecrackers, guns or ammunition, knives with blades longer than 3 inches, Mace, smoking, or suitcases. White House Visitor Center open daily 7:30–4.

HOW TO GET THERE

The White House is at 1600 Pennsylvania Ave. NW, in downtown Washington, DC. Closest Metro station: Federal Triangle on Blue and Orange lines.

CONTACTS

The White House (c/o President's Park, National Capital Region, 1100 Ohio Dr. SW, Room 344, Washington, DC 20242, tel. 202/208–1631, www.nps.gov/whho or www.whitehouse.gov).

See Also

Sewall-Belmont House National Historic Site, in Other National Parklands.

FLORIDA

Big Cypress National Preserve

In the southern part of the state, near Ochopee

The preserve conserves and protects the natural scenic, floral and faunal, and recreational values of the Big Cypress Watershed. The importance of this watershed to the Everglades National Park (see separate entry) was a major consideration for its establishment. The name Big Cypress does not refer to the size of the trees, but to the vast number of cypress that cover about one-third of the 729,000-acre preserve. The preserve is also home to the endangered Florida panther and red-cockaded woodpecker. The preserve was authorized on October 11, 1974.

WHAT TO SEE & DO

Bicycling, bird and wildlife viewing, fishing, hiking, hunting, off-road-vehicle driving, picnicking, scenic driving. **Facilities:** 2 visitor centers: Big Cypress Welcome Center (33000 Tamiami Trail E, Ochopee) and Oasis (52105 Tamiami Trail E, Ochopee), scenic loop roads, trails. Bookstore, picnic areas. **Programs & Events:** Ranger-led wet walks, biking, canoeing excursions, campfire programs. **Tips & Hints:** The preserve's climate is subtropical, with mild winters and hot, wet summers. Wear long sleeves, pants, sturdy shoes, and bug repellent when hiking. Allow at least two hours to drive the Loop Rd., an hour for the Turner River–Birdon Rd. loop. Visitor centers have information on closures that may be in effect. Go in winter (dry season) for best hiking conditions along Florida Trail. Busiest Dec.–Apr., least crowded June and Sept.

FOOD, LODGING & SUPPLIES

Camping: 6 campgrounds in the park: Bear Island (northern end of Hwy. 839; 40 sites; $16; no water, vault toilets), Burns Lake (14 sites; $16; no water, vault toilets), Midway (1 mile east of Oasis Visitor Center; 36 sites; $16–$19; flush toilets), Mitchell's Landing (½ mile west of Pinecrest; 15 sites; $16; no water), Monument (5 miles west of Oasis Visitor Center; 36 sites; $16; flush toilets, cold showers), Pinecrest (1½ miles east of Pinecrest; 10 sites; $16; no water). Backcountry camping allowed. **Hotels:** None in park. In Everglades City: Ivey House (107 Camellia St., tel. 239/695–3299, www.iveyhouse.com; 29 rooms, 1 cottage; $89–$229). **Restaurants:** None in park. In Everglades City: Oyster House (Chokoloskee Causeway, Hwy. 29 S, tel. 239/695–2073, www.oysterhouserestaurant.com; $7–$24). **Groceries & Gear:** None in park. In Everglades City: Everglades Station (31990 Tamiami Trail E, tel. 239/695–3340), Gator Express (203 Collier Ave., tel. 239/695–3937).

FEES, HOURS & REGULATIONS

Free. Off-road-vehicle permits: $50 a year, vehicle inspection required. Florida state fishing and hunting license required. Park open daily. Visitor centers open daily 9–4:30.

HOW TO GET THERE

The Oasis Visitor Center is halfway between Naples and Miami. Big Cypress Welcome Center is 4 miles east of Rte. 29. Closest airports: Ft. Myers International (70 miles), Miami International (75 miles).

CONTACTS

Big Cypress National Preserve (33100 Tamiami Trail E, Ochopee, FL 34141, tel. 239/695–1201, www.nps.gov/bicy). Everglades City Chamber of Commerce (Box 130, at corner of Rte. 29 and U.S. 41, Everglades City, FL 34139, tel. 239/695–3941, www.evergladeschamber.com).

Biscayne National Park

In the southeast part of the state, near Homestead

The 173,000-acre park, 95% of which is water, is a wonderful place to boat, sail, fish, snorkel, dive, and camp. The park protects a deep green forest of mangroves, and its water provides habitat for the Florida spiny lobster, shrimp, fish, sea turtles, and manatees. Its stunning emerald islands, fringed with mangroves, contain tropical hardwood forests, and its coral reefs support a kaleidoscope of fish, plants, and other animals. The park was established as a national monument in 1968 and redesignated a park in 1980.

WHAT TO SEE & DO

Boating (rentals, Miami and Key Largo), canoeing (Convoy Point), diving, fishing, sailing, snorkeling, viewing videos in English and Spanish. **Facilities:** Dante Fascell Visitor Center (Convoy Point, 9 miles east of Homestead), nature trails on keys. Book sales area, grills, picnic tables. **Programs & Events:** Ranger-led talks, walks and canoe trips; art exhibits; videos in English and Spanish; glass-bottom boat excursions; snorkeling and scuba-diving trips. Family Fun Fest (Dec.–Apr.). **Tips & Hints:** To see the park, either bring your own boat or make reservations (tel. 305/230–1100) to go on boat tours or snorkel or dive trips. Busiest Jan.–Apr., least crowded May–Dec.

FOOD, LODGING & SUPPLIES

Camping: 2 campgrounds in the park: Boca Chita (accessible by boat only; tent camping area; $15–$20; pit toilets), Elliott Key (waterside and forested camping areas on a 7-mile-long island accessible by boat only; tel. 305/230–7275; 20 sites; $15–$20; flush toilets, cold showers). **Hotels:** None in park. In Homestead: Redland Hotel (5 S. Flagler Ave., tel. 305/246–1904, redlandhotel.com; 13 rooms; $90–$200). **Restaurants:** None in park. In Homestead: El Toro Taco (1 S. Krome Ave., tel. 305/245–8182; $10–$20). **Groceries & Gear:** None in park. In Florida City: Walmart (33501 S. Dixie Hwy., tel. 305/242–4447).

FEES, HOURS & REGULATIONS

Free. Glass-bottom boat trips, kayak rentals, snorkel and scuba trips: call 305/230–1100 for fees and reservations. Florida state fishing license required. Leashed pets only at Convoy Point and Elliott Key. No pets on all other islands or mainland, on boats moored to the islands, or in the shallow waters around the islands. No skateboards, roller skates, or in-line skates. Visitor center open daily 9–5. Adams Key open daily sunrise–sunset. Elliott Key, Boca Chita Key, and all park waters open daily.

HOW TO GET THERE

9 miles east of Homestead on S.W. 328th St. (N. Canal Dr.). Closest airport: Miami International Airport (35 miles).

CONTACTS

Biscayne National Park (9700 S.W. 328th St., Homestead, FL 33033, tel. 305/230–7275, fax 305/230–1190, www.nps.gov/bisc). Greater Homestead–Florida City Chamber of Commerce (455 N. Flagler Ave., Homestead, FL 33030, tel. 305/247–2332, www.chamberinaction.com). Greater Miami Convention & Visitors Bureau (701 Brickell Ave., Suite 2700, Miami, FL 33131, tel. 305/539–3000, www.miamiandbeaches. com). Tropical Everglades Visitor Association (160 U.S. 1, Florida City, FL 33034, tel. 305/245–9180, www.tropicaleverglades.com).

Canaveral National Seashore

In the east-central part of the state, near Titusville

The longest stretch of preserved coastline on the east coast of Florida is at this seashore. Besides its recreational appeal, the 24-mile seashore is on a barrier island and protects 57,662 acres of undeveloped beach and wetlands. The park offers sanctuary to 1,000 species of plants and 300 species of birds, including 14 threatened or endangered species. The seashore was established on January 3, 1975.

WHAT TO SEE & DO

Beachcombing, bird and wildlife viewing, boating, canoeing (rentals, outside North District), fishing, hiking, surfing, swimming, visiting Eldora State House, Turtle Mound and Seminole Rest Trail historical sites. **Facilities:** Information center (North District, New Smyrna Beach), Eldora State House. Bookstore. **Programs & Events:** Ranger-led walks, talks, canoe and pontoon boat tours. Sea Turtle Watch programs (June and July). **Tips & Hints:** Visit Oct.–Mar. for best island camping. Beaches busiest Apr.–Aug., least crowded Oct. and Jan.

FOOD, LODGING & SUPPLIES

Camping: Limited backcountry beach and island camping allowed. Near Titusville: Manatee Hammock Campground (7275 S. U.S. 1, tel. 321/264–5083, www.campingspacecoast.com; 183 sites; $7–$28; flush toilets, showers, hookups). **Hotels:** None in park. In Titusville: Clarion Inn (4951 S. Washington Ave., tel. 321/269–2121, www. clarionhotel.com; 117 rooms; $74–$200). **Restaurants:** None in park. In Titusville: Dixie Crossroads (1475 Garden St., tel. 321/268–5000; $8–$28). ☂ **Groceries & Gear:** None in park. In Titusville: Publix (3265 Garden St., tel. 321/383–0511).

FEES, HOURS & REGULATIONS

Entrance fee: $5 per vehicle. Backcountry permit required ($10–$20 per night; tel. 386/428–3384 Ext. 10). Reservations required (tel. 386/428–3384 Ext. 10) for ranger-led canoe trips, pontoon boat rides, and Sea Turtle Watch programs. Lifeguards on duty Memorial Day–Labor Day. No beach camping in summer. Park usually closes when parking lots are full, which occurs during most summer weekends at the North District. Seashore open Nov.–Mar., daily 6–6; Apr.–Oct., daily 6 AM–8 PM. Information center open daily 9–4:30. South District (Titusville) closes three days before a shuttle launch at Kennedy Space Center and reopens the day after a successful launch.

HOW TO GET THERE

North District: Take I–95, Exit 84 on Rte. 44 to Rte. A1A in New Smyrna Beach. South District: Take I–95, Exit 80 on Rte. 406–402. Closest airports: Daytona Airport (50 miles), Orlando International Airport (50 miles).

CONTACTS

Canaveral National Seashore (212 S. Washington Ave., Titusville, FL 32796, tel. 321/267–1110, www.nps.gov/cana). Titusville Chamber of Commerce (2000 S. Washington Ave., Titusville, FL 32780, tel. 321/267–3036, www.titusville.org).

Castillo de San Marcos National Monument

In the northeast part of the state, in St. Augustine

Castillo de San Marcos was for many years the northernmost outpost of Spain's vast New World empire. Begun in 1672 and completed in 1695, it's the oldest masonry fort and the best-preserved example of a Spanish colonial fortification in the continental United States. The site was proclaimed a national monument on October 15, 1924.

WHAT TO SEE & DO

Attending living-history reenactments, self-guided tours. **Facilities:** Interpretive exhibits inside the fort. Bookstore, gift shop. **Programs & Events:** Ranger presentations (daily). Cannon-firing demonstrations (Fri., Sat., and Sun. year-round). Confederate encampment (Jan.); Union encampment (Mar.); Spanish "Nightwatch" (June); Change of Flags ceremony (July); Siege of 1702 reenactment (Nov.); British "Nightwatch," Christmas open house (Dec.). **Tips & Hints:** Busiest Apr.–July, least crowded Oct.–Jan.

FEES, HOURS & REGULATIONS

Entrance fee: $7 adults, free ages 16 and under. Leashed dogs only on grounds. No pets in fort. No alcohol. Grounds are open 5:30 AM–midnight; fort interior is open 8:45–4:45.

HOW TO GET THERE

The monument is in the center of St. Augustine, on Matanzas Bay. Closest airport: Jacksonville (40 miles).

CONTACTS

Castillo de San Marcos National Monument (1 S. Castillo Dr., St. Augustine, FL 32084, tel. 904/829–6506, fax 904/823–9388, www.nps.gov/casa). St. Augustine, Ponte Vedra, and The Beaches Visitor & Convention Bureau (29 Old Mission Ave., St. Augustine, FL 32084, tel. 800/653–2489, www.floridashistoriccoast.com).

De Soto National Memorial

On Tampa Bay south shore, in Bradenton

The memorial commemorates the expedition led by Hernando de Soto, who reached Florida's Gulf Coast in May 1539. This was the first large-scale European expedition into what is now the interior southern United States. De Soto traveled 4,000 miles during his four-year mission and had a significant influence on the course of North American history. The memorial was authorized on March 11, 1948.

WHAT TO SEE & DO

Hiking, walking. **Facilities:** Visitor center, 20-minute orientation film, self-guided trail through mangrove swamp, outdoor exhibit. Bookstore. **Programs & Events:** *Hernando de Soto in America* film (hourly, 9–4). Costumed ranger-led living-history programs (late Dec.–mid-Apr., daily), crossbow and musket firing (late Dec.–mid-Apr.). **Tips & Hints:** Busiest Mar. and Apr., least crowded Aug.–Sept.

FEES, HOURS & REGULATIONS

Free. Leashed pets only. No bikes on trail. Park grounds open daily sunrise–sunset. Parking lots close at 5 PM. Visitor center open daily 9–5.

HOW TO GET THERE

2½ miles north of Manatee Ave. (Rte. 64) on 75th St. NW in Bradenton. Closest airports: Sarasota–Bradenton International (12 miles), Tampa International (55 miles).

CONTACTS

De Soto National Memorial (Box 15390, Bradenton, FL 34280, tel. 941/792–0458, fax 941/792–5094, www.nps.gov/deso). Manatee County Tourist Information Center (5461 Factory Shops Blvd., Ellenton, FL 34222, tel. 941/729–7040, www.see-florida.com).

Dry Tortugas National Park

In the south, 70 nautical miles west of Key West, FL

Known for its famous marine and bird life and military history, the park includes a cluster of seven islands, or "keys," amid 100 square miles of shoals, water, and coral gardens. Fort Jefferson, its main cultural feature, is one of the largest 19th-century American coastal forts. The park was proclaimed as Fort Jefferson National Monument in 1935 and redesignated as Dry Tortugas National Park in 1992.

WHAT TO SEE & DO

Fishing, picnicking, sailing, scuba diving, snorkeling, touring historic structures. **Facilities:** Visitor center (Fort Jefferson). Book and chart sale areas, grills, picnic tables. **Programs & Events:** Guided tours daily 11 am, occasional ranger-led tours, moat walks. **Tips & Hints:** Go mid-Mar.–mid-May for migrating birds, June–Aug. for calmest weather. Busiest Mar.–June, least crowded Sept.–Nov.

FOOD & LODGING

Camping: In the park: Garden Key Campground (10 sites; $3 per person; composting toilets). No backcountry camping. **Hotels:** None in park. In Key West: Ambrosia Key West (622 Fleming St., tel. 305/296–9838 or 800/535–9838, www.ambrosiakeywest.com; 20 rooms; $189–$649). **Restaurants:** None in park. In Key West: Pepe's Café & Steak House (806 Caroline St., tel. 305/294-7192, www.pepescafe. net; $6–$19).

FEES, HOURS & REGULATIONS

Entrance fee: $5. Florida saltwater fishing license required. Fort Jefferson open daily dawn–dusk. Grounds outside fort open daily. Bush Key closed to visitors Jan. 15–Oct. 15 to protect nesting sooty terns and brown noddies. Visitor center open daily 8–5.

HOW TO GET THERE

70 miles west of Key West, FL. A ferry makes a daily round-trip to the park, and an air-taxi service offers daily trips to the park. Closest airport: Key West International.

CONTACTS

Dry Tortugas National Park (40001 State Rd. 9336, Homestead, FL 33034, tel. 305/242–7700, fax 305/242–7728, www.nps.gov/drto). Key West Chamber of Commerce (402 Wall St., Key West, FL 33041, tel. 305/294–2587, www.keywestchamber.org).

Everglades National Park

In the southern part of the state, west of Homestead

The 1.5-million-acre park is the largest subtropical wilderness in the continental United States. It has extensive fresh-, estuarine, and salt-water areas, open Everglades prairies, hardwood tree islands, cypress domes, pinelands, and mangrove forests. It's the only place in the world where the American alligator and crocodile coexist. The park was authorized on May 30, 1934; dedicated on December 6, 1947; and designated an International Biosphere Reserve on October 26, 1976; a World Heritage Site on October 26, 1979; and a Wetland of International Importance on June 4, 1987.

WHAT TO SEE & DO

Bicycling (rentals, Shark Valley, Flamingo), boating, boat touring (Flamingo, Gulf Coast), canoeing (rentals, Flamingo, Gulf Coast), fishing, hiking, kayaking (rentals, Flamingo, Gulf Coast), picnicking. **Facilities:** 5 visitor centers: Ernest F. Coe (main entrance, west of Homestead–Florida City), Royal Palm (4 miles west of Coe), Flamingo (38 miles southwest of main entrance), Shark Valley (U.S. 41, north side of park), and Gulf Coast (Everglades City); interpretive displays, trails, roadside interpretive exhibits, amphitheaters, boat-launch areas. Book sale areas, gift shops, fire pits, gasoline (daytime only, Flamingo). **Programs & Events:** Guided walks, talks (Royal Palm), boat tours (Flamingo, Gulf Coast), tram tours (Shark Valley). Guided walks, talks, evening programs (Long Pine Key, Flamingo campgrounds), bicycle tours (Shark Valley, Royal Palm), canoe tours (Flamingo, Gulf Coast), slough slogs (Shark Valley, Royal Palm). All late Dec.–early Apr. **Tips & Hints:** Go Dec.–Apr. for best wildlife viewing. Busiest Dec.–Apr., least crowded May–Nov.

FOOD, LODGING & SUPPLIES

⚠ **Camping:** 2 campgrounds in the park: Flamingo (end of main park road; 278 sites; $16; flush toilets, showers), Long Pine Key (7 miles from the main entrance off main road; 108 sites; $16; flush toilets). Backcountry camping allowed. 🏨 **Hotels:** None in park. In Homestead: Hotel Redland (5 S. Flagler Ave., tel. 305/246-1904, www.redlandhotel.com; 13 rooms; $90–$200). ✕ **Restaurants:** None in park. In Homestead: El Toro Taco (1 S. Krome Ave., tel. 305/245–8182; $10–$20). ⛁ **Groceries & Gear:** In the park: The Marina Store (1 Flamingo Lodge Hwy., tel. 239/695–3101 Ext. 304).

FEES, HOURS & REGULATIONS

Entrance fee: $5 per person on foot, bicycle, or motorcycle; $10 per vehicle. Backcountry camping permits ($10 plus $2 per person per night) available at Flamingo, Gulf Coast visitor centers. Boat-launch fees are $5 ($3 for nonmotorized). Boat tours at Flamingo and Gulf Coast vary in price (Flamingo Marina, tel. 239/695–3101; Everglades National Park Boat Tours, tel. 239/695–2591). Shark Valley tram tours: $19 adults, $12 ages 12 and under, $18 seniors (tel. 305/221–8455). Reservations recommended for all tours Dec.–Apr. Florida state fishing license required. No hunting. No pets on trails or in backcountry. Leashed pets only in campgrounds. Bicycles on selected trails only. No motorized vehicles on trails. Motorized boat use restricted. No airboats. Main park entrance open all the time. Shark Valley Visitor Center open daily mid-Dec.–mid-Apr., 8:45–5:15; mid-Apr.–mid-Dec., 9:15–5:15. Ernest Coe Visitor Center open daily Nov.–Apr., 8–5; May–Oct., 9–5. Royal Palm Visitor Center open daily 8–4:15. Flamingo Visitor Center open daily mid-Nov.–Apr., 8–4:30; May–mid-Nov. 9–4:30. Gulf Coast Visitor Center open mid-Nov.–mid-Apr., daily 8–4:30; mid-Apr.–mid-Nov., daily 9–4:30.

HOW TO GET THERE

The park is in South Florida, southwest of Miami. Access points are Gulf Coast, in the northwest corner of the park, reached via U.S. 41 south of Naples and Fort Myers; Shark Valley, on the north side of the park, reached via U.S. 41 west of Miami or south of Naples–Fort Myers; and the main park entrance, reached via Rte. 9336 west of Homestead and Florida City. Closest airports: Miami (45 miles northeast of main entrance), Fort Myers (70 miles northwest of Gulf Coast).

CONTACTS

Everglades National Park (40001 State Rd. 9336, Homestead, FL 33034-6733, tel. 305/242–7700, www.nps.gov/ever). Everglades Area Chamber of Commerce (Box 130, Everglades City, FL 34139, tel. 239/695–3941, www.evergladeschamber.com). Greater Homestead–Florida City Chamber of Commerce (455 N. Flagler Ave., Homestead, FL 33030, tel. 305/247–2332, www.chamberinaction.com). Greater Miami Convention & Visitors Bureau (701 Brickell Ave., Suite 2700, Miami, FL 33131, tel. 305/539–3000, www.miamiandbeaches.com). Tropical Everglades Visitor Association (160 U.S. 1, Florida City, FL 33034, tel. 305/245–9180, www.tropicaleverglades.com).

Fort Caroline National Memorial

In the northeast part of the state, in Jacksonville

The memorial pays tribute to the colony the French tried to establish near the mouth of the St. Johns River in 1564. The colony was plagued with hardship and conflicts with the Spanish, who were uneasy about a French settlement that was near the routes used by their treasure ships. The memorial was authorized on September 21, 1950.

WHAT TO SEE & DO

Hiking, picnicking, walking to Fort Caroline exhibit. **Facilities:** Visitor center, fort exhibit, trails, Spanish Pond area, Ribault Column. Bookstore, picnic area. **Programs & Events:** Ranger programs (call ahead for schedule). **Tips & Hints:** Bring insect repellent. Visit in spring and fall. Busiest Jan. and Feb., least crowded Dec. and July.

FEES, HOURS & REGULATIONS

Free. No hunting or fishing. Leashed pets only on trails. No bicycles on trails. Visitor center and memorial open daily 9–5.

HOW TO GET THERE

13 miles east of downtown Jacksonville. Closest airport: Jacksonville (25 miles).

CONTACTS

Fort Caroline National Memorial (12713 Ft. Caroline Rd., Jacksonville, FL 32225, tel. 904/641–7155, fax 904/641–3798, www.nps.gov/foca). Visit Jacksonville (208 N. Laura St., Suite 102, Jacksonville, FL 32202, tel. 904/798–9111, www.visitjacksonville.com).

Fort Matanzas National Monument

In the northeast part of the state, south of St. Augustine

Fort Matanzas ("slaughter" in Spanish) marks the site where, on September 29 and October 12, 1565, almost 250 Huguenot soldiers from the nearby French Fort Caroline were killed by the Spaniards in a battle for supremacy in the New World. The fort itself is a masonry fortification built by the Spanish between 1740 and 1742 to guard the "back door" to St. Augustine at the south end of Matanzas Inlet. The site was proclaimed a national monument in 1924.

WHAT TO SEE & DO

Picnicking, riding ferry to fort, swimming, touring fort, walking on boardwalk trails, wildlife viewing. **Facilities:** Visitor center, fort, interpretive exhibits, boardwalk. Bookstore–gift shop. **Programs & Events:** Year-round ferry service to the fort, ranger presentations (every hour on the half hour 9:30–4:30), living-history reenactments and nature programs monthly. **Tips & Hints:** Busiest Feb.–Apr., least crowded Sept. and Jan.

FOOD, LODGING & SUPPLIES

Camping: None in park. In St. Augustine: Ocean Grove RV Resort (4225 A1A S, tel. 800/342–4007, www.oceangroveresort.com; 141 sites; $50–$60; flush toilets, showers, hookups). **Hotels:** None in park. In St. Augustine: Best Western Historical Inn (2010 N. Ponce De Leon Blvd., tel. 904/829-9088, www.bestwestern.com; 39 rooms, $110). **X Restaurants:** None in park. In St. Augustine: Zaharias (3945 Rte. A1A S, tel. 904/471–4799, www.zahariasrestaurant.com; $9–$18). **Groceries & Gear:** Kangaroo (8880 A1A S, St. Augustine, tel. 904/471–6501).

FEES, HOURS & REGULATIONS

Free. Leashed pets only; pets not allowed on boat or in fort. No alcohol. No driving or walking on sand dunes. Park open daily 9–5:30; visitor center open daily 9–4:30. Ferry runs 9:30–4:30, weather permitting.

HOW TO GET THERE

The park is on Anastasia Island, 14 miles south of St. Augustine on Rte. A1A. Closest airports: Jacksonville (50 miles), Daytona (60 miles), Orlando (100 miles).

CONTACTS

Fort Matanzas National Monument (8635 A1A S, St. Augustine, FL 32080, tel. 904/471–0116, fax 904/471–7605, www.nps.gov/foma). St. Augustine, Ponte Vedra, and The Beaches Visitor & Convention Bureau (29 Old Mission Ave., St. Augustine, FL 32084, tel. 800/653–2489, www.floridashistoriccoast.com).

Gulf Islands National Seashore

In the northwest part of the state, near Pensacola, and in southeast Mississippi, near Ocean Springs

These offshore islands offer sparkling white-sand beaches, historic forts and structures, nature trails, and adjacent open waters. On the mainland are salt marshes and bayous in the Mississippi District, and the Naval Live Oaks Reservation and military forts in the Florida District. Research, monitoring, and mitigation programs preserve, protect, and restore the natural and cultural resources within the park. The seashore was authorized on January 8, 1971.

WHAT TO SEE & DO

Bird-watching, bicycling (rentals, Gulf Breeze, Pensacola Beach), boating (rentals, Gulf Breeze, Pensacola Beach, Perdido Key), fishing, picnicking, swimming, touring forts, walking. **Facilities:** 4 visitor centers: Naval Live Oaks (U.S. 98 east of Gulf Breeze, FL), Fort Pickens (Santa Rosa Island west of Pensacola Beach), Fort Barrancas (on Pensacola Naval Air Station), William M. Colmer (Ocean Springs, MS); Fort Pickens Museum, forts, auditoriums, nature trails, interpretive display boards. Book and map sale areas, boat launch, picnic areas, shelters. **Programs & Events:** Tours at Fort Pickens (daily at 2) and Fort Barrancas (daily at 2), Advanced Redoubt (Sat. at 11). Guided tours of Fort Massachusetts on West Ship Island, MS (late Mar.–Oct., daily 10:30), candlelight tours. Special events scheduled throughout year. **Tips & Hints:** Don't swim alone in unguarded waters. Be cautious about sun exposure, rip currents, jellyfish, Portuguese men-of-war, and barnacle-covered rocks. Be alert for sudden storms, and seek shelter during thunderstorms. Watch your step while exploring the forts and batteries. Go Apr.–Oct. for good weather and blooms, late Mar.–mid-May and Sept. and Oct. for migrating birds. Busiest May–July, least crowded Jan. and Feb.

FOOD, LODGING & SUPPLIES

Camping: In the park: Davis Bayou (south of Ocean Springs; tel. 228/875–3962; 52 sites; $14–$16; flush toilets, showers, hookups), Naval Live Oak (U.S. 98, east of Gulf Breeze; tel. 850/934–2622; group site; $20–$30; flush toilets, cold showers). Primitive camping allowed on East Ship, Horn, and Petit Bois Islands, and public sections of Cat Island, in MS, and Perdido Key, FL. **Hotels:** None in park. In

Ocean Springs, MS: Days Inn (7305 Washington Ave., tel. 228/872–8255, www.daysinn.com; 62 rooms; $86). ✕ **Restaurants:** In the park: snack bars and stores. In Pensacola: Fish House (600 South Barracks St., tel. 850/470–0003, www.goodgrits.com; $9–$15). ⌂ **Groceries & Gear:** In the park: Fort Pickens campground store (1400 Fort Pickens Rd., tel. 850/934–2622).

FEES, HOURS & REGULATIONS

Entrance fee: $3 per person on foot, bicycle, or motorcycle, $8 per vehicle. Park passes available. Florida or Mississippi state fishing license required. Primitive camping permit for Perdido Key required (free, must apply in person). No glass containers on beaches. No motor vehicles off roads. No metal detectors. No pets on beaches in Florida, on Horn and Petit Bois Islands, or in swimming area of Ship Island, on tour boats, and in historic structures. Leashed pets elsewhere. Don't feed or disturb wildlife. Seashore open daily 8–sunset. Fort Barrancas Visitor Center open Nov.–Feb., daily 8:30–3:45; Mar.–Oct., daily 9:30–4:45. Fort Pickens Visitor Center open daily 8:30–4. Fort Pickens Museum open daily 9–4. Naval Live Oaks Visitor Center open daily 8:30–4:30. William M. Colmer Visitor Center open daily 8:30–4:30.

HOW TO GET THERE

Mississippi District: the offshore access to Ship Island is provided by concession boats from Gulfport, MS (Mar.–Oct.). Private boats may dock near Ft. Massachusetts on West Ship Island during the day. Boats provide access to Horn, Petit Bois, Cat, and East Ship Islands. Follow the signs on U.S. 90 for the seashore to Davis Bayou, MS. Florida District, Johnson Beach (Perdido Key): take Rte. 292 southwest from Pensacola; for Naval Museum and historic forts: use the main entrance of Pensacola Naval Air Station off Barrancas (Rte. 295); for Naval Live Oaks and the Fort Pickens and Santa Rosa areas: take U.S. 98 from downtown Pensacola across the Pensacola Bay Bridge. Fort Pickens Road can flood; call 850/934–2656. Closest airports: Florida District—Pensacola (20 miles), Mississippi District—Gulfport (30 miles).

CONTACTS

For the Mississippi District: Gulf Islands National Seashore (3500 Park Rd., Ocean Springs, MS 39564; tel. 228/875-0821, 228/875–3962 campgrounds, fax 228/872–2954, www.nps.gov/guis). For the Florida District: Gulf Islands National Seashore (1801 Gulf Breeze Pkwy., Gulf Breeze, FL 32563, tel. 850/934–2600, fax 850/932–9654, www.nps.gov/guis). Biloxi Visitors Center (1050 Beach Blvd., Biloxi, MS 39530, tel. 228/374–3105, www.biloxi.ms.us). Emerald Coast Convention & Visitors Bureau (1540 Miracle Strip Pkwy., Fort Walton Beach, FL 32549-0609, tel. 850/651–7131 or 800/322–3319, www.emeraldcoastfl.com). Ocean Springs Area Chamber of Commerce (1000 Washington Ave., Ocean Springs, MS 39564, tel. 228/875–4424, www.oceanspringschamber.com). Pensacola Bay Area Convention & Visitors Bureau (1401 E. Gregory St., Pensacola, FL 32501, tel. 800/874–1234, www.visitpensacola.com). Pensacola Beach Visitors Information Center (735 Pensacola Beach Blvd., Pensacola Beach, FL 32561, tel. 850/932–1500 or 800/635–4803, www.visitpensacolabeach.com).

Timucuan Ecological & Historic Preserve

In the northeast part of the state, in Jacksonville

The preserve protects 46,000 acres of estuarine natural resources and historic and prehistoric sites between the Lower St. Johns and Nassau Rivers. The site includes four areas: Fort Caroline National Memorial (see separate entry), Kingsley Plantation, the Theodore Roosevelt Area, and Cedar Point. The Kingsley Plantation includes the oldest remaining plantation house in Florida. The 18th- and 19th-century structures include the planter's home, kitchen house, barn, and 23 of the original 32 slave quarters. The Theodore Roosevelt Area preserves a maritime hammock forest and evidence of the Timucua Indians who once inhabited northeast Florida. The Cedar Point area is undeveloped but has informal hiking trails, a small boat ramp, and restrooms. The preserve was authorized on February 16, 1988.

WHAT TO SEE & DO

Bird and wildlife viewing, boating, hiking, kayaking, picnicking, touring Kingsley Plantation and Fort Caroline. **Facilities:** Visitor centers and bookstores at Fort Caroline and Kingsley Plantation. Fort Caroline includes a large-scale fort exhibit commemorating the French colony, a 1-mile nature trail, and picnic area. The Theodore Roosevelt Area offers an observation tower at the marsh's edge, plus 3½ miles of trails. **Programs & Events:** Ranger talks at Kingsley Plantation, occasional ranger programs at the Theodore Roosevelt Area and Fort Caroline. **Tips & Hints:** Busiest Feb. and Mar., least crowded Aug. and Sept.

FEES, HOURS & REGULATIONS

Free. No hunting. Leashed pets only. No pets in buildings. No bicycles on trails. Fort Caroline National Memorial and visitor center open daily 9–5. Kingsley Plantation open daily 9–5. Theodore Roosevelt Area open daily sunrise–sunset.

HOW TO GET THERE

The preserve is in northeast Jacksonville. From I–95, exit on Heckscher Dr. (Rte. 105). Follow Heckscher east to I-295. For Kingsley Plantation, continue on Heckscher Dr. for 9 miles, turn left at the park sign onto Fort George Island, and follow signs to plantation; for Theodore Roosevelt Area and Fort Caroline National Memorial, from Heckscher Dr. turn south onto I-295, take the Monument Rd. exit, and at the traffic light turn left and follow the signs to Fort Caroline National Memorial and Theodore Roosevelt; for Cedar Point, from Heckscher Dr. go ¼ mile to the next light (New Berlin Rd.), turn left at the light and follow New Berlin Rd. to the intersection with Cedar Point Rd., turn right on Cedar Point Rd. and follow it to the end. The four sites are about 35 minutes driving time apart. Closest airport: Jacksonville (20 miles).

CONTACT

Timucuan Ecological and Historic Preserve (12713 Ft. Caroline Rd., Jacksonville, FL 32225, tel. 904/641–7155, www.nps.gov/timu).

See Also

Florida National Scenic Trail and Wekiva River, in Other National Parklands.

GEORGIA

Andersonville National Historic Site

In central Georgia, in Andersonville

Andersonville, or Camp Sumter, was the largest Confederate military prison established during the Civil War. More than 45,000 Union soldiers were confined in the camp during 14 months, and nearly 13,000 died from disease, poor sanitation, malnutrition, overcrowding, and exposure. The site serves as a memorial to all Americans ever held as prisoners of war and contains the National Prisoner of War Museum. The 514 acres include the Andersonville National Cemetery, with more than 20,000 interments, and the partially reconstructed prison site. The historic site was authorized on October 16, 1970.

WHAT TO SEE & DO

Hiking, picnicking, driving tour of cemetery and prison, walking. **Facilities:** National Prisoner of War Museum, visitor center, cemetery, prison, monuments. Bookstore, picnic area. **Programs & Events:** Ranger-guided cemetery walks and prison-site talks (most weekends). Living History Weekend (2nd weekend in Mar.), Memorial Day ceremony (last Sun., May). **Tips & Hints:** Plan to stay at least two hours. Wear comfortable clothing and walking shoes. Summers are hot and humid, winters are mild and rainy. Busiest Feb.–May and Aug.–Nov., least crowded Dec. and Jan.

FOOD, LODGING & SUPPLIES

Camping: None in park. In Elko, near Perry: Twin Oaks RV Park (305 Hwy. 26 E, tel. 478/987–9361, twinoaksrvpark.com; 73 sites; $38; flush toilets, showers, hookups). **Hotels:** None in park. In Americus: Best Western Plus Windsor Hotel (125 W. Lamar St., tel. 229/924–1555, www.windsor-americus.com; 53 rooms; $110–$225). **Restaurants:** None in park. In Andersonville: Andersonville Restaurant (213 W. Church St., tel. 229/928–8480; $7–$9). **Groceries:** None in park. In Andersonville: One Stop Store (211 Ellaville St., tel. 229/924–3070).

FEES & HOURS

Free; donations accepted. Driving tour audio: free. Park grounds open daily 8–5. Visitor center–museum open daily 9–5.

HOW TO GET THERE

From I–75 northbound, exit at Cordele, take U.S. 280 west to Americus and Rte. 49 north for 10 miles to park entrance on right. Closest airports: Columbus (60 miles), Macon (60 miles), Atlanta (175 miles).

CONTACTS

Andersonville National Historic Site (496 Cemetery Rd., Andersonville, GA 31711, tel. 229/924–0343, fax 229/928–9640, www.nps.gov/ande). Americus-Sumter Chamber of Commerce (409 Elm Ave., Suite A, Americus, GA 31709, tel. 229/924–2646, www.americus-sumterchamber.com).

Chattahoochee River National Recreation Area

Near Atlanta

The recreation area has 17 units along a 48-mile stretch of the Chattahoochee River. In addition to fishing, hiking, picnicking, and boating, the park contains a wide variety of natural habitats, flora and fauna, 19th-century historic sites, and Native American archaeological sites. The site was established on August 15, 1978.

WHAT TO SEE & DO

Boating, fishing, hiking, picnicking, rafting. **Facilities:** Visitor contact station (Island Ford), more than 75 miles of hiking trails. Bookstores, picnic areas, and pavilion (reservations tel. 678/538–1200). **Programs & Events:** Ranger-led interpretive talks. **Tips & Hints:** Busiest June–Aug., least crowded Nov. and Jan.

FOOD & LODGING

Camping: None in park. Near Buford: U.S. Army Corps of Engineers Sawnee Campground (3200 Buford Dam Rd., Lake Lanier, tel. 770/887–0592 or 877/444–6777; 57 sites; $22–$32; flush toilets, showers, hookups). **Hotels:** None in park. In Roswell: Holiday Inn Express (2950 Mansell Rd., tel. 770/552–0006 or 888/465–4329, www.hiexpress.com; 70 suites; $81–$100). **Restaurants:** None in park. In Sandy Springs: Fratelli di Napoli (8879 Roswell Rd., tel. 770/552–8784, www.northrivertavern.com; $6–$17).

FEES, HOURS & REGULATIONS

Free. Parking fee ($3 daily, $25 annual). Georgia fishing license and trout stamp required for ages 16 and over. Park open dawn to dusk year-round. Visitor contact station open daily 9–5.

HOW TO GET THERE

Visitor contact station: From I–285, take Rte. 400 north to Exit 6 (Northridge Rd.). Stay in right lane and follow signs. Closest airport: Atlanta (22 miles).

CONTACT

Chattahoochee River National Recreation Area (1978 Island Ford Pkwy., Sandy Springs, GA 30350, tel. 678/538–1200, fax 770/399–8087, www.nps.gov/chat). Atlanta Convention & Visitors Bureau (233 Peachtree St. NE, Suite 1400, Atlanta, GA 30303, tel. 404/521–6600, fax 404/577–3293, www.atlanta.net).

Chickamauga & Chattanooga National Military Park

In northwestern Georgia, and in southeastern Tennessee, near Chattanooga

On the fields and mountain slopes of this park in the fall of 1863, more than 150,000 Union and Confederate soldiers clashed in a series of battles remembered as some of the harshest fighting of the Civil War. The fighting ended with Union control of Chattanooga, the gateway to the Deep South. The park was established on August 19, 1890, and transferred from the War Department to the National Park Service on August 10, 1933.

WHAT TO SEE & DO

Scenic drives, walking. **Facilities:** 2 visitor centers: Chickamauga Battlefield (Fort Oglethorpe, GA) and Lookout Mountain Battlefield (Lookout Mountain, TN), Cravens House and Ochs Museum (both at Lookout Mountain, TN), trails. Bookstores, picnic areas. **Programs & Events:** Chickamauga Battlefield: 23-minute orientation film (shown hourly); car tours (Memorial Day–Aug., daily at 10 and 2); living-history demonstrations (Memorial Day-Aug.). Lookout Mountain: Cravens House tours (Memorial Day–Aug.); guided walks (Memorial Day–Aug., weekends at 11, 1, and 3). **Tips & Hints:** Visit in spring and fall. Busiest June and July, least crowded Jan. and Feb.

FOOD, LODGING & SUPPLIES

Camping: None in park. In Rising Fawn: Cloudland Canyon State Park (122 Cloudland Canyon Park Rd., tel. 706/657–4050, www.koa.com; 72 sites; $15–$28; flush toilets, hookups). **Hotels:** None in park. In Chattanooga, TN: Sheraton Read House (827 Broad St., tel. 423/266–4121, www.starwoodhotels.com; 241 rooms; $179–$259). In Fort Oglethorpe: Best Western Battlefield Inn (2120 Lafayette Rd., tel. 706/866–0222, www.bestwestern.com; 39 rooms; $69–$89). **✗ Restaurants:** None in park. In Chattanooga, TN: Southside Grill (1400 Coward St., tel. 423/266–9211; $8–$13; closed Sun.). In Fort Oglethorpe: O'Charley's (2542 Battlefield Pkwy., tel. 706/861–5520; $11–$13). **Groceries & Gear:** In Fort Oglethorpe: Kmart (526 Battlefield Pkwy., tel. 706/866–1337).

FEES, HOURS & REGULATIONS

Chickamauga Battlefield: free. Point Park at Lookout Mountain: $3 adults, free ages 15 and under. No bicycles on trails. No hunting. No in-line skating, roller-skating, or skateboarding. No metal detecting. Park open daily 6–dusk. Chickamauga Battlefield Visitor Center open daily 8:30–5; Lookout Mountain Visitor Center open daily Sept.–May, 9–5; June–Aug., 9–6.

HOW TO GET THERE

The Chickamauga Battlefield Visitor Center is in Fort Oglethorpe, on LaFayette Rd., south of Chattanooga, TN. The Lookout Mountain Battlefield Visitor Center is on Lookout Mountain, which may be reached from downtown Chattanooga via the Scenic or Ochs highways. Closest airport: Chattanooga, TN (10 miles).

CONTACT

Chickamauga and Chattanooga National Military Park (Box 2128, Fort Oglethorpe, GA 30742, tel. 706/866–9241, fax 423/752–5215, www.nps. gov/chch). Catoosa County Chamber of Commerce (Box 52, Ringgold, GA 30736, tel. 706/965–5201, www.catoosachamberofcommerce.com).

Cumberland Island National Seashore

In southeastern Georgia, near St. Marys

The seashore offers outstanding opportunities for relaxation and solitude in an undisturbed island paradise. One of the largest undeveloped barrier islands in the southeastern United States, the seashore contains federally designated wilderness and one of the largest maritime forests remaining in the United States. It also preserves several culturally significant sites including Plum Orchard and Dungeness, both built by the Thomas Carnegie family, the American industrialists who once owned most of the island. The seashore was established in 1972 and designated a Biosphere Reserve in 1986.

WHAT TO SEE & DO

Biking (rentals, Sea Camp Ranger Station), bird-watching, fishing, swimming. **Facilities:** On mainland: visitor center–park headquarters, bookstore, museum. On island: Sea Camp Ranger Station (exhibits), Ice House at Dungeness Dock (exhibits), Plum Orchard mansion, trails. **Programs & Events:** Ranger-guided tours (twice daily, Dungeness Dock), naturalist program (Sea Camp Ranger Station), mansion tour (Plum Orchard), beach and marsh ecology program (intermittently), deer and hog hunts (Oct.–Feb). **Tips & Hints:** Access by boat and ferry only. Watch for ticks. Best time to visit: spring and fall. Busiest Mar.–May, least crowded Dec. and Jan.

FOOD, LODGING & SUPPLIES

Camping: In the park: Sea Camp (tel. 877/860–6787; 18 sites; $4; flush toilets, cold showers), 4 backcountry sites. **Hotels:** In park: Greyfield Inn (tel. 904/261–6408 or 866/401–8581; 12 rooms; $395–$595). In St. Marys: Spencer House Inn (200 Osborne St., tel. 912/882–1872, spencerhouseinn.com; 14 rooms; $135–$245). **Restaurants:** None in park. In St. Marys: El Potro Mexican Restaurant (1923 Osborne Rd., tel. 912/882–0900, www.elpotrorestaurant.com; $6–$13). **Groceries & Gear:** None in park. In St. Marys: Walmart (6586 Rte. 40 E, tel. 912/882–3096).

FEES, HOURS & REGULATIONS

User fee: $4 per person. Round-trip ferry fee (reservations required, tel. 912/882–4335 or 877/860–6787): $20 adults, $14 ages 12 and under, $18 ages 65 and over. Backcountry permits ($2) available on island; reserve in advance. No motorized vehicles or pets allowed. No bicycles on wilderness trails or on beach. Participants in deer and hog hunts (tel. 912/882–4336) allowed on a first-come, first-served basis. Park open daily 8–4:30. Ferry doesn't operate Dec.–Feb., Tues. and Wed.

HOW TO GET THERE

Seashore access at St. Marys, 10 miles east of I–95, Exit 1 or Exit 3. Closest airport: Jacksonville, FL (34 miles).

CONTACTS

Cumberland Island National Seashore (101 Wheeler St., St. Marys, GA 31558, tel. 912/882–4336, fax 912/882–6284, www.nps.gov/cuis). Kingsland Tourist & Convention Bureau (Box 1928, 1190 E. Boone Ave., Kingsland, GA 31548, tel. 800/433–0225, www.visitkingsland. com). St. Marys Convention & Visitors Bureau (111 Osborne St., St. Marys, GA 31558, tel. 800/868–2199).

Fort Frederica National Monument

On St. Simons Island

Fort Frederica's ruins are a reminder of the struggle for empire between Spain and Great Britain. James Edward Oglethorpe founded the Georgia colony and built the fort on St. Simons Island, where it flourished in the 1740s. The southernmost post of the British colonies in North America, the fort protected Georgia and South Carolina from the Spanish in Florida. The park is known for its exceptional beauty and the antiquity of the tabby ruins. Stately oaks, exceptionally large grapevines, and Spanish moss lend an air of antiquity that is unequaled on the coast. The park was authorized on May 26, 1936.

WHAT TO SEE & DO

Ranger-led or self-guided walking tour of town ruins. **Facilities:** Visitor center, trail, wayside exhibits. Museum store. **Programs & Events:** 23-minute film *History Uncovered*, ranger-led tours, costumed interpretive programs. Frederica Festival (Feb.), Holiday Open House (Dec.). **Tips & Hints:** Plan to spend two hours at the monument. Sand gnats and mosquitoes are present year-round. Biting flies are worst in May and Sept. Busiest Feb. and Mar., least crowded Dec. and Jan.

FOOD & LODGING

Camping: None in park. On Jekyll Island: Jekyll Island Campground (1197 Riverview Dr., tel. 912/635–3021; 206 sites; $21–$35; flush toilets, showers, hookups). **Hotels:** None in park. On Jekyll Island: Days Inn (60 S. Beach View Dr., tel. 912/635–9800, www.daysinn. com; 124 rooms; $170–$205). In Brunswick: Best Western (126 Venture Dr., tel. 912/265–1114, www.bestwestern.com; 72 rooms; $90).

✕ **Restaurants:** None in park. On St. Simons Island: Putter's Club Dining Room (510 N. Windward Rd., tel. 912/638–3351; $5–$10).

FEES, HOURS & REGULATIONS

Entrance fee: $3 per person. No vehicles or bikes allowed in town site. Monument open daily 8:30–5. Visitor center open 9–5.

HOW TO GET THERE

On St. Simons Island, 12 miles from Brunswick, accessible from I–95 and U.S. 17 via the F.J. Torras (Brunswick–St. Simons) Causeway. Directional signs to the park are on all major roads to the island. The fort is on Frederica Rd. near Christ Church Episcopal Church.

CONTACTS

Fort Frederica National Monument (6515 Frederica Rd., St. Simons Island, GA 31522-9710, tel. 912/638–3639, www.nps.gov/fofr).

Fort Pulaski National Monument

Near Savannah

On April 11, 1862, national defense strategy changed forever when a Union-rifled cannon overcame a masonry fortification after only 30 hours of bombardment. Named for Revolutionary War hero Count Casimir Pulaski, the fort took 18 years to build. Preparing the ground for the fort was Robert E. Lee's first military assignment. This remarkably intact example of 19th-century military architecture, with its estimated 25 million bricks and 7½-foot-thick walls, is preserved for future generations as a reminder of the elusiveness of invincibility. The monument contains 5,623 acres, including some of the most pristine and scenic marshland on the Georgia coast. The monument was proclaimed in 1924 and transferred to the Park Service in 1933.

WHAT TO SEE & DO

Biking; bird-, wildlife, and ship viewing; fishing; hiking; picnicking; self-guided touring of fort and nature trail. **Facilities:** Visitor center, fort, lighthouse, nature trails. Bookstore, picnic areas. **Programs & Events:** Ranger-led talks and demonstrations; *The Battle of Fort Pulaski*, a 17-minute film; troop encampments, special programs, and demonstrations (holiday weekends). **Tips & Hints:** Plan to spend at least two hours. Busiest Apr.–Aug., least crowded Dec. and Jan.

FOOD, LODGING & SUPPLIES

⚠ **Camping:** None in park. On Tybee Island: River's End Campground and RV Park (915 Polk St., tel. 912/786–5518; 100 sites; $29–$64; flush toilets, showers, hookups). ▥ **Hotels:** None in park. In Savannah: Best Western Central Inn (45 Eisenhower Dr., tel. 912/355–1000, www. bestwestern.com; 126 rooms; $90–$100). ✕ **Restaurants:** None in park. On Tybee Island: Crab Shack (40 Estill Hammock Rd., tel. 912/786–9857, www.thecrabshack.com; $6–$24), A.J.'s Dockside Restaurant (1315 Chatham Ave., tel. 912/786–9533, ajsdocksidetybee.com; $7–$16). ⚑ **Gear:** None in park. On Tybee Island: Chu's Convenience Mart (304 1st St., tel. 912/786–5247).

FEES, HOURS & REGULATIONS

Entrance fee: $5 adults, free ages 15 and under. A 1½-mile round-trip hike takes you near, but not actually to, Cockspur Island Lighthouse. No bikes on trails leading to fort. Monument open daily 9–5, extended hours in summer.

HOW TO GET THERE

15 miles east of Savannah on U.S. 80. Follow signs for Fort Pulaski, Tybee Island, and beaches. Closest airport: Savannah (30 miles).

CONTACT

Fort Pulaski National Monument (Box 30757, U.S. 80E, Savannah, GA 31410-0757, tel. 912/786–5787, www.nps.gov/fopu). Savannah Convention & Visitors Bureau (101 E. Bay St., Savannah, GA 31401, tel. 912/644–6401, www.savannahvisit.com).

Jimmy Carter National Historic Site

In central Georgia, in Plains

The rural southern culture of Plains revolves around farming, church, and school and molded the character of the 39th U.S. president. The site includes President Carter's residence, boyhood home, school, and the railroad depot, which served as his campaign headquarters during the 1976 election. The area surrounding the residence is under the protection of the Secret Service and is not open to the public. The site was authorized on December 23, 1987.

WHAT TO SEE & DO

Touring by car or bicycle, visiting boyhood farm and campaign head-quarters. **Facilities:** Visitor center (Plains High School), historic farm and home. Bookstore, picnic area in town park. **Programs & Events:** 26-minute film, audio tour. Plains Peanut Festival (last Sat. in Sept.). Blacksmithing demonstrations (monthly). **Tips & Hints:** Plan to spend two to three hours visiting places associated with the Carters. Busiest Mar. and Apr., least crowded Dec. and Jan.

FOOD, LODGING & SUPPLIES

⚑ **Camping:** None in park. In Cordele: Georgia Veterans State Park (2459 U.S. Hwy. 280 W, tel. 800/864–7275; 76 sites; $25–$28; hook-ups). ⚑ **Hotels:** None in park. In Plains: Plains Historic Inn (106 Main St., tel. 229/824–4517, www.plainsinn.net; 7 rooms; $75–$110). ✗ **Restaurants:** None in park. In Americus: Waffle House (1207 Martin Luther King Jr. Blvd., tel. 229/931–0300, www.wafflehouse.com; $5–$8). ⚑ **Groceries:** None in park. In Plains: USA Food Mart Peanut Gallery (205 W. Church St., tel. 229/824–7734).

FEES & HOURS

Free. Visitor center open daily 9–5. Plains Depot open daily 9–4:30. Boyhood Farm open daily 10–5.

HOW TO GET THERE

From I–75 northbound, take Exit 33 (Cordele) and U.S. 280 west to Plains. From Columbus, take U.S. 280 east to Plains. Boyhood farm is 2 miles west of Plains on U.S. 280. Closest airport: Columbus (55 miles).

CONTACT

Jimmy Carter National Historic Site (300 N. Bond St., Plains, GA 31780, tel. 229/824–4104, fax 229/824–3441, www.nps.gov/jica).

Kennesaw Mountain National Battlefield Park

Between Kennesaw and Marietta, near Atlanta

Eleven miles of earthworks are preserved within the 2,923-acre park, which commemorates two Civil War battles where, during Sherman's 1864 Atlanta Campaign, Union general William T. Sherman met Confederate general Joseph E. Johnston. The site was authorized as a national battlefield in 1917, transferred to the Park Service in 1933, and redesignated in 1935.

WHAT TO SEE & DO

Hiking, picnicking, scenic drives. **Facilities:** Visitor center, battlefield and earthworks, auto tour roads, more than 16 miles of trails. Bookstore, grills. **Programs & Events:** 19-minute film *Kennesaw Mountain and the Atlanta Campaign,* ranger program, living-history programs (June–Oct., weekends). **Tips & Hints:** Allow two to three hours for visit. Take shuttle bus to mountaintop on weekends and major holidays. Stay on trails. Busiest Oct. and Apr., least crowded Jan. and Feb.

FEES, HOURS & REGULATIONS

Free. Leashed pets only. No bicycles on trails. Park open daily 7:30– dusk. Visitor center open daily 8:30–5.

HOW TO GET THERE

3 miles north of Marietta. From I–75, take Exit 269 and follow the brown-and-white park signs. Closest airport: Atlanta (35 miles).

CONTACTS

Kennesaw Mountain National Battlefield Park (900 Kennesaw Mountain Dr., Kennesaw, GA 30152, tel. 770/427–4686, fax 770/528–8399, www.nps.gov/kemo).

Martin Luther King Jr. National Historic Site

In Atlanta

In this two-block area, Atlanta honors the life, legacy, and teachings of Martin Luther King Jr., the civil rights leader who was assassinated on April 4, 1968, at age 39. The site contains the home where King was born, Ebenezer Baptist Church, Martin Luther King Jr. Center for Nonviolent Social Change, King's gravesite, Fire Station #6 Museum, and the residential and commercial districts of the "Sweet Auburn" community. The site was established in 1980.

WHAT TO SEE & DO

Touring the site. **Facilities:** Visitor center (450 Auburn Ave. NE), Birth Home of Martin Luther King Jr. (501 Auburn Ave. NE), Ebenezer Baptist Church (407 Auburn Ave. NE), King Center Freedom Hall exhibits and King gravesite (449 Auburn Ave. NE), Fire Station #6 Museum (39 Boulevard NE), wayside exhibits in neighborhood. Bookstores and gift shops. **Programs & Events:** Ranger-led tours of King's birth home, talks on historic role of black churches, orientation video. King Week Celebration (Jan.), Black History Month (Feb.), King Remembrance Day (Apr. 4), March on Washington Anniversary (Aug.), National Historic Site Anniversary (Oct. 10). **Tips & Hints:** The best months to visit are Oct.–Dec. Busiest Jan. and Feb., least crowded Mar. and Dec.

FEES & HOURS

Free. Site and visitor center open Memorial Day–Labor Day, daily 9–6; Labor Day–Memorial Day, daily 9–5.

HOW TO GET THERE

1½ miles east of downtown Atlanta. Closest airport: Atlanta.

CONTACTS

Martin Luther King Jr. National Historic Site (450 Auburn Ave. NE, Atlanta, GA 30312, tel. 404/331–5190, fax 404/730–3112, www.nps.gov/malu). Atlanta Convention & Visitors Bureau (233 Peachtree St. NE, Suite 1400, Atlanta, GA 30303, tel. 404/521–6600, fax 404/577–3293, www.atlanta.net).

Ocmulgee National Monument

In Macon

Around 17,000 years of human habitation, from Ice Age "Paleo" hunters to the Muscogee (Creek) Confederacy of historic times, are on display at this monument. People of the Early Mississippian Period Macon Plateau culture 1,000 years ago built a large town, which is now protected here. Huge earthen mounds and a unique ceremonial earth lodge, reconstructed over the original hand-molded clay floor, are reminders of this ancient agricultural society. One of two temple mounds at the Lamar site is the only remaining "spiral" mound. The British built a trading post at the site in the late 1600s. The Dunlap House and an earthen gun emplacement date from the Civil War battle that was fought here. The monument was authorized in 1936.

WHAT TO SEE & DO

Bird-watching, fishing, hiking, jogging, picnicking, touring the museum, walking to earth lodge and mounds. **Facilities:** Visitor center with archaeological museum, theater with 17-minute movie, 6-mile trail. Gift shop. **Programs & Events:** Lantern light tours (Mar.), field trip to Lamar Mounds and Village, children's summer workshops (July), Ocmulgee Indian Celebration (3rd weekend, Sept.). **Tips & Hints:** Visit in spring and fall. Busiest Sept.–Nov., least crowded Dec. and Jan.

FEES, HOURS & REGULATIONS

Free. Lamar Mounds can be seen only on occasional ranger-guided tours; call for dates and times. Georgia state fishing license required. Stay on trails. No bikes on trails. No climbing on mounds. No hunting. No kite flying. Leashed pets only. Park and visitor center open daily 9–5.

HOW TO GET THERE

On the east edge of Macon, off I–16 Exit 2. Closest airports: Macon (12 miles), Atlanta (90 miles).

CONTACTS

Ocmulgee National Monument (1207 Emery Hwy., Macon, GA 31217, tel. 478/752–8257, fax 478/752–8259, www.nps.gov/ocmu). Macon–Bibb County Convention & Visitors Bureau (450 Martin Luther King Jr. Blvd., Macon, GA 31201, tel. 478/743–1074, www.maconga.org).

See Also

Appalachian National Scenic Trail, West Virginia. *Augusta Canal National Heritage Area, Overmountain Victory National Historic Trail, and Trail of Tears National Historic Trail,* in Other National Parklands.

HAWAII

Haleakala National Park

In east Maui

The park preserves the outstanding volcanic landscape of the upper slopes of Haleakala (10,023 feet) and protects the fragile ecosystems of Kipahulu Valley, the scenic pools along Oheo Gulch, and many rare and endangered species. Hike through rain forests or a cinder desert or picnic near a 400-foot waterfall in this park of extremes. Haleakala originally was one of two units of Hawaii National Park (along with Hawaii Volcanoes National Park; see separate entry). It was redesignated as a separate park in 1961 and designated a Biosphere Reserve in 1980.

WHAT TO SEE & DO

Bird-watching, bicycling, hiking, picnicking, stargazing, sunrise and sunset watching, swimming, walking, whale-watching. **Facilities:** 3 visitor centers: Park Headquarters (mile 11, Crater Rd.), Haleakala (mile 21, Crater Rd.), and Kipahulu (mile 42, Rte. 31). Interpretive exhibits, pre-contact Hawaiian structures (before 1778), historic walls, Sugar Mill dam ruins, trails. Bookstores. **Programs & Events:** Guided walks and programs on geological, natural, and cultural history, guided cloud-forest hike (Mon. and Thurs. at 8:45, reservations recommended), Star programs (May–Sept.). **Tips & Hints:** Wear sturdy, comfortable shoes and lightweight, layered clothing that will keep you warm in wet weather at the summit. Temperatures range from 40°F to 65°F but can be below freezing with wind chill year-round. At Summit, watch for altitude sickness, hypothermia, and black ice on roads in winter. At Kipahulu, watch for flash floods, strong ocean currents, rockfalls, hypothermia, and mosquitoes. Bring binoculars to stargaze. Bring plenty of water. Go to Halemauu Trail and the Summit for sunsets. Busy year-round.

FOOD, LODGING & SUPPLIES

⚠ **Camping:** 2 campgrounds in the park: Hosmer Grove (Summit area; tent camping area; free; pit toilets), Kipahulu Campground (near Kipahulu Visitor Center; tent camping area; free; pit toilets). 3 cabins and 2 tent sites in the backcountry. 🏨 **Hotels:** None in park. In Hana: Hana Accommodations (Hana Hwy., tel. 808/248–7868 or 800/228–4262; www.hana-maui.com; 4 cottages; $95–$195) , Travaasa Hana (5031 Hana Hwy., tel. 808/248–8211, www.travaasa.com/hana; 70 rooms). ✕ **Restaurants:** None in park. In Hana: Paniolo Lounge (5031 Hana Hwy., tel. 808/248–8255; $12–$45). ⛁ **Groceries:** In Pukalani: Pukalani Superette (15 Makawao Ave., tel. 808/572–7616).

FEES, HOURS & REGULATIONS

Entrance fee: $5 per person on foot, bicycle, or motorcycle, $10 per vehicle. Backcountry camping permits (free) required. Hikers can reserve and wilderness cabins online up to 90 days in advance. Fishing at Kipahulu must be done in accordance with state fishing regulations. Bicycling restricted to roads. No skateboarding, skating, or hang gliding. No pets on trails. Leashed pets allowed in campground only. Park open daily. Park headquarters open daily 7–3:45. Haleakala Visitor Center open daily sunrise–3. Kipahulu Visitor Center open daily 9–5.

HOW TO GET THERE

The park's summit area is a 1½-hour drive (38 miles) from Kahului via Rtes. 37, 377, and 378. Kipahulu is a three- to four-hour drive (61 miles) from Kahului via Rtes. 36, 360, and 31. Closest airport: Kahului.

CONTACTS

Haleakala National Park (Box 369, Makawao, HI 96768, tel. 808/572–4400, fax 808/572–1304, www.nps.gov/hale). Hawaii Visitors & Convention Bureau (2270 Kalakaua Ave., Suite 801, Honolulu, HI 96815, tel. 800/464–2924, www.gohawaii.com).

Hawaii Volcanoes National Park

On the southeast side of the island of Hawaii

The park preserves the natural setting of Mauna Loa (13,677 feet), the world's most massive volcano, and Kilauea (the world's most active). It contains lush rain forests, raw craters, acid deserts, and great areas covered by lava flows. The park was established in 1916 and designated a Biosphere Reserve in 1980 and a World Heritage Site in 1987.

WHAT TO SEE & DO

Bird-watching, hiking, scenic driving. **Facilities:** Kilauea Visitor Center, art center, museum, trails, overlooks. Book and map sale areas, gift shop. **Programs & Events:** Ranger talks and walks (daily), evening programs (Tues. and Wed., 2 to 3 times a month). Cultural Festival (2nd weekend, July). **Tips & Hints:** Be prepared for anything from cold and wet weather to high winds to heat exhaustion. Bring rain gear, light sweaters, windbreakers, sturdy shoes, hats, water bottles, sunglasses, and sunscreen. Call 808/935–8555 for weather forecasts. Stay on trails and don't enter lava tubes (except Thurston Lava Tube). Avoid volcanic fumes. Busiest July and Aug., least crowded Apr. and Sept.

FOOD, LODGING & SUPPLIES

🏕 **Camping:** 2 campgrounds in park: Namakanipaio (off Rte. 11, near summit; tent camping area; free; flush toilets), Kulanaokuaiki (Hilina Pali Rd.; 3 sites; free; vault toilets). Backcountry camping allowed. 🏨 **Hotels:** In the park: Kilauea Military Camp (tel. 808/967-7315, www.kmc-volcano.com; active-duty and retired military personnel only; 90 cottages). In Volcano: Volcano Mist Cottage (11-3932 9th St., tel. 808/895–8359, www.volcanomistcottage.com; 1 cottage; $325). Check website for details of Volcano House reopening. ✕ **Restaurants:** None in park. In Volcano Village: Volcano's Lava Rock Café (Old Volcano Hwy., tel. 808/967–8526; $5–$8). ⚱ **Groceries:** In Volcano Village: Kilauea General Store (Old Volcano Hwy., tel. 808/967–7555).

FEES, HOURS & REGULATIONS

Entrance fee: $5 per person on foot, bicycle, or motorcycle, $10 per vehicle. Backcountry camping permit required (free). Park open daily. Visitor center open daily 7:45–5. Jaggar Museum open daily 8:30–5.

HOW TO GET THERE

From Hilo, go 30 miles southwest on Rte. 11; from Kailua-Kona, travel 96 miles southeast on Rte. 11 or 125 miles through Waimea and Hilo via Rtes. 19 and 11. Closest airport: Hilo.

CONTACTS

Hawaii Volcanoes National Park (Box 52, Hawaii National Park, HI 96718-0052, tel. 808/985–6000, fax 808/967–8186, www.nps.gov/havo). Hawaii Visitors and Convention Bureau (2270 Kalakaua Ave., Suite 801, Honolulu, HI 96815, tel. 800/464–2924, www.gohawaii.com).

Kalaupapa National Historical Park

On north shore of Molokai

Kalaupapa and Kalawao, the historic Hansen's disease (leprosy) settlements, are preserved in this park. Today, Kalaupapa is still home for many former patients. A means of rendering the disease inactive was proven successful by the 1940s, and paved the way for repealing the 104-year-old forced isolation statute in 1969. In Kalawao are the churches of Siloama, established by missionaries in 1866, and St. Philomena associated in part with the work of Joseph De Veuster (Saint Damien). Kalaupapa peninsula was inhabited by a native Hawaiian community before the establishment of the quarantine settlement at Kalawao in 1866. Evidence of this ancient and historic occupation found across all three *ahupuaʻa* (land divisions) is relatively undisturbed and represents one of the richest archaeological preserves in Hawaii. The 10,725-acre park contains spectacular sea cliffs, narrow valleys, a volcanic crater, a rain forest, lava tubes and caves, and offshore islands and waters. The park was authorized on December 22, 1980.

WHAT TO SEE & DO

Touring Kalaupapa and Kalawao settlements. **Facilities:** Wayside exhibits. Bookstore and sales shop. **Programs & Events:** Tours of Kalaupapa and Kalawao (Mon.–Sat.). **Tips & Hints:** Access to the Kalaupapa peninsula is by advance reservation through Damien Tours. Make reservations for commercial tours of the settlement and mule rides on the Pali Trail. Go Nov.–Mar. to see whales and migratory birds from Alaska.

FOOD, LODGING & SUPPLIES

🔥 **Camping:** None in park. Near Kualapuu: Palaau State Park (end of Kalae Rd. Rte. 47, tel. 808/567–6923; tent camping area; free; flush toilets; permit required). 🏨 **Hotels:** None in park. In Kaunakakai: Hotel Molokai (1300 Kamehameha V Hwy., tel. 877/553-5347, www. hotelmolokai.com; 54 rooms; $159–$259). ✘ **Restaurants:** None in park. In Kaunakakai: Kanemitsu Bakery & Restaurant (79 Ala Malama St., tel. 808/553–5855; $2–$5; closed Tues.). ♨ **Groceries:** None in park. In Kaunakakai: Friendly Market Center (90 Ala Malama St., tel. 808/553–5595).

FEES, HOURS & REGULATIONS

Free. Reservations and fees required for commercial tours, mule rides, and air flights. Contact Damien Tours (tel. 808/567–6171) for tour reservations and Molokai Mule Rides (tel. 808/567–6088 or 800/567–7550) for mule ride reservations. Flights to Kalaupapa from Oahu or Molokai are through Makani Kai Airlines (tel. 808/834–5813). Access to the Kalaupapa peninsula is limited to small scheduled tour groups. No one under 16 allowed. No hunting or firearms. No pets. No photographs of patients without their written permission. Park open daily. Commercial tours operate Mon.–Sat.

HOW TO GET THERE

The Kalaupapa Peninsula is at the base of a 1,600-foot cliff. There's no road access from the rest of Molokai. Visitors must hike or ride a trail by mule down the cliff or fly into the airport in the park. Tour buses run by Damien Tours pick up visitors at the bottom of the mule trail or at the airport. Closest airport: Kalaupapa (2 miles).

CONTACTS

Kalaupapa National Historical Park (National Park Service, Box 2222, Kalaupapa, HI 96742, tel. 808/567–6802, www.nps.gov/kala). Molokai Visitors Association (Box 960, Kaunakakai, HI 96748, tel. 808/553–3876, www.molokai-hawaii.com).

Kaloko-Honokohau National Historical Park

On west coast of island of Hawaii, near Kailua Kona

Kaloko-Honokohau preserves traditional native Hawaiian activities and culture. It's the site of an ancient Hawaiian settlement with four different *ahupua'a*, or traditional sea-to-mountain land divisions. Resources include fishponds, house-site platforms, petroglyphs, and a religious site. The park was established on November 10, 1978.

WHAT TO SEE & DO

Bird-watching, fishing, hiking, picnicking, snorkeling, surfing, swimming. **Facilities:** Visitor center (off Rte. 19). **Programs & Events:** Interpretive programs (occasionally). **Tips & Hints:** Busiest June and July, least crowded Sept. and Oct.

FOOD, LODGING & SUPPLIES

Camping: None in park. Near Kawaihae: Samuel M. Spencer Beach Park (Rte. 270, tel. 808/961–8311; tent camping area; $6; flush toilets, showers; permit required). **Hotels:** None in park. In Kailua-Kona: Outrigger Kanaloa at Kona (78–261 Manukai St., tel. 808/322–9625, www.outrigger.com; 166 units; $200–$365). **Restaurants:** None in park. In Kailua: Baci Bistro (30 Aulike St., tel. 808/262–7555, www.bacibistro.com; $5–$16), Kona Inn Restaurant (75-5744 Alii Dr. in the Kona Inn Shopping Village, tel. 808/329–4455; $8–$16). **Groceries & Gear:** In Waimea: Kawaihae Market & Deli (613665 Akoni Pule Hwy., tel. 808/880–1611).

FEES, HOURS & REGULATIONS

Free. No collecting artifacts, plants, rocks, or coral. Kaloko road gate open daily 8–5. Visitors are welcome in the park after 5, but vehicles need to be out before gate closes. Visitor center open daily 8:30–4.

HOW TO GET THERE

At the base of Hualalai Volcano along the Kona coast, 3 miles north of Kailua-Kona and south of the airport on Rte. 19 (Queen Kaahumanu Hwy.). The Kaloko gate is across the highway from the Kaloko New Industrial Park across from Kona Trade Center building. The park can also be accessed from the south end, by way of the Honokohau small boat harbor. Closest airport: Keahole-Kona (3 miles).

CONTACTS

Kaloko-Honokohau National Historical Park (73–4786 Kanalani St., #14, Kailua-Kona, HI 96740, tel. 808/326–9057, www.nps.gov/kaho/). Big Island Visitors Bureau (250 Keawe St., Hilo, HI 96720, tel. 808/961–5797, www.gohawaii.com/big-island).

Pu'uhonua o Honaunau National Historical Park

In southwest of the island of Hawaii, near Honaunau

Until 1819 this park was a sanctuary for vanquished Hawaiian warriors, noncombatants, and kapu breakers. The park includes prehistoric house sites, royal fishponds, coconut groves, and spectacular shore scenery. The 420-acre park was authorized as City of Refuge National Historical Park in 1955 and renamed in 1978.

WHAT TO SEE & DO

Fishing, hiking, picnicking, self-guided tours, watching crafts demonstrations. **Facilities:** Visitor center, restored temple, trail. Picnic area.

Programs & Events: Hawaiian Cultural Festival (June). **Tips & Hints:** Be alert for unexpected high waves. Watch for falling coconuts and coconut fronds off the trail. Busiest Feb. and July, least crowded Dec. and Jan.

FOOD, LODGING & SUPPLIES

Camping: None in park. See Kaloko-Honokohau National Historical Park. **Hotels:** None in park. In Captain Cook: Manago Hotel (826155 Mamalahoa Hwy., tel. 808/323–2642, www.managohotel. com; 64 rooms; $36–$78). **Restaurants:** None in park. In Captain Cook: Manago Hotel Restaurant (826155 Mamalahoa Hwy., tel. 808/ 323–2642, www.managohotel.com; $5–$14; closed Mon.). **Groceries:** None in park. In Captain Cook: Choice Mart (82-6066 Mamalahoa Hwy., Kealakekua Ranch Center, tel. 808/323–3994).

FEES & HOURS

Entrance fee: $3 per person on foot, bicycle, or motorcycle, $5 per vehicle. Park open daily 7–6. Visitor center open daily 8:30–4:30.

HOW TO GET THERE

From the airport, take Rte. 19 to Kailua, then Rte. 11 to Honaunau, then Rte. 160 to the park. Closest airport: Kona (30 miles).

CONTACTS

Pu'uhonua o Honaunau National Historical Park (Box 129, Honaunau, HI 96726, tel. 808/328–2326, www.nps.gov/puho). Kona-Kohala Chamber of Commerce (75–5737 Kuakini Hwy., Suite 208, Kailua-Kona, HI 96740, tel. 808/329–1758, www.kona-kohala.com).

Pu'ukohola Heiau
National Historic Site

In northwest of island of Hawaii, near Kawaihae

High on a hill above the Pacific Ocean sits Pu'ukohola Heiau, the last major religious structure of the ancient Hawaiian culture. Kamehameha I rebuilt the "Temple on the Hill of the Whale" between 1790 and 1791 during his rise to power and dedicated it to his family war god, Kukailimoku. The 85-acre site was authorized on August 17, 1972.

WHAT TO SEE & DO

Bird-watching, guided and self-guided tours of historical sites, hiking, shark- and whale-watching. **Facilities:** Visitor center, trails. **Programs & Events:** Interpretive talks, guided tours, Hawaiian programs. Arts-and-crafts demonstrations (once weekly, Mar.–Aug.). Pacific Islander Day (May). Hawaiian Cultural Festival (Aug.). **Tips & Hints:** Hike only if you are prepared for a long and rugged trail. Make guided-tour reservations two weeks in advance (tel. 808/882–7218 Ext. 1011). Busiest Dec.-Mar., least crowded Oct. and Nov.

FOOD, LODGING & SUPPLIES

None in park. See Kaloko-Honokohau National Historical Park.

FEES & HOURS

Free. Park gate closes at 5. Visitor center open daily 7:45–4:45.

HOW TO GET THERE

On the northwest shore of the island of Hawaii in the district of South Kohala. The visitor center is off Rte. 270, ¼ mile north of Rte. 19 intersection. Closest airport: Kailua-Kona (32 miles).

CONTACTS

Pu'ukohola Heiau National Historic Site (62-3601 Kawaihae Rd., Kawaihae, HI 96743, tel. 808/882–7218, fax 808/882–1215, www.nps. gov/puhe). Kona-Kohala Chamber of Commerce (75–5737 Kuakini Hwy., Suite 208, Kailua-Kona, HI 96740, tel. 808/329–1758, www. kona-kohala.com).

World War II Valor in the Pacific National Monument

In Hawaii, at Pearl Harbor

Originally named the USS *Arizona* Memorial, this monument grew out of a wartime desire to honor those who died in the December 7, 1941, attack. The memorial is the final resting place for many of the *Arizona*'s 1,177 crewmen who lost their lives that day. Their names are inscribed on the memorial. Other features include the USS *Oklahoma* Memorial and USS *Utah* Memorial (the latter accessible only by those with military base credentials). The park was established on September 9, 1980, and renamed in December 2008.

WHAT TO SEE & DO

Taking shuttle boat to memorial, touring memorial and museum. **Facilities:** Visitor center, theaters, memorial, museum. Bookstore. **Programs & Events:** Tours (daily 8–3). **Tips & Hints:** Reserve tickets in advance or arrive early to avoid a long wait. Plan for a three-hour visit. It's a good idea to secure all valuables in your hotel, because the visitor center is in a high-theft area. Bags can also be checked near the visitor center entrance for $3. Because of security regulations, backpacks, fanny packs, purses, diaper bags, shopping bags, large camera bags, luggage, and any other items that offer concealment are not allowed. Busiest June–Aug., least crowded Dec.–Feb.

FEES, HOURS & REGULATIONS

Free; donations encouraged. Audio guides ($7.50) available in English, Japanese, Mandarin Chinese, Korean, German, French, and Spanish. No baby strollers, carriages, or baby backpacks in the theaters or on the boats. Beach or swimwear is discouraged. No pets. The memorial is open daily 7–5.

HOW TO GET THERE

The memorial is a half-hour drive from Waikiki. Take Rte. 1 west to Arizona Memorial–Stadium Exit 15A, then Rte. 99 to the visitor center. Access is also available via a one-hour ride on Bus 20 or Bus 42 from Waikiki. Closest airport: Honolulu (3 miles).

CONTACTS

World War II Valor in the Pacific National Monument (1 Arizona Memorial Pl., Honolulu, HI 96818, tel. 808/422–3399, www.nps.gov/valr). Hawaii Visitor & Convention Bureau (2270 Kalakaua Ave., Suite 801, Honolulu, HI 96815, tel. 808/923–1811, www.gohawaii.com).

IDAHO

City of Rocks National Reserve

In southern Idaho, 45 miles south of Burley

In this reserve are historic pioneer trails in the midst of geologic grandeur. The name "City of Rocks" refers to massive granite rock formations—up to 2.5 billion years old and 600 feet high—that reminded California-bound emigrants in the 1800s of city buildings. The park also has world-class rock climbing and a diversity of habitat, wildlife, and vegetation. City of Rocks, which is cooperatively managed by the National Park Service and the State of Idaho, was designated on November 18, 1988.

WHAT TO SEE & DO

Bicycling, bird-watching, cross-country skiing, hiking, horseback riding (rentals, Almo), hunting, picnicking, rock climbing, snowmobiling, snowshoeing. **Facilities:** Visitor center (Almo), trails, wayside exhibits, kiosk. Gift shop, grills, picnic tables. **Programs & Events:** Interpretive talks, guided hikes, cultural demonstrations (Memorial Day–Labor Day, Fri. and Sat. nights). Stargazing (May–Oct.), City of Rocks Trail Ride (June–Oct.). **Tips & Hints:** Go late May–early June for wildflowers, May–June for birds, late Sept.–early Oct. for fall colors. Busiest May and June, least crowded Jan. and Feb.

FOOD, LODGING & SUPPLIES

Camping: In the park: City of Rocks Campground (64 individual and group sites scattered throughout park; $13, plus $11 reservation fee; vault toilets). Backcountry camping allowed. In Almo: Castle Rocks State Park Smoky Mountain Campground (729 E. Smoky Mountain Dr., tel. 888/922–6743; 37 campsites; $22; flush toilets, showers, hookups, yurts, lodge, and bunkhouse also available). **Hotels:** None in park. In Almo: Almo Creek Inn (3020 Elba-Almo Rd., tel. 208/824–5577; 8 rooms, 3 cabins; $100). In Burley: Best Western Plus Burley Inn (800 N. Overland Ave., Exit 208 off I–84, tel. 208/678-3501 or 800/401–6338, www.bestwestern.com; 126 rooms; $84–$90). **Restaurants:** None in park. In Almo: Almo Creek Outpost Steakhouse (3020 Elba-Almo Rd., tel. 208/824–5577; $6–$12). In Burley: Charlie's Café (615 E. Main St., tel. 208/678–0112; $6–$9). **Groceries & Gear:** None in park. In Almo: Tracy Mercantile Store (3001 Elba-Almo Rd., tel. 208/824–5570).

FEES, HOURS & REGULATIONS

Free. Permit required (free) for backcountry camping and backpacking; tel. 888/922–6743 for reservations for regular campsites. Leashed dogs only. Hunting in designated areas only. Idaho state hunting license required. Bikes and horses on designated trails only. No motorized ve-

151

hicles or equipment on trails or road. Reserve is open year-round, but some roads may be impassable Nov.–Apr. You can hike, ski, snowmobile, or snowshoe into the park. Visitor center open Apr.–Oct., daily 8–4:30; Nov.–Mar., weekdays 8–4:30.

HOW TO GET THERE

In Almo, ID, on the Idaho–Utah border. From Boise and west, take I–84 to Declo, Exit 216 (Rte. 77) to Almo. Closest airport: Twin Falls (85 miles).

CONTACTS

City of Rocks National Reserve (Box 169, Almo, ID 83312, tel. 208/ 824–5901, fax 208/246–2447, www.nps.gov/ciro). Castle Rocks State Park (3035 S. Elba-Almo Rd., Almo, ID 83312, tel. 208/ 824–5901, fax 208/246–2447, www.parksandrecreation.idaho.gov).

Craters of the Moon National Monument & Preserve

In south-central Idaho, southwest of Arco

The monument preserves approximately 1,100 square miles of strangely beautiful volcanic landscape encompassing almost all of the volcanic rift zone known as the Great Rift. It includes three lava fields: Craters of the Moon, Wapi, and Kings Bowl. There are more than 25 cones and 60 lava flows that range in age from 15,000 to 2,000 years old. The park contains one of the largest basaltic cinder cones in the world (Big Cinder Butte) and some of the best examples of spatter cones in the world. The north end of the monument contains a portion of Goodale's Cutoff, which is part of the Oregon Trail. The monument was proclaimed on May 2, 1924.

WHAT TO SEE & DO

Bird-watching, bicycling, caving, hiking, scenic drives, skiing, snowshoeing, telemarking. **Facilities:** Visitor center, overlooks, trails, wayside exhibits, amphitheater. Bookstore, picnic tables. **Programs & Events:** Guided walks, evening programs (mid-June–Labor Day), guided snowshoe hikes (Jan. and Feb., weekends, reservations required). **Tips & Hints:** Bring sturdy ground cloth to protect tent bottoms. Go in mid-June for peak flower display, in late summer and fall for most ice-free caving. Busiest July and Aug., least crowded Dec. and Jan.

FOOD, LODGING & SUPPLIES

⛺ **Camping:** In the park: Craters of the Moon Lava Flow Campground (51 sites; $10; flush toilets). Backcountry camping allowed (free). In Arco: KOA (2424 N. 3000 W, tel. 208/527–8513, www.koa. com; 61 sites; $25–$43; flush toilets, showers, hookups; closed Nov.–Apr.), Mountain View RV Park (705 W. Grand Ave., tel. 208/527–3707, www.mountainviewrvarco.com; 34 sites; $20–$30; flush toilets, showers, hookups; closed Nov.–Apr.). 🏨 **Hotels:** None in park. In Arco: D-K Motel (316 S. Front St., tel. 208/527–8282 or 800/231–0134, www.dkmotel.com; 25 rooms, 6 suites; $42-$66). ✗ **Restaurants:** In the park: snacks at visitor center. In Arco: Pickle's Place (440 S. Front St., tel. 208/527–9944, www.picklesplacerestaurant.com). ⚴ **Groceries & Gear:** None in park. In Arco: A&A Market, 218 N. Idaho St., tel. 208/527–8594).

FEES, HOURS & REGULATIONS

Entrance fee: $4 per person on foot or bicycle, $8 per vehicle. Caving permit, backcountry camping permit and permit to enter north section of monument required (free). Bikes allowed on roads and on Goodale's Cutoff. No hunting within original boundaries of monument; hunting permitted in expanded portions. No off-road vehicle travel. No pets on trails. Park road closed in winter. Park open daily. Visitor center open Memorial Day–Labor Day, daily 8–6; Labor Day–Memorial Day, daily 8–4:30.

HOW TO GET THERE

18 miles southwest of Arco on U.S. 20/26/93. Closest airport: Hailey/Sun Valley (60 miles).

CONTACTS

Craters of the Moon National Monument & Preserve (Box 29, Arco, ID 83213, tel. 208/527–1335, fax 208/527–3073, www.nps.gov/crmo). Butte County Chamber of Commerce (P.O. Box 837, Arco, ID 82313, tel. 208/527–3060, www.buttecountychamber.com). Lost River Valley Chamber of Commerce (Box 46, 159 N. Idaho St., Arco, ID 82313, tel. 208/527–3060, www.thelostrivervalley.com).

Hagerman Fossil Beds National Monument

In south-central Idaho, in Hagerman

Here are the world's richest known deposits from the late Pliocene era, roughly 3.5 million years ago. The collection includes the largest concentration of fossil horses in North America and more than 100 other animal species. The monument provides a glimpse of life that existed before the Ice Age and the earliest appearance of modern flora and fauna. This is one of only three units in the national park system that contains a portion of the Oregon National Historic Trail. The site was authorized in 1988.

WHAT TO SEE & DO

Hiking, scenic drives. **Facilities:** Visitor center, self-guided driving tour (year-round), trails (both hiking and equestrian), outdoor exhibits, amphitheater. Bookstore, overlooks. **Programs & Events:** Junior Ranger program. Paleo Porch Program, Junior Paleontologist Camp, and other educational programs (call for schedule). **Tips & Hints:** Best time to visit is April–Oct. Go in Dec. to see migratory waterfowl.

FOOD, LODGING & SUPPLIES

⛺ **Camping:** None in park. In Hagerman: Hagerman RV Village (18049 U.S. 30, tel. 208/837–4906 or 800/707–4906, www.hagermanrvvillage.com; 68 sites; $25; flush toilets, showers, hookups). 🏨 **Hotels:** None in park. In Hagerman: Hagerman Valley Inn (661 Frogs Landing, tel. 208/837–6196, fax 208/837–4568, www.hagermanvalleyinn.com; 16 rooms; $65). ✕ **Restaurants:** None in park. In Hagerman: Snake River Grill (611 Frogs Landing, tel. 208/837–6227, www.snakeriver-grill.com; $7–$24). ♿ **Groceries & Gear:** None in park. In Hagerman: Oasis Stop and Go (361 S. State St., tel. 208/837–4025), Chappell's Market (180 S. State St., tel. 208/837–6600).

FEES, HOURS & REGULATIONS

Free. Collection of fossils, artifacts, rocks, plants, animals, or any other object within the monument is prohibited. Monument open daily, closes at dusk. Many areas closed to public. Visitor center open Memorial Day–Sept., daily 9–5; Oct.–Memorial Day, Thurs.–Mon. 9–5.

HOW TO GET THERE

From I-84, take Hagerman Rd. west to U.S. 30 south; follow for approximately 2 miles. Park headquarters and visitor center are in Hagerman, on N. State St., across from the high school. Closest airports: Twin Falls (45 miles), Boise (90 miles).

CONTACTS

Hagerman Fossil Beds National Monument (221 N. State St., Box 570, Hagerman, ID 83332, tel. 208/933–4100, fax 208/837–4857, www.nps.gov/hafo). Hagerman Valley Chamber of Commerce (380 N. State St., Box 599, Hagerman, ID 83332, tel. 208/837–9131, www.hagermanvalleychamber.com). Hagerman Valley Historical Society Museum (100 S. State St., Hagerman, ID 83332, tel. 208/837–6288, www.hagermanmuseum.com).

Minidoka National Historic Site

In south-central Idaho, between Jerome and Twin Falls

The historic site commemorates the hardships and sacrifices of Japanese Americans incarcerated here during World War II. The Minidoka Relocation Center, as it was called during the war, operated from August 1942 until October 1945. It comprised 33,000 acres with 600 buildings. About 13,000 individuals from Washington, Oregon, and Alaska were held here in violation of their civil and constitutional rights. The site preserves a portion of the camp's original acreage and buildings. It was authorized on January 17, 2001.

WHAT TO SEE & DO

Viewing original barracks, root cellar, fire station, mess hall, warehouse, and other buildings. **Programs and Events:** 1.6-mile interpretive trail with outdoor exhibits, ranger-led walking tours, self-guided tours, Junior Ranger program. Annual Civil Liberties Symposium and Pilgrimage (June). **Tips & Hints:** The park is under development. There is no on-site visitor center, but information is available at the Hagerman Fossil Beds National Monument Visitor Center. Call 208/933–4100 before visiting. Summer temperatures average about 87°F. Visit in spring or fall for best weather.

FOOD, LODGING & SUPPLIES

Camping: None in park. In Jerome: Jerome–Twin Falls KOA (5431 U.S. 93, tel. 208/324–4169, www.koa.com; 92 sites, 8 cabins; $30–$45; flush toilets, showers, hookups). **Hotels:** None in park. In Twin Falls: Shilo Inns Suites (1586 Blue Lakes Blvd. N, tel. 208/733–7545 or 800/222-2244, fax 208/736-2019, www.shiloinns.com; 128 suites; $90–$120). **Restaurants:** None in park. In Twin Falls: Jakers Bar & Grill (1598 Blue Lakes Blvd. N, tel. 208/733–8400; $8–$19). **Groceries & Gear:** None in park. In Twin Falls: Fred Meyer (705 Blue Lakes Blvd. N, tel. 208/736–5340).

FEES, HOURS & REGULATIONS

Free. Collection of artifacts, rocks, plants, animals, or other objects is prohibited. Open daily dawn–dusk.

HOW TO GET THERE

Take I–84 to U.S. 93 north, follow for 5 miles, then head east on Rte. 25 for 9½ miles, then north on Hunt Rd. for about 2 miles. The park is 21 miles east of Jerome and 17 miles northeast of Twin Falls. Closest airports: Twin Falls and Boise.

CONTACTS

Minidoka National Monument (Box 570, Hagerman, ID 83332, tel. 208/933–4100, fax 208/837–4857, www.nps.gov/miin). Jerome Chamber of Commerce (104 W. Main St., Box 835, Jerome, ID 83338, tel. 208/324–2711, www.visitjeromeidaho.com).

Nez Perce National Historical Park

In north-central Idaho, near Lewiston; and in Washington, Oregon, and Montana

Nez Perce culture, traditions, and history are commemorated and celebrated in this park's 38 sites, which are in four states. Sites range from small roadside pullouts to village sites and battlefields. The Nez Perce National Historic Trail follows the route the Nez Perce took in the 1877 War and runs from the Wallowa Valley of northeast Oregon to Bear Paw Battlefield in north-central Montana. The park was authorized on May 15, 1965.

WHAT TO SEE & DO

Fishing, picnicking, walking. **Facilities:** Visitor center in Spalding, ID, trails, museums, interpretive display boards. Book and map sales areas, picnic tables. **Programs & Events:** Tours and walks, interpretive talks, cultural demonstrations. Commemorations of Nez Perce War of 1877 (White Bird, June; Big Hole, Aug.; Bear Paw, Oct.; website has exact dates). **Tips & Hints:** Park sites stretch more than 1,500 miles. Be prepared for extreme changes in climate and elevation. Busiest May and Aug., least crowded Nov. and Feb.

FOOD, LODGING & SUPPLIES

Camping: None in park. In Harpster: Harpster Riverside RV Park (off Rte. 13, 13 miles north of Grangeville, tel. 208/983–2312; 33 sites, 6 yurts; $6-$40; flush toilets, showers, hookups). **Hotels:** None in park. In Lewiston: Red Lion Hotel (621 21st St., tel. 208/799-1000 or 800/232-6730, www.redlionlewiston.com; 181 rooms; $100–$110). ✗ **Restaurants:** None in park. In Lapwai: Donald's Family Dining (304 N. U.S. 95, tel. 208/843–7273; $5–$8). In Lewiston: Bojack's Broiler Pit (311 Main St., tel. 208/746–9532, www.bojacksbroilerpit.com; $9–$18; closed Sun.). **Groceries & Gear:** None in park. In Lapwai: Valley Foods (204 U.S. 95 N, tel. 208/843–2070).

FEES, HOURS & REGULATIONS

Free. Idaho state fishing license required. Nez Perce Reservation permit required for steelhead fishing. Leashed pets only. No hunting. Spalding unit open during daylight. Spalding Visitor Center open Memorial Day–Labor Day, daily 8–5; Labor Day-mid-Nov., daily 8–4:30; mid-Nov.-mid-Mar., daily 9–4; mid-Mar.–Memorial Day, daily 8–4:30.

HOW TO GET THERE

Spalding visitor center is at 39063 U.S. 95, 11 miles east of Lewiston. Closest airport: Lewiston.

CONTACTS

Nez Perce National Historical Park (39063 U.S. 95, Lapwai, ID 83540, tel. 208/843–7009, fax 208/843–7003, www.nps.gov/nepe). Lewis Clark Valley Chamber of Commerce (111 Main St., Suite 120, Lewiston, ID 83501, tel. 208/743–3531 or 800/473–3543, www.lcvalleychamber.org).

See Also

Yellowstone National Park, Wyoming. *California National Historic Trail, Continental Divide National Scenic Trail, Lewis & Clark National Historic Trail, Nez Perce National Historic Trail, and Oregon National Scenic Trail*, in Other National Parklands.

ILLINOIS

Lincoln Home
National Historic Site

In central Illinois, in Springfield

Abraham Lincoln bought this house in the spring of 1844 for his wife and son, and it was the only home the family ever owned. They lived in it for 17 years, during which time Lincoln built his law practice and began a political career that would lead him to the presidency in 1861. The house has been restored to its 1860s appearance. It stands in the midst of a four-block historic neighborhood that the National Park Service is restoring so the neighborhood, like the house, will appear much as Lincoln would have remembered it. The site was authorized in 1971 and established in 1972.

WHAT TO SEE & DO

Touring the home and neighborhood. **Facilities:** Visitor center (426 S. 7th St.), sculptures, film, neighborhood houses (2 with self-guided museums). Bookstore. **Programs & Events:** Guided home tours, interpretive programs, walks. Lincoln's Birthday (Feb.), Christmas in Mr. Lincoln's Neighborhood (Dec.). **Tips & Hints:** Watch your footing on slippery boardwalks. Busiest May and July, least crowded Dec. and Jan.

FEES, HOURS & REGULATIONS

Free. Visitor parking lot fee ($2 per hour). No vehicles in the site's four city blocks. Leashed pets only. Park grounds open daily to pedestrians. Visitor center open daily 8:30–5.

HOW TO GET THERE

In downtown Springfield, at the intersection of 7th and Jackson Sts. Closest airport: Springfield (5 miles).

CONTACTS

Lincoln Home National Historic Site (visitor center: 426 S. 7th St.); 413 S. 8th St., Springfield, IL 62701, tel. 217/391–3226, fax 217/544–8771, www.nps.gov/liho). Springfield Convention & Visitors Bureau (109 N. 7th St., Springfield, IL 62701, tel. 217/789–2360 or 800/545–7300, fax 217/544–8700, www.visit-springfieldillinois.com).

See Also

Lewis & Clark National Historic Trail, Mormon Pioneer National Historic Trail, and Trail of Tears National Historic Trail, in Other National Parklands.

INDIANA

George Rogers Clark National Historical Park

In southwestern Indiana, in Vincennes

The park, including a classical memorial building, is on the site of the Revolutionary War Battle of Vincennes. The memorial commemorates the capture of the fort from the British by Lieutenant Colonel George Rogers Clark and his men on February 25, 1779, and the subsequent settlement of the region north of the Ohio River. The site was authorized in 1966.

WHAT TO SEE & DO

Picnicking, touring Clark Memorial. **Facilities:** Visitor center with 30-minute film about the Battle of Vincennes, memorial building, 26 acres of landscaped lawns. Book and gift shop, picnic tables. **Programs & Events:** Spirit of Vincennes Rendezvous (Memorial Day weekend), July 4 fireworks. **Tips & Hints:** Busiest May and July, least crowded Jan. and Feb.

FOOD, LODGING & SUPPLIES

Camping: None in park. In Vincennes: Ouabache Trails Park (3500 N. Lower Fort Knox Rd., tel. 812/882–4316, www.knoxcountyparks. com; 44 sites, 4 cabins; $10–$18; flush toilets, showers, hookups). **Hotels:** None in park. In Vincennes: Holiday Inn Express (2720 Battery Rd., tel. 812/886–5000, www.hiexpress.com; 73 rooms; $110–$140). **Restaurants:** None in park. In Vincennes: Old Thyme Diner (331 Main St., tel. 812/886–0333; $4–$7; no dinner Mon.–Thurs. and Sat., closed Sun.). **Groceries & Gear:** None in park. In Vincennes: Walmart (650 Kimmel Rd., tel. 812/886–0312).

FEES, HOURS & REGULATIONS

Free. Leashed pets only. Park and visitor center open daily 9–5.

HOW TO GET THERE

In downtown Vincennes. Take Willow or 6th St. Exit off U.S. 41 or 6th St. Exit off U.S. 50. Closest airport: Evansville (60 miles).

CONTACTS

George Rogers Clark National Historical Park (401 S. 2nd St., Vincennes, IN 47591, tel. 812/882–1776, fax 812/882–7270, www.nps.gov/gero). Knox County Chamber of Commerce (Box 553, Vincennes, IN 47591, tel. 812/882–6440 or 888/895–6622, fax 812/882–6441, www. knoxcountychamber.com). Vincennes/Knox County Convention & Visitors Bureau (779 S. 6th St., Vincennes, IN 47591, tel. 812/886–0400 or 800/886–6443, www.vincennescvb.com).

Indiana Dunes
National Lakeshore

In northwestern Indiana between Gary and Michigan City, along the southern shore of Lake Michigan

The 15,000-acre park preserves four main dune ridges that run parallel to Lake Michigan's shoreline. The younger dunes, which rise 180 feet, are still open and sandy, but the 8,000- to 12,000-year-old dune ridges are covered with oak and maple forests. Beaches, bogs, marshes, swamps, prairie remnants, and a farm and homestead dating to 19th-century fur trading and pioneer agriculture are also open to the public. The lakeshore was authorized on November 5, 1966.

WHAT TO SEE & DO

Bicycling (rentals, Chesterton), bird-watching, boating, cross-country skiing, fishing, hiking, horseback riding, picnicking, swimming. **Facilities:** 2 visitor centers: Dorothy Buell (1215 N. State Rd. 49, Porter) and Bailly-Chellberg (Mineral Spring Rd. and U.S. 20, Porter). Paul H. Douglas Center for Environmental Education (100 N. Lake St., Gary), beaches, biking and hiking trails, amphitheater. Bookstore, bathhouse, picnic pavilions, and shelters. **Programs & Events:** Ranger-guided hikes and programs, musicals (3rd Fri. of the month), ranger-guided Pinhook Bog tours (May–Oct., some weekends), Chellberg Farm and Bailly Homestead house tours and historic demonstrations (July and Aug., Sat. 1–4), campfire programs (June–Aug., Sat. evening). Maple Sugar Time Festival (1st 2 weekends, Mar.), Summer Solstice Celebration (June), Duneland Christmas (Dec.). **Tips & Hints:** Watch for rip currents. Don't walk on shoreline shelf ice. Go in spring for migrating birds and wildflowers, summer for swimming and wildflowers, fall for fall colors and prairie wildflowers. Busiest June–Aug., least crowded Dec. and Jan.

FOOD, LODGING & SUPPLIES

Camping: In the park: Dunewood Campground (78 sites; $15; flush toilets, showers). **Hotels:** None in park. In Michigan City: Red Roof Inn (110 W. Kieffer Rd., tel. 219/874-5251, www.redroof.com; 79 rooms; $75). **Restaurants:** None in park. In Chesterton: Lakeshore Café (371 Indiana Boundary Rd., tel. 219/926-6363; $6–$9). **Groceries & Gear:** None in park. In Beverly Shores: Jannsen's Dunes Mart (U.S. 12 and Broadway, tel. 219/879–8048).

FEES, HOURS & REGULATIONS

Parking fee: $6 per vehicle for day use at West Beach (Memorial Day–Labor Day). Indiana state fishing license required. Smelt fishing permit required. No dune buggies or snowmobiles. No hunting. No open fires except in campground. Leashed pets are allowed in most areas of the national lakeshore except the beaches west of Indiana Dunes State Park and on the Ly-co-ki-we and Great Marsh trails. Park open daily dawn–dusk. Visitor centers open Memorial Day–Labor Day, daily 8:30–6; Labor Day–Memorial Day, daily 8:30–4:30.

HOW TO GET THERE

Take I–80, I–90, or I–94 to Rte. 49 in Chesterton or Rte. 249 in Portage at Burns Harbor. From Chesterton, take Rte. 49 north and then either U.S. 20 or U.S. 12 to park. From Portage, take Rte. 249 to U.S. 12 east to the Dorothy Beull Visitor Center. Closest airports: Chicago's Midway (45 miles), Gary (10 miles).

CONTACTS

Indiana Dunes National Lakeshore (Dorothy Buell Memorial Visitor Center, 1215 N. State Rd. 49, Porter, IN 46304, tel. 219/926–7561, www.nps.gov/indu). Chesterton Duneland Chamber of Commerce (220 Broadway, Chesterton, IN 46304, tel. 219/926–5513, fax 219/926–7593, www.chestertonchamber.org). Indiana Dunes Tourism (1215 N. State Rd. 49, Porter, IN 46304, tel. 219/926–2255, www.indianadunes. com).

Lincoln Boyhood National Memorial

In southwestern Indiana, in Lincoln City

On this southern Indiana farm, Abraham Lincoln spent his young adulthood, from the ages of 7 to 21. He worked the land with his father, developed his love of reading and his curiosity for knowledge, and experienced the death of his mother, Nancy Hanks Lincoln, when he was nine years old. The memorial was authorized in 1962.

WHAT TO SEE & DO

Picnicking, touring living-historical farm, visiting Nancy Hanks Lincoln's grave and Cabin Site Memorial. **Facilities:** Visitor Center (3027 E. South St.) with 2 Memorial Halls, living-historical farm, museum, auditorium, gravesite, cabin site, trails. Bookstore, picnic tables, post office. **Programs & Events:** Interpretive programs (June–Aug.). Lincoln Day (Sun. preceding Feb. 12). **Tips & Hints:** Visit May–Sept., when living-historical farm is open. Busiest July and Aug., least crowded Jan. and Feb.

FOOD, LODGING & SUPPLIES

Camping: None in park. In Lincoln City: Lincoln State Park (Rte. 162 off U.S. 231, tel. 812/937–4710 or 866/622–6746, www.camp.in. gov; 150 sites; $10–$36; flush toilets, showers, hookups). **Hotels:** None in park. In Dale: Budget Hosts Stone's Motel (I–64 and U.S. 231, tel. 812/937–4448, www.budgethoststonesmotel.com; 33 rooms; $80). **Restaurants:** None in park. In Dale: Los Dos Charros Mexican Restaurant (410 S. Washington St., tel. 812/937–3775; $6–$9). **Groceries & Gear:** None in park. In Dale: Circle S (4 N. Washington St., tel. 812/937–2964).

FEES, HOURS & REGULATIONS

Entrance fee: $3 adults, free ages 15 and under, $5 per family. Leashed pets only. No bicycles or motorized equipment on trails. Visitor center open Mar.–Nov., daily 8–5, Dec.–Feb., daily 8–4:30. Grounds open daily 8–dusk. Farm open mid-Apr.–Sept., daily 8–5.

HOW TO GET THERE

In Lincoln City, 8 miles south of I–64 via U.S. 231 and Rte. 162. Closest airports: Evansville (45 miles), Louisville, KY (80 miles).

CONTACTS

Lincoln Boyhood National Memorial (2916 E. South St., Box 1816, Lincoln City, IN 47552, tel. 812/937–4541, fax 812/937–9929, www.nps.gov/libo). Spencer County Visitors Bureau (Box 202, Santa Claus, IN 47579, tel. 812/937–4199 or 888/444–9252, www.legendaryplaces.org).

IOWA

Effigy Mounds National Monument

In northeastern Iowa, near Marquette

More than 200 prehistoric burial and ceremonial mounds, some in the shapes of bears and birds, are preserved here. Woodland Native Americans built the mounds between 500 BC and AD 1300. The land was untouched by the glaciers of the Ice Age, so it provides a rugged terrain that includes bluffs towering 300–400 feet above the Mississippi River. Located where the eastern hardwood forest meets the midwestern prairie, the monument includes forests, prairies, rivers, and ponds. It was established on October 25, 1949.

WHAT TO SEE & DO

Hiking, snowshoeing, viewing mounds. **Facilities:** Visitor center, museum, and auditorium (3 miles north of Marquette), wayside exhibits, trails. Bookstore. **Programs & Events:** Ranger-guided walks (Memorial Day–Labor Day), bird walks (June–Sept., once each month), film festival (Jan.–Mar., weekends). Iowa Archaeology Month (Sept. or Oct.), Hawk Watch (first weekend in Oct.). **Tips & Hints:** Go in spring and late Sept. for bird migrations, in winter to see bald eagles. Busiest Aug. and Oct., least crowded Dec. and Jan.

FOOD, LODGING & SUPPLIES

⚠ **Camping:** None in park. In Prairie du Chien, WI: Big River Campground (106 W. Paquette St., tel. 608/326–2712; 108 sites; $18–$22; flush toilets, showers, hookups). 🏨 **Hotels:** None in park. In Prairie du Chien: Country Inn & Suites (1801 Cabela's La., tel. 608/326–5700 or 800/830–5222, www.countryinns.com; 64 rooms; $128-$150). ✗ **Restaurants:** None in park. In Prairie du Chien: Hungry House Cafe (531 N. Marquette Rd., tel. 608/326–4346, www.hungryhousecafe.com; $5–$12). ⛽ **Groceries & Gear:** None in park. In Prairie du Chien: Family Dollar (700 E. Blackhawk Ave., tel. 608/326–5453).

FEES, HOURS & REGULATIONS

Free. No bicycles or motorized vehicles on trails. Leashed pets only. Visitor center open Memorial Day–Labor Day, daily 8–6 (sometimes later); Labor Day–Memorial Day, daily 8:30–4:30. Trails open daily 8–dark.

HOW TO GET THERE

3 miles north of Marquette, IA, on Rte. 76. Closest airports: Prairie du Chien, WI (8 miles), Dubuque (60 miles), La Crosse, WI (70 miles).

CONTACTS

Effigy Mounds National Monument (151 Hwy. 76, Harpers Ferry, IA 52146, tel. 563/873–3491, www.nps.gov/efmo). McGregor–Marquette Chamber of Commerce (146 Main St., Box 105, McGregor, IA 52157, tel. 563/873–2186 or 800/896–0910, www.mcgreg-marq.org). Prairie Du Chien Chamber of Commerce (211 S. Main St., Box 326, Prairie du Chien, WI 53821, tel. 800/732–1673, www.prairieduchien.org).

Herbert Hoover National Historic Site

In east-central Iowa, in West Branch

This 187-acre park, flanked by 81 acres of tallgrass, encompasses the birthplace, gravesite, and boyhood neighborhood of Herbert Hoover, the 31st president of the United States. The park also contains a 19th-century blacksmith shop like the one operated by Hoover's father and preserves the town's first schoolhouse and the Friends Meetinghouse where the Hoovers worshipped. First Lady Lou Henry Hoover is buried alongside the president. The Herbert Hoover Presidential Library and Museum is administered by the National Archives and Records Administration. Congress authorized the historic site on August 12, 1965.

WHAT TO SEE & DO

Cross-country skiing, hiking, picnicking, touring buildings and library-museum. **Facilities:** Visitor center (Parkside Dr.–Main St. intersection), library-museum, birthplace cottage and other buildings, gravesite, wayside exhibits, 81-acre reconstructed tallgrass prairie, trails. Picnic shelters, gift shop. **Programs & Events:** Ranger-guided tours, Junior Ranger programs, self-guided and audio tours, blacksmith demonstrations, prairie walks; library-museum exhibits (all year). Hoover's Hometown Days (1st weekend, Aug.), Christmas Past (1st weekend, Dec.). **Tips & Hints:** Be careful on slippery boardwalks during frosty or wet weather. Not crowded most of the year.

FOOD, LODGING & SUPPLIES

Camping: None in park. In West Liberty: West Liberty Campground (1961 Garfield Ave., tel. 319/627–2676 or 800/562–7624; 50 sites; $28; flush toilets, showers, hookups). **Hotels:** None in park. In West Branch: Presidential Motor Inn (711 S. Downey Rd., Exit 264 off I–80, tel. 319/643–2526 or 877/643-2526, www.presidentialinn.biz; 35 rooms; $45–$50). **Restaurants:** None in park. In West Branch: Hoover House (102 W. Main St., tel. 319/643–5420; $5–$20). **Groceries & Gear:** None in park. In West Branch: Dewey's Jack & Jill (115 W. Main St., tel. 319/643–2611).

FEES, HOURS & REGULATIONS

Free. Presidential Library and Museum: $6 adults, $3 ages 62 and over, free ages 15 and under. Picnic shelter reservations available ($25, tel. 319/643–2541). Leashed pets only. No skateboarding. Bikes in designated areas only. Park and visitor center open daily 9–5.

HOW TO GET THERE

The visitor center is at the intersection of Parkside Dr. and Main St., ½ mile north of Exit 254 off I–80. Closest airport: Cedar Rapids (28 miles).

CONTACTS

Herbert Hoover National Historic Site (110 Parkside Dr., Box 607, West Branch, IA 52358, tel. 319/643–2541, www.nps.gov/heho). West Branch Chamber of Commerce (110 N. Poplar St., Box 218, West Branch, IA 52358, tel. 319/643–5888, fax 319/643–2305, www.westbranchiowa.org).

See Also

California National Historic Trail, Lewis & Clark National Historic Trail, and Mormon Pioneer National Historic Trail, in Other National Parklands.

KANSAS

Brown v. Board of Education National Historic Site

In Topeka, 61 miles west of Kansas City

In the former Monroe Elementary School building, once a segregated school for African American children, this site commemorates the landmark Supreme Court decision that made segregation in public schools illegal. On May 17, 1954, the U.S. Supreme Court unanimously declared that "separate but equal educational facilities are inherently unequal." Such facilities violate the 14th Amendment to the U.S. Constitution, which guarantees all citizens "equal protection of the laws," the court said. The lead plaintiff's daughter, Linda, was one of the two children among the 20 involved who attended Monroe Elementary School when *Brown v. Board of Education* of Topeka was initially filed in 1951. The site was established on October 26, 1992.

WHAT TO SEE & DO

Touring museum. **Facilities:** Visitor center with interpretive displays. **Tips & Hints:** Busiest Sept.–Apr., least crowded June–Aug.

FEES & HOURS

Free. Visitor center open daily 9–5.

HOW TO GET THERE

The park office and Monroe School (1515 Monroe St.) are in downtown Topeka. Closest airport: Kansas City (70 miles).

CONTACTS

Brown v. Board of Education National Historic Site (1515 S.E. Monroe St., Topeka, KS 66612, tel. 785/354–4273, fax 785/354–7213, www.nps.gov/brvb). Greater Topeka Chamber of Commerce (120 S.E. 6th Ave., Suite 110, Topeka, KS 66603-3515, tel. 785/234–2644, www.topekachamber.org).

Fort Larned National Historic Site

In west-central Kansas, west of Larned

Fort Larned was built in 1859 to protect travelers on the Santa Fe Trail from conflicts with Native Americans. In the 1860s the fort served as an agency of the Indian Bureau. Nine original buildings dating from 1866 still exist in a relatively undisturbed setting at a bend in the Pawnee River. Now that the parade ground, the flagpole, and most of the buildings have been restored or reconstructed, Fort Larned is one of the best surviving examples of an Indian Wars–era fort. A separate unit of the park contains a 44-acre plot of virgin prairie where you can see wagon ruts from the Santa Fe Trail and a prairie-dog town. The site was authorized in 1964 and established in 1966.

WHAT TO SEE & DO

Hiking, picnicking, touring buildings and grounds. **Facilities:** Visitor center, slide show, museum, 1½-mile nature trail, wayside exhibits. Bookstore, picnic tables with fire grills. **Programs & Events:** Guided tours by appointment; living-history programs (Memorial Day–Labor Day). Fort Larned Old Guard Roll Call (1st weekend, May), Candlelight Tour (2nd Sat., Oct., reservations essential), Christmas Open House (2nd Sat., Dec.). **Tips & Hints:** The best living-history programs take place on Memorial Day, July 4, and Labor Day weekends. Busiest June and July, least crowded Dec. and Jan.

FOOD, LODGING & SUPPLIES

Camping: None at site. In Kinsley: 4 Aces RV Park (1004 Massachusetts St., tel. 620/659-2321, www.4acesrvpark.com; 36 sites; flush toilets, showers, hookups; $30). **Hotels:** None at site. In Larned: Townsman Inn (123 E. 14th St., tel. 620/285–3114, www.townsmaninnlarned.com; 44 rooms; $45–$60), Rodeway Inn (802 E. 14th St., tel. 620/285–2300, fax 620/285–2250, www.rodewayinn.com; 40 rooms; $68–$73). **Restaurants:** None at site. In Larned: El Dos de Oros (417 W. 14th St., tel. 620/285–6238, $7–$10), Pizza Hut (126 W. 14th St., tel. 620/285–3101, $8–$15). **Groceries & Gear:** None at site. In Larned: Dillons (433 Main St., tel. 620/285-3171).

FEES, HOURS & REGULATIONS

Free. Leashed pets only. No hunting or relic hunting. Park and visitor center open Labor Day–Memorial Day, daily 8:30–4:30.

HOW TO GET THERE

6 miles west of Larned, via Rte. 156. Closest airports: Great Bend (28 miles), Wichita (136 miles).

CONTACTS

Fort Larned National Historic Site (1767 KS Hwy. 156, Larned, KS 67550-9321, tel. 620/285–6911, fax 620/285–3571, www.nps.gov/fols). Larned Area Chamber of Commerce (502 Broadway, Larned, KS 67550, tel. 620/285–6916 or 800/747–6919, www.larnedks.org).

Fort Scott National Historic Site

In southeastern Kansas, in Fort Scott

Established in 1842, Fort Scott guarded the Permanent Indian Frontier and kept settlers and Native Americans out of each other's territory. As the frontier was pushed westward, Fort Scott became obsolete.

Abandoned in 1853, the fort then became a town and was drawn into the violence of "Bleeding Kansas" and the Civil War. Today, the site has been restored to its 1840s appearance. It contains 20 major historic structures in which 33 rooms are furnished with original and reproduction 19th-century items, plus a parade ground and 5 acres of restored tallgrass prairie. The site was authorized in 1978.

WHAT TO SEE & DO

Touring buildings, walking trail. **Facilities:** Visitor center, museum. Bookstore, picnic tables. **Programs & Events:** Self-guided and cell phone tours year-round; guided tours (Memorial Day–Labor Day, daily at 1); living-history programs, reenactments, and demonstrations (Memorial Day, July 4, and Labor Day weekend). Civil War Encampment (Apr.), Good Ol' Days (June), American Indian Heritage Weekend (Sept.), Candlelight Tour (Dec., reservations essential). **Tips & Hints:** Watch footing on uneven walkways and steep stairs. Allow one–two hours to tour site. Busiest May and June, least crowded Jan. and Feb.

FOOD, LODGING & SUPPLIES

Camping: None in park. In Fort Scott: Gunn RV Park (1010 Park Ave., tel. 620/223–0550; 14 RV sites, grassy area for tents; $4–$8; flush and portable toilets, hookups), Fort Scott Mobile Home & RV Park (2162 Native Rd., tel. 620/223–3440 or 800/538–0216; 50 sites; $12–$19; flush toilets, showers, hookups). **Hotels:** None in park. In Fort Scott: Fort Scott Inn (101 State St., tel. 620/223–0100 or 888/800–3175; 76 rooms; $59–$70). **Restaurants:** None in park. In Fort Scott: Sugarfoot and Peaches BBQ (1601 E. Wall St., tel. 620/224–2888; $4–$5). **Groceries & Gear:** None in park. In Fort Scott: Walmart (2500 S. Main St., tel. 620/223–2867).

FEES, HOURS & REGULATIONS

Free. No pets indoors; no unleashed pets outdoors. No plant or artifact collecting. No metal detecting. Site and visitor center open Apr.–Oct., daily 8–5; Nov.–Mar., daily 9–5.

HOW TO GET THERE

Near the intersection of U.S. 54 and U.S. 69, in downtown Fort Scott, 90 miles south of Kansas City via U.S. 69, 60 miles from Joplin via Rte. 43 north to U.S. 54. Closest airports: Fort Scott, Joplin, Kansas City.

CONTACTS

Fort Scott National Historic Site (Old Fort Blvd., Box 918, Fort Scott, KS 66701, tel. 620/223–0310, fax 620/223–0188, www.nps.gov/fosc). Fort Scott Area Chamber of Commerce (231 E. Wall St., Fort Scott, KS 66701, tel. 620/223–3566 or 800/245–3678, fax 620/223–3574, www.fortscott.com).

Nicodemus National Historic Site

In northwestern Kansas, in Nicodemus

The town of Nicodemus was established in 1877 and settled by African Americans during Reconstruction after the Civil War. It's the site of one of the oldest reported post offices supervised by African Americans in the United States. Five historic buildings are within the 161-acre site: the First Baptist Church, built in 1907; the African-Methodist-Episcopal Church, built between 1885 and 1907; Township Hall, built in 1939; St. Francis Hotel, built in 1881; and Nicodemus District No. 1 School, built in 1918. The site was established as a National Historic Landmark in 1976 and as a National Historic Site in 1996.

WHAT TO SEE & DO

Biking, scenic drives, touring Township Hall, walking around grounds. **Facilities:** Visitor center, Historical Society museum. Bookstore, picnic tables. **Programs & Events:** Ranger-led guided tours year-round. Emancipation Day–Homecoming (last weekend, July), Pioneer Days (2nd weekend, Oct.). **Tips & Hints:** Township Hall serves as a temporary visitor center. The other historic buildings on site are privately owned and not open to the public.

FOOD, LODGING & SUPPLIES

Camping: None in park. In Stockton: Webster State Park (1210 9 Rd., tel. 785/425–6775; 155 primitive campsites, 77 utility sites; $8 plus $4.20 per vehicle; flush and pit toilets, showers, hookups). **Hotels:** None in park. In Hill City: Western Hills Motel (802 W. Main St., tel. 785/421–2141; 24 rooms; $50). **Restaurants:** None in park. In Hill City: Sub Station (602 W. Main St., tel. 785/421–3433; $4–$9). In Stockton: The Duck Blind Bar & Grill (323 Main St., tel. 785/425–6700; $6–$12; closed Sun.). **Groceries & Gear:** None in park. In Hill City: Casey's General Store (516 W. Main St., tel. 785/421–6460).

FEES & HOURS

Free. Park, visitor center, Township Hall, and bookstore open daily 9–4:30, though hours may vary.

HOW TO GET THERE

Nicodemus is 12 miles east of Hill City and 19 miles west of Stockton on U.S. 24. From Hays, take U.S. 183 north to Stockton. Closest airports: Hill City, Hays (50 miles).

CONTACTS

Nicodemus National Historic Site (510 Washington Ave., Suite B-1, Nicodemus, KS 67625, tel. 785/839–4321, fax 785/839–4325, www.nps.gov/nico). Hill City Chamber of Commerce (801 W. Main St., Hill City, KS 67642, tel. 785/421–5621, www.discoverhillcity.com).

Tallgrass Prairie National Preserve

In east-central Kansas, near Strong City

This site in the Flint Hills region of Kansas protects 17 square miles of the once vast tallgrass prairie ecosystem that once covered much of North America. Several 19th-century buildings listed as National Historic Landmarks, including a ranch house, limestone barn, and one-room schoolhouse, plus the cultural resources of the Spring Hill–Z Bar Ranch, are also part of the preserve. The Nature Conservancy, a non-profit organization, owns most of the land but shares in the management of it with the National Park Service. The site was authorized on November 12, 1996.

WHAT TO SEE & DO

Hiking trails, touring historic buildings in groups, touring preserve by bus, touring ranch headquarters. **Facilities:** Visitor center, information kiosks, interpretive wayside exhibits, orientation video, more than 40 miles of nature and hiking trails. Bookstore. **Programs & Events:** Self-guided tours of ranch headquarters and nature trail. Guided tours of ranch house (as staffing permits). Bus tours of tallgrass prairie (end of Apr.–Oct., daily at 11, as staffing permits). **Tips & Hints:** Watch for poisonous snakes, poison ivy, biting insects, ticks, and uneven terrain. Go mid-Apr.–June for wildflowers, Oct. to see the tallgrass at peak height. Reservations advised for bus tours. Park busiest June–Oct., least crowded Jan.–Mar.

FOOD, LODGING & SUPPLIES

Camping: None in park. In Cottonwood Falls: Swope Park (220 Broadway, tel. 620/273–6666; 6 RV sites; $10; hookups). **Hotels:** None in park. In Emporia: Best Western Hospitality House (3021 W. U.S. 50, tel. 620/342–7587, fax 620/342–9271 or 800/362–2036, www. bestwestern.com; 55 rooms; $85), Days Inn (3032 W. U.S. 50 Business, tel. 620/342–1787, www.daysinn.com; 39 rooms; $60–69). **✗ Restaurants:** None in park. In Emporia: Bruff's Bar & Grill (2640 W. 18th St., tel. 620/342–1223, bruffs.com; $6–$13). In Cottonwood Falls: Emma Chase Café (317 Broadway, tel. 620/273–6020, www.emmachasecafe. com; $7–$9), Grand Central Hotel & Grill (215 Broadway, tel. 620/ 273–6763, www.grandcentralhotel.com; $5–$17; closed Sun.). **Groceries & Gear:** In Strong City: Strong City Grocery (322 Cottonwood Ave., tel. 620/273–8639). In Cottonwood: Casey's General Store (424 N. Walnut St., tel. 620/273–8468)

FEES, HOURS & REGULATIONS

Free. No horses or bicycles on nature trails. Main parking lot, nature and hiking trails, and all other outdoor areas are open 24 hours. Ranch House, Ranch Barn and Visitor Center are open 8:30–4:30. One-room schoolhouse open May, June, Sept., and Oct. weekends noon–4, as staffing permits.

HOW TO GET THERE

The ranch headquarters area is 2 miles north of Strong City on Rte. 177. Closest airports: Emporia (18 miles), Wichita (80 miles), Kansas City (100 miles).

CONTACTS

Tallgrass Prairie National Preserve, 2480 B Hwy. 177, Strong City, KS 66869, tel. 620/273–8494, www.nps.gov/tapr). Chase County Chamber of Commerce (318 Broadway, Box 362, Cottonwood Falls, KS 66845, tel. 620/273–8469 or 800/431–6344, www.chasecountychamber. org). Emporia Area Chamber & Visitors Bureau (719 Commercial St., Emporia, KS 66801, tel. 800/279–3730 or 620/342–1600, www. emporiakschamber.org).

See Also

California National Historic Trail, Lewis & Clark National Historic Trail, Oregon National Historic Trail, Pony Express National Historic Trail, and Santa Fe National Historic Trail, in Other National Parklands.

KENTUCKY

Abraham Lincoln Birthplace National Historical Park

In southern Kentucky, south of Louisville

Abraham Lincoln, the 16th president of the United States, was born here on Sinking Spring Farm on February 12, 1809, and today nearly one-third of the farm is preserved at this National Historic Site. The memorial overlooks Sinking Spring, the water source for the original 348-acre property. In 1911 the Lincoln Farm Association added a neo-classical-style shrine for the symbolic birthplace cabin, and in 2001 the park designated the Abraham Lincoln Boyhood Home at Knob Creek, which preserves the site of Lincoln's home from ages 2 to 7. The park was authorized July 17, 1916, and declared a national historical site on September 8, 1959. It was redesignated as a national historical park in 2009.

WHAT TO SEE & DO

Hiking, picnicking, touring the grounds. **Facilities:** Visitor center, outdoor interpretive exhibits and signs, 15-minute movie, self-guided tours, hiking trails. Bookstore, covered picnic tables with fire grills, picnic tables. **Programs & Events:** Self-guided tours, daily interpretive talks. Musical tribute to Dr. Martin Luther King Jr. (Sun. before holiday in Jan. at 2), wreath-laying ceremony at symbolic birthplace cabin (Feb. 12, 1:30), anniversary of the founding of the National Park Service (Aug. 25), U.S. Constitution Week (Sept. 17). **Tips & Hints:** Go July–Aug. for the best weather; visit Dec. and Jan. to avoid crowds.

FOOD, LODGING & SUPPLIES

Camping: None at site. In Elizabethtown: Elizabethtown Crossroads Campground (209 Tunnel Hill Rd., tel. 270/737–7600 or 800/975-6521, www.elizabethtowncrossroadscampgroundky.com; 78 sites, 3 cabins; $25–$35, $40–50 cabins; flush toilets, showers, hookups). **Hotels:** None in park. In Elizabethtown: Best Western Atrium Gardens (1043 Executive Dr., tel. 270/769–3030 or 800/780–7234, www.bestwestern.com; 127 rooms; $79–$89). **Restaurants:** None in park. In Hodgenville: Lincoln Jamboree & Joel Ray's Restaurant (2579 Lincoln Farm Rd./U.S. 31 E, tel. 270/358–3545, www.lincolnjamboree.com; $5-$7). **Groceries & Gear:** None in park. In Hodgenville: Save-A-Lot Foodstore (102 Lincoln Dr., tel. 270/358–3108).

FEES, HOURS, & REGULATIONS

Free. No unleashed pets. No bikes, horses, or motorized equipment on trails. No hunting. Park and visitor center open Memorial Day–Labor Day, daily 8–6:45; Labor Day–Memorial Day, daily 8–4:45. Knob Creek open Apr.–Oct., daily 8:30–4:30.

HOW TO GET THERE

3 miles south of Hodgenville, on U.S. 31 E via Rte. 61. Closest airport: Louisville (55 miles).

CONTACTS

Abraham Lincoln Birthplace National Historical Park (2995 Lincoln Farm Rd., Hodgenville, KY 42748, tel./fax 270/358–3137, www. nps.gov/abli). LaRue County Chamber of Commerce (60 Lincoln Sq., Box 176, Hodgenville, KY 42748, tel. 270/358–3411, www. laruecountychamber.org).

Cumberland Gap National Historical Park

Junction of Kentucky, Virginia, and Tennessee, near Middlesboro, KY

This natural passageway across the Appalachian Mountains opened the west to 18th-century travelers and explorers. Native Americans first discovered the gap by following buffalo herds as they headed into the verdant hills of what is now Kentucky. Between 1775 and 1810, around 300,000 settlers passed through here, expanding the American frontier and opening new routes across the continent. Today you'll find wayside exhibits, a museum, and the abandoned old cabins of the former Hensley settlement, all with signage noting the area's historic significance. The park was authorized in 1940.

WHAT TO SEE & DO

Hiking, picnicking, scenic drives. **Facilities:** Visitor center, museum, hiking trails. Book-and-gift store, covered picnic tables with fire grills (reservations and fee), picnic tables. **Programs & Events:** Ranger-led walking tours (May–Aug.; reservations required), Gap (Cudjo's) Cave tours (Jan.–Mar., weekends 10 and 2; Apr. and May and Sept.–Dec. daily at 10, weekends at 2; Memorial Day–Aug., daily 9, 11:30, 3; reservations required). **Tips & Hints:** Go Apr.–May for wildflowers, in Sept. for great hiking, and in mid-Oct. for peak foliage. Busiest July–Oct., least crowded Jan. and Feb. Come prepared for variable weather all year. Pinnacle Overlook may close in winter because of bad weather.

FOOD, LODGING & SUPPLIES

⚠ **Camping:** In the park: Wilderness Road Campground (160 sites; $12–$17; flush toilets, showers, hookups). Backcountry camping allowed. 🛏 **Hotels:** None in park. In Middlesboro: Downtown Inn & Suites (1623 E. Cumberland Ave., tel. 606/248–5630, www. middlesboroinnandsuites.com; 100 rooms; $60), Holiday Inn Express (1252 N. 12th St./U.S. 25 E, tel. 606/248–6860 or 800/465–4329, www. hiexpress.com; 60 rooms; $89). ✕ **Restaurants:** None in park. In Middlesboro: Pelancho's (605 N. 12th St./U.S. 25 E, tel. 606/248–0303; $7–$9). In Pineville: Pine Mountain State Park Mountain View Restaurant (1050 State Park Rd., tel. 606/337–3066; $6–$12). 🛒 **Groceries &**

Gear: None in park. In Middlesboro: Kroger Grocery (515 N. 12th St., tel. 606/248–3410).

FEES, HOURS & REGULATIONS

Free. Pinnacle Overlook shuttle: $5. Hensley Settlement tour: $10 adults, $5 ages 12 and under. Gap (Cudjo's) Cave tour: $8 adults, $4 ages 12 and under. Picnic pavilions $30 per day, reservations required. Backcountry permits required (free). No vehicles over 20 feet on Pinnacle Rd. No unleashed pets, skateboards, or in-line skates. Bikes on paved roads and designated trails only. Do not feed animals. Park open daily dawn–dusk. Visitor center open daily 8–5.

HOW TO GET THERE

Via U.S. 25 east in Tennessee and Kentucky, and via U.S. 58 in Virginia. Closest airports: Middlesboro (3 miles), Knoxville (90 miles), Lexington (130 miles).

CONTACTS

Cumberland Gap National Historical Park (91 Bartlett Park Rd., Middlesboro, KY 40965, tel. 606/248–2817; 606/246–1075 activity reservations, fax 606/248–2818, www.nps.gov/cuga). Bell County Tourism Commission (2215 Cumberland Ave., Middlesboro, KY 40965, tel. 606/248–2482 or 800/988–1075, fax 606/248–0011, www.mountaingateway.com). Claiborne County Chamber of Commerce and Tourism (1732 Main St., Box 649, Tazewell, TN 37879, tel. 423/626–4149 or 800/332–8164, fax 423/626–1611, www.claibornecounty.com). Town of Cumberland Gap (330 Colwin St., Box 78, Cumberland Gap, TN 37724, tel. 423/869–3860, fax 423/869–8534, www.townofcumberlandgap.com).

Mammoth Cave National Park

In south-central Kentucky, northeast of Bowling Green

The Mammoth Cave network is the world's longest, extending for more than 390 miles beneath the hills of southern Kentucky. This incredible maze of underground passages, endless vertical shafts, and cold, black rivers also hides many unusual creatures: eyeless fish, cave spiders, white crayfish, and rare beetles, among many others. Above ground the park has 70 miles of backcountry hiking and horseback-riding trails, plus 31 miles of scenic shorelines along the Green and Nolin Rivers. The site was established in 1941, designated a World Heritage Site in 1981, and declared an International Biosphere Reserve in 1990.

WHAT TO SEE & DO

Bicycling, bird-watching, canoeing, cave touring, fishing, hiking, horseback riding, kayaking, picnicking. **Facilities:** Visitor center, hiking trails. Book-and-gift shop, covered picnic tables, picnic tables with fire grills. **Programs & Events:** Daily ranger-led cave tours and talks; ranger-led nature walks, evening programs (May–Oct.). Wildflower Day (Apr.), cemetery workshop (Oct.), Roots in the Cave (Nov.). **Tips & Hints:**

Wear comfortable walking shoes and bring a jacket for inside the cave. Go in spring for dogwood blooms, Aug. for wildflower peak. Busiest July and Aug., least crowded Dec. and Jan. Winter visits yield gorgeous icicle formations along the rivers, springs, and bluffs.

FOOD, LODGING & SUPPLIES

Camping: 3 campgrounds in the park: Mammouth Cave Campground (109 sites; $17; flush toilets), Houchins Ferry (12 sites; $12; pit toilets), Maple Springs (7 group sites; $30; pit toilets). Backcountry camping allowed. **Hotels:** In the park: Mammoth Cave Hotel (Rte. 70, tel. 270/758–2225 or 877/386-4383, www.mammothcavehotel.com; 62 rooms, 30 cottages; $99–$149; hotel cottages closed Nov.–mid-Mar., woodland cottages closed Oct.–mid-May). In Horse Cave: Country Hearth Inn (425 Flint Ridge Rd., tel. 270/786–2165, www.countryhearthhorsecave.com; 72 rooms; $55), Hampton Inn Horse Cave (750 Flint Ridge Rd., tel. 270/786–5000 or 800/426–7866, www.hamptoninn.com; 101 rooms; $89). **Restaurants:** In the park: Mammoth Cave Hotel (Rte. 70, tel. 270/758–2225; $4–$13). In Cave City: Sahara Steak House (413 E. Happy Valley Rd., tel. 270/773–3450; $6–$13). **Groceries & Gear:** In the park: Service Center–Caver's Camp Store (near Headquarters Campground, tel. 270/758–2232).

FEES, HOURS & REGULATIONS

Free. Scenic cave tours $5–$12, Introduction to Caving tour $24, Wild Cave Tour $48; children ages 6 or under not allowed on some tours. Backcountry camping permits (free) required. No pets on cave tours or off leash. Mountain bikes and in-line skates in designated areas only. No fireworks. No personal watercraft on river. No off-road motorized equipment. Park open year-round, with daily cave tours (except Dec. 25). Visitor center open Jan. and Feb., daily 9–5; Mar.–mid-June and Labor Day–Dec., daily 9–5; mid-June–Labor Day, daily 7–7.

HOW TO GET THERE

Via I–65 to Cave City or Park City exits, then head west on Rte. 70 or Mammoth Cave Parkway. Closest airports: Louisville, KY (90 miles), Nashville, TN (100 miles).

CONTACTS

Mammoth Cave National Park (1 Mammoth Cave Pkwy., Box 7, Mammoth Cave, KY 42259, tel. 270/758–2180, 877/444–6777 for activities requiring reservations or online at www.recreation.gov, fax 270/758–2447, www.nps.gov/maca). Cave City Chamber of Commerce (Box 460, 502 Mammoth Cave St., Cave City, KY 42127, tel./fax 270/773–5159, www.cavecitychamber.com). Edmonson County Tourist Commission (Box 628, Brownsville, KY 42210, tel. 800/624–8687, www.cavesandlake.com).

See Also

Big South Fork National River and Recreation Area, Tennessee. *Trail of Tears National Historic Trail*, in Other National Parklands.

LOUISIANA

Cane River Creole National Historical Park

In west-central Louisiana, near Natchitoches

Two sprawling plantations are joined in this historic park area: Oakland Plantation, founded in 1785, and Magnolia Plantation, settled in 1735 and founded in 1835. Both sites illustrate the gradual continuum from 18th-century land grants to mid-20th-century occupation and use by the same families who owned the plantations—as well as by many of the families who worked for them, first as slaves and later as tenants and sharecroppers. The Oakland unit includes the 1820s main house, 1850s slave and tenant houses, and most of the original outbuildings. The Magnolia unit has eight brick cabins from the 1850s, a blacksmith shop, the overseer's house, and wooden ginning and pressing equipment for cotton. The park was authorized on November 2, 1994.

WHAT TO SEE & DO

Touring plantations. **Facilities:** Magnolia Plantation (5549 Hwy. 119, Derry). Oakland Plantation (4386 Hwy. 494, Natchez). **Programs & Events:** Daily ranger-guided tours of Oakland (at 1 PM) and Magnolia (ranger available Sat. and Sun.; 24-hour advance reservations for groups); also self-guided and cell phone tours. **Tips & Hints:** Expect to spend about 1½ hours on each tour. Wear comfortable walking shoes. Busiest May–Sept., least crowded Jan.–Mar.

FOOD, LODGING & SUPPLIES

Camping: None in park. In Natchitoches: Nakatosh Campground (5428 Hwy.6, tel. 318/352–0911, www.nakatoshcamp.com; 25 tent sites, 41 RV sites; $31-$33). **Hotels:** None in park. In Natchitoches: Quality Inn (5362 University Pkwy., tel. 318/352–7500, www.qualityinn.com; 59 rooms; $88), Hampton Inn (5300 University Pkwy., tel. 318/354–0010 or 800/426–7866, www.hamptoninn.com; 74 rooms; $110-$124). **Restaurants:** None in park. In Natchitoches: Almost Home (5841 Hwy. 1 Bypass, tel. 318/352–2431; $7–$11; no dinner Mon.–Thurs., closed Sat.), Lasyone's Meat Pie Restaurant (622 2nd St., tel. 318/352–3353; $7–$12; closed Sun.). **Groceries & Gear:** None in park. In Natchitoches: Brookshires (318 Dixie Plaza, tel. 318/352–4000).

FEES, HOURS & REGULATIONS

Free. Park open for self-guided tours daily 8–4; ranger-led tours at 1 PM. Office open weekdays 8–4:30.

HOW TO GET THERE

Oakland Plantation: 8 miles south of Natchitoches on Hwy. 494; Magnolia Plantation: 10 miles farther south on Hwy. 119. Closest airports: Alexandria (45 miles) and Shreveport (75 miles).

CONTACTS

Cane River Creole National Historical Park (400 Rapides Dr., Natchitoches, LA 71457, tel. 318/356–8441, fax 318/352–4549, www.nps.gov/cari). Natchitoches Area Convention and Visitor's Bureau (781 Front St., Natchitoches, LA 71457, tel. 800/259–1714, www.natchitoches.net).

Jean Lafitte National Historical Park & Preserve

In southern Louisiana, between Eunice and New Orleans

The rich history of Louisiana's Mississippi River Delta is the focus of this diverse park's six sites. Relics of Acadian/Cajun history and culture are on exhibit at the Lafayette, Thibodaux, and Eunice sites, and boardwalks meander through the forest, swampland, and marshy environments of the Barataria Preserve near Crown Point, just south of New Orleans. Chalmette Battlefield was the site of the 1815 Battle of New Orleans, and Chalmette National Cemetery holds the graves of veterans from the Civil to the Vietnam wars. One site, smack in the New Orleans French Quarter, follows the history and culture of the city and the Mississippi Delta. The Chalmette Monument and Grounds, established in 1907, was transferred to the Park Service in 1933, renamed a national historical park in 1939, and incorporated into Jean Lafitte National Historical Park & Preserve in 1978.

WHAT TO SEE & DO

Attending cultural demonstrations and educational programs; canoeing; hiking; touring grounds, battlefields, and cemetery. **Facilities:** 6 visitor centers: Acadian (501 Fisher Rd., Lafayette), Prairie Acadian (250 W. Park Ave., Eunice), Wetlands Acadian (314 St. Mary St., Thibodaux), Barataria (6588 Barataria Blvd. Marrero, near Crown Point, 17 miles south of New Orleans), Chalmette (8606 W. St. Bernard Hwy., Chalmette), and French Quarter (419 Decatur St., New Orleans); movies; self-guided tours; hiking trails. Bookstores at each site. **Programs & Events:** Acadian: film 9–4, hourly; Prairie Acadian: *Rendez-vous des Cajun,* live radio show hosted by Park Service at Liberty Theater, adjacent to the cultural center, every Sat.; demonstrations Sat. 3–6, live music Sat. 6–8 PM; Wetlands Acadian: music Mon. 5:30–7 PM; Barataria: natural-history walks Fri.–Mon. at 10 AM, group walks (reservation only); Chalmette: ranger talks daily at 2:45, occasional living-history demonstrations, Battle of New Orleans anniversary (Jan.); French Quarter: walking tours daily at 9:30, folklife demonstrations occasional Sat. 11–3. All sites have films shown on request. **Tips & Hints:** Be aware that there are snakes and alligators in Barataria Preserve. Visit in spring and fall for best weather; summer is hot and humid. Busiest Mar., Apr., and Oct.; least crowded July–Sept. and Dec. and Jan.

LODGING

🏕 **Camping:** None in park. Near Barataria Preserve: Bayou Segnette State Park (7777 Westbank Expressway, Westwego, tel. 504/736–7140 or 888/677–2296; 98 sites; $26; flush toilets, showers, hookups). Near Chalmette Battlefield: St. Bernard State Park (501 St. Bernard's Pkwy., Braithwaite, tel. 504/682–2101 or 888/677–7823; 51 sites; $20; flush toilets, showers, hookups). 🏨 **Hotels:** None in park. In Eunice: Best Western (1531 W. Laurel Ave., tel. 337/457–2800 or 800/962–8423, www.bestwesternlouisiana.com; 35 rooms; $89). 🛒 **Groceries & Gear:** None in park. In Eunice: Winn-Dixie (1800 W. Laurel Ave., tel. 337/457–0878).

FEES & HOURS

Free. Acadian Lafayette open daily 8–5; Prairie Acadian open Tues.–Fri. 8–5, Sat. 8–6; Wetlands open Fri.–Sun. 9–5, Mon. 9–7, Tues.–Thurs. 9–6; Barataria daily 9–5; Chalmette Battlefield (daily 9–4:30), and French Quarter open daily 9–5. All sites except Prairie Acadian Cultural Center closed for Mardi Gras.

HOW TO GET THERE

Between Eunice and New Orleans via 210 miles of I–10 and U.S. 90. Closest airports: Lafayette (½ mile from Acadian Cultural Center), New Orleans (10 miles from French Quarter Visitor Center).

CONTACTS

Jean Lafitte National Historical Park and Preserve (419 Decatur St., New Orleans, LA 70130, tel. 504/589–3882, fax 504/589–3851, www.nps.gov/jela). Acadian Cultural Center (501 Fisher Rd., Lafayette, LA 70508-2033, tel. 337/232–0789); Barataria Preserve (6588 Barataria Blvd., Marrero, LA 70072, tel. 504/589–2330); Chalmette Battlefield (8606 St. Bernard Hwy., Chalmette, LA 70043, tel. 504/281–0510); French Quarter Visitor Center (419 Decatur St., New Orleans, LA 70130, tel. 504/589–2636); Prairie Acadian Cultural Center (250 W. Park Ave., Eunice, LA 70535, tel. 337/457–8499); Wetlands Acadian Cultural Center (314 St. Mary St., Thibodaux, LA 70301, tel. 985/448–1375). New Orleans Metropolitan Convention & Visitors Bureau (2020 St. Charles Ave., New Orleans, LA 70130, tel. 504/566-5011 or 800/672–6124, www.neworleanscvb.com).

New Orleans Jazz National Historical Park

In southeastern Louisiana, in New Orleans

This fascinating, musically oriented park serves up the sights, sounds, and settings of the place where jazz first evolved in America. Elaborate exhibits on the origins, early history, development, and progression of jazz are found throughout the site. The park offers a variety of programming and live performances, and visitors are invited to participate in ranger-led interpretive music programs. The park was authorized on October 31, 1994.

WHAT TO SEE & DO

Attending concerts, participating in music programs, watching parades and demonstrations. **Facilities:** Visitor center (916 N. Peters St., New Orleans, tel. 504/589–4841), movies. Book-and-gift shop. **Programs & Events:** Jazz workshops, conferences, guest lectures, live concerts. **Tips & Hints:** Check out the monthly calendar on the park website, as programs are always changing. Busiest Oct. and Apr.; least crowded July and Aug.

FEES & HOURS

Free. Visitor center open Tues.–Sat. 9–5.

HOW TO GET THERE

In New Orleans via I–10 to Exit 236 Esplanade, south to Decatur St., and west to N. Peters St., or via I–10 to Exit 235 Canal, south to Decatur St., and east to N. Peters St.

CONTACTS

New Orleans Jazz National Historic Park (419 Rue Decatur, New Orleans, LA 70130, tel. 504/589–4806, fax 504/589–3865, www.nps.gov/jazz). New Orleans Metropolitan Convention & Visitors Bureau (2020 St. Charles Ave., New Orleans, LA 70130, tel. 800/672–6124 or 504/566–5011, www.neworleanscvb.com).

Poverty Point National Monument/State Historic Site

In northeastern Louisiana, near Epps

Owned and funded by the Louisiana Office of State Parks, this 402-acre site offers an interpretation of the culture of the peoples who constructed prehistoric earthworks here between 1700 and 700 BC. A museum, an archaeological laboratory, interpretive trails, and audiovisual programs tell the stories of these ancient local residents. Tram tours and craft workshops bring Native American cultural traditions to life. The site was designated a national monument on October 31, 1988.

WHAT TO SEE & DO

Touring museum and site. **Facilities:** Visitor center, museum, outdoor interpretive exhibits, movies, hiking trails. **Programs & Events:** Guided open-air tram tours (Mar.–Oct.), occasional basket-weaving workshops, night hikes, flint-knapping workshops. Fall School Days (last Fri., Sept.). **Tips & Hints:** In the summer, tour in the morning to avoid heat. Busiest Oct., Apr., and May; least crowded Jan. and Feb.

FOOD, LODGING & SUPPLIES

🔥 **Camping:** None in park. In Delhi: Poverty Point Reservoir and State Park (1500 Poverty Point Pkwy., tel. 318/878–7536 or 800/479–0392; 54 campsites, 8 cabins; campsites $16–$26, cabins $100–$150; flush toilets, showers, hookups; 15-day maximum; open year-round). 🏨 **Hotels:** None in park. In Delhi: Best Western Delhi Inn (135 Snider Rd., tel. 318/878–5126 or 800/780–7234, www.bestwesternlouisiana.com; 45 rooms; $89–$99). In Tallulah: Tallulah Days Inn (143 Hwy. 65 S, tel. 318/574–5200, www.daysinn.com; 34 rooms; $81). ✗ **Restaurants:** None in park. In Delhi: Fox's Pizza Den (620 1st St., tel. 318/878–8888, www.foxspizza.com; $8). ⛁ **Groceries & Gear:** In Delhi: Family Dollar (807 Broadway Dr., tel. 318/878–5073).

FEES & HOURS

Admission fee: $4 per person, free ages 12 and under and 62 and older. Park and visitor center open daily 9–5.

HOW TO GET THERE

Near Epps: From I–20 take Exit 153 (Hwy. 17) north to Epps, head east on Hwy. 134 for 5 miles, then north on Hwy. 577 for 1 mile. Closest airports: Monroe (55 miles), Jackson, MS (75 miles).

CONTACTS

Poverty Point National Monument (Box 276, Epps, LA 71266, tel. 318/926–5492 or 888/926–5492, www.nps.gov/popo). Epps Town Hall (120 Maple St., Epps, LA 71237, tel. 318/926–5224).

See Also

....

Vicksburg National Military Park, Mississippi.

MAINE

Acadia National Park

On the northeastern coast of Maine and on Mount Desert Island

Acadia's glaciated coastal and island landscape embraces towering mountains, shimmering lakes, and thick hardwood and evergreen forests. Its rich cultural history, provided by various indigenous peoples and successive waves of French and English immigrants, can be traced back 5,000 years. The Sieur de Monts Spring nature center near Bar Harbor and the Islesford Historical Museum on Little Cranberry Island explore the area's natural beauty and cultural ties. Walking trails and 45 miles of carriage roads cut through gorgeous countryside, and ranger-led programs explain the importance of the surrounding scenery. The park was proclaimed as Sieur de Monts National Monument on July 8, 1916, established as Lafayette National Park on February 26, 1919, and changed to Acadia National Park on January 19, 1929.

WHAT TO SEE & DO

Bicycling and boating (rentals in Bar Harbor, Northeast Harbor, Southwest Harbor), cross-country skiing (rentals in Bar Harbor), fishing, hiking, rock climbing, swimming. **Facilities:** Visitor center: Hulls Cove (3 miles north of Bar Harbor, off Rte. 3), Sieur de Monts Spring Nature Center (1½ miles south of Bar Harbor, off Rte. 3), Islesford Historical Museum (Little Cranberry Island), museum, guided and self-guided tours, hiking trails. Book and map sales, picnic tables with fire grills. **Programs & Events:** Daily ranger-guided walks, hikes, talks, demonstrations, amphitheater programs, and boat cruises (late May–mid-Oct.). **Tips & Hints:** Avoid touring 10–2 in summer because of crowds. Visit late May–early June for wildflowers and migrating warblers, or first half of Oct. for fall foliage and raptor migration. Basic snacks are available, and a shuttle bus runs through the park. Busiest July and Aug., least crowded Jan. and Feb.

FOOD, LODGING & SUPPLIES

Camping: 3 campgrounds in the park: Blackwoods (Mount Desert Island; 300 sites; $20; flush toilets Apr.–Nov., pit toilets Dec.–Mar.; reservations suggested May–Oct.), Seawall (Mount Desert Island; 200 sites; $20; flush toilets; closed Oct.–mid-May), Isle au Haut (5 lean-tos; $25; pit toilet; closed mid-Oct.–mid-May). In Bar Harbor: Bar Harbor/Oceanside KOA (136 County Rd., tel. 207/288–3520 or 888/562–5605; 200 sites; $70–$160; flush toilets, showers, hookups; closed Nov.–May). **Hotels:** None in park. In Bar Harbor: Quality Inn (40 Kebo St., tel. 207/288–5403 or 877/424–6423, www.qualityinn.com; 77 rooms; $169), Anchorage Motel (51 Mt. Desert St., tel. 207/288–3959 or 800/366-3959, www.anchoragebarharbor.com; 50 rooms; $109–$129), Belle Isle Motel (910 Hwy. 3, tel. 207/288–5726, www.belleislemotel.net;

26 rooms; $73). ✗ **Restaurants:** In the park: Jordan Pond House Restaurant (tel. 207/276–3316; $9–$18; closed late Oct.–mid-May); snacks at Cadillac Mountain, Thunder Hole. In Bar Harbor: Terrace Grille (Newport Dr., tel. 207/288-3351 or 800/248-3351, www.barharborinn. com; $10–$25; open mid-May–mid-Oct.). ♿ **Groceries & Gear:** In Bar Harbor: Hannaford (86 Cottage St., tel. 207/288–5680).

FEES, HOURS & REGULATIONS

Entrance fee: $20 per vehicle for a 7-day pass. Permit ($25) required to camp at Isle au Haut. Write for lean-to reservations; written forms must be postmarked on or after Apr. 1. Maine fishing license ($11 for one day, $23 for three, and $43 for seven) required for freshwater fishing. Rock climbing permit (free) required for groups of six or more at Otter Cliff. No hunting. No pets on beaches or ladder trails, leashed pets on the rest. No bikes on hiking trails. No motorized vehicles on trails; only foot traffic, horses (most roads), bicycles, strollers, and electric wheelchairs on carriage roads. Park open daily but most scenic roads close in winter. Hulls Cove Visitor Center open mid-Apr.-June, Sept., and Oct., daily 8–4:30; July and Aug., daily 8–6. Park headquarters open year-round, Mon.–Fri. 8–4:30. Sieur de Monts Nature Center open May, weekends 9–5; June–Sept., daily 9–5. Islesford Historical Museum open mid-June–Sept., daily 10–3:30.

HOW TO GET THERE

3 miles north of Bar Harbor via Rte. 3. Closest airports: Trenton (12 miles), Bangor (45 miles).

CONTACTS

Acadia National Park (Box 177, Bar Harbor, ME 04609, tel. 207/288–3338; 877/444–6777 for Blackwoods and Seawall campgrounds reservations; 207/288–3338 group camping and Isle au Haut reservations, fax 207/288–8813, www.nps.gov/acad). Bar Harbor Chamber of Commerce (1201 Bar Harbor Rd., Trenton, ME 04605, seasonal office in Bar Harbor at Harbor Place Pier, mid-May–Oct., tel. 207/288–5103 or 800/345-4617, www.barharborinfo.com). Mount Desert Chamber of Commerce (18 Harbor Dr., Box 675, Northeast Harbor, ME 04662, tel. 207/276-5040, www.mountdesertchamber.org). Southwest Harbor–Tremont Chamber of Commerce (329 Main St., Box 1143, Southwest Harbor, ME 04679, tel. 207/244–9264, www.acadiachamber.com).

St. Croix Island International Historic Site

Northeastern Maine, near Calais

Pierre Dugua Sieur de Mons and his company of 78 men attempted to establish a French settlement on St. Croix Island in 1604–05. Preceding Jamestown (1607) and Plymouth (1620), Sieur de Mons's outpost was one of the earliest European settlements on the North Atlantic coast of North America. The settlement was short-lived. In the summer of 1605 the French moved to a more favorable location where they established the Port Royal Habitation on the shores of the present-day Annapolis Basin, Nova Scotia. The first international historic site in the National Park System was authorized as a national monument in 1949 and redesignated in 1984.

WHAT TO SEE & DO

Picnicking, walking to interpretive shelter with view of island. **Facilities:** Interpretive trail with six bronze statues of Native Americans and French, scale model of island from 1604, hiking trails, visitor contact station. **Programs & Events:** Ranger-guided walks, talks, cultural demonstrations, basket-weaving demonstrations, interpretive programs (June–mid-Sept.). **Tips & Hints:** Plan to spend a half hour; dress warmly for constant breezes. Summer temperatures average around 75°F.

FOOD, LODGING & SUPPLIES

⚴ **Camping:** None in park. In Robbinston: Hilltop Campground (317 Ridge Rd., tel. 207/454–3985 or 866/454–3985, www. hilltopcampgroundmaine.com; 84 RV sites; $32–38; flush toilets, showers, hookups). ⛺ **Hotels:** None in park. In Princeton: Bellmard Inn & Cabins (86 Main St., tel. 207/796–2261, www.bellmardinn. com; 7 rooms, 2 cabins; $40–$50). In Robbinston: Redclyffe Shore Motor Inn (U.S. 1, tel. 207/454–3270, fax 207/454-8723, www. redclyffeshoremotorinn.com; 16 rooms; $85–$95; closed Nov.–mid-May). ✘ **Restaurants:** None in park. In Calais: Down East Pizza (183 North St., tel. 207/454–2509; $6–$10), Yancy's Restaurant (332 North St., tel. 207/ 454–8200; $5–$11).

FEES, HOURS & REGULATIONS

Free. No fires. Site open daily dawn–dusk; visitor contact center open daily mid-May–Columbus Day.

HOW TO GET THERE

120 miles north of Bar Harbor via U.S. 1; from Bangor, take Rte. 9 to Calais, then U.S. 1 south for 8 miles. Access to island by private boat only. Closest airport: Bangor (90 miles).

CONTACTS

Saint Croix Island International Historic Site (Box 40, Calais, ME 04619, tel. 207/454–3871, www.nps.gov/sacr). St. Croix Valley Chamber of Commerce (39 Union St., Calais, ME 04619, tel. 207/454–2308 or 888/422–3112, fax 207/454-2308, www.visitcalais.com).

See Also

Appalachian National Scenic Trail, West Virginia.

MARYLAND

Antietam National Battlefield

In northwestern Maryland, near Sharpsburg

Antietam is one of the best-preserved Civil War battlefields in the nation. On these fields on September 17, 1862, the Union army stopped the northern advance of Confederate forces in the bloodiest single-day battle in American history. Wayside exhibits and tablets describe the battle, and cannons line the 8½-mile driving tour. A stop along the route at a tower offers a view of the ¼-mile stretch known as "Bloody Lane," where 5,600 Union and Confederate soldiers were killed, wounded, or captured in three hours—more casualties than occurred during the entire eight years of the American Revolution. The site was established as a national battlefield in 1890 and transferred to the Park Service in 1933.

WHAT TO SEE & DO

Cross-country skiing, hiking, horseback riding, picnicking, scenic drives, walking. **Facilities:** Visitor center, outdoor interpretive exhibits, guided and self-guided tours, museum, movies, hiking trail. Bookstore. **Programs & Events:** Self-guided driving tour, one-hour documentary *Antiem* (daily at noon), orientation film (daily, every half hour except noon and 12:30), ranger programs. Concert and fireworks (1st Sat., July); battle anniversary hikes, tours, and programs (week of Sept. 17); Annual Memorial Illumination (1st Sat., Dec.). **Tips & Hints:** Recorded driving tour available (fee). Busiest July and Aug., least crowded Jan. and Feb.

FOOD, LODGING & SUPPLIES

Camping: In the park: Rohrbach (near Antietam Creek, off Burnside Bridge Rd.; reservations required; 10 sites; $25; closed Dec.-Mar.). In Boonsboro: Greenbrier State Park (21843 National Pike, tel. 301/791–4767 or 888/432–2267 for reservations, www.dnr.state.md. us; 165 sites; $21–$27 plus $4.50 reservation fee; flush toilets, showers, some hookups). **Hotels:** None in park. In Shepherdstown, WV: Comfort Inn (70 Maddex Square Dr., tel. 304/876–3160, www.comfortinn.com; 51 rooms; $99). In Hagerstown, MD: Clarion Hotel (901 Dual Hwy./U.S. 40, tel. 301/733-5100, www.clarionhotel.com; 114 rooms; $99). **Restaurants:** None in park. In Shepherdstown, WV: Bavarian Inn & Lodge (164 Shepherd Grade Rd., tel. 304/876-2551, www.bavarianinnwv.com; $8–$14). In Sharpsburg: Battleview Market & Diner (5331 Sharpsburg Pike, tel. 301/432–2676, www. battleviewmarket.com; $3–$11). **Groceries & Gear:** None in park. In Shepherdstown, WV: Food Lion (85 Maddex Square Dr., tel. 304/876–0601).

FEES, HOURS & REGULATIONS

Entrance fee: $4 adults, free ages 15 and under, $6 per family. No open water for horses; spigots only. Horseback-riding groups of five or more must sign in at visitor center; groups of more than 10 require a special use permit. No hunting, metal detecting, or relic hunting. Leashed pets only. Crop fields, pastures, reforested areas, barns, and other farm areas closed to public. No climbing on monuments or cannons. Bikes on roads only. No kite flying, ball games, sunbathing, model airplane or rocket flying, or Frisbees. Park open daily dawn–dusk. Visitor center open Memorial Day–Labor Day, daily 8-6; Labor Day–Memorial Day, daily 8:30-5.

HOW TO GET THERE

1 mile north of Sharpsburg, MD, on Rte. 65.

CONTACTS

Antietam National Battlefield (visitor center: 5831 Dunker Church Rd., Box 158, Sharpsburg, MD 21782, tel. 301/432–5124, fax 301/432–4590, www.nps.gov/anti). Hagerstown–Washington County Convention & Visitors Bureau (16 Public Sq., Hagerstown, MD 21740, tel. 301/791–3246 or 800/257–2600, www.marylandmemories.org).

Assateague Island National Seashore

In southeastern Maryland, near Ocean City; also in eastern Virginia within the Chincoteague National Wildlife Refuge

The 37-mile-long shoreline is one of the few protected and undeveloped barrier islands on the East Coast. This dynamic seashore environment provides refuge to wild horses, as well as to abundant and specialized flora, fauna, and marine life. It was authorized on September 21, 1965.

WHAT TO SEE & DO

Bicycling (rentals in park), clamming, crabbing, fishing, hiking, hunting, kayaking (rentals in park), off-road driving, swimming, viewing exhibits and aquariums. **Facilities:** 3 visitor centers: Assateague Island (Maryland district), Chincoteague National Wildlife Refuge, and Toms Cove (Virginia district); guided and self-guided tours, hiking trails. Bookstores, picnic tables with fire grills. **Programs & Events:** Ranger-led crabbing, clamming, and surf-fishing demonstrations, beach walks, marsh walks, bay exploring, kayak trips (reservations required), Junior Ranger and campfire programs. Pony penning in Chincoteague, VA (last Wed. and Thurs., July). **Tips & Hints:** Bring insect repellent, screen tents, sunscreen, and sand stakes. Proper food storage strictly enforced. Bike and kayak rentals available June–Aug., daily; April, May, Sept., and Oct., weekends. No roads connect north and south entrances to Assateague Island. Busiest July and Aug., least crowded Jan. and Feb.

FOOD, LODGING & SUPPLIES

🐾 **Camping:** In the park: 153 sites scattered around the park (tel. 877/444–6777; $20–$25; portable toilets, cold showers. In Berlin, MD: Assateague State Park (7307 Stephen Decatur Hwy., tel. 410/641–2918, www.dnr.state.md.us/publiclands/eastern/assateague.asp; 350 sites; $28–$40; flush toilets, some hookups). In Chincoteague, VA: Maddox Family Campgrounds (6742 Maddox Blvd., tel. 757/336–3111, www.chincoteague.com/maddox; 550 sites; $35–$43; flush toilets, showers, some hookups). 🛏 **Hotels:** None in park. In Ocean City, MD: Dunes Manor Hotel (2800 Biltmore Ave., tel. 410/289–1100 or 800/523-2888, www.dunesmanor.com; 170 rooms; $169–$254). In Berlin, MD: Holland House Bed & Breakfast Inn (5 Bay St., tel. 410/641–1956, www.hollandhousebandb.com; 6 rooms; $110–$140). ✕ **Restaurants:** None in park. Concession stand at Maryland State Park (May–Sept.). In Ocean City, MD: Waterman's Seafood Co. (12505 Ocean Gateway, tel. 410/213-1020, www.crabsoc.com; $7–$13). ♨ **Groceries & Gear:** None in park. In Ocean City, MD: Superfresh (12741 Ocean Gateway, tel. 410/213–0410). In Berlin, MD: Food Lion (10138 Old Ocean City Blvd., tel. 410/ 629–1576).

FEES, HOURS & REGULATIONS

Entrance fee: $15 per vehicle for seven-day pass; free for people on foot or bicycle (VA); $3 per person in a bus or taxi, free for people on foot or bicycle (MD). Ranger-led kayak trips: $10 per paddler (reservations required; apply in person at Assateague Island Visitor Center). Camping available year-round, mid-Apr.-mid-Oct. by reservation (tel. 877/444–6777, www.recreation.gov). Backcountry camping permit ($6 per person ages 16 and over) required. Off Road Vehicle Permit ($90 annual, restrictions apply) required. Hunting permitted Sept.–Jan.; Maryland state hunting license ($45 for three days) required. Blocking traffic on roads to view horses is prohibited. No feeding or touching wild horses. Leashed pets only in limited areas at Assateague; no pets in Virginia areas. Maryland District: Seashore open daily. Assateague Island Visitor Center open daily 9–5. Virginia District: Toms Cove Visitor Center open May-Sept., daily 9-5; Oct.–Apr., daily 9–4; tel. 757/336–6577. Chincoteague National Wildlife Refuge: Refuge open May–Sept., daily 5 AM–10 PM; Apr. and Oct., daily 6 AM–8 PM; Nov.–Mar., daily 6–6. Visitor centers open May–Sept., daily 9-5; Oct.–Apr., daily 9–4.

HOW TO GET THERE

Offshore of Maryland and Virginia: Maryland district 8 miles south of Ocean City via Rte. 611; Virginia district entrance at Chincoteague via U.S. 13 and Rte. 175. Closest airport: Salisbury (40 miles west of Ocean City, 45 miles northwest of Chincoteague, VA).

CONTACTS

Assateague Island National Seashore (7206 National Seashore La., Berlin, MD 21811, tel. 410/641–1441 visitor center, 410/641–3030 ranger station, 877/365–6777 camping reservations, fax 410/641–1099, www.nps.gov/asis). Chincoteague Chamber of Commerce (6733 Maddox Blvd., Box 258, Chincoteague, VA 23336, tel. 757/336-6161, www. chincoteaguechamber.com). Ocean City Convention and Visitors Bureau (4001 Coastal Hwy., Ocean City, MD 21842, tel. 410/723–8610 visitor center direct or 800/626-2326, www.ococean.com).

Catoctin Mountain Park

In northern Maryland, near Thurmont

The eastern hardwood forests of the Catoctin Mountains are rich with opportunities for camping, picnicking, fishing, and hiking. Created during the Great Depression, the park was built by the Works Progress Administration and the Civilian Conservation Corps as a set of neighborhood recreational areas and camps for federal employees. One of these camps eventually became Camp David, the presidential retreat that is closed to the public. Catoctin Recreation Demonstration Area was transferred to the Park Service in 1936 and renamed in 1954.

WHAT TO SEE & DO

Cross-country skiing, fishing, hiking, horseback riding (rentals, Gettysburg), picnicking, rock climbing, wildlife-watching. **Facilities:** Visitor center, hiking trails. Bookstore. **Programs & Events:** Interpretive programs; campfire programs (weekends June–Aug.). Fall Color Walks (weekends mid-Oct.). **Tips & Hints:** Plan to spend 30 minutes in visitor center. Hikes vary from 30 minutes to seven hours; average is two–three hours. Busiest July, Aug., and Oct. weekends, least crowded Jan. and Feb.

FOOD, LODGING & SUPPLIES

Camping: 5 campgrounds in the park: Adirondack Shelter (free), Camp Greentop (12 cabins; $900; flush toilets, showers; closed late Oct.-mid-Apr.), Camp Misty Mount (26 cabins, 3 lodges; $55–$75 cabins, $75–$185 lodges; flush toilets, showers; closed late Oct.–mid-Apr.), Camp Round Meadow (4 dormitories; $175-$700; flush toilets, showers), Owens Creek (51 sites; $16; flush toilets, showers; closed late Nov.–mid-Apr.), Poplar Grove (3 group sites; $30; pit toilets; reservations required; closed Mar.–mid-Apr.). **Hotels:** None in park. In Thurmont: Cozy Country Inn (103 Frederick Rd./Rte. 806, tel. 301/271-4301, www.cozyvillage.com; 16 rooms, 5 cottages; $67–$78), Super 8 (300 Tippin Dr., tel. 301/271–7888; 46 rooms; $80-$92). **Restaurants:** None in park. In Thurmont: Cozy Country Inn (105 Frederick Rd./Rte. 806, tel. 301/271–7373; $6–$17), Mountain Gate Family Restaurant (133 Frederick Rd., tel. 301/271–4373, www. mountaingatefamilyrestaurant.com; $7–$10). **Groceries & Gear:** None in park. In Thurmont: Food Lion (U.S. 15 and Tippin Dr., tel. 301/271–9949). In Frederick: Trail House (17 S. Market St., tel. 301/694–8448).

FEES, HOURS & REGULATIONS

Free. Park Central Rd. and part of Manahan Rd. closed in winter for cross-country skiing. Permits (free) required for Adirondack Shelter and rock climbing. Maryland State fishing license ($20.50) required. Park open daily. Visitor center open Mon.–Thurs. 10–4:30, Fri. 10–5, weekends 8:30–5. Closed Wed. in winter.

HOW TO GET THERE

18 miles from Frederick via U.S. 15 north and Rte. 77 west. Closest airports: Dulles (60 miles), Baltimore (65 miles).

CONTACTS

Catoctin Mountain Park (6602 Foxville Rd., Thurmont, MD 21788, tel. 301/663-9388, www.nps.gov/cato). Tourism Council of Frederick County, Inc. (51 S. East St., Frederick, MD 21701, tel. 301/600–2888 or 800/999–3613, www.fredericktourism.org).

Chesapeake & Ohio Canal National Historical Park

Parallels 185 miles of the Potomac River from Georgetown (in Washington, DC) to Cumberland, MD

This waterway, built between 1828 and 1850 and used until 1924, preserves the history of the C&O Canal and its related structures. The system's 74 lift locks raised the boats traveling the canal from near sea level to an elevation of 605 feet; today, the locks, dams, aqueducts, and other structures provide several short and widely separated stretches of water perfect for canoeists, kayakers, and anglers. Its towpath offers a nearly level byway for hikers and bicyclists. The canal was established as a national historical park on January 8, 1971.

WHAT TO SEE & DO

Biking (rentals in Cumberland and Hancock, MD; Harpers Ferry, WV; and Washington, DC), boating and canoeing (rentals in Harpers Ferry and Washington, DC), hiking, picnicking, viewing Great Falls in Potomac, MD. **Facilities:** 7 visitor centers with interpretive displays: Georgetown (1057 Thomas Jefferson St. NW, Washington, DC), Brunswick (40 W. Potomac St., Brunswick, MD), Great Falls (11710 MacArthur Blvd., Potomac, MD), Ferry Hill (16500 Shepherdstown Pike, Sharpsburg, MD), Williamsport (205 West Potomac St., Williamsport, MD), Hancock (439 E. Main St., Hancock, MD), and Cumberland (13 Canal St., Cumberland, MD); outdoor interpretive exhibits throughout the park. Covered picnic tables. **Programs & Events:** Ranger programs (vary at each location). Replica canal boats at Georgetown, Great Falls, and Williamsport (typically May–early Nov.). Heritage Days in Cumberland, MD (June), Summerfest in Oldtown, MD (June), Barge Bash in Hancock, MD (June), Bluegrass at the Bowles House in Hancock, MD (3rd Sat. of month, June–Oct.), Retreat Through Williamsport (1st weekend in July), Williamsport Days in Williamsport, MD (3rd weekend in Aug.), Canal Apple Festival in Hancock, MD (mid-Sept.), Brunswick Railroad Days (early Oct.). **Tips & Hints:** Avoid towpath after heavy rains and during heavy winds. Busiest June–Aug., least crowded Jan. and Feb.

FOOD, LODGING & SUPPLIES

🏕 **Camping:** In park: 6 campgrounds ($10 individual sites, $20 group sites; pit toilets, water mid-Apr.–mid-Nov.): Antietam Creek (mile 69; 20 sites), Fifteen Mile Creek (mile 140.9; 10 sites), McCoys Ferry (mile 110.4; 14 sites), Paw Paw (mile 156.1; 8 sites), Spring Gap (mile 173.3; 19 sites), Marsden Tract (mile 11.5; group campsite; $20; permit required). 30 primitive campsites (free) along the canal approximately every 5–7 miles from Swains Lock (mile 16.6) to Evitts Creek (mile 180.1). In Flintstone: Rocky Gap State Park (12500 Pleasant Valley Rd. NE, tel. 301/722–1480, www.dnr.state.md.us/publiclands/western/rockygap.asp; 278 sites; $23–$29; flush toilets, showers, hookups). 🏨 **Hotels:** None in park. In Cumberland: Holiday Inn (100 S. George St., tel. 301/724-8800, www.hicumberland.com; 130 rooms; $127–$139). ✗ **Restaurants:** None in park. In Cumberland: Kramer's Restaurant & Deli (13 Canal St., tel. 301/722-8003, www.kramersdelionline.com; $3–$8; closed Sun.). 🛒 **Groceries & Gear:** None in park. In Cumberland: Martin's Food Market (739 Park St., tel. 301/777–7656).

FEES, HOURS & REGULATIONS

Free. Entrance fee for Great Fall $3 per person on foot or bicycle, $5 per vehicle. Canal boat rides $8, free ages 3 and under. Reservations required for Carderock picnic pavilion. Maryland or Washington, DC, fishing license required. No gas-powered boats in park. Electric motors allowed in Big Pool, Little Pool, and canal waters from Lock 68 to Town Creek. No motorized vehicles, mopeds, or dirt bikes on towpath. Bike riding on towpaths only. Leashed pets only. No hunting. Towpath open daily dawn–dusk. Georgetown Visitor Center open mid-June–Sept., Wed.–Sun. 9:30–4:30. Great Falls Visitor Center open daily 9–4:30. Brunswick Visitor Center open Thurs. and Fri. 10–2, Sat. 10–4, Sun. 1–4. Williamsport Visitor Center open Wed.–Sun. 9–4:30. Hancock Visitor Center open May–Oct., Fri.–Tues. 9–4:30. Cumberland Visitor Center open daily 9–5.

HOW TO GET THERE

From Cumberland: I–68 to Hancock, then I–70 to Frederick, then I–270 to Capital Beltway (I–495). Take Exit 41, Clara Barton Pkwy. west, then left onto MacArthur Blvd. The visitor center is at the intersection with Falls Rd. (Rte. 189).

CONTACTS

Chesapeake & Ohio Canal National Historical Park (Headquarters: 1850 Dual Hwy., Suite 100, Hagerstown, MD 21740, tel. 301/739-4200, www.nps.gov/choh).

Clara Barton National Historic Site

In southwestern Maryland, in Glen Echo, northwest of Washington, DC

Clara Barton, humanitarian and founder of the American Red Cross, lived in Glen Echo the last 15 years of her life. From 1897 to 1904, her 30-plus-room mansion also served as the Red Cross headquarters and as a warehouse for disaster relief supplies. From here she organized and directed relief efforts for victims of natural disasters and war. Today the home has numerous exhibits detailing her work, and the picnic grounds adjacent to Glen Echo Park make a pleasant break after touring the grounds. The site was authorized on October 26, 1974.

WHAT TO SEE & DO

Picnicking, touring house. **Facilities:** Indoor interpretive exhibits, guided tours. Bookstore, picnic tables. **Programs & Events:** Guided tours (hourly 10–4). **Tips & Hints:** Allow 30–45 minutes for tour. Busiest on weekend afternoons, least crowded mornings.

FEES, HOURS & REGULATIONS

Free. Guided tours only. Site open daily.

HOW TO GET THERE

9 miles northwest of Georgetown via MacArthur Blvd. and Oxford Rd. to Clara Barton Pkwy., and via I–495/I–95 (Beltway) to Clara Barton Pkwy. (watch for signs to Glen Echo Park). Public transportation via Montgomery County Transit Authority Ride-on-Bus 29 from Friendship Heights metro station (Red Line) or by taxi. Closest airports: Reagan Washington National (11 miles), Dulles (22 miles).

CONTACT

Clara Barton National Historic Site (5801 Oxford Rd., Glen Echo, MD 20812, tel. 301/320–1410, www.nps.gov/clba).

Fort McHenry National Monument & Historic Shrine

In central Maryland, in Baltimore

The American resistance to a British naval attack against Fort McHenry on September 13–14, 1814, prevented the capture of Baltimore during the War of 1812. A large flag was raised over the fort after the 25-hour battle, and the v ictory inspired Francis Scott Key to write "The Star-Spangled Banner." Today, visitors experience interactive electronic exhibits, a dynamic big-screen movie, and displays highlighting the War of 1812 and role of the flag and the anthem in American culture. The restored fort includes furnished rooms, an electronic battle map, and displays of original artifacts. In the summer, "soldiers" from the War of 1812 form the fort's garrison. The fort was authorized as a national park under the War Department in 1925, transferred to the Park Service in 1933, and redesignated in 1939.

WHAT TO SEE & DO

Bicycling, jogging, picnicking, touring fort. **Facilities:** Visitor center, guided and self-guided tours, museum, movie. Book-and-gift shop, picnic tables. **Programs & Events:** Flag changing programs (twice daily, weather permitting), living-history programs (Memorial Day-Labor Day, weekends noon-4), bird walks (year-round). Flag Day Program (June 14), Star-Spangled Banner Weekend Celebration (2nd weekend Sept.). Veterans' Day program (Nov.). **Tips & Hints:** Visit in spring and fall for best weather. Busiest May and June, least crowded Jan.–Mar.

FEES, HOURS & REGULATIONS

Entrance fee: $7 adults, free ages 15 and under. No pets in fort, leashed pets only elsewhere. No climbing on cannons or earthworks. No skates or skateboards. No fishing off seawall. No public docking. No food or drink in buildings. Visitor center and fort open Memorial Day–Labor Day, daily 8–7:45; rest of year, daily 8-4:45.

HOW TO GET THERE

3 miles southeast of the Baltimore Inner Harbor via I–95 to Exit 55 Key Hwy. and Lawrence St.; turn left, then left on E. Fort Ave. and continue 1 mile (follow blue-green FORT McHENRY signs along all major routes to the park). From the Inner Harbor, take Light St. south to Key Hwy., turn left, then follow Fort McHenry signs to Lawrence St. Closest airport: Baltimore, 10 miles from the fort.

CONTACT

Fort McHenry National Monument & Historic Shrine (end of E. Fort Ave., Baltimore, MD 21230-5393, tel. 410/962–4290, fax 410/962–2500, www.nps.gov/fomc).

Fort Washington Park

In central Maryland, in Fort Washington, south of Washington, DC

Built between 1814 and 1824, the fort that stands here today replaced the original Fort Washington, which was built in 1808 and destroyed during the War of 1812. Constructed to protect the water approach to Washington, DC, the fort was the only permanent fortification guarding the nation's capital until the Civil War. The fort was garrisoned by the U.S. Coast Artillery and armed until 1917. After the guns were removed, the fort was used as a training facility until 1946, when it became a national park.

WHAT TO SEE & DO

Bird-watching, fishing, hiking, picnicking, touring fort and grounds. **Facilities:** Visitor center, hiking trail. Bookstore, picnic tables with fire grills. **Programs & Events:** Fort tours (by request). Artillery firings

(Apr.–Oct., first Sun. monthly); living-history programs (schedules vary). **Tips & Hints:** Fort Washington offers great views of Mt. Vernon and the skyline of Washington, DC. Expect to spend 30–60 minutes on tour. Busiest May and June, least crowded Dec.–Mar.

FEES & HOURS

Entrance fee: $3 per person on foot, bicycle, or bus; $5 per vehicle. Fort and visitor center open Apr.–Sept., daily 9–5; Oct.–Mar., daily 9–4:30. Park grounds open daily 9–dusk.

HOW TO GET THERE

In Fort Washington, MD, via the Capital Beltway (I–495) to Exit 3A Indian Head Hwy. or Rte. 210 south; continue to Fort Washington Rd., turn right, and follow to park entrance. Closest airport: Washington, DC (Reagan Washington National, 15 miles).

CONTACT

Fort Washington Park (13551 Fort Washington Rd., Fort Washington, MD 20744, tel. 301/763–4600, fax 301/763–1389, www.nps.gov/fowa).

Greenbelt Park

In central Maryland, in Greenbelt

This 1,176-acre park provides a green oasis between Washington, DC, and Baltimore, MD. A refuge for native plants and animals, it's a favorite local spot for camping, hiking, and picnicking. The park was transferred from the Public Housing Authority on August 3, 1950.

WHAT TO SEE & DO

Bicycling, hiking, jogging, picnicking, walking. **Facilities:** Information kiosk, 10 miles of trails. Picnic tables. **Programs & Events:** Natural, service, and cultural resource programs. National Trails Day events (1st Sat., June), Potomac River Watershed Cleanup (early Apr.), National Park Week (late Apr.), Public Lands Day (Sept.). **Tips & Hints:** Busiest Memorial Day weekend, least crowded in Jan. and Feb.

LODGING

Camping: In the park: Greenbelt Campground (southwestern part of the park, end of Park Central Rd.; 174 sites; $16; flush toilets, showers; tel. 877/444–6777).

FEES & HOURS

Free. Headquarters open weekdays 8–4. Self-registration campground open daily.

HOW TO GET THERE

12 miles from Washington, DC, 18 miles from Baltimore via I–95 to Exit 23 (Kenilworth Ave. S); turn left on Greenbelt Rd. E; park is on right. Closest Metro subway stop is Greenbelt Station (2½ miles). Closest airports: Washington, DC (Reagan Washington National, 17 miles), Baltimore (21 miles).

CONTACT
Greenbelt Park (6565 Greenbelt Rd., Greenbelt, MD 20770, tel. 301/344–3948 picnic area reservations, 301/344–3944 ranger station, 877/444-6777 camping reservations, fax 301/344–3736, www.nps.gov/gree).

Hampton National Historic Site

In central Maryland, in Towson

Hampton preserves and interprets the core of what once was a vast agricultural and commercial estate owned by one family for more than 150 years. It was supported by a large workforce, including indentured servants and slaves. The mansion is the centerpiece of the formerly 24,000-acre property, which also had an iron foundry, farm, formal grounds, and gardens. Today, some 20 buildings and 40,000 artifacts survive, including the mansion, slave quarters, family cemetery, farm, and outbuildings. The site was designated in 1948.

WHAT TO SEE & DO
Touring the mansion, outbuildings, grounds, and formal gardens. **Facilities:** Visitor center. Book-and-gift shop. **Programs & Events:** Guided mansion tours (daily 9–4, on the hour), guided grounds tours (Memorial Day–Labor Day), self-guided tours; special programs include carriage rides, music performances, and lectures (2nd Sun. of each month). **Tips & Hints:** Busiest Apr. and May, least crowded Jan. and Feb.

FEES & HOURS
Free. Park and visitor center open daily 9–5. Gift shop open Mar.–early Jan.

HOW TO GET THERE
Near the Baltimore Beltway (I–695) via Exit 27B. Closest airport: Baltimore (40 miles from estate).

CONTACTS
Hampton National Historic Site (535 Hampton La., Towson, MD 21286, tel. 410/823–1309, fax 410/823–8394, www.nps.gov/hamp). Baltimore County Tourism & Promotion (400 Washington Ave., Towson, MD 21204, tel. 410/887–2849, www.visitbacomd.com).

Monocacy National Battlefield

In central Maryland, near Frederick

Known as the "Battle That Saved Washington," the Battle of Monocacy on July 9, 1864, was the last Confederate attempt to carry the Civil

War into the north. Although Confederate general Jubal A. Early defeated the Union forces under Major General Lew Wallace, the latter commander's effort delayed Early long enough to marshal a successful defense of Washington, DC. The site was authorized as Monocacy National Military Park in 1934, with no land acquisition until 1976, when the name was changed to Monocacy National Battlefield.

WHAT TO SEE & DO

Hiking, scenic drives. **Facilities:** Visitor center with interactive map (4801 Urbana Pike, Frederick), hiking trail. Bookstore. **Programs & Events:** Ranger-led programs (Memorial Day–Labor Day); living-history programs and special events (monthly, Apr.–Aug.). **Tips & Hints:** Busiest July and Aug., least crowded Dec. and Jan.

FEES, HOURS, & REGULATIONS

Free. Leashed pets only. No hunting or relic collecting. No bikes on trail. Visitor center open year-round, 8:30–5.

HOW TO GET THERE

2½ miles south of Frederick via Rte. 355; from I–70, take Market Street/Rt. 85 south toward Buckeystown, then turn south at the second traffic light onto Rt. 355 (Urbana Pike). The Monocacy National Battlefield Visitor Center is on the left, at 5201 Urbana Pike. Closest airports: Dulles (45 miles), Reagan (50 miles).

CONTACTS

Monocacy National Battlefield (4632 Araby Church Rd., Frederick, MD, 21704, tel. 301/662–3515, fax 301/662–3420, www.nps.gov/mono). Tourism Council of Frederick County (151 S. East St., Frederick, MD 21701, tel. 301/600–2888 or 800/999-3613, www.fredericktourism.org).

Piscataway Park

In southern Maryland, near Accokeek

This attractive park stretches 6 miles along the Potomoc River from Piscataway Creek to Marshall Hall, part of a plan to preserve the river view from Mount Vernon as it was in George Washington's day. The park also has serene spots to picnic, bird-watch, view the mansion across the Potomac, and tour the working reproduction of an 18th-century National Colonial Farm. Preservation efforts began in 1952, and the park was authorized on October 4, 1961.

WHAT TO SEE & DO

Backcountry hiking, bird-watching, fishing, picnicking, touring farm. **Facilities:** Picnic area. **Tips & Hints:** Farm tours run by Accokeek Foundation. Busiest Apr.–Oct., least crowded Dec. and Jan.

FEES & HOURS

Free. Park open daily dawn–dusk. National Colonial Farm open mid-Mar.–Nov., Tues.–Sun. 10–4; Dec.–mid-Mar., weekends 10–4.

HOW TO GET THERE

14 miles south of Washington, DC, via I–95 (Capital Beltway) to Exit 3A to Rte. 210 south (Indian Head Hwy.); drive 10 miles to intersection in Accokeek, turn right on Bryan's Point Rd.; park is 4 miles ahead on the Potomac River. Closest airport: Washington, DC (Reagan, 21 miles).

CONTACTS

Piscataway Park (c/o Fort Washington Park, 13551 Fort Washington Rd., Fort Washington, MD 20744, tel. 301/763–4600, www.nps.gov/pisc). Accokeek Foundation (tel. 301/283-2113, www.accokeek.org).

Thomas Stone National Historic Site

In southern Maryland, near Port Tobacco

Haberdeventure plantation was the home of Thomas Stone, one of Maryland's four signers of the Declaration of Independence. Stone was a delegate to the Continental Congress between 1775 and 1777 and again between 1783 and 1784. As a member of the Continental Congress, he served on the 13-member committee that drafted the country's first system of government under the Articles of Confederation. Today the 322-acre site contains Stone's five-part tidewater plantation house and several outbuildings typical of an 18th- and 19th-century Maryland plantation. The site was authorized on November 10, 1978.

WHAT TO SEE & DO

Taking guided tour, viewing exhibits. **Facilities:** Visitor center with movie. Bookstore. **Programs & Events:** Ranger-led tours (10–4), audiovisual programs. Seasonal activities and special events available. **Tips & Hints:** Plan to spend an hour visiting site, 20 minutes on tour. Busiest June and July, least crowded Jan. and Feb.

FOOD, LODGING & SUPPLIES

Hotels: None at site. In La Plata: Best Western Plus (6900 Crain Hwy., tel. 301/934–4900 or 877/356-4900, www.bestwesternmaryland.com; 73 rooms; $109). **Restaurants:** None at site. In La Plata: Casey Jones Pub (417 E. Charles St., tel. 301/392-5116, www.casey-jones.com; $6–$16; closed Sun.). **Groceries & Gear:** None at site. In La Plata: Safeway (40 Shining Willow Way, tel. 301/392–1875).

FEES & HOURS

Free. Site open June–Labor Day, daily 9–5; Labor Day–June, Wed.–Sun. 9–5.

HOW TO GET THERE

30 miles south of Washington, DC, via U.S. 301 to Rte. 6, or via Rte. 225 to Rose Hill Rd., near Port Tobacco. Closest airport: Washington, DC (Reagan, 30 miles).

CONTACTS

Thomas Stone National Historic Site (6655 Rosehill Rd., Port Tobacco, MD 20677, tel. 301/392–1776, fax 301/934–8793, www.nps.gov/thst). Charles County Chamber of Commerce (101 Centennial St., Suite A, La Plata, MD 20646, tel. 301/932–6500, www.charlescountychamber. org).

See Also

Appalachian National Scenic Trail, West Virginia. *George Washington Memorial Parkway,* Virginia. *Harpers Ferry National Historical Park,* West Virginia. *Potomac Heritage National Scenic Trail,* District of Columbia.

MASSACHUSETTS

Adams National Historical Park

In eastern Massachusetts, in Quincy

The birthplace and home of John Adams and John Quincy Adams—the nation's second and sixth presidents—are preserved in this park. A free trolley-bus service takes visitors to the 17th-century saltbox houses where these great men were born. The tour also includes a visit to the "Old House" at "Peace field," which from 1788 to 1927 was the family home of four Adams generations. A visit to the nearby United First Parish Church, final resting place of both presidents and first ladies, completes the experience. The site was designated on December 9, 1946, and redesignated by Congress in 1998.

WHAT TO SEE & DO

Touring the three homes, church, and grounds. **Facilities:** Main visitor center (1250 Hancock St.) and Carriage House (135 Adams St.). Bookstore (1250 Hancock St.). **Programs & Events:** Interpretive tours (mid-Apr.–mid-Nov., daily); special programs, reenactments, lecture series. **Tips & Hints:** Parking free at President's Place garage with validation stamp from main visitor center. Go Apr.–Aug. for garden blooms, Sept.–Nov. for fall foliage. Busiest July and Aug.

FEES, HOURS & REGULATIONS

Park entrance fee and tour: $5 adult. United First Parish Church: $5. No backpacks, strollers, photography, or video cameras in homes. No pets. Park open mid-Apr.–mid-Nov., daily 9–5. Main visitor center open limited hours in off-season. Carriage House visitor orientation center open mid-Apr.–mid-Nov., daily 9–5. Last full tour departs at 3:15; no tours mid-Nov.–mid-Apr. Visitors should first go to the main visitor center and board a bus to tour other sites; other sites are not open to the public without a tour.

HOW TO GET THERE

South of downtown Boston via the Red Line to Quincy Center Station; cross to Hancock St. and Galleria for Visitor Center. Closest airport: Boston (8 miles).

CONTACTS

Adams National Historical Park (135 Adams St., Quincy, MA 02169, tel. 617/770–1175, fax 617/472–7562, www.nps.gov/adam).

Boston African American National Historic Site

In Boston

Fifteen pre–Civil War structures here preserve the history of Boston's 19th-century free African American community. Located in the Beacon Hill neighborhood and linked by the 1.6-mile-long Black Heritage Trail, the collection of buildings includes the African Meeting House, the oldest standing African American church in the United States, and the Abiel Smith School. Also on site is Augustus Saint-Gaudens' memorial to Robert Gould Shaw, the white officer who led the 54th Regiment, the first African American regiment recruited from the North by the U.S. government during the Civil War. The site was authorized on October 10, 1980.

WHAT TO SEE & DO

Walking the Black Heritage Trail. **Facilities:** Indoor and outdoor interpretive exhibits and signs, park office in Museum of African American History (partner). **Programs & Events:** Self-guided and ranger-led walking tours, historic talks in the African Meeting House. **Tips & Hints:** Walking tour maps and guides free at the African Meeting House. Tour participants meet at the Shaw monument (northeast corner of Boston Common, near Park and Beacon Sts.). Park busiest July and Aug., least crowded Dec. and Jan.

FEES, HOURS & REGULATIONS

Entrance fee: $5 for adults, $3 for children 13-17 and seniors over 62). Donations support the Museum of African American History, which is open Mon.–Sat. 10–4. Guided walking tours of site and Black Heritage Trail (Memorial Day–Labor Day, daily at 10, noon, and 2; Labor Day–Memorial Day, Mon. and Sun. at 2).

HOW TO GET THERE

In Boston via I–90 (Massachusetts Tpke.) to Copley Sq. exit and Stuart St., then left on Charles St. (Rte. 28) to Boston Common; or via I–93 to Storrow Dr. and Copley Sq. exit, then left on Beacon St., right on Arlington St., left on Boylston St., and left on Charles St. (Rte. 28). Several parking garages are close by. Closest MBTA subway stops are Park St. on the Red and Green lines and Bowdoin Sq. on the Blue Line. Closest airport: Boston (4 miles).

CONTACTS

Boston African American National Historic Site (14 Beacon St., Suite 401, Boston, MA 02108, tel. 617/742–5415, fax 617/720–0848, www. nps.gov/boaf).

Boston Harbor Islands National Recreation Area

In Boston Harbor

The park encompasses 34 islands that range in size from less than an acre to more than 243. As a system of islands, this submerged glacial drumlin field is unique in the United States. Six of the islands are accessible by seasonal public ferry. Interactive videos, exhibit boards, and the information kiosk at Long Wharf provide all the details. The area was authorized in 1996.

WHAT TO SEE & DO

Beachcombing, boating, fishing, hiking, kayaking, picnicking, sailing. **Facilities:** Fan Pier visitor center (U.S. Courthouse), Spectacle Island visitor center, information booth, dock. Book-and-gift shop. **Programs & Events:** Nature walks, living-history programs, marine ecology programs (May–Oct.). Family Fun Days interactive performances, music, and historic activities on Georges Island (July and Aug., Sat.); Civil War Encampment (mid-July); Halloween program (Oct.). **Tips & Hints:** Plan on 90-minute round-trip ferry ride to Georges Island. Bring food and water for visit to park; sustenance is available only on Georges Island.

FOOD, LODGING & SUPPLIES

Camping: Primitive camping on Bumpkin, Grape, Lovells, and Peddocks islands (32 family tent sites, 3 group sites; site fee $6 per night; pit toilets; closed mid-Oct.–Apr.; reservations and permit required, see below). **Restaurants:** Snack bars on Spectacle and Georges Islands (open weekends early May-early June and early Sept.-early Oct., daily early June-early Sept.) **Groceries & Gear:** Gift shop with camping supplies on Georges Island.

FEES, HOURS & REGULATIONS

Free. Islands open year-round; ferry service seasonal. Ferry to Georges and Spectacle Islands ($15) from Long Wharf, with additional summer departures from Hingham Shipyard Pier in Hingham and Pemberton Point Pier in Hull; interisland shuttle free. Departures: May–late June, roughly every two hours 9:45–5; late June–Labor Day, hourly 9–6; Labor Day–Columbus Day, Mon.–Wed., hourly 10:30–4:30, Thurs.–Sun., roughly every two hours 9:30–5. Camping permit (free) must be secured at least 48 hours and up to six months in advance of visit; a one-time reservation transaction fee ($9.25) will be assessed on all permits. No bikes except on Deer Island, Nut Island, and World's End. No motorized equipment, pets, or alcohol. Island visitor centers open Memorial Day–Columbus Day, weekends 10–5. Information kiosk open Memorial Day–Labor Day, daily 9–4:30.

HOW TO GET THERE

Via ferry from Long Wharf and other locations around Boston. Closest airport: Boston (5 miles).

CONTACTS

Boston Harbor Islands National Recreation Area (408 Atlantic Ave., Suite 228, Boston, MA 02110-3350, tel. 617/223–8666, fax 617/223–8671, www.nps.gov/boha). Boston Harbor Island Alliance (408 Atlantic Ave., Suite 228, Boston, MA 02110, tel. 617/223–8672, fax 617/223-8671, www.islandalliance.org). Boston Harbor Islands Visitor Pavillion (191 W. Atlantic Ave., tel. 617/223–8667, www.bostonharborislands. org). Boston's Best Cruises (116 E. Howard St., Quincy, MA 02169; tel. 617/770—0040, www.bostonsbestcruises.com). Greater Boston Convention and Visitors Bureau (2 Copley Pl., Suite 105, Boston, MA 02116, tel. 617/536–4100 or 888/733–2678, fax 617/424–7664, www. bostonusa.com).

Boston National Historical Park

In Boston

The 2½-mile Freedom Trail stretches past the relics of the revolutionary generation of Bostonians who blazed a trail from colonialism to independence. On the way are the Old State House, Old South Meeting House, Faneuil Hall, Paul Revere House, Old North Church, Bunker Hill Monument, and Charlestown Navy Yard, where the USS *Constitution* ("Old Ironsides") is berthed. The park was authorized on October 1, 1974.

WHAT TO SEE & DO

Touring historic sites, walking tour trail. **Facilities:** 2 visitor centers: Downtown (1 Faneuil Hall Sq.) and Charlestown Navy Yard (55 Constitution Rd.), Battle of Bunker Hill Museum (43 Monument Sq.). Book and museum shops. **Programs & Events:** Ranger-led historical talks at Faneuil Hall and Bunker Hill Monument, self-guided and guided (mid-Apr.–Thanksgiving) tours of World War II destroyer USS *Cassin Young*, self-guided and U.S. Navy–led (year-round) tours of USS *Constitution* (year-round), ranger-led walking tours of the Freedom Trail (mid-Apr.–Nov.). Boston's Harborfest (July 4 weekend). **Tips & Hints:** Sites are accessible by public transport. The downtown visitor center is close to the State St. stop on the Blue and Orange lines and the Haymarket stop on the Green and Orange lines. Water transport connects downtown Boston (Long Wharf) and the Charlestown Navy Yard. Busiest July and Aug., least crowded Jan. and Feb. Tours fill up quickly in summer.

FEES & HOURS

Free admission to federally owned sites (Bunker Hill Monument, Bunker Hill Museum, USS *Constitution*, Dorchester Heights Monument), and to ranger-led programs on the Freedom Trail and at Faneuil Hall. Battle of Bunker Hill Museum open daily 9–5. A discounted Freedom Trail ticket, sold at Faneuil Hall Visitor Center, offers savings on other sites. Fees collected at privately owned and operated sites: Old South

Meeting House ($6 adults, $5 ages 62 and over and students with ID, $1 ages 6–18, free ages 5 and under), Old State House ($7.50 adults, $6 ages 62 and over and students with ID, $3 ages 6–18, free ages 5 and under), Paul Revere House ($3.50 adults, $3 ages 62 and over and per student with ID, $1 ages 5–17, free ages 4 and under). Downtown visitor center open daily 9–5. Charlestown Navy Yard visitor center open daily 9–5. Most historic sites open mid-Apr.–Labor Day, daily 9:30–5; Labor Day–mid-Apr., daily 10–4. USS *Constitution* open Apr.–Oct., Tues.–Sun. 10–4; Nov.–Mar., Thurs.–Sun. 10–4; tours every half hour 10:30–3:30.

HOW TO GET THERE

Near downtown Boston via U.S. 1 and I–93 north or south; follow signs to Charlestown Navy Yard. Closest airport: Boston (4 miles).

CONTACTS

Boston National Historical Park (Charlestown Navy Yard, Boston, MA 02129-4543, tel. 617/242–5601, www.nps.gov/bost).

Cape Cod National Seashore

On outer Cape Cod, off the eastern coast of Massachusetts, southeast of Boston

More than 43,000 acres of pristine beaches and grassy, wind-swept uplands fill this gorgeous seaside park, which stretches from Chatham to Provincetown on the state's Outer Cape. (The park area mainly encompasses land in the towns of Provincetown, Truro, Wellfleet, and Eastham.) The main 40-mile band of shoreline draws many visitors to its mesmerizing ocean views, but further explorations uncover little embers of local history in statuesque lighthouses, charming Cape Cod–style dwellings, and weathered lifesaving stations. It's a wonderful walking area, with dozens of clear, deep, freshwater kettle ponds pocketing the land, salt marshes, wild cranberry bogs, and pleasant trails threaded throughout fields, forests, and dunes. The site of the former Marconi Wireless Station, where in 1903 Guigelmo Marconi transmitted the first wireless message across the Atlantic, from President Theodore Roosevelt to King George of England, is also found here. The park was authorized in 1961 and established in 1966.

WHAT TO SEE & DO

Bicycling, bird-watching, boating (rentals nearby, see below), fishing, hiking, whale-watching, picnicking, swimming, touring historic sites. **Facilities:** Salt Pond Visitor Center ((Nauset Rd. and U.S. 6, Eastham) and Province Lands Visitor Center (Race Point Rd., Provincetown), movies, indoor and outdoor exhibits, 12 self-guided nature trails, 3 bike trails, 6 swimming beaches. Bookstores. **Programs & Events:** Ranger-led hikes, canoe tours, beach walks, historic-house tours. Ranger-led interpretive programs (May–Oct.), campfire programs (July and Aug.). **Tips & Hints:** Plan on at least a half-day visit. Busiest July and Aug., least crowded Jan. and Feb.

FOOD, LODGING & SUPPLIES

⚲ **Camping:** None in park. In Brewster: Nickerson State Park (3488 Main St., Rte 6A, tel. 508/896–3491, 877/422–6762 reservations; 403 sites, 6 yurts; $15–$17, $40 yurts; flush toilets, showers; closed Columbus Day–mid-Apr.). 🏨 **Hotels:** In park: Nauset Knoll Motor Lodge (237 Beach Rd., East Orleans, MA 02643; tel. 508/255–2364, www.capecodtravel.com/nausetknoll; 12 rooms; $145–$185; closed late Oct.-mid-Apr.). In Truro: Outer Reach Resort (535 Rte. 6, N. Truro, MA 02652; tel. 508/487–9090 or 800/942–5388, www.outerreachresort.com; 58 rooms; $119–$159). In Provincetown: Surfside Hotel and Suites (543 Commercial St., tel. 508/487–1726 or 866/757–8616, www.surfsideinn.cc; 83 rooms; $99–$250). In North Eastham: Captain's Quarters Motel & Conference Center (U.S. 6, tel. 508/255–5686 or 800/327-7769, www.captains-quarters.com; 75 rooms; $99–$135; closed Dec.–Mar.). ✖ **Restaurants:** In park: Herrring Cove Snack Bar (Herring Cove Beach, Rte. 6, Provincetown, MA, no phone). Highland Links Golf Course (10 Highland Light Rd., Truro MA 02666, tel. 508/487–9201, www.trurolinks.com; $3–$7). In Provincetown: Lobster Pot (321 Commercial St., tel. 508/487–0842, www.ptownlobsterpot.com; $9–$20; closed Dec.–Mar.). ♨ **Groceries & Gear:** None in park. In Eastham: Cumberland Farms (4460 Hwy. 6, tel. 508/ 255–1162).

FEES, HOURS & REGULATIONS

Entrance fee: $15 per vehicle; $3 per bicyclist or walk-in at lifeguard-protected swimming beaches (Memorial Day–late June, weekends; late June–Labor Day, daily; Labor Day–Columbus Day, weekends). Seasonal pass $45. Permits required for beach campfires and overnight parking while fishing. Oversand driving permits: $50 for 7 days, $150 for the season. Self-contained vehicle permit for overnight camping: $75 for 7 days. Parking lots open daily 6–midnight. Salt Pond Visitor Center open June–mid-Oct., daily 9–5; mid-Oct.–June, daily 9–4:30. Province Lands Visitor Center open May–Oct., daily 9–5.

HOW TO GET THERE

Near Provincetown, via Rte. 3 south; from Boston via Sagamore Bridge in Bourne, then along U.S. 6 east to Eastham and Provincetown; from Providence, RI, via I–95 north to I–195 east, then along U.S. 6 east as above. Closest airports: Hyannis (35 miles), Boston (120 miles).

CONTACTS

Cape Cod National Seashore (99 Marconi Station Site Rd., Wellfleet, MA 02667, tel. 508/771–2144, fax 508/349–9052, www.nps.gov/caco). Cape Cod Chamber of Commerce (5 Patti Page Way, Centerville, MA 02632, tel. 508/362–3225 or 888/332–2732, www.capecodchamber.org).

Frederick Law Olmsted National Historic Site

In eastern Massachusetts, in Brookline

The site preserves the home and office of America's leading landscape architect, Frederick Law Olmsted, who created some 5,000 public and private landscapes—including Boston's Emerald Necklace, New York's Central Park, and the U.S. Capitol grounds in Washington, DC. In 1883, Olmsted opened the Brookline office that would be inherited by his sons, associates, and successors, and that would eventually become a vital part of America's national heritage. More than 1 million landscape design documents were produced at Olmsted's home and office, and the grounds are now a living exhibit of the artist's design ideals. The site was established in 1979.

WHAT TO SEE & DO

Touring historic grounds. **Facilities:** Visitor center with film. Bookstore. **Programs & Events:** Interpretive tours (Fri.–Sun. 10–4:30), ranger-led tours of Olmsted-designed landscapes in Boston area. Holiday Open House (Dec.). **Tips & Hints:** Parking is limited. Busiest May and June, least crowded Nov.–Jan.

FEES, HOURS & REGULATIONS

Free. No smoking or pets inside historic buildings. Site open Fri.–Sun. 10–4:30.

HOW TO GET THERE

Near Brookline, 3 miles from downtown Boston via MBTA Bus 60 (exit at intersection of Boylston and Warren Sts. in Brookline, then follow Warren St. ⅛ mile to Olmsted NHS), MBTA Riverside "D" Green Line subway (exit at Brookline Hills station, turn right, follow sidewalk to Cypress St. and across Boylston St. intersection, turn right on Walnut St., left on Warren St., and continue to intersection with Warren and Dudley Sts.). Closest airport: Boston (8 miles).

CONTACTS

Frederick Law Olmsted National Historic Site (99 Warren St., Brookline, MA 02445, tel. 617/566–1689, fax 617/232–4073, www.nps.gov/frla). Brookline Chamber of Commerce (251 Harvard St., Suite 1, Brookline, MA 02446, tel. 617/739–1330, www.brooklinechamber.com).

John Fitzgerald Kennedy National Historic Site

In eastern Massachusetts, in Brookline

The site preserves the house where the 35th president of the United States was born in 1917. This was the first home shared by the president's father and mother, Joseph P. and Rose Fitzgerald Kennedy, and represents the social and political beginnings of one of the world's most prominent political families. The nine-room house was restored in the 1960s, under the direction of Rose Kennedy as a memorial to her son. Included are household furnishings, photographs, and significant family mementos representing the Kennedy family lifestyle. The site was established in 1969.

WHAT TO SEE & DO

Touring the home. **Facilities:** Visitor center. Bookstore. **Programs & Events:** Self-guided and ranger-led home tours (late May–Oct., Wed.–Sun. 9:30–5), guided walking tours of neighborhood (June–Aug., Thurs.-Sun. at 1). Kennedy Birthday Weekend (last weekend in May). **Tips & Hints:** No on-site parking. Busiest July and Aug.

FEES, HOURS & REGULATIONS

Free. No smoking or pets in building. Park and visitor center open May–Oct., Wed.–Sun. 9:30–5.

HOW TO GET THERE

In Brookline, 3 miles from Boston via MBTA Green Line ("C" – Cleveland Circle) train; exit at intersection of Beacon and Harvard Sts. (Coolidge Corner), walk 4 blocks north on Harvard St., turn right onto Beals St. and continue ¾ block. Closest airport: Boston (7 miles).

CONTACTS

John Fitzgerald Kennedy National Historic Site (83 Beals St., Brookline, MA 02446, tel. 617/566–7937, fax 617/730–9884, www.nps.gov/jofi). Brookline Chamber of Commerce (251 Harvard St., Suite 1, Brookline, MA 02446, tel. 617/739–1330, www.brooklinechamber.com).

Longfellow House– Washington's Headquarters National Historic Site

Near Boston, in Cambridge

Henry Wadsworth Longfellow raised a family and wrote many of his most beloved poems here between 1837 and his death in 1882. The house, built in 1759, also served as George Washington's headquarters early in the American Revolution. Handsomely furnished rooms exhibit an array of American and European decorative arts, paintings, and sculptures, as well as Longfellow's personal library of 12,000 books. The house is an outstanding example of mid-Georgian architecture, surrounded by formal gardens where the Longfellows entertained some of the world's famous writers and artists. The site was authorized in 1972.

WHAT TO SEE & DO

Touring the house and gardens. **Facilities:** Visitor center, museum. Bookstore. **Programs & Events:** Self-guided tours of grounds and neighborhood, guided tours of house (June–Oct., Wed.–Sun. at 10, 11, 12, 1, 2, 3, and 4), guided tours of neighborhood (June–Aug.). Longfellow Summer Festival of Music & Poetry (June–Aug.). **Tips & Hints:** No on-site parking. Busiest July and Aug.

FEES & HOURS

Entrance fee: Free. House and visitor center open June–Oct., Wed.–Sun. 9:30–5. Garden and grounds open year-round, daily dawn–dusk.

HOW TO GET THERE

In Cambridge, 3 miles from Boston via MBTA Red Line (Alewife) train outbound; exit at Harvard Sq., follow signs for Church St., continue to Brattle St., turn right, and walk 7–10 minutes. Closest airport: Boston (9 miles).

CONTACTS

Longfellow House-Washington's Headquarters National Historic Site (105 Brattle St., Cambridge, MA 02138, tel. 617/876–4491, fax 617/497–8718, www.nps.gov/long). Cambridge Chamber of Commerce (859 Massachusetts Ave., Cambridge, MA 02139, tel. 617/876–4100, www.cambridgechamber.org).

Lowell National Historical Park

In northeast Massachusetts, in Lowell

America's Industrial Revolution is commemorated at this park, which includes the Wannalancit Mill turbine exhibit and authentic "mill girl" boardinghouse. The main attraction is the Boott Cotton Mills Museum, which encloses a weave room of 88 operating looms. Altogether, the informative exhibits document the Northeast's transition from farm to factory, as well as the history of immigrant labor. The site was authorized on June 5, 1978.

WHAT TO SEE & DO

Taking tours. **Facilities:** Visitor center (246 Market St., Lowell), Boott Cotton Mills Museum (115 John St., Lowell), movie. **Programs & Events:** Exhibits, guided and self-guided tours, trolley tours (Mar.–Nov.), boat and walking tours (weekends late May–late June, daily late June–mid-Oct.; reservations required), museum talks (late May–mid-Oct.). Kids Weeks (Feb., Apr.), Lowell Women's Week (1st week, Mar.), Lowell Folk Festival (last full weekend, July), Lowell Summer Music Festival (July and Aug.), National Park Day (Aug. 25), Banjo and Fiddle Contests (Sept.). **Tips & Hints:** Tours go out rain or shine. Busiest May–July, least crowded Dec.–Feb.

FEES, HOURS & REGULATIONS

Free. Canal tours: $8 adults, $6 ages 6–16, $7 ages 62 and over, free ages 5 and under. Trolley tours free. Boott Cotton Mills Museum: $6 adults, $3 ages 6–16, $4 ages 62 and over, free ages 5 and under. No eating, drinking, or smoking in buildings. Visitor center open late June–Aug., daily 9–5:30; Sept.–late June, daily 9–5 (sometimes closes early in winter). Boott Cotton Mills Museum open daily 9:30–4:30 (call ahead for winter hours).

HOW TO GET THERE

In Lowell, via the Lowell Connector from either I–495 or Rte. 3; exit on Thorndike St. north, turn right on Dutton St. to marked parking lot. Closest airport: Boston (25 miles).

CONTACTS

Lowell National Historical Park (67 Kirk St., Lowell, MA 01852, tel. 978/970–5000, fax 978/275–1762, www.nps.gov/lowe). Greater Lowell Chamber of Commerce (131 Merrimack St., Lowell, MA 01852, tel. 978/459–8154, fax 978/452–4145, www.greaterlowellchamber. org). Greater Merrimack Valley Convention & Visitors Bureau (40 French St., 2nd Fl., Lowell, MA 01852, tel. 978/459–6150, www. merrimackvalley.org).

Minute Man National Historical Park

In eastern Massachusetts, in Concord, Lincoln, and Lexington

Preserved here are the historic sites, structures, and landscapes associated with the events of April 19, 1775, and the beginning of the American Revolution. The North Bridge, Minute Man Statue, and Battle Road are global symbols of hummanity's universal struggle for freedom and independence. The park also celebrates the 19th-century literary Renaissance at the Wayside, home of Nathaniel Hawthorne, Louisa May Alcott, and Margaret Sidney. The Battle Road Trail winds through the area, and Hartwell Tavern explores the more raucous side of 18th-century life. The park was authorized on September 21, 1959.

WHAT TO SEE & DO

Biking, canoeing (rentals in Concord), cross-country skiing (Battle Road Trail), hiking, picnicking, touring historic buildings and sites. **Facilities:** 2 visitor centers: Minute Man (Lexington) and North Bridge (Concord); interpretive signs, movie, hiking trails. Bookstores, picnic tables. **Programs & Events:** Ranger-led programs, self-guided tours, colonial reenactments, fife-and-drum demonstrations, military encampments, musket firings (late May–Oct.). Patriots' Day weekend (mid-Apr.). **Tips & Hints:** Begin visit by watching multimedia presentation at Minute Man Visitor Center. Busiest July and Oct., least crowded Dec.–Feb.

FOOD, LODGING & SUPPLIES

▥ Hotels: None in park. In Concord: Concord's Colonial Inn (48 Monument Sq., tel. 978/369–9200 or 800/370–9200, www.concordscolonialinn.com; 45 rooms, 7 suites; $154–$194). In Lexington: Quality Inn & Suites (440 Bedford St., tel. 781/861–0850, fax 781/861-0821, www.choicehotels.com; 204 rooms; $99). **✗ Restaurants:** None in park. In Concord: Liberty Restaurant at Concord's Colonial Inn (48 Monument Sq., tel. 978/369–2373, www.concordscolonialinn.com; $11–$17), Papa Razzi (768 Elm St., tel. 978/371-0030, www.paparazzitrattoria.com; $8–$16). In West Concord: Nashoba Brook Bakery and Cafe (152 Commonwealth Ave., tel. 978/318–1999, www.slowrise.com; $7–$8). **⚱ Groceries & Gear:** None in park. In West Concord: White Hen Pantry (1224 Main St., tel. 978/369–1434).

FEES, HOURS & REGULATIONS

Free. The Wayside: $5 adults, free ages 16 and under. No campfires or hunting. No horses or recreational vehicles on Battle Road Trail. Leashed dogs only. North Bridge Visitor Center open Apr.–Oct., daily 9–5; Nov. and Dec., daily 9–4; Jan.–Mar., daily 11–3. Minute Man Visitor Center open late March–Oct., daily 9–5; Nov., daily 9-4; closed Dec.-late Mar. The Wayside open late May-Oct., Weds.-Sun., daily 9:30-5:30; guided tours May–Oct., Wed.–Sun. 10, 11, 1, 2, 3, 4:30; Sept., Fri.–Sun. 9:30–5:30. Hartwell Tavern open late May–Oct., daily 9:30–5:30. Battle Road Trail open daily sunrise–sunset.

HOW TO GET THERE

The park stretches between the towns of Lexington and Concord, along Rte. 2A and Lexington Rd. From I–95, take Exit 30B to Minute Man Visitor Center on Rte. 2A in Lexington. Closest airports: Boston (22 miles), Manchester, NH (40 miles).

CONTACTS

Minute Man National Historical Park (174 Liberty St., Concord, MA 01742, tel. 978/369–6993, fax 978/318–7800, www.nps.gov/mima). Concord Chamber of Commerce (15 Walden St., Suite 7, Concord, MA 01742, tel. 978/369–3120, www.concordchamberofcommerce.org). Concord Visitor Center (58 Main St., Concord, MA, tel. 978/369–3120).

New Bedford Whaling National Historical Park

In southeastern Massachusetts, in New Bedford

This site commemorating whaling and its effect on American history is unique in the National Park System. The 13-block, 34-acre National Historic Landmark District is home to such intriguing sights as the working waterfront, the Seamen's Bethel, and the 1894 schooner *Ernestina*. The New Bedford Whaling Museum brings northeastern whaling and seafaring traditions to life while showing their importance to the region's economy. The Rotch-Jones-Duff House and Garden Museum are also open for viewing. The park was authorized on November 12, 1996.

WHAT TO SEE & DO

Touring historic district. **Facilities:** Visitor center, living-history exhibits, museums, movie. **Programs & Events:** Guided and self-guided tours (seasonally), walking tours of historic district (July and Aug., daily), evening concerts (Thurs. 6:30), maritime craft demonstrations (July and Aug., Sat. noon–2). Art, History, and Architecture night (2nd Thurs. monthly, 5–9). **Tips & Hints:** Plan to stay a full day. Elm St. Garage one block from visitor center. Busiest July and Aug., least crowded Jan. and Feb.

FOOD, LODGING & SUPPLIES

Hotels: In New Bedford: Fairfield Inn & Suites (185 MacArthur Dr., tel. 774/634–2000, fax 774/634–2001, www.marriott.com; 82 rooms, 24 suites; $179–$219). In Fall River/Westport: Hampton Inn (53 Old Bedford Rd., tel. 508/675–8500, fax 508/675–0075, www.hamptoninn.com; 133 rooms; $179–$199). ✗ **Restaurants:** In New Bedford: Freestone's City Grill (41 William St., tel. 508/993–7477, www.freestonescitygrill.com; $7–$10), No Problemo (813 Purchase St., tel. 508/984–1081, www.noproblemotaqueria.com; $5–$7). Davy's Locker (1480 E. Rodney French Blvd., tel. 508/992–7359, www.davyslockerrestaurant.com; $5–$12).

FEES & HOURS

Free. Rotch-Jones-Duff House and Garden Museum: $6 adults, $5 students and ages 65 and over, $3 ages 4–12, free ages 3 and under. New Bedford Whaling Museum: $14 adults, $12 ages 59 and over, $9 for students with ID, $6 ages 6–14, free ages 5 and under. Visitor center open daily 9–5 (9–9 2nd Thurs. of each month).

HOW TO GET THERE

In New Bedford, 30 miles east of Providence, RI, via I–195 (take Exit 15, drive 1 mile to the downtown exit, turn right on Elm St. and right into Elm St. parking garage; 20 miles west of Cape Cod via I–195; 50 miles south of Boston via I–93 to Rte. 24 to Rte. 140. Closest airports: New Bedford (4 miles), Warwick, RI (40 miles), Boston (60 miles).

CONTACTS

New Bedford Whaling National Historical Park (33 William St., New Bedford, MA 02740, tel. 508/996–4095, fax 508/984–1250, www.nps.gov/nebe). *Ernestina* schooner (New Bedford State Pier, Box 2010, New Bedford, MA 02741-2010, tel. 508/992–4900, www.ernestina.org). New Bedford Whaling Museum (Old Dartmouth Historical Society, 18 Johnny Cake Hill, New Bedford, MA 02740, tel. 508/997–0046, www.whalingmuseum.org). Rotch-Jones-Duff House and Garden Museum (396 County St., New Bedford, MA 02740, tel. 508/997–1401, www.rjdmuseum.org). Seamen's Bethel (New Bedford Port Society, 15 Johnny Cake Hill, New Bedford, MA 02740, tel. 508/992–3295, www.portsociety.org). New Bedford Office of Tourism (133 William St., New Bedford, MA 02740, tel. 508/979–1400, www.newbedford-ma.gov).

Salem Maritime National Historic Site

In northeastern Massachusetts, in Salem

The port town of Salem was a major northeast trading point for early America, and this historic park restores the exciting days when creaky wooden schooners cruised up to the docks beneath billowing sails. Bounding the water are authentic 18th- and 19th-century wharves, where such buildings as the Custom House, the West India Goods Store, and the 17th-century Narbonne House are open for exploration. The Public Stores are stocked with sundries of the times, and the home of 18th-century merchant E.H. Derby shows off the lavish tastes of the era's top traders. You can also tour the *Friendship,* the North Shore's tallest Tall Ship, a full-size replica of a 342-ton merchant ship built in Salem in 1797. The site was designated on March 17, 1938.

WHAT TO SEE & DO

Touring the wharves, historic buildings, neighborhoods, and 18th-century merchant sailing ship, visiting 18th-century garden. **Facilities:** Visitor center (2 New Liberty St.), orientation center (193 Derby St.). Bookstores. **Programs & Events:** Guided and self-guided tours year-round. Salem Maritime Festival (July–early Aug.). **Tips & Hints:** Allow a full day for Salem, and at least another to see historic and cultural attractions of Essex County. Busiest July and Oct., least crowded Jan. and Feb.

FEES & HOURS

Free. Ranger-led historic tours: $5 adults, $3 ages 6–16 and 62 and over, free ages 5 and under. Site open daily 9–5. Street and garage parking is available, as is public transportation.

HOW TO GET THERE

In Salem, 15 miles north of Boston via Rte. 128 north to Rte. 114 east; via Newburyport–Rockport Commuter Line train from Boston's North Station; via Bus 455 or 450 from Boston's Haymarket Square or South Station to Salem rail depot. From Boston's Logan International Airport, take Rte. 1A north. Closest airport: Boston (17 miles).

CONTACTS

Salem Maritime National Historic Site (193 Derby St., Salem, MA 01970, tel. 978/740–1650, www.nps.gov/sama.

Saugus Iron Works National Historic Site

In northeastern Massachusetts, in Saugus

This open-air park along the Saugus River is the site of the first integrated ironworks in North America. In use from 1646 to 1668, the complex houses the reconstructed blast furnace, a forge, a rolling mill, a blacksmith shop, and a restored 17th-century dwelling. The museum, which sits on a ridge above the river in a tidal basin, has working waterwheels and machinery. The park was authorized on April 5, 1968.

WHAT TO SEE & DO

Touring museum, historic house, and industrial site; walking nature trail. **Facilities:** Visitor center, museum, movie, hiking trail. Book and map sales. **Programs & Events:** Ranger-led tours (Apr.–Oct.), self-guided tours, occasional evening concerts and movies (July–Aug.). Saugus Founder's Day (Sept.). **Tips & Hints:** Plan to spend two hours. Busiest June–Aug., least crowded Apr. and Oct.

FEES & HOURS

Free. Site open Apr.–Oct., daily 9–5.

HOW TO GET THERE

10 miles south of Salem and 10 miles north of Boston via I–95 or U.S. 1 to Exit 43–Walnut St. (drive east toward the town of Lynn and follow signs to park), or via U.S. 1 to Main St. Saugus exit. Closest airport: Boston (10 miles).

CONTACT

Saugus Iron Works National Historic Site (244 Central St., Saugus, MA 01906, tel. 781/233–0050, fax 781/231–7345, www.nps.gov/sair).

Springfield Armory National Historic Site

In western Massachusetts, in Springfield

The nation's first national armory, authorized by President George Washington, was created here in 1794. Fifty-five acres are dotted with original armory buildings, as well as a museum that maintains one of the world's most extensive and unique collections of small firearms. Also on exhibit are examples of the largest collection of experimental and standard military arms in the United States. Displays depict weapons manufacturing processes, with details about their inventors and the women who worked here. The site was authorized in 1974 and established in 1978.

WHAT TO SEE & DO

Touring the museum and grounds. **Facilities:** Information booth, indoor interpretive exhibits, museum. Bookstore. **Programs & Events:** Ranger talks, film and video presentations, self-guided tours; exhibits year-round. National Park Week (late Apr.), Military Encampment (June). **Tips & Hints:** Go in fall to view the foliage. Busiest June–Aug., least crowded Dec. and Jan.

FEES, HOURS & REGULATIONS

Free. Leashed pets outside only. Site and museum open year-round, daily 9–5.

HOW TO GET THERE

In Springfield via I–91, take Broad St. exit to Technical Community College campus on corner of State and Federal Sts. Closest airport: Windsor Locks, CT (17 miles).

CONTACTS

Springfield Armory National Historic Site (1 Armory Sq., Suite 2, Springfield, MA 01105-1299, tel. 413/734–8551, fax 413/747–8062, www.nps.gov/spar). Greater Springfield Convention & Visitors Bureau (1441 Main St., Springfield, MA 01103, tel. 413/787–1548 or 800/723–1548, fax 413/781-4607, www.valleyvisitor.com).

See Also

Appalachian National Scenic Trail, West Virginia. *Blackstone River Valley National Heritage Corridor and Essex National Heritage Area,* in Other National Parklands.

MICHIGAN

Isle Royale National Park

*In Lake Superior, near the Michigan–Minnesota and
United States–Canada borders*

Isle Royale is actually an archipelago of more than 200 islands, all of
which are clustered around one huge chunk of forested wilderness.
Measuring 9 miles by 45 miles, this central island is the largest in Lake
Superior, and it's home to a variety of wildlife. Moose may have found
the island by swimming here in the early 1900s, and wolves probably arrived here by crossing a rare ice bridge from Canada in the late
1940s. Although sightings of these animals are special events, there are
many other mammals and birds commonly found along the park trails.

Visitor centers at Windigo and Rock Harbor have informative staff,
and the Edisen Fishery, Rock Harbor Lighthouse, and McCargoe
Cove are also on-site. The park was authorized in 1931 and designated
a Biosphere Reserve in 1980.

WHAT TO SEE & DO

Backpacking, boat cruising, canoeing (rentals in park), diving (charters available), hiking, kayaking, powerboating (rentals in park), sailing.
Facilities: 3 visitor centers: Houghton (800 E. Lakeshore Dr.), Rock
Harbor (northeast section of park), and Windigo (southwest section of
park); outdoor interpretive exhibits, hiking trails. Book and map sales,
picnic tables. **Programs & Events:** Guided tours, evening programs at
Rock Harbor and Windigo, interpretive program at Daisy Farm (twice
weekly), daily guided walks and dockside talks at Windigo and Rock
Harbor, living-history fishing demonstration at Edisen Fishery (twice
weekly): all available mid-June–Labor Day. **Tips & Hints:** Come prepared for variable weather, which tends to be cool and wet Apr.–early
June and Sept.–Oct. Go June–Aug. for flowers, May and Sept. for
migrating birds. Bring repellent, netting, long-sleeve shirts, and long
pants to avoid bites from mosquitoes, flies, gnats, and other insects.
Busiest July and Aug., least crowded in May and Oct.

FOOD, LODGING & SUPPLIES

Camping: In the park: 36 campgrounds with 112 sites and 50
shelters scattered throughout the park (free; pit toilets; closed Nov.–
mid-Apr.). Backcountry camping allowed. Rock Harbor Marina has
electrical hookups and boat pump-out. In Grand Portage, MN: Grand
Portage Marina & Campground (Marina Rd., adjacent to Grand Portage Lodge, tel. 218/475–2476, www.grandportage.com; 29 RV sites,
tent camping area; $15–$30; flush toilets, showers, hookups; closed
Nov.–Apr.). **Hotels:** In the park: Rock Harbor Lodge (tel. 906/337–
4993, 866/644–2003 in winter; 60 rooms, 20 cabins; $200–$300; closed
early Sept.–late May). In Copper Harbor, MI: Keeweenaw Mountain

Lodge (U.S. 41, tel. 906/289-4403, www.atthelodge.com; 8 rooms, 24 cottages, $95–$129; closed mid-Oct.–mid-May). In Grand Portage, MN: Grand Portage Lodge & Casino (off U.S. 61, tel. 218/475–2401 or 800/543-1384, www.grandportage.com; 100 rooms; $95–$115). In Hancock, MI: Ramada Hancock (99 Navy St., tel. 906/482-8400, www. ramadahancock.com; 51 rooms; $90). In Houghton, MI: Country Inn & Suites (919 Razorback Dr., tel. 906/487-6700 or 800/830–5222, www.countryinns.com; 75 rooms, 23 suites; $129–$139). ✘ **Restaurants:** In the park: Rock Harbor Complex (tel. 906/337–4993; $8–$16; closed early Sept.–late May). In Copper Harbor, MI: Mariner North (245 Gratiot St., tel. 906/289-4637, www.manorth.com; $8–$12; closed weekdays Nov. and Apr.). In Houghton, MI: Suomi Restaurant (54 Huron St., tel. 906/482–3220; $4–$7). ♨ **Groceries & Gear:** None in park. In Houghton, MI: Econofoods (1000 W. Sharon Ave., tel. 906/ 295–4558).

FEES, HOURS & REGULATIONS

User fee: $4 adults, free ages 11 and under. Park access summer only via ferry service, floatplane, or private boat. Private boats can access the island mid-Apr.–late Oct. Public transportation to island available mid-May–mid-Oct. from Grand Portage, MN (tel. 651/ 653–5872), Houghton (tel. 906/482–0984), and Copper Harbor (tel. 906/289–4437). Seaplane service available from Houghton (tel. 906/ 482–0984). Camping permits (free from Windigo and Rock Harbor and Houghton visitor centers) required for all camping and boating. Motorboat permits ($4 per person, per day). Houghton Visitor Center open mid-June–late Aug., Mon.–Sat. 8–6; Sept.–mid-June, weekdays 8–4:30. Rock Harbor Visitor Center open June–Labor Day, daily 8–8; intermittently Apr.–May and Labor Day–Oct. Windigo Visitor Center open June–Labor Day, daily 8–6; intermittently Apr.–May and Labor Day–Oct.

HOW TO GET THERE

Via ferry: 22 miles east of Grand Portage, MN; 56 miles northwest of Copper Harbor; and 73 miles north of Houghton. Closest airport: Houghton–Hancock (10 miles from downtown).

CONTACTS

Isle Royale National Park (800 E. Lakeshore Dr., Houghton, MI 49931, tel. 906/482–0984, fax 906/487–7170, www.nps.gov/isro). Keweenaw Convention & Visitors Bureau (56638 Calumet Ave., Calumet, MI 49913, tel. 906/337–4579 or 800/338–7982, www.keweenaw.info).

Keweenaw National Historical Park

Upper Peninsula of Michigan, in Calumet

Copper mining has taken place on the Keweenaw Peninsula for 7,000 years, and many of the processes developed within these parklands were fundamental to the success of mining in the United States. Here, 1,870 acres of private land are split into two units: Quincy, home of the world's largest steam hoist, and Calumet, home of one of the most productive copper mines in world history. In addition to self-guided historic tours, there are scenic drives, hiking trails, and ski and snowmobile tracks for exploring. A trackless trolley makes stops around the Calumet unit, and tour boats ply the Keweenaw waterway in summer. The park was established on October 27, 1992.

WHAT TO SEE & DO

Bicycling; cross-country skiing; hiking; mountain biking; snowmobiling; touring fort, mines, museums, and historic buildings. **Facilities:** National Park Visitor Center and Museum (Calumet) with three floors of exhibits, park information desk at Quincy Mine site, outdoor interpretive exhibits, museum, hiking trails. **Programs & Events:** Ranger-led tours, self-guided tours. **Tips & Hints:** Go early in day July and Aug. to buy tickets for Quincy mine tour. Plan to spend three days to visit all cooperating sites. Go late Sept.–early Oct. for fall foliage. Expect snow between Thanksgiving and Easter. Busiest July and Aug., least crowded Jan. and Feb.

FOOD, LODGING & SUPPLIES

Camping: None at site. In Hancock: Hancock Recreation Area Beach and Campground (Rte. 203, tel. 906/482–7413, www. cityofhancock.com; 56 RV sites, 15 tent sites; $14–$22; flush toilets, showers, hookups; closed Nov.–May 1). Backcountry camping in Porcupine Mountains. **Hotels:** None in park. In Calumet: AmericInn Lodge & Suites (56925 S. 6th St., tel. 906/337–6463 or 800/ 634–3444, www.americinn.com; 67 rooms, 15 suites; $95), Arcadian Acres Motel (51950 U.S. 41, tel. 906/482–0288; 13 rooms; $49–$55). **Restaurants:** None in park. In Calumet: The Hut Inn (58540 Wolverine St./U.S. 41, tel. 906/337–1133, www.hutinn.com; $5–$10; closed Mon.), Jim's Pizza & Family Restaurant (117 6th St., tel. 906/ 337–4440; $4–$9), Michigan House (300 6th St., tel. 906/337–1910, www.michiganhousecafe.com; $5–$11). **Groceries & Gear:** None in park. In Houghton: Down Wind Sports (308 Sheldon Ave., tel. 906/ 482–2500). In Hancock: Keweenaw Co-Op Natural Foods & Groceries (1035 Ethel Ave., tel. 906/482–2030).

FEES, HOURS & REGULATIONS

Free. Entrance fees to individual sites vary. Quincy mine and hoist tour: $15 adults, $8 ages 6–12, free ages 5 and under. Permit required for backcountry camping at Porcupine Mountains Wilderness state park ($14 per night, tel. 906/885–5275). Motor vehicle pass ($8 daily, $29 annually) required for Fort Wilkins Historic State Park and Porcupine Mountains Wilderness.

HOW TO GET THERE

Quincy: 1 mile north of Hancock via U.S. 41; Calumet: 8 miles north of Quincy via U.S. 41. Directions available from Keweenaw Tourism Council. Closest airport: Houghton (6 miles).

CONTACTS

Keweenaw National Historical Park (25970 Red Jacket Rd., Calumet, MI 49913, tel. 906/483–3176, fax 906/337–3169, www.nps.gov/kewe). Keweenaw Convention & Visitors Bureau (56638 Calumet Ave., Calumet, MI 49913, tel. 906/337–4579 or 800/338–7982, www.keweenaw. info). Upper Peninsula Travel and Recreation Association (Box 400, Iron Mountain, MI 49801, tel. 906/774–5480 or 800/562–7134, www. uptravel.com).

Pictured Rocks
National Lakeshore

Upper Michigan, between Munising and Grand Marais

Only 5 miles across at its widest point, this 73,236-acre park hugs the Lake Superior shoreline for 40 miles and shows off some of Michigan's most attractive landscapes. Multicolored sandstone cliffs, rocky beaches, and gently sloping sand dunes decorate the park's fringes, and the inland areas are filled out by thundering waterfalls, placid lakes, and northern hardwood forests that shelter a multitude of animal species. The lakeshore was authorized on October 15, 1966.

WHAT TO SEE & DO

Backpacking, boating, canoeing, cross-country skiing, fishing, hiking, hunting, ice fishing, kayaking, picnicking, snowmobiling, snowshoeing, wildlife-watching. **Facilities:** 4 visitor centers: Pictured Rocks National Lakeshore (Hiawatha National Forest, 400 E. Munising Ave., junction of Rte. 28 and Rte. 58, Munising), Grand Sable Visitor Center (E21090 Rte. 58, 1 mile west of Grand Marais), Munising Falls Visitor Center (1505 Sand Point Rd., Munising), and Miners Castle Information Station (N9310 Miners Castle Rd., near Munising); information kiosk, interpretive exhibits, hiking trails. Bookstores, picnic tables with fire grills. **Programs & Events:** Guided and self-guided tours, Au Sable Light Station tours (July–Labor Day, Tues.–Sun.; $3 per adult, under 6 free), Artist-in-Residence public programs (generally two weeks in fall). **Tips & Hints:** Expect summer highs near 90°F, with much cooler evenings and below-freezing temperatures in winter. Watch for Lake Superior storms year-round. Bring layered clothing and rain gear. Use caution when hiking cliff trails and while swimming, wading, or boating. Bring insect repellent in late spring or early summer, when black flies and mosquitoes are out in force. Busiest July and Aug., least crowded Oct.–May.

FOOD, LODGING & SUPPLIES

⚠ **Camping:** 3 campgrounds ($14-$16; pit toilets) in the park: Hurricane River (21 sites; closed Nov.–mid-May), Little Beaver Lake (8 sites; closed Nov.–mid-May), Twelvemile Beach (36 sites; closed Nov.–mid-May). Backcountry camping allowed. In Munising: Wandering Wheels Campground (E10160 Rte. 28 E, tel. 906/387–3315, www.wanderingwheelscampground.net; 215 sites; $22–$35; flush toilets, showers, hookups; closed mid-May–mid-Oct.). 🏨 **Hotels:** None in park. In Munising: Cherrywood Lodge of Munising (E10160 Hwy. M28 E, tel. 906/387–4864 or 855/255–1901, www. cherrywoodlodgemunising.com; 80 rooms; $89). In Grand Marais: Voyageurs Motel (20914 E. Wilson St., tel. 906/494–2389, voyageursmotel.grandmaraismichigan.com; 10 rooms; $95). ✕ **Restaurants:** None in park. In Au Train: Brownstone Inn (E4635 Rte. 28, tel. 906/892–8332, www.brownstoneinn.net; $5–$14; closed 1st 2 weeks in Nov. and Mon. from Labor Day to Memorial Day). In Grand Marais: West Bay Diner & Delicatessen (corner of Veterans and Woodruff Sts., tel. 906/494–2607; $4–$12). ♿ **Groceries & Gear:** None in park. In Munising: Bob's IGA (131 W. Superior St., tel. 906/387–4073).

FEES, HOURS & REGULATIONS

Free. Backcountry permit ($5 per person per night) required for backcountry camping. Backcountry advanced reservation fee: $15. Reservations by fax or mail only (Box 40, Munising, MI 49862-0040, fax 906/387–4457). Drive-in camping fee: $14 per night at Hurricane River and Little Beaver Lake, $16 per night for lakeside sites at Twelvemile Beach. Michigan state hunting and fishing license ($7 for one day fishing, $15 for seasonal hunting. Daily summer boat tours of park (late May–mid-Oct., tel. 906/387–2379) depart from Munising. Altran runs summer backpacker shuttle service (reservation required, tel. 906/387–4845; $20 per person, $75 groups of 4; Mon., Thurs., Sat. runs). No motorized or wheeled vehicles, pets, or domestic pack animals in backcountry. Leashed pets only in day-use areas and drive-in campgrounds. No hunting Apr.–Labor Day. No hunting in visitor-use areas. Park open daily. Park headquarters open weekdays 8–4:30. Munising Interagency Visitor Center open daily 9–4:30, Memorial Day–Labor Day, daily 8–6. Grand Sable Visitor Center open Memorial Day–Labor Day, daily 9–5. Miners Castle Information Station and Munising Falls open Memorial Day–Labor Day, daily 9–5:30.

HOW TO GET THERE

Via Rte. 58 between Munising and Grand Marais; reach Munising via Rte. 28 and Grand Marais via Rte. 77. Closest airports: Marquette (55 miles), Escanaba (65 miles).

CONTACTS

Pictured Rocks National Lakeshore (Box 40, N8391 Sand Point Rd., Munising, MI 49862-0040, tel. 906/387–3700 information; 906/387–2607 headquarters, www.nps.gov/piro). Alger County Chamber of Commerce (129 E. Munising Ave., Munising, MI 49862, tel. 906/387–2138, www.algercounty.org). Grand Marais Chamber of Commerce (Box 139, Grand Marais, MI 49839, tel. 906/494–2447, www.grandmaraismichigan.com).

River Raisin National Battlefield Park

In southeastern Lower Michigan, in the city of Monroe.

Perched on the western shoreline of Lake Erie, River Raisin is the site of the devastating January 1813 Battles of Frenchtown that occurred during the War of 1812. The battlefield illustrates the multinational struggle for supremacy in the old Northwest between the United States, Indian nations, and the British Empire. The combined forces of Tecumseh's Confederation of Native American peoples, aligned with British forces, demonstrated their strength by inflicting the largest number of United States combat fatalities of the war. The resulting rally cry "Remember the Raisin" spurred America's successful retaking of the Northwest Territories. River Raisin was declared a National Battlefield Park in October 2010.

WHAT TO SEE & DO

Scavenger hunts for youngsters, touring battlefield, viewing exhibits and map-light show at visitor center depicting sites of battles. **Facilities:** Visitor center; interpretive, hiking, and biking trails. Gift shop, picnic areas. **Programs & Events:** River Raisin Heritage Trail Visa program takes hikers and bicyclists on a 9-mile adventure through the battlefield, the town of Monroe, and Sterling State Park; ranger-guided tours and programs upon request, living-history demonstrations and reenactment of battle (Sat. closest to anniversary of attack Jan. 22, 1813); open house with special programming and children's games (mid-May). **Tips & Hints:** Check out the wonderful woodlands picnic area and pavilion. Visit during the week for smaller crowds, June–Oct. for best weather. Busiest June and July, least crowded Dec.–Feb.

FOOD & LODGING

Camping: None in park. In Monroe: Sterling State Park (2800 State Park Rd., Monroe, MI 48162, tel. 734/289-2715, reservations 800/447-2757; 256 sites; $24–$33; flush toilets, showers, hookups). **Hotels:** None in park. In Monroe: Hampton Inn (1565 N. Dixie Hwy., tel. 734/289-5700, www.hamptoninn.com; 74 rooms; $99–$130). **Restaurants:** None in park. In Monroe: Michigan Bar & Grill (40 S. Monroe St., tel. 734/243-6690; $10–$29. Joe's French-Italian (2896 N. Dixie Hwy., tel. 734/289-2800, www.joesfrenchitalian.com; $8–$19).

FEES, HOURS & REGULATIONS

Free. Visitor center open daily 10–5. Visitors must remain on marked trails. No prospecting for artifacts.

HOW TO GET THERE

From the south, take I–75 to Exit 14 and travel west into Monroe. Closest airport: Detroit (20 miles).

CONTACTS

River Raisin National Battlefield Park (1403 E. Elm Ave., Monroe, MI 48162, tel. 734/243–7136, fax 734/244–5501, www.nps.gov/rira). Monroe County Chamber of Commerce (1645 N. Dixie Hwy. 2, Monroe, MI 48162, tel. 734/384-3366, www.monroemi.usachamber.com).

Sleeping Bear Dunes National Lakeshore

Northwestern lower Michigan, near Empire

Massive sand dunes rise like smooth mountains above the Lake Michigan coasts here, protecting 35 miles of shoreline and edging acres of gorgeous inland terrain. Beech-maple forests shimmer with light in the summer, and months later their cheery autumn hues are reflected in dozens of clear lakes and quiet rivers. Grassy bluffs rise up to 460 feet, providing sweeping views of Lake Michigan's two offshore wilderness islands, as well as a wetland environment filled with birds and mammals. The area's history is showcased at the Boat Museum and the Maritime Museum in Glen Haven; a cannery is also open for touring. The park was authorized in 1970 and established in 1977.

WHAT TO SEE & DO

Apple and mushroom picking, bicycling, bird-watching, canoeing (rentals in and near park), cross-country skiing (rentals in Traverse City), dune climbing, fishing, hang gliding, hunting, picnicking, scenic drives, scuba diving (rentals in Traverse City), snowshoeing (rentals in Glen Arbor, Traverse City), swimming, tubing (rentals in and near park), walking beaches. **Facilities:** 2 visitor centers: Empire (9922 Front St.) and South Manitou Island; 2 museums, outdoor interpretive exhibits, hiking trails. Covered picnic tables with fire grills. **Programs & Events:** Guided walks and campfire programs (late June–Labor Day), snowshoe hikes (Dec.–Mar., weekends), lyle-gun firing (mid-June–Labor Day, weekly). Special events (Apr–mid-Sept.). **Tips & Hints:** Expect summer highs near 90°F with much cooler evenings, and below-freezing temperatures in winter. Bring layered clothing and rain gear. Use caution when hiking trails near sand cliffs. Bring insect repellent in warmer months to combat black flies and mosquitoes. No food or lodging available on islands. Make ferry reservations in advance for travel to the Manitou Islands. Busiest July and Aug., least crowded Nov.–Apr.

FOOD, LODGING & SUPPLIES

Camping: In the park: D.H. Day (87 sites; $12; vault toilets; closed late Nov.–early Apr.), Platte River (tel. 231/325–5881; 179 sites; $16–$24; flush toilets, showers, some hookups). Backcountry camping ($5 per night up to 4 people) available at Valley View, White Pine, and on North and South Manitou islands. **Hotels:** None in park. In Thompsonville: Crystal Mountain Resort & Spa (12500 Crystal Mountain Dr., tel. 231/378–2000 or 800/968–7686, www.crystalmountain.com; 180

rooms, 181 suites; $179-$189). In Frankfort: Harbor Lights Resort (15 2nd St., tel. 231/352–9614 or 800/346–9614; 75 rooms; $119–$145). ✕ **Restaurants:** In Glen Arbor: Western Avenue Bar and Grill (6410 Western Ave., tel. 231/334–3362, www.tcgrills.com; $7–$15). ⚑ **Groceries & Gear:** None in park. In Empire: Deering's Food Market (10233 Front St., tel. 231/326–5249).

FEES, HOURS & REGULATIONS

$5 per person on foot, bicycle, or motorcycle; $10 per vehicle. Permits required for all ($5–$23) backcountry campers. Summer: Obtain Valley View permit from D.H. Day, obtain White Pine permit from Platte River. Permit required (free) for hang gliding and nonpowered-model flying. Ferries $35 round-trip adults, $20 round-trip ages 12 and under. Michigan state fishing and hunting licenses ($7–$14 per day) required. Stay on established trails, especially on dunes. No pets on Dune Climb, islands, swim beaches, or ski trails. Leashed pets elsewhere. No boat motors on most inland lakes. No glass on beaches. Park open daily. Philip A. Hart Visitor Center in Empire open Memorial Day–Labor Day, daily 8–6; Labor Day–Memorial Day, daily 8:15–4. South Manitou Island Visitor Center open Memorial Day–Labor Day, when rangers are available. Scenic drive open mid-Apr.–mid-Nov. Maritime Museum buildings open Memorial Day–Labor Day, daily 11–5; Labor Day–mid-Oct., weekends with varying hours. Manitou Islands ferry runs from Leland May–Oct.

HOW TO GET THERE

25 miles north of Frankfort via Rte. 22, and 25 miles west of Traverse City via Rte. 72. Closest airport: Traverse City (30 miles).

CONTACTS

Sleeping Bear Dunes National Lakeshore (9922 Front St., Empire, MI 49630, tel. 231/326-5134, fax 231/326–5382, www.nps.gov/slbe). Manitou Island Transit (tel. 231/256–9061, fax 231/256–2352, www.manitoutransit.com). Benzie County Chamber of Commerce & Visitors Bureau (826 Michigan Ave., Box 204, Benzonia, MI 49616, tel. 231/882–5801, fax 231/882–9249, www.benzie.org). Empire Chamber of Commerce (Box 65, Empire, MI 49630, www.empirechamber.com). Leelanau Peninsula Chamber of Commerce (5046 S. West Bay Shore Dr., Suite G, Suttons Bay, MI 49682, tel. 231/271–9895, fax 231/271–9896, www.leelanauchamber.com).

See Also

Automobile National Heritage Area and North Country National Scenic Trail, in Other National Parklands.

MINNESOTA

Grand Portage National Monument

In northeastern Minnesota

The partially reconstructed stockade area appears as it did in the 1790s, when it was the North West Company's fur-trading headquarters on Lake Superior's western shore. The 8½-mile portage was a vital link on one of the principal routes for Native Americans, explorers, missionaries, and fur trappers heading for the Northwest. It was part of the ancient Grand Portage Trail, which had been used for centuries before the fur traders arrived. Today, daily boat service runs to Isle Royale National Park in summer. The site was designated a national historic site in 1951 and became a national monument in 1958.

WHAT TO SEE & DO

Hiking, picnicking, snowshoeing, touring post. **Facilities:** Outdoor interpretive exhibits, movies, hiking trails. Bookstore, picnic tables, dock. **Programs & Events:** Interpretive talks, living-history demonstrations, cultural demonstrations, daily boat trips to Isle Royale National Park in Michigan (mid-June–Labor Day); see separate entry. Grand Portage Rendezvous and Grand Portage Pow Wow (both 2nd full weekend, Aug.). **Tips & Hints:** Visit mid-June–mid-Sept. for most activities and services. Busiest July and Aug., least crowded Jan. and Feb.

FOOD, LODGING & SUPPLIES

Camping: In the park: 2 backcountry sites at Fort Charlotte (free; pit toilets). In Grand Portage: Grand Portage Marina & Campground (Marina Rd., adjacent to Grand Portage Lodge & Casino, tel. 218/475-2476, www.grandportage.com; 29 RV sites, tent camping area; $15–$30; flush toilets, showers, hookups; closed Nov.–Apr.). **Hotels:** None in park. In Grand Marais: Best Western Plus Superior Inn & Suites (104 ist Ave./U.S. 61 E, tel. 218/387–2240 or 800/780–7234, www.bestwesternminnesota.com; 66 rooms; $130–$190). In Grand Portage: Grand Portage Lodge & Casino (U.S. 61, tel. 218/475–2401 or 800/543–1384, www.grandportage.com; 100 rooms; $95–$115), Ryden's Border Store, Cafe & Hotel (9301 Ryden Rd., tel. 218/475–2330; 4 rooms; $46; closed mid-Oct.–Apr.). **Restaurants:** None in park. In Grand Portage: Island View Dining (Grand Portage Lodge, U.S. 61, tel. 218/475–2401; $6–$12), Ryden's Border Store, Cafe & Hotel (9301 Ryden Rd., tel. 218/475-2330; $5–$10; closed mid-Oct.–mid-Mar.). **Groceries & Gear:** None in park. In Grand Marais: Cook County Whole Foods Co-Op (20 E. 1st St., tel. 218/387–2503).

FEES, HOURS & REGULATIONS

Entrance fee: Free. Parking fee at marina: $3 to leave car while visiting Isle Royale. Backcountry camping permits (free at trailheads and Grand Portage Heritage Center) required. No hunting. No motorized vehicles or bikes on trail. Leashed pets only on trail. No pets in buildings or within stockade. Heritage Center and Historic Depot open daily, dawn–dusk. Park facilities open Memorial Day–mid-Oct., daily 9–5.

HOW TO GET THERE

36 miles northeast of Grand Marais via U.S. 61. Closest airports: Thunder Bay, Canada (45 miles), Duluth, MN (156 miles).

CONTACTS

Grand Portage National Monument (Headquarters: 170 Mile Creek Rd., Grand Portage, MN 55604, tel. 218/475–0123 or 218/475–0174; Site: Box 426, 211 Mile Creek Rd., Grand Portage, MN 55605, www.nps.gov/grpo). Grand Marais Area Tourism Association (13 N. Broadway Ave., Box 1048, Grand Marais, MN 55604, tel. 218/387-2524 or 888/922–5000, www.grandmarais.com).

Mississippi National River & Recreation Area

In the Minneapolis–St. Paul area, from Dayton and Ramsey to Hastings

Museums, cultural centers, and natural and historical attractions stretch along 72 miles of the Mississippi River corridor, representing the dynamic history of the great, 2,350-mile-long waterway. Twenty-five communities are settled along this 54,000-acre section of river, each unique in its attractions, which range from quiet rural parks to bustling metropolitan riverfronts. Numerous exhibits and museums are points of interest in each town, notably the Minnesota History Center and the Science Museum of Minnesota in St. Paul, the Sibley House Historic Site in Mendota, and the Mill City Museum in Minneapolis. The area was established on November 18, 1988.

WHAT TO SEE & DO

Bicycling, boating, paddle boat touring, canoeing, cross-country skiing, fishing, guided and self-guided tours, hiking, paddling, and picnicking. **Facilities:** 6 visitor centers: Mississippi River (lobby of Science Museum of Minnesota, St. Paul), Coon Rapids Dam East (9750 Egret Blvd., Coon Rapids), Coon Rapids Dam West (10360 W. River Rd., Brooklyn Park), Fort Snelling State Park (1 Post Rd., St. Paul), North Mississippi Regional Park (4900 Mississippi Court, Minneapolis), Carpenter Nature Center (12805 St. Croix Trail S, Hastings) museums, hiking trails. **Programs & Events:** Informational talks, museum events, interpretive centers, stewardship programs. **Tips & Hints:** Best time to visit, May–Oct. Least crowded Dec.–Mar., when river typically freezes.

FOOD, LODGING & SUPPLIES

🏕 **Camping:** None in park. In Coon Rapids: Bunker Hill Campground (Hwy. 242 and Foley Blvd., tel. 763/862-4970, www.anokacountyparks. com; 44 sites; $17–$25 plus $5 reservation fee; flush toilets, showers, some hookups; closed early Oct.–late May). 🏨 **Hotels:** None in the park. In St. Paul: Super 8 St. Paul (1739 Old Hudson Rd., tel. 651/ 771–5566 or 800/800-8000, www.staystpaul.com; 100 rooms; $84). In Hastings: AmericInn Lodge & Suites (2400 Vermillion St., tel. 651/ 437-8870 or 800/634–3444; 52 rooms; $80–$100). 🍴 Restaurants: None in park. In Coon Rapids: Harvest Grill (12800 Bunker Prairie Rd., tel. 763/755–1234, www.harvestgrillmn.com; $6–$20). In Prescott, WI: Muddy Waters Bar and Grill (231 N. Broad St., tel. 715/262-5999, www.muddywatersbarandgrill.biz; $7-$12). ♿ **Groceries & Gear:** None in park. In Hastings: Coborns (225 33rd St. W, tel. 651/437–2066).

FEES, HOURS & REGULATIONS

Free. Fees to enter two parks in corridor: Coon Rapids Dam East ($5) and Fort Snelling State Park ($5). Pay to park required in certain areas. Minnesota fishing license ($8.50 for one day) required. Area open daily 24 hours. Mississippi River Visitor Center open early June–Aug., Sun.–Thurs. 9:30–5, Fri. and Sat. 9:30–9; early Sept.–early June, Sun. and Tues.–Thurs. 9:30–5, Fri. and Sat. 9:30–9. Closed one week in early Sept.; shorter hours on some holidays. Other visitor center hours vary by site.

HOW TO GET THERE

The park covers a 72-mile stretch of the Mississippi River from Dayton and Ramsey, through the Minneapolis–St. Paul metro region, to south of Hastings. Closest airport: Minneapolis–St. Paul (10 miles).

CONTACTS

Mississippi National River & Recreation Area (111 Kellogg Blvd. E, Suite 105, St. Paul, MN 55101, 651/290–4160, fax 651/290–3214, www. nps.gov/miss). Mississippi River Visitor Center: Science Museum of Minnesota, 120 W. Kellogg Blvd., St. Paul, MN 55102, tel. 651/293–0200). East Coon Rapids Dam (9750 Egret Blvd., Coon Rapids, MN 55433, tel. 763/757–4700, www.anokacountyparks.com). West Coon Rapids Dam (10360 West River Rd., Brooklyn Park, MN 55444, tel. 763/694–7790, www.threeriversparks.org). Fort Snelling State Park (1 Post Rd., St. Paul, MN 55111, tel. 612/725-2724, www.dnr.state. mn.us). North Mississippi Regional Park (5114 N. Mississippi Dr., Minneapolis, MN 55430, tel. 612/230–6400, www.minneapolisparks. org). Explore Minnesota Tourism (121 7th Pl. E, Metro Square Suite 100, St. Paul, MN 55101, tel. 651/296–5029 or 888/868–7476, www. exploreminnesota.com).

Pipestone National Monument

In southwestern Minnesota, near Pipestone

For centuries, Native Americans obtained stone from these lands to make pipes for ceremonial and social uses, and today the 282-acre site preserves the noted Pipestone Quarries in their natural prairie setting. The Pipestone Indian Shrine Association, which is headquartered at the monument, has locally made items on display and for sale. About 160 acres of the area are bluestem prairie, an important remnant of the once-abundant grasslands typical of the region. The monument was established in 1937.

WHAT TO SEE & DO

Hiking through prairie and quarries, picnicking, taking self-guided tour, touring museum, watching pipe-making and crafts demonstrations. **Facilities:** Visitor center, cultural center, interpretive exhibits, museum, movies, hiking trail. Picnic tables with fire grills. **Programs & Events:** Pipe-making and cultural demonstrations (Apr.–Oct.), ranger-led trail walks (June–Aug.). Founders Day (Aug. 25). **Tips & Hints:** Busiest July and Aug., least crowded Jan. and Feb.

FOOD, LODGING & SUPPLIES

Camping: None in park. In Pipestone: Pipestone RV Campground (919 N. Hiawatha Ave., tel. 507/825-2455, www.pipestonervcampground.com; 66 RV sites, 9 tent camping sites; $20–$32; flush toilets, showers, hookups; closed Nov.–mid-Apr.). Hotels: None in park. In Pipestone: Historic Calumet Inn (104 W. Main St., tel. 507/825–5871 or 800/535–7610, www.calumetinn.com; 40 rooms; $100). **Restaurants:** None in park. In Pipestone: Historic Calumet Restaurant (104 W. Main St., tel. 507/825–5871; $6–$8; no dinner Sun.). **Groceries & Gear:** None in park. In Pipestone: Coborn's (115 2nd Ave. NE, tel. 507/825–4201), Hank's Foods (504 7th St. SW, tel. 507/825–3652).

FEES, HOURS & REGULATIONS

Entrance fee: $3 per person, children 15 and under free. No hunting or fishing. Leashed pets only on trail. No bikes, skateboards, or in-line skates on trail. Park and trail open daily. Visitor center open daily 8–5.

HOW TO GET THERE

On the northern edge of Pipestone via U.S. 75 or Rtes. 23 or 30. Closest airport: Sioux Falls, SD (45 miles).

CONTACTS

Pipestone National Monument (36 N. Reservation Ave., Pipestone, MN 56164, tel. 507/825-5464 Ext. 214, fax 507/825–5466, www.nps.gov/pipe). Pipestone Area Chamber of Commerce (117 8th Ave. SE, Box 8, Pipestone, MN 56164, tel. 507/825–3316 or 800/336–6125, www.pipestoneminnesota.com).

Voyageurs National Park

In northeastern Minnesota, near International Falls

Water dominates the landscape of this 218,000-acre park, nearly half of which is covered with more than 30 glacier-carved lakes. It got its name from the French Canadian *voyageurs* (or "travelers"), who once plied these waters in birch-bark canoes on their way to trade furs, food, and medicine with the resident Indian tribes along the "voyageurs highway" that stretches from the Great Lakes into the interior of the Pacific Northwest. Although birch-bark canoes have essentially disappeared, the most popular park activities still include sailing, kayaking, and houseboating on lakes Rainy, Kabetogama, Namakan, and Sand Point. Bears roam the fragrant pine forests while eagles soar over the meadows by day; after dark, listen for loons and wolves. It's a place to explore scenic nature, learn about local geology, and step back into the fascinating history of the region's fur-trading economy. The park was authorized in 1971 and established in 1975.

WHAT TO SEE & DO

Canoeing, cross-country skiing, fishing, hiking, houseboating, kayaking, motorboating, picnicking, sailing, snowmobiling, snowshoeing. **Facilities:** 3 visitor centers: Rainy Lake (11 miles east of International Falls), Kabetogama Lake (9924 Gappa Rd.), and Ash River (9899 Meadwood Rd.); outdoor interpretive displays. Book and map sales, picnic tables with fire grills, docks. **Programs & Events:** Canoe trips, boat tours (daily mid-June–Sept.), Junior Ranger programs, Ice Box Days (International Falls, 3rd week in Jan.). **Tips & Hints:** Primary access to park, campsites, hotel, and restaurant by watercraft in summer and snowmobile in winter. Visitor centers and boat tours accessible by car. Go Jan. and Feb. for snowmobiling, year-round for fishing, June for wildflowers, May–Sept. for eagles, and mid-Sept. for fall color. Busiest July and Aug., least crowded Nov.–Apr.

FOOD, LODGING & SUPPLIES

Camping: In the park: 244 tent and houseboat sites throughout the park (free; pit toilets). In Bearhead Lake State Park: Woodenfrog Campground (off U.S. 169, tel. 218/365–7229, www.dnr.state.mn.us; 61 sites; $12; pit toilets). **Hotels:** In the park: Kettle Falls Hotel & Resort (tel. 218/240–1726 or 218/240–1724, www.kettlefallshotel.com; 12 rooms, 4 suites; $70; closed Oct.–Apr.). In International Falls: Days Inn (2331 U.S. 53 S, tel. 218/283-9441, www.daysinn.com; 57 rooms; $99), AmericInn hotel & Suites (1500 U.S. 71, tel. 218/283–4451 or 800/539–0036, www.americinn.com; 96 rooms, 7 suites; $100–$140). **Restaurants:** In the park: Kettle Falls Hotel & Resort (tel. 218/240–1726; $5–$14; closed Oct.–Apr.). **Groceries & Gear:** None in park. In Kabetogama: Gateway General Store (9378 Hwy. 53, tel. 218/875–2121). In International Falls: Loon's Nest (3552 Hwy. 11 E, tel. 218/286–5850), Outdoorsman Headquarters (1100 3rd Ave., tel. 218/283–9337).

FEES, HOURS & REGULATIONS

Entrance fee: Free. Tour boats (reservations recommended, tel. 877/444–6777, www.recreation.gov) $15–$50. Camping permit required (free). No personal watercraft. Minnesota state fishing license ($8.50 for one day) required. No hunting or trapping. No mountain bikes on trails. No off-road vehicles. Leashed pets in front country only. No pets on trails (except Oberholtzer Trail). Snowshoes (free) and cross-country ski equipment ($5 per day) available at Rainy Lake Visitor Center. Snowmobiles on main lakes and designated safety portages only. Park open daily. Main park inaccessible mid-Nov.–Dec. because of thin ice, Apr.–early May because of thaws. Rainy Lake Visitor Center open early May–early Sept., daily 9–5; mid-Sept.–Apr., Wed.–Sun. 9–4. Kabetogama Lake Visitor Center open mid-May–Sept., daily 9–5. Ash River Visitor Center open mid-May–Sept., Thurs.–Sun. 9–5.

HOW TO GET THERE

Rainy Lake Visitor Center is 11 miles east of International Falls via U.S. 53, 160 miles north of Duluth via U.S. 53., and 300 miles north of Minneapolis via I–35 and U.S. 53. Closest airport: International Falls (15 miles).

CONTACTS

Voyageurs National Park (360 Hwy. 11 E, International Falls, MN 56649, tel. 218/283–6600, www.nps.gov/voya). Ash River Trail Tourism (10418 Ash River Tr., Orr, MN 55771, tel. 800/950–2061, www.ashriver.com). Crane Lake Tourism Bureau (7238 Handberg Rd., Crane Lake, MN 55725, tel. 800/362–7405, www.visitcranelake.com). International Falls Convention and Visitors Bureau (301 2nd Ave., International Falls, MN 56649, tel. 800/325–5766, www.rainylake.org). Kabetogama Tourism Bureau (10124 Timber Wolf Tr., Lake Kabetogama, MN 56669, tel. 800/524–9085, www.kabetogama.com).

See Also

Saint Croix National Scenic Riverway, Wisconsin. *North Country National Scenic Trail,* in Other National Parklands.

MISSISSIPPI

Brices Cross Roads
National Battlefield Site

In northeastern Mississippi, near Baldwyn

Comprising just an acre of historic grounds, this memorial site commemorates a famous Civil War battle. On June 10, 1864, Confederate General Nathan Bedford Forrest won a tactical victory over a superior federal force, but was unsuccessful in achieving a more important objective: disrupting a key Union supply route. His victory at Brices Cross Roads went down in history as a prime example of winnning the battle but losing the war. The site was established in 1929 and transferred to the Park Service in 1933.

WHAT TO SEE & DO

Reading interpretive panels and commemorative granite marker, viewing battlefield and cannons. **Facilities:** Visitor center (mile 266, Tupelo), interpretive signs. **Programs & Events:** Visitor center. **Tips & Hints:** Informational folder available at the site or from Natchez Trace Parkway Visitor Center. Busiest Oct.–Apr., least crowded Dec. and Jan.

FOOD, LODGING & SUPPLIES

Camping: See Natchez Trace Parkway. In Tupelo: Campground at Barnes Crossing (125 Rd. 1698, tel. 662/844–6063, www.cgbarnescrossing.com; 54 RV sites; $32; flush toilets, showers, hookups). **Hotels:** None in park. In Tupelo: Comfort Inn (1190 N. Gloster St., tel. 662/842–5100 or 866/539–0036, www.comfortinn.com; 83 rooms; $109–$119), Holiday Inn Express & Suites (1612 McClure Dr., tel. 662/620–8184 or 877/859–5095, fax 662/620-8181, www.hiexpress.com; 101 rooms; $90–$99). **Restaurants:** None in park. In Baldwyn: Bumper's Drive-In (618 N. 4th St., tel. 662/365–8834, www.bumpersdrivein.com; $4–$8). In Saltillo: Bishop's Barbeque & Grill (2546 Hwy. 145 N, tel. 662/869–8351, www.bishopsbbqgrill.com; $4–$10). **Groceries & Gear:** None in park. In Baldwyn: Food Giant (218 Hwy. 45 N, tel. 662/365–7411). In Tupelo: Kroger (960 W. Main St., tel. 662/840–8448).

FEES & HOURS

Entrance fee: Free. Visitor center open daily 8–5.

HOW TO GET THERE

6 miles west of Baldwyn via Rte. 370. Closest airports: Memphis, TN (104 miles), Tupelo (20 miles).

CONTACTS

Brices Cross Roads National Battlefield Site, Natchez Trace Parkway, 2680 Natchez Trace Pkwy., Tupelo, MS 38804, tel. 662/680–4027, fax 662/680–4041, www.nps.gov/brcr).

Natchez National Historical Park

In southwestern Mississippi, in Natchez

One of the greatest collections of significant antebellum properties in the United States is found in Natchez, Mississippi. This park celebrates the history of the city, as well as its historic roles in the settlement of the old Southwest, the Cotton Kingdom, and the antebellum South. Here, the 18th-century Fort Rosalie was built by the French and later occupied by the British, Spanish, and Americans. The William Johnson House was the home of William Johnson, a free black man, whose diary tells the story of everyday life in antebellum Natchez. The Melrose Estate once belonged to John T. McMurran, who rose from being a middle-class lawyer to a position of wealth and power before the Civil War. The estate also contains a slave cabin and a slavery exhibit. The park was authorized on October 7, 1988.

WHAT TO SEE & DO

Touring historic buildings and modern exhibits. **Facilities:** Three visitor centers: Natchez Visitor Center (640 S. Canal St.), Melrose Estate (1 Melrose/Montebello Pkwy.), and William Johnson House (210 State St.); hiking trails. Bookstores. **Programs & Events:** Guided tours of Melrose (hourly 10–4). Walking tours of historic district and gardens (Memorial Day–Labor Day, Sat.). Historic Natchez Conference (Jan.), Natchez Literary and Cinema Celebration (Feb.). **Tips & Hints:** Plan to spend about one hour viewing exhibits and film at the Natchez Visitor Center; two hours touring the Melrose home, grounds, and outbuildings; and one hour at the William Johnson House. Busiest Apr.–Oct., least crowded Jan. and Feb.

FOOD, LODGING & SUPPLIES

Camping: None in park. In Natchez: Natchez State Park (230B Wickliff Rd., off Hwy. 61 N, tel. 601/442-2658, www.mdwfp.com; 50 RV sites, 8 tent sites, 10 cabins; $18–24 for RV sites, $77–87 for cabins; flush toilets, showers, hookups). **Hotels:** None in park. In Natchez: Monmouth Plantation (36 Melrose Ave., tel. 601/442–5852 or 800/828-4531, www.monmouthplantation.com; 15 rooms, 15 suites; $195–$235), Natchez Eola Hotel (110 N. Pearl St., tel. 601/445–6000 or 866/445-3652, www.natchezeola.com; 131 rooms; $107–118). **Restaurants:** None in park. In Natchez: Biscuits & Blues (315 Main St., tel. 601/446-9922, www.biscuitsblues.com; $6–$9; closed Mon.), Magnolia Grill (49 Silver St., tel. 601/446-7670, www.magnoliagrill.com; $10–$16). **Groceries & Gear:** None in park. In Natchez: Natchez Market

(280 John R. Junkin Dr., tel. 601/442–9156), Sports Center (305 Sgt. Prentiss Dr., tel. 601/442–7951).

FEES, HOURS & REGULATIONS

Free. Melrose mansion tour: $10 adults, $5 ages 63 and over and ages 6–17, free ages 5 and under. No flash photography in historic houses. Natchez Visitor Reception Center open Mon.–Sat. 8:30–5, Sun. 9–4. Melrose and William Johnson House open daily 8:30–5.

HOW TO GET THERE

80 miles north of Baton Rouge, LA, via U.S. 61 north; 70 miles south of Vicksburg via U.S. 61 south; and 100 miles southeast of Jackson via I–20, the Natchez Trace Pkwy., and U.S. 61 to Melrose Montebello Pkwy. Closest airport: Baton Rouge (70 miles).

CONTACTS

Natchez National Historical Park (640 S. Canal St., Box E, Natchez, MS 39120, tel. 601/442–7047, www.nps.gov/natc). Natchez Convention & Visitors Bureau (640 S. Canal St., Natchez, MS 39120, tel. 800/647–6724, www.visitnatchez.org).

Natchez Trace National Scenic Trail

From southwestern Mississippi, in Natchez, through northwestern Alabama to north-central Tennessee, near Nashville

Five segments of this trail have been constructed within the boundaries of the Natchez Trace Parkway. The parkway is a 444-mile park and motor road commemorating the historic Natchez Trace network of trails created by local Native American tribes and later used by explorers, missionaries, and settlers. Potkopinu is a 3-mile segment north of Natchez; Rocky Spring is a 10-mile segment near Port Gibson, MS; Yockanookany is a 24-mile segment near Ridgeland, MS, near Jackson; Blackland Prairie is a 6-mile segment near Tupelo, MS; and Highland Rim is a 20-mile segment south of Franklin, TN, near the community of Leipers Fork. The trail was established on March 28, 1983.

WHAT TO SEE & DO

Hiking, horseback riding. **Facilities:** Visitor center, hiking trails.

FOOD, LODGING & SUPPLIES

⛺ **Camping:** See Natchez Trace Parkway. 🏨 **Hotels:** See Brices Cross Roads National Battlefield Site for Tupelo/Baldwyn area, Natchez National Historical Park for Natchez area. ✗ **Restaurants:** See Brices Cross Roads National Battlefield Site for Tupelo/Baldwyn area, Natchez National Historical Park for Natchez area. ⛁ **Groceries & Gear:** See Brices Cross Roads National Battlefield Site for Tupelo/Baldwyn area, Natchez National Historical Park for Natchez area.

FEES & HOURS

Free. Trail open sunrise to sunset.

HOW TO GET THERE

All trail segments are along Natchez Trace Parkway: Potkopinu is between mileposts 17 and 20; Rocky Springs is between mileposts 52 and 59; Yockanookany is between mileposts 108 and 131; Blackland Prairie is between mileposts 261 and 266; and Highland Rim is between mileposts 408 and 427. The Natchez Trace Visitor Center is at milepost 266, at the Blackland Prairie trailhead (about 6 miles north of Tupelo). Closest airports: Tupelo (7 miles from visitor center), Jackson, MS (195 miles from visitor center), and Nashville, TN (200 miles from visitor center).

CONTACT

Natchez Trace National Scenic Trail (c/o Natchez Trace Pkwy., 2680 Natchez Trace Pkwy., Tupelo, MS 38804, tel. 662/680–4027 or 800/305–7417, fax 662/680–4034, www.nps.gov/natt).

Natchez Trace Parkway

From southwestern Mississippi, in Natchez, through northwestern Alabama, to central Tennessee, in Nashville

The 444-mile parkway commemorates the historic Natchez Trace, a series of trails used by Natchez, Choctaw, Chickasaw, Creek, and Cherokee peoples. The Trace later served European explorers, boatmen, settlers, soldiers, outlaws, itinerant preachers, and missionaries as a trade and transportation route, helping to form the old Southwest. The unit was established as a National Park Service unit on May 18, 1938.

WHAT TO SEE & DO

Bicycling, driving, fishing, hiking, horseback riding. **Facilities:** Mount Locust Visitor Center (mile 15.5), Parkway Information Cabin (mile 102.4), Parkway Visitor Center (mile 266), Meriwether Lewis Site (mile 385.9). Book and map sales. **Programs & Events:** 12-minute film at Parkway Visitor Center, ranger-led tours of Mount Locust (call for hours); ranger-led programs at Parkway Information Cabin and Parkway Visitor Center (dates and times vary). **Tips & Hints:** Pick up parkway map, guide, and bicycle information packet at visitor center. Check for parkway detours; last 16 miles on north end may close during inclement weather. Go Mar.–Apr. for wildflowers, Oct.–Nov. for fall colors. Busiest in Apr. and Oct., least crowded Dec.–Jan.

FOOD, LODGING & SUPPLIES

🏕 **Camping:** 3 campgrounds (free; flush toilets, drinking water) in the park: Jeff Busby (mile 193.1; 18 sites), Meriwether Lewis (mile 385.9 in Tennessee; 32 sites), Rocky Springs (mile 54.8; 22 sites). Several federal, state, and private campgrounds are found along the parkway (see Brices Cross Roads National Battlefield Site for Tupelo/Baldwyn area,

Natchez National Historical Park for Natchez area). 🏨 **Hotels:** See Brices Cross Roads National Battlefield Site for Tupelo/Baldwyn area, Natchez National Historical Park for Natchez area. ✖ **Restaurants:** See Brices Cross Roads National Battlefield Site for Tupelo/Baldwyn area, Natchez National Historical Park for Natchez area. ♿ **Groceries & Gear:** Camp store at Jeff Busby (mile 193.1). See Brices Cross Roads National Battlefield Site for more in Tupelo/Baldwyn area, Natchez National Historical Park for more in Natchez area.

FEES, HOURS & REGULATIONS

Free. Mississippi, Alabama, or Tennessee state fishing license required. No hunting. Leashed pets only. No bicycling or motorized vehicles on trails. The Natchez Trace Parkway is a designated bike route; motorists must allow at least 3 feet while passing cyclists. Speed limit 50 mph unless otherwise posted. No commercial vehicles. Parkway open daily. Parkway Visitor Center, at milepost 266 in Tupelo, MS, open daily 8–5. Mount Locust Visitor Center open daily 9-4:30. Parkway Information Cabin open Wed.–Sun. 9–4:30.

HOW TO GET THERE

Parkway Visitor Center is in Tupelo, MS, about 100 miles south of Memphis, TN, via U.S. 78. Closest airport: Tupelo (7 miles), Nashville, TN (200 miles), Jackson, MS (195 miles).

CONTACTS

Natchez Trace Parkway (2680 Natchez Trace Pkwy., Tupelo, MS 38804, tel. 662/680–4025 or 800/305–7417; 800/305–7417 closures and detours, fax 662/680–4041, www.nps.gov/natr). Jackson Convention & Visitors Bureau (111 E. Capitol St., Suite 102, Jackson, MS 39201, tel. 601/960–1891 or 800/354–7695, www.visitjackson.com). Nashville Area Convention & Visitors Bureau (150 4th Ave. N, Suite G-250, Nashville, TN 37219, tel. 800/657–6910, www.visitmusiccity. com). Natchez Convention & Visitors Bureau (640 S. Canal St., Natchez, MS 39120, tel. 800/647–6724, www.visitnatchez.org). Tupelo Convention & Visitors Bureau (399 E. Main St., Tupelo, MS 38804, tel. 662/841–6521 or 800/533–0611, www.tupelo.net). Vicksburg Convention & Visitors Bureau (1221 Washington St., Vicksburg, MS 39183, tel. 800/221–3536, www.visitvicksburg.com). Williamson County–Franklin Chamber of Commerce (1164 Columbia Ave., Box 156, Franklin, TN 37065-0156, tel. 615/794–1225 or 800/356–3445, www.williamson-franklinchamber.com).

Tupelo National Battlefield

In northeastern Mississippi, in Tupelo

The Battle of Tupelo, which was part of a larger strategy by Union General William Tecumseh Sherman to protect his railroad supply line, occurred on July 13 and 14, 1864, when Union troops under General A. J. Smith fought Confederate soldiers under General Nathan Bedford Forrest. Both sides also battled the heat that ultimately forced the Federal retreat. A monument marks the event, and the park is dotted with old cannons and interpretive placards. The 1-acre Tupelo National Battlefield Site was established in 1929, transferred to the Park Service in 1933, and redesignated in 1961.

WHAT TO SEE & DO

Visiting site and monument. **Facilities:** Interpretive signs. **Tips & Hints:** Busiest in Apr. and Oct., least crowded Dec. and Jan.

FOOD, LODGING & SUPPLIES

Camping: See Brices Cross Roads National Battlefield Site. **Hotels:** See Brices Cross Roads National Battlefield Site. **Restaurants:** See Brices Cross Roads National Battlefield Site. **Groceries & Gear:** See Brices Cross Roads National Battlefield Site.

FEES & HOURS

Free. Park open daily sunrise to sunset.

HOW TO GET THERE

In Tupelo via Rte. 6, just over 1 mile west of intersection with U.S. 45 and 1 mile east of Natchez Trace Pkwy. Closest airports: Tupelo (4 miles), Memphis, TN (100 miles).

CONTACTS

Tupelo National Battlefield (c/o Natchez Trace Parkway, 2680 Natchez Trace Pkwy., Tupelo, MS 38804, tel. 601/680–4027 or 800/305–7417, www.nps.gov/tupe). Tupelo Convention & Visitors Bureau (399 E. Main St., Tupelo, MS 38804, tel. 800/533–0611, www.tupelo.net).

Vicksburg National Military Park

In western Mississippi, in Vicksburg

A key battle of the Civil War—including the campaign, siege, and defense of Vicksburg from April 29 to July 4, 1863—is commemorated at this park. Battles at Port Gibson, Raymond, Jackson, Champion Hill, and Big Black River were all part of the Vicksburg campaign, as was the 47-day Union siege against the city. Located high on the bluffs, Vicksburg was known as "the Gibraltar of the Confederacy" and guarded the Mississippi River; with its surrender, the Union regained control of the lower Mississippi River and split the Confederacy in two. Today, more than 1,300 monuments and markers are scattered throughout the grounds, as are reconstructed trenches and earthworks, an antebellum structure, more than 125 emplaced cannons, and the Vicksburg National Cemetery. The USS *Cairo* Museum and Gunboat is also on the grounds. A 16-mile scenic drive winds past many of the significant historic sites. The park was established in 1899 and transferred to the Park Service in 1933.

WHAT TO SEE & DO

Bird-watching, hiking, scenic drives, touring museum and cemetery, viewing restored gunboat, walking. **Facilities:** Visitor center, interpretive signs, USS *Cairo* Museum and Gunboat (mile 7.9). Bookstore, picnic tables. **Programs & Events:** Guided battlefield tours, self-guided driving tours. ranger talks, black powder demonstration, living-history program, and cannon-firing demonstrations (all mid-June–mid-Aug.). **Tips & Hints:** Wear comfortable clothing and walking or hiking shoes. Audiotapes available for driving tours. Best weather Mar.–May. Busiest Apr. and May, least crowded Nov. and Dec.

FOOD, LODGING & SUPPLIES

Camping: None in park. In Vicksburg: Ameristar RV Campground (725 Lucy Bryson St., 601/638–1000 or 800/667–3386; 67 sites; flush toilets, showers, hookups; $24–28). **Hotels:** None in park. In Vicksburg: Ameristar Casino Hotel (4155 Washington St., tel. 601/638–1000 or 800/700–7770; 149 rooms; $89–$159), Battlefield Inn (4137 I–20 N. Frontage Rd., tel. 601/638–5811 or 800/359–9363, www.battlefieldinnsms.com; 118 rooms; $65–$85), Hampton Inn & Suites (3330 Clay St., 601/636–6100 or 800/847–0372, www.vicksburghamptoninn.com; 123 rooms, 34 studio suites; $149). ✕ **Restaurants:** None in park. In Vicksburg: Roca Restaurant & Bar (127 Country Club Dr., tel. 601/638–0800, www.rocarestaurant.com; $9–$15; closed Mon., no lunch Sat., no dinner Sun.), Walnut Hills (1214 Adams St., tel. 601/638–4910, www.walnuthillsms.com; $7–$15; closed Sat., no dinner Sun.). **Groceries & Gear:** None in park. In Vicksburg: Family Dollar (1305 Mission 66, tel. 601/638–8048).

FEES, HOURS & REGULATIONS

Entrance fee: $8 per vehicle, $4 per bus passenger. Guided battlefield tour: $40 per car, $60 per van, $80 per bus; reservations available. No hunting. No metal detectors. No fires or cooking. Park open Apr.–Sept., daily 7–7, Oct.–Mar., daily 8–5. Visitor center open daily 8–5. Cairo Museum open Nov.–Mar., daily 8:30–5; Apr.–Oct., daily 9:30–6.

HOW TO GET THERE

In Vicksburg off I–20/U.S. 61 at Exit 4B; take Clay St. (U.S. 80) west for ¼ mile to park. Closest airport: Jackson (50 miles).

CONTACTS

Vicksburg National Military Park (3201 Clay St., Vicksburg, MS 39183, tel. 601/636–0583; 601/636–3827 battlefield tour, fax 601/636–9497, www.nps.gov/vick). Vicksburg Convention & Visitors Bureau (3300 Clay St., Box 110, Vicksburg, MS 39181, tel. 601/636-9421 or 800/221–3536, www.visitvicksburg.com).

See Also

Gulf Islands National Seashore, Florida.

MISSOURI

George Washington Carver National Monument

In southwestern Missouri, near Diamond

George Washington Carver, who was born here around 1864, ascended to national prominence as a scientist, educator, and humanitarian. The park preserves the historic 1881 home where he lived and a cemetery from the same era (though Carver himself is not buried there). Kids have fun at the hands-on discovery center, and talks on local history and nature are held year-round at the multipurpose classroom facility. The monument was authorized in 1943 and established in 1953. This was the first unit of the National Park Service established to honor the contributions of an African American.

WHAT TO SEE & DO

Hiking, picnicking, touring home and cemetery. **Facilities:** Visitor center, museum, movie, outdoor interpretive exhibits. Book-and-gift shop, picnic tables. **Programs & Events:** Ranger-guided tours; interpretive, living-history, cultural, and nature programs; educational field trips. Black Heritage Month and fourth-grade Art & Essay Contest (Feb.), Art in the Park (Apr.), Carver Day Celebration (July), Prairie Day Celebration (Sept.), Holiday Open House (Dec.). **Tips & Hints:** Busiest in May and July, least crowded Dec. and Jan.

FOOD, LODGING & SUPPLIES

Camping: None at site. In Carthage: Ballard's Campground (13969 Ballard Loop, ¼ mile south of I–44, tel. 417/359–0359; 30 sites; $17–$23; flush toilets, showers, hookups). **Hotels:** None in park. In Carthage: Best Western Precious Moments Hotel (2701 Hazel Ave., tel. 417/359–5900 or 800/780–7234, www.bestwesternmissouri.com; 121 rooms; $77–$79), Carthage Inn (2244 Grand Ave., tel. 417/358–2499 or 888/454–2499, www.carthageinn.com; 40 rooms; $65). **Restaurants:** None in park. In Joplin: Undercliff Grill & Bar (6385 Old U.S. 71, tel. 417/623–8382, www.undercliff.net; $5–$13; closed Mon. and Tues.; no dinner Sun.). The Joplin Eagle Drive-In (4224 S. Main St., tel. 417/623–2228; $5–$13.) **Groceries & Gear:** None in park. In Diamond: Casey's General Store (101 N. Washington St., tel. 417/325–7114).

FEES, HOURS & REGULATIONS

Free. No hunting or fishing. No motorized or mechanized equipment on trails. Leashed pets only. Monument and visitor center open daily 9–5.

HOW TO GET THERE

10 miles east of Joplin via I–44, take Exit 11A to U.S. 71 south, then the Diamond exit 4 miles east and travel ½ mile south. Closest airport: Joplin (15 miles).

CONTACTS

George Washington Carver National Monument (5646 Carver Rd., Diamond, MO 64840, tel. 417/325–4151, fax 417/325–4231, www.nps. gov/gwca). Carthage Chamber of Commerce (402 S. Garrison Ave., Carthage, MO 64836, tel. 417/358–2373, fax 417/358–7479, www. carthagechamber.com). Joplin Convention & Visitors Bureau (602 S. Main St., Joplin, MO 64801, tel. 417/625–4789 or 800/657–2534, www. visitjoplinmo.com). Neosho Chamber of Commerce (308 W. Spring St., Box 605, Neosho, MO 64850, tel. 417/451–1925, www.neoshocc. com).

Harry S Truman National Historic Site

In west-central Missouri, near Independence

Preserved at this historic site is a remarkably complete collection of structures and objects associated with the life of Harry S Truman, 33rd president of the United States. Five properties and associated structures stand within it: the Truman Home (219 N. Delaware St.), Frank Wallace House (601 W. Truman Rd.), George Wallace House (605 W. Truman Rd.), Noland House (216 N. Delaware St.), and Truman Farm (Grandview, ½ mile west of U.S. 71 on Blue Ridge Blvd.). Truman lived on the farm for 11 years before moving to the 219 N. Delaware house in 1919 after his marriage to Bess Wallace, whose family lived there. He returned to the Delaware St. home after his term ended in 1953. The Trumans lived there until his death in 1972 and her death in 1982. The 219 N. Delaware St. site was authorized in 1983. The other three homes and the farm were acquired in 1991 and 1994.

WHAT TO SEE & DO

Touring the home, farm, and surrounding National Historic Landmark District. **Facilities:** Visitor center, outdoor interpretive exhibit. Bookstore. **Programs & Events:** Slide program, guided tours of the Truman Home (Memorial Day–Oct., daily 9–4:45; Nov.–Memorial Day, daily 9–4), Farm Home tours (Memorial Day–Labor Day, Fri.–Sun., every half hour 9:30–4, tickets required). **Tips & Hints:** Same-day Truman Home tour tickets available at 8:30 from the visitor center; tickets are first-come, first-served, and groups are limited to eight people. Same-day Farm Home tour tickets, available on-site at 9:30, are limited to groups of six people. Go Nov.–Mar. to avoid crowds. Busiest June and July, least crowded Jan. and Feb.

FEES, HOURS & REGULATIONS

Truman Home and Truman Farm home tour: $4 adults 16 and older, free ages 15 and under; tickets required for all. Truman Farm Home: tickets required. No advance tour reservations accepted. No diaper bags, backpacks, cameras, camera bags, or cell phones permitted on either home tour. No pets in buildings. Leashed pets allowed on grounds of farm only. No smoking or picnicking. No vehicles off paved roads or parking lots. Visitor center open daily 8:30–5. Truman Farm grounds open daily dawn–dusk.

HOW TO GET THERE

From Independence via I–70, take Noland Rd. north to Truman Rd., turn left, drive two blocks to visitor center. Via I–435, take Truman Rd. exit east to corner of Truman Rd. and Main St.. Reach Truman Farm via U.S. 71 to Grandview, then exit west onto Blue Ridge Blvd. and drive ½ mile. Closest airport: Kansas City (31 miles).

CONTACTS

Harry S Truman National Historic Site (223 N. Main St., Independence, MO 64050, tel. 816/254–9929, fax 816/254–4491, www.nps.gov/hstr). Grandview Chamber of Commerce (1200 Main St., Grandview, MO 64030, tel. 816/316–4800, www.grandview.org). Independence Chamber of Commerce (210 W. Truman Rd., Box 1077, Independence, MO 64050, tel. 816/252–4745, www.independencechamber.org).

Jefferson National Expansion Memorial

In east-central Missouri, in St. Louis

The memorial commemorates St. Louis's role in the westward growth of the United States from 1803 through 1890. Important buildings here include the city's Old Courthouse, built between 1839 and 1862, and the Gateway Arch, an internationally renowned 1965 structure designed by Eero Saarinen. The fascinating Museum of Westward Expansion, underneath the Gateway Arch, chronicles the region's growth westward during the 19th century. The memorial was established on December 20, 1935.

WHAT TO SEE & DO

Riding to the top of the arch, touring museum and courthouse. **Facilities:** Visitor center, museum, accessibility kiosks, information kiosks, movies. Book-and-gift shops. **Programs & Events:** Ranger-guided tours, riverboat cruises, bike tours, helicopter tours. African-American Heritage Month (Feb.), St. Louis Storytelling Festival (1st weekend, May), Patriotic 4th of July, Victorian Christmas (Thanksgiving–Dec.), programs surrounding Fair St. Louis (July). **Tips & Hints:** Park in garage at north end of grounds on Washington Ave. Gateway Arch is not wheelchair accessible and requires climbing at least 96 nonstandard steps. Inform ticket center beforehand if you have a fear of heights or confined spaces. Arrive ½ to 1 hour ahead of reservation time for security check. Busiest July and Aug., least crowded Jan. and Feb. Advanced tickets recommended to ensure availability.

FEES, HOURS & REGULATIONS

Free. Additional programs: $3 adults, free ages 16 and under; $6 per family. Separate charges for arch ride and films. Old Courthouse free. Leashed pets only on grounds. No in-line skating, skateboarding, or other recreational activities, except walking and jogging. Gateway Arch and visitor center open Memorial Day–Labor Day, daily 8 AM–10 PM; Labor Day–Memorial Day, daily 9–6. Old Courthouse open year-round, daily 8–4:30.

HOW TO GET THERE

In St. Louis, visitor center at base of Gateway Arch. Closest airport: St. Louis (8 miles).

CONTACTS

Jefferson National Expansion Memorial (11 N. 4th St., St. Louis, MO 63102, tel. 314/655–1700, fax 314/655–1642, www.nps.gov/jeff). St. Louis Convention & Visitors Commission (701 Convention Plaza, Suite 300, St. Louis, MO 63101, tel. 800/325–7962, www.explorestlouis. com).

Ozark National Scenic Riverways

In southeastern Missouri, near Van Buren

Around 134 miles of waterways along the Current and Jacks Fork Rivers provide scenic settings for hiking, canoeing, tubing, fishing, and swimming. More than 300 springs pour millions of gallons of clear, cold water into the streams, while forests and meadows fill in the surrounding hills and valleys. Ozark culture also is preserved throughout the 80,790-acre park. The park was authorized in 1964 and established in 1972.

WHAT TO SEE & DO

Boating, canoeing (rentals in park and in Eminence and Van Buren), fishing, hiking, hunting, swimming, tubing. **Facilities:** 5 visitor centers: Watercress Headquarters (Van Buren), Alley Mill (Alley Spring, near Eminence), Round Spring (Van Buren), Pulltite (above Round Spring), and Akers (above Pulltite); outdoor interpretive exhibits. Covered picnic tables. **Programs & Events:** Evening programs (Memorial Day–Labor Day, weekends), Round Spring Cave tours (Memorial Day–Labor Day, daily at 10 and 2), occasional events (June–Aug., weekends). **Tips & Hints:** Wear life jackets on river (required for children 12 and under). Canoeing possible any time of year. Busiest July and Aug., least crowded Jan. and Feb.

FOOD, LODGING & SUPPLIES

 Camping: In the park: 5 campgrounds ($14; flush toilets, showers): Alley Spring (162 sites), Big Spring (181 sites), Pulltite (55 sites), Round Spring (56 sites), Two Rivers (19 sites). Near Salem: Montauk State Park Campgrounds (Rte. 5, tel. 573/548–2201, 877/422–6766 reservations, www.montaukpark.com; 154 sites; $13–$26; flush toilets, showers, some hookups). **Hotels:** In the park: Big Spring Cabins (Rtes. 103 and Z, off U.S. 60, near Van Buren, tel. 573/323–4332; 14 cabins; $65–$120; closed late Nov.–mid-Mar., 1 cabin open year-round). In Doniphan: Days Inn Doniphan (100 Oak Tree Village, at Hwys. 160 and 21, tel. 573/996–2400 or 800/225–3297; 46 rooms; $69). ✗ **Restaurants:** In the park: Big Spring Historic Dining Lodge (Rtes. 103 and Z, off U.S. 60, tel. 573/323–4332; $4–$7; closed Labor Day–Memorial Day). In Van Buren: Float Stream Restaurant (102 Main St., tel. 573/323–9606; $6–$18). Stray Dog BBQ (Hwys. 60 and 103, tel. 573/323–0020, www.straydogbbq.net; $5–$8). **Groceries & Gear:** Camp stores at Akers Ferry, Alley Spring, Round Spring, Pulltite, and Two Rivers.

FEES, HOURS & REGULATIONS

Free. Cave tours $5 adults, $2 ages 12 and under. Missouri state fishing and hunting licenses ($5–$11 for one day) required. No inboard motors. No personal watercraft. Horsepower limits apply. Leashed pets only. Park open daily. Alley Mill Visitor Center open Memorial Day–Labor Day, daily 9–4:30; Labor Day–mid-Oct., weekends 9–4:30. Park Headquarters Visitor Center open Memorial Day–Labor Day, daily 8–4:30; Labor Day-Memorial Day, weekdays 8–4:30.

HOW TO GET THERE

175 miles south of St. Louis and 250 miles southeast of Kansas City via Rte. 19 to Akers Ferry, Pulltite, and Round Spring; from Eminence via Hwy. 106 to Alley Spring and Two Rivers; and 4 miles from Van Buren via Rte. 103 to Big Spring. Closest airports: Springfield (166 miles), St. Louis (176 miles).

CONTACT

Ozark National Scenic Riverways (404 Watercress Dr., Box 490, Van Buren, MO 63965, tel. 573/323–4236, fax 573/323–4140, www.nps.gov/ozar).

Ulysses S. Grant
National Historic Site

In east-central Missouri, in St. Louis

The 9.6-acre heart of the former 1,000-acre plantation owned by Ulysses and Julia Grant is preserved at this National Historic Site. The site is significant for its association with the apparently "average" man who led the army that saved the Union, served two terms as president, and wrote one of the most important military commentaries of modern times. The property includes the main house, summer kitchen, chicken house, ice house, and barn. The site was authorized on October 2, 1989.

WHAT TO SEE & DO

Touring buildings and grounds. **Facilities:** Visitor center, museum. Book-and-gift shop. **Programs & Events:** Daily ranger-led tours, daily Junior Ranger program, guest lectures, living-history demonstrations, children's programs. Special events are listed on the park website. **Tips & Hints:** Walking is required to fully experience the park. Watch for uneven ground and slippery surfaces. Busiest July and Aug., least crowded Jan. and Feb.

FEES, HOURS & REGULATIONS

Free. Reservations suggested for special events. Leashed pets only. Site open daily 9–5.

HOW TO GET THERE

In south St. Louis County via Gravois Rd. (Rte. 30) and Watson Rd. (Rte. 366). Closest airport: St. Louis (20 miles).

CONTACTS

Ulysses S. Grant National Historic Site (7400 Grant Rd., St. Louis, MO 63123, tel. 314/842–1867, fax 314/842–1659, www.nps.gov/ulsg). Missouri Tourism Welcome Center (I-270 at Riverview Dr., Box 38182, St. Louis, MO 63138, tel. 314/869–7100, www.visitmo.com). St. Louis Convention & Visitors Commission (701 Convention Plaza, Suite 300, St. Louis, MO 63102, tel. 800/325–7962).

Wilson's Creek National Battlefield

In southwestern Missouri, near Springfield

On August 10, 1861, the first major Civil War engagement west of the Mississippi River was fought at this site. It was a battle of more than 5,000 Union troops and 12,000 Confederates; the former lost General Nathanial Lyon, the first Union general killed in battle, and the latter emerged victorious. Today, with the exception of the vegetation, the 1,971-acre battlefield has changed little from its historic setting. Major sites include a 5-mile tour road, the restored 1852 Ray House, and "Bloody Hill," the scene of the major battle. The site was authorized as a national battlefield park in 1960 and redesignated in 1970.

WHAT TO SEE & DO

Biking, hiking, touring battlefield and Ray House. **Facilities:** Visitor center, outdoor interpretive exhibits, guided and self-guided tours, hiking trails. Bookstore, covered picnic tables. **Programs & Events:** Self-guided driving tour, self-guided tours of Bloody Hill; living-history programs and Ray House tours (weekends Memorial Day–Labor Day).

Battle anniversary (Aug. 10). **Tips & Hints:** Plan to spend at least two hours. Busiest May–Aug., least crowded Jan.–Mar.

FOOD, LODGING & SUPPLIES

⊞ **Hotel:** None in park. In Springfield: Quality Inn & Suites Chesterfield Village (3930 S. Overland Ave., tel. 417/888–0898, www. qualityinn.com; 50 rooms; $75). ✕ **Restaurants:** None in park. In Springfield: Hemingway's Blue Water Café (1935 S. Campbell Ave., 4th fl., Bass Pro Shop, tel. 417/891–5100, www. hemingwaysbluewatercafe.com; $5–$13; no dinner Sun.), Zio's Italian Kitchen (1249 E. Kingsley St., tel. 417/889–1919, www.zios.com; $6–$10). ⌂ **Groceries & Gear:** None in park. In Springfield: Bass Pro Shops (1935 S. Campbell Ave., tel. 417/887–7334). In Republic: Price Cutter (1013 U.S. 60 E, tel. 417/732–2828).

FEES & HOURS

Entrance fee: $5 adults, free ages 16 and under, $10 per vehicle. Park open daily 8–5; extended hours in summer. Visitor center open daily 8–5.

HOW TO GET THERE

10 miles southwest of Springfield and 3 miles east of Republic. From I–44, take Exit 70 south to U.S. 60. Cross U.S. 60 and drive ¾ mile to Wilson's Creek Blvd. The battlefield is 1 mile south. From U.S. 60 and U.S. 65, take the James River Freeway to FF Highway, then south to M Highway. Follow M west to Wilson's Creek Blvd. The park entrance is 1 mile south. Closest airport: Springfield (15 miles).

CONTACTS

Wilson's Creek National Battlefield (6424 W. Farm Rd. 182, Republic, MO 65738, tel. 417/732–2662, fax 417/732–1167, www.nps.gov/wicr). Springfield Convention & Visitors Bureau (815 E. St. Louis St., Springfield, MO 65806, tel. 417/881-5300 or 800/678–8767, www. springfieldmo.org).

See Also

California National Historic Trail, Lewis & Clark National Historic Trail, Oregon National Historic Trail, Pony Express National Historic Trail, Santa Fe National Historic Trail, and Trail of Tears National Historic Trail, in Other National Parklands.

MONTANA

Big Hole National Battlefield

In southwestern Montana, near Wisdom

One of the West's most tragic stories played out on this battlefield. In 1877 the U.S. Army was charged with forcing resistant Nez Perce Indians onto a reservation in Idaho. In the same year, a few Nez Perce warriors killed several white settlers as retribution for Nez Perce deaths and mistreatment at the hands of white people. The bloodshed provoked a massive manhunt and the beginning of a 1,500-mile odyssey. The Nez Perce fled north from their homeland in central Idaho, pursued by the U.S. Army. The tribe engaged 10 separate U.S. commands in 13 battles and skirmishes. One of the fiercest of these took place at Big Hole Battlefield, where both sides suffered serious losses. The site was established as a national monument in 1910, transferred to the Park Service in 1933, and changed to a National Battlefield in 1963.

WHAT TO SEE & DO

Cross-country skiing, fishing, picnicking, snowshoeing, touring battlefield. **Facilities:** Visitor center, museum, movie, guided tours, hiking trails. Book and map sales, picnic tables. **Programs & Events:** Guided hikes, interpretive talks (June–Aug.). Big Hole Battle Annual Commemoration (weekend near Aug. 9). **Tips & Hints:** Busiest July and Aug., least crowded Dec. and Jan.

FOOD, LODGING & SUPPLIES

Camping: None at site. In Beaverhead-Deerlodge National Forest: May Creek Campground (Rte. 43, 17 miles west of Wisdom, tel. 406/689–3243, www.fs.usda.gov/bdnf; 21 sites; $7; pit toilets; closed Labor Day–July). **Hotels:** None in park. In Jackson: Jackson Hot Springs Lodge (108 Jardine Ave., tel. 406/834–3151, www.jacksonhotsprings. com; 24 rooms and cabins; $45–$126). In Wisdom: Nez Perce Motel (509 Rte. 43, tel. 406/689–3254; 8 rooms; $55). **Restaurants:** None in park. In Wisdom: Antler's Saloon (43 Hwy. 43, tel. 406/689–9393; $9–$14), Crossing Bar & Grill (327 County Rd., tel. 406/689–3260, www.thecrossingbarandgrill.com; $8–$13). **Groceries & Gear:** None in park. In Wisdom: Conover's Trading Post (317 Hwy. 43 W, tel. 406/689–3272), Wisdom Market (Main St. at Hwy. 43, tel. 406/689–3271).

FEES, HOURS & REGULATIONS

Free. Montana state fishing license ($8–$10) required. Pets in parking areas only; must be leashed. No hunting. Trails open until dusk. Visitor center open Memorial Day–Labor Day, daily 9–5; Labor Day–Memorial Day, daily 10–5.

HOW TO GET THERE

10 miles west of Wisdom via Rte. 43. Closest airport: Butte (80 miles).

CONTACT

Big Hole National Battlefield (16425 Hwy. 43 W, Wisdom, MT 59761, tel. 406/689–3155, fax 406/689–3151, www.nps.gov/biho).

Bighorn Canyon
National Recreation Area

South-central Montana, near Hardin, to north-central Wyoming, near Lovell

The most compelling attraction here is the geology of the canyon, which is several thousand feet deep in places. Naturally, Bighorn Canyon also has plenty of bighorn sheep, and it's the site of the nation's first wild horse range, the Bad Pass Trail. The scenic road in the Wyoming end of the area winds past wildife habitat and several historic ranches. Look for the Bighorn River, below the Yellowtail Dam. The area was established in 1966.

WHAT TO SEE & DO

Boating (rentals, lake marina), fishing, hiking, hunting, ice fishing, skiing, swimming, touring canyon. **Facilities:** 2 visitor centers: Yellowtail Dam (Fort Smith, MT) and Bighorn Canyon (Lovell, WY); outdoor interpretive exhibits, hiking trails. Bookstores, picnic tables with fire grills. **Programs & Events:** Canoe trips, interpretive talks, campfire programs (June–Aug.). Mustang Days fireworks at Horseshoe Bend (Sun. before July 4). **Tips & Hints:** Watch for rattlesnakes and fragile edges near drop-offs. Be aware of and respect Crow Indian Reservation boundaries. Bighorn Canyon is a relatively undiscovered treasure, with few visitors there at any time.

FOOD, LODGING & SUPPLIES

🏕 **Camping:** 5 campgrounds ($5) in the park: Afterbay Lake (40 sites; vault toilets), Black Canyon (17 boat-in sites; vault toilets), Horseshoe Bend (59 sites; flush toilets), Medicine Creek (6 boat-in or hike-in sites; vault toilets), Trail Creek (15 sites; vault toilets). In Yellowtail, MT: Cottonwood Camp (3 miles north of Fort Smith, tel. 406/666–2391; 16 RV sites, tent camping area, 19 cabins; $10–$65; flush toilets, showers, hookups). 🏨 **Hotels:** None in park. In Hardin, MT: Super 8 (201 14th St. W, tel. 406/665–1700 or 800/800–8000, www.hardinmontanasuper8. com; 63 rooms; $94), Lariat Motel (709 N. Center Ave., tel. 406/665–2683; 18 rooms; $49). In Lovell, WY: Econo Inn (595 E. Main, tel. 307/548–2725; 34 rooms; $65). ✘ **Restaurants:** In the park: grill and staples at Ok-A-Beh Marina. In Lovell, WY: Switchback Grill (384 W. Main St., tel. 307/548–9595; $8–$12). In Powell, WY: El Tapatio Mexican Restaurant (112 N. Bent St., tel. 307/754–8085; $7–$13; closed Sun.). 🛒 **Groceries & Gear:** None in park. In Lovell, WY: Red Apple (9 E.

Main St., tel. 307/548–2224). In Powell, WY: Blair's Market (331 W. Coulter Ave., tel. 307/754–3122).

FEES, HOURS & REGULATIONS

Entrance fee: $5 per vehicle. Montana ($8–$10) or Wyoming ($6–$14) state fishing license required. No hunting in restricted areas. Leashed pets only. No motorized or mechanical vehicles off paved or dirt roads. Park open daily. Yellowtail Dam Visitor Center open Memorial Day–Labor Day, daily 9–5. Bighorn Canyon Visitor Center open year-round, daily 8–6.

HOW TO GET THERE

North Unit (Montana side) 1 mile west of Fort Smith; South Unit (Wyoming side) 14 miles northeast of Lovell. Closest airports: Cody, WY (50 miles), Billings (90 miles from North District).

CONTACTS

Bighorn Canyon National Recreation Area, North Unit (Box 7458, Fort Smith, MT 59035, tel. 406/666–2412, fax 406/666–2415, www.nps.gov/bica). Bighorn Canyon National Recreation Area, South Unit (20 U.S. 14A E, Lovell, WY 82431, tel. 307/548–2251, fax 307/548–7826). Hardin Area Chamber of Commerce (10 E. Railway St., Box 446, Hardin, MT 59034, tel. 406/665–1672, fax 406/665–3577, www.thehardinchamber.org). Lovell Area Chamber of Commerce (287 E. Main St., Box 295, Lovell, WY 82431, tel. 307/548–7552, www.lovellchamber.com).

Glacier National Park

In northwestern Montana, near West Glacier

This ruggedly beautiful park, considered one of the most ecologically intact temperate areas in the world, offers spectacular mountain scenery and the chance for a true wilderness experience. Within the boundaries of the 1-million-acre park are 25 glaciers, 6 10,000-foot peaks, and numerous lakes and waterways set amid expansive meadows and steep ravines. Grizzly bears, mountain lions, gray wolves, moose, and bighorn sheep are but a few of the creatures that can be seen in the vast forests, while swift, shallow rivers shelter beaver, otters, muskrats, raccoons, and a variety of other small mammals. Look overhead to spot bald eagles, hawks, falcons, and other birds of prey; the marshy lakeshores and riverbanks are also home to numerous waterfowl. The area has many Native American ties as well, and the visitor centers host summer programs by Blackfeet, Salish, and Kooterai tribal members. The park was established in 1910, authorized as part of the Waterton-Glacier International Peace Park in 1932, and designated a Biosphere Reserve in 1976 and a World Heritage Site in 1995.

WHAT TO SEE & DO

Backpacking (rentals in Columbia Falls and West Glacier), bicycling (rentals in East Glacier and outside West Glacier), boating (rentals in Apgar, Lake McDonald, Many Glacier, Two Medicine), cross-country skiing (rentals in Essex), fishing, golfing (in East and West Glacier, Columbia Falls), hiking, horseback riding, picnicking, rafting (trips from West Glacier), snowshoeing, touring park in vintage buses, wildlife watching. **Facilities:** 3 visitor centers: Apgar (west side of park), Logan Pass (Going-to-the-Sun Rd.), St. Mary (east side of park); Vintage Red Buses, outdoor interpretive exhibits, movies, guided and self-guided tours, more than 700 miles of hiking trails. Book and map sales, book-and-gift shops, picnic tables. **Programs & Events:** Ranger-led hikes and talks, slide shows, boat tours, guided walks, and daylong hikes. Native America Speaks series by Blackfeet, Salish, and Kooterai tribal members (July and Aug.). **Tips & Hints:** Be aware of water and snow hazards and the dangers of altitude sickness and hypothermia. Ticks are prevalent throughout the woods. Do not bother or feed wild animals, and know what to do if confronted by a bear or mountain lion. Bear-proof storage boxes are provided for front-country campgrounds, but bring 25 feet of rope to hoist food up into trees in the backcountry. Go in Sept. to avoid crowds. Busiest July and Aug., least crowded Nov. and Dec.

FOOD, LODGING & SUPPLIES

Camping: 13 campgrounds in the park (1,000 sites; $10–$23; some flush toilets, some pit toilets, some showers). Backcountry camping available. **Hotels:** In the park: Apgar Village Lodge (tel. 406/888–5484, www.westglacier.com; 20 rooms; $125–$145; closed early Oct.–mid-May), Glacier Park Lodge (tel. 406/892–2525 or 866/875–8456, www.nationalparkreservations.com; 161 rooms; $145; closed late Sept.–mid-May), Granite Park Chalet (tel. 888/345–2649, www.graniteparkchalet.com; 12 rooms; $179; closed mid-Sept.–June), Lake McDonald Lodge and Cabins (tel. 406/892–2525 or 406/888–5431, www.glacierparkinc.com; 100 rooms; $127–$134; closed Oct.–mid-May), Many Glacier Hotel (tel. 406/892–2525 or 402/732–4411, www.glacierparkinc.com; 214 rooms, 8 suites; $149; closed late Sept.–early June), Prince of Wales Hotel (Waterton, Canada, tel. 406/892–2525 or 866/875–8456, www.nationalparkreservations.com; 86 rooms; $234; closed mid-Sept.–early June), Rising Sun Motor Inn and Cabins (tel. 406/892–2525 or 406/732–5523, www.glacierparkinc.com; 72 rooms; $118–$134; closed mid-Sept.–mid-June), Sperry Chalet (tel. 888/345–2649, www.sperrychalet.com; 17 rooms; $215; closed mid-Sept.–mid-July), Swiftcurrent Motor Inn and Cabins (tel. 406/892–2525 or 406/732–5531, www.glacierparkinc.com; 88 rooms; $72–$118; closed mid-Sept.-early June), Village Inn at Apgar (tel. 406/892–2525 or 406/888–5632, www.glacierparkinc.com; 36 rooms; $135; closed Oct.–May), West Glacier Motel and Cabins (tel. 406/888–5462, www.westglacier.com; 9 rooms, 5 cabins; $95–$120; closed late Sept.–mid-May). **Restaurants:** In the park: Eddie's Café (in Apgar Village), Great Northern Dining Room (Glacier Park Lodge), Italian Gardens (Swiftcurrent Motor Inn), Jammer Joe's Grill & Pizzeria, Lucke's Lounge, Russell's Fireside Dining Room (Lake McDonald Lodge), Ptarmigan Dining Room (Many Glacier Hotel), Royal Stewart Dining Room (Prince of Wales Hotel), Two Dogs Flat Grill (Rising Sun Motor Inn). **Groceries & Gear:** In the park: Eddie's Groceries (in Apgar Village),

Swiftcurrent camp store (Many Glacier Valley), Rising Sun camp store (east part of the park), Two Medicine camp store (southeast part of the park), Lake MacDonald Lodge camp store. In West Glacier: West Glacier Mercantile (West Glacier Village, tel. 406/888–5362).

FEES, HOURS & REGULATIONS

Entrance fee: $12 per person on foot, bicycle, or motorcycle; $25 per vehicle. Backpacking permits ($5 per person per night, $30 additional fee for advance reservation). Backcountry camping permits required. Historic Red Bus tours ($40–$75 adults, $20–$37.50 children). Hiker shuttle ($10 adults, $5 children per segment). No vehicles wider than 8 feet or longer than 21 feet allowed on Logan Pass between Avalanche and Sun Point. No backcountry campfires in summer. No hunting. No pets or bikes on trails. No snowmobiles. Boats require inspection for invasive aquatic species. Park open daily. Logan Pass open mid-June–mid-Oct. Apgar Visitor Center open May–Oct., daily 8 AM–9 PM; Nov.–Apr., weekends 9–4:30. Logan Pass Visitor Center open mid-June–mid.-Oct., daily 9–7. St. Mary Visitor Center open mid-May–mid-Sept., daily 8 AM–9 PM.

HOW TO GET THERE

West entrance, near West Glacier, 19 miles east of Columbia Falls via U.S. 2; east entrance, in St. Mary, 22 miles northwest of Browning via U.S. 89. Closest airport: Kalispell (25 miles from west entrance)

CONTACTS

Glacier National Park (West Glacier, MT 59936, tel. 406/888–7800, 877/444–6777 camping reservations, www.nps.gov/glac). Glacier Park, Inc., sightseeing buses and shuttles (tel. 406/892–2525, www. glacierparkinc.com). Columbia Falls Area Chamber of Commerce (Box 312, Columbia Falls, MT 59912, tel. 406/892–2072, www. columbiafallschamber.com). Cut Bank Area Chamber of Commerce (725 E. Main St., Box 1243, Cut Bank, MT 59427, tel. 406/873–4041, www.cutbankchamber.com). Flathead Convention & Visitor Bureau (Box 237, Bigfork, MT 59911, tel. 406/756–9091 or 800/543–3105, www.fcvb.org). Glacier Country (140 N. Higgins, Suite 204, Missoula, MT 59802, tel. 406/532–3234 or 800/338–5072, www.glaciermt.com).

Grant-Kohrs Ranch National Historic Site

In southwestern Montana, in Deer Lodge

Established by Canadian fur trader John Grant and expanded by cattle baron Conrad Kohrs, the site was the headquarters for one of the largest 19th-century range ranches in the country. The 2,000-acre park is maintained today as a working ranch, and the 90 historic structures serve as a living museum of the frontier cattle industry of the 1860s–1930s. The site was authorized in 1972.

WHAT TO SEE & DO

Observing ranch life, with its cattle, poultry, and horses; touring ranch and outbuildings; walking nature trail. **Facilities:** Visitor center, guided and self-guided tours, hiking trails. Bookstore. **Programs & Events:** Ranger-led ranch house tours, self-guided walks of ranch outbuildings; demonstrations of blacksmithing, chuck-wagon cooking, 1890s cowboy life (May–Sept.). Ranch Days (last full weekend, July). **Tips & Hints:** Plan two–four hours for visit. Busiest July and Aug., least crowded Jan. and Feb.

FOOD, LODGING & SUPPLIES

Camping: None in park. In Deer Lodge: Indian Creek RV Park (745 Maverick La., tel. 406/846–3848; 63 sites; $15–$29; flush toilets, showers, hookups). **Hotels:** None in park. In Deer Lodge: Western Big Sky Inn (210 Main St., tel. 406/846–2590, www.westernbigskyinn. com; 20 rooms; $64). **Restaurants:** None in park. In Deer Lodge: Broken Arrow Steakhouse (317 Main St., tel. 406/846–3400; $15–$25), Scharf's Family Restaurant (819 Main St., tel. 406/846–3300; $7–$14). **Groceries & Gear:** None in park. In Deer Lodge: Ace Hardware (506 2nd St., tel. 406/846–2461), Valley Foods IGA (711 Main St., tel. 406/846–2684).

FEES, HOURS & REGULATIONS

Free. No smoking or pets beyond parking lot or visitor center areas. Site open June–Aug., daily 9–5:30; Sept.–May, daily 9–4:30.

HOW TO GET THERE

Via I–90 to Deer Lodge (Exit 184); follow signs, park at north end of town. Closest airports: Butte (36 miles), Helena (60 miles), Missoula (80 miles).

CONTACTS

Grant-Kohrs Ranch National Historic Site (266 Warren La., Deer Lodge, MT 59722, tel. 406/846–2070, fax 406/846–3962, www.nps. gov/grko). Powell County–Deer Lodge Chamber of Commerce (1109 Main St., Deer Lodge, MT 59722, tel. 406/846–2094, www. powellcountymontana.com).

Little Bighorn Battlefield National Monument

In southeastern Montana, near Hardin

One of the last armed efforts of the Northern Plains people to preserve their way of life is memorialized here. On June 25 and 26, 1876, in the valley of the Little Bighorn River, more than 260 soldiers and attached personnel of the U.S. Army met defeat and death at the hands of several thousand Lakota and Cheyenne warriors. Among the dead were Lieutenant Colonel George Armstrong Custer and every member of his immediate command. Although the Native Americans won the battle, they subsequently lost the war against the expansion of Euro-

Americans into the Northern Plains. In 2003 a memorial was dedicated to the Sioux, Cheyenne, Arapaho, Arikara, and Crow who fought at the battle. The battlefield was designated a national cemetery in 1879 and a national monument in 1946.

WHAT TO SEE & DO

Touring battlefield by car. **Facilities:** Visitor center, museum, outdoor interpretive exhibits, hiking trails. Bookstore. **Programs & Events:** Ranger talks (Memorial Day–Labor Day). Battle Anniversary (June 25). **Tips & Hints:** Cell phone audio program (free) guides you on walking or driving tours. Research library open by appointment. Visit Sept.–May for good weather and fewer crowds. Busiest June–Aug., least crowded Dec. and Jan.

FOOD, LODGING & SUPPLIES

See Bighorn Canyon National Recreation Area.

FEES, HOURS & REGULATIONS

Entrance fee: $5 per person, $10 per vehicle. No pets. Park and visitor center open mid-Apr.–Memorial Day, daily 8–6; Memorial Day–July, daily 8 AM–9 PM; Aug.–Labor Day, daily 8–8; Labor Day–Sept., Labor Day–mid-Apr., daily 8–4:30.

HOW TO GET THERE

18 miles southeast of Hardin, near junction of I–90 and U.S. 212. Closest airport: Billings (60 miles).

CONTACTS

Little Bighorn Battlefield National Monument (Box 39, Crow Agency, MT 59022, tel. 406/638–3204, fax 406/638–2623, www.nps.gov/libi). Bighorn County Historical Museum and Visitor Center (1163 3rd St. E, Hardin, MT 59034, tel. 406/665–1671, www.bighorncountymuseum. org). Hardin Area Chamber of Commerce (10 E. Railway, Box 446, Hardin, MT 59034, tel. 406/665–1672, www.thehardinchamber.org).

See Also

Fort Union Trading Post National Historic Site, North Dakota. *Nez Perce National Historical Site,* Idaho. *Yellowstone National Park,* Wyoming. *Continental Divide National Scenic Trail, Flathead River, Lewis and Clark National Historic Trail,* and *Nez Perce National Historic Trail,* in Other National Parklands.

NEBRASKA

Agate Fossil Beds National Monument

In northwestern Nebraska, north of Scottsbluff

Animal fossils in beds of sedimentary rock, formed about 19 million years ago by the compression of mud, clay, and eroded materials deposited by water and wind, are concentrated under the grass-covered hills at this monument along the Niobrara River. Native American artifacts document the visits of Lakota Chief Red Cloud and others to pioneer rancher James Cook's property from 1890 to 1940. The monument was authorized on June 5, 1965.

WHAT TO SEE & DO

Attending ranger talks, fishing, hiking, picnicking, touring historic quarry sites, viewing exhibits. **Facilities:** Visitor center, museum, outdoor interpretive exhibits, movie, hiking trails. Bookstore. **Programs & Events:** Ranger-guided tours; guided walks, talks, and cultural demonstrations (Memorial Day–Labor Day). **Tips & Hints:** Go late May–Sept. for wildflowers. Busiest June and July, least crowded Dec. and Feb.

FOOD, LODGING & SUPPLIES

Camping: None in park. In Crawford: Fort Robinson State Park (3 miles west of Crawford on U.S. 20, tel. 308/665–2900; 6 tent sites, 51 RV sites; $12–$24; flush toilets, showers, some hookups). **Hotels:** None in park. In Crawford: Fort Robinson State Park Lodge (U.S. 20, 3 miles west of Crawford, tel. 308/665–2900; 16 lodge rooms, 34 cabins; $50–$120; closed mid-Nov.-mid-Apr.), High Plains Homestead (263 Sand Creek Rd., tel. 308/665–2592 or 888/365–2592, www.highplainshomestead.com; 6 rooms; $78). **Restaurants:** None in park. In Crawford: Frontier Bar & Restaurant (342 2nd St., tel. 308/665–1872; $6–$10). In Scottsbluff: Whiskey Creek Steakhouse (1802 E. 20th Pl., tel. 308/632–4900; $10–$20). **Groceries & Gear:** None in park. In Scottsbluff: Main Street Market (401 S. Beltline Hwy. W, tel. 308/632–5303).

FEES, HOURS & REGULATIONS

Free. Nebraska state fishing license ($7.50–$9.50) required. No hunting. Leashed pets only. No motorized or mechanized equipment except wheelchairs on trails or off roads. Monument open daily dawn–dusk. Visitor center open Memorial Day–Labor Day, daily 8–6; Labor Day–Memorial Day, daily 8–4.

HOW TO GET THERE

Between Harrison and Mitchell via Rte. 29. Closest airport: Scottsbluff (50 miles).

CONTACTS

Agate Fossil Beds National Monument (301 River Rd., Harrison, NE 69346-2734, tel. 308/668–2211, fax 308/668–2318, www.nps.gov/agfo). Scotts Bluff County Tourism (1825 10th St., Scottsbluff, NE 69361, tel. 308/633–1808 or 800/788–9475, fax 308/632–7128, www.visitscottsbluff.com).

Homestead National Monument of America

In southeastern Nebraska, near Beatrice

The monument memorializes the Homestead Act of 1862, which encouraged pioneers to settle the American West by granting 160 acres of land to any household head who would live, work, and build on the land. It encompasses the site of the Daniel Freeman homestead, one of the very first claimed on January 1, 1863—the first day the act took effect. The Homestead Act remained in place through 1976 in the continental United States, and until 1986 in Alaska. The monument includes 100 acres of restored tallgrass prairie, the restored Palmer-Epard cabin, and the Freeman School, an original one-room prairie schoolhouse. The site was established in 1936.

WHAT TO SEE & DO

Cross-country skiing, hiking, picnicking, touring facilities. **Facilities:** Education center, Homestead Heritage Center, museum, guided and self-guided tours, hiking trails. Bookstore, picnic tables. **Programs & Events:** Ranger-led interpretive talks and walks. Homestead Days (June), American Indian History Month (Nov.), Winter Festival of Prairie Cultures (Thanksgiving–Jan. 1), Monumental Fiddling Championship (Sat., Memorial Day weekend), Heartland Storytelling Festival (early May), campfire programs (Sat. in July and Aug.). **Tips & Hints:** Go Aug. and Sept. to see tallgrass prairie at full height; May–Sept. for wildflowers; and Mar.–May, Sept. and Oct. for migrating birds. Busiest May and June, least crowded Jan. and Feb.

FOOD, LODGING & SUPPLIES

Camping: None in park. In Fairbury: Rock Creek Station State Historical Park (57426 710th Rd., tel. 402/729–5777; 13 sites; $40; flush toilets, showers, hookups). **Hotels:** None in park. In Beatrice: Holiday Inn Express (4005 N. 6th St., tel. 402/228–7000 or 888/465–4329, www.hiexpress.com; 70 rooms; $100), New Victorian Inn (3721 N. 6th St., tel. 402/228–8808, www.newvictorianinn.com; 56 rooms; $80). ✗ Restaurants: None in park. In Beatrice: The Black Crow Restaurant and Bar (405 Court St., tel. 402/228–7200; $5–$10; closed Sun. and Mon.). **Groceries & Gear:** None in park. In Beatrice: Sun Mart (1815 E. Court St., tel. 402/223–5207).

FEES, HOURS & REGULATIONS

Free. No hunting. No bikes or motorized vehicles on trails. Leashed pets in designated areas only. No smoking on trails, on the prairie, or in forested areas. Trails open daily sunrise–sunset. Heritage center, museum, and education centers open Memorial Day–Labor Day, daily 8:30–6; Labor Day–Memorial Day, weekdays 8:30–5, weekends 9–5.

HOW TO GET THERE

4 miles west of Beatrice via Rte. 4. Closest airport: Lincoln (49 miles).

CONTACTS

Homestead National Monument of America (8523 W. Rte. 4, Beatrice, NE 68310, tel. 402/223–3514, fax 402/228–4231, www.nps.gov/home). Beatrice Chamber of Commerce–Gage County Visitors Bureau (205 N. 4th St., Beatrice, NE 68310, tel. 402/223–2338, www.beatricechamber.com).

Missouri National Recreational River

From Niobrara, Nebraska, to southeastern South Dakota, near Yankton, to northeastern Nebraska, near Ponca

The recreational waterway includes two reaches of the Missouri River, west and east of Lewis and Clark Lake along the Nebraska–South Dakota border, as well as 20 miles of the lower Niobrara River and 8 miles of its tributary, Verdigre Creek. The rivers represent the environment that existed when Lewis and Clark made their journey about 200 years ago. High chalk bluffs, stands of cottonwood, marshy areas, and wide plains dominate the area. Farming is practiced by landowners, and descendants of European immigrants and Plains Indians maintain a rich cultural heritage. The park unit was authorized in 1978 and expanded in 1991.

WHAT TO SEE & DO

Bicycling (rentals: Lewis and Clark Lake Yankton, SD), bird-watching, boating, canoeing (rentals: Lewis and Clark Lake, Yankton, SD), fishing, hiking, horseback riding, swimming at state parks. **Facilities:** No National Park Service facilities; park office in downtown Yankton. Rangers staff the Army Corps of Engineers Lewis and Clark Visitor Center at Gavins Point dam; Nebraska state visitor centers at Niobrara and Ponca state parks. **Programs & Events:** Ranger-led interpretive programs at Army Corps of Engineers visitor center and Yankton Riverside Park (Memorial Day–Labor Day). **Tips & Hints:** Most surrounding land is private; respect owners' property rights. Visit May–Oct. for best on-river activities, although July and Aug. can be very hot and windy. Busiest July and Aug., least crowded Dec. and Jan.

FOOD, LODGING & SUPPLIES

Camping: None in park. In Niobrara: Niobrara State Park (89261 522nd Ave., tel. 402/857–3373; 38 RV sites; $18; flush toilets, showers, hookups). In Ponca: Ponca State Park (88090 Spur 26 E, 68770, tel. 402/755–2284; 57 sites; $18; flush toilets, showers, hookups). **Hotels:** None in park. In Niobrara: Whitetail River Lodge (89140 Hwy. 14, tel. 402/857–3564, www.whitetailriverlodge.com; 5 rooms; $67). In Yankton, SD: Best Western Kelly Inn (1607 E. U.S. 50, tel. 605/665-2906 or 800/635–3559, www.bestwesternyankton.com; 123 rooms; $90–$109). ✕ **Restaurants:** None in park. In Niobrara: FlyWay Cafe (89141 Rte. 14, tel. 402/857–3544; $6–$7; closed Tues.). **Groceries & Gear:** None in park. In Pickstown, SD: Fort Randall Bait & Tackle (U.S. 281, tel. 605/487–7760). In Yankton, SD: Hy-Vee Food Store (2100 Broadway Ave., tel. 605/665–3412).

FEES, HOURS & REGULATIONS

Free. Facilities along corridor may charge fees. Nebraska or South Dakota state hunting and fishing licenses required. Landowner permission needed for hunting. No trespassing on private land. No restrooms. Area open daily. Army Corps of Engineers Lewis and Clark Visitor Center open Memorial Day–Labor Day, Sun.–Thurs. 8–6, Fri. and Sat. 8–7; Labor Day–Nov., daily 8–4:30; Nov.–mid-Apr., weekdays 8–4:30; mid-April–Memorial Day, daily 8–4:30. Ponca State Park Visitor Center open Memorial Day–Labor Day, daily 8–8; Labor Day–Memorial Day, daily 8–5.

HOW TO GET THERE

Along the Missouri River east and west of Yankton, SD. Closest airports: Sioux City, IA (106 miles east of Niobrara); Sioux City, SD (95 miles east of Niobrara).

CONTACTS

Missouri National Recreational River (508 E. 2nd St., Yankton, SD, 57078, tel. 605/665–0209, www.nps.gov/mnrr). Niobrara State Park (89261 522 Ave., Niobrara, NE 68760, tel. 402/857–3373). Ponca State Park Visitor Center (tel. 402/755–2284). Yankton Area Chamber of Commerce (803 E. 4th St., Yankton, SD 57078, tel. 605/665–3636 or 800/888–1460, www.yanktonsd.com).

Niobrara National Scenic River

In north-central Nebraska, near Valentine

Eastern deciduous, western pine, and northern boreal forest ecosystems merge with sandhills, tallgrass, and mixed-grass prairie in the beautiful Niobrara River valley. Soaring sandstone cliffs stand guard along the western banks; the eastern portion of the river gives way to a broader valley with some cattle ranches. The upper portion of the

76-mile stretch of waterway is excellent for canoeing. The scenic river was authorized on May 24, 1991.

WHAT TO SEE & DO

Canoeing, kayaking and tubing (rentals in Valentine and along river). **Facilities:** Visitor center at wildlife refuge and Smith Falls State Park, hiking trails. **Programs & Events:** Niobrara River Cleanup (May), ranger programs (June–Aug.). **Tips & Hints:** Go weekdays to avoid crowds; May–Oct. to run river; May, June, Oct., and Nov. for migrating waterfowl; June for wildflowers; and late Sept.–mid-Oct. for fall colors. Most common canoeing section of river begins east of Valentine and runs downstream 30 miles. Much of river frontage is privately owned; respect landowners' property rights. Busiest on July and Aug. weekends, least crowded Nov.–Mar.

FOOD, LODGING & SUPPLIES

Camping: In park: Berry Bridge Campground (90281 Berry Bridge Rd., Valentine, tel. 402/376–3474, www.niobraracamping.com; 20 tent sites, 8 RV sites; $7–$22; flush toilets, showers, some hookups). Near Valentine: Smith Falls State Park (Rte. 12, 15 miles east of Valentine, tel. 402/376–1306; 18 tent sites; $4 per adult; vehicle permit $4 per day; flush and pit toilets, showers). **Hotels:** None in park. In Valentine: Comfort Inn (101 S. Main St., tel. 402/376–3300 or 800/478–3307, www.comfortinn.com; 50 rooms; $119), Dunes Lodge and Suites (340 E. Hwy. 20, 402/376–3131 or 800/357–3131, www.duneslodge.com; 72 rooms, $100–$110), Super 8 Valentine (223 E. Hwy. 20, tel. 402/376–1250 or 877/976–1250, valentinesuper8.com; 32 rooms; $96). **Restaurants:** None in park. In Valentine: Jordan's Sports Bar & Café (404 E. Hwy. 20, tel. 402/376–1255, www.jordansfinedining.com; $5–$15). **Groceries & Gear:** None in park. In Valentine: Henderson's IGA (710 E. Hwy. 20, tel. 402/376–1144), Yucca Dune Outdoor Adventure Gear (148 E. 1st St., tel. 402/376–3330).

FEES & HOURS

Free. River access fee $1 per person at wildlife refuge. Smith Falls State Park daily parking fee ($5). River accessible daily, but may freeze in winter. Wildlife refuge visitor center open Memorial Day–Labor Day, daily 8–4:30; Labor Day–Memorial Day, weekdays 8–4:30.

HOW TO GET THERE

Valentine is off U.S. 83, 76 miles south of I–90 and 130 miles north of 1–80. River access points are in Fort Niobrara Refuge, Smith Falls State Park, and the Middle Niobrara Natural Resource District. Closest airports: North Platte, NE (126 miles), Rapid City, SD (215 miles).

CONTACTS

Niobrara National Scenic River Headquarters (214 W. Hwy. 20, Valentine, NE 69201, tel. 402/376–1901, www.nps.gov/niob). Valentine Chamber of Commerce–Cherry County Tourism (239 S. Main St., Valentine, NE 69201, tel. 402/376-2969 or 800/658–4024, www.visitvalentine.com).

Scotts Bluff National Monument

In western Nebraska, near Gering

A prominent natural landmark for emigrants on the Oregon Trail, the 800-foot-high Scotts Bluff, along with Mitchell Pass and the adjacent prairie lands, are set aside in a 3,000-acre national monument. This site preserves the memory of the historic Oregon, California, Mormon, and Pony Express Trails, remnants of which still can be seen. The monument museum contains exhibits about the area's natural and cultural history, and houses a unique collection of watercolor paintings by the frontier photographer and artist William Henry Jackson. The site was proclaimed on December 12, 1919.

WHAT TO SEE & DO

Driving or hiking to bluff summit, hiking to remnants of the Oregon Trail and covered wagons, touring museum. **Facilities:** Visitor center (Summit Rd., off Old Oregon Trail), museum, outdoor interpretive signs, guided tours, hiking trails. Book-and-gift shop. **Programs & Events:** Local art show, Spring Up the Bluff relay race (mid-Apr.); summit shuttle, living-history programs, interpretive walks and talks (Memorial Day–Labor Day); Music at the Monument (June, Sun.); amphitheater program (mid-June–mid-Aug., Sat.). Christmas on the Prairie (1st Sat., Dec.). **Tips & Hints:** Carry plenty of water when hiking in summer. Watch for rattlesnakes. Go in spring for prairie flowers, fall for cooler temperatures and fewer people. Busiest July and Aug., least crowded Dec. and Jan.

FOOD, LODGING & SUPPLIES

Camping: None in park. In Scottsbluff: Riverside Campground (1514 S. Beltline Hwy. W, tel. 308/632–6342; 50 sites; $10–$20; flush toilets, showers, hookups; closed Oct.–Apr.). **Hotels:** None in park. In Gering: Monument Inn & Suites (1130 M St., tel. 308/436–1950 or 877/342–6099; 61 rooms; $78). In Scottsbluff: Holiday Inn Express (1821 Frontage Rd., tel. 308/632–1000 or 888/465–4329, www. hiexpress.com; 70 rooms; $109). **Restaurants:** None in park. In Scottsbluff: El Charrito Restaurant & Lounge (802 21st Ave., tel. 308/632–3534; $4–$9; closed Mon.). **Groceries & Gear:** None in park. In Scottsbluff: Safeway (601 Broadway Blvd., tel. 308/635–1232).

FEES, HOURS & REGULATIONS

Entrance fee: $5 per car. Stay on trails. Leashed pets only. No hunting. No rock, plant, or animal gathering. No off-road usage. No vehicles longer than 25 feet or taller than 11 feet, 7 inches on summit road. Monument open daily dawn–dusk. Visitor center open Memorial Day–Labor Day, daily 8–7; Labor Day–Memorial Day, daily 8–5.

HOW TO GET THERE

3 miles west of Gering on Old Oregon Trail. Closest airport: Scottsbluff (10 miles).

CONTACTS

Scotts Bluff National Monument (Box 27, Gering, NE 69341, tel. 308/436–9700, fax 308/436–7611, www.nps.gov/scbl). Scotts Bluff County Tourism (2930 Old Oregon Trail, Gering, NE 69341, tel. 308/633–1808 or 800/788–9475, fax 308/632–7128, www.visitsscottsbluff.com).

See Also

California National Historic Trail, Chimney Rock National Historic Site, Lewis & Clark National Historic Trail, Mormon Pioneer National Historic Trail, Oregon National Scenic Trail, and Pony Express National Historic Trail, in Other National Parklands.

NEVADA

Great Basin National Park

In east-central Nevada, near Baker

In Great Basin National Park, high-desert terrain yields to numerous small streams and lakes, interspersed with dramatic mountains, including 13,063-foot-high Wheeler Peak. Roads and trails lead to the rim of the peak's cirque. The park also has trails to an ancient bristlecone-pine forest and the 75-foot-high Lexington Arch. Lehman Caves, which have been attracting visitors since the 1880s, feature many unusual limestone formations. The park was established as Lehman Caves National Monument in 1922. In 1986, 77,000 acres of surrounding forest land was added to the monument to create Great Basin National Park.

WHAT TO SEE & DO

Cave touring, caving, fishing, hiking, picnicking, scenic drives. **Facilities:** Visitor centers (Lehman Caves and Great Basin), scenic drive, wayside exhibits, nature trails, amphitheaters. Bookstores, mail drop, picnic area. **Programs & Events:** Year-round cave tours, slide show, and movie. Ranger-led hikes, walks, talks, and evening programs; scenic drive to Wheeler Peak (mid-June–mid-Aug.). **Tips & Hints:** Watch for altitude sickness. Wear good walking shoes or boots in cave. No pets. Visit year-round for caves, June–Sept. to explore landscape and bristlecone pines. Busiest May and July, especially during holiday weekends; least crowded Dec. and Jan.

FOOD, LODGING & SUPPLIES

Camping: In the park: 4 campgrounds ($12; pit toilets): Baker Creek (32 sites; closed Sept.–mid-May), Lower Lehman Creek (11 sites); Upper Lehman Creek (22 sites; closed Sept.–mid-May; sections may be closed for improvements until 2015), Wheeler Peak (37 sites; closed Sept.–May). Primitive campsites along Strawberry Creek Rd. and Snake Creek Rd. (free). Backcountry camping allowed. In Baker: Border Inn (U.S. 6/50, tel. 775/234–7300, www.greatbasinpark. com/borderinn.htm, 22 sites; $15; flush toilets, showers, hookups). **Hotels:** In Baker: Border Inn (U.S. 6/50, tel. 775/234–7300, www. greatbasinpark.com/borderinn.htm; 29 rooms; $55–$65). **Restaurants:** In the park: Lehman Caves Café (Hwy. 488, 775/234–7221; closed mid-Oct.-mid-Apr.; no dinner). In Baker: T & D's Country Store, Restaurant & Lounge (1 Main St., tel. 775/234–7264; $5–$10; closed Mon. and Tues.). **Groceries & Gear:** In park: Lehman Caves Café (775/234–7221; closed mid-Oct.-mid-Apr.). In Baker: T & D's Country Store, Restaurant & Lounge (1 Main St., tel. 775/234–7264).

FEES, HOURS & REGULATIONS

Free. Cave tours $8–$10 adults, $5 ages 5–16, free ages 4 and under. Backcountry registration strongly recommended. Wild caving permits required two weeks in advance. Nevada state fishing license ($9–$18) required. No bikes on trails. No fireworks. No guns. No pets on trails or in caves; leashed pets elsewhere. Vehicles over 24 feet long not permitted on Scenic Dr. Lehman Campground to Wheeler Peak. No watercraft on lakes. Park open daily. Lehman Caves Visitor Center open year-round, daily 8–4:30. Great Basin Visitor Center open May–Sept., daily 8–4:30.

HOW TO GET THERE

5 miles west of Baker on Rte. 488 and 68 miles east of Ely via U.S. 6/50. Closest airports: Ely (68 miles), Salt Lake City (234 miles), Las Vegas (300 miles).

CONTACTS

Great Basin National Park (Baker, NV 89311, tel. 775/234–7517; 775/234–7331 cave tour reservations; 775/234–7561 wild caving permits, www.nps.gov/grba). White Pine Chamber of Commerce (636 Aultman St., Ely, NV 89301, tel. 775/289–8877, www.whitepinechamber.com). White Pine County Tourism and Recreation Board (150 6th St., Ely, NV 89301, tel. 775/289–3720 or 800/496–9350, www.elynevada.net).

Lake Mead National Recreation Area 👓

Near Las Vegas, in southern Nevada and northwestern Arizona

The 1.5-million-acre national recreation area, the nation's first, draws nearly 8 million visitors a year. Boating, fishing, and swimming are available on the two huge lakes formed by the Hoover and Davis dams. Three of America's four desert ecosystems—the Mojave, Great Basin, and Sonoran deserts—meet at Lake Mead. Desert bighorn sheep, mule deer, coyotes, kit foxes, eagles, cottontails, jackrabbits, bobcats, ringtail cats, desert tortoise, numerous lizards, and snakes all can be found in the recreation area. The area is administered under agreements with the Bureau of Reclamation signed in 1936 and 1947. It was established as a national recreation area in 1964.

WHAT TO SEE & DO

Boating (rentals available), canoeing, fishing, hiking, kayaking, picnicking, sailing, scenic drives, scuba diving, sunbathing, swimming, waterskiing. **Facilities:** Visitor center (4 miles northeast of Boulder City, NV, on U.S. 93), marinas, trails. Bookstore, fuel. **Programs & Events:** Ranger-led programs and hikes, paddle-wheel tour boats to Hoover Dam, rafting tours. **Tips & Hints:** Summer temperatures reach 120°F in the shade. Go Oct.–May for best hiking weather. Busiest June and July, least crowded Nov. and Dec.

FOOD, LODGING & SUPPLIES

🏕 **Camping:** 8 campgrounds ($10; flush toilets) in the park: Boulder Beach (154 sites), Callville Bay (80 sites), Las Vegas Bay (89 sites), Cottonwood Cove (149 sites), Katherine Landing (173 sites), Echo Bay (166 sites), Temple Bar (153 sites), Willow Beach (38 sites). Backcountry camping allowed. 🏨 **Hotels:** In the park: Cottonwood Cove Resort & Marina (tel. 702/297–1464; 24 rooms; $115), Lake Mohave Resort (Katherine Landing, tel. 928/754–3245; 49 rooms; $95–$125), Temple Bar Marina (tel. 928/767–3211; 18 rooms, 4 cabins; $60–$130). ✕ **Restaurants:** In the park: Snack bars or restaurants at all marinas. ♨ **Groceries & Gear:** Grocery and supply stores at all marinas.

FEES & HOURS
Entrance fee: $5 per person, $10 per vehicle; $16 per vessel for lake use. Recreation area open daily. Visitor center open daily 8:30–4:30.

HOW TO GET THERE
The visitor center is 27 miles east of Las Vegas via U.S. 93. Other lake access available via I–15 north of Las Vegas, U.S. 95 south of Las Vegas, and U.S. 93 in Arizona. Closest airports: Las Vegas (27 miles), Bullhead City, AZ (82 miles).

CONTACTS
Lake Mead National Recreation Area (601 Nevada Way, Boulder City, NV 89005, tel. 702/293–8907; 702/293–6180 paddle-boat tours, fax 702/293–8936, www.nps.gov/lake.

See Also

Death Valley National Monument, California. *California National Historic Trail and Pony Express National Historic Trail,* in Other National Parklands.

NEW HAMPSHIRE

Saint-Gaudens
National Historic Site

In western New Hampshire, in Cornish

This renowned artist's retreat in the New Hampshire hills was the home and studio of Augustus Saint-Gaudens (1848–1907), one of America's most popular and talented sculptors. Centered on Saint-Gaudens's 19th-century Federal-style house, Aspet, combines secluded studios, galleries, and gardens where the artist's works are on display. A stable building houses a collection of antique carriages. The site was established in 1964.

WHAT TO SEE & DO

Hiking; picnicking; touring gardens, house, and galleries. **Facilities:** Information booth, movie, guided and self-guided tours, hiking trails. Picnic tables. **Programs & Events:** Interpretive tours of house, art exhibits. Sunday concert series (July–mid-Aug.). **Tips & Hints:** Walking tours last one hour. Turning around is difficult for large RVs towing vehicles. Busiest July and Aug., least crowded May and June.

FOOD, LODGING & SUPPLIES

Camping: None in park. In Ascutney, VT: Running Bear Camping Area (6248 U.S. 5, tel. 802/674–6417; 100 sites; $25–$34; flush toilets, showers, hookups). **Hotels:** None in park. In West Lebanon, NH: Baymont Inn (45 Airport Rd., tel. 603/298-8888, www.baymontinns.com; 56 rooms; $110). In Newport, NH: Newport Motel (467 Sunapee St., tel. 603/863–1440 or 800/741–2619; 18 rooms; $75–$99, www.newportmotelnh.com). **Restaurants:** None in park. In Windsor, VT: Windsor Diner (135 Main St., tel. 802/674–5555; $5–$12). **Groceries & Gear:** None in park. In Claremont: Hannaford Supermarket (220 Washington St., tel. 603/543–1681).

FEES, PERMITS & REGULATIONS

Entrance fee: $5 adults, free ages 15 and under. No snowmobiles or off-road vehicles. Buildings and grounds open late May–Oct., daily 9–4:30; grounds also open Nov.–late May, daily dawn–dark.

HOW TO GET THERE

9 miles north of Claremont via Rte. 12A; 2 miles from Windsor, VT, via I–91 to Exit 8 or 9; or via I–89 to Exit 20, heading 12 miles south on Rte. 12A. Note that the bridge between Windsor, VT, and Cornish, NH, isn't accessible to RVs or buses. Closest airports: Lebanon, NH (11 miles), Manchester, NH (80 miles), Windsor Locks, CT (125 miles).

CONTACTS

Saint-Gaudens National Historic Site (139 Saint Gaudens Rd., Cornish, NH 03745, tel. 603/675–2175, fax 603/675–2701, www.nps.gov/saga). Greater Claremont Chamber of Commerce (24 Opera House Sq., Moody Bldg., Suite 102, Claremont, NH 03743, tel. 603/543–1296, www.claremontchamber.org).

See Also

Appalachian National Scenic Trail, West Virginia. *Lamprey Wild & Scenic River,* in Other National Parklands.

NEW JERSEY

Great Egg Harbor National Scenic & Recreational River

In southern New Jersey, near Atlantic City

The Great Egg Harbor River, a 129-mile waterway with 17 tributaries, drains 304 miles of pristine marshes into the heart of New Jersey's Pinelands National Reserve. Fallen leaves and cedar roots tint the water the color of tea, and the river's mix of freshwater and tidal wetlands draws waterfowl throughout the year. The Fox Nature Center reveals other creatures hidden amid the wetlands, as well as the park's cultural background. The cooperatively managed river (the National Park Service owns no land here) was designated in 1992.

WHAT TO SEE & DO

Bicycling, bird-watching, boating, canoeing, fishing, hiking, visiting historic sites. **Tips & Hints:** River runs primarily through private property. There are no National Park Service facilities, but you can go to the Fox Nature Center in Estell Manor County Park (tel. 609/625–1897, building open weekdays 8–4:30, weekends 8–4; grounds open dawn–dusk) for visitor information.

FOOD, LODGING & SUPPLIES

⚠ **Camping:** None in park. In Mays Landing, NJ: Lake Lenape (6303 Harding Hwy., tel. 609/625–8219; closed Nov.–Mar.; 18 sites; $17; pit toilets), Estelle Manor Park (109 Hwy. 50, tel. 609/625–8219; closed Nov.–Mar.; 8 sites; $17; pit toilets). In Woodbine: Belleplain State Forest (1 Henkinsifkin Rd., tel. 609/861–2404; 169 sites; $20–$25; flush toilets, showers). 🏨 **Hotels:** None in park. In Ocean City: Ocean 7 (870 E. 7th St., tel. 609/398-2200, www.ocean7motel.com; 80 rooms; $180–$270; closed mid-Oct.–mid-Apr., min. stay in high season). In Absecon: Clarion Inn & Suites Atlantic City North (342 E. White Horse Park, tel. 609/272–8700, www.clarionatlanticcityhotel.com; 60 rooms; $79–159). ✕ Restaurants: None in park. In Somers Point: Crab Trap (2 Broadway, tel. 609/927-7377, www.thecrabtrap.com; $7–$14). ⛏ **Groceries & Gear:** None in park. In Mays Landing: Acme Market (4454 Black Horse Pike, tel. 609/6625–4710).

FEES, HOURS & REGULATIONS

Free. Corridor open daily. New Jersey state fishing license ($9–$22.50) required. Fox Nature Center open weekdays 8–4:30, weekends 8–4.

HOW TO GET THERE

Take the Garden State Pkwy. to the Great Egg Harbor Bay near Somers Point.

CONTACTS

Great Egg Harbor National Scenic & Recreational River (National Park Service, Northeast Regional Office, Custom House, 3rd fl., 200 Chestnut St., Philadelphia, PA 19106, tel. 215/597–9175, fax 215/597–5747, www.nps.gov/greg). Atlantic County Parks (109 Hwy. 50, Mays Landing, NJ 08330, tel. 609/645–1897, www.aclink.org/parks). Fox Nature Center (Estell Manor County Park, 109 Hwy. 50, Mays Landing, tel. 609/625–1897).

Morristown National Historical Park

In northern New Jersey, near Morristown

During two winters, Morristown sheltered the main encampment of the Continental Army. General George Washington held his troops together and rebuilt his forces here through the winter of 1777 and encountered one of the greatest tests of his leadership during the winter of 1779–80, when starvation and cold drove his men to mutiny. Displays at the Jockey Hollow Visitor Center, Washington's Headquarters, the Ford Mansion, the Wick Farm House, and the park museum interpret the events and various settings from the era. The site was authorized in 1933.

WHAT TO SEE & DO

Hiking, picnicking, touring museum and buildings. **Facilities:** Visitor center, museum, guided and self-guided tours, hiking trails. Book and map sales. **Programs & Events:** Guided tours of Ford Mansion, interpretive talks, soldier-life demonstrations, living-history demonstrations at Wick Farm House. National Trails Day (1st Sat., June), reading of the Declaration of Independence (July 4). **Tips & Hints:** Busiest May–July and mid-late Oct. for fall foliage season, least crowded Dec. and Jan.

FEES, HOURS & REGULATIONS

Entrance fee: $4 adults, free ages 16 and under. No bikes on trails. No motorized or mechanized equipment on trails. No unleashed pets. Visitor center and museum open daily 9–5. Wick House open daily 9:30–4:30 (varies depending on staff availability).

HOW TO GET THERE

Via I–287 to Exits 30B (Jockey Hollow) and 36 (Washington Headquarters and Museum). Closest airport: Newark (18 miles).

CONTACTS

Morristown National Historical Park (30 Washington Pl., Morristown, NJ 07960, tel. 973/539–2016 Ext. 210, fax 973/451–9212, www.nps.gov/morr). Morris County Chamber of Commerce (325 Columbia Tpke., Suite 101, Florham Park, NJ 07932, tel. 973/539–3882, fax 973/539–3960, www.morrischamber.org). Morris County Tourism Bureau (6 Court St., Morristown, NJ 07960, tel. 973/631–5151, www.morristourism.org).

Paterson Great Falls National Historical Park

In downtown Paterson, NJ, in the northeastern corner of the state

After being harnessed to generate the power for new commerce more than two centuries ago, the Great Falls of the Passaic River, one of the nation's most stunning waterfalls, played a pivotal role in the formation of America's Industrial Revolution. Today, it is among the youngest units in the National Park Service system. The Great Falls of Paterson, NJ, became a National Natural Landmark in 1967. It was designated a National Historical Park on November 7, 2011.

WHAT TO SEE & DO

Hiking, taking self-guided tours, visiting the Great Falls Historic District Cultural Center and the Paterson Museum. **Facilities:** Paterson Museum (2 Market St., tel. 973/321-1260, www.patersonmuseum. com), Great Falls Historic District Cultural Center (65 McBride Ave., tel. 973/279-9587, www.patersonnj.gov). **Programs & Events:** Call the park to check on availability of programs. **Tips & Hints:** This is an urban park, with a stunning waterfall. Visitors may visit the Paterson Museum and its companion Cultural Center to learn more about the falls' role in the Industrial Revolution, as well as the immigrants who lived and worked in the region.

FEES, HOURS & REGULATIONS

Free. Paterson Museum: $2 for adults, children free; open Tues.–Fri. 10-4, weekends 12:30-4:30. Great Falls Historic District Cultural Center: free, open weekdays 9–5, weekends 12:30–4:30.

HOW TO GET THERE

From I-80 West, take Exit 57 B-A to downtown Paterson, turn left onto Cianci St. and left on Market St., then turn right onto Spruce and, one block later, take another right onto McBride Ave. Extension. Park at the Great Falls Overlook parking area. Closest airport: Newark (22 miles).

CONTACT

Paterson Great Falls National Historical Park (72 McBride Ave., Paterson, NJ 07501, 973/523–5295, www.nps.gov/pagr).

Thomas Edison National Historical Park

In northeastern New Jersey, in West Orange

Thomas Edison's lab and estate, Glenmont, were home to the inventor from 1887 until his death in 1931. At his "Invention Factory," he developed the phonograph, invented the movie camera and the nickel-iron-alkaline battery, and was awarded more than half of his 1,093 patents. The laboratory complex includes his chemistry lab, machine shop, and library, and a replica of the world's first motion picture studio. The graves of Thomas and Mina Edison are on the Glenmont grounds. The Edison Home National Historic Site was designated in 1955, the Edison Laboratory National Monument was proclaimed in 1956, and the sites were combined as Thomas Edison National Historical Park in 2009.

WHAT TO SEE & DO

Touring lab complex and 15.5-acre Glenmont Estate. **Facilities:** Visitor center, movies, audio tour. Bookstore. **Tips & Hints:** Parking is on Main St., across from the lab. Tickets for the Glenmont Estate are distributed on a first-come, first-served basis the day of the tour and often sell out by early afternoon.

FEES, PERMITS & REGULATIONS

Entrance fee for Laboratory Complex and Glemnont: $7 for adults, free for children under 16. Laboratory Complex open Wed.–Sun. 9–5. Glenmont open Fri.–Sun. noon–5; tickets for Glenmont Estate must be obtained at the Laboratory Complex before entering.

HOW TO GET THERE

15 miles west of New York City, in West Orange, via the Garden State Pkwy. to Exit 145 or via the New Jersey Tpke. to Exit 15W; from either, take I–280 west to Exit 10, then the first right off the ramp, go to end of street and make a left onto Main St., and continue ¾ mile. From the west, take I–280 east to Exit 9 and make a left at end of ramp, then a left onto Main St. at second light. Public transportation available via New Jersey Transit (800/772–2222). Closest airport: Newark (20 miles).

CONTACT

Thomas Edison National Historical Park (211 Main St., West Orange, NJ 07052, tel. 973/736–0550, fax 973/736–8496, www.nps.gov/edis).

NEW MEXICO

Aztec Ruins National Monument

In northwestern New Mexico, in Aztec

Numerous and varied structures of the Ancestral Pueblo people are preserved at this intriguing World Heritage Site. Recent evidence suggests that the settlement was planned sometime in the late 1000s, and that the community's design remained intact until the group moved away two centuries later. The enormous West Ruin, a pueblo of 400 rooms, is open to the public through an 800-yard, self-guided trail. The reconstructed Great Kiva is one of the walk's highlights. The site was proclaimed a national monument January 24, 1923, and designated a World Heritage Site in 1987.

WHAT TO SEE & DO

Hiking. **Facilities:** Visitor center with museum and interpretive exhibits, movie, self-guided tours. Bookstore, picnic area. **Programs & Events:** Interpretive talks (daily Memorial Day–Labor Day; less frequently May, Sept., and Oct.). **Tips & Hints:** Busiest July and Aug., least crowded Dec. and Jan. Visit in May for wildflowers and Oct. for fall colors.

FOOD, LODGING & SUPPLIES

Camping: None in park. In Farmington: Riverside Mobile Park (120 S. Gooding La., tel. 505/327–2566; 11 RV sites; $19). **Hotels:** None in park. In Farmington: Red Lion Hotel (700 Scott Ave., tel. 505/327–5221, redlion.rdln.com; 192 rooms; $69–$79). In Aztec: Step Back Inn (123 W. Aztec Blvd., tel. 505/334–1200 or 800/334-1255, www.stepbackinn.com; 39 rooms; $72–$98). **Restaurants:** None in park. In Aztec: Aztec Restaurant (107 E. Aztec Blvd., tel. 505/334–9586; $5–$7), Hiway Grill (401 N.E. Aztec Blvd., tel. 505/334–6533, www.hiwaygrill.com; $6–$15; closed Sun.). **Groceries & Gear:** None in park. In Aztec: Frontier Sports (300 N.E. Aztec Blvd., tel. 505/334-0009, www.frontiersports2.com), Safeway (415 N. Main St., tel. 505/334–7334).

FEES, HOURS & REGULATIONS

Entrance fee: $5 adults, free ages 15 and under. Leashed pets in picnic area, no pets on trail. Monument and visitor center open Memorial Day–Labor Day, daily 8–6; Labor Day–Memorial Day, daily 8–5.

HOW TO GET THERE

10 miles east of Farmington and 35 miles south of Durango, CO, via U.S. 550, ½ mile south of Ruins Rd. Closest airports: Farmington (15 miles), Albuquerque (180 miles).

CONTACTS

Aztec Ruins National Monument (84 County Rd. 2900, Aztec, NM 87410, tel. 505/334–6174, fax 505/334–6372, www.nps.gov/azru). Aztec Chamber of Commerce & Visitor's Center (110 N. Ash St., Aztec, NM 87410, tel. 505/334–9551 or 888/543–4629, www.aztecnm.com).

Bandelier National Monument

In north-central New Mexico, near Los Alamos

Pajarito Plateau is rich with archaeological sites, which were the homes of ancestral Pueblo people from the 12th through the 16th century. Trails afford access to crumbling beige cliffs, forested mesas, and deep gorges, all within a dramatic landscape formed by a huge volcanic eruption more than 1 million years ago. Two-thirds of the 32,737-acre park is wilderness. The park was proclaimed on February 11, 1916, and transferred from the Forest Service on February 25, 1932.

WHAT TO SEE & DO

Cross-country skiing, guided and self-guided walks, hiking, picnicking. **Facilities:** Visitor center, museum, guided and self-guided tours, hiking trails. Book and map sales, book-and-gift shop, picnic tables. **Programs & Events:** Guided walks, interpretive talks, evening campfire programs and walks, cultural and craft demonstrations (all June–Sept.). **Tips & Hints:** Visit in Apr., May, Sept., and Oct. for moderate temperatures and less chance of snow. Busiest July and Aug., least crowded Dec. and Jan.

FOOD, LODGING & SUPPLIES

Camping: 2 campgrounds in the park: Juniper (66 sites; $12; flush toilets), Ponderosa (2 group sites; $35; pit toilets). Backcountry camping available. **Hotels:** None in park. In Los Alamos: Hampton Inn (124 Hwy. 4, tel. 505/672–3838, www.hamptoninn.hilton.com; 72 rooms; $115-$125), Holiday Inn Express (60 Entrada Dr., tel. 505/661–2646 or 877/859–5095, www.hiexpress.com; 86 rooms; $109). **Restaurants:** In the park: café in gift shop. In Los Alamos: Hill Diner (1315 Trinity Dr., tel. 505/662–9745, www.hilldiner.com; $8–$13). **Groceries & Gear:** None in park. In Los Alamos: Smith's Food & Drug (31 Sherwood Blvd., tel. 505/672–3811).

FEES, HOURS & REGULATIONS

Entrance fee: $6 per person for 7-day permit. Through 2015, access to the Frijoles Canyon, which contains the visitor center and most of the park's attractions, will be limited to free shuttle buses operated by Los Alamos County Atomic City Transit. They depart daily 9–6 from the parking lot at the corner of Rover Blvd. and Hwy. 4 in White Rock. Backcountry camping permit required (free, must be obtained in person at visitor center). New Mexico state fishing license required. No bikes or motorized or mechanized equipment on trails. No firewood gathering. No hunting. No pets on trails or in backcountry. Leashed pets only in campground, picnic area, parking areas, along roadways. Park open 7–7. Visitor center open Memorial Day–Labor Day, daily 8–6; Labor Day–mid.-Oct. and mid-Apr.–Memorial Day, daily 9–5:30; mid-Oct.–mid-Apr., daily 9–4:30.

HOW TO GET THERE

10 miles south of Los Alamos via Rtes. 501 and 4; 8 miles southwest of White Rock via Rte. 4; 47 miles northwest of Santa Fe via U.S. 84/285 and Rtes. 502 and 4. Closest airports: Santa Fe (50 miles), Albuquerque (100 miles).

CONTACTS

Bandelier National Monument (15 Entrance Rd., Los Alamos, NM 87544, tel. 505/672–3861 Ext. 517, fax 505/672–9607, www.nps.gov/band). Bandelier Visitor Center (Park Headquarters, Frijoles Canyon, 3 miles from entrance station). Los Alamos County Atomic City Transit (tel. 505/661–7433, www.losalamosnm.us/transit). Los Alamos County Chamber of Commerce and Visitor Center (109 Central Park Sq., Box 460, Los Alamos, NM 87544, tel. 505/662–8105 or 800/444–0707, www.visit.losalamos.com). White Rock Tourist Information Center (35 Rover Blvd., White Rock, NM 87544, tel. 505/672-3183).

Capulin Volcano National Monument

In northeastern New Mexico, east of Raton

Capulin Volcano, named for the capulin (chokecherry) plants that grow on its slopes, is a cinder cone formed by a volcanic eruption that occurred between 56,000 and 62,000 years ago. The 1,082-foot mountain that remains consists mostly of loose cinders and ash, and is one of the most accessible cinder cones in the United States. The pinyon-juniper woodland and brush-covered slopes in the High Plains ecosystem of the Raton-Clayton Volcanic Field provide habitat for a number of animal species. The monument was proclaimed August 9, 1916, as Capulin Mountain National Monument, then changed to Capulin Volcano National Monument on December 31, 1987.

WHAT TO SEE & DO

Driving, hiking, picnicking. **Facilities:** Visitor center, movies, guided and self-guided tours, hiking trails. Book and map sales, picnic tables with fire grates. **Programs & Events:** Ranger-led volcano talks (daily June–Aug.). **Tips & Hints:** Avoid rim trail during threatening weather. Go in June and July for wildflower bloom peaks and ladybugs swarming on rim trail. Visit in May, late Aug., and Sept. for best weather with few visitors. Busiest June and July, least crowded Jan. and Feb.

FOOD, LODGING & SUPPLIES

Camping: None in park. In Raton: Sugarite Canyon State Park (Hwy. 526, 2 miles north of Hwy. 72, tel. 505/476–3355; 41 sites; flush toilets, showers, some hookups; $10–18). In Capulin: Capulin RV Park (Hwys. 64/87 and 325, tel. 575/278–2921; 30 sites; flush toilets, showers, hookups; $17–$27). ⊞ **Hotels:** None in park. In Raton: Holiday Inn Express Hotel & Suites (101 Card Ave., tel. 575/445–1500, www. hiexpress.com; 80 rooms; $108–132). ✕ **Restaurants:** None in park. In Raton: Oasis Rrestaurant (1445 S. 2nd St., tel. 575/445–2766; $5–$12). ♧ **Groceries & Gear:** None in park. In Trinidad, CO: Safeway (457 W. Main St., tel. 719/846–2246).

FEES, HOURS & REGULATIONS
Entrance fee: $5 per vehicle. No hunting. No off-trail hiking. No pets or strollers on trails. No trailers, towed vehicles, pedestrians, or bikes on volcano road when open to traffic. Park and visitor center open Memorial Day–Labor Day, daily 8–5:30; Labor Day–Memorial Day, daily 8–4:30.

HOW TO GET THERE
3 miles north of Capulin via Rte. 325; 37 miles east of Raton or 61 miles west of Clayton via U.S. 64/87. Closest airport: Raton.

CONTACTS
Capulin Volcano National Monument (Box 40, Capulin, NM 88414, tel. 575/278–2201, fax 575/278–2211, www.nps.gov/cavo). Raton Chamber of Commerce (100 Clayton Rd., Raton, NM 87740, tel. 575/445–3689, www.raton.info).

Carlsbad Caverns National Park

In southeastern New Mexico, near Carlsbad

The underground passageways of Carlsbad Cavern contain an incomparable realm of huge subterranean chambers, trickling limestone icicle forests of stalactites and stalagmites, and beautiful cave formations. The main attractions aren't just the enormous caverns—which include the nation's deepest limestone cave (1,604 feet); this is also the haunt for thousands of Mexican free-tail bats (more accurately known as Brazilian free-tailed bats), which stream out in black clouds from the large natural entrance at dusk. More than 117 caves are threaded beneath the desert and rocky cliff faces. The park was proclaimed Carlsbad Cave National Monument on October 25, 1923, established as Carlsbad Caverns National Park on May 14, 1930, and became a World Heritage Site on December 6, 1995.

WHAT TO SEE & DO
Attending ranger talks and cave tours (year-round) and bat-flight programs (May–Oct.), hiking, picnicking. **Facilities:** Visitor center, guided tours, hiking trails. Book-and-gift shop. **Programs & Events:** Daily ranger-guided tours. Evening bat programs (May–Oct.). Bat Flight Breakfast Program (usually July). **Tips & Hints:** Go May–late Oct. to see bats. It's damp and very chilly inside the caves; wear rubber-soled

shoes and bring jacket or sweater. Be prepared for 75-story descent on Natural Entrance Route. Reservations recommended for ranger-led cave tours (877/444–6777 or www.recreation.gov). Busiest June and July, least crowded Nov. and Jan.

FOOD, LODGING & SUPPLIES

🐪 **Camping:** None in park. Backcountry camping available. 🏨 **Hotels:** None in park. In White's City: Rodeway Inn (6 Carlsbad Caverns Hwy., tel. 575/785–2296, www.rodewayinn.com; 62 rooms; $90–$95). In Carlsbad: Days Inn (3910 National Parks Hwy., tel. 575/887–7800, www.daysinn.com; 50 rooms; $90). Motel 6 (3824 National Parks Hwy., tel. 575/885–0011, www.motel6.com; 80 rooms; $50–$60). ✕ **Restaurants:** In the park: restaurant in the visitor center and lunchroom in cave. In Carlsbad: No Whiner Diner (1801 S. Canal St., tel. 575/234–2815, www.nowhinerdiner.com; $6–$10; closed weekends), Red Chimney Pit Bar-B-Que (817 N. Canal St., tel. 505/885–8744, www.redchimneypitbarbque.com; $7–$11; closed weekends). 🛒 **Groceries & Gear:** None in park. In Carlsbad: Walmart (401 S. Canal St., tel. 575/885–0727).

FEES, HOURS & REGULATIONS

Cave entry fee: $6 adults, free ages 15 and under. Fee includes two options of arriving at Big Room (Natural Entrance and Big Room routes, both 1 mile each). Audio-guide rental: $5. Ranger-guided King's Palace tour $8 adults, $4 ages 6–15. No children under 4. Ranger-guided Slaughter Canyon Cave tour (reservations required) $15 adults, $7.50 ages 8–15. No children under 8. Ranger-led cave tours $7–$20. To prevent White-Nose Syndrome, a disease fatal for hibernating bats, no clothing, footwear, or other items that have been in other caves or mines. Permit required (free) for all backcountry camping. Visitor center open Memorial Day–Labor Day, daily 8–7; Labor Day–Memorial Day, daily 8–5. Self-guided tours Memorial Day–Labor Day, daily 8:30–5 (Natural Entrance closes at 3:30); Labor Day–Memorial Day, daily 8:30–3:30 (Natural Entrance closes at 2).

HOW TO GET THERE

20 miles south of Carlsbad via U.S. 62/180, 150 miles northeast of El Paso, TX; visitor center (near Carlsbad Cavern entrance) 7 miles from White's City, NM. Closest airports: Carlsbad, El Paso, TX.

CONTACTS

Carlsbad Caverns National Park (727 Carlsbad Cavern Hwy.; 3225 National Parks Hwy., Carlsbad, NM 88220, tel. 575/785–2232, www.nps.gov/cave). Carlsbad Convention and Visitors Bureau (302 S. Canal St., Box 910, Carlsbad, 88220, tel. 575/887–6516 or 800/221–1224, www.carlsbadchamber.com).

Chaco Culture National Historical Park

In northwestern New Mexico, between Grants and Bloomfield

This World Heritage Site preserves the extraordinary architecture and cultural legacy of the Chacoan people, the Ancestral Puebloans whose culture flourished in Chaco Canyon from the mid-9th century to the mid-13th century. The area was the cultural hub for a group of communities linked by an elaborate network of trails running throughout the present Four Corners region. The site was proclaimed Chaco Canyon National Monument on March 11, 1907, redesignated and renamed in 1980, and designated a World Heritage Site on December 8, 1987.

WHAT TO SEE & DO

Biking and hiking 9-mile loop road and to backcountry archaeological sites, picnicking, taking self-guided and ranger-led tours. **Facilities:** Visitor center with interpretive displays and videos, outdoor interpretive signs, guided and self-guided tours, hiking trails. Bookstore, book and map sales, book-and-gift shop. **Programs & Events:** Daily video programs. Ranger-guided tours, evening night sky programs (Apr.–Oct.); guided hikes and campfire programs (May–Sept.). **Tips & Hints:** Call ahead for road conditions in inclement weather. Access to park from the north (via U.S. 550) requires driving 13 miles on graded dirt road; if you come from the south (via Hwys. 9 and 57), you'll drive 20 miles on dirt road. Both roads can be impassable in bad weather. The site is very remote, with no food, gas, or other supplies.

FOOD, LODGING & SUPPLIES

Camping: In the park: Gallo Campground (49 sites; $10; flush toilets). **Hotels:** None in park. In Farmington: America's Best Value Inn (600 E. Broadway St., tel. 505/325–2288, www.americasbestvalueinn.com; 149 rooms; $64). **Restaurants:** None in park. In Cuba: El Bruno's (U.S. 550 at Rte. 126, tel. 575/289–9429, www.elbrunos.com; $8–$18). **Groceries & Gear:** None in park. In Farmington: Safeway (730 W. Main St., tel. 505/325-8732).

FEES, HOURS & REGULATIONS

Entrance fee: $4 per person on bicycle or motorcycle, $8 per vehicle. Backcountry hiking permit (free) required. No collecting, disturbing, or removing pottery or artifacts. No firearms or hunting. No motorized or mechanized equipment on trails. No touching, defacing, or chalking petroglyphs or rock paintings. Leashed pets permitted on backcountry trails. Mountain bikes on three designated trails only. Park open daily. Visitor center open daily 8–5. Loop drive closes at sunset.

HOW TO GET THERE

24 miles southeast of Nageezi via U.S. 550 to Rte. 7900, then follow signs 21 miles to park. Closest airport: Albuquerque (168 miles).

CONTACTS

Chaco Culture National Historical Park (Box 220, Nageezi, NM 87037, tel. 505/786–7014 Ext. 221, fax 505/786–7061, www.nps.gov/chcu). Farmington Convention and Visitors Bureau (3041 E. Main St., Farmington, NM 87402, tel. 505/326–7602 or 800/448–1240, www.farmingtonnm.org).

El Malpais National Monument

In west-central New Mexico, near Grants

El Malpais means "the badlands" in Spanish, and here volcanic lava flows and cinder cones, pressure ridges, and complex lava-tube systems dominate the harsh landscape. Sandstone bluffs and mesas border the eastern side of the monument, providing access to vast wilderness. Historic and archaeological sites provide reminders of the 10,000 years of human habitation in the area, while cultural resources are kept alive by the spiritual and physical presence of contemporary Native Americans. Here the Puebloan peoples of the Acoma, Laguna, and Zuni, and Ramah Navajo tribes continue their ancestral uses of El Malpais by gathering herbs and medicines, paying respect, and renewing ties. El Malpais is managed jointly by the National Park Service and the Bureau of Land Management. The site was established on December 31, 1987.

WHAT TO SEE & DO

Backpacking, bird-watching, caving, hiking, mountain biking, picnicking. **Facilities:** 2 visitor centers (Northwest New Mexico Visitor Center, El Malpais Information Center), movies, hiking trails. Bookstores, picnic tables. **Programs & Events:** Ranger-led hikes and programs. Evening bat flights (June–Aug.). **Tips & Hints:** Weather can be unpredictable. Never go hiking alone. Use extreme caution and wear sturdy boots when hiking on lava terrain. Carry a daypack with water, snacks, rain gear, first-aid kit, and sunscreen. Bring topographical maps and compass or global-positioning devices for backcountry exploration. Busiest July and Aug., least crowded Dec. and Jan.

FOOD, LODGING & SUPPLIES

🏕 **Camping:** In the park: backcountry camping available. In Grants: Grants–Cibola Sands KOA (Rte. 53, ½ mile south of I–40, tel. 505/287–4376, 888/562–5608 reservations, www.koa.com; 5 tent sites, 43 RV sites; $28–$46; flush toilets, showers, hookups). Campgrounds also at El Morro National Monument (see below). 🏨 **Hotels:** None in park. In Grants: Days Inn (1504 E. Santa Fe Ave., tel. 505/287–8883, www.daysinn.com; 62 rooms; $80), Holiday Inn Express (1512 E. Santa Fe Ave., tel. 505/287–9252 or 877/859–5095, www.hiexpress.com; 76 rooms; $127). ✗ **Restaurants:** None in park. In Grants: La Ventana Steakhouse (110½ Geis St., tel. 505/287–9393; $9–$14; closed Sun.).

🛒 **Groceries & Gear:** In Grants: Smith's Food & Drug Center (700 E. Roosevelt Ave., tel. 505/285–6336).

FEES, HOURS & REGULATIONS

Free. Backcountry camping permit (free) recommended for backcountry camping. Cave exploration requires a free permit. High-clearance and four-wheel-drive vehicles only on backcountry dirt roads. No mechanized vehicles in wilderness areas. Monument open daily. Sandstone Bluffs Overlook closes at dusk. Visitor Center open daily 8–5. Information center open daily 8:30–4:30.

HOW TO GET THERE

Visitor center 23 miles south of Grants via Rte. 117 (I–40, Exit 89) and Rte. 53 (I–40, Exit 81); Northwest New Mexico Visitor Center 1 mile south of Grants via 1–40 at Exit 85. Closest airport: Albuquerque (72 miles).

CONTACTS

El Malpais National Monument (Headquarters: 123 E. Roosevelt Ave., Grants, NM 87020, tel. 505/285–4641, fax 505/285–5661; Information Center: 11000 Ice Caves Rd., tel./fax 505/783–4774, www.nps.gov/elma). Northwest New Mexico Visitor Center (1900 E. Santa Fe Ave., Grants, NM 87020, tel. 505/876–2783). Grants Chamber of Commerce (100 Iron St., Box 297, Grants, NM 87020, tel. 505/287–4802 or 800/748–2142, www.grants.org).

El Morro National Monument

In western New Mexico, near Grants

Rising some 200 feet above the valley floor, El Morro's massive sandstone mesa dominates the land. A natural basin at the foot of El Morro held the area's only water for Native Americans, explorers, and travelers, who gathered here as early as the turn of the first millennium. Petroglyphs carved by the prehistoric Ancestral Puebloans are the oldest inscriptions on El Morro, probably dating from AD 1000 to AD 1400; the earliest-known European inscription is that of Don Juan de Onate, in 1605. The monument's most significant prehistoric pueblo site, however, is the 13th- to 14th-century village of Atsinna atop El Morro, which is part of the Zuni Indian tradition and folklore. The monument was proclaimed on December 8, 1906.

WHAT TO SEE & DO

Hiking to inscriptions and ruins, picnicking. **Facilities:** Visitor center, video, self-guided tours, hiking trail. Book and map sales, picnic tables with fire grills. **Programs & Events:** Ranger-led programs and talks. **Tips & Hints:** Headland trail may be closed during bad weather in winter. Visit in Oct. for better weather and fewer crowds. Busiest July and Aug., least crowded Dec. and Jan.

FOOD, LODGING & SUPPLIES

Camping: 1 primitive campground in the park (9 sites; $5 May–Nov., free Dec.–Apr.; pit toilets, water May–Nov.). Near El Morro: El Morro RV Park and Cabins (Hwy. 53, tel. 505/783–4612, www.elmorro-nm.com; 4 tent sites, 22 RV sites, 6 cabins; $12-$25, $79 cabins; flush toilets, showers, hookups). **Hotels:** None in park. In Grants: Cimarron Rose B&B (689 Oso Ridge Rte., tel. 800/856–5776, www.cimarronrose.com; 3 suites; $125–$145). In Zuni: Inn at Halona (23B Pia Mesa Rd., tel. 505/782–4547 or 800/752–3278, www.halona.com; 8 rooms; $79). ✗ **Restaurants:** Near El Morro: Ancient Way Café (Hwy. 53, tel. 505/783–4612, www.elmorro-nm.com; $7–$12; closed Wed.). In Milan: Wow Diner (1300 Motel Dr., tel. 505/287–3801; $7–$12; closed Mon.). **Groceries & Gear:** None in park. In Thoreau: Family Dollar (70 Hwy. 371, tel. 505/862–0278).

FEES, HOURS & REGULATIONS

Entrance fee: $3 adults, free ages 15 and under. Leashed pets only on trails. No mountain bikes, trail bikes, motorized equipment on trails. Park trails open daily 9-4 in winter, 9-6 in summer. Visitor center open daily 9–5 in winter, 9–7 in summer.

HOW TO GET THERE

56 miles from Gallup via Rte. 602 south and Rte. 53 east through Ramah. Closest airport: Albuquerque (120 miles).

CONTACTS

El Morro National Monument (Rte. HC 61, Box 43, Ramah, NM 87321, tel. 505/783–4226, fax 505/783–4689, www.nps.gov/elmo). Gallup-McKinley Chamber of Commerce (106 W. Historic Hwy. 66, Gallup, NM 87301, tel. 505/722–2228 or 800/380–4989, www.thegallupchamber.com). Grants Chamber of Commerce (100 Iron St., Box 297, Grants, NM 87020, tel. 505/287–4802 or 800/748–2142, www.grants.org).

Fort Union National Monument

In northeastern New Mexico, near Watrous

Fort Union was established in 1851 to guard the Santa Fe Trail, and during its 40-year history three different fortifications were constructed. The third Fort Union, the largest such structure in the American Southwest, functioned as a military garrison, territorial arsenal, and military supply depot. A 1½-mile trail leads visitors past the ruins of the last two forts. Wagon ruts along the Santa Fe Trail are visible here. The monument was established on April 5, 1956.

WHAT TO SEE & DO

Picnicking, touring the ruins. **Facilities:** Visitor center, museum, guided and self-guided tours, hiking trails. Book and map sales, picnic tables. **Programs & Events:** Self-guided tours. Guided tours and interpretative walks (Memorial Day–Labor Day, daily at 11 and 2; Labor Day-Memorial Day, weekends at 11). Living-history demonstrations (during special events), Junior Ranger Camps (June), Cultural Encounters on the Santa Fe Trail (June), First Fort Site and Arsenal Tour (July and Sept.), An Evening at Fort Union–Candlelight Tours (Aug.). **Tips & Hints:** Plan to spend two hours. Self-guided 1½-mile walking tour takes 1½ hours. Busiest July and Aug., least crowded Dec. and Jan.

FOOD, LODGING & SUPPLIES

Camping: None in park. In Las Vegas: Storrie Lake State Park (Rte. 518, tel. 505/425–7278 or 877/664–7787; 45 sites; $10–$14; flush toilets, showers, some hookups). **Hotels:** None in park. In Las Vegas, NM: Comfort Inn (2500 N. Grand Ave., tel. 505/425-1100, www.comfortinn.com; 101 rooms; $90), Historic Plaza Hotel (230 Plaza Pk., tel. 505/425–3591 or 800/328–1882, www.plazahotel-nm.com; 72 rooms; $79). ✗ **Restaurants:** None in park. In Las Vegas: El Rialto Restaurant & Lounge (141 Bridge St., tel. 505/454–0037; $7–$20; closed Sun. and Mon.). ☖ **Groceries & Gear:** None in park. In Las Vegas: Family Dollar (208 Mills Ave., tel. 505/454–8877).

FEES, HOURS & REGULATIONS

Entrance fee: $3 adults, free ages 16 and under. Don't climb on walls or foundations of ruins. Stay on trail to avoid rattlesnakes in the tall grass. Except for two scheduled tours in July and Sept., First Fort Arsenal site closed to public. No pets in buildings, leashed pets permitted on trails only. Monument open Memorial Day–Labor Day, daily 8–6; Labor Day-Memorial Day, daily 8–4.

HOW TO GET THERE

8 miles north of I–25 (Exit 366) at end of Rte. 161. Closest airport: Las Vegas (20 miles), Albuquerque (153 miles).

CONTACTS

Fort Union National Monument (Box 127, Watrous, NM 87753, tel. 505/425–8025, fax 505/454–9272, www.nps.gov/foun). Las Vegas–San Miguel County Chamber of Commerce (1244 Railroad Ave., Box 128, Las Vegas, NM 87701, tel. 505/425–8631 or 800/832–5947, fax 505/425–3057, www.lasvegasnewmexico.com).

Gila Cliff Dwellings National Monument

In southwestern New Mexico, north of Silver City

A glimpse of 13th-century ancient Puebloan life can be seen at these well-preserved cliff dwellings. Homes rise up into the sheer, pale rock faces, looking much as they did when they were inhabited from around 1280 through the early 1300s. The Gila Wilderness surrounding the cliffs has numerous hiking trails, horseback-riding paths, and backcountry campsites. The monument was proclaimed in 1907 and transferred to the National Park Service in 1933.

WHAT TO SEE & DO

Bird-watching, fishing, hiking, horseback riding, touring cliff dwellings. **Facilities:** Visitor center, guided tours, hiking trail, video. Bookstore. **Programs & Events:** Daily guided tour. **Tips & Hints:** Call ahead for winter hours and road hazards, and in summer for wilderness fire conditions. To reach park, U.S. 180 east option is 25 miles longer but in much better condition than Rte. 15. Busiest Mar., July, summer holiday weekends; least crowded Dec. and Jan.

FOOD, LODGING & SUPPLIES

Camping: None in park. In Silver City: Gila Hot Springs RV Park and Campground (Rte. 15, 4½ miles south of monument, tel. 505/536–9551, www.gilahotspringsranch.com; 34 tent and RV sites; $5–$20; flush toilets, showers, hookups). **Hotels:** None in park. In Silver City: Holiday Inn Express (1103 Superior St., tel. 575/538–2525 or 877/859–5095, www.hiexpress.com; 60 rooms; $109). **Restaurants:** None in park. In Lake Roberts: Spirit Canyon Café (684 Hwy. 35, mile marker 22, tel. 575/536–9459, www.spiritcanyon.com; $5–$7). **Groceries & Gear:** None in park. In Silver City: Doc Campbell's Post (Gila Hot Springs Ranch, Rte. 15, 4½ miles south of monument, tel. 505/536–9551).

FEES, HOURS & REGULATIONS

Entry fee: $3 adults, free ages 15 and under, $10 per family. Trailers over 20 feet or large motor homes must take Rte. 35 to reach monument. Monument open daily 9–4. Visitor center open daily 8–4:30.

HOW TO GET THERE

44 miles north of Silver City on Rte. 15, or via U.S. 180 east to Rte. 152, then Rte. 35 to Rte. 15. Closest airport: Silver City (64 miles).

CONTACTS

Gila Cliff Dwellings National Monument (HC 68, Box 100, Silver City, NM 88061, tel. 575/536–9461, fax 575/536–9344, www.nps.gov/gicl). Silver City–Grant County Chamber of Commerce (3 Rio de Arenas, Arenas Valley, NM 88022, tel. 575/538–3785 or 800/548–9378, www. silvercity.org).

Pecos National Historical Park

In northeastern New Mexico, near Pecos

Two separate historic areas are preserved in this important park: the ruins of the 15th-century Pueblo of Pecos, and the site of the Civil War battle at Glorieta Pass. Several old buildings are the attractions of Pecos, including the remains of two 17th- and 18th-century Spanish colonial missions. Sections of the Santa Fe Trail are threaded throughout the terrain, and the area also includes the former Forked Lightning cattle ranch and Kowlowski's Trading Post. Pecos National Monument was authorized in 1965 and redesignated as a national historical park in 1990.

WHAT TO SEE & DO

Hiking; fishing; picnicking; touring ranch, ruins, and battlefield. **Facilities:** Visitor center, guided and self-guided tours, 1¼-mile hiking trail around Pueblo of Pecos, 2¼-mile hiking trail in Battle of Glorieta area. Bookstore, picnic area. **Programs & Events:** Tours of battlefield and ruins. Cultural demonstrations (Memorial Day–Labor Day, every other weekend); night sky and full moon programs (summer, dates vary). Feast Day Mass (1st Sun., Aug.). **Tips & Hints:** Plan a half-day or full-day visit. Advanced reservations recommended for tours of Arrowhead, Battlefield, and Lightning Ranch House. Busiest July and Aug., least crowded Jan. and Feb.

FOOD, LODGING AND SUPPLIES

Camping: None in park. In Santa Fe: KOA (934 Old Las Vegas Hwy., tel. 505/466–1419 or 800/562–1514, www.koa.com; 15 tent sites, 44 RV sites; $25–$46; flush toilets, showers, hookups; closed mid-Nov.–Feb.). **Hotels:** None in park. In Silver City: Holiday Inn Express (1103 Superior St., tel. 575/538–2525 or 877/859–5095, www.hiexpress.com; 60 rooms; $109). **Restaurants:** None in park. In Pecos: Pancho's (9 S. Main St., tel. 505/757–2620, www.panchosinpecos.com; $6–$9), Frankie's at the Casanova (Rte. 63, tel. 505/757–3322; $7–$9; no dinner Sun.). **Groceries & Gear:** None in park. In Pecos: Adelo's Town and Country Store (13 Pecos Hwy., tel. 505/757–8565).

FEES & HOURS

Entrance fee: $3 per person. Park open Memorial Day–Labor Day, daily 8–6; Labor Day–Memorial Day, daily 8–5. Visitor center open Memorial Day–Labor Day, daily 8–6; Labor Day–Memorial Day, daily 8–4:30.

HOW TO GET THERE

2 miles south of Pecos via Rte. 63, and 28 miles southeast of Santa Fe via I–25 to Exit 299 (if traveling north) or Exit 307 (if traveling south).

CONTACTS

Pecos National Historical Park (Box 418, Pecos, NM 87552, tel. 505/757–7241, fax 505/757–7207, www.nps.gov/peco).

Petroglyph National Monument

In central New Mexico, on the west side of Albuquerque

More than 20,000 petroglyphs carved by Ancestral Puebloans, Hispanic sheepherders, and early settlers stretch along this 17-mile volcanic escarpment. Hiking trails wind through the gorgeous Boca Negra

Canyon, many to petroglyphs and associated archaeological sites relating the 12,000-year story of human habitation on Albuquerque's West Mesa. The park was authorized on June 27, 1990.

WHAT TO SEE & DO

Hiking, viewing petroglyphs. **Facilities:** Visitor center (4001 Unser Blvd., Albuquerque), guided and self-guided tours, hiking trails. Book and map sales, picnic tables. **Programs & Events:** Ranger-led tours (weekends Memorial Day–mid-Oct., otherwise by reservation), cultural demonstrations (weekends Memorial Day–Labor Day). **Tips & Hints:** Before hiking, get maps at visitor center. Come in spring for cactus and wildflower blooms, Sept. and Oct. for best weather. Watch for rattlesnakes. Busiest May–Oct., least crowded Dec. and Jan.

FEES, HOURS & REGULATIONS

Free. Canyon parking fee: $1 per car weekdays, $2 weekends. No hunting. No motorized equipment. No pets at Boca Negra Canyon, leashed pets only on trails at Rinconada Canyon and Volcanoes day-use area. Stay on designated paths. Park and visitor center open daily 8–5.

HOW TO GET THERE

3 miles north of I–40, on Unser Blvd. NW at Western Trail. Closest airport: Albuquerque (12 miles).

CONTACTS

Petroglyph National Monument (6001 Unser Blvd. NW, Albuquerque, NM 87120, tel. 505/899–0205, fax 505/899-0207, www.nps.gov/petr).

Salinas Pueblo Missions National Monument

In central New Mexico, near Mountainair

This site was a major trade center and one of the most populous regions of the Pueblo world during the early 17th century. Built between 1622 and 1660 by the Tompiros and Tiwa people, it comprises three distinct sections—the Abó, Quarai, and Gran Quivira missions—all of which were abandoned in the 1670s after a devastating drought. The Gran Quivira mission was proclaimed a national monument in 1909, and in 1981 the Abó and Quarai missions were added to create Salinas Pueblo Missions National Monument.

WHAT TO SEE & DO

Picnicking, touring ruins and museum. **Facilities:** Visitor center (in Mountainair), guided and self-guided tours, museum, movie, hiking trails. Picnic area. **Programs & Events:** Ranger-led tours (by request), self-guided tours. **Tips & Hints:** Busiest Apr.–Sept., least crowded Dec. and Jan.

FOOD, LODGING & SUPPLIES

🏕 **Camping:** None in park. In Bernardo: Kiva RV Park and Horse Motel (21 Old Hwy. 60 W, tel. 505/861–0693, www.kivarvparkandhorsemotel.com; 36 RV sites, tent camping area; $10–$28; flush toilets, showers, hookups). ▦ **Hotels:** None in park. In Mountainair: The Rock Motel (901 U.S. 60 W, tel. 505/847–2577; 17 rooms; $60–$80), Turner Inn & RV Park (303 U.S. 60 E, tel. 505/847–0248 or 888/847–0170, www.turnerinnandrvpark.com; 12 rooms; $55–$65. ✗ **Restaurants:** None in park. In Mountainair: Alpine Alley (201 Summit Ave. N, tel. 505/847–2478, www.alpinealley.com; $4–$7). ⟁ **Groceries & Gear:** None in park. In Mountainair: B Street Market (204 W. Broadway, tel. 505/847–2223).

FEES & HOURS

Free. Monument open Memorial Day–Labor Day, daily 9–6; Labor Day–Memorial Day, daily 9–5. Visitor center in Mountainair open year-round, daily 8–5.

HOW TO GET THERE

Visitor center is at the corner of Ripley Ave. and Broadway in Mountainair, one block west of Rte. 55. From the visitor center, the Abó mission is 9 miles west via U.S. 60 and ½ mile north on Rte. 513; Quarai is 8 miles north on Rte. 55 and 1 mile west on CR B076; to reach Gran Quivira, head 26 miles south on Rte. 55. Closest airport: Albuquerque (75 miles).

CONTACTS

Salinas Pueblo Missions National Monument (Box 517, Mountainair, NM 87036, tel. 505/847–2585, fax 505/847–2441, www.nps.gov/sapu).

White Sands National Monument

In southern New Mexico, near Alamogordo

The glistening white sands of the world's largest gypsum dunefield are partially protected by this fascinating park. Spread over 176,000 acres, the hills rise to 60 feet in some places, providing a harsh environment for the hardy species of flora and fauna that survive here today. You can catch glimpses of the desert's plants and animals at the newly renovated visitor center at the beginning of Dunes Drive. Full-moon shows at the amphitheater offer spectacular moonlit views over the dunes (monthly May–Oct.). The monument was proclaimed on January 18, 1933.

WHAT TO SEE & DO

Hiking, photography, picnicking, sand sledding, scenic drives. **Facilities:** Visitor center, hiking trails. Book-and-gift shop, picnic tables with grill fires. **Programs & Events:** Daily sunset nature walks, guided and self-guided tours, Lake Lucero tours (year-round, monthly). Full-moon hikes (monthly, May–Oct.), mammal identification programs (daily, Memorial Day–Labor Day), full-moon bike rides (Apr. and Oct.). **Tips & Hints:** Bring water, hat, sunscreen, sunglasses, and high-energy snacks if hiking. Call ahead to see if park is closed for White Sands

Missile Range testing. Motorcyclists should be aware that 6 miles of the Scenic Dunes Dr. has a rough and loose gypsum surface. Go in fall and winter for best weather, spring for whitest dunes (because of winds), May for wildflowers, late May–mid-June for yucca blooms. Busiest July and Aug., least crowded Nov.–Jan.

FOOD, LODGING & SUPPLIES

🏕 **Camping:** In the park: backcountry camping. In Alamogordo: Desert Paradise (1090 U.S. 70 west, tel. 575/434–2266, www.desert-paradise-rv.com; 30 RV sites; $25–$30; flush toilets, showers, hookups). 🏨 **Hotels:** None in park. In Alamogordo: Best Western Desert Aire (1021 S. White Sands Blvd., tel. 575/437–2110 or 800/780–7234, www.bestwestern.com; 92 rooms; $79), Quality Inn (1401 S. White Sands Blvd., tel. 575/437–7100, www.qualityinn.com; 108 rooms; $84). ✕ **Restaurants:** In the park: snacks at visitor center. In Alamogordo: Margo's Mexican Food (504 E. 1st St., tel. 575/434–0689, www.margosmexicanfood.com; $5.25–$10), Pizza Patio (2203 E. 1st St., tel. 575/434–0689; $5–$7). 🛒 **Groceries & Gear:** None in park. In Alamogordo: J&J Mini Market (2126 N. Florida Ave., tel. 575/437–7793).

FEES, HOURS & REGULATIONS

Entrance fee: $3 adults, free ages 15 and under. Backcountry camping permits ($3 per night) required. Lake Lucero tours and full-moon bike ride: $3 adults, $1.50 ages 15 and under. Advanced reservations required. No hunting. No vehicles or bikes on trails or off roads. Leashed pets on trails. Dunes Dr. open Memorial Day–Labor Day, daily 7 AM–9 PM; Labor Day–Memorial Day, daily 7–sunset. Closed during missile range testing. Visitor center open Memorial Day–Labor Day, daily 8–7; Labor Day–Memorial Day, daily 8–5.

HOW TO GET THERE

15 miles southwest of Alamogordo and 52 miles northeast of Las Cruces via U.S. 70. Closest airport: El Paso, TX (90 miles).

CONTACTS

White Sands National Monument (U.S. 70, Box 1086, Holloman AFB, NM 88330-1086, tel. 575/479–6124, fax 575/479–4333, www.nps.gov/whsa). Alamogordo Chamber of Commerce (1301 N. White Sands Blvd., Alamogordo, NM 88310, tel. 575/437–6120 or 800/826–0294, www.alamogordo.com).

See Also

Continental Divide National Scenic Trail and Santa Fe National Historic Trail, in Other National Parklands.

NEW YORK

African Burial Ground National Monument

In New York City

In 1991, during an excavation for construction of a federal building, workers discovered the skeletal remains of more than 400 free and enslaved Africans buried in a 6.6-acre area in Lower Manhattan. The memorial honors the estimated 15,000 Africans buried at this site during the 17th and 18th centuries. It's been called the most important urban archaeological discovery in the United States. The monument was authorized in February 2006.

WHAT TO SEE AND DO

Touring ancestral chamber, wall of remembrance. **Facilities:** Visitor center with exhibits, replicas of burial artifacts, and commemorative art. **Programs & Events:** Movies; ranger-led 90-minute walking tours of Lower Manhattan, focusing on the African American presence in early New York in places like Fort Amsterdam and the Slave Market on Wall Street and tracing the rise of abolitionism in the neighborhood known as Little Africa. Tours begin on the steps of Federal Hall National Memorial (26 Wall St.). Call for tour schedule and to make reservations (tel. 212/637–2019).

FEES, HOURS & REGULATIONS

Free. Visitor center open Tues.–Sat. 9–5, except for holidays. Because the visitor center is in a federal office building, visitors must go through airport-style screening before entering. The memorial is open May–Oct., daily 9–5; Nov.–Apr., daily 9–4.

HOW TO GET THERE

The monument is in Lower Manhattan, close to Foley Square and just north of City Hall. The African Burial Ground National Monument is on the first floor of the Ted Weiss Federal Building, just north of City Hall at 290 Broadway. The memorial is behind the Weiss Building at the corner of Duane St. and Elk St. Public transportation is recommended. The west-side 1, 2, 3, A, C subways stop at Chambers St.; Broadway R and W trains stop at City Hall. East-side 4, 5, 6 subways stop at Brooklyn Bridge–City Hall. If you are driving from the east side of Manhattan, take Franklin Delano Roosevelt (FDR) Dr. at the City Hall exit and proceed west to Broadway. If you're on the west side, take the West Side Highway/West St. to Chambers St., and then drive east to Broadway. Closest airports: LaGuardia (11 miles), JFK (19 miles), Newark, NJ (13 miles).

CONTACTS

African Burial Ground National Monument (290 Broadway, 1st fl., New York, NY 10007, tel. 212/637–2019, www.nps.gov/afbg/).

Castle Clinton
National Monument

In New York City

The site preserves the fort built between 1807 and 1811 to defend New York City during the War of 1812. In 1815 the Southwest Battery, constructed on the rocks off the tip of Manhattan, was renamed Castle Clinton in honor of DeWitt Clinton, mayor of New York City from 1803 to 1807. The fort later became a restaurant and entertainment center, opera house, and theater, an immigrant-landing depot where 7 million people entered the United States, and finally the New York City Aquarium. It closed in 1941. The monument was authorized on August 12, 1946.

WHAT TO SEE & DO

Self- and ranger-guided tours of the site. **Facilities:** Museum, fortification. Bookstore, ticket booth for ferries to Liberty Island and Ellis Island. **Programs & Events:** Ranger-led programs and tours. Concert series (Thurs., July and Aug.). **Tips & Hints:** Use mass transit. Plan on 30 minutes to tour site. Busiest July and Aug. and late Nov.–late Dec., least crowded Jan. and Feb.

FEES & HOURS

Free. Monument open daily 8:30–5.

HOW TO GET THERE

The monument is in Battery Park at the southern tip of Manhattan. Public transportation is recommended. The west-side 1 subway train stops at South Ferry station in Battery Park. The east-side 4 trains stop at Bowling Green station adjacent to Battery Park. The Broadway R trains stop at Whitehall St. station adjacent to Battery Park. Frequent bus service to South Ferry is provided by routes M-5, M-15, and M-20. Closest airports: LaGuardia (14 miles), JFK (23 miles), Newark, NJ (14 miles).

CONTACT

Castle Clinton National Monument (Battery Park, New York, NY 10007, tel. 212/344–7220, www.nps.gov/cacl).

Eleanor Roosevelt National Historic Site

In New York's Hudson River Valley, in Hyde Park

Eleanor Roosevelt used Val-Kill Cottage in her younger years as a retreat and in her later years as her home, where she entertained heads of state. It was built as a factory building for Val-Kill Industries before being converted to a house in 1937. The site was authorized on May 26, 1977.

WHAT TO SEE & DO

Touring home and grounds. **Facilities:** Val-Kill Cottage, playhouse with introductory film, Rose Garden, Cutting Garden, The Stone Cottage, exhibits, walkways and trails. **Programs & Events:** Guided tours. **Tips & Hints:** Allow one hour for film and tour, more for viewing landscaped grounds and walking trail. Busiest in Aug. and Oct., least crowded Jan. and Feb.

FOOD, LODGING & SUPPLIES

Camping: None at site. In Rhinebeck: Interlake RV Park (428 Lake Dr., tel. 845/266–5387, www.interlakervpark.com; 159 sites; $41–$55; flush toilets, showers, hookups). **Hotels:** None at site. In Hyde Park: Golden Manor (4100 Albany Post Rd./U.S. 9, tel. 845/229–2157, www. goldenmanorhydepark.com; 40 rooms; $65–$85), Quality Inn (4142 Albany Post Rd./U.S. 9, tel. 845/229–0088, www.qualityinn.com; 61 rooms; $120). **Restaurants:** None at site. In Hyde Park: Eveready Diner (3184 Albany Post Rd./U.S. 9, tel. 845/229–8100; $5–$12), Hyde Park Brewing Co. (4076 Albany Post Rd./U.S. 9, tel. 845/229–8277, www.hydeparkbrewing.com; $9–$13; no lunch Mon. and Tues.). **Groceries & Gear:** None at site. In Hyde Park: Super Stop & Shop (5 St. Andrews Rd., tel. 845/229–9615).

FEES & HOURS

Free. Guided tour: $8 adults, free ages 15 and under. Site open May–Oct., daily 9–5; Nov.–Apr., Thurs.–Mon. 9–5. Grounds open daily until sunset.

HOW TO GET THERE

In Hyde Park, about 90 miles north of New York City and 70 miles south of Albany on Rte. 9G. From U.S. 9, make a right onto St. Andrews Rd. (Rte. 40A). Turn left onto Rte. 9G. Home is on the right. Closest airports: Newburgh (24 miles), Albany (78 miles).

CONTACTS

Eleanor Roosevelt National Historic Site (4097 Albany Post Rd., Hyde Park, NY 12538, tel. 845/229–9422, fax 845/229–7115, www.nps.gov/ elro). Dutchess County Tourism Promotion Agency (3 Neptune Rd., Poughkeepsie, NY 12601, tel. 845/463–4000 or 800/445–3131, www. dutchesstourism.com).

Federal Hall National Memorial

In New York City

This graceful building occupies the site of the original Federal Hall, where the trial of John Peter Zenger, involving freedom of the press, was held in 1735. The Stamp Act Congress convened here in 1765, and the Second Continental Congress met here in 1785. George Washington took the oath as first U.S. president and the Bill of Rights was adopted here in 1789. The present building was completed in 1842. The statue of Washington is by John Quincy Adams Ward. The site was designated as Federal Hall Memorial National Historic Site in 1939 and redesignated in 1955.

WHAT TO SEE & DO

Attending ranger-led tours and programs, taking self-guided tours of museum. **Facilities:** Museum. Museum shop. **Programs & Events:** Self-guided tours, ranger-led programs and tours, 2 orientation videos (daily). Seasonal activities and special events available. **Tips & Hints:** Use mass transit to get to memorial. Busiest July and Aug., least crowded Jan. and Feb.

FEES & HOURS

Free. Memorial open weekdays 9–5.

HOW TO GET THERE

The west-side 2 and 3 subway trains stop at Wall and William Sts., one block east of Federal Hall. The east-side 4 and 5 subway trains stop at Wall St. and Broadway, one block west of Federal Hall. On weekdays, the Nassau St. J and Z subway trains stop at Wall and Broad Sts. Frequent bus service is provided by route M-5 on Broadway, one block to the west, and by route M-15 on Water St., three blocks to the east. Closest airports: LaGuardia (12 miles), JFK (21 miles), Newark, NJ (14 miles).

CONTACT

Federal Hall National Memorial (26 Wall St., New York, NY 10005, tel. 212/668–2561, fax 212/668–2899, www.nps.gov/feha).

Fire Island National Seashore

In southeastern New York, on Long Island's south shore

The seashore's 32-mile-long barrier island contains extensive salt marshes, a 300-year-old American holly forest, and the only federally protected wilderness in New York State. It includes the Fire Island Light Station, which now displays the 16-foot-tall rotating beacon that signaled to mariners from 1858 to 1932; Sailors Haven; Watch Hill; the Wilderness Visitor Center at Smith Point; and the 612-acre estate of William Floyd, a signer of the Declaration of Independence, in Mastic Beach, Long Island. The seashore was authorized in 1964.

WHAT TO SEE & DO

Boating, canoeing, fishing, hiking, house and tower touring, kayaking, picnicking, swimming. **Facilities:** 3 visitor centers: Watch Hill, Sailors Haven, Wilderness. Fire Island Lighthouse; William Floyd Estate (Mastic Beach); marinas, trails. Book sale areas, gift shops, grills, picnic tables. **Programs & Events:** Tours of Fire Island Lighthouse. Guided nature walks (Sailors Haven and Watch Hill, July and Aug.), birdwatching treks (year-round), wilderness program (year-round), canoe program (Watch Hill, July and Aug.), house tours (William Floyd Estate, Memorial Day–Oct.). **Tips & Hints:** Island has no roads and is accessible only by boat or passenger ferry, or by driving to Robert Moses State Park or Smith Point County Park and walking in. Bring adequate food, water, and supplies for day trips. Go in late Apr., May, Sept., or Oct. for songbird migration; Sept. and Oct. for hawk migration; May–Aug. for wildflower blooms. Busiest July and Aug., least crowded Jan. and Feb.

FOOD, LODGING & SUPPLIES

⚠ **Camping:** Watch Hill Campground (tel. 631/567–6664, www. watchhillfi.com; 26 sites; $25, minimum stay on weekends; reservations required; closed mid-Oct.–mid-May; flush toilets, drinking water, grills, picnic tables, public phone). Backcountry camping available (year-round). 🏨 **Hotels:** None in park. In Bellport: Springhill Suites Long Island Brookhaven (2 Sawgrass Dr., tel. 631/924–0090 or 888/236–2427, www.springhillsuites.com; 128 rooms; $149–$189). ✕ **Restaurants:** In the park: snack bar and restaurant at Watch Hill (tel. 631/597–3109; Thurs.–Sun., summer only); snack bar at Sailors Haven (tel. 631/597–6171; summer only). ⛁ **Groceries & Gear:** None in park. In Sayville: Super Stop & Shop (191 Montauk Hwy., tel. 631/589–9677).

FEES, HOURS & REGULATIONS

Free. Ferry fees vary. Fee charged for parking at Robert Moses State Park and at Smith Point County Park. Fire Island Lighthouse Tower tour: $7 adults, $4 ages 62 and over, $3.50 ages 11 and under. Backcountry permits required (free). Leashed pets only; pets prohibited on beaches mid-March–Labor Day. No skating, bicycling, or skateboarding. No mechanical equipment or metal detectors. Sailors Haven Visitor Center open mid-May–late June, weekends 10–4; late June–Labor Day, daily 10–5; Labor Day–mid-Oct., weekends 10–2. Watch Hill Visitor Center open mid-May–late June, weekends 9–5; late June–Labor Day, daily 9–5; Labor Day–mid-Oct., weekends 9–5. William Floyd Estate open Memorial Day–Veterans Day, weekends and holidays 9–5; Old Mastic House tours Memorial Day–Veterans Day, weekends and holidays, every half hour 10–4. Fire Island Lighthouse open Apr.–mid-Nov., daily 9:30–5; mid-Nov.–mid-Dec., daily 9:30–4; Jan.–Mar., daily noon–4. Wilderness Visitor Center open daily 9–4.

NEW YORK

HOW TO GET THERE

The seashore is accessible by ferry or boat off the south shore of Long Island (there are ferry terminals in Bayshore, Patchogue and Sayville). You can also drive to Robert Moses State Park (via Robert Moses Pkwy.) or Smith Point County Park (via William Floyd Pkwy.) and walk to the island. Closest airport: Islip, (6 miles from the Watch Hill ferry terminal in Patchogue).

CONTACTS

Fire Island National Seashore (120 Laurel St., Patchogue, NY 11772, tel. 631/687–4750, 631/321–7028 lighthouse tours; 631/567–6664 camping reservations, fax 631/289–4898, www.nps.gov/fiis). Watch Hill Visitor Center (tel. 631/597–6455). Fire Island Tourism Bureau (40 Main St., Sayville, NY 11782, www.fireisland.com).

Fort Stanwix National Monument

In central New York, in Rome

The British built a fort at the site in 1758 during the French and Indian War to protect the Oneida Carry, a six-mile-long portage that linked the Mohawk River and Wood Creek. Fort Stanwix was rebuilt by the Americans during the Revolutionary War in 1776. The British attacked the fort in August 1977 before retreating to Canada. The fort has been almost entirely reconstructed to its 1777 appearance. The site was authorized in 1935. It became a National Historic Landmark in 1963 and was listed on the National Register of Historic Places in 1984.

WHAT TO SEE & DO

Touring the fort. **Facilities:** Visitor center, fort, museum, living-history quarters, trail. Bookstore. **Programs & Events:** Ranger-guided tours, interpretive programs, living-history demonstrations (weekends in April, May, Sept., and Oct.); occasional reenactments; orchestra concert (last Sat., July). **Tips & Hints:** Busiest July and Aug., least crowded Nov., Dec., and Apr.

FOOD, LODGING & SUPPLIES

Camping: None in park. Near Rome: Delta Lake State Park (8797 Rte. 46, tel. 315/337–4670; 800/456–2267 reservations; 101 sites; $13–$19; flush toilets, showers; closed Columbus Day–early May). **Hotels:** None in park. In Rome: The Beeches Inn and Conference Center (7900 Turin Rd., tel. 315/336–1776 or 800/765–7251, www.thebeeches.com; 75 rooms; $72–$89), Quality Inn (200 S. James St., tel. 315/336–4300, www.qualityinn.com; 104 rooms; $89–$150). **Restaurants:** None in park. In Rome: The Beeches Inn and Conference Center (7900 Turin Rd., tel. 315/336–1776 or 800/765–7251, www.thebeeches.com; $6–$15; closed Mon., no lunch Sat.). **Groceries & Gear:** None in park. In Rome: Herb Philipson's Army & Navy (300 W. Dominick St., tel. 315/336–1300), Price Chopper (1919 Black River Blvd., tel. 315/339–1919).

FEES, HOURS & REGULATIONS

Free. Fort open Apr.–Dec., daily 10–4. Monument grounds open daily, 24 hours. Visitor center open daily 9–5. No pets in fort buildings; leashed pets elsewhere.

HOW TO GET THERE

The monument is in downtown Rome on Rte. 49 north. Closest airport: Syracuse (50 miles).

CONTACTS

Fort Stanwix National Monument (James St. and Erie Blvd. W, tel. 315/338–7730, fax 315/334–5051, www.nps.gov/fost). Rome Area Chamber of Commerce (139 W. Dominick St., Rome, NY 13440, tel. 315/337–1700, www.romechamber.com).

Gateway National Recreation Area

In New York City and northeastern New Jersey, on Sandy Hook peninsula

Gateway, one of two major urban national parks in the country, offers visitors a national-park experience with diverse cultural, historical, and recreational opportunities. It is the nation's fourth most-visited national park site, with more than 8 million visitors each year. The recreation area includes three units: Jamaica Bay in Queens and Brooklyn; Staten Island; and Sandy Hook in New Jersey. The park was authorized on October 27, 1972.

WHAT TO SEE & DO

Attending educational programs, beachcombing, bicycling, bird-watching, fishing, hiking, jogging, kayaking, participating in organized sports, sunbathing, swimming, touring forts and lighthouses, walking. **Facilities:** 3 visitor centers: William Fitts Ryan Visitor Center at Floyd Bennett Field, Jamaica Bay Wildlife Refuge, and Sandy Hook. At Jamaica Bay Unit: picnic areas, gift shop, marina, car-top boating ramp (Floyd Bennett Field). At Staten Island Unit: picnic areas, gift shop, marina and boat-launching ramp (Great Kills Park). At Sandy Hook Unit: picnic areas, gift shop, beach concessions, and ferry service (seasonal). **Programs & Events:** Ranger-led programs and walks (several times weekly, weekends). Outdoor programs (May–Oct.). At Jamaica Bay Unit: Canarsie Pier Concert Series (June–Aug.), Fort Tilden Concert Series (June–Aug.). At Staten Island Unit: New York City Five Borough Bike Tour (May), Metropolitan Opera Concert (June), New York Philharmonic Orchestra Concert (July), New York City Half Marathon (Oct.), New York City Marathon (Nov.). At Sandy Hook Unit: Beach Concert Series (June–Aug.). **Tips & Hints:** Watch for deer ticks and poison ivy. Get to Sandy Hook beach early on summer weekends. Access can be limited or closed between 10 and 3. Best weather: Apr.–Oct. Go in spring and fall to see migrating bird species, and Sept. and Oct. to see monarch butterflies. Busiest July and Aug., least crowded Jan. and Feb.

FOOD, LODGING & SUPPLIES

⚠ **Camping:** In park: Floyd Bennett Field (tel. 877/444–6777, www. recreation.gov; 35 tent sites, 6 RV sites; $20; pit toilets). Near Matawan, NJ: Cheesequake State Park (300 Gordon Rd., tel. 732/566–2161; 53 sites; $20; flush toilets, showers; closed Nov.–Mar.). 🏨 **Hotels:** None in park. ✗ **Restaurants:** In Jamaica Bay Unit: snack bar at Riis Park Boardwalk (Memorial Day–Labor Day). In Staten Island Unit: seasonal snack bar and roving meal mobiles at Miller Field and Great Kills. In Sandy Hook Unit: Meals at Seagull's Nest Restaurant (tel. 732/872–0025; $6–$14, summers only), seasonal snack bars at beach houses. ⚠ **Groceries & Gear:** None in park.

FEES, HOURS & REGULATIONS

Free. Sandy Hook parking fee Memorial Day–Labor Day: $15 daily. $50 annual fee for anglers to use designated parking lots. Jacob Riis parking fee Memorial Day–Labor Day: $10 daily. Leashed dogs only. No pets on swimming beaches at Sandy Hook or Great Kills Park, mid-Mar.–Labor Day. Permit required to drive on beach at Breezy Point. No off-road bicycling in park. No horse trails. No pets or alchohol at overnight camping. Park open daily sunrise–sunset except in designated fishing–beach areas that are covered under a permit. Visitor center hours: At Jamaica Bay, Ryan Visitor Center at Floyd Bennett Field open daily 8:30–5; Canarsie Pier open daily 9–4:30; Jamaica Bay Wildlife Refuge open daily 8:30–5. At Staten Island Unit, Fort Wadsworth open Memorial Day–Labor Day.

HOW TO GET THERE

Breezy Point District is on Rockaway Peninsula in Queens. Take Flatbush Ave. (Exit 11S) off Belt Pkwy. over the Marine Park Bridge. The Jamaica Bay District is in Brooklyn. Take Flatbush Ave. (Exit 11S) off Belt Pkwy. The Jamaica Bay Wildlife Refuge is in Queens. Take Cross Bay Blvd. (Exit 17S) off Belt Pkwy. Closest airports: JFK and LaGuardia Airports. Staten Island Unit: Fort Wadsworth is on Staten Island. Take Verrazano Narrows Bridge–Staten Island Expressway to Bay St. exit and follow signs. Miller Field is on Staten Island. Take New Dorp La. off Hylan Blvd. Great Kills Park is on Staten Island off Hylan Blvd. south of New Dorp La. Closest airport: Newark, NJ (10 miles). The Sandy Hook Unit is on Sandy Hook Peninsula in NJ. Take the Garden State Pkwy. to Exit 117, then Rte. 36 east past Highlands, NJ. Closest airport: Newark, NJ (25 miles).

CONTACTS

Gateway National Recreation Area (Public Affairs Office, 210 New York Ave., Staten Island, NY 10305, tel. 718/354–4606, fax 718/354–4605, www.nps.gov/gate). Jamaica Bay Unit Visitor Center (Floyd Bennett Field, Bldg. 69, Brooklyn, NY 11234, tel. 718/338–3799). Staten Island Unit, Fort Wadsworth Visitor Center (120 New York Ave., Staten Island, NY 10305, tel. 718/354–4504). Sandy Hook Unit Visitor Center (Box 530, Highland, NJ 07732, tel. 732/872–5970). New York State Tourism (Box 2603, Albany, NY 12220–0603, tel. 800/225–5697, www. iloveny.com). New Jersey Department of Tourism and Travel (Box 826, 20 W. State St., Trenton, NJ 08625, tel. 800/537–7397, www.visitnj.org).

General Grant National Memorial

In New York City

The memorial, popularly known as Grant's Tomb, is the final resting place of Ulysses S. Grant and his wife, Julia Dent Grant. After serving as Union commander during the Civil War, Grant served two terms as president before entering business on Wall Street. As president, Grant signed an act on March 1, 1872, establishing Yellowstone as the nation's first national park. His tomb, designed by architect John Duncan, is constructed of 8,000 tons of granite and marble. The 150-foot-tall memorial is the largest mausoleum in North America. It was dedicated in 1897 and authorized to be transferred to federal ownership and Park Service administration in 1958.

WHAT TO SEE & DO

Touring memorial and visitor center. **Facilities:** Visitor center, memorial, museum. Museum shop. Bookstore. **Programs & Events:** Self-guided tours available Mon.–Sun., 10–11, 12–1, 2–3, and 4–5. Informational talks at visitor center, Mon.–Sun., 11:15, 1:15, and 3:15. **Tips & Hints:** Plan on 20–30 minutes for tours and programs. Busiest July and Aug., least crowded Jan. and Feb.

FEES & HOURS

Entrance fee: Free. Memorial open daily 10–11, 12–1, 2–3, and 4–5.

HOW TO GET THERE

The memorial is at Riverside Dr. and 122nd St. in Manhattan in New York City. West-side subway train 1 stops at the W. 116th St. Station at Columbia University, two blocks east and six blocks south of Grant's Tomb. Bus service is provided on Riverside Dr. up to 120th St. by route M-5. Closest airports: LaGuardia (9 miles), JFK (21 miles), Newark, NJ (24 miles).

CONTACT

General Grant National Memorial (Headquarters: 26 Wall St., New York, NY 10005, tel. 212/666–1640, www.nps.gov/gegr).

Governors Island National Monument

In Upper New York Bay, off the southern tip of Manhattan, in New York City

This 172-acre island was a U.S. Army base from 1794 to 1966, then a Coast Guard base from 1966 to 1996. The monument includes two early-19th-century fortifications: Castle Williams and Fort Jay. From the island, you can see views of Manhattan, the Statue of Liberty, and New York Harbor. The island is open to the public May and Sept., and tours are offered at other times by reservation. The island is managed in partnership with the Trust for Governors Island, which operates the ferry service from Manhattan. A portion of the island (approximately 22 acres) was designated a National Monument in 2001 and transferred to the Park Service on January 31, 2003.

WHAT TO SEE & DO

Bicycling, taking guided tour of forts and historic sections of island. **Facilities:** Two historic forts. **Programs & Events:** Ranger-guided tours (May–Sept., reservations required for other times). **Tips & Hints:** Hours and accessibilty vary; check for current information. Expect to spend 10 minutes on the ferry and about two hours on the tour.

FEES & HOURS

Free. Park open mid-May-Sept. (varies from year to year); open access typically on weekends, limited access on other days.

HOW TO GET THERE

Island accessible by ferry (free) from Lower Manhattan (Slip 7 at the Battery Maritime Building, 10 South St.) and sometimes from Brooklyn. Closest airports: Newark, NJ (15 miles), LaGuardia (about 12 miles), JFK (about 21 miles).

CONTACTS

Governors Island National Monument (10 South St., New York, NY 10004, tel. 212/825–3045, fax 212/825–3055, www.nps.gov/gois).

Hamilton Grange National Memorial

In New York City

Alexander Hamilton—Caribbean immigrant, American patriot, Revolutionary War officer, co-author of the *Federalist Papers,* and first U.S. treasury secretary—built the Grange in the village of Harlem in 1802. The Grange, named after the Hamilton family's ancestral home in Scotland, served as his home for two years. On July 11, 1804, Hamilton was fatally wounded in a duel with his political rival, Aaron Burr. The memorial was authorized on April 27, 1962.

WHAT TO SEE & DO

Touring the house and exhibit room, viewing exterior of building and grounds. **Facilities:** Fully renovated house, exhibit room, visitor center. Museum shop. **Programs & Events:** Ranger-guided tours (hourly), period music. Hamilton's Birthday (Sun. nearest Jan. 11). **Tips & Hints:** Busiest June and July, least crowded Jan. and Feb.

FEES & HOURS

Free. Visitor center and museum open Wed.–Sun. 9–5.

HOW TO GET THERE

In Manhattan's St. Nicholas Park, the house is at 414 W. 141st St., between Convent Ave. and St. Nicholas Ave. From I–87 (Major Deegan Expressway), take Exit 4 to 145th St., then head south on St. Nicholas Ave. The 1 subway train, which runs along 7th Ave./Broadway, stops at the W. 137th St. station at City College, two blocks west and five blocks south of Hamilton Grange. The A, B, C, and D subway trains stop at the W. 145th St. station on St. Nicholas Ave., four blocks north of Hamilton Grange. The M-3 bus runs along St. Nicholas Ave., the M-4 and M-5 run along Broadway, the M-100 and M-101 run along Amsterdam Ave., and the BX-19 runs crosstown on 145th St. Closest airports: LaGuardia (8 miles), JFK (19 miles), Newark, NJ (24 miles).

CONTACT

Hamilton Grange National Memorial (414 W. 141st St., New York, NY 10032, tel. 646/548–2310, www.nps.gov/hagr).

Home of Franklin D. Roosevelt National Historic Site

In southeastern New York, in Hyde Park

Springwood was the birthplace and lifetime residence of the 32nd president. The gravesites of Franklin Delano Roosevelt and Eleanor Roosevelt are in the Rose Garden. Also on-site is the FDR Presidential Library and Museum. Tours to Top Cottage, built in 1938, are available from here. The site was designated on January 15, 1944.

WHAT TO SEE & DO

Touring home and adjacent library and museum. **Facilities:** Visitor center, introductory film, furnished home, memorial Rose Garden, icehouse, stables, grounds, trails. Museum store, café. **Programs & Events:** Ranger-led tours of house, self-guided tours of grounds and museum. Shuttle bus access to Top Cottage (May–Oct., fee). **Tips & Hints:** Allow one to two hours to see house and grounds, one to two more hours to see adjoining FDR Presidential Library and Museum (usually about 3 hours total), and 1½ hours for Top Cottage tour and tour of Hyde Park. Busiest Aug. and Oct., least crowded Jan. and Feb.

FOOD, LODGING & SUPPLIES

See Eleanor Roosevelt National Historic Site.

FEES & HOURS

Free. FDR Presidential Library and Museum: $14 adults, free ages 15 and under. Visitor center open Apr.–Oct., daily 9-6; Nov.–Mar., daily 9–5. Grounds open daily 7–sunset. Top Cottage open May–Oct., daily, by shuttle bus only.

HOW TO GET THERE

The site is on U.S. 9 in Hyde Park, just north of Poughkeepsie, 90 miles north of New York City and 70 miles south of Albany. Closest airport: Newburgh (28 miles).

CONTACTS

Home of Franklin D. Roosevelt National Historic Site (4097 Albany Post Rd., Hyde Park, NY 12538, tel. 845/229–9115, 877/444–6777 tour reservations, fax 845/229–7115, www.nps.gov/hofr). Henry A. Wallace Visitor and Education Center (tel. 845/486–7770 or 800/337–8474, www.fdrlibrary.marist.edu). Dutchess County Tourism Promotion Agency (3 Neptune Rd., Suite M17, Poughkeepsie, NY 12601, tel. 845/463–4000 or 800/445–3131, www.dutchesstourism.com).

Martin Van Buren
National Historic Site

In east-central New York, in Kinderhook

The 36-room mansion and farm of Martin Van Buren, the nation's eighth president, is at this 300-acre site. Van Buren bought the Federal-style home in 1839. He hired architect Richard Upjohn to remodel the home and build an Italianate addition. The mansion has been restored to the Van Buren period. The site was authorized on October 26, 1974.

WHAT TO SEE & DO

Touring home and grounds, picnicking. **Facilities:** Visitor center, orientation video, home, grounds, wayside exhibits, nature trails. Bookstore. **Programs & Events:** Ranger-led tours of home. Interpretive talks, bicycle tours, farm tours (weekends, reservations required), hikes, living-history programs, crafts demonstrations. Harvest Day celebration (on a weekend in Sept.). **Tips & Hints:** Plan to spend 1½ to 2 hours touring home and grounds. House isn't air-conditioned and some activities are outdoors. Busiest July and Aug., least crowded Sept. and Oct.

FOOD, LODGING & SUPPLIES

Hotels: None in park. In Hudson: St. Charles Hotel (16–18 Park Pl., tel. 518/822–9900, www.stcharleshotel.com; 34 rooms, 2 suites; $89–$119). In Valatie: Blue Spruce Inn & Suites (3093 U.S. 9, tel. 518/758-9711 or 888/261–9823, www.bluespruceinnsuites.com; 22 rooms, 4 suites; $85–$105). ✗ **Restaurants:** None in park. In Hudson: Cascades (407 Warren St., tel. 518/822-9146, www.thecascadeshudson.com; $6-$9; no dinner, closed Sun.). In Valatie: Four Brothers Pizza Inn (2960 Rte. 9, tel. 518/758–7151, www.fourbrotherspizzainn.com; $5–$12), Main Street Diner (3032 Main St., tel. 518/758–1233; $4–$8). ⛺ **Groceries & Gear:** None in park. In Valatie: Hannaford Supermarket & Pharmacy (2967 Rte. 9, tel. 518/758–8800).

FEES, HOURS & REGULATIONS

Entrance fee: $5 adults, free ages 15 and under. No strollers or video cameras. Still photography with no flash only. Visitor center open Memorial Day–Oct., daily 9–4:30; Nov. 1–Apr. closed. House open by guided tour only with sign-up at ranger station.

HOW TO GET THERE

Site is on Rte. 9H in Kinderhook. From I–90 east, take Exit B1 to U.S. 9 south. Bear right on Rte. 9H to site 5 miles on right. From I–90 west, take Exit 12 onto U.S. 9 south and follow directions above. From I–87 south (New York State Thruway), take Exit 21 to Rte. 23 east. Cross Rip Van Winkle Bridge (toll), turn left on Rte. 9H north. Site is 15 miles north on left. Be careful not to confuse U.S. 9 and Rtes. 9J, 9G, and 9W, all of which are near site, with Rte. 9H, which is the location of the site.

CONTACTS

Martin Van Buren National Historic Site (1013 Old Post Rd., Kinderhook, NY 12106, tel. 518/758–9689, fax 518/758–6986, www.nps. gov/mava). Columbia County Chamber of Commerce (1 N. Front St., Hudson, NY 12534, tel. 518/828–4417, www.columbiachamber-ny. com).

Sagamore Hill
National Historical Site

On Long Island, near Oyster Bay

With the exception of the eight years he spent in the White House (1901–09), Sagamore Hill was Theodore Roosevelt's home from 1885 until his death in 1919. The rambling 23-room, Queen Anne–style house reflects the many roles this man played: cowboy, conservationist, big-game hunter, scientist, politician, naval strategist, orator, soldier, family man, and Nobel Peace Prize winner. (The home is currently closed for rehabilitation and is expected to reopen in 2015.) Also on the 83-acre site are the outbuildings of the Sagamore Hill Farm and Old Orchard Museum, the former home of Roosevelt's son, Brigadier General Theodore Roosevelt Jr., winner of the Medal of Honor. The site was authorized in 1962.

WHAT TO SEE & DO

Hiking nature trails, touring grounds and museum. **Facilities:** Visitor center (12 Sagamore Hill Rd., Oyster Bay), Theodore Roosevelt home, Old Orchard Museum. Bookstore. **Programs & Events:** Ranger-guided tours of the grounds, nature trail, woodlands and beach areas (year-round). Ranger talks (daily). Sagamore Hill Day (3rd weekend, Oct.). July 4th Celebration. **Tips & Hints:** The best times to visit are early summer weekdays or weekday afternoons in spring and fall. Go early Oct. to early Nov. for fall foliage. Busiest July and Aug., least crowded Jan. and Feb.

FEES, HOURS & REGULATIONS

Free. Leashed pets only. Bicycles and vehicles on entry road and parking area only. Grounds open daily dawn–dusk. Visitor center open daily 9–5. Old Orchard Museum open Memorial Day–Labor Day, daily 10-5; Labor Day–Memorial Day, Wed.–Sun. 10–5.

HOW TO GET THERE

2 miles east of Oyster Bay via Cove Rd. and Cove Neck Rd. The Long Island Railroad connects with Amtrak from New York City's Pennsylvania Station at 7th Ave. and 33rd St. Get off at Oyster Bay Station (on the Oyster Bay Line) or Syosset Station (on the Port Jefferson Line). Take taxi to site. By car, take either Exit 41N from I–495/Long Island Expressway or Exit 35N from the Northern State Pkwy. to Rte. 106 north. Follow Sagamore Hill signs. Closest airports: LaGuardia (27 miles), JFK (28 miles), MacArthur (30 miles).

CONTACTS

Sagamore Hill National Historic Site (20 Sagamore Hill Rd., Oyster Bay, NY 11771, tel. 516/922–4788, fax 516/922–4792, www.nps.gov/sahi). Long Island Convention and Visitors Bureau (330 Motor Pkwy., Suite 203, Hauppauge, NY 11788, tel. 877/386–6654, www.discoverlongisland.com). Oyster Bay Chamber of Commerce (Box 21, Oyster Bay, NY 11771, tel. 516/922–6464, www.visitoysterbay.com).

Saint Paul's Church National Historic Site

In southeastern New York, in Mount Vernon

Located on the former village green of Eastchester, the park contains a 5-acre burial ground dating to 1704, an 18th-century church associated with the American Revolution, and a site museum. The site was designated in 1943 and transferred to the Park Service in 1980.

WHAT TO SEE & DO

Touring church, burial ground, and museum. **Facilities:** Visitor center, church, burial ground, museum, 1830 organ, 1758 church bell. **Programs & Events:** Site tours (weekdays), burial-ground tours (second Sat. of month, noon–4), tower walks (Apr.–Oct., Fri. 3 PM, conditions permitting), living-history programs, costumed interpretation programs with special activities for children, Black History Month (2nd Sat., Feb.), Women's History Month (2nd Sat., Mar.), military encampment and reenactment commemorating 1776 Battle of Pell's Point (2nd or 3rd Sat., Oct.). **Tips & Hints:** Visit Apr.–Oct. Busiest June and July, least crowded Jan. and Feb.

FEES & HOURS

Free. Site and visitor center open weekdays 9–5; also year-round, 2nd Sat. every month, noon–4.

HOW TO GET THERE

From the Hutchinson River Pkwy., take Exit 7, turn left onto Boston Post Rd., take Boston Post Rd. to Pelham Pkwy., and make a right; 4 stoplights later make left onto S. Columbus Ave. Closest airports: LaGuardia (13 miles), JKF (20 miles), Newark, NJ (30 miles).

CONTACTS

Saint Paul's Church National Historic Site (897 S. Columbus Ave., Mount Vernon, NY 10550, tel. 914/667–4116, fax 914/667–3024, www. nps.gov/sapa). Mount Vernon Chamber of Commerce (86 Mt. Vernon Ave., Box 351, Mount Vernon, NY 10550, tel. 888/716–2460, www. mtvernonchamber.org).

Saratoga National Historical Park

In east-central New York, in Stillwater

The Battles of Saratoga, the first significant American military victory during the American Revolution, have been called the most important in world history. Here, in 1777, American forces overwhelmingly defeated an invading British army—a victory so powerful that it drew international allies and turned the tide to ultimately win independence for a new nation. The park comprises four units—the Battlefield in Stillwater, the General Philip Schuyler House in Schuylerville, the 155-foot-tall Saratoga Monument, and Victory Woods. The park was authorized on June 1, 1938.

WHAT TO SEE & DO

Bicycling, cross-country skiing and snowshoeing, guided touring of Schuyler House, hiking, picnicking, scenic drives, visiting monument, walking, wildlife-watching. **Facilities:** Battlefield visitor center, tour road (audio tour purchase), 4.2-mile Wilkinson National Historic Trail, 6 miles of historic trails, wayside exhibits, Neilson House (1777). Bookstore and sales area, picnic areas. **Programs & Events:** Guided tours of Schuyler House and Saratoge Monument (Memorial Day weekend–Labor Day), Frost Faire (Jan.). Battle Anniversary Commemoration (Sept.), Schuyler House Candlelight Tour (mid-Oct.). July 4 Celebration. **Tips & Hints:** Plan to stay overnight in area to visit battlefield and other sites. Make lodging and dining reservations early if you plan to visit during Saratoga horse-racing season (late July and Aug.). Busiest July and Aug., least crowded Dec. and Feb.

FOOD, LODGING & SUPPLIES

Hotels: None in park. In Saratoga Springs: Holiday Inn (232 Broadway, tel. 518/584–4550 or 800/465–4329, www.saratogahi.com; 168 rooms; $179–$339), Hampton Inn & Suites (25 Lake Ave., tel. 518/584–2100 or 800/426–7866, www.hamptoninn.com; 123 rooms; $150–$339). **X Restaurants:** None in park. In Saratoga Springs: Olde Bryan Inn (123 Maple Ave., tel. 518/587–2990, www.oldebryaninn.com; $6–

$15), Mrs. London's Bakery and Café (464 Broadway, tel. 518/581–1652, www.mrslondons.com; $7–$13), Panza's Restaurant (510 Rte. 9P, tel. 518/584–6882; $5–$12). ♿ **Groceries & Gear:** None in park. In Stillwater: Stewart's (781 Hudson Ave., tel. 518/664–9083).

FEES & HOURS

Free for General Philip Schuyler House, Saratoga Monument, and Victory Woods. Battlefield: $3 per person on foot or bicycle, $5 per vehicle, ages 15 and under free. Visitor center open daily 9–5. Tour road usually open Apr.–mid-Nov. Schuyler House open for guided tours Memorial Day–Labor Day. Saratoga Monument and Neilson House open Memorial Day–Labor Day, hours vary.

HOW TO GET THERE

35 miles north of Albany and 10 miles southeast of Saratoga Springs on U.S. 4/Rte. 32. From I–87 (Northway), take Exit 12 (if heading north) right to Rte. 67, left onto U.S. 9, right onto Rte. 9P, right onto Rte. 423, left on Rte. 32, right to battlefield; or Exit 14 (if headed south). Head east on Rte. 29 and south on U.S. 4 or Rte. 32 to park. Closest airport: Albany (29 miles).

CONTACTS

Saratoga National Historical Park (648 Rte. 32, Stillwater, NY 12170, tel. 518/664–9821 Ext. 1777, fax 518/664–3349, www.nps.gov/sara). Saratoga County Tourism Department and Chamber of Commerce (28 Clinton St., Saratoga Springs, NY 12866, tel. 800/526–8970 or 518/584–3255, www.saratoga.org).

Statue of Liberty National Monument

In New York Harbor and off Jersey City shoreline

The 152-foot-tall copper statue bearing the torch of freedom was a gift from the French people to the United States in 1886 to commemorate the alliance of the two nations during the American Revolution. Designed by Frederic Bartholdi, the statue became a symbol of freedom for the nearly 12 million immigrants who arrived at nearby Ellis Island between 1892 and 1954. The main building on Ellis Island is now a museum dedicated to the history of immigration. The statue was proclaimed a national monument in 1924, transferred to the Park Service in 1933, and designated a World Heritage Site in 1984. Ellis Island was incorporated into the national monument in 1965.

WHAT TO SEE & DO

Taking ferry to Liberty and Ellis islands, touring museums. **Facilities:** Statue, Ellis Island Main Building, museums, Ellis Island library and oral-history collection, Ellis Island documentary. **Programs & Events:** Ranger-led tours (when staffing permits at Ellis and Liberty Islands). **Tips & Hints:** You may have to wait in line an hour or more for the ferry to the islands; you may have to wait another hour or more to enter the monument. Drink plenty of fluids in summer. Dress warmly in winter. Arrive early in the day for shorter lines. Busiest mid-Apr.–Sept., least crowded Jan. and Feb.

FOOD

✕ **Restaurants:** In the park: cafeterias on Liberty Island and Ellis Island.

FEES & HOURS

Free. Separate tickets are required to enter the crown of the statue ($3 person, limited to 240 people per day) and the monument (free, limited to 2,800 people per day). Round-trip ferry fee: $17 adults, $14 ages 62 and over, $9 ages 3–12, free ages 2 and under. Fee includes visits to both islands; reserved times only. Monument open daily, hours vary.

HOW TO GET THERE

Islands accessible by ferry only. Ferries (tel. 201/604–2800, www. statuecruises.com) leave Battery Park in Lower Manhattan and Liberty State Park in Jersey City, NJ. Closest airports: LaGuardia (about 13 miles to Battery Park), JFK (20 miles to Battery Park), and Newark, NJ (10 miles to Liberty State Park).

CONTACT

Statue of Liberty National Monument (Liberty Island, New York, NY 10004, tel. 212/363–3200, fax 212/363–8347, www.nps.gov/stli). The Statue of Liberty–Ellis Island Foundation (17 Battery Pl., Suite 210, New York, NY 10004-3507, tel. 212/561–4500, www.statueofliberty.org).

Theodore Roosevelt Birthplace National Historic Site

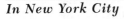

In New York City

Theodore Roosevelt, apostle of the strenuous life, larger-than-life hero to millions of Americans, and 26th president of the United States, was born in a brownstone house on this site on October 27, 1858. His family lived here until he was 14. The house was demolished in 1916, reconstructed in 1923, and furnished by the Women's Roosevelt Memorial Association with the assistance of the president's widow and sisters. The site was authorized on July 25, 1962.

WHAT TO SEE & DO

Touring period rooms. **Facilities:** Five Victorian-era rooms furnished and decorated as they were during Roosevelt's occupancy, museum gallery. Museum gift shop. **Programs & Events:** Ranger-led programs and tours (throughout the day). **Tips & Hints:** Plan to spend 45 minutes at the site. House tours last 30 minutes and start on the hour; last tour begins at 4. Busiest in summer and Mar. and Apr., least crowded Sept. and Jan.

FEES & HOURS

Free. House open Tues.–Sat. 9–5, tours 10–4, no tour at noon.

HOW TO GET THERE

The reconstructed house is in Manhattan at 28 E. 20th St., between Broadway and Park Ave. S. Use mass transit to get to house because parking is scarce. The 6 subway train, which runs along Lexington Ave., stops at the E. 23rd St. station on Park Ave. S. The N and R subway trains stop at the E. 23rd St. station on Broadway. Frequent bus service is provided by the M-1 along Park Ave. S, the M-5 along 5th Ave., and the M-2 or M-3 along 5th Ave. and Park Ave. S. The M-23 operates crosstown on 23rd St. Closest airports: LaGuardia (9 miles), JFK (18 miles), Newark (14 miles).

CONTACT

Theodore Roosevelt Birthplace National Historic Site (28 E. 20th St., New York, NY 10003, tel. 212/260–1616, fax 212/677–3587, www.nps.gov/thrb).

Theodore Roosevelt Inaugural National Historic Site

In Buffalo

Theodore Roosevelt was sworn in here—at the home of his longtime friend Ansley Wilcox—on September 14, 1901, to become the 26th president of the United States after the assassination of William McKinley. The house, which was built in the 1830s as officers' quarters for the Buffalo Barracks, is an outstanding example of Greek Revival architecture. The site was designated in 1966 and opened in 1971.

WHAT TO SEE & DO

Taking guided walking tour, touring house and neighborhood, viewing interactive exhibits. **Facilities:** Visitor center, house, grounds. Museum shop, research library. **Programs & Events:** Guided house tours and architectural and historical walking tours (May-Sept., reservations required). Victorian Days Children's Program (July and Aug.), Teddy Bear Picnic (usually June-Aug.), Inaugural Commemoration (Sept.), Victorian Christmas (Dec.). **Tips & Hints:** Park in lot behind site on Franklin St. Busiest July, Aug., and Dec., least crowded Jan. and Feb.

FEES & HOURS

Entrance fee: $10 adults, $7 ages 62 and older, $5 ages 6–18, free ages 5 and under; $25 per family. Architectural and historical tours: $10 adults, $5 ages 6–14. Tours leave hourly, beginning at 9:30 on weekdays and 12:30 on weekends; last tour leaves at 3:30. Site open weekdays 9–5, weekends noon–5.

HOW TO GET THERE

1 mile north of downtown Buffalo. Closest airport: Buffalo (5 miles).

CONTACTS

Theodore Roosevelt Inaugural National Historic Site (641 Delaware Ave., Buffalo, NY 14202, tel. 716/884–0095, fax 716/884–0330, www.

nps.gov/thri). Buffalo Niagara Convention and Visitors Bureau (617 Main St., Suite 200, Buffalo, NY 14203, tel. 800/283–3256, www.visitbuffaloniagara.com).

Vanderbilt Mansion National Historic Site

In New York's Hudson Valley region, in Hyde Park

Once the country home of Frederick W. Vanderbilt, a grandson of industrialist and philanthopist Cornelius Vanderbilt, the Vanderbilt Mansion is a magnificent example of the great estates built by wealthy financial and industrial leaders between 1880 and 1900. The site was designated on December 18, 1940.

WHAT TO SEE & DO

Taking guided tours of home, taking self-guided tours of formal garden and grounds. **Facilities:** Visitor center, furnished home of Frederick Vanderbilt, grounds and gardens, trails. Bookstore, gift shop. **Programs & Events:** Ranger-led mansion tours. **Tips & Hints:** Allow one to two hours to see house and grounds. Busiest June–Aug., least crowded Jan. and Feb.

FOOD, LODGING & SUPPLIES

See Eleanor Roosevelt National Historic Site.

FEES & HOURS

Free. Guided tours: $8 adults, free ages 15 and under. Site open daily 9–5, guided tour only; grounds open daily 7 AM–sunset.

HOW TO GET THERE

About 90 miles north of New York City, 70 miles south of Albany on the east bank of the Hudson River. The site is on U.S. 9, 2 miles north of the Home of Franklin Delano Roosevelt National Historic Site (see separate listing). Closest airports: Newburgh (28 miles), Albany (77 miles).

CONTACTS

Vanderbilt Mansion National Historic Site (4097 Albany Post Rd., Hyde Park, NY 12538, tel. 845/229–9115, 800/967–2283 for house tours, fax 845/229–7115, www.nps.gov/vama). Dutchess County Tourism Promotion Agency (3 Neptune Rd., Suite M17, Poughkeepsie, NY 12601, tel. 845/463–4000 or 800/445–3131, www.dutchesstourism.com).

Women's Rights National Historical Park

In central New York, in Seneca Falls and Waterloo

Seneca Falls is the birthplace of the women's rights movement in the United States. The park includes the Wesleyan Chapel, the site of the first Women's Rights Convention in 1848; the Elizabeth Cady Stanton house, home of one of the founders of the movement; the Hunt House, where the convention organizers first met; the M'Clintock House, where the "Declaration of Rights and Sentiments" was written; and a visitor center with exhibits and a film. The park was authorized on December 28, 1980.

WHAT TO SEE & DO

Touring museum, historic buildings, district, and homes. **Facilities:** Visitor center (136 Fall St.), Elizabeth Cady Stanton home. Bookstore. **Programs & Events:** Wesleyan Chapel talks and Stanton House programs (daily). Ranger-guided programs at Wesleyan Chapel. Stanton House (daily, Mar.–Nov.), M'Clintock House (daily, June–Aug.). Women's History Month (Mar.), Convention Days (3rd weekend, July). **Tips & Hints:** Busiest Apr. and May, least crowded Jan. and Feb.

FOOD, LODGING & SUPPLIES

Camping: None in park. Near Seneca Falls: Cayuga Lake State Park (2678 Lower Lake Rd., tel. 315/568–5163; 800/456–2267, www. reserveamerica.com; 286 sites; $19–$25; flush toilets, showers, hookups; most sites closed mid-Oct.–Apr.). **Hotels:** None in park. In Waterloo: Holiday Inn (2468 Mound Rd., tel. 315/539–5011 or 800/957–4654, www.hiwaterloo.com; 147 rooms; $114–$139). In Seneca Falls: Microtel Inn & Suites (1966 Rtes. 5 and 20, tel. 315/539–8438 or 800/337–0050, www.senecafallsmicrotelinn.com; 69 rooms, 21 suites; $110). **Restaurants:** None in park. In Waterloo: Abigail's Restaurant (Waterloo–Seneca Falls Rd., tel. 315/539–9300, www. abigailsrestaurant.com; $5–$10; no lunch Sat.). **Groceries & Gear:** None in park. In Waterloo: Tops Friendly Market (1963 Kingdom Plaza, tel. 315/539–8866).

FEES, HOURS & REGULATIONS

Free. No pets in visitor center or any historic building (service animals excepted). Visitor center open daily 9–5, park grounds open daily dawn–dusk.

HOW TO GET THERE

Park visitor center is at 136 Fall St. (Rte. 5/U.S. 20), which is reached via Exit 41 off New York State Thruway (I–90), then Rte. 414 for 4 miles and Rte. 5/U.S. 20 east for 2 miles. Closest airports: Syracuse (48 miles), Rochester (55 miles).

CONTACTS

Women's Rights National Historical Park (136 Fall St., Seneca Falls, NY 13148, tel. 315/568–2991, fax 315/568–2141, www.nps.gov/wori). Seneca County Chamber of Commerce (2020 Rtes. 5 and 20 W, Box 70, Seneca Falls, NY 13148, tel. 315/568–2906 or 800/732–1848, www. senecachamber.org).

Blue Ridge Parkway

*The parkway follows the Blue Ridge and Southern
Appalachian mountains for 469 miles through western
Virginia and North Carolina.*

The parkway, which connects the Shenandoah and Great Smoky
Mountains National Parks, provides recreational opportunities and
scenic overlooks and preserves remnants of Appalachian culture from
the late 19th and early 20th centuries. With elevations ranging from
about 650 feet to nearly 6,050 feet, the parkway protects a wide variety
of plant and animal life. Within the park are 1,600 identified types
of vascular plants and more than 40 rare or endangered plants and
animals. Parkway construction began on September 11, 1935, with
funding from the National Industrial Recovery Act. The parkway was
established on June 30, 1936.

WHAT TO SEE & DO

Bicycling, camping, canoeing (rentals Julian Price Park, mile 295),
driving, fishing, hiking, picnicking. **Facilities:** 469-mile-long parkway
and 13 visitor centers: Humpback Rocks (mile 6), James River (mile
63), Peaks of Otter (mile 86), Blue Ridge Parkway Visitor Center at
Explore Park (mile 115), Rocky Knob (mile 169), Blue Ridge Music
Center (mile 213), Moses H. Cone Memorial Park (mile 294), Linn
Cove (mile 304), Linville Falls (mile 316), Museum of North Carolina
Minerals (mile 331), Craggy Gardens (mile 364), Blue Ridge Parkway
Visitor Center (mile 384), and Waterrock Knob (mile 451). The
Northwest Trading Post (mile 258) sells crafts and foods produced in
the northwestern North Carolina mountains, and the Folk Art Center
(mile 382) sells products from the Southern Highlands Craft Guild.
Trails, wayside exhibits, bulletin boards. Gift shops, picnic facilities,
sales outlets. **Programs & Events:** Ranger-led demonstrations and/or
interpretive talks at all major parkway locations (June–Oct.). Brinegar
Days at Brinegar Cabin (mile 238; Aug.), Mountain Music at Mabry
Mill (mile 176; May–Oct., Sun.), and Roanoke Mountain Campground
(mile 120; June–Sept., Sun.), outdoor concerts (Blue Ridge Music
Center, mile 213; June–Sept., daily). **Tips & Hints:** Speed limit is 45
mph. Go during the week to avoid traffic. Go Apr.–May for wildflowers,
mid-Oct. for fall leaf color. Winter weather can close sections for
long periods. Get gas beforehand, as there's none available on the
parkway. Busiest July–Oct., least crowded Jan. and Feb.

FOOD, LODGING & SUPPLIES

Camping: 9 campgrounds ($16; flush toilets; closed late Oct.–Apr.)
in the park: Otter Creek (mile 60, tel. 434/299–5125; 69 sites), Peaks
of Otter (mile 86, tel. 540/586–4357; 132 sites), Roanoke Mountain
(mile 120, tel. 540/767–2492; 105 sites), Rocky Knob (mile 167, tel.

540/745–9660; 109 sites), Doughton Park (mile 239, tel. 336/372–8568; 127 sites), Price Park (mile 297, tel. 828/963–5911; 197 sites), Linville Falls (mile 316, tel. 828/765–7818; 70 sites), Crabtree Falls (mile 339, tel. 828/675–0941; 93 sites), and Mount Pisgah (mile 408, tel. 828/456–8829; 128 sites). Backcountry camping allowed at Rocky Knob area at Rockcastle Gorge and Doughton Park area at Basin Cove (permit required, see below). ⌂ **Hotels:** In the park: Peaks of Otter (mile 86, tel. 540/586–1081; 63 rooms; $93–$125), Rocky Knob Cabins (mile 174, tel. 540/593–3503; 7 cabins; $54), Pisgah Inn (mile 409, tel. 828/235–8228; 51 rooms; $103; closed Nov.–Mar.). In Asheville: Crowne Plaza Hotel (1 Resort Dr., off I–240 at Exit 3B, tel. 828/254–3211 or 877/227–6963, www.ashevillecp.com; 272 rooms, 4 suites; $150–$172). In Brevard: Sunset Motel (415 S. Broad St., tel. 828/884–9106, www.thesunsetmotel.com; 19 rooms; $60). In Waynesville: Best Western Smoky Mountain Inn (130 Shiloh Tr., tel. 828/456–4402 or 800/218–2121, www.bestwestern.com; 58 rooms; $80–$110). ✘ **Restaurants:** 3 restaurants in park (closed Oct.–May): Peaks of Otter (mile 86, tel. 540/586–1081; $5–$10), Mabry Mill (mile 176, tel. 540/952–2947; $5–$10), Pisgah Inn (mile 409, tel. 828/235–8228; $6–$10). In Pisgah Forest: Pisgah Fish Camp (663 Deavor Rd., tel. 828/877–3129; $5–$15). ⛄ **Groceries & Gear:** None in park. In Asheville: Bi-Lo (801 Fairview Rd., tel. 828/299–1400).

FEES, HOURS & REGULATIONS

Free. Backcountry permits required (free; available in Basin Cove, tel. 336/372–8568, or Rockcastle Gorge, tel. 540/745–9660). Virginia or North Carolina state fishing license required. No hunting. Trails for foot travel only, except designated horse trails. Park motor road open daily except in bad weather. Ridge Parkway Visitor Center and Museum of North Carolina Minerals open year-round, daily 9–5. All other visitor centers open May–Oct., daily 9–5.

HOW TO GET THERE

Major cities along the Blue Ridge Parkway are Waynesboro (U.S. 250 and I–64) and Roanoke (U.S. 220, U.S. 460, and I–81) in Virginia, and Boone (U.S. 321 and U.S. 421), Asheville (I–40 and I–26, and U.S. 70, U.S. 74, and U.S. 23), and Waynesville (U.S. 19/23 and I–40) in North Carolina. Closest regional airports: Roanoke, VA; Asheville, NC.

CONTACTS

Blue Ridge Parkway (199 Hemphill Knob Rd., Asheville, NC 28803, tel. 828/298–0398 recorded information; 828/271–4779 for headquarters, www.nps.gov/blri). Boone Area Chamber of Commerce (870 W. King St., Suite A, Boone, NC 28607, tel. 828/264–2225, www.boonechamber.com). Greater Augusta Regional Chamber of Commerce (30 Ladd Rd., Box 1107, Fishersville, VA 22939, tel. 540/324–1133, www.augustava.com). Roanoke Valley Convention & Visitors Bureau, VA (101 Shenandoah Ave. NE, Roanoke, VA 24016, tel. 540/342–6025, www.visitroanokeva.com).

Cape Hatteras National Seashore

On the Outer Banks

The nation's first national seashore, Cape Hatteras preserves significant portions of North Carolina's famed barrier islands—Bodie, Hatteras, and Ocracoke. The Cape Hatteras Light, the tallest brick lighthouse in North America, harks back to the days when this stretch of ocean was known as the "Graveyard of the Atlantic" because of its treacherous currents and offshore shoals. The park was authorized in 1937.

WHAT TO SEE & DO

Beach-going, bird-watching, boardsailing, fishing, hiking, surfing, swimming, touring lighthouses. **Facilities:** 3 visitor centers: Bodie Island (8 miles south of U.S. 158/U.S. 64 intersection), Hatteras Island (Buxton, 45 miles south of U.S. 158/U.S. 64 intersection), and Ocracoke Island. Contact station at Whalebone Junction (U.S. 158/U.S. 64 intersection, Nags Head), lighthouses and restored keepers' homes, nature trails, wayside exhibits. Book sale areas, changing and shower facilities, picnic areas. **Programs & Events:** Guided beach walks, nature trail hikes, natural history programs, ecology demonstrations, lighthouse tours, ranger-led recreational demonstrations (mid-June–mid-Aug.). **Tips & Hints:** Guided Cape Hatteras Lighthouse tours (late Apr.–early Oct.) by timed ticket entry only with no advance reservations. Make sure to know rip current safety information. Arrive early to be sure to get tickets. Plan for a wait in summer for free 40-minute ferry from Hatteras to Ocracoke Island. Go Mar. and Apr., and Oct. and Nov. for bird migrations. Busiest July and Aug., least crowded Jan. and Feb.

FOOD, LODGING & SUPPLIES

Camping: 4 campgrounds ($20; flush toilets, cold showers) in the park: Cape Point (202 sites; closed Aug.–late May), Frisco (127 sites; closed mid-Oct.–mid-Apr.), Ocracoke (tel. 877/444–6777 reservations; 136 sites; $23; closed mid-Oct.–mid-Apr.), Oregon Inlet (120 sites; closed mid-Oct.–mid-Apr.). **Hotels:** None in park. In Hatteras: Seaside Inn (57321 Hwy. 12, tel. 252/986–2700; 10 rooms; $75–$105). ✗ **Restaurants:** None in park. In Waves: Down Under (25920 Rte. 12, tel. 252/987–2277, www.downunderrestaurant.com; $5–$13). In Frisco: Quarterdeck (54214 Rte. 12, tel. 252/986–2425, www.quarterdeckfamilyrestaurant.com; $2–$9). **Groceries & Gear:** None in park. In Avon: Food Lion (41934 Rte. 12, tel. 252/995–4488).

FEES, HOURS & REGULATIONS

Free. Lighthouse tours: $7 adults, $3.50 ages 13 and under (must be at least 42 inches tall) and 62 and over. Off-road vehicle permit required for beach driving. North Carolina state and U.S. federal migratory bird-hunting licenses required. North Carolina saltwater fishing license required. Group camping permit required. Leashed pets only.

No all-terrain vehicles. Access to some areas barred because of habitat-nesting and endangered species. Seashore open daily. Visitor centers open Sept.–May, daily 9–5; June–Aug., daily 9–6. Closed Dec. 25.

HOW TO GET THERE

Via U.S. 168–158 from the north, U.S. 64 from the west, and U.S. 70 and Cedar Island ferry from the south. Closest major airport: Norfolk, VA (85 miles).

CONTACTS

Cape Hatteras National Seashore (1401 National Park Dr., Manteo, NC 27954, tel. 252/473–2111; 800/365–2267 camping at Ocracoke, www.nps.gov/caha). Outer Banks Chamber of Commerce (Box 1757, 101 Town Hall Dr., Kill Devil Hills, NC 27948, tel. 252/441–8144, fax 252/441–0338, www.outerbankschamber.com). Outer Banks Visitors Bureau (1 Visitors Center Circle, Manteo, NC 27954, tel. 877/629–4386, www.outerbanks.org).

Cape Lookout National Seashore

In eastern North Carolina, near Beaufort

The 56-mile-long barrier islands of Cape Lookout National Seashore run from Ocracoke Inlet to Beaufort Inlet. They consist mostly of wide, bare beaches with low dunes, flat grasslands, and large expanses of salt marsh along the Core Sound. Attractions include the Cape Lookout lighthouse, historic Portsmouth Village, two lifesaving stations, and the Shackleford Banks horses, the oldest documented horse population in North America. The seashore was authorized in 1966.

WHAT TO SEE & DO

Beachcombing, boating, fishing, shelling, surfing, swimming. **Facilities:** 3 visitor centers: Cape Lookout (Harkers Island), Light Station Visitor Center, and Portsmouth Village; Keepers Quarters Museum (near Cape Lookout Lighthouse). Bookstores (Harkers Island Visitor Center and Light Station Visitor Center). **Programs & Events:** Lighthouse talks, guided walks, and Portsmouth Village programs (June–Aug.). **Tips & Hints:** Bring everything you'll need with you, including water, sunscreen, and insect repellent (none available in the park). Visit in spring and fall for best weather and smaller crowds. Busiest Aug. and Nov., least crowded Feb. and Mar.

FOOD, LODGING & SUPPLIES

Camping: Rental cabins near the park: Great Island Cabin Camp (25 cabins; $73–$168; closed early Dec.–Mar.), Long Point Cabin Camp (20 units; $112–$135; closed early Dec.–Mar.). Backcountry camping available on Core Banks and Shackleford Banks. **Hotels:** None in park. In Ocracoke: Pony Island Motel (785 Irvin Garrish Hwy., tel. 252/928–4411 or 866/928–4411, www.ponyislandmotel.com; 50 rooms; $112–$125). **Restaurants:** None in park. At Harker's

Island: Captain's Choice (977 Island Rd., tel. 252/728–7122; $5–$10; closed late Dec.–early Jan., Mon. year-round). ♿ **Groceries & Gear:** None in park. At Harker's Island: Best Supermarket (1016 Island Rd., tel. 252/728–4393).

FEES, HOURS & REGULATIONS

Free. Public ferries: $15 per person. Park open daily. Cape Lookout Visitor Center open daily 9–5. Light Station, Portsmouth visitor centers open Memorial Day–Labor Day, daily 9–5. Cape Lookout Lighthouse open mid-May–late Sept.; adults $8, seniors 62 and above $4, children 12 and younger $4. Children must be 44 inches tall to enter the lighthouse.

HOW TO GET THERE

21 miles from Beaufort, NC. From U.S. 70 east, take right on Harkers Island Rd. to Harkers Island. Ferry services depart from Beaufort and Harkers Island. Closest airport: New Bern (45 miles).

CONTACTS

Cape Lookout National Seashore (1800 Island Rd., Harkers Island, NC 28531, tel. 252/728–2250, www.nps.gov/calo). Crystal Coast Tourism Authority (3409 Arendell St., Morehead City, NC 28557, tel. 252/726–8148 or 800/786–6962, www.crystalcoastnc.org).

Carl Sandburg Home National Historic Site

In western North Carolina, in Flat Rock

The site preserves Connemara, the 264-acre farm where Pulitzer Prize–winning author and poet Carl Sandburg (1878–1967) and his family lived the last 22 years of his life. The farm consists of a 22-room house, barns, sheds, rolling pastures, mountainside woods, trails, two small lakes, a trout pond, flower and vegetable gardens, and an orchard. The site was authorized on October 17, 1968.

WHAT TO SEE & DO

Bird-watching, hiking, picnicking, touring house and grounds. **Facilities:** Visitor information station, historic home, trails, outdoor amphitheater. Bookstore. **Programs & Events:** Guided house tours, self-guided walking tours of grounds, barn, and Chikaming goat herd. Ranger-led programs and walks (June–Aug. and Oct.), plays (late June–mid-Aug.), Poetry Celebration (Apr.), Sandburg Folk Music Festival (Memorial Day), Christmas at Connemara (Dec.). Book signings, special presentations by noted authors and historians (dates vary). **Tips & Hints:** Plan to spend at least two hours. Be prepared for rain. Temperatures are moderate. Weather is unpredictable in spring and fall. Busiest July and Oct., least crowded Jan. and Feb.

FOOD, LODGING & SUPPLIES

🏕 **Camping:** None at site. In Saluda: Orchard Lake Campground (460 Orchard Lake Rd.; tel. 828/749–3901, www.orchardlakecampground. com; 115 sites; $32–$40; flush toilets, showers, hookups). 🏨 **Hotels:** None at site. In Flat Rock: Holiday Inn Express (111 Commercial Blvd., tel. 828/698–8899 or 800/465–4329, www.hiexpress. com; 65 rooms; $95–$130). ✕ **Restaurants:** None at site. In Fletcher: Blue Sky Café (3987 Hendersonville Rd., tel. 828/684–1247, www. iloveblueskycafe.com; $6–$8). 🍴 **Groceries & Gear:** None at site. In Flat Rock: Ingles Market (220 Highland Lake Rd., tel. 828/692–1335).

FEES, HOURS & PERMITS

Guided house tour: $5 adults, $3 senior citizens, free ages 16 and under. Site open daily 9–5.

HOW TO GET THERE

Take U.S. 225 south for 5 miles from Hendersonville, turn on Little River Rd. at the Flat Rock Playhouse. From Asheville, take I–26 south for 26 miles to Upward Rd. exit and follow park signs. Closest airport: Asheville.

CONTACTS

Carl Sandburg Home National Historic Site (81 Carl Sandburg La., Flat Rock, NC 28731, tel. 828/693–4178, fax 828/693–4179, www.nps. gov/carl). Hendersonville Visitor Information Center (201 S. Main St., Hendersonville, NC 28792, tel. 828/693–9708 or 800/828–4244, www. historichendersonville.org).

Fort Raleigh National Historic Site

On Roanoke Island in northeastern North Carolina

Supported by Sir Walter Raleigh, a community of 116 colonists landed on Roanoke Island in 1587 to begin the first English settlement of the New World. When a supply ship arrived three years later, the settlement was deserted and the colonists could not be found. Their fate remains a mystery. The park includes a reconstruction of an earthen fort built by the English. The formal Elizabethan Gardens are nearby. The outdoor symphonic drama *The Lost Colony* has been performed here since 1937. The park also tells the story of the island's Native American culture, its role in the American Civil War, the Freedmen's Colony that was established here, and the activities of radio pioneer Reginald Fessenden. The site was designated on April 5, 1941.

WHAT TO SEE & DO

Attending outdoor drama, touring fort and gardens, walking trails. **Facilities:** Visitor center, restored earthen fort, Waterside Theater, trails, gardens. Gift shop. **Programs & Events:** Video, ranger-led interpretive programs and trail walks. The 2½-hour *Lost Colony* drama (mid-June– Aug., Mon.–Sat. nights; tel. 252/473–3414 or 800/488–5012). Virginia

Dare birthday commemoration (Aug. 18). Dare was the first child born to English parents (1587) in the New World. **Tips & Hints:** Plan to spend two hours to view the exhibits and video, and to tour the grounds. Bring insect repellent if you plan to attend outdoor drama. Busiest June and July, least crowded Dec. and Jan.

FOOD, LODGING & SUPPLIES

⚑ **Camping:** None at site. In Wanchese: The Refuge on Roanoke Island (2881 Hwy. 345, tel. 252/473–1096, www.therefuge-roanokeisland.com; 59 sites; $60; flush toilets, showers, hookups). 🏨 **Hotels:** None at site. In Roanoke Rapids: Hampton Inn (85 Hampton Blvd., tel. 252/537–7555 or 800/426–7866, www.hamptoninn.com; 126 rooms; $110–$130). ✕ **Restaurants:** None at site. In Manteo: Full Moon Café & Grille (208 Queen Elizabeth St., tel. 252/473–6666, www.thefullmooncafe.com; $8-$13). ⚑ **Groceries & Gear:** None at site. In Manteo: Piggly Wiggly (118 S. U.S. 64/264, tel. 252/473–3727).

FEES & HOURS

Free. *The Lost Colony* drama (tel. 252/473–3414; $16–$20 adults, $15 ages 62 and over, $8 ages 11 and under). Site open June–Aug., daily 9–6; Sept.–May, daily 9–5. Elizabethan Gardens: $8, $5 ages 6–17.

HOW TO GET THERE

On Roanoke Island, off U.S. 64/264 and about 3 miles north of Manteo, 92 miles southeast of Norfolk, VA, and 197 miles east of Raleigh. Closest airport: Dare County Municipal Airport (2 miles), Manteo (2 miles), Norfolk, VA (100 miles).

CONTACTS

Fort Raleigh National Historic Site (c/o Cape Hatteras National Seashore, 1401 National Park Dr., Manteo, NC 27954, tel. 252/473–5772, fax 252/473–2595, www.nps.gov/fora, www.thelostcolony.org). See Cape Hatteras National Seashore for additional contacts.

Guilford Courthouse National Military Park

Midstate, in Greensboro

The battle fought here on March 15, 1781, was the largest, most hotly contested action of the Revolutionary War's climactic Southern Campaign. The loss of British soldiers at Guilford Courthouse foreshadowed the final American victory at Yorktown seven months later. The site includes 28 monuments, including the graves of two signatories of the Declaration of Independence. The park was established in 1917 and transferred to the Park Service in 1933.

WHAT TO SEE & DO

Bicycling, hiking, scenic drives, viewing animated battle map program. **Facilities:** Visitor center with museum exhibits, battlefield, animated map, 30-minute orientation film, 2¼-mile tour road, bike and foot trails, interpretive displays, monuments. Bookstore. **Programs & Events:** Self-guided audio tours, ranger-led programs. Battle Anniversary (Mar. 15). **Tips & Hints:** Busiest May and July, least crowded Dec. and Jan.

FEES, HOURS & REGULATIONS

Free. Leashed pets only. Bicycling only in bike lanes. No motorized or mechanized equipment or bicycles on walking trails. No climbing on cannons or monuments. Park and visitor center open daily 8:30–5.

HOW TO GET THERE

In northwestern Greensboro, from U.S. 220 (Battleground Ave.), turn east on New Garden Rd. to reach entrance. Closest airport: Piedmont Triad International (6 miles).

CONTACTS

Guilford Courthouse National Military Park (2332 New Garden Rd., Greensboro, NC 27410-2355, tel. 336/288–1776, fax 336/282–2296, www.nps.gov/guco). Greensboro Area Convention & Visitor Bureau (2200 Pinecroft Rd., Suite 200, Greensboro, NC 27401, tel. 336/274–2282 or 800/344–2282, www.visitgreensboronc.com).

Moores Creek National Battlefield

In southeastern North Carolina, near Wilmington, in Currie

The 88-acre park commemorates the decisive American Revolution victory at the Battle of Moores Creek Bridge on February 27, 1776. The battle ended British Royal Governor Josiah Martin's hopes of regaining control of the colony and scuttled plans by the British to land an invasionary force in Brunswick, about 50 miles to the south. The decisive win raised morale throughout the colonies. The colony of North Carolina voted to declare independence from the British on April 12, 1776. The site was established as a national military park in 1926, transferred to the Park Service in 1933, and redesignated in 1980.

WHAT TO SEE & DO

Bird- and wildlife watching, picnicking, touring battlefield by walking trails. **Facilities:** Visitor center, video, trails. Bookstore, grills, picnic areas, shelter, tables. **Programs & Events:** Talks, walks, and demonstrations (Memorial Day–Labor Day, weekends), battle anniversary commemoration (last full weekend, Feb.). "Celebrating the Constitution" (Sept. 17). **Tips & Hints:** Plan to spend an hour touring visitor center, exhibits, and trails, and watching video. Busiest May and June, least crowded Dec. and Jan.

FOOD, LODGING & SUPPLIES

🏕 **Camping:** None in park. In Carolina Beach: Carolina Beach State Park (1010 State Park Rd., tel. 910/458–8206 or 877/722–6762, www. reserveamerica.com; 71 sites; $17; pit toilets, showers). 🏨 **Hotels:** None in park. In Wilmington: Carolinian Inn (2916 Market St., tel. 910/763–4653, www.thecarolinianinn.com; 61 rooms; $80), Hampton Inn and Suites (1989 Eastwood Rd., tel. 910/256–9600 or 800/426–7866, www.hamptoninn.com; 90 rooms, 30 suites; $129–$159). ✗ **Restaurants:** None in park. In Wilmington: Front Street Brewery (9 N. Front St., tel. 910/251–1395, www.frontstreetbrewery.com; $7–$12), Rucker Johns (5564 Carolina Beach Rd., tel. 910/452–1212, www. ruckerjohns.com; $7–$10). ⛽ **Groceries & Gear:** None in park. In Atkinson: Family Dollar (410 W. Church St., tel. 910/283–6188).

FEES & HOURS

Free. Site open daily 9–5.

HOW TO GET THERE

20 miles northwest of Wilmington via U.S. 421 and Rte. 210. From I–40, take Rte. 210 west for 15 miles to park. Closest airport: New Hanover International (25 miles).

CONTACTS

Moores Creek National Battlefield (40 Patriots Hall Dr., Currie, NC 28435, tel. 910/283–5591, fax 910/283–5351, www.nps.gov/mocr). Wilmington and Beaches Convention & Visitors Bureau (505 Nutt St., Unit A, Wilmington, NC 28401, tel. 877/406–2356, www.wilmingtonandbeaches.com).

Wright Brothers National Memorial

In Kill Devil Hills on the Outer Banks

The first successful, sustained, controlled, powered flights in a heavier-than-air machine were made here by Wilbur and Orville Wright on December 17, 1903. The site includes a 60-foot-tall granite monument perched atop 90-foot-tall Kill Devil Hill, reconstructed living quarters and hangar, the First Flight trail area, and a Centennial Pavilion. The site was authorized in 1927, and transferred to the Park Service in 1933.

WHAT TO SEE & DO

Air touring; touring visitor center, reconstructed living quarters, and hangar building; viewing reproduction of the 1902 Wright Glider and the 1903 Wright Flyer; walking First Flight grounds to the Wright Monument. **Facilities:** Visitor center, Centennial Pavilion, wayside exhibits, monument. Bookstore. **Programs & Events:** Ranger talks (daily at 10, 11, noon, 2, 3, and 4), ranger-led interpretive children's programs on kite building, First Flight tours (mid-June–Aug.). First Flight Anniversary Celebration (Dec. 17), National Aviation Day and Orville

Wright's Birthday (Aug. 19). **Tips & Hints:** Allow one–two hours to visit site. Watch for cacti and sandspurs. Stay on walkway. Busiest July and Aug., least crowded Jan. and Feb.

FOOD, LODGING & SUPPLIES

🏕 **Camping:** None at site. In Kill Devil Hills: Joe and Kay's Campground (1193 Collington Rd., tel. 252/441–5468; 15 tent sites; $25; flush toilets, showers). 🏨 **Hotels:** None at site. In Kill Devil Hills: Quality Inn Carolina Oceanfront (401 N. Virginia Dare Trail, tel. 252/480–2600, www.qualityinn.com; 118 rooms; $129–$140; minimum stay in high season). ✗ **Restaurants:** None at site. In Kitty Hawk: The Good Life (3712 N. Croatan Hwy., tel. 252/480–2855, www.goodlifegourmet.com; $7–$10). ♨ **Groceries & Gear:** None at site. In Kill Devil Hills: Food Lion (1720 N. Croatan Hwy., tel. 252/480–1016).

FEES, HOURS & REGULATIONS

Entrance fee: $3 adults, free ages 16 and under; $4 per vehicle. Leashed pets only. No motorized vehicles or skateboards on trails. Airstrip daylight use only. 24-hour parking limit for planes. Park and visitor center open mid-June–Labor Day, daily 9-6; Labor Day–mid-June, daily 9–5.

HOW TO GET THERE

At mile 7.5 on U.S. 158. Closest airports: Manteo (7 miles); Norfolk, VA (85 miles).

CONTACTS

Wright Brothers National Memorial (c/o Cape Hatteras National Seashore, 1401 National Park Dr., Manteo, NC 27954, tel. 252/441–7430, fax 252/441–7730, www.nps.gov/wrbr). See Cape Hatteras National Seashore for additional contacts.

See Also

Appalachian National Scenic Trail, West Virginia. *Great Smoky Mountains National Park,* Tennessee. *Overmountain Victory National Historic Trail and Trail of Tears National Historic Trail,* in Other National Parklands.

NORTH DAKOTA

Fort Union Trading Post National Historic Site

In northwestern North Dakota, near Williston

The park is a reconstruction of the most significant fur-trading post on the upper Missouri River. John Jacob Astor's American Fur Company built Fort Union in 1828. In its heyday, the post employed as many as 100 people to trade beaver furs and buffalo robes. In 1867 the fort was dismantled by the army for materials to expand nearby Fort Buford. The site was authorized in 1966.

WHAT TO SEE & DO

Bird-watching, picnicking, touring the trading post. **Facilities:** Visitor center, trading post, wayside exhibits. Book sales area, picnic area, reproduction trade goods for sale. **Programs & Events:** Ranger-guided tours (mid-May–mid-Sept. on request), educational programs, audiovisual presentation. Rendezvous (3rd weekend, June), Indian Arts Showcase (mid-Aug.), Living History Weekend (Labor Day), Winter Camp (Dec.). **Tips & Hints:** Busiest June and July, least crowded Dec. and Jan.

FOOD & LODGING

Camping: None at site. Nearby: Fort Buford State Historic Site (Rte. 1804, 23 miles southwest of Williston, tel. 701/572–9034; open area of primitive sites; free; vault toilets; closed mid-Sept.–mid-May). **Hotel:** None at site. In Williston: El Rancho Motor Hotel (1623 2nd Ave. W, tel. 701/572–6321 or 800/433–8529, www.elranchomotel. net; 92 rooms; $120). **Restaurant:** None at site. In Williston: Dakota Farms Family Restaurant (1906 2nd Ave. W, tel. 701/572–4480, $8–$15).

FEES, HOURS & REGULATIONS

Free. No hunting. Leashed pets only. Park and visitor center open Memorial Day–Labor Day, daily 8–6:30; Labor Day–Memorial Day, daily 9–5:30.

HOW TO GET THERE

On Rte. 1804, 25 miles southwest of Williston. Closest airport: Williston.

CONTACTS

Fort Union Trading Post National Historic Site (15550 Rte. 1804, Williston, ND 58801, tel. 701/572–9083, fax 701/572–7321, www.nps.gov/fous). Williston Area Chamber of Commerce (10 Main St., Williston, ND 58801, tel. 701/577–6000, www.willistonchamber.net).

Knife River Indian Villages National Historic Site

Midstate, near Stanton

Remnants of historic and prehistoric Native American villages are preserved at this 1,759-acre site, which was last occupied in 1845 by the Hidatsa and Mandan. An array of artifacts of the Plains Native American culture and a full-scale furnished earth lodge are on exhibit. The area also was the home of Sacagawea, who accompanied Lewis and Clark on their expedition to the Northwest. The site was authorized in 1974.

WHAT TO SEE & DO

Bird-watching, canoeing, cross-country skiing, fishing, hiking, picnicking, touring the site. **Facilities:** Visitor center, museum, trails, interpretive panels. Bookstore, picnic tables. **Programs & Events:** Guided tours of earth lodge (Memorial Day–Labor Day). Northern Plains Indian Culture Fest (last full weekend, July). **Tips & Hints:** Visit June–Aug. for programs. Busiest June–Aug., least crowded Nov. and Dec. Park is on Mountain Time.

FOOD, LODGING & SUPPLIES

Camping: None in park. In Lake Sakakawea State Park (Rte. 200, 1 mile north of Pick City, tel. 701/487–3315 or 800/ 807–4723): Elbowoods (50 sites; $20; flush toilets, showers, hookups), Sanish (29 sites; $20; flush toilets, showers, hookups), Van Hook (36 sites; $20; flush toilets, showers, hookups). **Hotels:** None in park. In Hazen: Roughrider Motor Inn (707 8th Ave. NE, tel. 701/748–2209; 57 rooms; $68). **Restaurants:** None in park. In Stanton: Cafe DuMond (Rte. 31, tel. 701/745–3535; $6). **Groceries & Gear:** None in park. In Hazen: Teresa's Grocery and Bakery (10 Main Rd., 701/487-3000).

FEES, HOURS & REGULATIONS

Free. North Dakota fishing license required. Leashed pets only on trails. No hunting. No mountain bikes, trail bikes, motorized or mechanized equipment on trails. Earth lodge unfurnished Nov.–Mar. Trails open daily 6 AM–10 PM. Park and visitor center open Labor Day–Memorial Day, daily 8–4:30; Memorial Day–Labor Day, daily 8–6.

HOW TO GET THERE

Rte. 37, ½ mile north of Stanton. Closest airport: Bismarck (60 miles).

CONTACTS

Knife River Indian Villages National Historic Site (Box 9, Stanton, ND 58571, tel. 701/745–3300, fax 701/745–3708, www.nps.gov/knri). Hazen Chamber of Commerce (146 E. Main St., Hazen, ND 58545, tel. 701/748–6848, www.hazennd.org).

Theodore Roosevelt National Park

In western North Dakota, near Medora (South Unit) and Watford City (North Unit)

Theodore Roosevelt first came to Dakota Territory in September 1883 to hunt bison. Before returning home to New York, he became interested in the cattle business and became a partner in the Maltese Cross Ranch partnership. The next year he returned to the badlands and started a second open-range ranch, the Elkhorn. Roosevelt witnessed the decline in wildlife and saw the grasslands destroyed because of overgrazing. He became an avid conservationist and eventually established the U.S. Forest Service. In his lifetime, Roosevelt signed into law 5 national parks, 150 national forests, 51 federal bird reservations, 18 national monuments, 24 reclamation projects, 7 conservation conferences and commissions, and 4 national game preserves, totaling about 230,000,000 acres of protected land. Today the colorful North Dakota badlands provide the scenic backdrop to the park that memorializes the 26th president for his enduring contributions to the conservation of our nation's resources. The Little Missouri River winds through the 70,447-acre park, which was established as a memorial park in 1947 and became a national park in 1978.

WHAT TO SEE & DO

Bird and wildlife viewing, canoeing, hiking, horseback riding, picnicking, scenic drives, skiing. **Facilities:** 3 visitor centers: Medora (South Unit entrance), Painted Canyon (7 miles east of Medora on I–94), and North Unit (near entrance); Maltese Cross Cabin, wayside exhibits, trails, scenic drives. Book and map sales, picnic sites with fire grates. **Programs & Events:** Orientation films, evening campfire programs, nature walks and hikes. Tours of Maltese Cross Cabin (mid-June–early Sept.). **Tips & Hints:** Be prepared for variable weather in summer. Go May–Sept. for the best weather. Busiest July and Aug., least crowded Dec. and Jan.

FOOD, LODGING & SUPPLIES

Camping: 2 campgrounds in the park: Cottonwood (South Unit; 76 sites; $10; flush toilets), Juniper (North Unit; 50 sites; $10; flush toilets). In Medora: Red Trail Campground (250 E. River Rd. S, off Pacific Ave., tel. 701/623-4317, www.redtrailcampground.com; 104 sites; $24–$34; flush toilets, showers, hookups; closed Oct.–Apr.). **Hotels:** None in park. In Medora: AmericInn Motel & Suites (75 E. River Rd. S, tel. 701/623–4800 or 800/634–3444, www.americinn.com; 55 rooms, 8 suites; $134–$269). In Watford City: Roosevelt Inn & Suites (600 2nd Ave. SW, tel. 701/842–3686, www.rooseveltinn.com; 44 rooms; $110). **Restaurants:** None in park. In Medora: Little Missouri Saloon & Dining (440 3rd St., tel. 701/623–4404; $10–$15; closed Sun. in winter). **Groceries & Gear:** None in park. In Medora: Medora Convenience Store (200 Pacific Ave., tel. 701/623–4479).

FEES, HOURS & REGULATIONS

Entrance fee: $5 per person, $10 per vehicle. Backcountry permits (free) required for all backcountry camping. No hunting. No pets on trails or in backcountry. Leashed pets elsewhere. No bikes on trails. No horses in campground or on nature trails. Weed-free horse feed required. Park open daily. Scenic drives sometimes closed in winter. South Unit Visitor Center open mid-June–Labor Day, daily 8–6 Mountain Time; Labor Day–mid-June, daily 8–4:30 Mountain Time. Painted Canyon Visitor Center open Apr.–Memorial Day, daily 8:30–4:30 Mountain Time; Memorial Day–Labor Day, daily 8:30–6 Mountain Time; Labor Day–mid-Nov., daily 8:30–4:30 Mountain Time. North Unit Visitor Center open Apr.–mid-Nov, daily 9–5:30 Central Time, mid-Nov.–March, Fri.–Sun. 9–5:30 Central Time.

HOW TO GET THERE

South Unit: 1 mile north of Medora, off I–94. North Unit: 15 miles south of Watford City via U.S. 85. Closest airports: Dickinson (35 miles from Medora), Williston (60 miles from North Unit), Bismarck (167 miles from North Unit, 133 miles from South Unit).

CONTACTS

Theodore Roosevelt National Park (Box 7, Medora, ND 58645, tel. 701/623–4466 South Unit; tel. 701/842–2333 North Unit, fax 701/623–4840, www.nps.gov/thro). Dickinson Convention & Visitors Bureau (72 E. Museum Dr., Dickinson, ND 58601, tel. 701/483–4988 or 800/279–7391, www.visitdickinson.com). McKenzie County Tourism Bureau (Box 699, Watford City, ND 58854, tel. 701/444–5804 or 800/701–2804, www.4eyes.net). Medora Area Convention & Visitors Bureau (475 4th St., Medora, ND 58645, tel. 701/623–4829, www.medorand.com).

See Also

International Peace Garden, Lewis & Clark National Historic Trail, and North Country National Scenic Trail, in Other National Parklands.

OHIO

Cuyahoga Valley National Park

In northeastern Ohio, between Cleveland and Akron

The area preserves 33,000 acres of pastoral valley along 22 miles of the Cuyahoga River. It includes the river and its floodplain, steep and gentle valley walls forested by deciduous and evergreen woods, and numerous tributaries and their ravines. Of this area, approximately 18,000 acres are owned by the National Park Service. Local public agencies own 9,000 of the remaining acres, and the balance is privately owned. Cuyahoga Valley was authorized as a National Recreation Area on December 27, 1974. The park's name was changed to Cuyahoga Valley National Park on October 11, 2000.

WHAT TO SEE & DO

Bicycling (rentals), cross-country skiing (rentals), hiking, scenic railroad, snowshoeing (rentals). **Facilities:** 5 visitor centers: Boston Store Visitor Center (1550 Boston Mills Rd., Peninsula) has canal boat-building exhibits; Canal Visitor Center (7104 Canal Rd., Valley View) focuses on life along the canal; Hunt Farm Visitor Information Center (2045 Bolanz Rd., Peninsula) has kid-friendly exhibits; Peninsula Depot Visitor Center (1630 Mill St., Peninsula) has general information; Frazee House is closed for repairs until further notice; 183 miles of hiking trails, 54 miles of bridle trails, 20 miles of Ohio & Erie Towpath Trail. Book-and-gift shops, meeting rooms, reservable picnic shelters. **Programs & Events:** Interpretive programs year-round. **Tips & Hints:** Busiest June–Aug. and Oct., least crowded Dec.–Feb.

FEES, HOURS & REGULATIONS

Free. Some interpretive programs, picnic shelters, and meeting rooms have fees. Leashed pets only. No hunting. Bikes on designated trails only. Park open daily. Some areas close at dusk. Boston Store Visitor Center open June-Aug., daily 8-6; Sept.–May, daily 10–4. Canal Visitor Center open Nov.–Apr., weekends 10–4; May, Sept., and Oct., Wed.–Sun. 10-4; June-Aug., daily 10–4. Hunt Farm Visitor Information Center and Peninsula Depot Visitor Center hours vary seasonally.

LODGING

Hotels: In the park: Inn at Brandywine Falls (8230 Brandywine Rd., Sagamore Hills, tel. 330/467–1812 or 888/306–3381; 3 rooms, 3 suites; $139–$325.

HOW TO GET THERE

The park is east of I–77, between Cleveland and Akron. Closest airports: Cleveland (15 miles), Akron (20 miles).

CONTACTS

Cuyahoga Valley National Park (1550 Boston Mills Rd., Peninsula, OH 44264, tel. 330/657–2752, fax 440/546–5989, www.nps.gov/cuva). Ohio Office of Travel & Tourism (77 S. High St., Box 1001, Columbus, OH 43216, tel. 800/282-5393, consumer.discoverohio.com).

Dayton Aviation Heritage National Historical Park

In western Ohio, in Dayton

The park preserves sites associated with Wilbur and Orville Wright and the early development of aviation. It also honors the life and work of African American poet Paul Laurence Dunbar. The park, a cooperative effort between the National Park Service and four other organizations, includes five sites: Huffman Prairie Flying Field and Interpretive Center; the Wright Cycle Company Complex, which includes the Wright brothers' print shop building; the 1905 Wright Flyer III (in Dayton History's Carillon Historical Park); the Paul Laurence Dunbar House State Memorial; and Hawthorn Hill, Orville Wright's 1914–48 residence. The park was authorized on October 16, 1992.

WHAT TO SEE & DO

Touring five sites. **Facilities:** 2 visitor centers: Huffman Prairie Flying Field Interpretive Center and the Wright Cycle Company Complex, museum, exhibits at Paul Laurence Dunbar State Memorial, Carillon Historical Park, and Hawthorn Hill. Bookstores. **Programs & Events:** Interpretive talks on aviation, early transportation history, African American history, and accomplishments of Paul Laurence Dunbar and Wilbur and Orville Wright. **Tips & Hints:** Plan to spend at least an hour touring the Wright Cycle Company Complex, an hour at the Paul Laurence Dunbar State Memorial, an hour at the Huffman Prairie Flying Field, and 30 minutes at Wright Hall in Carillon Historical Park. Exploring all of Carillon Historical Park takes 2–3 hours. Guided tours of Hawthorn Hill take 60–90 minutes. Travel between park units can take 20–30 minutes. Busiest June and July, least crowded Jan. and Feb.

FEES &HOURS

Entrance fees: Wright Cycle Company Complex and Huffman Prairie Flying Field: free. Paul Laurence Dunbar State Memorial: $6 adults, $5 seniors, $3 ages 6–12 and members; free ages 5 and under. Wright Hall–Carillon Historical Park: $8 adults, $7 ages 60 and older, $5 ages 3–17, free for members and ages 2 and under. Hawthorn Hill: $12. Huffman Prairie visitor center open daily 8:30–5. Wright Cycle Company Complex open daily 8:30–5. Paul Laurence Dunbar State Memorial open Memorial Day–Labor Day, Thurs.–Sat. 9:30–5, Sun. noon–5; Apr., May, Sept., and Oct., Sat. 9:30–5, Sun. noon–5. Huffman Prairie Flying Field open daily 8–6, when the Wright-Patterson Air Force Base is open. Wright Hall–Carillon Historical Park open Apr.–Oct.,

Mon.–Sat. 9:30–5, Sun. noon–5. Hawthorn Hill, pre-reserved tours
Wed. and Sat. at 10:30 and noon.

HOW TO GET THERE

To reach the Wright Cycle Company Complex, exit I–75 at 3rd St. in
downtown Dayton. Cross the Miami River and turn left at the second
stoplight on the west side of the river on S. Williams St. The building
is on the left. From I–70 or U.S. 35, exit onto I–75 and follow above
directions. Huffman Prairie Flying Field and Interpretive Center is
near the intersection of Kauffman Rd. and Rte. 444; access from I–675
or Rte. 4. Closest airport: Dayton (10 miles).

CONTACTS

Dayton Aviation Heritage National Historical Park (16 S. Williams St.,
Dayton, OH 45402, tel. 937/225–7705, fax 937/222–4512, www.nps.
gov/daav). Carillon Historical Park, Dunbar House, and Hawthorn
Hill (1000 Carillon Blvd., Dayton, OH 45409, tel. 937/293–2841, www.
daytonhistory.org). Dayton-Montgomery County Convention & Visitors Bureau (1 Chamber Plaza, Suite A, Dayton, OH 45402, tel. 937/
226–8211 or 800/221–8235, www.daytoncvb.com). Greene County
Convention & Visitors Bureau (1221 Meadowbridge Dr., Suite A,
Beaver Creek, OH 45434, tel. 937/429–9100, www.greenecountyohio.
org). Huffman Prairie Flying Field and Interpretive Center (tel. 937/
425–0008).

First Ladies National Historic Site

In Canton, in northeastern Ohio

Two properties, the home of First Lady Ida Saxton McKinley and the
Education and Research Center, are preserved in this park, which
commemorates the role of the First Lady in American history. The
site, managed in cooperation with the National First Ladies' Library,
was authorized on October 11, 2000.

WHAT TO SEE & DO

Touring house and library. **Facilities:** Saxton McKinley House (331
Market Ave. S), Education and Research Center (205 Market Ave. S).

FEES & HOURS

Entrance fees: $7 adults, $6 seniors, $5 children. Reservations for tours
recommended for all, required for groups of six or more.

HOW TO GET THERE

Take I–77 to the Tuscarawas St. exit. Drive east to Market Ave. and
head south on Market to 4th St. Nearest airport: Akron-Canton Regional Airport (11 miles).

CONTACT

First Ladies National Historic Site (331 Market Ave. S, Canton, OH
44702, tel. 330/452–0876, fax 330/456–3414, www.nps.gov/fila).

Hopewell Culture National Historical Park

In south-central Ohio, near Chillicothe

Archaeological remnants of earthwork and mound complexes built by the Hopewell, who inhabited the Ohio River valley between 200 BC and AD 500, are preserved in this park. The Mound City Group, a 13-acre rectangular earth enclosure with at least 24 mounds, provides insight into the social, ceremonial, political, and economic life of the Hopewell people. The site was proclaimed the Mound City Group National Monument in 1923 and renamed in 1992.

WHAT TO SEE & DO

Picnicking, touring earthworks. **Facilities:** Visitor center, interactive computer program with in-depth cultural and archaeological information, museum, trails, video. Book sales area, picnic area. **Programs & Events:** Crafts demonstrations, nature and archaeology walks. Ranger-guided tours (Memorial Day–Labor Day, daily). National Parks week (3rd week, May), Ohio Archaeology week (3rd. week, June), Hopewell Discovery Days (2nd Sat. in Oct.). **Tips & Hints:** Busiest July and Aug., least crowded Dec. and Jan.

FEES, HOURS & REGULATIONS

Free. Leashed pets only. No bicycles on trails. Park open daily sunrise–sunset. Visitor center open June–Aug., daily 8:30-6; Sept.–May, daily 8:30–5.

HOW TO GET THERE

3 miles north of Chillicothe on Rte. 104. Closest airport: Columbus (50 miles).

CONTACTS

Hopewell Culture National Historical Park (16062 Rte. 104, Chillicothe, OH 45601, tel. 740/774–1125, fax 740/774–1140, www.nps.gov/hocu). Ross–Chillicothe Convention & Visitors Bureau (Box 353, Chillicothe, OH 45601, tel. 740/702–7677 or 800/413-4118, www.visitchillicotheohio.com).

James A. Garfield National Historic Site

In northeast Ohio, in Mentor

The Victorian-era home of the 20th president of the United States is preserved at this site. The estate was nicknamed Lawnfield during the 1880 presidential campaign. The site was authorized in 1980.

WHAT TO SEE & DO

Touring visitor center (a restored carriage barn), home, and grounds of Lawnfield; viewing interpretive displays and artifacts. **Facilities:** Visitor center, family home, wayside exhibits, video, grounds. Gift shop. **Programs & Events:** Interpretive talks, lectures, and home tours. Presidents' Day (Feb.), Civil War Encampment (June–Aug.), Cleveland Shakespeare Festival (June–Aug.). **Tips & Hints:** Busiest July and Aug., least crowded Jan. and Feb.

FEES & HOURS

Entrance fee: $5 adults; free ages 16 and under. Park and visitor center open May–Oct., Mon.–Sat. 10–5, Sun. noon–5; Nov.–Apr., weekends noon–5. Last tour of home at 4:15 PM.

HOW TO GET THERE

25 miles east of Cleveland, off I–90 on Mentor Ave. (U.S. 20). Closest airport: Cleveland (35 miles).

CONTACTS

James A. Garfield National Historic Site (8095 Mentor Ave., Mentor, OH 44060, tel. 440/255–8722, fax 440/974–2045, www.nps.gov/jaga). Lake County Visitors Bureau (35300 Vine St., Suite A, Eastlake, OH 44095, tel. 800/368–5253 or 440/975–1234, www.lakevisit.com). Mentor Area Chamber of Commerce (7547 Mentor Ave., Suite 302, Mentor OH 44060, tel. 440/946–2625, www.mentorchamber.org).

Perry's Victory & International Peace Memorial

On South Bass Island in Lake Erie

The memorial column that rises 352 feet above Lake Erie commemorates war and peace. Oliver Hazard Perry's victory over a British fleet in the Battle of Lake Erie served as a turning point in the War of 1812. The monument was built between 1912 and 1915, established as a national monument in 1936, and redesignated in 1972.

WHAT TO SEE & DO

Fishing; kite flying; sunbathing; touring memorial, rotunda, and observation deck. **Facilities:** Visitor center, interpretive exhibits, video. Bookstore. **Programs & Events:** Ranger talks (mid-June–Aug.), costumed presentations and musket firings (mid-June–Aug.). Battle Anniversary (weekend after Labor Day), concerts, and ceremonies. **Tips & Hints:** Plan to spend two hours visiting the memorial. In summer, expect to wait in line for the elevator to the observation deck. Spring on Lake Erie is cool and windy into June. Busiest July and Aug., least crowded Dec.–Mar.

FOOD, LODGING & SUPPLIES

⚠ **Camping:** None at memorial. In Put-in-Bay: South Bass Island State Park (Box 326, tel. 866/644–6727, www.ohiostateparks.com; 135

sites, 10 with hookups; $27–$32; flush toilets, showers). ⊞ **Hotels:** None at memorial. In Put-in-Bay: Park Hotel (234 Delaware Ave., tel. 419/285–3581, www.parkhotelpib.com; 25 rooms; $147; closed Nov.– Apr.). ✗ **Restaurant:** None at memorial. In Put-in-Bay: The Boardwalk (Bay View Ave., tel. 419/285–3695, www.the-boardwalk.com; $8–$27; closed Oct.–Apr.). ⚖ **Groceries:** None at memorial. In Put-in-Bay: Press House Corner Market (1400 Catawba Ave., tel. 419/285–2716).

FEES & HOURS

Entrance fee: $3 adults, free ages 15 and under. Memorial open late Apr.–mid-May and Sept.–mid-Oct., daily 10–5; mid-Oct.–Apr. and mid-May–Aug., daily 9–7.

HOW TO GET THERE

On South Bass Island in the village of Put-in-Bay. Access to the island by boat or plane only. Miller Boat Line (tel. 800/500–2421) provides ferry service Mar.–Nov. from Catawba Point, near Port Clinton. Put-in-Bay Boat Lines–Jet Express (tel. 800/245–1538) provides ferry service seasonally from Port Clinton to Put-in-Bay. Closest airports: Cleveland (85 miles), Toledo (50 miles), Detroit, MI (75 miles).

CONTACTS

Perry's Victory and International Peace Memorial (93 Delaware Ave., Box 549, Put-in-Bay, OH 43456, tel. 419/285–2184, fax 419/285–2516, www.nps.gov/pevi). Put-in-Bay Chamber of Commerce (Box 250, Put-in-Bay, OH 43456, tel. 419/285–2832, www.put-in-bay.com).

William Howard Taft National Historic Site

In Cincinnati

William Howard Taft is the only person in U.S. history to have served as both president (1909–13) and Chief Justice of the United States (1921–30). He was born and raised in this 1840s Greek Revival–style home. Four furnished rooms have been restored to depict the lifestyle of Taft and his family during the 1860s. The site was authorized on December 2, 1969.

WHAT TO SEE & DO

Taking ranger-guided and self-guided tours of home. **Facilities:** Home, Taft Education Center with interactive displays, orientation film. Bookstore, gift shop. **Programs & Events:** Ranger-guided and self-guided tours. New Year's Open House (Jan.), Constitution Day and Taft's Birthday (Sept.), Father Christmas (Dec.), Christmas Decoration Workshop (Dec.). **Tips & Hints:** Busiest July and Aug., least crowded Nov. and Jan.

FEES, HOURS & REGULATIONS

Free. No smoking, pets, food, or drink in house. House open daily 8–4.

HOW TO GET THERE

The Taft House is at 2038 Auburn Ave., in the Mount Auburn section of Cincinnati. From I–71 north, take Exit 2 (Reading Rd.). Make a left onto Dorchester St. Turn right on Auburn and drive 1½ blocks to the home. From I–71 south, take Exit 3 (Taft Rd.) to Auburn Ave. Turn left to home. Closest airport: Cincinnati (10 miles).

CONTACTS

William Howard Taft National Historic Site (2038 Auburn Ave., Cincinnati, OH 45219, tel. 513/684–3262, fax 513/684–3627, www.nps.gov/wiho). Cincinnati Convention & Visitors Bureau (525 Vine St., Cincinnati, OH 45202, tel. 513/621–2142, www.cincyusa.com).

See Also

David Berger National Memorial, North Country National Scenic Trail, and Ohio & Erie Canal National Heritage Corridors, in Other National Parklands.

OKLAHOMA

Chickasaw National Recreation Area

In south-central Oklahoma, near Sulphur

This recreation area was named in honor of the Chickasaw, the land's longtime inhabitants. Numerous springs, streams, and lakes attract nature lovers and adventure seekers from all over the state. Sulphur Springs Reservation was authorized in 1902, renamed and redesignated Platt National Park in 1906, combined with Arbuckle National Recreation Area, and renamed and redesignated in 1976.

WHAT TO SEE & DO

Boating, fishing, hiking, hunting, picnicking, scenic drives, swimming, waterskiing. **Facilities:** Information and nature center with live exhibits, 20 miles of trails, scenic roads. Bookstore, picnic pavilions. **Programs & Events:** Ranger-led nature walks, campfire programs (Memorial Day–Labor Day, weekends). Bald Eagle Watch (Jan. and Feb.), Historic Candlelight Tour (late Nov. or early Dec.). **Tips & Hints:** Busiest June and July, least crowded Jan. and Feb.

FOOD, LODGING & SUPPLIES

Camping: 6 campgrounds in park: Buckhorn (off Buckhorn Rd. in the southeast portion of the recreation area; 135 sites; $14–$22; flush toilets, showers, hookups), Central (near the junction of U.S. Hwy. 177 and State Hwy. 7; 10 group sites; $30), Cold Springs (near the junction of U.S. Hwy. 177 and State Hwy. 7; 63 sites; $12; flush toilets; closed early Oct.–early May), Guy Sandy (north of State Hwy. 110, on the recreation area's western edge; 40 sites; $14; portable toilets; closed Sept.–Apr.), Rock Creek (south of Broadway Ave. off 12th St. west of the Bromide Pavilion; 106 sites; $14–$24; flush toilets), the Point (south on Cooper Memorial Rd. in the south-central part of the recreation area; 55 sites; $14–$24; flush toilets, showers, hookups). **Hotels:** None in park. In Sulphur: Super 8 (2116 W. Broadway, tel. 580/622–6500, www.super8.com; 39 rooms; $65–$95). In Davis: Inn at Treasure Valley (I–35 and Hwy. 7, tel. 580/369–3223, www.treasurevalleycasino.com; 49 rooms, 10 suites; $89–$129). **Restaurants:** None in park. In Sulphur: The Bricks (2118 W. Broadway Ave., tel. 580/622–3125; $6–$8). **Groceries:** None in park. In Sulphur: Sooner Foods (815 W. Broadway Ave., tel. 580/622–2828).

FEES, HOURS & REGULATIONS

Free. Boat launching permit required ($4 per day). Picnic pavilion reservation fee ($30). Boat launch and camping fees taken through automated machines; cash and credit cards accepted. Park open daily. Travertine Information and Nature Center open Memorial Day–Labor Day, daily 9-5:30; Labor Day–Memorial Day, daily 9–4:30.

HOW TO GET THERE

On U.S. 177, south of Sulphur, 90 miles south of Oklahoma City, and 120 miles north of Dallas, TX. From I–35 south, take Exit 55 to Rte. 7. From I–35 north, take Exit 51 to Rte. 7. After Sulphur (10 miles), turn south on Rte. 177. Closest airports: Oklahoma City, Dallas, TX.

CONTACTS

Chickasaw National Recreation Area (1008 W. 2nd St., Sulphur, OK 73086, tel. 580/622-3161, www.nps.gov/chic). Davis Chamber of Commerce (100 E. Main St., Davis, OK 73030, tel. 580/369–2402, www. davisok.org). Sulphur Chamber of Commerce (717 W. Broadway, Sulphur, OK 73086, tel. 580/622–2824, www.sulphurokla.com).

Washita Battlefield National Historic Site

In western Oklahoma, near Cheyenne

The park preserves the site of the Battle of the Washita (November 27, 1868), one of the most controversial engagements between Plains tribes and the U.S. Army—called by some a massacre and others a major victory. Lieutenant Colonel George A. Custer attacked a sleeping Cheyenne village and killed about 50 men, women, and children, including tribe leader Peace Chief Black Kettle. The events symbolize the struggle of the southern Great Plains tribes to maintain their traditional way of life and not to submit to reservation confinement. The park was authorized on November 12, 1996.

WHAT TO SEE & DO

Viewing battlefield historic site from overlook, walking on trails. **Facilities:** Visitor center (Hwy. 47A) features museum exhibits, 27-minute film about the Washita attack. Overlook with historical plaque, commemorative monument, panel indicating approximate route, approach, and attack of Custer; 1½ miles of trails. Bookstore. **Programs & Events:** Ranger-led walks and talks (Memorial Day–Labor Day). **Tips & Hints:** Visit in spring and fall; summers are very hot.

FOOD, LODGING & SUPPLIES

Camping: None at site. In Black Kettle Recreation Area: 2 campgrounds with primitive sites (10 miles northwest of Cheyenne on U.S. 283, tel. 580/497–2143; free; pit toilets). **Hotels:** None at site. In Cheyenne: Cheyenne Motel (U.S. 283 N, tel. 580/497–3383; 68 rooms; $65). **Restaurants:** None at site. In Cheyenne: Odes Drive-In (1st and Broadway, tel. 580/497–2393; $3–$7; closed Sun., no lunch Sat.). **Groceries & Gear:** None at site. In Cheyenne: Market Square Thriftway (300 S. L. L. Males, tel. 580/497–2600).

FEES, HOURS & REGULATIONS

Free. No hunting. No pets on trail. Site open daily dawn–dusk. Park visitor center open daily 8–5.

HOW TO GET THERE

2 miles west of Cheyenne on Rte. 47A and 30 miles north of I–40 via U.S. 283. Closest airports: Oklahoma City, Amarillo, TX (both 140 miles).

CONTACTS

Washita Battlefield National Historic Site (18555 Hwy. 47A, Ste. A, Cheyenne, OK 73628, tel. 580/497–2742, fax 580/497–2712, www.nps.gov/waba). Cheyenne Chamber of Commerce (Box 57, Cheyenne, OK 73628, tel. 580/497–3318 or 877/497–3318, www. cheyenneokchamber.org).

See Also

Fort Smith National Historic Site, Arkansas. Santa Fe National Historic Trail and Trail of Tears National Historic Trail, in Other National Parklands.

OREGON

Crater Lake National Park

*In southern Oregon, 60 miles northwest of
Klamath Falls*

Crater Lake is one of the most famous lakes on Earth, principally because of its unusual blue color and its mountain setting. With a depth
of 1,943 feet, Crater Lake is the deepest lake in the United States and
is among the deepest in the world, and it holds the world record for
natural water clarity. The mature forests that surround Crater Lake are
largely untouched. The park was established on May 22, 1902.

WHAT TO SEE & DO

Boat tours, cross-country skiing (rentals, Klamath Falls, Medford),
hiking, scenic drives. **Facilities:** 2 visitor centers: Steel and Rim Village, wayside exhibits, film. Book sale areas, picnic areas, post office.
Programs & Events: Campfire programs, geology and natural-history
walks (late June–Labor Day, daily), boat tours (late June–mid-Sept.),
snowshoe walks (late Nov.–Apr., weekends), trolley tours around the
rim, daily (early July-early Oct.). **Tips & Hints:** Go early July–late Sept.
to avoid snow, mid-July–early Aug. for wildflowers. Busiest July and
Aug., least crowded Dec.–Mar.

FOOD, LODGING & SUPPLIES

Camping: 2 campgrounds in the park: Lost Creek (on the road to
Pinnacles Overlook, in the southwestern corner of the park; 16 tent
sites; $10; flush toilets; closed Oct.–June), Mazama (off State Hwy. 62,
near Mazama Village in the south-central part of the park; 211 sites;
$19–$25; flush toilets, showers, hookups; closed early Oct.–mid-June).
Backcountry camping allowed. In Fort Klamath: Crater Lake Resort
(50711 Rte. 62, tel. 541/381–2349; 15 sites; $30–$40; flush toilets,
showers, hookups). **Hotels:** In the park: Crater Lake Lodge (tel.
541/830–8700; 71 rooms; $204; closed mid-Oct.–mid-May), Mazama
Village Motor Inn (tel. 541/830–8700; 40 rooms; $138; closed early
Oct.–late May). **Restaurants:** In the park: Dining Room at Crater
Lake Lodge (tel. 541/594–2255; $10–$15; closed mid-Oct.–mid-May).
Groceries & Gear: In the park: Mazama Village (tel. 541/594–2255
Ext. 3703).

FEES, HOURS & REGULATIONS

Entrance fee: $5 person on foot or bicycle; $10 per car. Backcountry
permits required (free). No bicycles or off-road vehicles allowed off
paved roads. Leashed pets allowed in front country only. No private
boats. No wildlife feeding or hunting. No climbing or hiking inner caldera walls except on Cleetwood Cove Trail. Park open daily. Steel Visitor Center open mid-Apr.–early Nov., daily 9–5; early Nov.–mid-Apr.,
daily 10–4. Rim Village Visitor Center open June–Sept., daily 9:30–5.

HOW TO GET THERE

Take Rte. 62, 60 miles northwest of Klamath Falls and 80 miles north-east of Medford. Closest airports: Medford, Klamath Falls.

CONTACT

Crater Lake National Park (Box 7, Crater Lake, OR 97604, tel. 541/594–3100, fax 541/594–3010, www.nps.gov/crla).

Lewis & Clark National Historical Park

In northwestern Oregon, near Astoria

After their epic journey across the West, the 33-member Lewis and Clark Expedition spent the winter of 1805–06 at Fort Clatsop. In 1955 local citizens built a replica of the explorers' fort in a lush spruce and hemlock forest that is the focal point of the park. The first replica burned down in 2005, but a new fort was built in 2007. The Salt Works site in nearby Seaside commemorates where the explorers set up a camp to boil seawater to produce salt for use at the fort and on the return trip. The memorial was authorized on May 29, 1958.

WHAT TO SEE & DO

Canoeing, picnicking, touring fort replica, walking trails. **Facilities:** Visitor center, 6½-mile fort-to-sea trail, trailside interpretive panels, replica of stone oven (Seaside). Bookstore, covered picnic tables. **Programs & Events:** Audiovisual programs. Interactive living-history programs (mid-June–Labor Day). Newfoundland Dog Day (July), National Park Service Founders Day (Aug. 25), Explorers' Christmas at Fort Clatsop (Dec. 26–Jan. 1). **Tips & Hints:** Fort replica floors are slippery and uneven. Go in winter for more authentic expedition weather. Busiest July and Aug., least crowded Jan. and Feb.

FOOD, LODGING & SUPPLIES

Camping: None in park. In Warrenton: Fort Stevens State Park (100 Peter Iredale Rd., tel. 503/861–1671 park, 800/452–5687 reservations; 519 sites; $17–$22; flush toilets, showers, hookups). **Hotels:** None in park. In Astoria: Astoria Dunes (288 W. Marine Dr., tel. 503/325–7111 or 800/441–3319, www.astoriadunes-motel.com; 58 rooms; $65–$155). **Restaurants:** None in park. In Astoria: Columbian Café (1114 Marine Dr., tel. 503/325–2233; $6–$12; closed Mon. and Tues.), Pig 'N' Pancake (146 W. Bond St., tel. 503/325–3144; $8–$20), Ship Inn (1 2nd St., tel. 503/325–0033; $8–$16). **Groceries & Gear:** None in park. In Warrenton: Fred Meyer (695 S. U.S. 101, tel. 503/861–3000).

FEES, HOURS & REGULATIONS

Entrance fee: $3 adults, free ages 15 and under. No hunting or fishing. Bikes allowed on a few trails. No skateboards. No pets in fort rooms or visitor center. Leashed pets elsewhere. Park and visitor center open mid-June–Labor Day, daily 9-6; Labor Day–mid-June, daily 9–5.

HOW TO GET THERE

6 miles southwest of Astoria, off U.S. 101. Closest airport: Portland (100 miles).

CONTACTS

Lewis & Clark National Historical Park (92343 Fort Clatsop Rd., Astoria, OR 97103, tel. 503/861–2471, fax 503/861–2585, www.nps.gov/lewi). Astoria–Warrenton Chamber of Commerce (111 W. Marine Dr., Astoria, OR 97103, tel. 503/325–6311, www.oldoregon.com). Seaside Chamber of Commerce (7 N. Roosevelt Dr., Seaside, OR 97138, tel. 503/738–6391, www.seasidechamber.com).

John Day Fossil Beds National Monument

In north-central Oregon, near Dayville, Mitchell, and Clarno

The heavily eroded volcanic deposits of the scenic John Day River basin house a well-preserved fossil record of plants and animals that spans more than 40 of the 65 million years of the Cenozoic Era, or Age of Mammals. The monument is composed of three widely separated units: Sheep Rock, Painted Hills, and Clarno. The monument was authorized in 1974 and established in 1975.

WHAT TO SEE & DO

Scenic drives, self-guided trail tours, visiting fossil museum at Sheep Rock Unit. **Facilities:** Thomas Condon Paleontology Center with fossil museum, visitor center, James Cant Ranch cultural museum, theater. Bookstore, picnic tables. **Programs & Events:** Self-guided tours, ranger-led talks in fossil museum, ranger-led trail hikes. **Tips & Hints:** Go to Clarno in morning, Sheep Rock in early afternoon, and Painted Hills in late afternoon for best light for scenic views and photography. Go mid-Apr.–mid-May for wildflowers at Painted Hills. Busiest July and Aug., least crowded Jan. and Feb.

FOOD & LODGING

Camping: None in park. Near Mitchell: Ochoco Divide (U.S. 26, 15 miles west of Mitchell, tel. 541/416–6500; 26 sites; $13). **Hotels:** None in park. In John Day: Americas Best Value Inn (390 W. Main St., tel. 541/575–1462 or 800/452–4899, www.americasbestvalueinn.com; 43 rooms; $60), Best Western Inn (315 W. Main St., tel. 541/575–1700, www.bestwestern.com; 40 rooms; $85). **Restaurants:** None in park. In John Day: Grub Steak Mining Company (149 E. Main St., tel. 541/575–1970; $6–$8), Outpost Pizza Pub & Grill (201 W. Main St., tel. 541/575–0250; $9).

FEES, HOURS & REGULATIONS

Free. No collecting or disturbing fossils or geologic or biological resources. No public telephones at sites. Park trails, overlooks, and grounds open sunrise–sunset. Thomas Condon Paleontology Center (with visitor center and fossil museum) open daily 9–5. James Cant Ranch (with cultural museum) open weekdays 9–4.

HOW TO GET THERE

Paleontology Center and Cant Ranch at Sheep Rock Unit, 9 miles west of Dayville, near intersection of U.S. 26 and Rte. 19. Painted Hills Unit is 10 miles west of Mitchell off U.S. 26. Clarno Unit is 18 miles west of Fossil on Rte. 218. Closest airports to Sheep Rock Unit: Redmond (80 miles), Boise, ID (240 miles), Portland (250 miles).

CONTACTS

John Day Fossil Beds National Monument (32651 Rte. 19, Kimberly, OR 97848-9701, tel. 541/987–2333, fax 541/987–2336, www. nps.gov/joda). Grant County Chamber of Commerce (281 W. Main St., John Day, OR 97845, tel. 541/575–0547 or 800/769–5664, www. gcoregonlive.com). Prineville–Crook County Chamber of Commerce (390 N.E. Fairview, Prineville, OR 97754, tel. 541/447–6304, www. visitprineville.org).

Oregon Caves National Monument

In southwestern Oregon, near Cave Junction

Belowground at this monument is a marble cave created by natural forces more than 1.5 million years in one of the world's most diverse geologic realms. Aboveground is 480 acres of wilderness, including a remnant of an old-growth coniferous forest that's crisscrossed with hiking trails. In addition to its unique geologic setting, Oregon Caves has Pleistocene mammal fossils and a large assortment of endemic cave life. The monument was proclaimed in 1909 and transferred to the National Park Service in 1933.

WHAT TO SEE & DO

Cave touring, hiking. **Facilities:** Visitor center with interpretive displays, trails. Book sales area. **Programs & Events:** Ranger-guided walks, day programs (Memorial Day–Labor Day). **Tips & Hints:** Entrance to caves by guided tour only; tours offered late Mar.–early Nov. No reservations. Come early to avoid crowds. Wear tennis shoes or boots and a jacket for cave tours. Temperature is 44°F in cave. Don't take tour if you have breathing or heart problems. Cave trail is 1 mile with ascent of 230 feet; there are more than 500 stairs. To help curtail white-nose syndrome, a fatal disease in bats, do not wear clothing, footwear, or gear used in caves east of the Rocky Mountains or in Europe. Tour takes about 1½ hours. Large RVs not recommended on road to park. Go mid-May to mid-July for wildflowers. Busiest July and Aug., least crowded Labor Day–Memorial Day.

FOOD, LODGING & SUPPLIES

Camping: None in park. In Siskiyou National Forest: Cave Creek (Rte. 46, 16 miles east of Cave Junction, tel. 541/592–2166; 18 sites;

$10; vault toilets; closed mid-Sept.–mid-May), Grayback (Rte. 46, 12 miles east of Cave Junction, tel. 541/592–4440; 37 sites; $16; flush toilets; closed late Sept.–Memorial Day). In Cave Junction: Country Hills Resort (7901 Caves Hwy., tel. 541/592–3406, www.countryhillsresort. com; 25 sites; $16–$23; flush toilets, showers, hookups). ⊞ **Hotels:** In the park: Oregon Caves Chateau (20000 Caves Hwy., tel. 541/592–3400; 22 rooms, 3 suites; $90–$160; closed Nov.–Apr.). In Cave Junction: Out 'N' About (300 Page Creek Rd., tel. 541/592–2208, www. treehouses.com; 3 cabins, 12 tree houses; $120–$280). ✕ **Restaurant:** In the park: Oregon Caves Chateau (20000 Caves Hwy., tel. 541/592–3400; $6–$11; closed Nov.–Apr.). ⚱ **Groceries:** None in park. In Cave Junction: Shop Smart (205 Watkins St., tel. 541/592–3333).

FEES, HOURS & REGULATIONS

Free. Cave tour: $8.50 adults, $6 ages 16 and under. Free tour of first room for families with small children. Cave restrictions: children must be at least 42 inches tall and able to climb a set of test stairs unassisted. No infants. No child care available. Canes allowed in first cave room only. Only first room is wheelchair accessible. No pets on trails, leashed pets elsewhere. Mountain bikes on existing roads only. No motor vehicles on trails. Monument open daily. Visitor center open spring and fall, daily 9:30-5; summer, daily 8:30–6. Hours for cave tours vary, so call ahead.

HOW TO GET THERE

20 miles southeast of Cave Junction via Rte. 46. Closest airport: Medford (80 miles).

CONTACT

Oregon Caves National Monument (19000 Caves Hwy., Cave Junction, OR 97523, tel. 541/592–2100, fax 541/592–3981, www.nps.gov/orca).

See Also

Nez Perce National Historical Park, Idaho. *California National Historic Trail, Lewis & Clark National Historic Trail, McLoughlin House National Historic Site, Oregon National Historic Trail, and Pacific Crest National Scenic Trail,* in Other National Parklands.

PENNSYLVANIA

Allegheny Portage Railroad National Historic Site

In central Pennsylvania, 10 miles west of Altoona

Preserved here are the remains of the first railroad to cross the Allegheny Mountains, including the first railroad tunnel built in the United States. The 36-mile-long Portage Railroad, completed in 1834, used a series of 10 inclined planes to lift canal boats loaded on railroad-type flatcars across the mountains between Hollidaysburg and Johnstown. The railroad, in conjunction with the Pennsylvania Main Line Canal, reduced the time to travel the 390 miles between Philadelphia and Pittsburgh to four or five days from three weeks. The site was authorized on August 31, 1964.

WHAT TO SEE & DO

Cross-country skiing (rentals in Altoona), hiking, picnicking, viewing the historic sites, walking. **Facilities:** Visitor center, film, interpretive displays at Engine House No. 6, Historic Lemon House Tavern, wayside exhibits. Book sale area, picnic pavilion with grills, tables. **Programs & Events:** Interpretive tours of Lemon House. Costumed demonstrations, including log hewing, stonecutting, and lifestyles of the past (June–Aug.). Evening on the Summit outdoor concert ($2) and guest lectures (Sat. nights in summer), guided hikes and van tours to lesser-known areas of the railroad (June–Aug., Sun.; reservations required, tel. 814/886–6150). **Tips & Hints:** Go Apr. and May for wildflowers, Oct. for fall colors. Busiest weekdays in May because of school groups, least crowded Dec. and Jan.

FOOD, LODGING & SUPPLIES

Camping: None in park. In Duncansville: Wright's Orchard Station (2381 Plank Rd., tel. 814/695–2628, www.wrightscampground. com; 40 sites; $27–$35; flush toilets, hookups). **Hotels:** None in park. In Altoona: Hampton Inn (180 Charlotte Dr., tel. 814/941–3500, www.hamptoninn.hilton.com; 111 rooms; $129–$149). In Ebensburg: Comfort Inn (111 Cook Rd., tel. 814/472–6100 or 800/424–6423, www.comfortinn.com; 78 rooms; $81–$150). **Restaurants:** None in park. In Altoona: Jethro's (417 Parkview La., tel. 814/942–2178, www.jethros4u.com; $9–$20). **Groceries & Gear:** None in park. In Altoona: Walmart Supercenter (2600 Plank Rd. Commons, tel. 814/949–8980).

FEES, HOURS & REGULATIONS

Entrance fee: $4 per person. Bikes restricted to hard-surface roads. No hunting. Leashed pets only. Visitor center open daily 9–5.

HOW TO GET THERE

10 miles west of Altoona, 15 miles east of Ebensburg on U.S. 22 (Gallitzin exit). Nearest airports: Martinsburg (20 miles), Johnstown (30 miles), Pittsburgh (80 miles).

CONTACTS

Allegheny Portage Railroad National Historic Site (110 Federal Park Rd., Gallitzin, PA 16641, tel. 814/886–6150, fax 814/884–0206, www.nps.gov/alpo). Allegheny Mountains Convention & Visitors Bureau (tel. 814/943–4183 or 800/842–5866, fax 814/943–8094, www. alleghenymountains.com). Greater Johnstown–Cambria Convention & Visitors Bureau (111 Market St., Johnstown, PA 15901, tel. 814/536–7993 or 800/237–8590, www.visitjohnstownpa.com).

Delaware Water Gap National Recreation Area

The Delaware River on the Pennsylvania–New Jersey border, from East Stroudsburg to Milford

The recreation area contains 67,000 acres of forest, mountain ridge, and floodplain along a 40-mile stretch of the Delaware River; the geologically significant water gap, a mile-wide cut in the Kittatinny Ridge created by the Delaware River; and thousands of acres of woodland open to hiking and other recreational activities. One of the last free-flowing rivers on the East Coast, the river is home to threatened and endangered plants and animals. Significant prehistoric and historic sites are located throughout the park. The park was authorized on September 1, 1965.

WHAT TO SEE & DO

Boating, canoeing (rentals), cross-country skiing, fishing, hiking, hunting, picnicking, snowshoeing, swimming. **Facilities:** 3 visitor centers: Kittatinny Point (off Exit 1, I–80 in New Jersey), Bushkill (U.S. 209), Dingman's Falls (U.S. 209); trails, roadside radio interpretation, bulletin boards. Picnic areas with tables. **Programs & Events:** Nature study programs (weekends, Pocono Environmental Education Center, 5 miles south of Dingman's Falls Visitor Center). Guided hikes, children's programs, waterfall walks, campfire programs (June–Sept., weekends); cultural history demonstrations (May–Oct., weekends; Millbrook Village). Delaware River Sojourn (mid- to late June); Peter's Valley Craft Fair (last weekend, Sept.); Millbrook Days Folk Life Festival (1st full weekend, Oct.); Van Campen Day (3rd Sun. in Oct.). **Tips & Hints:** Bring your own cookstove or grill. Go in fall for hawk-watching, winter for eagles. Busiest July and Aug., least crowded Jan. and Feb.

FOOD, LODGING & SUPPLIES

Camping: In the park: Dingman's Campground (1006 Rte. 209, Dingman's Ferry, tel. 570/828–1551 or 877/829–1551; 133 sites; $32–

$40; flush toilets, showers, campground store). Worthington State Forest Campground (Old Mine Rd., tel. 908/841–9575; 72 sites; $20; flush toilets, showers; closed Jan.–Mar.). Backcountry camping for Appalachian Trail users only. ⛺ **Hotels:** In the park: Cliff Park Inn (155 Cliff Park Rd., tel. 570/426–2418; 14 rooms; $136–$263). In East Stroudsburg: Echo Valley Cottages (1 Lower Lakeview Dr., tel. 570/223–0662, www.echovalleycottages.com; 9 cottages; $275–$600 weekly). ✗ **Restaurants:** In the park: Cliff Park Inn (155 Cliff Park Rd., tel. 570/426–2418; no dinner Sun.–Wed.; $8–$16). In East Stroudsburg: Arlington Diner (834 N. 9th St., tel. 570/421–2329; $7–$15). ⚒ **Groceries & Gear:** At Dingman's Campground. In Delaware Water Gap: Pack Shack Adventures (88 Broad St., tel. 570/424–8533). In West Hazleton: Weis Market (100 Weis La., tel. 570/455–0612).

FEES, HOURS & REGULATIONS

Free. Smithfield, Bushkill, Dingman's, and Milford beaches: $10 weekends, $7 weekdays per vehicle. No pets in Worthington State Forest Campground, leashed pets only elsewhere. Bicycling in designated areas only. Pedestrian traffic only on trails. No ground fires. Kittatinny Point Visitor Center open Memorial Day–Labor Day, daily 9–5; Labor Day–Columbus Day, weekends 9–5. Bushkill Visitor Center open Memorial Day–Labor Day, daily 9–5; Labor Day–Columbus Day, weekends 9–5. Millbrook Village open Labor Day–Columbus Day, Fri.–Sun. 9–5. Dingman's Falls Visitor Center reopening in 2013.

HOW TO GET THERE

The recreation area is on the Pennsylvania–New Jersey border from I–80 (Delaware Water Gap) to I–84 (just north of Milford). Closest airport: Lehigh Valley International Airport near Allentown (44 miles from town of Delaware Water Gap).

CONTACTS

Delaware Water Gap National Recreation Area (River Rd., Bushkill, PA 18324, tel. 570/426–2452, fax 570/426–2402, www.nps.gov/dewa). Kittatinny Point Visitor Center (in the Water Gap, off Interstate 80 in NJ, tel. 908/496–4458). Dingman's Falls Visitor Center (off Johnny Bee Rd., intersecting PA Rt. 209 near milepost 14, tel. 570/828–6125).

Edgar Allan Poe National Historic Site

In Philadelphia

The life and work of Edgar Allan Poe, one of America's most gifted authors, are explored in a three-building complex at 532 N. 7th St., where he lived from 1843 to 1844. The site was authorized on November 10, 1978.

WHAT TO SEE & DO

Touring home, viewing exhibits. **Facilities:** Sales area. **Programs & Events:** Ranger-guided and self-guided home tours. Edgar Allan Poe's literary legacy tours, Poetry Month (Apr.). **Tips & Hints:** Busiest July and Oct., least crowded Jan. and Feb.

FEES & HOURS

Free. Site open Wed.–Sun. 9–5.

HOW TO GET THERE

At 532 N. 7th St., 1 mile from the visitor center at the Independence National Historical Park (see separate entry). Closest airport: Philadelphia.

CONTACTS

Edgar Allan Poe National Historic Site (532 N. 7th St., Philadelphia, PA 19123, tel. 215/597–8780, fax 215/597–1901, www.nps.gov/edal). Independence Visitor Center (6th and Market Sts., tel. 215/965–7676).

Eisenhower National Historic Site

In Gettysburg, in south-central Pennsylvania

The 690-acre site preserves the former home and farm of Dwight D. Eisenhower, the 34th president of the United States, and his wife, Mamie. The farm served as a weekend retreat, a refuge in time of illness, and a gathering place for political groups and the Eisenhower family. Premier Khrushchev, Chancellor Adenauer, President de Gaulle, and other VIPs trooped over its fields and toured the cattle barns and fields during Eisenhower's terms as president, when he used the farm for his personal style of diplomacy. From 1961 to 1969, the farm served as the couple's retirement home, and the First Lady continued to live here until her death in 1979. The site was designated on November 27, 1967.

WHAT TO SEE & DO

Touring home, farm, and cattle barns. **Facilities:** Reception center, home, barns, farm. Bookstore. **Programs & Events:** Tours of grounds and home, Junior Secret Service Program (daily). Tours and interpretive talks (Apr.–Oct.), cattle show barn (Apr.–Oct.), Mamie Remembers Gettysburg (May), World War II Weekend (Sept.), Christmas with the Eisenhowers (Dec.). **Tips & Hints:** Go Apr.–Oct., when all facilities are open and tours and programs scheduled. Busiest June and Oct., least crowded Jan. and Feb.

FOOD & LODGING

⛺ **Camping:** None in park. 🏨 **Hotels:** None in park. In Gettysburg: Battlefield B&B (2264 Emmittsburg Rd., tel. 717/334–8804, www.gettysburgbattlefield.com; 9 rooms, 1 cottage; $175–$299), Comfort Inn (871 York Rd., tel. 717/337–2400, www.comfortinn.com; 78 rooms, 2 suites; $110–$140). 🍴 **Restaurants:** None in park. In Gettysburg: Dobbin House (89 Steinwehr Ave., tel. 717/334–2100, www.

dobbinhouse.com; $7–$14), Farnsworth House Inn (401 Baltimore St., tel. 717/334–8838, www.farnsworthhouseinn.com; $8–$15).

FEES, HOURS & REGULATIONS

Admission: $7.50 adults, $5 ages 6–12, free ages 5 and under. All visits by shuttle bus. No on-site parking. No pets. Park open daily.

HOW TO GET THERE

Via shuttle bus from Gettysburg National Military Park Visitor Center, 1 mile south of Gettysburg, PA, 1195 Baltimore Pike (State Rte. 97). Closest airport: Harrisburg (60 miles).

CONTACTS

Eisenhower National Historic Site (1195 Baltimore Pike, Ste. 100, Gettysburg, PA 17325, tel. 717/338–9114, fax 717/338–0821, www. nps.gov/eise). Gettysburg Convention & Visitors Bureau (35 Carlisle St., Gettysburg, PA 17325, tel. 717/334–6274, fax 717/334–1166, www. gettysburg.travel).

Flight 93
National Memorial

In southwestern Pennsylvania, north of Shanksville.

This memorial commemorates the passengers and crew of United Airlines Flight 93. On the morning of September 11, 2001, Flight 93 took off from Newark International Airport bound for San Francisco. When it neared Cleveland, hijackers on board commandeered the plane and redirected it toward Washington, DC. Passengers and crew members on board are believed to have acted together to crash the plane in a remote field in rural Pennsylvania before it reached the capital. On a memorial plaza, the names of those who died are emblazoned on a massive wall of white marble, situated on the plane's flight path. Interpretive panels describe the fateful day.

The crash site was established as a national memorial on September 24, 2002.

WHAT TO SEE & DO

Viewing crash site, visiting memorial plaza. **Facilities:** Memorial plaza. Visitor center scheduled for completion in 2014.

FEES, HOURS & REGULATIONS

Free. Memorial Plaza open Apr.–Oct., daily 9–7 with last entry at 6:30; Nov.–Mar., daily 9–5 with last entry at 4:30. Park rangers and volunteers are on hand to answer questions during park hours.

HOW TO GET THERE

From U.S. 219, take the Stoystown–Jennerstown exit onto U.S. 30 east. Closest airport: Pittsburgh (97 miles).

CONTACTS

Flight 93 National Memorial (6424 Lincoln Hwy., Stoystown, PA 15563, tel. 814/893–6322, www.nps.gov/flni). Somerset County Chamber of Commerce (601 N. Center Ave., Somerset, PA 15501, tel. 814/445–6431, www.somersetcountychamber.com).

Fort Necessity National Battlefield

In southwestern Pennsylvania, southeast of Uniontown

On July 3, 1754, the opening battle of the French and Indian War took place at a palisade fort built here by a 22-year-old George Washington. He was forced to surrender to an enemy for the first and only time in his military career. The fort has been reconstructed on the site. The completely furnished 1830 Mount Washington Tavern is one of the highlights of a visit. The site was established as a national battlefield in 1931, transferred to the Park Service in 1933, and redesignated in 1961.

WHAT TO SEE & DO

Cross-country skiing; hiking; picnicking; touring fort, historic tavern, grave site, military encampments, and glen. **Facilities:** Interpretive and education center, visitor center, tavern, wayside exhibits, grave, trails. Bookstore, grills, pavilions, picnic area. **Programs & Events:** Cell-phone tour, ranger-guided walks, daily historic weapons and cannon demonstrations, hands-on ranger-led interpretive programs on Native American culture and fur trade. Soldier-life programs (mid-June–mid-Aug.), military encampments (summer weekends). National Road Festival (3rd weekend, May), Battle Anniversary Memorial Program (July 3). **Tips & Hints:** Go in summer for interpretive programs, fall for foliage. Busiest July and Aug., least crowded Dec. and Jan.

FOOD, LODGING & SUPPLIES

Camping: None in park. In Ohiopyle: Ohiopyle State Park (400 Kentuck Rd., off Rte. 381, tel. 888/727–2757; 207 tent sites, 6 cottages; $19–$57; flush toilets, showers, hookups). **Hotels:** None in park. In Chalk Hill: Lodge at Chalk Hill (U.S. 40, tel. 724/438–8880 or 800/833–4283, www.thelodgeatchalkhill.com; 60 rooms, 6 suites; $78–$84). **Restaurants:** None in park. In Hopwood: Sun Porch (U.S. 40, tel. 724/439–5734; $8–$12; closed Mon., no lunch Sat.). **Groceries & Gear:** None in park. In Hopwood: Adrians Market (1776 National Pike E, tel. 724/438–4304). In Ohiopyle: Falls Market (69 Main St., tel. 724/329–4973).

FEES, HOURS & REGULATIONS

Entrance fee: $5 adults, free ages 16 and under. No hunting. Leashed pets only. No motorized or mechanized equipment on trails. Visitor center open daily 9–5. Fort open daily sunrise–sunset. Mount Washington Tavern open daily 9–5. Jumonville Glen open May–Oct., daily. Braddock Grave site open daily.

HOW TO GET THERE

On U.S. 40, 11 miles east of Uniontown. Closest airports: Connellsville (16 miles), Morgantown, WV (37 miles), Pittsburgh (75 miles).

CONTACTS

Fort Necessity National Battlefield (1 Washington Pkwy., Farmington, PA 15437, tel. 724/329–5512, fax 724/329–8682, www.nps.gov/fone). Fayette County Chamber of Commerce (65 W. Main St., Uniontown, PA 15401, tel. 724/437–4571, www.fayettechamber.com). Laurel Highlands Convention & Visitors Bureau (120 E. Main St., Ligonier, PA 15658, tel. 724/238–5661, www.laurelhighlands.org).

Friendship Hill National Historic Site

In southwestern Pennsylvania, near Point Marion

This site, on the Monongahela River, preserves the brick, frame, and stone home that belonged to Albert Gallatin, secretary of the treasury from 1801 to 1814 under presidents Jefferson and Madison. It was authorized in 1978.

WHAT TO SEE & DO

Cross-country skiing, hiking, picnicking, touring Gallatin House. **Facilities:** Visitor center, mansion, trail, wayside exhibits. Bookstore, picnic area, and pavilion. **Programs & Events:** Guided and self-guided tours, special talks (Memorial Day–Labor Day). FestiFall (3rd weekend, Sept.). **Tips & Hints:** Busiest May–Sept., least crowded Jan. and Feb.

FOOD, LODGING & SUPPLIES

None in park. See Fort Necessity National Battlefield.

FEES, HOURS & REGULATIONS

Free. No hunting or metal detecting. Leashed pets only. No cars or bikes on trails. No off-trail hiking. Gallatin House and visitor center open daily 9–5; weekends only Nov.–Mar. Park grounds open daily sunrise to sunset.

HOW TO GET THERE

On Rte. 166, 3 miles north of Point Marion. Closest airports: Morgantown, WV (10 miles), Pittsburgh (60 miles).

CONTACTS

Friendship Hill National Historic Site (1 Washington Pkwy., Farmington, PA 15437, tel. 724/725–9190, fax 724/725–1999, www.nps.gov/frhi). Fayette County Chamber of Commerce (65 W. Main St., Uniontown, PA 15401, tel. 724/437–4571 or 800/916–9365, www.fayettechamber.com). Laurel Highlands Convention & Visitors Bureau (120 E. Main St., Ligonier, PA 15658, tel. 800/333–5661, www.laurelhighlands.com).

Gettysburg National Military Park

Near Gettysburg, in south-central Pennsylvania

The Civil War battle fought here on July 1–3, 1863, resulted in a Union victory that repelled the second Confederate invasion of the North, a major turning point in the war. More than 51,000 soldiers were killed, wounded, or captured in this battle, making it the bloodiest of the war. The Soldiers' National Cemetery at Gettysburg contains more than 7,000 interments, of which 3,500 are from the Civil War. President Abraham Lincoln delivered his immortal Gettysburg Address here on November 19, 1863. You can visit the David Wills House, where Lincoln stayed and finished writing his famous speech. The park was established in 1895 and transferred to the Park Service in 1933.

WHAT TO SEE & DO

Bicycling; horseback riding; touring battlefield, cemetery, museum, David Wills House. **Facilities:** Gettysburg National Military Park Museum and Visitor Center (1195 Baltimore Pike, Gettysburg); auditorium; battlefield; cemetery; cyclorama; hiking and horse trails; 1,300 monuments, markers, and memorials. Bookstore. **Programs & Events:** Interpretive programs on battle, national cemetery, and Gettysburg Address (Apr.-Oct.); guided walking tours (Apr.–Oct., rest of year as staffing permits); campfire programs (mid-June–mid-Aug.), living-history demonstrations (Apr.–Oct., weekends). Memorial Day Ceremony, Battle Anniversary (July 1–3), Gettysburg Address Anniversary (Nov. 19), Remembrance Day (closest Sat. to Nov. 19). **Tips & Hints:** Plan to spend at least a full day at the site. Since 2013 is the 150th anniversary of the battle, plan your visit and make reservations well in advance. Busiest July and Aug., least crowded Jan. and Feb.

FOOD & LODGING

Camping: In the park: group campground for organized youth groups only (tel. 717/334–1124 Ext. 3131; reservations required). **Hotels:** See Eisenhower National Historic Site. **✗ Restaurants:** See Eisenhower National Historic Site.

FEES, HOURS & REGULATIONS

Free. Cyclorama, film, and museum tickets: $12.50 adults, $8.50 ages 6–12, free ages 5 and under. Reservations highly recommended for licensed battlefield guides (tel. 877/874–2478). Off-road biking not allowed. Park grounds and roads open Apr.–Oct., daily 6 AM–10 PM; Nov.–Mar., 6 AM–7 PM. Visitor center and museum open Apr.-Oct., daily 8–6; Nov.-Mar., daily 8–5.

HOW TO GET THERE

From U.S. 15, follow signs to park. For visitors traveling west on U.S. 30, exit onto U.S. 15 south and follow park signs. For those traveling east on Rte. 30, turn left at Lincoln Sq. onto Baltimore St. and follow signs. Closest airport: Harrisburg (60 miles).

CONTACTS

Gettysburg Foundation (www.gettysburgfoundation.org; for film, cyclorama, and museum experience tickets, and for licensed battlefield guides reservations). Gettysburg National Military Park (1195 Baltimore Pike, Gettysburg, PA 17325, tel. 717/334–1124, www.nps.gov/gett). Gettysburg Convention & Visitors Bureau (571 W. Middle St., Gettysburg, PA 17325, tel. 717/334–6274, www.gettysburg.travel).

Hopewell Furnace National Historic Site

In southeastern Pennsylvania, near Elverson

This rural American 19th-century iron plantation is home to a blast furnace, the ironmaster's mansion, and auxiliary structures. Hopewell Furnace was founded in 1771 by Ironmaster Mark Bird and operated until 1883. The site was designated in 1938 and renamed in 1985.

WHAT TO SEE & DO

Biking, hiking, touring museum displays. **Facilities:** Visitor center, furnace complex and buildings, charcoal hearth, tour trail, wayside exhibits, audio stations. Bookstore. **Programs & Events:** Self-guided tours. Living-history programs, sheep shearing (May), molding and casting demonstrations (July–Labor Day), apple sales (Sept.). Establishment Day (1st weekend, Aug.), Apple Harvest Day (Sept.), Amidst the Storm: the Civil War Homefront (Oct.), Iron Plantation Christmas (Dec.). **Tips & Hints:** Plan to stay up to two hours. Busiest Aug. and Sept., least crowded Jan. and Feb.

FOOD, LODGING & SUPPLIES

🔺 **Camping:** None in park. In Elverson: French Creek State Park (843 Park Rd., tel. 610/582–9680; 201 sites; $19–$29; flush toilets, showers, hookups). 🏨 **Hotels:** None in park. In Pottstown: Comfort Inn (99 Robinson St., tel. 610/326–5000, www.comfort.inn; 119 rooms; $99–$129). ✗ **Restaurants:** None in park. In Phoenixville: Sly Fox Brewing Co. (Rte. 113, tel. 610/935–4540, www.slyfoxbeer.com; $9–$17). ⛄ **Groceries & Gear:** None in park.

FEES & HOURS

Free. Site open daily 9–5. Visitor center and historic buildings open Wed.–Sun. 9–5.

HOW TO GET THERE

5 miles south of Birdsboro on Rte. 345 and 10 miles from the Morgantown interchange on the PA Tpke. (I–76) via Rtes. 23 east and 345 north. Closest airports: Reading (21 miles), Allentown (41 miles), Philadelphia (53 miles), Harrisburg (79 miles).

CONTACT

Hopewell Furnace National Historic Site (2 Mark Bird La., Elverson, PA 19520, tel. 610/582–8773, fax 610/582–2768, www.nps.gov/hofu).

Independence National Historical Park

In Philadelphia

Here are the Liberty Bell, an international symbol of freedom, and Independence Hall, where the nation's founders drafted both the Declaration of Independence and the U.S. Constitution. The park, which spans 54 acres in downtown Philadelphia, includes Carpenter's Hall, Christ Church, and 17 other buildings open to the public. The park was authorized in 1948. Independence Hall was designated a World Heritage Site in 1979.

WHAT TO SEE & DO

Touring historic buildings, using interactive exhibits, viewing films. **Facilities:** Independence Visitor Center (6th and Market Sts.). Museum shops. **Programs & Events:** Guided tours of Independence Hall (every 15–20 minutes), tours of Todd House and Bishop White House, ranger programs at other sites. Seasonal activities available. **Tips & Hints:** Visit Dec.–early Mar. to avoid crowds. Busiest June and July, least crowded Jan. and Feb.

FEES, HOURS & REGULATIONS

Free. Tickets to Independence Hall can be picked up at the visitor center on day of tour. Tour reservations ($1.50) are available at 877/444-6777 or www.recreation.gov. Buildings generally are open daily 9–5; some are open later June–Aug. Visitor center open daily 9–6.

HOW TO GET THERE

The visitor center is at 6th and Market Sts., in Philadelphia's downtown. From I–95, follow signs for the Central Philadelphia/I–676/Independence Hall exit. Stay to the right and follow the signs to Callowhill St. Continue straight to 6th St. Turn left onto 6th St.; the garage entrance is on the left side, just past Arch St. Closest airport: Philadelphia.

CONTACTS

Independence National Historic Park (313 Walnut St., Philadelphia, PA 19106, tel. 800/537–7676, www.nps.gov/inde). Independence Visitor Center (6th and Market Sts., tel. 215/965–7676). Philadelphia Convention and Visitors Bureau (1700 Market St., Suite 3000, Philadelphia, PA 19102, tel. 215/636-3300, www.philadelphiausa.travel).

Johnstown Flood National Memorial

In southwestern Pennsylvania, in St. Michael

Johnstown, a steel-company town with a population of 30,000 in 1889, was built on a floodplain at the fork of the Little Conemaugh and

Stony Creek Rivers. When an old dam broke on May 31, 1889, after a night of heavy rains, 20 million tons of water devastated the town and killed more than 2,200 people. The memorial was authorized on August 31, 1964.

WHAT TO SEE & DO

Hiking, touring house and visitor center. **Facilities:** Visitor center (Lake Rd.), Historic Unger House, trails. Bookstore, picnic area. **Programs & Events:** Film (hourly year-round), ranger presentations (summer). Memorial program, luminaria commemorating flood victims (on or about May 31). **Tips & Hints:** Busiest July and Aug., least crowded Jan. and Feb.

FOOD, LODGING & SUPPLIES

Camping: None in park. In Patton: Prince Gallitzin State Park (966 Marina Rd., tel. 814/674–1000 or 888/727–2757, www.visitpaparks.com; 400 sites; $21–$31; flush toilets, showers, hookups). **Hotels:** None in park. In Johnstown: Holiday Inn (250 Market St., tel. 814/535–7777, www.holidayinn.com; 159 rooms; $135–$139). **Restaurants:** None in park. In Johnstown: Em's Original Subs (434 Main St., tel. 814/535–5919; $4–$9). **Groceries & Gear:** None in park. In Johnstown: Ideal Market (Centertown Mall, Walnut St., tel. 814/539–4680).

FEES & HOURS

Entrance fee: $4 adults, free ages 15 and under. Visitor center open daily 9–5.

HOW TO GET THERE

10 miles northeast of Johnstown. Take U.S. 219 to the St. Michael–Sidman exit. Head east on Rte. 869 for 1½ miles. Turn left on Lake Rd. at the memorial sign. Follow Lake Rd. 1½ miles to visitor center on the right. Closest airport: Johnstown.

CONTACTS

Johnstown Flood National Memorial (733 Lake Rd., South Fork, PA 15956, tel. 814/495–4643, www.nps.gov/jofl). Greater Johnstown Cambria County Convention & Visitors Bureau (416 Main St., Suite 100, Johnstown, PA 15901, tel. 814/536–7993 or 800/237–8590, fax 814/539–3370 or 800/237–8590, www.visitjohnstownpa.com).

Middle Delaware National Scenic River

In northeastern Pennsylvania and northwestern New Jersey

The river flows 40 miles through the Delaware Water Gap National Recreation Area (see separate listing). The scenic river was established November 10, 1978.

WHAT TO SEE & DO

Boating, fishing, swimming. See Delaware Water Gap National Recreation Area.

CONTACT

Middle Delaware National Scenic River (c/o Delaware Water Gap National Recreation Area, River Rd., Bushkill, PA 18324, tel. 570/426–2452, www.nps.gov/dewa).

Steamtown
National Historic Site

In northeastern Pennsylvania, in Scranton

In the former Scranton Yards of the Delaware, Lackawanna & Western Railroad, this site interprets the story of steam railroading and its effect on the country. Included are an operating roundhouse, locomotive shop, museum, seasonal train tours, and excursions. The park was authorized in 1986.

WHAT TO SEE & DO

Picnicking; riding steam train; touring museum, locomotive shop, and roundhouse. **Facilities:** Visitor center, museum, locomotive shop, roundhouse, theater. Museum store, picnic tables. **Programs & Events:** Ranger tours, walking tours. Two-hour steam train excursion (reservations recommended, tel. 570/340–5204), train tours (late Apr.–Nov.). National Park Week (3rd week, Apr.); RailFest (Labor Day weekend). **Tips & Hints:** Visitor center and museums are climate controlled. The rest of the site is outdoors. Trains have heat but no air-conditioning. Busiest Aug. and Oct., least crowded Jan. and Feb.

FEES, HOURS & REGULATIONS

Free. Museum entrance fee: $7 adults, free ages 16 and under. No pets, food, drink, or tobacco in any building. Food and drink allowed on excursion, but no pets or tobacco. Leashed pets only elsewhere. No alcohol. Bicycles on park roads only. Site open Apr.–Dec., daily 9–5; Jan.–Apr., daily 10–4.

HOW TO GET THERE

In downtown Scranton via Exit 185 (Central Scranton Expressway) off I-81.

CONTACTS

Steamtown National Historic Site (150 S. Washington Ave., Scranton, PA 18503, tel. 570/340–5200 or 888/693–9391, www.nps.gov/stea). Lackawanna County Convention & Visitors Bureau (99 Glenmaura National Blvd., Moosic, PA 18507, tel. 570/496-1701 or 800/229–3526, www.visitnepa.org).

Thaddeus Kosciuszko National Memorial

In Philadelphia

Thaddeus Kosciuszko, Polish-born patriot and hero of the American Revolution, is commemorated at 301 Pine St., Philadelphia. His efforts on behalf of the fight for independence in America and Poland are remembered at the small town house where he rented a room during the winter of 1797–98. The memorial, the smallest in the national park system, was authorized on October 21, 1972.

WHAT TO SEE & DO

Viewing exhibits. **Facilities:** House. Sales area. **Programs & Events:** Film (in English and Polish), exhibits (Wed.-Sun. noon–4). Thaddeus Kosciuszko Birthday (Feb. 4). **Tips & Hints:** Busiest July and Aug., least crowded Dec. and Jan.

FEES & HOURS

Free. Memorial open Wed.–Sun. noon–4.

HOW TO GET THERE

At 301 Pine St., five blocks from the Independence Visitor Center (see separate entry for Independence National Historical Park). Closest airport: Philadelphia (10 miles).

CONTACTS

Thaddeus Kosciuszko National Memorial (143 S. 3rd St., Philadelphia, PA 19106, tel. 215/597–8787, fax 215/597–1416, www.nps.gov/thko). Philadelphia Convention & Visitors Bureau (1515 Market St., Philadelphia, PA 19102, tel. 215/636–1666, fax 215/636–3327, www.philadelphiausa.travel).

Upper Delaware Scenic & Recreational River

In southeastern New York and northeastern Pennsylvania, along the states' borders

The 73-mile stretch of free-flowing river between Hancock and Sparrowbush, New York, includes the Roebling Bridge, believed to be the oldest existing wire-cable suspension bridge, and the Zane Grey home and museum. The park was authorized on November 10, 1978.

WHAT TO SEE & DO

Boating, eagle watching, fishing, kayaking. **Facilities:** Summer visitor center (Narrowsburg, NY), Zane Grey Museum (Lackawaxen, PA), Roebling's Delaware Aqueduct and Tollhouse (Minisink Ford, NY), bulletin boards at river accesses; traveler's information radio station (1610 AM). **Programs & Events:** Seasonal activities. Delaware River

Sojourn (June), Zane Grey Days (July), Fall Foliage Sightseeing (Oct.).
Tips & Hints: Respect rights of private property owners who own most of the land along the river. Wear a life vest. Busiest July and Aug., least crowded Dec. and Feb.

FOOD, LODGING & SUPPLIES

Camping: In the park: Buckhorn Natural Area (at Stairstep Rapids, tel. 570/685–4871; 10 canoe-in sites; free; no water; permit required). In Barryville, NY: Kittatinny Campground (3854 Rte. 97, tel. 845/557–8611, www.kittatinny.com; 350 sites; $14–25; flush toilets, showers, store, hookups). **Hotels:** None in park. In Barryville, NY: Carriage House (25 Rte. 55, tel. 845/557–0400; 28 rooms; $70–$150). In Eldred, NY: Eldred Preserve (1040 Rte. 55, tel. 845/557–8316 or 800/557–3474, www.eldredpreserve.com; 26 rooms; $75–$95). **✕ Restaurants:** In Eldred, NY: Eldred Preserve (1040 Rte. 55, tel. 845/557–8316, www.eldredpreserve.com; $8–$13). In Lackawaxen: Lackawaxen Inn (188 Scenic Dr., tel. 570/685–7061, www.theinnatlackawaxen.com; $6–$10). **Groceries & Gear:** None in park. In Barryville: River Market (3385 State Rte. 97, tel. 845/557–3663). In Narrowsburg: Pecks Market (120 Kirk Rd., tel. 845/252–3016).

FEES, HOURS & REGULATIONS

Free. New York or Pennsylvania state hunting and fishing license required. Permit required (free) for backcountry camping at Stairway Rapids (tel. 570/685–4871). Public river access open daily 5 AM–10 PM. Visitor facilities open Memorial Day–Labor Day. Zane Grey Museum open Memorial Day–Labor Day, daily 9–4:30; Labor Day–mid-Oct., Wed.–Sun. 9–4:30.

HOW TO GET THERE

From New York or Pennsylvania, take I–84 to Port Jervis (Exit 1), then U.S. 6 west to Rte. 97 north, which parallels most of the river. Northern sections may be reached off NY Rte. 17. Closest airports: Wilkes-Barre–Scranton (45 miles); Stewart International, Newburgh, NY (85 miles).

CONTACTS

Upper Delaware Scenic & Recreational River (274 River Rd., Beach Lake, PA 18405-9737, tel. 570/685–4871, fax 570/685–4874, www.nps.gov/upde). Zane Grey Museum (Scenic Dr., Lackawaxen, PA, tel. 570/685–4871).

Valley Forge National Historical Park

In southeastern Pennsylvania, in Valley Forge

Protected here is the site of the third winter encampment of George Washington's Continental Army. The army lived here from December 19, 1777, to June 19, 1778, during the American Revolution, and 2,000 soldiers died here from disease caused by shortages of food, blankets, and clothing needed to protect them from the bitter cold. Local residents now use the park for recreation, and visitors tour the park for its history. You can visit the newly restored 1913 Valley Forge Train Station. The park was authorized on July 4, 1976.

WHAT TO SEE & DO

Bicycling, bird-watching, canoeing, fishing, hiking, horseback riding, jogging, picnicking, scenic drives. **Facilities:** Visitor center, museum, train station, historic buildings, 10-mile driving tour, 6-mile hiking trail, encampment store, interpretive wayside exhibits. Bookstore, picnic areas. **Programs & Events:** Interpretive programs (mid-June–Labor Day), walking tours and commander-in-chief talks (mid-June–Labor Day), 90-minute guided trolley tour (Memorial Day–Labor Day daily, Labor Day–Memorial Day weekends). George Washington's Birthday (Presidents' Day weekend, Feb.), French Alliance Day (weekend closest to May 6), March-Out of the Continental Army (weekend closest to June 19), March-In of Washington's Army (Dec. 19, 6:30–9 PM), trolley tours (daily in summer, varied schedule off-season). **Tips & Hints:** Visit Washington Memorial Chapel, a privately owned facility within the park. Be careful during driving tours when crossing three busy state roads. Go Apr. and early May for dogwood blooms, late Oct. and early Nov. for fall foliage. Busiest July and Aug., least crowded Dec. and Jan.

FOOD, LODGING & SUPPLIES

⚠ **Camping:** None in park. In Elverson: French Creek State Park (843 Park Rd., tel. 610/582–9680; 201 sites; $19–$29; flush toilets, showers, hookups). 🏨 **Hotels:** None in park. In King of Prussia: Best Western Plus (127 S. Gulph Rd., tel. 610/265–4500, www.bestwestern.com; 168 rooms; $99–$139), Comfort Inn–Valley Forge (550 W. DeKalb Pike at U.S. 202 N, tel. 610/962–0700; 121 rooms; $95–$149). ✗ **Restaurants:** None in park. In Malvern: General Warren Inn (Old Lancaster Hwy., tel. 610/296–3637; $12–$16). ⛁ **Groceries & Gear:** None in park. In King of Prussia: Acme Supermarket (320 W. De Kalb Pike, tel. 610/768–4100).

FEES, HOURS & REGULATIONS

Free. Guided trolley tours $16 adults, $8 children 11 and under. Pennsylvania state fishing license required. No hunting. Leashed pets only. Bikes and horseback riding on designated paths and areas only. No motorized vehicles off tour road. No in-line skating or skateboarding. Park open daily dawn–dusk. Visitor center and Washington Headquarters open daily 9–5. Varnum's Quarters open mid-June–Labor Day, weekends noon–4.

HOW TO GET THERE

20 miles west of Philadelphia, at the intersection of Rte. 23 and N. Gulph Rd. Closest airport: Philadelphia.

CONTACTS

Valley Forge National Historical Park (1000 N. Outer Line Dr., King of Prussia, PA 19406, tel. 610/783–1000, fax 610/783–1053, www.nps.gov/vafo). Valley Forge Convention & Visitors Bureau (1000 First Ave., Ste.

101, King of Prussia, PA 19406, tel. 610/834–1550, fax 610/834-0202, www.valleyforge.org).

See Also

Potomac Heritage National Scenic Trail, District of Columbia. *Appalachian National Scenic Trail,* West Virginia. *Benjamin Franklin National Memorial, Delaware & Lehigh, Gloria Dei (Old Swedes') Church National Historic Site, North Country National Scenic Trail, Southwestern Pennsylvania Industrial Heritage Route, Steel Industry American Heritage Area, and White Clay Creek,* in Other National Parklands.

RHODE ISLAND

Roger Williams National Memorial

In northern Rhode Island, in Providence

The memorial commemorates the life of Roger Williams, the founder of Rhode Island. A champion of religious freedom, Williams was banished from Massachusetts and settled Providence in 1636. This colony served as a refuge where all could come to worship freely. The memorial is on a common lot of the original settlement and includes 4½ acres of landscaped park. The memorial was designated on October 22, 1965.

WHAT TO SEE & DO

Picnicking, viewing exhibits, walking. **Facilities:** Visitor center (N. Main and Smith Sts.), video, wayside exhibits. Bookstore. **Programs & Events:** Junior Ranger program. **Tips & Hints:** Combine visit with trips to Rhode Island State House and Historic Benefit Street. Go in June and Sept. for the best weather, Sept. and Oct. for fall foliage. Busiest May and Oct., least crowded Jan. and Feb.

FEES, HOURS & REGULATIONS

Free. Leashed pets only. Memorial and visitor center open Memorial Day–Columbus Day, daily 9–5; Columbus Day–Memorial Day, daily 9–4:30.

HOW TO GET THERE

From I–95 South take the downtown Providence exit 22A. Turn left onto Francis St., right at Gaspee St., right onto Smith St., right onto Canal St. Entrance to parking lot is on the left. Closest airport: Warwick (10 miles).

CONTACTS

Roger Williams National Memorial (282 N. Main St., Providence, RI 02903, tel. 401/521–7266, fax 401/521–7239, www.nps.gov/rowi). Providence and Warwick Convention & Visitors Bureau (1 Westminster St., Providence, RI 02903, tel. 401/456–0200 or 800/556-2484, www.goprovidence.com). Rhode Island Economic Development Corp. (1 W. Exchange St., Providence, RI 02903, tel. 800/556-2484, fax 401/273–8270, www.visitrhodeisland.com).

See Also

Blackstone River Valley National Heritage Corridor and Touro Synagogue National Historic Site, in Other National Parklands.

SOUTH CAROLINA

Charles Pinckney National Historic Site

In southeastern South Carolina, northeast of Charleston

Charles Pinckney (1754–1824) was a statesman, an officer in the American Revolution, and a principal framer of the U.S. Constitution. He served four terms as governor of South Carolina and in the State Assembly. He also served in the U.S. Senate, the House of Representatives, and as President Jefferson's minister to Spain. His ancestral home, Snee Farm, once consisted of 715 acres, 28 of which are today preserved at this site. Archaeological remains of brick foundations from the Pinckney era and an 1820s tidewater cottage also are maintained. The site was authorized on September 8, 1988.

WHAT TO SEE & DO

Touring facility and grounds. **Facilities:** Visitor center, wayside exhibits. Bookstore, picnic tables. **Programs & Events:** Self-guided walking tours through the house and grounds. Constitution Week (3rd week, Sept.). **Tips & Hints:** Go late Mar.–mid-Apr. for azalea and camellia blooms.

FEES, HOURS & REGULATIONS

Free. No hunting. No mountain or trail bikes. Leashed pets only. Park and visitor center open daily 9–5.

HOW TO GET THERE

The park is at 1254 Longpoint Rd., off U.S. 17 in Mount Pleasant, northeast of Charleston. Closest airport: Charleston (10 miles).

CONTACTS

Charles Pinckney National Historic Site (c/o Fort Sumter National Monument, 1214 Middle St., Sullivan's Island, SC 29482, tel. 843/881–5516, fax 843/881–7070, www.nps.gov/chpi). Charleston Convention & Visitors Bureau (423 King St., Charleston, SC 29403, tel. 843/853–8000, www.charlestoncvb.com).

Congaree National Park

In central South Carolina, near Hopkins

The 26,000-acre park contains the last significant tract of old-growth bottomland hardwood forest in the United States. The park, most of which is managed as wilderness, is home to more than 90 tree species, including state and national champion trees, and abundant wildlife that includes the endangered red-cockaded woodpecker. The monument was authorized as Congaree Swamp National Monument in 1976 and designated an International Biosphere Reserve in 1983. It was designated a national park in 2003.

WHAT TO SEE & DO

Bird-watching, camping, canoeing, fishing, hiking, kayaking, picnicking. **Facilities:** Visitor center, film, 25 miles of hiking trails, 27-mile canoe trail, 2½-mile boardwalk. Bookstore, picnic tables. **Programs & Events:** Self-guided walks, ranger-guided walks and canoe trips. Owl prowls, Swampfest (1st Sat. in Oct.), Campfire Chronicles (early Nov.), living history event. **Tips & Hints:** Plan to stay at least two to four hours. Longer trails can take eight hours to explore. Canoe trips can vary in duration from four hours to overnight. Busiest Mar. and Apr., least crowded Aug.

FOOD & LODGING

Camping: In the park: Long Leaf Campground (off the entrance road, in the north portion of the park; 8 sites; free; portable toilets), Bluff Campground (off the entrance road, in the north portion of the park; 6 sites; free). Backcountry camping allowed. Near Columbia: Sesquicentennial State Park (9574 Two Notch Rd., off I–20, tel. 803/788–2706; 85 sites; $16; flush toilets, showers, hookups). **Hotels:** None in park. In Columbia: Columbia Marriott (1200 Hampton St., tel. 803/771–7000, www.marriott.com; 300 rooms; $185), Roadway Inn (1301 Main St., tel. 803/779–7790; 60 rooms, 15 suites; $60–$169). **Restaurants:** None in park. In Columbia: Motor Supply Co. Bistro (920 Gervais St., tel. 803/256–6687; $9–$25; closed Mon.), Mr. Friendly's New Southern Café (2001-A Greene St., tel. 803/254–7828; $11–$25). **Groceries & Gear:** None in park. In Columbia: Piggly Wiggly, 4711 Forest Dr., Exit 9 on I–77; tel. 803/790-0037.

FEES, HOURS & REGULATIONS

Free, donations accepted. Reservations for some guided programs should be made in advance. Backcountry permits required (free from visitor center). South Carolina state fishing license required. Park open daily dawn–dusk. Visitor center open daily; hours vary by season.

HOW TO GET THERE

From I–77, take Exit 5 east onto Rte. 48 (Bluff Rd.), and follow signs. Closest airport: Columbia (25 miles).

CONTACTS

Congaree National Park (100 National Park Rd., Hopkins, SC 29061, tel. 803/776–4396, fax 803/783–4241, www.nps.gov/cong). Columbia Convention & Visitors Bureau (1101 Lincoln St., Columbia, SC 29201, tel. 803/545–0000 or 800/264–4884, fax 803/545–0013, www.columbiacvb.com).

Cowpens National Battlefield

In northwestern South Carolina, near Chesnee

The battlefield commemorates a decisive Revolutionary War battle that helped turn the tide of war in the South. On this field on January 17, 1781, Daniel Morgan led his army of tough Continentals, militia, and cavalry to a brilliant victory over Banastre Tarleton's larger force of British regulars. Walking trails, monuments, and an 1828 log cabin are available. Cowpens was established as a national battlefield site in 1929, transferred to the Park Service in 1933, and redesignated in 1972.

WHAT TO SEE & DO

Biking, bird and wildlife viewing, hiking, jogging, picnicking, scenic drives, walking. **Facilities:** Visitor center, fiber-optic battle program, 1828 log cabin, tour roads and trails, wayside exhibits, overlooks, monuments. Bookstore, picnic area. **Programs & Events:** *Cowpens: A Battle Remembered* presentation (daily 9–4, hourly). Battle anniversary (weekend nearest Jan. 17). **Tips & Hints:** Plan to stay at least two hours. Busiest June and July, least crowded Nov. and Dec.

FOOD & LODGING

Camping: None in park. **Hotels:** None in park. In Gaffney: Quality Inn (143 Corona Dr., tel. 864/487–4200, www.qualityinn.com; 83 rooms; $52–$70). In Spartanburg: Days Inn (115 Rogers Commerce Blvd., tel. 864/814–0560, www.daysinn.com; 40 rooms; $58). **Restaurants:** None in park. In Chesnee: Bantam Chef (418 S. Alabama Ave., tel. 864/461–8403; $6–$11). **Groceries & Gear:** None in park. In Gaffney: Ingles Market (1627 W. Floyd Baker Blvd.; tel. 864/489-2479).

FEES, HOURS & REGULATIONS

Free. Battlefield open daily 9–5.

HOW TO GET THERE

At the intersection of Rtes. 11 and 110, 3 miles east of Chesnee, 10 miles west of Gaffney and I–85 via Exit 92, and 17 miles northeast of Spartanburg via U.S. 221. From I–26, take Exit 5 to Rte. 11 east. Closest airports: Greenville–Spartanburg (45 miles), Charlotte, NC (60 miles).

CONTACTS

Cowpens National Battlefield (Box 308, Chesnee, SC 29323, tel. 864/461–2828, fax 864/461–7795, www.nps.gov/cowp). Spartanburg Convention & Visitors Bureau (298 Magnolia St., Spartanburg, SC 29306, tel. 864/594–5050 or 800/374–8326, fax 864/594–5052, www.visitspartanburg.com).

Fort Sumter
National Monument

In southeastern South Carolina, in Charleston Harbor and on Sullivan's Island

Fort Sumter was one of many coastal fortifications built by the United States after the War of 1812. The first shots of the Civil War were fired here on April 12, 1861, during a Confederate two-day bombardment that ended with the Union troops' withdrawal. Fort Moultrie, administered with Fort Sumter, is the site of the first Patriot victory over the British Navy in the American Revolution, a victory that contributed to British reluctance to invade the South. The fort played a major role for the Confederate Army during the opening battle of the Civil War and the siege of Charleston. The monument was authorized in 1948. Fort Moultrie was transferred to the National Park Service in 1961.

WHAT TO SEE & DO

Touring the forts. **Facilities:** Fort Sumter: museum, wayside exhibits. Fort Moultrie: visitor center, 22-minute film, wayside exhibits. Bookstores. **Programs & Events:** Fort Sumter: ranger orientation and history talks, battle anniversary and living-history programs (Apr. 12). Fort Moultrie: self-guided walking tours, Carolina Day (late June), battle anniversary and living-history programs (June 28). **Tips & Hints:** Fort Sumter: Get to boat departure area at least 30 minutes early. Go Sept. and Oct. for best weather and smaller crowds. Fort Moultrie: Allow two hours for tour. Busiest Apr. and July, least crowded Dec. and Jan.

FEES, HOURS & REGULATIONS

Fort Sumter: free. Tour boat fees apply (tel. 843/722–2628). No pets. Fort open Mar. and Sept.–Nov., daily 10–4; Apr.–Labor Day, daily 10–5:30; hours vary rest of year. Fort Moultrie: $3 adults, $1 ages 15 and under, $5 per family. No pets. Fort open daily 9–5.

HOW TO GET THERE

Fort Sumter is in Charleston Harbor and accessible only by boat. Departures at Fort Sumter National Monument Visitor Education Center at Liberty Square (340 Concord St., Charleston) and Patriots Point Naval and Maritime Museum (40 Patriots Point Rd., Mount Pleasant). Fort Moultrie is on Sullivan's Island. From Mount Pleasant, take Rte. 703 to Middle St. Closest airport: Charleston (20 miles).

CONTACTS

Fort Moultrie (1214 Middle St., Sullivan's Island, SC 29482, tel. 843/883–3123, fax 843/883–3910, www.nps.gov/fomo). Fort Sumter National Monument (1214 Middle St., Sullivan's Island, SC 29482, tel. 843/883–3123, fax 843/883–3910, www.nps.gov/fosu). Charleston Convention & Visitors Bureau (423 King St., Charleston, SC 29403, tel. 843/853–8000).

Kings Mountain National Military Park

In north-central part of the state, near Blacksburg

Preserved in this park is the site of a pivotal American Revolution battle, which was fought here on October 7, 1780. After a series of British victories, patriots from Virginia, the Carolinas, and Georgia defeated British Major Patrick Ferguson at Kings Mountain. The U.S. victory forced British General Charles Cornwallis to retreat back into South Carolina for the winter and helped turn the tide of the war against the British. The park, located in South Carolina near the North Carolina border, was established in 1931.

WHAT TO SEE & DO

Hiking, touring battlefield, viewing museum exhibits. **Facilities:** Visitor center, amphitheater, film, trail, wayside exhibits. Bookstore. **Programs & Events:** Living-history encampments (occasionally). Evening programs and concerts (May–Oct.), musket and rifle demonstrations (May–Oct., weekends). Battle anniversary (Oct. 7). **Tips & Hints:** Best times to visit are spring and fall. Go in spring and summer for wildflowers, Oct. for fall foliage. Busiest May and June, least crowded Dec. and Jan.

FOOD, LODGING & SUPPLIES

Camping: In the park: Backcountry camping allowed (check-in at visitor center required). In Blacksburg: Kings Mountain State Park (1277 Park Rd., tel. 803/222-3209, www.southcarolinaparks.com; 125 sites; $12–$18; flush toilets, showers, hookups). **Hotels:** See Cowpens National Battlefield. **Restaurants:** See Cowpens National Battlefield. **Groceries & Gear:** In Kings Mountain, NC: Food Lion (610 E. King St., tel. 704/739–7458).

FEES, HOURS & REGULATIONS

Free. No hunting, mountain biking, or ATV use. No metal detecting. Leashed pets only. Park open daily 9–5.

HOW TO GET THERE

On Rte. 216, 4 miles southeast of I–85 via Exit 2 (just over the border in NC). Closest airports: Charlotte, NC (40 miles); Greenville, SC (50 miles).

CONTACT

Kings Mountain National Military Park (2625 Park Rd., Blacksburg, SC 29702, tel. 864/936–7921, fax 864/936–9897, www.nps.gov/kimo).

Ninety Six
National Historic Site

In southern South Carolina, near Greenwood

Among several theories of how Ninety Six got its name is one saying that 18th-century English traders thought the stopping place was 96 miles from the Cherokee village of Keowee. The park commemorates the role the settlement played during British settlement of the frontier and the southern campaign of the American Revolution. It also offers historic roads and paths, the earthen British-built Star Fort (circa 1781), and the partially reconstructed Stockade Fort. Archaeological complexes abound, including the underground remains of two villages, plantations, houses, and forts. The site was authorized on August 16, 1976.

WHAT TO SEE & DO

Fishing, hiking interpretive trail, picnicking, viewing museum exhibits. **Facilities:** Visitor center, auditorium, video, 18-mile hiking trail, wayside exhibits. Book sales area, picnic tables. **Programs & Events:** Ranger-led activities, walks, and tours (May–Sept.). Lifeways of the Cherokee Indians and Colonial Settlers (1st weekend in Apr., even-number years), Revolutionary War Days Encampment (1st weekend in Apr., odd-number years), Living History Saturdays (3rd Sat. of month, May–Sept.). Independence Day Celebration (closest weekend to July 4), Annual Autumn Candlelight Tour (2nd Sat. in Oct.). **Tips & Hints:** Visit in spring and fall when temperatures are cooler. Busiest in May and Oct., least crowded Jan. and Feb.

FOOD, LODGING & SUPPLIES

Camping: None in park. In Greenwood: Lake Greenwood State Park (302 State Park Rd., tel. 864/543–3535; 125 units; $18–$23; flush toilets, showers, hookups). **Hotels:** None in park. In Greenwood: Hampton Inn (1624 Bypass 72 NE, tel. 864/388–9595, www.hamptoninn.hilton.com; 75 rooms, 2 suites; $109–$179). Holiday Inn Express (110 Birchtree Dr., tel. 864/223–2296, www.holidayinn.com; 46 rooms, 24 suites; $99–$159). **Restaurants:** None in park. In Greenwood: Mill House (237 Maxwell Ave., tel. 864/323–0321; $11–$19). **Groceries & Gear:** None in park. In Ninety Six: Piggly Wiggly (204 N. Cambridge, tel. 864/543–3918).

FEES, HOURS & REGULATIONS

Free. Donations accepted. South Carolina state fishing license required. Leashed pets only. No hunting. No mechanized equipment on trails (except that used by visitors with disabilities). No bicycles on walking trail; no skateboards. Park is open daily dawn–dusk. Visitor center open daily 9–5.

HOW TO GET THERE

2 miles south of the town of Ninety Six, which is on Rte. 34, 10 miles east of Greenwood. Closest airport: Greenville (65 miles).

CONTACTS

Ninety Six National Historic Site (1103 Hwy. 248, Ninety Six, SC 29666, tel. 864/543–4068, fax 864/543–2058, www.nps.gov/nisi). Ninety Six Chamber of Commerce (97 Main St. E, Ninety Six, SC 29666, tel. 864/543-2047, www.ninetysixsc.blogspot.com).

See Also

Historic Camden, Overmountain Victory National Historic Trail, and South Carolina National Heritage Corridor, in Other National Parklands.

SOUTH DAKOTA

Badlands National Park

In southwestern South Dakota, near Wall

The 244,000-acre park is well known for its outstanding geological features—steep canyons, sharp ridges, gullies, sawtooth spires, and knobs—and its rich paleontological resources, especially Oligocene-era mammal fossils. But it also contains the largest protected mixed-grass prairie in the National Park Service, 64,000 acres of wilderness, and the site of the reintroduction of the black-footed ferret, one of the most endangered land mammals in North America. The Stronghold Unit, which is managed under an agreement with the Oglala Sioux Tribe, includes the sites of the 1890s Ghost Dances. The site was authorized as a national monument in 1939 and redesignated a national park in 1978.

WHAT TO SEE & DO

Hiking, horseback riding, scenic drives. **Facilities:** 2 visitor centers: Ben Reifel (Cedar Pass, Rte. 240 northeast of Interior) and White River (Stronghold Unit); loop roads, trails. Book and map sale areas, gift shop, picnic tables. **Programs & Events:** Guided walks, talks, and multimedia programs (mid-June–Labor Day). **Tips & Hints:** Bring hats and sunglasses to protect against bright sun, and carry water. Watch for cactus. Give bison plenty of room. Busiest July and Aug., least crowded Dec. and Jan.

FOOD, LODGING & SUPPLIES

Camping: 2 campgrounds in the park: Cedar Pass (100 sites; $16–$28; flush toilets, pit toilets), Sage Creek (primitive camping area; free; pit toilets). Backcountry camping allowed. In Interior: Badlands White River KOA (20720 Rte. 44, 4 miles south of Interior, tel. 605/433–5337; 134 sites, 10 cabins; $18–$36, $46–$82; flush toilets, showers, hookups; closed Oct.–mid-Apr.). In Wall: Arrow Camp (515 Crown St., tel. 605/279–2112; 100 sites; $17–$29; flush toilets, showers, hookups). **Hotels:** In the park: Cedar Pass Lodge (20681 Hwy. 240, tel. 605/433–5460, www.cedarpasslodge.com; 28 cabins; $85–$150; closed Oct.–mid-Apr.). In Interior: Badlands Ranch & Resort (Rte. 44, tel. 605/433-5599, badlandsranchandresort.com; 4 rooms, 7 cabins; $58–$68, $78–$110 cabins). **Restaurants:** In the park: Cedar Pass Lodge (20681 Hwy. 240, tel. 605/433–5460, www.cedarpasslodge.com; $5–$16; closed Oct.–mid-Apr.). In Wall: Western Art Gallery Restaurant (510 Main St., tel. 605/279–2175; $5–$23). **Groceries & Gear:** None in park. In Interior: Badlands Grocery (101 Main St., tel. 605/433–5445). In Wall: Wall Drug Store (510 Main St., tel. 605/279–2175).

FEES, HOURS & REGULATIONS

Entrance fee: $7.50 per person, $15 per vehicle. No hunting, collecting, open campfires, off-road travel. Backcountry campers must be at least a half-mile away from roads and trails, not visible, and leave no trace. Bicycling on established roads only. Pets allowed on roads and established campgrounds only and must be on a leash. Park open daily. Ben Reifel Visitor Center open daily 8–4, extended hours in summer. White River Visitor Center open early June–late Aug., daily 10–4.

HOW TO GET THERE

The park loop road (Rte. 240) can be accessed from I–90 via Exits 110 or 131. Follow signs to visitor center. Closest airport: Rapid City (80 miles).

CONTACTS

Badlands National Park (Box 6, Interior, SD 57750, tel. 605/433–5361, fax 605/433–5404, www.nps.gov/badl). South Dakota Tourism (711 E. Wells Ave., Pierre, SD 57501, tel. 605/773–3301 or 800/732–5682, www.travelsd.com).

Jewel Cave National Monument

In southwestern South Dakota, near Custer

With more than 160 miles surveyed, Jewel Cave is recognized as the second-longest cave in the world. Air flow inside the cave's passages indicates a vast area yet to be explored. Cave tours provide opportunities for viewing this pristine cave system and its wide variety of speleothems, including stalactites, stalagmites, draperies, flowstone, frostwork, boxwork, and hydromagnesite balloons. The cave is an important hibernaculum for four species of bats. Above ground the monument protects Hell and Lithograph canyons, a ranger cabin listed on the National Register of Historic Structures, and some of the last unlogged ponderosa pine forest in the Black Hills. The monument was established in 1908 and transferred to the Park Service in 1933.

WHAT TO SEE & DO

Hiking surface trails, picnicking, touring caves. **Facilities:** Visitor center, Historic Area Ranger Station, trails. Book sales areas, picnic tables. **Programs & Events:** Ranger-led scenic cave tours (daily, reservations strongly recommended), ranger-led lantern tours (June–Labor Day, daily; reservations strongly recommended), wild caving tours (June–Aug., daily except Tues. and Fri.; reservations required). **Tips & Hints:** Make reservations, especially June–Aug., to avoid a two- to three-hour wait for cave tours. Call Black Hills Central Reservations at 866/601–5103 or visit online at www.blackhillsvacations.com, which can book your tour up to a year in advance. Cave is 49°F year-round. Busiest July and Aug., least crowded Dec. and Jan.

FOOD, LODGING & SUPPLIES

⚠ **Camping:** None in park. In Custer: Beaver Lake Campground (12005 W. U.S. 16, tel. 605/673–2464, www.beaverlakecampground. net; 92 sites; $26–$38; flush toilets, showers, laundry, store, hookups),

Comanche Park (U.S. 16, 6 miles west of Custer, tel. 605/574–4402; 877/444–6777 reservations; 35 sites; $14; vault toilets; closed mid-Sept.–mid-May). 🏨 **Hotels:** None in park. In Custer State Park: Blue Bell Lodge & Resort (Rte. 87, tel. 605/255–4531 or 888/875–0001; 29 cabins; $130–$240), State Game Lodge & Resort (U.S. 16A, tel. 605/255–4541 or 800/658–3530; 47 rooms, 22 cabins; $89–$215, $75–$315 cabins). In Custer: Americas Best Value Dakota Cowboy Hotel (208 W. Mt. Rushmore Rd., tel. 605/673–4659, www.americasbestvalueinn.com; 48 rooms; $55–$80; closed mid-Oct.–Apr.). ✗ **Restaurants:** None in park. In Custer State Park: State Game Lodge & Resort (U.S 16A, tel. 605/255–4541; $15–$28). In Custer: Cattleman's Steakhouse and Fish Market (140 W. Mt. Rushmore Rd., tel. 605/673-4402; $5–$10; closed mid-Oct.–Apr.). 👍 **Groceries & Gear:** None in park. In Custer: Lynn's Dakota Mart (800 Mt. Rushmore Rd., tel. 605/673–4463), True Value Hardware (529 Mt. Rushmore Rd., tel. 605/673–2227).

FEES, HOURS & REGULATIONS

Free. Scenic cave tour fees: $8 adults, $4 ages 6–16, free ages 5 and under. No children under 6 on some tours. Wild caving tour fees: $27 per person; no children under 16. No pets, tripods, food, bags/purses, or walking sticks in cave. No pets in visitor center or on trails. No mountain or trail bikes, motorized or mechanized equipment on trails. No hunting or open fires. Check site for hours.

HOW TO GET THERE

13 miles west of Custer and 24 miles east of Newcastle, WY, via U.S. 16. Closest airport: Rapid City (53 miles).

CONTACTS

Jewel Cave National Monument (11149 U.S. 16, Bldg. B12, Custer, SD 57730, tel. 605/673–8356, fax 605/673–8397, www.nps.gov/jeca). Custer County Chamber of Commerce (615 Washington St., Custer, SD 57730, tel. 605/673–2244 or 800/922–9818, fax 605/673–3726, www.custersd.com). Newcastle Chamber of Commerce (1323 Washington St., Newcastle, WY 82701, tel. 307/746–2739, www.newcastlewyo.com).

Minuteman Missile National Historic Site

In southwestern South Dakota, in Interior

The history of the Cold War is the focus of this park unit. The site consists of a launch control center, an aboveground facility attached to an underground launch center, and a launch facility, known as a missile silo. The site was established on December 2, 1999.

WHAT TO SEE & DO

Touring site. **Facilities:** Visitor center (off Interstate 90, Exit 131).

FEES, HOURS & REGULATIONS

Free. Visitor center open daily 8–4:30. Tours Memorial Day–Labor Day, daily at 9 AM and 1:30 PM; Labor Day–Memorial Day, daily at 10 AM. Tours of site are available daily on first-come, first-served basis. Tour spaces are extremely limited.

HOW TO GET THERE

Take I–90 to Exit 131.

CONTACT

Minuteman Missile National Historic Site (c/o Badlands National Park, Box 6, Interior, SD 57750, tel. 605/433–5361, 605/433–5552 for tour information, fax 605/433–5248, www.nps.gov/mimi).

Mount Rushmore National Memorial

In southwestern South Dakota, near Keystone

The faces of four U.S. presidents—George Washington, Thomas Jefferson, Abraham Lincoln, and Theodore Roosevelt—are carved into the southeast side of the granite mountain. Sculptor Gutzon Borglum and 400 workers spent 14 years (1927–41) carving the images that collectively represent the birth, growth, preservation, and development of the first 150 years of the United States. The memorial was authorized in 1925.

WHAT TO SEE & DO

Climbing, hiking, viewing the memorial. **Facilities:** Information center, Lincoln Borglum Museum, Sculptors Studio, amphitheater, theaters, trails. Bookstore. **Programs & Events:** Guided walks, studio talks at Sculptors Studio, evening lighting ceremony (summer season), religious services (June–Aug.). July 4 Celebration. **Tips & Hints:** Visit in the early morning for the best light and enjoy breakfast with the presidents. Busiest June–Sept., least crowded Dec. and Feb.

FOOD & LODGING

⛺ **Camping:** None in park. In Hill City: Palmer Gulch (Rte. 244, tel. 605/574–2525, www.palmergulch.com; 445 sites, 55 cabins; $21–$81; flush toilets, showers, hookups; closed Oct.–Apr.). See also Jewel Cave National Monument. 🏨 **Hotels:** None in park. In Hill City: Lodge at Palmer Gulch (12620 Rte. 244, tel. 605/574–2525 or 800/562–8503, www.palmergulch.com; 62 rooms, 30 cabins; $60–$215). See also Jewel Cave National Monument and Wind Cave National Park. ✘ **Restaurants:** In park: Carvers Cafe (Rte. 244, tel. 605/574–2515; $7–$13). In Hill City: Alpine Inn (225 Main St., tel. 605/574–2749; $10–$12; closed Sun.).

FEES, HOURS & REGULATIONS

Free. Parking fees: $11 (good for one calendar year). No pets. Trails for walking only. No off-road travel. Park open daily. Information center and museum open Memorial Day–Labor Day, daily 8 AM–10 PM; Labor Day–Memorial Day, daily 8–5; call or check website to confirm.

HOW TO GET THERE

The memorial, which is surrounded by the Black Hills National Forest, is 25 miles southwest of Rapid City via U.S. 16 and 3 miles from Keystone via U.S. 16A and Rte. 244. Closest airport: Rapid City.

CONTACTS

Mount Rushmore National Memorial (13000 Hwy. 244, Bldg. 1, Ste. 1, Keystone, SD 57751, tel. 605/574–2523, fax 605/574–2307, www.nps. gov/moru). Keystone Chamber of Commerce (110 Swanzey St., or Box 653, Keystone, SD 57751, tel. 605/666-4896, www.keystonechamber. com). Rapid City Chamber of Commerce (Box 747, Rapid City, SD 57709, tel. 605/343–1744, www.visitrapidcity.com). South Dakota Department of Tourism (711 E. Wells Ave., Pierre, SD 57501, tel. 605/ 773–3301 or 800/732–5682, www.travelsd.com).

Wind Cave National Park

In southwestern South Dakota, near Hot Springs

Wind Cave, in the scenic Black Hills, is one of the longest and most complex caves in the world, and the first cave protected by the federal government. It contains beautiful boxwork—a rare cave formation—in greater variety and profusion than any other cave in the world. In 2011, the park was expanded by 5,556 acres (slated to be opened to the public around 2014) with acquisition of a historic homestead ranch dating to 1881 and a prehistoric buffalo jump dating to 1030 A.D. The 33,851-acre park's rolling mixed-grass prairie, pine-covered hills, and woodland ravines also are home to a diverse mix of eastern and western plant and wildlife species, including bison, elk, pronghorn, mule deer, coyotes, and prairie dogs. The park was established on January 9, 1903.

WHAT TO SEE & DO

Cave touring, hiking, picnicking, wildlife viewing. **Facilities:** Visitor center, Cave Elevator Building with exhibits, amphitheater, self-guided nature trails, wayside exhibits, fire lookout tower. Bookstore, fire grates, picnic tables. **Programs & Events:** Cave tours (daily). Interpretive talks and campfire programs (June–Aug.). **Tips & Hints:** Wear walking shoes and sweater or jacket in cave. Cave temperature is 53°F. Stay away from bison and prairie dogs and their burrows, which harbor rattlesnakes. Mornings are usually less crowded for cave tours. Go in spring or fall to avoid crowds. Busiest July and Aug., least crowded Dec. and Jan.

FOOD, LODGING & SUPPLIES

⚑ **Camping:** In the park: Elk Mountain (65 sites; $12, $6 in winter; flush toilets; no running water Oct.–Apr.). See also Jewel Cave National Monument. 🏨 **Hotels:** None in park. In Hot Springs: Best Western (737 S. 6th St., tel. 605/745–7378 or 877/664–7378, www. bestwesternhotsprings.com; 51 rooms, 9 suites; $60–180), Americas

Best Value Inn (602 N.W. River St., tel. 605/745–4292 or 888/605–4292, www.americasbestvalueinn.com; 32 rooms, 3 cabins; $40–$90). See also Jewel Cave National Monument. ✗ **Restaurants:** None in park. In Hot Springs: Dale's Family Restaurant (745 Battle Mountain Ave., tel. 605/745–5443; $6–$12). In Pringle: Hitchrail Bar and Restaurant (110 Earl St., tel. 605/673–2697; $8–$18). See also Jewel Cave National Monument. ⛄ **Groceries & Gear:** In Hot Springs: Family Thrift (505 S. 6th St., tel. 605/745–3203).

FEES, HOURS & REGULATIONS

Free. Cave tour fees: $7–$9 adults, free ages 5 and under. Wild cave tour: $23, no children under 16. Reservations (tel. 605/745–4600) available up to a month in advance. Backcountry permits (free from visitor center or Centennial Trail trailheads) required for all backcountry camping. No hunting. No pets on trails or in backcountry. Leashed pets elsewhere. Bikes allowed on roads open to vehicle traffic. Fires in campground fire grates and picnic area only. No food, drink, or camera tripods in caves. Park open daily. Visitor center open May and Sept., daily 8–6; June–Aug., daily 8–7; Oct.–Apr., daily 8–4:30.

HOW TO GET THERE

7 miles north of Hot Springs and 20 miles south of Custer via U.S. 385. Closest airport: Rapid City (60 miles).

CONTACTS

Wind Cave National Park (2611 Hwy. 385, Hot Springs, SD 57747, tel. 605/745–4600, fax 605/745–4207, www.nps.gov/wica). Custer County Chamber of Commerce (615 Washington St., Custer, SD 57730, tel. 605/673–2244 or 800/922–9818, www.custersd.com). Hot Springs Area Chamber of Commerce (801 S. 6th St., Hot Springs, SD 57747, tel. 800/325–991, www.hotsprings-sd.com).

See Also

Missouri National Recreational River and Niobrara National Scenic Riverway, Nebraska. *Lewis & Clark National Historic Trail,* in Other National Parklands.

TENNESSEE

Andrew Johnson National Historic Site

In northeastern Tennessee, in Greeneville

At this site are two homes, the tailor shop, and the burial site of Andrew Johnson, who became president in 1865 after Abraham Lincoln was assassinated. Guided tours explore the presidential homestead, which belonged to Johnson from 1851 until his death in 1875. The site was authorized as a national monument on August 29, 1935; established on April 27, 1942; and redesignated a national historic site on December 11, 1963.

WHAT TO SEE & DO

Touring the facilities. **Facilities:** Visitor center with museum, orientation film, and tailor shop, early Johnson home with museum, president's homestead, national cemetery where Johnson is buried. Book sales area. **Programs & Events:** Ranger-guided tours (daily at 9:30, 10:30, 11:30, 1:30, 2:30, 3:30, and 4:30). Memorial Day program (late May). **Tips & Hints:** Busiest May and Oct., least crowded Jan. and Feb.

FOOD, LODGING & SUPPLIES

Camping: None in park. Near Greeneville: Horse Creek (Horse Creek Rd., off Rte. 107, tel. 423/638-4109, www.fs.usda.gov/cherokee; 15 sites; $10; flush toilets, showers), Old Forge (Old Forge Rd., off Horse Creek Rd., tel. 423/638–4109; 10 sites; $7), Paint Creek (off Rte. 70, tel. 423/638–4109; 19 sites; $10; flush toilets, showers, hookups). **Hotels:** None in park. In Greeneville: Jameson Inn (3160 E. Andrew Johnson Hwy., tel. 423/638–7511, www.jamesoninns.com; 55 rooms; $84). **Restaurants:** None in park. In Greeneville: Olde Tusculum Eatery (905 Erwin Hwy., tel. 423/638–9210; $5–$12, closed weekends, no dinner). **Groceries & Gear:** None in park. In Greeneville: Food City (905 Snapps Ferry Rd., tel. 423/638–1271).

FEES, HOURS & REGULATIONS

Free. Leashed pets only. Site open daily 9–5.

HOW TO GET THERE

In downtown Greeneville, at the corner of College and Depot Sts. Closest airport: Tri-Cities (40 miles).

CONTACTS

Andrew Johnson National Historic Site (121 Monument Ave., Greeneville, TN 37744-1088, tel. 423/639–3711, fax 423/798–0754, www.nps.gov/anjo). Greene County Partnership–Chamber of Commerce (115 Academy St., Greenville, TN 37743, tel. 423/638–4111, fax 423/638–5345, www.greenecountypartnership.com).

Big South Fork National River & Recreation Area

In northeastern Tennessee and south-central Kentucky

The free-flowing Big South Fork of the Cumberland River and its tributaries pass through 90 miles of scenic gorges and valleys containing a range of natural and historic features. Recreational opportunities abound. Planning and development by the U.S. Army Corps of Engineers was authorized in 1974, Park Service management was authorized in 1976, and transfer to the Park Service was completed in 1991.

WHAT TO SEE & DO

Biking, canoeing (rentals in Whitley City), fishing, hiking, horseback riding, hunting, kayaking, rafting (rentals in Whitley City), swimming. **Facilities:** 2 visitor centers: Bandy Creek (15 miles west of Oneida, TN, off Rte. 297); Kentucky center (off Hwy. 1651, Blue Heron), outdoor museum (Blue Heron Mining Community, KY), hiking and horse trails, overlooks, pool (Bandy Creek area; $3). Bookstores. **Programs & Events:** Astronomy programs, dulcimer concerts. Evening programs (Memorial Day–Sept., Sat.). Spring Planting Festival (Apr.), Storytelling and Craft Festival (Sept.), Pioneer Encampments (Oct.). **Tips & Hints:** Use caution when crossing rivers on foot or horseback. Be careful when swimming in rivers, approaching overlooks, and in weather when hypothermia is a risk. Busiest Sept. and Oct., least crowded Jan. and Feb.

FOOD, LODGING & SUPPLIES

Camping: 3 campgrounds in the park: Alum Ford (end of Rte. 700; 7 sites; $5; pit toilets), Bandy Creek (off Rte. 297; 149 sites; $19–$22; flush toilets, showers, hookups), Blue Heron (off Rte. 742; 45 sites; $17; flush toilets, showers, hookups). Backcountry camping and horse campsites available. **Hotels:** In the park: Charit Creek Lodge (tel. 865/429–5704; 2 cabins, 2 lodge rooms; $129; hike or ride in only). In Jamestown: Big South Fork Lodge & Horse Campground (3607 Leatherwood Ford Rd., tel. 931/879–4230; 6 rooms, 1 cabin; $49–$85). **Restaurants:** None in park. In Oneida: Preston's Steakhouse (17987 Alberta St., tel. 423/569-4158; $7-20).

Groceries & Gear: None in park. In Corbin, KY: Sheltowee Trace Outfitters (2001 Hwy. 90, tel. 800/541–7238). In Parkers Lake, KY: Sheltowee Trace Outfitters (1943 Hwy. 90, 606/376–5567, www.ky-rafting. com).

FEES, HOURS & REGULATIONS

Free. Guided horseback rides available (tel. 423/286–7433). Big South Fork Scenic Railway offers train excursions from Stearns, KY, to the Blue Heron Mining Community (tel. 800/462–5664). Backcountry permit required ($5–$25). Hunting and fishing allowed in recreation area. Tennessee or Kentucky state hunting and fishing licenses required. Park open daily. Bandy Creek Visitor Center open Nov.–May, daily 9–

5:30; June–Oct., daily 8–6. Kentucky Visitor Center open Apr.–Nov., daily 9–5:30.

HOW TO GET THERE

The Tennessee visitor center is 15 miles west of Oneida, off Rte. 297. The Kentucky visitor center is in Blue Heron. Park headquarters is 9 miles west of Oneida on Rte. 297. Closest airports: Knoxville (80 miles), Nashville (150 miles), Lexington, KY (261 miles).

CONTACT

Big South Fork National River & Recreation Area (Park Headquarters, 4564 Leatherwood Rd., Oneida, TN 37841, tel. 423/569–9778 or 423/286-7275, 606/376–5073 in KY, www.nps.gov/biso).

Fort Donelson National Battlefield

In northwestern Tennessee, near Dover

Fort Donelson was created to preserve and interpret the remains of the Battle of Fort Donelson, the 1862 Civil War conflict. The park includes the fort, river batteries, outer defense earthworks, Surrender House (Dover Hotel), and a national cemetery. The historical significance of the park centers on three major themes: Union commander Ulysses S. Grant ("Unconditional Surrender" Grant) and his capture of the fort and 13,000 Confederate prisoners; the use of ironclad gunboats on inland rivers; and the beginning of the Union Army's control of the north-to-south inland waters of the Tennessee and Cumberland Rivers. The park was established as a national military park on March 26, 1928, transferred to the Park Service in 1933, and redesignated in 1985.

WHAT TO SEE & DO

Hiking, picnicking, scenic drives, visiting museum. **Facilities:** Visitor center, Surrender House, museum, wayside exhibits, trails, cell-phone tours. Book and map sale area, picnic tables. **Programs & Events:** Introductory movie. **Tips & Hints:** Go Apr.–June for flowers, Sept.–Mar. for smaller crowds. Busiest June and July, least crowded Jan. and Feb.

FOOD, LODGING & SUPPLIES

⚑ **Camping:** None in park. Near Dover: Piney Campground (Land Between the Lakes National Forest, 621 Fort Henry Rd., tel. 931/232–5556; 384 sites, 9 cabins; $12–$32; flush toilets, showers, hookups). ▦ **Hotels:** None in park. In Clarksville: Riverview Inn (50 College St., tel. 931/552–3331, www.theriverviewinn.com; 147 rooms, 11 suites; $99). ✘ **Restaurants:** None in park. In Dover: Bauer's (2148 Donelson Pkwy., tel. 931/232–4817; $7–$10). ⛿ **Groceries & Gear:** None in park. In Dover: Piggly Wiggly (1536 Donelson Pkwy., tel. 931/232–7024).

FEES, HOURS & REGULATIONS

Free. Leashed pets only. No metal detectors, skating, skateboards, vehicles on trails, hunting. Park open Memorial Day–Labor Day, daily 8–

8; Labor Day–Nov., daily 8–6, Nov.-Memorial Day, daily 8-4:30. Visitor center open daily 8–4:30. Surrender House open daily 9–4.

HOW TO GET THERE

1 mile west of Dover, off U.S. 79. Closest airport: Nashville (90 miles).

CONTACTS

Fort Donelson National Battlefield (Box 434, Dover, TN 37058, tel. 931/232–5706, fax 931/232–6331, www.nps.gov/fodo). Dover–Stuart County Chamber of Commerce (Box 147, Dover, TN 37058, tel. 931/232-8290, www.stewartcountychamberofcommerce.com).

Great Smoky Mountains National Park

In eastern Tennessee, near Gatlinburg; and western North Carolina, near Cherokee

The 521,621-acre forested park is world renowned for the diversity of its plants and animals, the beauty of its ancient mountains, the quality of its remnants of American pioneer culture, and the depth and integrity of the wilderness sanctuary within its boundaries. It's one of the largest protected areas in the East. The park was authorized in 1926 and designated a Biosphere Reserve in 1976 and a World Heritage Site in 1983.

WHAT TO SEE & DO

Bicycling (rentals in Cades Cove), fishing, hiking, horseback riding, picnicking, tubing. **Facilities:** 3 visitor centers: Sugarlands (2 miles south of Gatlinburg, TN, on U.S. 441), Oconaluftee (1 mile north of Cherokee, NC), and Cades Cove (near Townsend, TN); Mountain Farm Museum, orientation film at Sugarlands, scenic drives, 800 miles of trails. Bookstores, picnic areas. **Programs & Events:** Ranger-led interpretive walks and talks, video presentations, and campfire programs (June–Sept.). Storytelling, living-history programs, Old Timers' Day, Quilt Show, Women's Work, Mountain Life Festival, Sorghum Molasses and Apple Butter Making (all May–Oct.); Cosby in the Park (3rd Sat. in May), Festival of Christmas Past (2nd Sat. in Dec.). **Tips & Hints:** Expect temperatures to be 10–20 degrees cooler on mountaintops (up to 6,643 feet). Summers are hot and humid at lower elevations; frost begins in late Sept.; the driest weather is in the fall. Busiest July, Aug., and Oct., least crowded Jan. and Feb.

FOOD, LODGING & SUPPLIES

Camping: 10 campgrounds in the park (all with flush toilets): Abrams Creek (16 sites; $14; closed Nov.–mid-May), Balsam Mountain (46 sites; $14; closed mid-Oct.–mid-May), Big Creek (12 tent sites; $14; closed Nov.–Mar.), Cades Cove (159 sites; $17–$20), Cataloochee (27 sites; $20; closed Nov.–Feb.), Cosby (157 sites; $14; closed Nov.–mid-Mar.), Deep Creek (92 sites; $17; closed Nov.–Mar.), Elkmont (220 sites; $17–$23; closed Dec.–mid-Mar.), Look Rock (68 sites; $14;

closed Nov.–mid-May), Smokemont (140 sites; $17–$20). Backcountry camping in designated sites only. 🛏 **Hotels:** In the park: LeConte Lodge (tel. 865/429–5704; 60 beds; $121 per person; closed mid-Nov.–late Mar.). In Gatlinburg: Brookside Resort (463 E. Parkway, tel. 865/436–5611 or 800/251–9597, www.brooksideresort.com; 115 rooms, 3 suites, 8 cottages; $75–$300). ✕ **Restaurants:** None in park. In Gatlinburg: Atrium (432 Parkway, tel. 865/430–3684; $6–$9), Greenbrier Restaurant (370 Newman Rd., tel. 865/436–6318; $14–$22). ⛽ **Groceries & Gear:** None in park. In Gatlinburg: Food City (1219 E. Parkway, tel. 865/430–3116).

FEES, HOURS & REGULATIONS

Free. Fees charged at developed campgrounds. Reservations mandatory mid-May–Oct. for Cades Cove, Elkmont, and Smokemont (tel. 877/444–6777, www.recreation.gov). Reservations available for five horse camps (tel. 877/444–6777, www.recreation.gov). Reservations and permit required for backcountry camping (865/436–1297). Workshops at Great Smoky Mountains Institute at Tremont (tel. 865/448–6709). Weekend workshops at Smoky Mountain Field School (tel. 800/284–8885). Tennessee or North Carolina fishing license required. No pets on most trails. Leashed pets elsewhere. Sugarlands and Oconaluftee visitor centers are open daily 9–4, longer hours in summer. Cades Cove is open Jan., daily 9–4; Feb. and Nov., daily 9–5; Mar., Sept. and Oct., daily 9–6; Apr.–Aug. daily 9–7; Dec., daily 9–4:30.

HOW TO GET THERE

The park has three main entrances. From I–40 east in TN, take Exit 407 (Sevierville) to Rte. 66 south, continue to U.S. 441 south, follow U.S. 441 to park. From I–40 west in TN, take Exit 386B in Knoxville to U.S. 129 south to Alcoa–Maryville. At Maryville proceed on U.S. 321 east through Townsend. Continue straight on Rte. 73 into park. From I–40 in NC, take U.S. 19 west through Maggie Valley. Proceed to U.S. 441 north at Cherokee into the park. From Atlanta and points south, follow U.S. 23 north to U.S. 441 north. Closest airports: Knoxville, TN (50 miles), Asheville, NC (60 miles).

CONTACT

Great Smoky Mountains National Park (107 Park Headquarters Rd., Gatlinburg, TN 37738, tel. 865/436–1200, fax 865/436–1220, www.nps.gov/grsm).

Obed Wild & Scenic River

In east-central Tennessee, near Wartburg

Clear and Daddy's Creeks, about 45 miles of free-flowing streams on the Obed and Emory Rivers, are protected in this park. The river provides some of the most rugged scenery in the Southeast and has spectacular gorges 500 feet deep. The river was authorized on October 12, 1976.

WHAT TO SEE & DO

Fishing, hiking, hunting, picnicking, rock climbing, swimming, white-water boating. **Facilities:** Visitor center (Wartburg), trails. Bookstore. **Programs & Events:** Ranger-led talks and walks, video presentations (on request). **Tips & Hints:** Be aware of changing weather conditions if boating or climbing. White-water conditions suitable for experienced boaters only. Go Jan.–Apr. for best white-water boating. Call park for water levels and float information.

FOOD, LODGING & SUPPLIES

Camping: In the park: Rock Creek (off Catoosa Rd., near Nemo Bridge; 11 sites; $7; no water). Near Wartburg: Frozen Head State Park (964 Flat Fork Rd., tel. 423/346–7732; 20 sites; $13; showers and bathhouse). **Hotels:** None in park. In Crossville: Motel 6 (4083 U.S. 127, tel. 931/484–7581, www.motel6.com; 88 rooms; $40). In Harriman: Days Inn (120 Childs Rd., tel. 865/882-6200, www.daysinn.com; 50 rooms; $72–$80). Quality Inn (1845 S. Roane St., tel. 865/882–5340, www.qualityinn.com; 80 rooms; $70–$80). **Restaurants:** None in park. In Harriman: Gondolier Pizza (1822 Roane State Hwy., tel. 865/717–0277; $6–$17). In Wartburg: Angie's Restaurant (107 N. Kingston St., tel. 423/346–7000; $12–$26). **Groceries & Gear:** None in park. In Wartburg: Darnell's Food Market (1014 Main St., tel. 423/346–3344).

FEES, HOURS & REGULATIONS

Free. No glass bottles at river access points. No alcohol. Tennessee hunting and fishing licenses required. Visitor center open daily 9–5.

HOW TO GET THERE

From I–40, follow U.S. 27 north or U.S. 127 north. From the south, follow I–75 north to I–40 west. From the north, take I–75 to Rte. 63 west to U.S. 27 south. Closest airport: Knoxville (50 miles).

CONTACT

Obed Wild and Scenic River (208 N. Maiden St., Box 429, Wartburg, TN 37887, tel. 423/346–6294, www.nps.gov/obed).

Shiloh National Military Park

In southwestern Tennessee, near Savannah

The largest battle of the 1862 Civil War campaign for possession of the railroads of the western Confederacy and military control of the lower Mississippi River occurred on this site. The park includes 4,000 acres of preserved battlefield, with more than 150 monuments, 217 cannons, 450 iron interpretive tablets, and the historic Peach Orchard, Hornets Nest, and Bloody Pond. Shiloh also protects an extensive Native American mound complex. The park was established in 1894 and transferred to the Park Service in 1933.

WHAT TO SEE & DO

Biking, genealogy and military research, hiking, scenic drives, touring museum, walking. **Facilities:** 2 visitor centers: Shiloh Battlefield Visitor and Corinth Civil War Interpretive centers, museum and film, 450 tablets, 151 monuments, 14 wayside panels, and 5 audio boxes. Bookstore, fire pits and grates, pavilion, picnic tables. **Programs & Events:** Film (daily, hourly), ranger-guided tours and talks (occasionally), living-history demonstrations (occasionally); guided hikes, interpretive talks, cultural demonstrations (May–Aug.); Shiloh anniversary (closest weekend to Apr. 6–7). Memorial Day Service (May). **Tips & Hints:** Observe 25-mph speed limit. Watch for pedestrians, bicyclists, and wildlife. Face traffic when hiking on road. Watch for snakes. Go in early spring when crowds are smaller and historic Peach Orchard is blooming, fall for foliage. Busiest Apr. and May, least crowded Dec. and Jan.

FOOD, LODGING & SUPPLIES

🏕 **Camping:** None in park. In Pickwick Dam: Pickwick Landing State Park (Rte. 57 S, tel. 731/689–3129 or 800/250–8615; 48 sites; $20; flush toilets, showers, hookups). 🏨 **Hotels:** None in park. In Pickwick Dam: Pickwick Landing (Rte. 57 S, tel. 731/689–3135 or 800/250–8615; 100 rooms, 5 suites, 13 cabins; $68–$230). ✗ **Restaurants:** None in park. In Shiloh: Catfish Hotel (1140 Hagy La., tel. 731/689–3327, www.catfishhotel.com; $12–$16; closed Mon.). ♿ **Groceries & Gear:** None in park. In Counce: Ray & Sandy's Store (6309 Hwy. 57, tel. 731/689–3292).

FEES, HOURS & REGULATIONS

Free. No hunting, metal detecting, or removing archaeological resources. Leashed pets only. Bicycles on pavement only. No in-line skating or skateboarding. Shiloh Visitor Center and Corinth Civil War Interpretive Center open daily 8–5. Grounds open until sunset.

HOW TO GET THERE

12 miles south of Savannah via U.S. 64 and Rte. 22, and 22 miles north of Corinth, MS, via U.S. 45 and Rte. 22. Closest airports: Hardin County (15 miles), Memphis (115 miles).

CONTACTS

Shiloh National Military Park (1055 Pittsburgh-Landing Rd., Shiloh, TN 38376, tel. 731/689–5696, fax 731/689–5450, www.nps.gov/shil). Hardin County Department of Tourism (507 Main St., Savannah, TN 38372, tel. 731/925–2364 or 800/552–3866, www.tourhardincounty.org).

Stones River National Battlefield

Midstate, in Murfreesboro

Between December 31, 1862, and January 2, 1863, the Union Army of the Cumberland and the Confederate Army of Tennessee fought here in a battle that cost each side nearly 30% in casualties. The battle was a key Union victory that marked the start of the campaign to take Chattanooga and Atlanta. Stones River National Cemetery, with more than 7,000 interments, of which more than 2,500 are unidentified, adjoins the battlefield. The cemetery was established in 1865, and the park was established in 1927.

WHAT TO SEE & DO

Cell-phone tours, self-guided bicycle and walking tours of the battlefield, self-guided drives. **Facilities:** Visitor center (1563 N. Thompson La., Murfreesboro), Fortress Rosecrans (Old Fort Park, off Rte. 96), interpretive wayside panels and exhibits along tour route and trails. Bookstore, picnic tables. **Programs & Events:** Film (year-round), interpretive walks and talks (June–Sept.), living-history demonstrations (June–Aug.). "Hallowed Ground" cemetery tour by lantern (June–Aug.), Battle Anniversary (weekend closest to Dec. 31–Jan. 2). **Tips & Hints:** Go to visitor center first. Go in spring and fall for best weather. Busiest July and Oct., least crowded Dec. and Jan.

FOOD, LODGING & SUPPLIES

Camping: None in park. In Lebanon: Cedars of Lebanon State Park (328 Cedar Forest Rd., tel. 615/443–2769; 117 sites; $20; flush toilets, showers, hookups). **Hotels:** None in park. In Murfreesboro: Americas Best Value Inn (1954 S. Church St., 800/992–2694, www.americasbestvalueinn.com; 115 rooms; $55–$80). **Restaurants:** None in park. In Murfreesboro: Slick Pig Bar-B-Que (1920 E. Main St., tel. 615/890–3583; $5–$7). **Groceries & Gear:** None in park. In Murfreesboro: Kroger (1776 W. Northfield Blvd., tel. 615/890–9873).

FEES, HOURS & REGULATIONS

Free. Stay on trails. No hunting. Leashed pets only. No metal detectors. No removing artifacts. No in-line skating, rollerblading, or skateboarding. Bikes on park roads only. Battlefield open daily 8–5, visitor center open daily 8–5, grounds open until dark for visitors on foot.

HOW TO GET THERE

Take I–24 to Exit 76, Medical Center Pkwy. to Thompson La. Go north on Thompson La. to entrance. Closest airport: Nashville (30 miles).

CONTACTS

Stones River National Battlefield (3501 Old Nashville Hwy., Murfreesboro, TN 37129, tel. 615/893–9501, fax 615/893–9508, www.nps.gov/stri). Lebanon-Wilson County Chamber of Commerce (149 Public Sq., Lebanon, TN 37087, tel. 615/444–5503 or 800/789–1327, fax 615/443–0596, www.lebanonwilsonchamber.com). Rutherford County Chamber of Commerce (3050 Medical Center Pkwy., Murfreesboro, TN 37129, tel. 615/893-6565 or 800/716–7560, fax 615/890-7600, www.rutherfordchamber.org).

See Also

Appalachian National Scenic Trail, West Virginia. *Chickamauga and Chattanooga National Military Park,* Georgia. *Cumberland Gap National Historical Park,* Kentucky. *Natchez Trace National Scenic Trail and Natchez Trace Parkway,* Mississippi. *Overmountain Victory National Historic Trail, Tennessee Civil War Heritage Area, and Trail of Tears National Historic Trail,* in Other National Parklands.

TEXAS

Alibates Flint Quarries National Monument

Texas Panhandle, north of Amarillo

Few prehistoric Native American archaeological sites in the Canadian River region of the Texas Panhandle are as dramatic as Alibates Flint Quarries. People quarried flint for tools here for 12,000 years, since before the time of the Ice Age Clovis culture, when Native Americans used Alibates flint for spear points to hunt the imperial mammoth. The monument was authorized as Alibates Flint Quarries and Texas Panhandle Pueblo Culture National Monument on August 21, 1965, and redesignated on November 10, 1978.

WHAT TO SEE & DO

Boating, guided tours. **Facilities:** Park headquarters (419 E. Broadway, Fritch). Picnic tables. **Programs & Events:** Guided tours by reservation, flint-chipping demonstrations, school tours. **Tips & Hints:** No entry without a guide. Call several days in advance Memorial Day–Labor Day for tour reservations. Busiest May and June, least crowded Dec. and Jan.

FOOD, LODGING & SUPPLIES

Camping: See Lake Meredith National Recreation Area. **Hotels:** None in park. In Fritch: Lonestar Inn (205 E. Broadway, tel. 806/857–3191; 20 rooms; $45). **Restaurants:** None in park. In Fritch: Tio Pancho's (311 W. Broadway St., tel. 806/857–5740; $6–$11. **Groceries & Gear:** None in park. In Fritch: B&R Thriftway (316 E. Broadway, tel. 806/857–2976).

FEES, HOURS & REGULATIONS

Free. Tour reservations required (tel. 806/857–3151). Boating permit for Lake Meredith $4 per day, $12 for 3 days, $40 per year. Park headquarters open weekdays 8–4:30.

HOW TO GET THERE

12 miles southwest of Fritch. Closest airport: Amarillo (40 miles).

CONTACTS

Alibates Flint Quarries National Monument (Box 1460, Fritch, TX 79036, tel. 806/857–3151, www.nps.gov/alfl). Amarillo Convention & Visitor Council (1000 S. Polk St., Amarillo, TX 79101, tel. 800/692–1338 or 806/374–1497, www.visitamarillotx.com). Texas Travel Information Center (9400 E. I–40, Amarillo, TX 79118, tel. 806/335–1441).

Amistad National Recreation Area

On the Rio Grande, north of Del Rio

Amistad—the name means "friendship"—is a 58,000-acre international recreation area on the United States–Mexico border. The Amistad Reservoir offers outstanding water sports and was created by the 6-mile-long Amistad Dam on the Rio Grande, a joint U.S.–Mexico project. Archaeological research shows that Native Americans lived in this area continuously for 10,000 years before the arrival of Europeans. The rock paintings they left are considered to be as significant as sites in Europe, Australia, and Baja California. The region also contains some of the oldest and best-preserved archaeological deposits in North America. The park is administered under a November 11, 1965, cooperative agreement with the International Boundary and Water Commission as Amistad Recreation Area and was authorized as Amistad National Recreation Area on November 28, 1990.

WHAT TO SEE & DO

Bird-watching, boating, camping, fishing, hiking, hunting, picnicking, scuba diving, swimming, visiting rock art sites, waterskiing. **Facilities:** Visitor Information Center (U.S. 90, west of Del Rio) with bookstore, visitor center (Rough Canyon), nature trails, fishing docks, boat ramps, amphitheater, interpretive panels, bank fishing. Book and map sales, picnic areas with grills, tables and shade shelters. **Programs & Events:** 10- and 30-minute videos on rock art, 35-minute video on Amistad, 38-minute video on Big Bend (on request) at Visitor Information Center, ranger-led guided bird walks (Oct.–Mar.), other interpretive programs (Dec.–Apr.). **Tips & Hints:** Get drinking water at Diablo East. Watch for strong lake winds. Go in spring for wildflower blooms. Busiest Jan.–Mar., least crowded Sept. and Oct.

FOOD, LODGING & SUPPLIES

Camping: 5 campgrounds in the park: Governor's Landing (15 sites; $8; vault toilets), San Pedro (35 sites; $4; vault toilets, no water), Spur 406 (6 sites; $4; vault toilets, no water), 277 North (17 sites; $4; vault toilets, no water), Rough Canyon (4 sites; $4; flush toilets). Backcountry camping allowed by boat. **Hotels:** None in park. In Del Rio: Best Western Inn (810 Veterans Blvd., tel. 830/775-7511, www.bestwestern.com; 62 rooms; $75), Laguna Diablo Resort (875 Sanders Point Rd., tel. 830/774–2422 or 866/227–7082; 10 apartments; $109–$129). **Restaurants:** None in park. In Ciudad Acuña, Mexico: Crosby's (195 Hidalgo, tel. 877/2–2020; $5–$16). In Del Rio: Kettle's Restaurant (2003 Veterans Blvd., tel. 830/775–6060; $7–$14), Memo's Restaurant (804 E. Losoya St., tel. 830/774–1583; closed Sun.; $8–$16). **Groceries & Gear:** None in park. In Del Rio: HEB Grocery (500 Pecan St., tel. 830/774–2596).

FEES, HOURS & REGULATIONS

Free. Lake-use permits required on U.S. side of Lake Amistad ($4 per day or $40 per year. Permits are available at the Amistad Visitor Information Center on State Hwy. 90W, or from automated fee machines at Diablo East, Rough Canyon, and Pecos. Group camping reservations available up to 180 days in advance (tel. 830/775–7491). Texas state and Mexico fishing license required in respective waters. Texas state hunting license and $20 park hunting permit required. Hunting allowed in five designated areas in certain seasons only. Leashed pets only. No off-road travel. Vehicle access to reservoir and boat launch sites restricted. Park open daily. Visitor Information Center open daily 8–5.

HOW TO GET THERE

Closest lake access: 8 miles west of Del Rio on U.S. 90 or 277. Closest airport: Del Rio.

CONTACTS

Amistad National Recreation Area (4121 Veterans Blvd., Del Rio, TX 78840, tel. 830/775–7491, fax 830/775–7299, www.nps.gov/amis). Del Rio Chamber of Commerce (1915 Veterans Blvd., Del Rio, TX 78840, tel. 830/775–3551, www.drchamber.com).

Big Bend National Park

In southwest Texas, near Marathon

The 801,163-acre park is a land of borders. Situated on the U.S.–Mexico border on the Rio Grande, it's a place where countries and cultures meet. It's also a place that merges natural environments from desert to mountains while offering a great diversity of plants and animals. The park was authorized in 1935, established in 1944, and designated an International Biosphere Reserve in 1976.

WHAT TO SEE & DO

Backpacking, biking (rentals, Study Butte–Terlingua), bird and wildlife viewing, hiking, rafting (rentals, Study Butte–Terlingua), scenic drives. **Facilities:** 5 visitor centers: Panther Junction, Persimmon Gap, Chisos Basin, Castolon, and Rio Grande Village; hiking and biking trails; paved and primitive roads. Bookstore, camp stores, gas station, laundry. **Programs & Events:** Nature walks, workshops, and evening programs. **Tips & Hints:** The park is very large and remote. Come prepared with food, water, and a full tank of gas. Plan to spend two days to see most of the park from the main roads or a week if hiking. Always carry drinking water. Busiest Mar. and Apr., least crowded June and July.

FOOD, LODGING & SUPPLIES

Camping: 4 campgrounds in the park: Chisos Basin (63 sites; $14; flush toilets), Cottonwood (31 sites; $14; pit toilets), Rio Grande Village (100 sites; $14; flush toilets, showers), Rio Grande RV Park (25 sites; $33; flush toilets, showers, hookups). Backcountry camping available throughout park (110 sites). **Hotels:** In the park: Chisos Mountain Lodge (tel. 432/477–2291; 72 rooms; $70–$100). In Lajitas: Lajitas Golf Resort & Spa (Rte. 170, tel. 432/424–5000, www.lajitasgolfresort.com; 103 rooms; $150–$760). ✘ **Restaurants:** In the park: Chisos Mountain Lodge (tel. 432/477–2291; $6–$17). In Lajitas: The Candlilla (Lajitas Golf Resort & Spa, Rte. 170, tel. 432/424–5000, www.lajitasgolfresort.com; $6–$20). ☖ **Groceries:** Rio Grande Village, Chisos Basin, and Cottonwood campgrounds.

FEES, HOURS & REGULATIONS

Entrance fee: $10 per person on foot, bicycle, motorcycle, or bus; $20 per vehicle. Permit required ($10) for backcountry camping. Trailers over 20 feet or RVs over 24 feet not recommended on the road to the Chisos Mountains Basin. High-clearance vehicles only on dirt roads. Leashed pets only on roads and in campgrounds; none on trails. Park open daily. Panther Junction Visitor Center open daily 8–6. Chisos Visitor Center open daily, hours vary. Persimmon Gap Visitor Center open daily, hours vary. Rio Grande Village generally open Nov.–Apr., daily 8:30–4:30. Castalon Visitor Center open Nov.–Apr., daily 10–5.

HOW TO GET THERE

Park headquarters is 70 miles south of Marathon via U.S. 385 and 108 miles from Alpine via Rte. 118. Closest airports: Midland-Odessa (230 miles), El Paso (325 miles).

CONTACT

Big Bend National Park (Box 129, Big Bend National Park, TX 79834, tel. 432/477–2251, www.nps.gov/bibe).

Big Thicket National Preserve

In southeast Texas, near Beaumont

The preserve protects an area of rich biological diversity where the eastern hardwood forests, the southern coastal wetlands, the western prairies, and the arid Southwest converge. It consists of nine land units and four water corridors encompassing over 100,000 acres. The preserve was authorized in 1974 and designated a Biosphere Reserve in 1981.

WHAT TO SEE & DO

Bicycling, bird-watching, boating, canoeing, fishing, hiking, horseback riding, hunting, picnicking, powerboating. **Facilities:** Visitor center, films, trails. Bookstore, picnic sites. **Programs & Events:** Guided walks, tours, off-site talks, and environmental education programs. **Tips & Hints:** Allow two hours to see the visitor center and hike the inside loop of the Kirby Nature Trail. Watch for flooded trails after rains and heavy releases from Steinhagen Reservoir that can flood popular campsites along the Neches River. Go in spring and fall for best weather. Wear comfortable sportswear and walking shoes, and carry rain gear. Rain, heat, and humidity are typical. Temperatures typically reach 85°F–95°F in summer, and 55°F in winter. Go Sept.–May for best hiking; Mar. and Oct. for wildflower identification; mid-Apr.–mid-

May for bird-watching; Apr.–Oct. for boating, fishing, and canoeing; Oct. and mid-Jan. for hunting. Busiest Apr. and Oct., least crowded Jan. and Feb.

FOOD, LODGING & SUPPLIES

Camping: In the park: Backcountry camping allowed. In Lumberton: Village Creek State Park (off Alma Dr., tel. 409/755–7322; 41 sites; $7–$15, plus $3 park entry fee; flush toilets, showers, hookups, dump stations). **Hotels:** None in park. In Beaumont: Holiday Inn–Beaumont Plaza (3950 I–10, tel. 409/842–5995, www.holidayinn.com; 253 rooms, 80 suites; $99–$259). **Restaurants:** In Beaumont: Chula Vista (1135 N. 11th St., tel. 409/898–8855; $6–$17). **Groceries & Gear:** In Kountze: Brookshire Brothers (90 W. Monroe St., tel. 409/246–3804).

FEES, HOURS & REGULATIONS

Free. All programs require reservations (free, tel. 409/951–6700). Backcountry camping permit required (free, tel. 409/951–6700). Texas state fishing, hunting, and trapping licenses required. Hunting and trapping by permit (free) only. No vehicles on trails. Leashed pets on trails. All-terrain bicycles and horses on Big Sandy Trail only. Visitor center open daily 9–5.

HOW TO GET THERE

Visitor center is at junction of U.S. 69 and Rte. 420. Major north–south access is via U.S. 69/287; major east–west access is via U.S. 190, U.S. 90, or I–10. Closest airports: Beaumont–Port Arthur (40 miles), Houston (90 miles).

CONTACTS

Big Thicket National Preserve (6044 Farm to Market Rd. 420., Kountze, TX 77625, tel. 409/951–6700, www.nps.gov/bith). Beaumont Convention & Visitors Bureau (801 Main St., Beaumont, tel. 409/880–3749 or 800/392–4401, www.beaumontcvb.com).

Chamizal National Memorial

In west Texas, in El Paso

Chamizal National Memorial commemorates the peaceful settlement of a century-old boundary dispute between Mexico and the United States. The Chamizal Treaty of 1963 was a milestone in the diplomatic relations between the two countries and is celebrated in parks across the river from each other. The memorial focuses on the arts and provides an avenue for cross-cultural understanding and enrichment that transcends barriers of race, ethnicity, and language. The park was authorized in 1966 and established in 1974.

WHAT TO SEE & DO

Attending indoor theater and outdoor amphitheater events, bicycling, jogging, picnicking, touring art gallery. **Facilities:** Visitor center (800 S. San Marcial St., between Paisano St. and Delta Dr.), indoor theater, trail, art galleries, outdoor amphitheater, outdoor comfort station. Bookstore, grills, picnic tables. **Programs & Events:** Plays, musicals, recitals, ballet (weekly). Siglo de Oro Spanish Drama Festival (1st week, Mar.), Music Under the Stars (June–Aug., Sun. evening), July 4 evening concert. **Tips & Hints:** Go May–Sept. for best weather. Busiest June and July, least crowded Jan. and Feb.

FEES, HOURS & REGULATIONS

Free. Leashed pets only. No motorized vehicles on trail. Park grounds open daily 5 AM–10 PM. Visitor center open Tues.–Sat. 8–5.

HOW TO GET THERE

In downtown El Paso at 800 S. San Marcial St., between Paisano and Delta Sts. Closest airport: El Paso.

CONTACTS

Chamizal National Memorial (800 S. San Marcial St., El Paso, TX 79905, tel. 915/532–7273, fax 915/532–7240, www.nps.gov/cham). El Paso Convention & Visitor Bureau (1 Civic Center Plaza, El Paso, TX 79901, tel. 915/534–0653, fax 915/532–2963). El Paso Hispanic Chamber of Commerce (2401 E. Missouri Ave., El Paso, TX 79903, tel. 915/566-4066, www.ephcc.org). Greater El Paso Chamber of Commerce (10 Civic Center Plaza, El Paso, TX 79901, tel. 915/534-0500, www.elpaso.org).

Fort Davis
National Historic Site

In west Texas, in Fort Davis

Soldiers from Fort Davis helped open the area to settlement and protected travelers, freight wagons, and mail carriers along the San Antonio–El Paso Road from 1854 to 1891. Today the fort is regarded as one of the best-preserved in the Southwest. The 474-acre site was authorized in 1961 and established in 1963 as a unit of the National Park Service.

WHAT TO SEE & DO

Hiking, picnicking, self-guided tours of 24 fort buildings and more than 100 ruins. **Facilities:** Visitor center, museum, fort buildings, video, ruins, and trails. Bookstore, picnic area. **Programs & Events:** Interpretive programs (Memorial Day, July 4, Labor Day), Junior Ranger program. Fort Davis Frontier Day (Sat. of Labor Day weekend). **Tips & Hints:** Plan to stay about three to six hours, depending on whether you hike. Busiest spring and summer, least crowded Dec. and Jan.

FOOD & LODGING

Camping: None in park. Near Fort Davis: Davis Mountains State Park (Rte. 118 off Rte. 17, 4 miles northwest of Fort Davis, tel. 432/426–3337; 100 sites; $15–$25, plus $5 park entry fee; flush toilets, showers, hookups). Hotels: None in park. In Fort Davis: Indian Lodge (Park Rd. 3, tel. 432/426–3254; 39 rooms; $95–$135), Hotel Limpia (Main St., tel. 432/426–3237 or 800/662–5517, www. hotellimpia.com; 31 rooms; $95–$189). ✗ **Restaurants:** None in park. In Fort Davis: Cueva de Leon Café (100 W. 2nd St., tel. 432/426–3801; $3–$12).

FEES & HOURS

Entrance fee: $3 adults, free ages 16 and under. Fort and facilities open daily 8–5.

HOW TO GET THERE

On the north edge of the town of Fort Davis on Rtes. 17 and 118. The site can be reached from the north via I–10, from the south via U.S. 90. The town of Marfa is 21 miles to the south. Closest airport: Midland-Odessa (165 miles).

CONTACTS

Fort Davis National Historic Site (Box 1379, Ft. Davis, TX 79734, tel. 432/426–3224, fax 432/426–3122, www.nps.gov/foda). Fort Davis Chamber of Commerce (Box 378, Fort Davis, TX 79734, tel. 800/524–3015, www.fortdavis.com).

Guadalupe Mountains National Park

In west Texas, near Pine Springs

The 86,416-acre park includes part of the Capitan Reef, one of the most extensive and significant noncoral Permian-period fossil reefs in the world. Guadalupe contains more than 1,000 identified plant species, 296 bird species, 58 mammal species, 56 reptile and amphibian species, and numerous archaeological sites. The park is also home to Guadalupe Peak, the highest point in Texas (8,749 feet), and McKittrick Canyon, which contains the park's only perennial stream. Also on view are relic forest and riparian areas, spectacular scenery, historic structures such as the Pinery, a remnant of the Butterfield overland mail route, and various cultural resources from prehistoric to pioneer ranching. The park was authorized in 1966 and established in 1972.

WHAT TO SEE & DO

Backpacking, bird and wildlife viewing, hiking, picnicking. **Facilities:** Visitor center (Pine Springs), visitor contact stations (McKittrick Canyon and Dog Canyon), museum (Frijole Ranch), trails, amphitheater. Bookstore, picnic tables. **Programs & Events:** Slide show; interpretive programs (Memorial Day–Labor Day). **Tips & Hints:** Watch for high winds and rapid weather changes. Prepare for steep, rocky trails. Carry plenty of water. Go in spring for birds, May–Sept. for wildflowers, late Oct.–early Nov. for fall colors. Busiest Mar. and Oct., least crowded Jan. and Feb.

FOOD, LODGING & SUPPLIES

Camping: 2 campgrounds in the park: Dog Canyon (off Rte. 137; 13 sites; $8; flush toilets), Pine Springs (behind visitor center; 39 sites; $8; flush toilets). 10 backcountry campgrounds available. **Hotels:** None in park. In Carlsbad: Days Inn (3910 National Parks Hwy, tel. 575/887–7800, www.daysinn.com; 50 rooms, 8 suites; $89-$109). In Whites City, NM: Rodeway Inn–Whites City Resort (6 Carlsbad Cavern Hwy., tel. 575/785–2291, www.rodewayinn.com; 62 rooms; $95). **Restaurants:** None in park. In Carlsbad, NM: Velvet Garter Restaurant and Saloon (17 Carlsbad Caverns Hwy., tel. 575/785–2291; $20–$25). **Groceries & Gear:** In Carlsbad, NM: Walmart (2401 S. Canal St., tel. 575/885–0727).

FEES, HOURS & REGULATIONS

Entrance fee: $5 per person. Backcountry camping permits required (free). No fishing or hunting. No open fires in park (including charcoal). No pets outside campgrounds, leashed pets only in campgrounds. No mountain bikes or trail bikes except on Williams Ranch Rd. No motorized or wheeled vehicles on trails. No pack and riding stock except on designated trails. No overnight use of stock in backcountry. No swimming, bathing, or wading. Park open daily. Visitor center open Memorial Day–Labor Day, daily 8-6; Labor Day–Memorial Day, daily 8–4:30. Highway gate to McKittrick Canyon open Apr.–Oct., daily 8–6; Nov.–Mar., daily 8–4:30.

HOW TO GET THERE

110 miles east of El Paso via U.S. 62/180, 65 miles north of Van Horn via Rte. 54, and 55 miles southwest of Carlsbad, NM, via U.S. 62/180. Closest airports: Carlsbad, NM, El Paso, TX.

CONTACTS

Guadalupe Mountains National Park (400 Pine Canyon Dr., Salt Flat, TX 79847, tel. 915/828–3251, fax 915/828–3269, www.nps.gov/gumo). Carlsbad Chamber of Commerce (Box 910, Carlsbad, NM 88220, tel. 505/887–6516, www.carlsbadchamber.com).

Lake Meredith National Recreation Area

Texas Panhandle, near Amarillo

Each year more than 1 million visitors come to this lake, which is the prime recreation area in the Texas Panhandle and was created by the Sanford Dam on the Canadian River. The 12-mile-long lake is bordered by the red beds of the Permian formations and the white dolomite of the Alibates formation. The lake has been administered in cooperation with the Bureau of Reclamation since 1965.

WHAT TO SEE & DO

Bird-watching, boating, fishing, horseback riding, hunting, motorcycle and off-road vehicle riding, picnicking, scuba diving, swimming. **Facili-**

ties: Park headquarters, Alibates contact station, lake. Sales areas, picnic areas. **Tips & Hints:** Go Feb.–May or Oct.–Dec. for bird migrations. Busiest June–Aug., least crowded Jan. and Feb.

FOOD, LODGING & SUPPLIES

Camping: 16 campgrounds in the park: (about 1,000 sites; free; some flush toilets, some hookups). Backcountry camping allowed. **Hotels:** None in park. In Fritch: Lonestar Inn (205 E. Broadway, tel. 806/857–3191; 20 rooms; $40). ✗ **Restaurants:** In Fritch: Tio Pancho's Restaurant (311 W. Broadway St., tel. 806/857-5740; $6–$11. **Groceries & Gear:** None in park. In Fritch: B&R Thriftway (316 E. Broadway, tel. 806/857–2976). In Borger: Walmart (1404 W. Wilson St., tel. 806/274–7257).

FEES, HOURS & REGULATIONS

Free. Boating fee: $4 per day. Texas state hunting and fishing licenses required. Leashed pets only. Some horse-riding restrictions. Off-road vehicles require state permit ($16 per year, tel. 806/379–8900). Park headquarters open weekdays 8–4:30.

HOW TO GET THERE

Park headquarters is on Rte. 136 in Fritch. Closest airports: Borger (20 miles), Amarillo (35 miles).

CONTACTS

Lake Meredith National Recreation Area (Box 1460, 419 E. Broadway, Fritch, TX 79036, tel. 806/857–3151, fax 806/857–2319, www.nps.gov/lamr). Amarillo Chamber of Commerce (Box 9480, 1000 S. Polk St., Amarillo, TX 79105, tel. 806/373-7800, www.amarillo-chamber.org). Texas Travel Information Center (9400 E. I–40, Amarillo, TX 79118, tel. 806/335–1441).

Lyndon B. Johnson National Historical Park

In south-central Texas, in Johnson City and Stonewall

Historically significant properties associated with Lyndon B. Johnson, the 36th president of the United States, are preserved here. In the Johnson City District are the President's Boyhood Home and the Johnson Settlement, a complex of restored historic structures that traces the evolution of the Texas Hill Country from the open-range cattle kingdom of President Johnson's grandfather Sam E. Johnson Sr. to the local ranching and farming of more recent times. At the LBJ Ranch in Stonewall, visitors can view the one-room schoolhouse attended by Johnson, his Reconstructed Birthplace, the Johnson Family Cemetery, where the president and Mrs. Johnson are buried, the Texas White House, and the ranching operation that continues today. The park was authorized in 1969 as a national historic site and enlarged and redesignated as a national historical park in 1980.

WHAT TO SEE & DO

Fishing, scenic drives, touring historic sites, viewing exhibits. **Facilities:** 2 visitor centers: (100 Ladybird La., Johnson City; LBJ State Historical Park, U.S. 290, near Stonewall), Hangar visitor center at the LBJ Ranch, ranch, home, settlement. Bookstores (both sites), picnic tables with grills, pool, softball field, tennis courts. **Programs & Events:** Films, ranger-guided tours of Boyhood Home (daily), self-guided driving tours of LBJ State Park and LBJ Ranch, guided tours of the Texas White House. LBJ 100 Bicycle Tour (Mar.), wreath laying at Johnson Family Cemetery (Aug. 27), Tree Lighting (Dec.). **Tips & Hints:** Dress casually. Summers can be very hot. Don't approach longhorn cattle or wildlife. Go in Mar., Apr., and Oct. for best weather. Go Mar. and Apr. for migratory birds and wildflowers. Busiest Mar. and Apr., least crowded Aug. and Dec.–Feb.

FOOD, LODGING & SUPPLIES

⚠ **Camping:** None in park. In Blanco: Blanco State Park (101 Park Rd. 23, tel. 512/389–8900; 31 sites, 7 shelters; $14–$21, plus $3 park entry fee; flush toilets, showers, hookups). In Johnson City: Padernales Falls State Park (Rte. 2766 and Rte. 3232, tel. 830/868-7304 or 512/389–8900; 69 sites; $20, plus $3 park entry fee; flush toilets, showers, hookups). 🏨 **Hotels:** None in park. In Fredericksburg: Sunday House Inn (501 E. Main St., tel. 830/997–4484, www.sundayhouseinn.com; 121 rooms; $70–$150). ✗ **Restaurants:** None in park. In Fredericksburg: Altdorf German Biergarten & Dining Room (301 W. Main St., tel. 830/997–7865, www.altdorfbiergarten-fbg.com; $14–$20). ⛏ **Groceries & Gear:** None in park. In Blanco: Lowes (111 Blanco Ave., U.S. 281, tel. 830/833–4521).

FEES, HOURS & REGULATIONS

Free. Texas White House tour: daily 10-4:30; $3 per person. No pets in buildings; leashed pets elsewhere. Johnson Settlement open daily 9–sunset. LBJ State Park & Historic Site visitor center open daily 8–5. Johnson City visitor center open daily 8:45–5. LBJ State Park and Historic Site visitor center open daily 8–5.

HOW TO GET THERE

The Johnson City District is at 100 Ladybird La., in Johnson City, 48 miles west of Austin on U.S. 290 and 65 miles north of San Antonio on U.S. 281. The LBJ Ranch and LBJ State Historical Park are on U.S. 290, 14 miles west of Johnson City and 16 miles east of Fredericksburg. Closest airports: Austin, San Antonio.

CONTACTS

Lyndon B. Johnson National Historical Park (Box 329, Johnson City, TX 78636, tel. 830/868–7128 Ext. 244, fax 830/868–0810, www.nps.gov/lyjo). Lyndon B. Johnson State Historical Park (Box 238, Stonewall, TX 78671, tel. 830/644–2252, fax 830/644–2430, www.tpwd.state.tx.us). Fredericksburg Convention & Visitor Bureau (302 E. Austin St., Fredericksburg, TX 78624, tel. 888/997-3600 or 830/997–6523, fax 830/997-8588, www.visitfredericksburgtx.com). Johnson City Chamber of Commerce (100 E. Main St., Johnson City, TX 78636, tel. 830/

868–7684, fax 830/868–5700, www.johnsoncity-texas.com). Stonewall Chamber of Commerce (250 Peach St., or P.O. Box 1, Stonewall, TX 78671, tel. 830/644–2735, www.stonewalltexas.com).

Padre Island National Seashore

In southeast Texas, near Corpus Christi

The seashore provides a rare opportunity for primitive beach recreation on 80 miles of the longest barrier island in the world. Padre Island is well known for its wide sandy beaches, excellent fishing, and abundant bird and marine life. The seashore was authorized in 1962 and established in 1968.

WHAT TO SEE & DO

Beachcombing, bird-watching, boating, fishing, picnicking, swimming, windsurfing (rentals, Bird Island Basin). **Facilities:** Maaquite Visitor Center (Park Rd. 22), boat launch ramp, nature trail. Book and map sale areas, gift shop. **Programs & Events:** Orientation video, ranger-led campfire programs, beach walks, deck talks, Junior Ranger program. Sea-turtle hatchling releases (June–Aug.), Adopt-A-Beach Cleanup (Apr. and Sept.), Center for Marine Conservation Cleanup (Apr. and Sept.). **Tips & Hints:** Go in spring for wildflowers, spring and fall for neotropical migratory birds. Go to Bird Island Basin in spring for windsurfing. Go May–Aug. to view nesting sea turtles. Go in winter to see winter waterfowl and fish for black drum and bull redfish. Watch for rattlesnakes. Busiest July and Aug., least crowded Sept. and Oct.

FOOD, LODGING & SUPPLIES

Camping: 5 campgrounds in the park: Bird Island Basin (primitive camping area; $5; pit toilets), Malaquite Beach (42 sites; $8; flush toilets, cold showers), North Beach (primitive camping area; free; no water), South Beach (primitive camping area; free; no water), Yarborough Pass (primitive camping area; free; no water). **Hotels:** None in park. In Corpus Christi: Days Inn (4302 Surfside Blvd., tel. 361/882–3297, www.daysinn.com; 55 rooms; $69–$119), Fortuna Bay B&B (15405 Fortuna Bay Dr., tel. 361/949–7554, www.fortunabaybnb.com; 10 suites; $140). **Restaurants:** In Corpus Christi: Crawdaddy's (414 Starr St., tel. 361/883–5432; $10–$12). **Groceries & Gear:** In Corpus Christi: HEB Grocery (3500 Leopard St., tel. 361/882–9864).

FEES, PERMITS & REGULATIONS

Entrance fee: $10 per vehicle (good for seven days). Bird Island day-use fee: $5 per day or $10 per year. Texas state fishing license and saltwater stamp required. Camping in designated areas only. No hunting, no vehicles in dunes. Leashed pets only. Park open daily. Visitor center open daily 9–5.

HOW TO GET THERE

On North Padre Island, 10 miles southeast of Corpus Christi via South Padre Island Dr., which turns into Park Rd. 22. Closest airport: Corpus Christi.

CONTACTS

National Park Service, Padre Island National Seashore (Box 181300, Corpus Christi, TX 78480, tel. 361/949–8068, fax 361/949–9951, www.nps.gov/pais). Corpus Christi Chamber of Commerce (1501 N. Chaparral St., Corpus Christi, TX 78401, tel. 361/881–1800 or 800/766–2322, www.corpuschristichamber.org).

Palo Alto Battlefield National Historical Park

In south Texas, near Brownsville

On May 8, 1846, the Battle of Palo Alto took place—the first major battle of the Mexican-American War (1846–48). General Zachary Taylor's 2,300-man U.S. Army of Occupation used its superior cannon and innovative artillery methods to outduel General Mariano Arista's 3,600-man force. At war's end, Mexico ceded claims to what are now Texas, New Mexico, Arizona, Utah, Nevada, and California to the United States. The most recent addition to the park is the Resaca de la Palma Battlefield, 5 miles south of Palo Alto. The site was authorized in 1978 and dedicated in 1993.

WHAT TO SEE & DO

Viewing exhibits. **Facilities:** Visitor center (7200 Paredes Line Rd., Brownsville), walking trail with interpretive signage leading to overlook. Book sales area. **Programs & Events:** Video; interpretive talks (periodically), living-history programs (monthly, Sept.–May), weekly tours during winter season. Anniversary celebration (Sat. closest to May 8), Memorial Illumination, Resaca de la Palma Battlefield (Nov.), Archeology Fair (Oct.). **Tips & Hints:** South Texas summer weather is generally hot and humid. Wear lightweight cotton clothing. Winter weather is generally mild, but expect cool mornings. Busiest Dec.–Apr.

FOOD, LODGING & SUPPLIES

Camping: None in park. In Rio Hondo: Adolph Thomae Park (37844 Marshall Hutts Rd., tel. 956/748–2044; 35 sites; $15–$30; flush toilets, showers, hookups). On South Padre Island: Isla Blanca Park (33174 State Park Rd. 100, tel. 956/761–5494; 594 sites; $15–$40; flush toilets, showers, hookups). **Hotels:** None in park. In Brownsville: Americas Best Value Inn (825 N. Expressway Dr., tel. 956/504–3331, www.americasbestvalueinn.com; 52 rooms, 1 suite; $50–$250). In Rancho Viejo: Rancho Viejo Resort (1 Rancho Viejo Dr., tel. 956/350–4000 or 800/531-7400, www.rvrcc.com; 60 rooms and villas; $98–$359). **Restaurants:** None in park. In Brownsville: Mi Pueblito, (Pablo Kisel St., tel. 956/793–7716; $6–$16). **Groceries & Gear:** None in park. In Brownsville: HEB Market (2155 Paredes Line Rd., tel. 956/574–9707).

FEES & HOURS

Free. Visitor center open daily 8–5. Park trail and battlefield overlook close at 4:30.

HOW TO GET THERE

In Brownsville on Rte. 1847 (Paredes Line Rd.), just north of the intersection with Rte. 511. Closest airport: Brownsville.

CONTACTS

Palo Alto Battlefield National Historical Park (1623 Central Blvd., Suite 213, Brownsville, TX 78520, tel. 956/541–2785, fax 956/541–6356, www.nps.gov/paal). Brownsville Convention & Visitors Bureau (Box 4697, Brownsville, TX 78523, tel. 956/546–3721, fax 956/546–3972, www.brownsville.org).

Rio Grande Wild & Scenic River

In southwest Texas, along the Rio Grande

This remote, undeveloped 196-mile strip on the American shore of the Rio Grande in the Chihuahuan Desert protects the river. It begins in Big Bend National Park and continues downstream to the Terrell–Val Verde county line. There are no facilities outside of Big Bend National Park (see separate entry). The wild and scenic river was authorized on November 10, 1978.

WHAT TO SEE & DO

See Big Bend National Park.

CONTACT

Rio Grande Wild & Scenic River (c/o Big Bend National Park, Box 129, Big Bend National Park, TX 79834, tel. 915/477–2251, www.nps.gov/rigr).

San Antonio Missions National Historical Park

In south-central Texas, in San Antonio

Preserved here are four 18th-century Spanish missions—Concepcion, San Jose, San Juan, and Espada—that were built along the San Antonio River to introduce Coahuiltecan Native Americans to Spanish society and Catholicism. These missions, along with their presidio and settlement, were the foundation of the city of San Antonio. The missions still serve as active parishes and represent a virtually unbroken link with the past. The park was authorized in 1978 and established in 1983.

WHAT TO SEE & DO

Picnicking, touring missions, viewing museum exhibits. **Facilities:** Visitor center (San Jose), 3 park contact stations (Concepcion, San Juan, Espada), trail. Sales outlets, picnic tables. **Programs & Events:** Ranger-guided walks and talks (daily), ranger-guided walk of Rancho de Las Cabras (1st Sat. each month). **Tips & Hints:** Prepare for summer heat. Watch for fire ants. Busiest July and Oct., least crowded Jan. and Feb.

FEES, HOURS & REGULATIONS

Free. No hunting. Leashed pets only. No bicycles in mission compounds. No motorized equipment on trails. Park and visitor center open daily 9–5.

HOW TO GET THERE

From I–37, exit on West Southcross, then turn left on Roosevelt to Mission San Jose. From I–10, exit south on Probandt and follow Park Service signs to Concepcion. Closest airport: San Antonio (15 miles).

CONTACTS

San Antonio Missions National Historical Park (6701 San Jose Dr., San Antonio, TX 78214, tel 210/932–1001, fax 210/534–1106, www.nps.gov/saan). South San Antonio Chamber of Commerce (7902 Challenger Dr., San Antonio, TX 78235, tel. 210/533–1600, fax 210/533–1611, www.southsachamber.org). Greater San Antonio Visitor Information Center (317 Alamo Plaza, San Antonio, TX 78205, tel. 210/270–8748 or 800/447–3372, fax 210/207–6842, visitsanantonio.com).

UTAH

Arches National Park

In southeastern Utah, near Moab

The 76,519-acre park contains one of the largest concentrations of natural sandstone arches in the world. The arches and numerous other extraordinary geologic features, including spires, pinnacles, pedestals, and balanced rocks, are highlighted in striking foreground and background views created by contrasting colors, land forms, and textures. The site was proclaimed a national monument in 1929 and redesignated in 1971.

WHAT TO SEE & DO

Hiking, picnicking, scenic drives. **Facilities:** Visitor center, scenic road, overlooks, trails. Book and map sale area, picnic areas. **Programs & Events:** Ranger-led walks, guided hikes, evening campfire programs (mid-Mar.–Oct.). Easter Sunrise Service. **Tips & Hints:** Plan on a half-day visit for basic road tour and stops at overlooks; add more time for hiking. Conditions are hot and dry in summer. Carry drinking water. Reserve hikes weeks to months in advance. Busiest Mar., least crowded Dec. and Jan.

FOOD, LODGING & SUPPLIES

Camping: In the park: Devil's Garden (52 sites; $20; flush toilets, pit toilets). **Hotels:** None in park. In Moab: Archway Inn (1551 N. U.S. 191, tel. 435/259–2599 or 800/341–9359, aarchwayinn.com; 80 rooms, 15 suites, 2 apartments; $159), Holiday Inn Express (1515 U.S. 191, tel. 435/259–1150 or 877/863–4784, www.hiexpress.com; 79 rooms; $179). **Restaurants:** None in park. In Moab: Jail House Café (101 N. Main St., tel. 435/259–3900; $5–$10). **Groceries & Gear:** None in park. In Moab: City Market (425 S. Main St., tel. 435/259–5181).

FEES, HOURS & REGULATIONS

Entrance fee: $10 per vehicle. Fiery Furnace backcountry permit $4 adults, $2 ages 5–12, children under 5 not permitted. Fiery Furnace guided walks $10 adults, $5 ages 5–12, under 5 not permitted. Walks are limited to 25 people and often fill weeks in advance. Guide companies offer four-wheel-drive, float, and photography tours. Park open daily. Visitor center open Apr.–Oct., daily 7:30–6:30; Nov.–Mar., daily 8–4:30 (hours may vary, call ahead).

HOW TO GET THERE

5 miles north of Moab on U.S. 191. Closest airports: Canyonlands (15 miles), Grand Junction, CO (120 miles), Salt Lake City (250 miles).

CONTACTS

Arches National Park (Box 907, Moab, UT 84532, tel. 435/719–2299, fax 435/719–2305, www.nps.gov/arch). Grand County Travel Council

(Box 550, Moab, UT 84532 or 40 N. 100 E, Moab, UT 84532, tel. 800/
635–6622, www.discovermoab.com).

Bryce Canyon National Park

In south-central Utah, near Tropic

The park is named for one of a series of horseshoe-shaped amphitheaters carved from the eastern edge of the Paunsaugunt Plateau. Erosion has shaped colorful Claron limestone, sandstones, and mudstones
into thousands of spires, fins, pinnacles, and mazes. These unique formations, called "hoodoos," are whimsically arranged and tinted with
many colors. Ponderosa pines, high-elevation meadows, and spruce-fir
forests border the rim of the plateau, and panoramic views of three
states spread beyond the park's boundaries. The park was proclaimed a
national monument on June 8, 1923; provisionally authorized as Utah
National Park on June 7, 1924; renamed on February 25, 1928; and
established in September 1928.

WHAT TO SEE & DO

Cross-country skiing (rentals, Ruby's Inn), guided trail rides (tel. 435/
679–8665), hiking, picnicking, scenic drives, snowshoeing, stargazing.
Facilities: Visitor center with auditorium, orientation film, overlooks,
trails. Publication sales, gift shop, picnic areas. **Programs & Events:**
Ranger-led walks and talks, canyon hikes, rim walks, geology talks, evening slide programs, Junior Ranger program, night sky programs, star
parties, moonlight hikes (all late May–Sept.). **Tips & Hints:** Use caution
if unaccustomed to altitude. Wear hiking boots to hike trails. Busiest
Aug. and Sept., least crowded Jan. and Feb.

FOOD, LODGING & SUPPLIES

Camping: 2 campgrounds in the park: North (102 sites; $15; flush
toilets), Sunset (tel. 877/444–6777; 102 sites; $15; flush toilets, show-
ers; group site; $30; flush toilets, showers; reservations required).
Backcountry camping allowed. In Bryce: Bryce Canyon Pines (2476 W.
Hwy. 12, 9 miles east of U.S. 89, tel. 800/892–7923; 50 sites; $20–$30;
flush toilets, showers, hookups; closed Nov.–Mar.). **Hotels:** In the
park: Bryce Canyon Lodge (tel. 435/834–5361, 888/297–2757 reservations; 70 rooms, 40 cabins, 3 suites; $156, $166 cabins and suites;
closed Nov.–Mar.). In Ruby's Inn: Best Western (Rte. 63, tel. 435/834–
5341 or 866/866–6616, www.bestwestern.com; 368 rooms; $59–$160).
Restaurants: In the park: Bryce Canyon Lodge (tel. 435/834–5361;
$8–$12; closed Nov.–Mar.), Bryce Canyon Pines Restaurant (Rte. 12,
tel. 435/834–5441; $5–$16). **Groceries & Gear:** In the park: Sunrise
Point General Store (tel. 435/834–5361 Ext. 757). In Panguitch: Joe's
Main St. Market (10 S. Main St., tel. 435/676–2361).

FEES, HOURS & REGULATIONS

Entrance fee: $25 per vehicle. Backcountry permits required ($15; visitor center). Shuttle bus service (free) available along roads in park. No
bikes on trails. No trailers beyond Sunset Campground. No hunting.

No pets on trails, leashed pets only otherwise. Park open daily. Visitor center open May–Sept., daily 8–8; Oct.–Apr., daily 8–4:30.

HOW TO GET THERE

From north or south on U.S. 89, turn east on Rte. 12 (7 miles south of Panguitch). Turn south on Rte. 63 and travel 3 miles to reach the park entrance. From the east, travel west on Rte. 12. Turn south on Rte. 63 to reach the park entrance. Closest airport: Bryce Canyon Airport, St. George (46 miles).

CONTACTS

Bryce Canyon National Park (Box 640201, Bryce Canyon, UT 84764, tel. 435/834–5322, fax 435/834–4102, www.nps.gov/brca). Garfield County Travel Council (Box 200, Panguitch, UT 84759, tel. 800/444–6689, www.brycecanyoncountry.com).

Canyonlands National Park

In southeast Utah, near Moab

At the intersection of the Green River and the Colorado River, this park preserves 527 square miles of colorful canyons, mesas, buttes, fins, arches, and spires. Ancestral Puebloan rock art and ruins dot the red-rock landscape. The mighty river canyons divide the park into three districts, each offering spectacular sightseeing and exploration opportunities. The park was established on September 12, 1964.

WHAT TO SEE & DO

Four-wheel-drive touring, hiking, mountain biking, river running, rock climbing. **Facilities:** 2 visitor centers: Island in the Sky (Rte. 313 off U.S. 191) and Needles (Rte. 211 off U.S. 191); information center (Maze, Hans Flat Ranger Station, dirt road off Rte. 24), trails, backcountry roads. Bookstores. **Programs & Events:** Junior Ranger program (ages 6–12), evening programs, overlook talks and other programs (Mar.–Oct.). **Tips & Hints:** Canyonlands is primarily a backcountry destination. Summer temperatures average 92°F, and winter temperatures average 39°F. Busiest Apr.–Oct., least crowded Dec. and Jan.

FOOD, LODGING & SUPPLIES

🏕 **Camping:** 2 campgrounds in the park: Squaw Flat (Needles district; 26 sites; $15; vault toilets), Willow Flat (Island in the Sky district; 12 sites; $10; vault toilets). Backcountry camping allowed. 🏨 **Hotels:** None in park. See Arches National Park. ✕ **Restaurants:** None in park. See Arches National Park. ⛁ **Groceries & Gear:** None in park. See Arches National Park.

FEES, HOURS & REGULATIONS

Entrance fee: $5 per person on bicycle or motorcycle, $10 per vehicle. Backcountry permit required ($5–$30, tel. 435/259–4351). No pets on trails or in backcountry, even in vehicles. No ATVs. No mountain bikes on hiking trails or off designated roads. Park open daily. Island in the Sky Visitor Center open Mar.–Oct., daily 8–6; Nov.–Feb., daily 9–5.

Needles Visitor Center open Mar.–May, daily 8–6; June–Oct., daily 8–5; Nov.–Feb., daily 9–4:30.

HOW TO GET THERE

Canyonlands is divided into three districts that are two to six hours apart by car. To reach Needles District from Moab, take U.S. 191 south and Rte. 211 west. To reach Island in the Sky District from Moab, take U.S. 191 north and Rte. 313 west. To reach the Maze District from Moab, take U.S. 191 north to I–70 west. Take Exit 147 off I–70 to Rte. 24 south, and then a graded dirt road east to the Hans Flat Ranger Station. Closest airports: Canyonlands (18 miles), Grand Junction, CO (115 miles), Salt Lake City (240 miles).

CONTACTS

Canyonlands National Park (2282 S.W. Resource Blvd., Moab, UT 84532, tel. 435/719–2313, www.nps.gov/cany). San Juan Visitor's Center (117 S. Main St., or Box 490, Monticello, UT 84535, tel. 800/574–4386).

Capitol Reef National Park

In south-central Utah, near Torrey

The park's Waterpocket Fold, a giant, sinuous wrinkle in the Earth's crust created approximately 65 million years ago, stretches for 100 miles with colorful cliffs, massive domes, soaring spires, and stark monoliths. The park also protects a section of the Fremont River, petroglyphs from the prehistoric Fremont culture, and fruit orchards and buildings from Mormon pioneer settlement. The site was proclaimed a national monument in 1937 and redesignated as a national park in 1971.

WHAT TO SEE & DO

Bird-watching, bicycling, hiking, picking fruit (in season), picnicking. **Facilities:** Visitor center, pioneer buildings, trails, wayside panels, amphitheater, orchards. Bookstore, sales outlet. **Programs & Events:** Geology and archaeology talks, ranger presentations, evening programs (May–Sept., daily as staffing allows). **Tips & Hints:** Go in spring or fall for best hiking weather and wildflowers, summer and fall for fruit harvest. Watch for thunderstorms and flash floods July–Sept. Busiest spring and fall, least crowded Dec. and Jan.

FOOD, LODGING & SUPPLIES

Camping: In the park: Fruita (71 sites; $10; flush toilets, picnic tables); 2 primitive campgrounds: Cathedral Valley (6 sites; free; pit toilets, no water), Cedar Mesa (5 sites; free; pit toilets, no water). Backcountry camping allowed. **Hotels:** None in park. In Torrey: Best Western Capitol Reef Resort (2600 E. Rte. 24, tel. 435/425–3761, www.bestwestern.com; 100 rooms; $77–$200), Boulder View Inn (385 W. Main St., tel. 435/425–3800; 11 rooms; $65). **Restaurants:** None in park. In Torrey: Café Diablo (599 W. Main St., tel. 435/425–3070; $7–$21; closed mid-Oct.–mid-Apr.), Capitol Reef Café (360 W. Main

St., tel. 435/425–3271; $7–$15). ⚲ **Groceries & Gear:** None in park. In Hanksville: Bull Mountain Market (30 E. 100 N., tel. 435/542–3249).

FEES, HOURS & REGULATIONS

Entrance fee: $5 for scenic drive. Backcountry permits (free) required for all backcountry camping. Utah state fishing license required. No hunting. No pets on trails, in buildings, or off roads. Carry water on hikes. No rock, plant, animal, or artifact collecting. No mountain bikes off roads. Park open daily. Visitor center open Labor Day-Memorial Day, daily 8–4:30; Memorial Day–Labor Day, daily 8-6.

HOW TO GET THERE

37 miles west of Hanksville and 10 miles east of Torrey on Rte. 24. Closest airports: Hanksville, Bicknell (18 miles), Grand Junction, CO (180 miles), Salt Lake City (195 miles).

CONTACTS

Capitol Reef National Park (HC 70, Box 15, 52 Scenic Dr., Torrey, UT 84775, tel. 435/425–3791, fax 435/425–3026, www.nps.gov/care). Wayne County Travel Council (Box 7, Teasdale, UT 84773, tel. 435/425–3365 or 800/858–7951, www.capitolreef.travel).

Cedar Breaks National Monument

In southwestern Utah, near Cedar City

The monument preserves a large, multicolored geologic amphitheater that is 2,500 feet deep and 3 miles across. The rim of the amphitheater sits at 10,500 feet above sea level and is lined with forests of spruce and fir and subalpine meadows full of wildflowers that are brilliant with color in the summer. The monument was proclaimed on August 22, 1933.

WHAT TO SEE & DO

Cross-country skiing, hiking, picnicking, scenic drives, snowmobiling, snowshoeing. **Facilities:** Cedar Breaks Visitor Center, natural amphitheater, 6-mile scenic drive, scenic overlooks, trails. Book sale area, fire grates, picnic tables. **Programs & Events:** Interpretive programs (Memorial Day–Columbus Day, daily 10–5), evening campfire programs (July 4–Labor Day, weekends), guided hikes. **Tips & Hints:** Come prepared for cool weather and high elevation (summertime high: 60°F, rim elevation: 10,000 feet). Visit late June–late Sept. Busiest July and Aug., least crowded Jan. and Feb.

FOOD, LODGING & SUPPLIES

⚲ **Camping:** In the park: Point Supreme (28 sites; $14; flush toilets, showers; closed Oct.–mid-June). In Dixie National Forest: Duck Creek (Rte. 14, tel. 877/444–6777, www.recreation.gov; 58 sites; $15–$30; flush toilets). 🏨 **Hotels:** None in park. In Cedar City: Abbey Inn (940 W. 200 N, tel. 435/586–9966 or 800/325–5411, www.abbeyinncedar.

com; 81 rooms; $75–$110). ✗ **Restaurants:** None in park. In Cedar City: Market Grill (2290 W. 200 N, tel. 435/586–9325; $7–$13). ⬧ **Groceries & Gear:** None in park. In Cedar City: Smith's (633 S. Main St., tel. 435/586–1203).

FEES, HOURS & REGULATIONS

Entrance fee: $4 per person. Utah state fishing license required. No hunting. Leashed pets only on roadsides, paved walkways, campground. No mountain bikes on trails. No motorized vehicles off paved roads. Visitor center open Memorial Day–Columbus Day, daily 9–6. Scenic drive open mid-May–mid-Nov.

HOW TO GET THERE

Cedar Breaks National Monument is along Rte. 148, between Rtes. 143 and 14. The visitor center is 23 miles from Cedar City via Rtes. 148 and 14, 8 miles from Brian Head via Rtes. 148 and 143, and 25 miles from Parowan via Rtes. 148 and 143. Closest airports: Cedar City, St. George.

CONTACTS

Cedar Breaks National Monument (2390 W. Rte. 56, Suite 11, Cedar City, UT 84720, tel. 435/586–9451, fax 435/586–3813, www.nps.gov/cebr). Cedar City Chamber of Commerce (581 N. Main St., Cedar City, UT 84720, tel. 435/586–4484, www.cedarcitychamber.org).

Golden Spike National Historic Site

In northwestern Utah, at Promontory Summit

The site commemorates the completion of the first transcontinental railroad on May 10, 1869, at Promontory Summit. On that day, a golden spike was symbolically tapped into a polished laurel-wood tie, and then a final iron spike was driven to complete the railroad, thus linking East and West for the first time. The site was established in 1965.

WHAT TO SEE & DO

Hiking, scenic drives, visiting historic site. **Facilities:** Visitor center, two 1869 steam locomotive replicas, museum. Bookstore. **Programs & Events:** Ranger talks (Memorial Day–Labor Day, daily), engine house tours (Apr.–Columbus Day), steam engine demonstrations (May–Columbus Day, daily), golden spike reenactment (mid-May–Labor Day, Sat. and holidays). Golden Spike Anniversary Celebration (May 10), Railroader's Festival (2nd Sat. in Aug.), Winter Film Festival and Steam Demonstration (last weekend, Dec.). **Tips & Hints:** Plan to spend two to three hours. Go anytime to see locomotives, but go May–early Oct. to see them operate. Busiest May–Aug., least crowded Dec. and Jan.

FOOD, LODGING & SUPPLIES

⬧ **Camping:** None in park. Near Brigham City: Willard Bay State Park: (Exit 357 off I–15, tel. 435/734-9494; 78 sites; $16–$25; flush toilets, vault toilets, showers, hookups). **Hotels:** None in park. In Brigham City: Crystal Inn (480 Westland Dr., tel. 435/723–0440 or 800/408–0440, www.crystalinnbrigham.com; 52 rooms; $85–$100), Galaxie Motel (740 S. Main St., tel. 435/723–3439 or 800/577–4315; 29 rooms; $39). ✕ **Restaurants:** None in park. In Brigham City: Maddox Ranch House (1900 S. U.S. 89, tel. 435/723–8545; $9–$23; closed Sun. and Mon.). ⛃ **Groceries & Gear:** None in park. In Brigham City: Smith's (156 S. Main St., tel. 435/734–2500). In Willard: Country Market (600 W. 750 N, tel. 435/723–5022).

FEES, HOURS & REGULATIONS

Entrance fee: May–Columbus Day, $4 per person, $7 per vehicle; rest of the year, $3 per person, $5 per vehicle. Steam locomotives run May–Labor Day, daily 10–4:30. No hunting. Leashed pets only. No mechanized recreational vehicles on trails. Park and visitor center open daily 9–5.

HOW TO GET THERE

In Promontory, 32 miles west of Brigham City via Rtes. 13 and 83. Closest airport: Salt Lake City (95 miles).

CONTACTS

Golden Spike National Historic Site (Box 897, Brigham City, UT 84302, tel. 435/471–2209, fax 435/471–2341, www.nps.gov/gosp). Bear River Chamber of Commerce (28 W. 100 N, Tremonton, UT 84337, tel. 435/257–7585, www.brvcc.com). Box Elder County Economic Development, Tourism Council (1 S. Main St., Brigham City, UT 84302, tel. 435/734–3300 or 877/390–2326, www.boxelder.org). Brigham City Chamber of Commerce (6 N. Main St., Brigham City, UT 84302, tel. 435/723–3931, www.bcareachamber.com).

Natural Bridges National Monument

In southeastern Utah, near Blanding

Owachomo Bridge, Sipapu Bridge, and Kachina Bridge depict the three phases in a natural bridge's history, as running water forms and then ultimately destroys these perforated rock walls. Utah's first National Park Service site also offers outstanding examples of geological and erosion processes and preserves numerous Ancestral Puebloan archaeological sites. The site was proclaimed on April 16, 1908.

WHAT TO SEE & DO

Bicycling, hiking, scenic drives. **Facilities:** Visitor center (Rte. 275 off Rte. 95), 9-mile drive, trails, overlooks. Book and map sales area. **Programs & Events:** Campfire programs (May–mid-Oct.), astronomy programs (May–Sept.). **Tips & Hints:** Carry plenty of water on hikes. Watch for flash floods and severe lightning July–Sept. Avoid midget prairie rattlesnakes. Respect cultural sites. Visit late Apr.–Oct. Busiest May–Sept., least crowded Dec.–Feb.

FOOD, LODGING & SUPPLIES

🏕 **Camping:** In the park: Natural Bridges (13 sites; $10; pit toilets). 🏨 **Hotels:** None in park. In Blanding: Gateway Inn (88 E. Center St., tel. 435/678–2278, www.gatewayinnblanding.com; 57 rooms; $60–$90), Super 8 (755 S. Main St., tel. 435/678–3880 or 800/800–8000; 55 rooms, 2 suites; $49–$89, $139 suites). ✗ **Restaurants:** None in park. In Fry Canyon: Fry Canyon Lodge Café (Rte. 95, tel. 435/259–5224; $11–$23). ⛓ **Groceries & Gear:** None in park. In Blanding: Clark's Market (820 S. Main St., tel. 435/678–2721).

FEES, HOURS & REGULATIONS

Entrance fee: $3 per person on bicycle or motorcycle, $6 per vehicle. No climbing on bridges. No pets on trails or in canyons. Leashed pets elsewhere. Bikes on paved roads only. No hunting or gathering of flora or fauna. Bridge View Dr. open 24 hours. Visitor center open May–Aug., daily 8–6; Sept.–Apr., daily 8–4:30.

HOW TO GET THERE

The visitor center is 38½ miles west of Blanding via Rtes. 95 and 275, 44 miles north of Mexican Hat via Rte. 261, and 50 miles east of Hite Marina on Lake Powell via Rte. 95. Closest airports: Cortez, CO (120 miles), Salt Lake City (353 miles), Phoenix, AZ (389 miles).

CONTACTS

Natural Bridges National Monument (HC 60 Box 1, Lake Powell, UT 84533, tel. 435/692–1234, fax 435/692–1111, www.nps.gov/nabr). Monticello Chamber of Commerce (Box 490, Monticello, UT 84535, tel. 435/587–2992, www.monticelloutah.org).

Rainbow Bridge National Monument

In south-central Utah, near Blanding

Rainbow Bridge is one of the world's largest natural bridges. The 275-foot-wide, 291-foot-tall bridge has inspired people throughout time—from the neighboring Native American tribes, who consider Rainbow Bridge sacred, to the 200,000 people from around the world who visit it each year. The monument was proclaimed on May 30, 1910.

WHAT TO SEE & DO

Boating (rentals), boat touring, day and backcountry hiking. **Facilities:** Ranger station with bulletin board (Dangling Rope Marina, 12 miles from bridge), outdoor exhibits, 1¼-mile trail. **Programs & Events:** Boat tours (May–Sept., daily; Oct.–Apr., intermittently), ranger-led natural- and cultural-history talks (mostly Memorial Day–Sept.). **Tips & Hints:** Plan on at least a five-hour round-trip to travel by boat to bridge (six hours from Lake Powell marinas). Wear lightweight, light-color clothing and a hat in summer, layers of clothing rest of year. Be prepared for summer temperatures up to 110°F with little, if any, shade; winter temperatures to 0°F; and windy springs. Respect the religious beliefs of Native American tribes or nations who claim Rainbow Bridge as a religious site. Busiest June–Sept., least crowded Jan. and Feb.

FOOD, LODGING & SUPPLIES

None in park. See Glen Canyon National Recreation Area, Arizona.

FEES, HOURS & REGULATIONS

Free. Fee is charged at Glen Canyon National Recreation Area. ARA-MARK (tel. 800/528–6154) provides boat tours to Rainbow Bridge May–Sept., daily, and intermittently rest of year; Antelope Point Marina (tel. 928/645–5900) also offers half-day boat tours to Rainbow Bridge. Half-day and full-day tours available at Wahweap. Hiking permit required (tel. 928/871–6647) from Navajo Nation to backpack around Navajo Mountain to Rainbow Bridge. No water-based recreation activities (swimming, fishing, waterskiing, and so forth) allowed within monument. Ranger station at Dangling Rope Marina staffed intermittently Mar.–Nov.

HOW TO GET THERE

The bridge is in San Juan County, UT, immediately adjacent to Navajo Mountain and the Navajo Reservation. Public access by boat via Lake Powell, through Arizona. Trips to the bridge may be made in private, rental, or tour boats. Courtesy dock available for short-term docking while people make the ½-mile walk to the bridge. By boat, 50 miles from Wahweap, Antelope Point, Bullfrog, or Halls Crossing to Rainbow Bridge. Closest airport: Page, AZ (7 miles).

CONTACTS

Rainbow Bridge National Monument (Box 1507, Page, AZ 86040, tel. 928/608–6404, www.nps.gov/rabr). Glen Canyon National Recreation Area (Box 1507, Page, AZ 86040, tel. 928/608–6404, www.nps.gov/glca).

Timpanogos Cave National Monument

In north-central Utah, near American Fork

Hansen Cave, Middle Cave, and Timpanogos Cave, three small but wonderfully decorated limestone caves, are the attractions at this monument. These exquisitely beautiful caverns are decorated with a dazzling display of helictites and anthodites in a variety of fantastic shapes. The monument was proclaimed in 1922 and transferred to the Park Service in 1933.

WHAT TO SEE & DO

Fishing, hiking, picnicking, touring caves. **Facilities:** Visitor center, video of cave tour, ¼-mile nature trail. Bookstore, fire grills, gift shop, picnic area. **Programs & Events:** Cave tours (May–Sept., daily), weekend evening programs. **Tips & Hints:** Buy cave tour tickets in advance or arrive early in the day. Bring a jacket or sweater. Cave temperature is 45°F. Bring water on three-hour cave hike. The 1½-mile trail rises 1,065 feet. Visit early in the morning or on weekdays. Busiest July–Aug., least crowded May and Sept.

FOOD, LODGING & SUPPLIES

Camping: None in park. In American Fork: Granite Flat (Rte. 92, tel. 877/444–6777; 67 sites; $14; flush and vault toilets), Little Mill (Rte. 92, tel. 877/444–6777; 78 sites; $12; vault toilets). **Hotels:** None in park. In Lehi: Best Western Plus Timpanogos (195 S. 850 E, tel. 801/768–1400, www.bestwestern.com; 59 rooms; $85–$130), Motel 6 (210 S. 1200 E, tel. 801/768–2668, www.motel6.com; 112 rooms; $44–$99). **X Restaurants:** None in park. In American Fork: JCW (580 E. State Rd., tel. 801/492–1762; $7–$8; closed Sun.). In Linden: Los Hermanos (395 N. State St., tel. 801/785–1715; $6–$15; closed Sun.). **Groceries & Gear:** None in park. In American Fork: Albertson's (135 E. Main St., tel. 801/756–1440).

FEES, HOURS & REGULATIONS

Entrance fee: $6 per vehicle. Cave tour tickets: $7 adults, $5 ages 6–15, $3 ages 3–5 or ages 62 and over. It's a good idea to book tours in advance (tel. 801/756–5238). State fishing license required. No cave tours in winter. No pets, strollers, or other wheeled vehicles on cave trail. Tours run 7–4:30. Picnic areas open dawn–dusk. Visitor center open May–Sept., daily 7–5:30; late Sept.–Oct., daily 8–5.

HOW TO GET THERE

24 miles south of Salt Lake City via Exit 284 (Alpine Highland) off I–15. Turn east on Rte. 92 for 10 miles to monument. Closest airport: Salt Lake City.

CONTACTS

Timpanogos Cave National Monument (R.R. 3, Box 200, American Fork, UT 84003, tel. 801/756–5238, fax 801/756–5661, www.nps.gov/tica). Uinta-Wasatch-Cache National Forest (88 W. 100 N, Provo, UT 84601, tel. 801/377–5780, www.fs.usda.gov/uwcnf). Utah Tourism & Recreation Information Center (300 N. State St., Salt Lake City, UT 84114, tel. 801/538–1030 or 800/200–1160). Utah Valley Convention and Visitors Bureau (51 S. University Ave., Suite 215, Provo, UT 84601, tel. 801/379–2555, www.utahvalley.com).

Zion National Park

In southwestern Utah, near Springdale

Protected within Zion's 229 square miles are a spectacular landscape of cliffs and canyons and a wilderness full of the unexpected. Colorful canyon and mesa scenery includes erosion and rock-fault patterns that create phenomenal shapes and landscapes. The park is home to Kolob Arch, one of the world's largest arches, with a span that measures 310 feet. Mule deer, golden eagles, and mountain lions also call Zion home. Mukuntuweap National Monument was proclaimed in 1909 and established as Zion National Park in 1919.

WHAT TO SEE & DO

Bicycling, bird and wildlife viewing, hiking, horseback riding, picnicking, scenic drives. **Facilities:** 2 visitor centers: Kolob Canyons (off I–15) and Zion Canyon (east of Springdale off Rte. 9); human history museum, trails. Picnic sites and tables. **Programs & Events:** Guided walks, evening programs, talks, and horseback rides (late Mar.–early Oct.); Junior Ranger program (May–Sept.). **Tips & Hints:** Don't hike alone. Stay on trails and stay out of drainage areas during thunderstorms. Watch for rockfalls and landslides. Free shuttle system (Apr.–Oct.) operates along the 6-mile Zion Scenic Drive. Parking lot at visitor center is often full 9–4: park in Springdale and ride the shuttle bus to the park entrance. Busiest June–Aug., least crowded Jan. and Feb.

FOOD, LODGING & SUPPLIES

Camping: 3 campgrounds in the park: Lava Point (6 sites; free; no water; closed mid-Oct.–May), South (126 sites; $16; flush toilets; closed Nov.–early Mar.), Watchman (183 sites; $16–$20; flush toilets, hookups). Backcountry camping allowed. **Hotels:** In the park: Zion Lodge (tel. 303/297–2757 or 435/772–3213; 121 rooms; $175–$185). In Springdale: Canyon Ranch Motel (668 Zion Park Blvd., tel. 435/772–3357, www.canyonranchmotel.com; 22 rooms; $69–$99), Cliffrose Lodge & Gardens (281 Zion Park Blvd., tel. 435/772–3234 or 800/243–8824, cliffroselodge.com; 35 rooms, 14 suites; $9–$145). **✗ Restaurants:** In the park: Zion Lodge (tel. 435/772–3213; $7–$13). In Springdale: Pioneer Lodge & Restaurant (838 Zion Park Blvd., tel. 435/772–3009; $8–$20), Switchback Grille & Trading Co. (1149 S. Zion Park Blvd., tel. 435/772–3777; $7–$14). **Groceries & Gear:** In Springdale: Sol Foods Market (95 Zion Park Blvd., tel. 435/772–0277).

FEES, HOURS & REGULATIONS

Entrance fee: $12 per person on foot, bicycle, or motorcycle; $25 per vehicle ($25 maximum per family). Extra $15 fee for oversize vehicles for Zion–Mt. Carmel tunnel. Permit required for hikes through Virgin River Narrows. Wilderness permits ($10–$20) required; restrictions apply, inquire at visitor center for details. Zion Scenic Drive limited to shuttle buses. All other park roads are open to private vehicles. No vehicles taller than 11 feet, 4 inches in Zion–Mt. Carmel Hwy. Tunnel.

HOW TO GET THERE

The Kolob Canyons visitor center can be reached via Exit 40 off I–15. The Zion Canyon visitor center is east of Springdale off Rte. 9. Closest airport: St. George (46 miles).

CONTACT

Zion National Park (Springdale, UT 84767-1099, tel. 435/772–3256, www.nps.gov/zion). Zion Canyon Visitor Bureau (www.zionpark.com).

See Also

Glen Canyon National Recreation Area, Arizona. *Dinosaur National Monument and Hovenweep National Monument,* Colorado. *California National Historic Trail, Mormon Pioneer National Historic Trail, Oregon National Historic Trail, and Pony Express National Historic Trail,* in Other National Parklands.

VERMONT

Marsh-Billings-Rockefeller National Historical Park

In east-central Vermont, in Woodstock

The park, the first in the system to focus on conservation history, protects the home of some of America's most distinguished conservationists. George Perkins Marsh, who grew up here, wrote *Man and Nature*, which was published in 1864. Frederick Billings created a progressive dairy farm and forest on the estate here in the late 1800s. His granddaughter Mary French Rockefeller and her husband, Laurance, who made enormous contributions to the national parks, lived here and donated the site to the National Park Service. The park contains one of the oldest professionally managed woodlands in the United States, and the mansion includes hundreds of artworks from influential 19th-century landscape painters. The site, which opened to the public in June 1998, is managed as a partnership between the National Park Service and the Woodstock Foundation, which operates the Billings Farm & Museum. The adjacent museum manages the farm as both a historic site and a working dairy farm. The park was established on August 26, 1992.

WHAT TO SEE & DO

Touring mansion, grounds, farm, forest, and museum. **Facilities:** Two visitor centers (Billings Farm & Museum, Carriage Barn), mansion and grounds, 1890 farmhouse, museum, 20 miles of trails and carriage roads. **Programs & Events:** Guided tours of mansion, gardens, and grounds; film; conservation stewardship programs. **Tips & Hints:** Expect to spend up to a full day at the park. Busiest Aug.–Oct., least crowded Nov.–Feb.

FOOD, LODGING & SUPPLIES

⛺ **Camping:** None in park. In Barnard: Silver Lake State Park (20 State Park Beach Rd., off Rte. 12, tel. 802/234–9451; 39 sites, 7 lean-tos; $16–$27; flush toilets, showers). 🏨 **Hotels:** None in park. In Woodstock: The Shire Riverview Motel (46 Pleasant St., tel. 802/457–2211; 42 rooms; $138–$228), Woodstock Inn & Resort (14 The Green, tel. 802/457–1100; 142 rooms, 7 suites, 1 house; $164–$723). ✗ **Restaurants:** None in park. In Woodstock: Bentleys (3 Elm St., tel. 802/457–3232; $9–$20), Woodstock Inn & Resort (14 The Green, tel. 802/457–1100; $23–$34). ⛏ **Groceries & Gear:** None in park. In Woodstock: F. H. Gillingham & Sons (16 Elm St., tel. 802/457–2100), Woodstock Farmers Market (468 Woodstock Rd., tel. 802/457–3658; closed Mon.).

FEES & HOURS

Billings–Rockefeller Mansion: $8 adults, free ages 15 and under, $4 ages 62 and over. Billings Farm & Museum: $12 adults, $11 ages

62 and over, $6 ages 5–15, $3 ages 3 and 4. Combination ticket: $17 adults, $13 seniors ages 62 and over. Grounds open daily. Park open Sat. of Memorial Day weekend (May)–Oct., daily 10–5. Visitor centers open daily 10–5. Billings Farm & Museum open May–Oct., daily 10–5.

HOW TO GET THERE

Off Rte. 12 in Woodstock, next to the Billings Farm & Museum. Closest airports: Lebanon, NH (17 miles), Burlington (95 miles), Manchester, NH (95 miles).

CONTACTS

Marsh-Billings-Rockefeller National Historical Park (54 Elm St., Woodstock, VT 05091, tel. 802/457–3368, fax 802/457–3405, www. nps.gov/mabi). Billings Farm & Museum (Box 489, Woodstock, VT 05091, tel. 802/457–2355, fax 802/457–4663, www.billingsfarm.org). Woodstock Area Chamber of Commerce (61 Central St., Box 486, Woodstock, VT 05091, tel. 802/457–3555 or 888/496–6378, www. woodstockvt.com).

See Also

Appalachian National Scenic Trail, West Virginia.

VIRGINIA

Appomattox Court House National Historical Park

In south-central Virginia, 25 miles east of Lynchburg

General Robert E. Lee surrendered the Confederate Army of Northern Virginia to Lieutenant General Ulysses S. Grant at this historic village and battleground, bringing an end to the Civil War, which killed approximately 618,000 people. The site was authorized as a national historic monument on August 13, 1935, and designated a national historic park on April 15, 1954.

WHAT TO SEE & DO

Touring historic village, walking tours of the battlefield. **Facilities:** Visitor center and museum in reconstructed courthouse building, furnished room exhibits throughout the historic village, self-guided walking tours, wayside exhibits in battlefield areas. Bookstore. **Programs & Events:** Audiovisual programs every half hour in visitor center, ranger-guided tours, living-history and other programs (Memorial Day–Labor Day). **Tips & Hints:** Plan a two-hour stay to see the park. Spend another six hours driving the associated Lee's Retreat Route, which covers 100 miles and has 26 wayside stops with radio messages. Go mid-Apr.–mid-May, Sept. and Oct. Busiest June and July, least crowded Jan. and Feb.

FOOD, LODGING & SUPPLIES

Camping: None in park. Near Appomattox: Holliday Lake State Park (2759 State Park Rd., tel. 434/248–6308; 37 sites; $27; flush toilets, showers, hookups). **Hotels:** None in park. In Appomattox: Babcock House B&B (250 Oakleigh Ave., tel. 434/352–7532, www.babcockhouse.com; 5 rooms; $110–$150). **Restaurants:** None in park. In Lynchburg: Big Lick Tropical Grill (4001 Murray Pl., tel. 434/528–3604; $8). **Groceries & Gear:** In Appomattox: Kroger (7789 Richmond Hwy. 460, tel. 434/352–0817), Wilbun's Supermarket (1974 Confederate Blvd., tel. 434/352–5165).

FEES, HOURS & REGULATIONS

Entrance fee: $4 per person, $10 per vehicle (Memorial Day–Labor Day); $3 per person, $5 per vehicle (Labor Day–Memorial Day), under 16 free. No pets in buildings, leashed pets otherwise. No vehicles, bikes, or horses on trails or historic roads. Park and visitor center open daily 8:30–5.

HOW TO GET THERE

25 miles east of Lynchburg and 2 miles north of Appomattox on Rte. 24. Closest airport: Lynchburg.

CONTACTS

Appomattox Court House National Historical Park (Box 218, Appo-mattox, VA 24522-0218, tel. 434/352–8987, fax 434/352–8330, www.nps.gov/apco). Appomattox County Chamber of Commerce (276 Court St., Box 704, Appomattox, VA 24522, tel. 434/352–2621, www.appomattoxchamber.org).

Arlington House, the Robert E. Lee Memorial

In northern Virginia, in Arlington

The house that Robert E. Lee lived in for 30 years today is a memorial to Lee, who gained the respect of Northerners and Southerners through his service in the Civil War. The antebellum home overlooks the Potomac River and Washington, DC. The memorial was authorized in 1925, transferred to the Park Service in 1933, designated the Custis-Lee Mansion in 1955, and restored to its original name, Arlington, in 1972.

WHAT TO SEE & DO

Touring the house. **Facilities:** House, slave quarters, museum, gardens. Bookstore. **Programs & Events:** Self-guided and guided tours. **Tips & Hints:** Busiest Mar.–Aug., least crowded Jan. and Feb.

HOW TO GET THERE

The memorial is accessible by shuttle bus or by a 10-minute walk from the Arlington National Cemetery Visitor Center parking area. Access from Washington, DC, is via the Memorial Bridge. Access from Virginia is from the George Washington Memorial Pkwy. The memorial is also accessible by the Blue line of the Metro subway system. Closest airport: Reagan.

FEES, HOURS & REGULATIONS

Free. Parking fee at Arlington National Cemetery ($1.75 per hr.). House open Apr. and May, daily 9-5; June–Aug., daily 9–5:30; Sept.–Mar., daily 9:30–4:30. Time entry on busy days.

CONTACT

Arlington House, the Robert E. Lee Memorial (c/o National Park Service, George Washington Memorial Pkwy., Turkey Run Park, McLean, VA 22101, tel. 703/235–1530, www.nps.gov/arho).

Booker T. Washington National Monument

In southwestern Virginia, 22 miles southeast of Roanoke

Booker T. Washington, educator, orator, and presidential adviser, was born into slavery, reared, and emancipated at this former plantation site. The park is one of the few places where visitors can see how slavery and the plantation system worked on a smaller scale. It provides a focal point for discussions about one of the most powerful African Americans in history and the evolving context of race in American society. It was authorized on April 2, 1956.

WHAT TO SEE & DO

Viewing exhibits, walking historic and nature trails. **Facilities:** Visitor center, wayside exhibits. Bookstore, picnic area. **Programs & Events:** Ranger-guided tours (Memorial Day–Labor Day, 11 and 2), audiovisual programs, living-history program and demonstrations (periodically). Christmas program and open house (1st Sat. in Dec.). **Tips & Hints:** Busiest Feb.–June, least crowded Dec. and Jan.

FOOD, LODGING & SUPPLIES

Camping: None in park. In Bedford: Peaks of Otter (Blue Ridge Pkwy., mile 86; tel. 540/586–4496; 141 sites; $16–$19; flush toilets). **Hotels:** None in park. In Bedford: Peaks of Otter Lodge (Blue Ridge Pkwy., mile 86; tel. 540/586–1081, www.peaksofotter.com; 63 rooms; $59–$147). **Restaurants:** None in park. In Bedford: Peaks of Otter Lodge (Blue Ridge Pkwy., mile 86, tel. 540/586–9263, www.peaksofotter.com; $9–$27). **Groceries & Gear:** None in park. In Moneta: Shop Rite (14600 Moneta Rd., on 122; tel. 540/297–6000).

FEES, HOURS & REGULATIONS

Free. Group tours and education programs (reservations required, tel. 540/721–2094). No hunting or bike riding. Leashed pets only. Park open daily 9–5.

HOW TO GET THERE

On Rte. 122, 16 miles northeast of Rocky Mount, 22 miles southeast of Roanoke via Rte. 116 south and Rte. 122 north, and 21 miles south of Bedford via Rte. 122 south. Closest airport: Roanoke.

CONTACTS

Booker T. Washington National Monument (12130 Booker T. Washington Hwy., Hardy, VA 24101, tel. 540/721–2094, fax 540/721–8311, www.nps.gov/bowa). Smith Mountain Lake Regional Chamber of Commerce (16430 Booker T. Washington Hwy., 2, Moneta, VA 24121, tel. 540/721–1203 or 800/676–8203, fax 540/721-7796, www.visitsmithmountainlake.com).

Cedar Creek & Belle Grove National Historical Park

In the northern Shenandoah Valley, near Middletown and Strasburg

This park, together with several on-site nonprofit preservation organizations, strives to commemorate the history of the land and structures within its boundaries. Most of the acreage within the park is closed to visitors, except two partner sites: Belle Grove Plantation, an 18th-century farm and limestone manor house, and the Cedar Creek Battlefield Foundation headquarters, a memorial to the 1864 Civil War battle. The national historical park encompasses approximately 3,500 acres within Shenandoah Valley Battlefields National Historic District. In Strasburg, the Hupp's Hill Civil War Museum displays original battlefield artifacts and shows a movie about the Battle of Cedar Creek. The park was established on December 19, 2002.

WHAT TO SEE & DO

Touring battlefield and museum, touring plantation farm and house. **Facilities:** Belle Grove Plantation, Cedar Creek Battlefield Foundation headquarters, Hupp's Hill Civil War Park Museum. **Programs & Events:** Guided and self-guided tours, battle reenactments at Cedar Creek (Oct.). **Tips & Hints:** There are no Park Service facilities in the park, although a visitor contact station is planned.

FOOD, LODGING & SUPPLIES

Camping: In the park: Battle of Cedar Creek Campground (8950 Valley Pk., tel. 540/869–1888; 61 sites; $10–$30; toilets, showers, hookups). **Hotels:** None in park. In Middletown: Wayside Inn (7783 Main St., tel. 540/869–1797, www.alongthewayside.com; 20 rooms, 2 suites; $99–$169). In Strasburg: Hotel Strasburg (213 S. Holliday St., tel. 540/465–9191 or 800/348–8327, www.hotelstrasburg.com; 29 rooms; $98–$190). **Restaurants:** None in park. In Middletown: Wayside Inn (7783 Main St., tel. 540/869–1797, www.alongthewayside.com; $16–$35). In Strasburg: Hotel Strasburg (213 S. Holliday St., tel. 540/465–9191, www.hotelstrasburg.com; $17–$25). **Groceries & Gear:** None in park. In Strasburg: Food Lion (794 Shopping Center Rd., off U.S. 11, tel. 540/465–5335).

FEES, HOURS & REGULATIONS

Belle Grove Plantation Manor House daily tours: $10 adults, $8 ages 6–12, free ages 5 and under. Cedar Creek Battlefield Foundation headquarters: free. Belle Grove Plantation open Apr.–Oct., daily 10-4, Sun. 1–5. Cedar Creek Battlefield Foundation headquarters open Apr.–Oct., Fri.–Mon. 10–4, Sun. 1–5; Nov.–Mar., by appointment. Hupp's Hill Civil War Park Museum ($5), Fri.-Tues. 9–5.

HOW TO GET THERE

At the junction of I–81 and I–66 in the northern Shenandoah Valley, exit onto the historic Valley Turnpike (U.S. 11), which runs through the park. Closest airport: Dulles (57 miles).

CONTACTS

Cedar Creek & Belle Grove National Historical Park (7718½ Main St., Middletown, VA 22645, tel. 540/868–9176 or 540/869–3051, www. nps.gov/cebe). Belle Grove Plantation (336 Belle Grove Rd., Middletown, VA 22645, tel. 540/869–2028, www.bellegrove.org). Cedar Creek Battlefield Foundation (8437 Valley Pk., Middletown, VA 22645, tel. 540/869–2064, www.cedarcreekbattlefield.org). Hupp's Hill Civil War Park Museum (33229 Old Valley Pk., Strasburg, VA 22641, tel. 540/ 465-5884, www.cedarcreekbattlefield.org).

Colonial National Historical Park

In southeastern Virginia, near Williamsburg

The park includes Historic Jamestowne, the site of the first permanent English settlement in North America; Yorktown Battlefield, the site of the last major battle of the American Revolution; and the 23-mile-long scenic Colonial Parkway that connects the two with Colonial Williamsburg. Also included is the Cape Henry Memorial, which marks the approximate site of the first landing of Jamestown's colonists in 1607. The park was authorized as a Colonial National Monument on July 3, 1930; proclaimed on December 30, 1930; and redesignated a Colonial National Historical Park on June 5, 1936.

WHAT TO SEE & DO

Bicycling, scenic drives, walking into historic Yorktown. **Facilities:** 2 visitor centers: Jamestown and Yorktown; wayside exhibits. At Jamestown: Visitor center with exhibits and theater presentations; archaeological excavation of original 1607 fort site; archaearium museum of excavation findings and original 1690s church tower; Glasshouse with exhibit on early glassblowers; 5-mile driving tour of island setting. Museum store. At Yorktown: Visitor center with exhibits and orientation film; battlefield driving tour, including Moore House and Surrender Field, with interpretive pavilion at actual surrender site; historic village with a dozen original and reconstructed 18th-century homes, including home of Thomas Nelson Jr., signer of the Declaration of Independence. **Programs & Events:** Ranger-guided tours (daily), living-history tours (Jamestown: Apr.). Lamb's Artillery Firing Program (Yorktown: Mar.– Oct., periodically); Jamestown Landing Day (mid-May); Memorial Day Weekend–Civil War Weekend (Yorktown: end of May); Independence Day Celebration (Yorktown: July 4); First Assembly Day Commemoration (Jamestown: late July); Yorktown Day (Yorktown: Oct. 19). **Tips & Hints:** Allow at least three hours to visit each site. Go in winter to avoid crowds. Busiest Apr.–July, least crowded Jan. and Feb.

FEES, HOURS & REGULATIONS

Entrance fees: $10 adults; under 16 free. Jamestown open daily 8:30– dusk. Historic Jamestowne Visitor Center open daily 9–5. Grounds open daily dawn–dusk, last entry at 4:30. Yorktown Visitor Center open daily 9–5.

HOW TO GET THERE

Off I–64, near Williamsburg, with sections in Jamestown and Yorktown and a parkway connecting the two. Closest airports: Newport News–Williamsburg (11 miles), Norfolk (37 miles), Richmond (56 miles).

CONTACTS

Colonial National Historical Park (Box 210, Yorktown, VA 23690, tel. 757/898–2410, fax 757/898–6346, www.nps.gov/colo). Greater Williamsburg Chamber & Tourism Alliance (421 N. Boundary St., Williamsburg, VA 23187, tel. 757/229–6511, fax 757/229–2047, www.williamsburgcc.com).

Fort Monroe
National Monument

Near Hampton, VA, in the extreme southeastern corner of the state

Designed by a French military engineer as a coastal defense in the aftermath of the War of 1812, Fort Monroe's history echoes the nation's colorful past. It remains the largest stone fortress ever built in the United States and the only fort in the country fully encircled by a wet moat. Until it was closed in 2011, the fortress was the third-oldest U.S. Army post in continuous active service. The 325-acre site became a National Historic Landmark in 1960. By presidential proclamation, it was designated a National Monument in November 2011.

WHAT TO SEE & DO

Taking a self-guided walking tour of the historic fortifications, visiting the nearby Casemate Museum of regional and military history. **Facilities:** Casement Museum. **Programs & Events:** Living-history demonstrations by the 99th New York State Volunteer Infantry Co. (begins at Casemate Museum, 3rd Sat., Apr.-Aug.). **Tips & Hints:** The Casemate Museum, within the fort, is a great place to get oriented and features Robert E. Lee's living quarters, Jefferson Davis's prison cell, and a collection of military uniforms and memorabilia.

FOOD & LODGING

⚠ **Camping:** None in park. In Virginia Beach: North Bay Shore Campground (3257 Colechester Rd., tel. 757/426-7911, www.northbayshorecampground.net, tel. 866/658–3021; 206 sites; $35–$50; flush toilets, showers, hookups; open May–Sept.). 🏨 **Hotels:** None in park. In Hampton: Crowne Plaza Hampton Marina (700 Settlers Landing Rd., tel. 757/727-9700, www.hamptonmarinahotel.com; 173 rooms and suites; $100–$329). ✕ **Restaurants:** In park: Paradise Ocean Club (490 Fenwick Rd., Fort Monroe, tel. 757/224–0290, www.paradiseoceanclub.com; $9–$11). In Hampton: The Chamberlin (2

Fenwick Rd., tel. 757/637-7200, www.historicchamberlin.com; $16–$20. Jason's Deli (39 Coliseum Crossing, tel. 757/825-1501; $6–$9).

FEES, HOURS & REGULATIONS

Free. Monument and Casemate Museum (20 Bernard Rd., Hampton, tel. 757/788-3391) open daily 10:30–4:30.

HOW TO GET THERE

Take I–64 to Hampton, Exit 268, then left onto S. Mallory St. Take right at next light onto E. Mellen St. and continue less than a mile to a small bridge leading into Fort Monroe. Closest airport: Newport News-Williamsburg (13 miles).

CONTACT

Fort Monroe National Monument (41 Bernard Rd., Fort Monroe, VA 23651, tel. 757/722-3678, www.nps.gov/fomr).

Fredericksburg & Spotsylvania County Battlefields Memorial National Military Park

In eastern Virginia, in Fredericksburg area

About 100,000 men became Civil War casualties in the four major battles fought in the vicinity of Fredericksburg—Fredericksburg, Chancellorsville, Wilderness, and Spotsylvania Court House. The park also includes the historic structures of Chatham, Ellwood, Salem Church, and the "Stonewall" Jackson Shrine and encompasses 8,000 acres, making it one of the largest military parks in the world. Fredericksburg National Cemetery, with 15,333 interments, 12,746 of them unidentified, is within the park. The park was established in 1927 and transferred to the Park Service in 1933.

WHAT TO SEE & DO

Touring battlefields by car and on foot. **Facilities:** 2 visitor centers: Fredericksburg and Chancellorsville; 2 exhibit shelters (Wilderness, Spotsylvania Court House), restored Ellwood historic structure, Chatham, Salem Church, "Stonewall" Jackson Shrine, tour roads, trails. Bookstores. **Programs & Events:** Guided tours. National Cemetery Luminaria (Memorial Day weekend), Memorial Day Commemorative Program (May), Battle of Fredericksburg Commemoration Ceremony (Dec.). **Tips & Hints:** Allow two days to tour all four battlefields. Busiest June and July, least crowded Jan. and Feb.

FOOD, LODGING & SUPPLIES

Camping: None in park. In Fredericksburg: KOA (7400 Brookside La., tel. 540/898–7252, www.koa.com; 117 sites; $31–$56; flush toilets, showers, hookups). **Hotels:** None in park. In Fredericksburg: Best Western (2205 Plank Rd., tel. 540/371–5050, www.bestwestern.com;

VIRGINIA

108 rooms; $75), Dunning Mills Inn (2305C Jefferson Davis Hwy., tel. 540/373–1256, www.dunningmills.com; 54 rooms; $69). ✘ **Restaurants:** None in park. In Fredericksburg: Goolrick's Pharmacy (901 Caroline St., tel. 540/373–9878; $3–$6; closed Sun.). ♿ **Groceries & Gear:** None in park. In Fredericksburg: Wegmans (2281 Carl D Silver Pkwy., tel. 540/322-4800).

FEES & HOURS

Free. $2 for films. Visitor centers open daily 9–5, extended hours in spring, summer, and fall. Park open daily.

HOW TO GET THERE

Fredericksburg is 50 miles south of Washington, DC; 60 miles north of Richmond; and 3 miles east of I–95. Fredericksburg Battlefield Visitor Center is at 1013 Lafayette Blvd. in Fredericksburg. Chancellorsville Battlefield Visitor Center is on Rte. 3, 8 miles west of I–95. Closest airport: Reagan (55 miles), Richmond (55 miles).

CONTACT

Fredericksburg and Spotsylvania County Battlefields Memorial National Military Park (120 Chatham La., Fredericksburg, VA 22405, tel. 540/371–0802, www.nps.gov/frsp).

George Washington Birthplace National Monument

In northeastern Virginia, near Colonial Beach

The park evokes the spirit of the 18th-century tobacco farm where Washington was born and includes a memorial mansion and gardens and the tombs of several generations of Washingtons. The historic buildings, groves of trees, livestock, gardens, rivers, and creeks evoke the earliest scenes of Washington's childhood. The site was established on January 23, 1930.

WHAT TO SEE & DO

Hiking, picnicking, touring site, wildlife viewing. **Facilities:** Visitor center, home site, colonial farm area, burial grounds, trails, beach. Bookstore. **Programs & Events:** Ranger-guided tours. A Washington Christmas at Pope's Creek (Dec.). George Washington's Birthday (Presidents' Day and Feb. 22). **Tips & Hints:** Plan one to two hours for the visit, and bring a picnic lunch. Busiest June and July, least crowded Dec. and Jan.

FOOD, LODGING & SUPPLIES

🏕 **Camping:** None in park. Near Montross: Westmoreland State Park (Rte. 3, tel. 804/493–8821 or 800/933–7275 for reservations; 133 sites; $20–$27; flush toilets, showers, hookups). 🏨 **Hotels:** None in park. In Montross: Inn at Montross (21 Polk St., tel. 804/493–8624, www.theinnatmontross.com; 5 rooms; $149). ✘ **Restaurants:** None in park. In Montross: Inn at Montross (21 Polk St., tel. 804/493–8624, www.

theinnatmontross.com; $8–$35, open Thurs.–Sun.). 👥 **Groceries & Gear:** None in park. In Montross: Food Lion (18044 Kings Hwy., tel. 804/493–7367).

FEES & HOURS

Free. Visitor center and historic area open daily 9–5.

HOW TO GET THERE

On the Potomac River, 38 miles east of Fredericksburg, and accessible via Rte. 3 to Rte. 204. Closest airport: Richmond (75 miles).

CONTACT

George Washington Birthplace National Monument (1732 Popes Creek Rd., Washington's Birthplace, VA 22443, tel. 804/224–1732, www.nps.gov/gewa).

George Washington Memorial Parkway

In northeastern Virginia, near McLean

Natural scenery along the Potomac River, across the water from Washington, DC, is preserved along this parkway. It connects the historic sites from Mount Vernon, where Washington lived, past the nation's capital, which he founded, to the Great Falls of the Potomac, where the president demonstrated his skill as an engineer. The parkway was authorized in 1930 and transferred to the Park Service in 1933.

WHAT TO SEE & DO

Bicycling, bird-watching, dancing, hiking, kayaking and canoeing, picnicking, sailing, scenic drives. **Facilities:** With nearly 7,200 acres, the parkway includes more than 25 historical, natural, and recreational sites, including Arlington House; the Robert E. Lee Memorial; Clara Barton National Historic Site; Lyndon Baines Johnson Memorial Grove on the Potomac; Theodore Roosevelt Island; the Arlington Memorial Bridge; Claude Moore Colonial Farm; Dyke Marsh Wildlife Preserve; Fort Hunt Park; Fort Marcy; Glen Echo Park; Great Falls Park (in Virginia); Netherlands Carillon; Turkey Run Park; U.S. Marine Corps War Memorial (commonly nicknamed the Iwo Jima Memorial); and the Women in Military Service to America Memorial. Boat ramps, marinas, picnic areas. **Programs & Events:** Interpretive programs, guided walks, tours, concerts, Junior Ranger program, children's programs and camps. Sunset Parade (U.S. Marine Corps War Memorial, early June–mid-Aug., Tues. evenings). **Tips & Hints:** Busiest spring and fall, least crowded Jan. and Feb.

FEES, HOURS & REGULATIONS

Entrance fees and hours vary depending upon site, although there is no charge to attend the majority of park sites. Reservations required for many interpretive programs offered at sites that are not regularly staffed. Reservations may be required for tours with groups of 10 or more, so call the park to inquire in advance. Permit required for group picnicking at Fort Hunt Park Apr.–Oct. Possession and consumption of alcohol on park property is prohibited except by permit or at designated concession facilities. No weapons. Contact the park for additional regulations that should be considered during your visit.

HOW TO GET THERE

The parkway runs parallel to the Potomac River north and south of Washington, DC, and is accessible from all major travel routes from the south and west, including I–495, I–95, and I–66. Closest airport: Reagan.

CONTACT

George Washington Memorial Parkway (700 George Washington Memorial Pkwy., McLean, VA 22101, tel. 703/289–2500, fax 703/289–2598, www.nps.gov/gwmp).

Maggie L. Walker National Historic Site

In southeastern Virginia, in Richmond

This row house, at 110½ E. Leigh St., was the home of Maggie Lena Walker (1867–1934), a prominent African American civic and fraternal leader who rose to prominence in post–Civil War Richmond. She is best known as the country's first woman bank president, founding the St. Luke Penny Savings Bank in 1903. This historic site is in the heart of Jackson Ward, an important and impressive historic African American neighborhood, once considered the Harlem of the South, where 2nd Street was "Black Wall Street." Today, you can see an awesome display of 1880s–1920s neoclassical architecture. Sadly, much of Jackson Ward was destroyed in the 1950s with the building of the interstates (I–95, I–64). But what's left is a wonderful reminder of a once thriving, prosperous, post-slavery black neighborhood that flourished during the Jim Crow South. The site was authorized in 1978.

WHAT TO SEE & DO

Touring house. **Facilities:** Visitor center with film, home, exhibit hall. Bookstore. **Programs & Events:** Ranger-guided tours (year-round, Mon.–Sat.). 2nd St. Festival (1st weekend, Oct.), Maggie Walker Birthday Celebration (mid-July). **Tips & Hints:** Busiest Feb.–May, least crowded Sept. and Jan.

FEES, HOURS & REGULATIONS

Free. No pets. Site and visitor center open Mar.–Oct., Mon.–Sat. 9–5; Nov.–Feb., Mon.–Sat. 9–4:30.

HOW TO GET THERE

In Richmond, at 600 N. 2nd St. via Exits 76A or B off I–95/I–64. Closest airport: Richmond (10 miles).

CONTACTS

Maggie L. Walker National Historic Site (600 N. 2nd St., Richmond, VA 23223, tel. 804/771–2017, fax 804/771–2226, www.nps.gov/mawa). Metro Richmond Convention & Visitors Bureau (401 N. 3rd St., Richmond, VA 23219, tel. 804/782–2777 or 800/370–9004, www.visitrichmondva.com).

Manassas National Battlefield Park

In northeastern Virginia, in Manassas

Two battles between Union and Confederate troops during the Civil War are commemorated here. Nearly 900 men lost their lives in July 1861, and another 3,300 died during a two-and-a-half-day battle in August 1862, which brought the Confederacy to the height of its power. The park was designated on May 10, 1940.

WHAT TO SEE & DO

Hiking, picnicking, scenic drives. **Facilities:** Visitor center (Henry Hill, Sudley Rd.); contact station (Brawner Farm, Pageland La.), interpretive trails. Bookstore, picnic areas. **Programs & Events:** Ranger-guided tours and programs, living-history demonstrations. Battlefield Hike (Apr. and Oct.). **Tips & Hints:** Use caution while driving heavily traveled roads that divide the park. Visit Apr.–Oct. for best weather. Busiest June and July, least crowded Dec.–Feb.

FOOD & LODGING

🏕 **Camping:** None in park. In Centreville: Bull Run Regional Park (7700 Bull Run Dr., tel. 703/631–0550; 150 sites; $2–$45; flush toilets, showers, hookups). In Haymarket: Greenville Farm Family Campground (14004 Shelter La., tel. 703/754–7944; 150 sites; $29–$38; flush toilets, showers). 🏨 **Hotels:** None in park. In Manassas: Best Western Battlefield Inn (10820 Balls Ford Rd., tel. 703/361–8000, www.bestwestern.com; 123 rooms; $109), Courtyard Manassas (10701 Battleview Pkwy., tel. 703/335–1300, www.marriott.com; 149 rooms; $99–$169). ✘ **Restaurants:** None in park. In Manassas: Carmello's & Little Portugal (9108 Center St., tel. 703/368–5522; $11–$30; no lunch weekends). 🛒 **Groceries & Gear:** None in park. In Manassas: Costco (10701 Sudley Manor Dr., tel. 703/368-7579).

FEES, HOURS & REGULATIONS

Entrance fee: $3 adults. No hunting. No bikes, motorized or mechanized equipment on trails. Leashed pets only. Park open daily dawn–dusk. Henry Hill visitor center open daily 8:30–5. Brawner Farm contact station open seasonally.

HOW TO GET THERE

The park is 26 miles west of Washington, DC. Henry Hill Visitor Center is 1 mile north of I–66, via Exit 47B and Rte. 234. Closest airports: Dulles (25 miles), Reagan (30 miles).

CONTACTS

Manassas National Battlefield Park (6511 Sudley Rd., Manassas, VA 20109, tel. 703/361–1339, fax 703/361–7106, www.nps.gov/mana). Manassas City Visitor Center (9431 West St., Manassas, VA 20110, tel. 703/361–6599, www.visitmanassas.org).

Petersburg National Battlefield

In southeastern Virginia, near Petersburg

Preserved in this park are three tracts associated with General Ulysses S. Grant's attack and siege of Petersburg during the Civil War. In the spring of 1864, after failing to defeat General Robert E. Lee's army and capture Richmond, the Confederate capital, Grant moved his army across the James River and attacked Petersburg. A 9½-month siege resulted, ending when the last supply lines to Lee's army and Richmond were cut. The site was established as a national military park in 1926, transferred to the Park Service in 1933, and changed to a national battlefield in 1962.

WHAT TO SEE & DO

Bicycling, hiking, horseback riding, picnicking, scenic drives. **Facilities:** 3 visitor centers: Eastern Front (5001 Siege Rd., Petersburg); Five Forks (9840 Courthouse Rd., Dinwiddie County); Grant's Headquarters at City Point (1001 Pecan Ave., Hopewell); interpretive signs, wayside exhibits. Gift shops, picnic area (Eastern Front). **Programs & Events:** 17-minute video, ranger-guided walks (mid-June–mid-Aug., daily). **Tips & Hints:** Visit in spring and fall for best weather. Go in Apr. for dogwood blooms, late Oct. for fall foliage. Busiest June and July, least crowded Jan. and Feb.

FOOD & LODGING

Camping: None in park. Near Chesterfield: Pocahontas State Park (10301 State Park Rd., tel. 804/796–4255 or 800/933–7277; 119 sites; $27; flush toilets, showers, hookups). **Hotels:** None in park. In Hopewell: Quality Inn (4911 Oaklawn Blvd., tel. 804/458–1500, www.qualityinn.com; 115 rooms; $99–$119). In Petersburg: Comfort Inn (11974 S. Crater Rd., tel. 804/732–2900, www.comfortinn.com; 96 rooms; $70–$80). **Restaurants:** None in park. In Hopewell: K&L's Barbecue (1410 Maple St., tel. 804/458–4241; $8–$10; closed weekends). In Petersburg: Alexander's (101 W. Bank St., tel. 804/733–7134; $11–$15; closed Sun. and Mon., no dinner Tues.).

FEES, HOURS & REGULATIONS

Entrance fee: $5 per vehicle. Stay off earthworks and on trails. No metal detectors or artifact hunting. No hunting. Leashed pets only. No mechanized equipment on trails. No horseback riding on paved trails. Park open daily 8–dusk. Visitor center hours: all are open daily 9–5.

HOW TO GET THERE

Eastern Front visitor center is 2½ miles east of central Petersburg on Rte. 36. Grant's Headquarters is at Appomattox Plantation on Pecan Ave. in Hopewell. From I–95 or I–295, take Rte. 10, then make a left on Appomattox St., and a left on Cedar La. Five Forks is on Courthouse Rd., off I–85 in Dinwiddie County. Closest airport: Richmond (30 miles).

CONTACTS

Petersburg National Battlefield (1539 Hickory Hill Rd., Petersburg, VA 23803, tel. 804/732–3531, ext. 200, fax 804/732–0835, www.nps. gov/pete).

Prince William Forest Park

In northeastern Virginia, near Triangle

The 15,000-acre park contains the largest example of an eastern piedmont forest in the National Park System and is a sanctuary for native plants and animals in a rapidly developing region. The park encompasses the Quantico Creek watershed and a heritage of land usage that includes colonial tobacco production, subsistence farming, iron pyrite mining, the Civilian Conservation Corps, and a World War II spy-training base. Congress created the Chopawamsic Recreational Demonstration Area in 1933. It was transferred to the Park Service in 1936 and renamed in 1948.

WHAT TO SEE & DO

Bird and wildlife viewing, fishing, hiking, on- and off-road biking, picnicking. **Facilities:** Visitor center, 11-mile scenic drive, 3-mile paved bike trail, 18 miles of fire roads for mountain biking, 35 miles of hiking trails. Map sale area. **Programs & Events:** Ranger-led tours and talks (weekends). **Tips & Hints:** Busiest June and Oct., least crowded Nov. and Jan.

FOOD, LODGING & SUPPLIES

⚠ **Camping:** 4 campgrounds in the park: Chopawamsic (8 hike-in sites; free; pit toilet), Oak Ridge (100 sites; $15; flush toilets), Travel Trailer Village (tel. 703/221–2474; 77 sites; $22–$25; flush toilets, showers, hookups), Turkey Run Ridge (tel. 703/221–7181; 6 group sites; $40; flush toilets). 5 cabin camps (tel. 703/221–5843; $30–$50; flush toilets, showers; reservations required). 🏨 **Hotels:** In Triangle: Ramada Inn Quantico (4316 Inn St., tel. 703/221–1181 or 800/272–6232, www. ramada.com; 135 rooms; $99–$139). ✗ **Restaurants:** None in park. In Dumfries: Montclair Family Restaurant (17001 Dumfries Rd., tel. 703/ 221–4097; $7–$13). ⛁ **Groceries & Gear:** None in park. In Dumfries: Food Lion (5050 Waterway Dr., Dumfries, tel. 703/897–9220).

FEES, HOURS & REGULATIONS

Entrance fee: $3 per person on foot or bicycle, $5 per vehicle. Backcountry permit (free) required for all backcountry camping. Park open daily dawn–dusk. Registered campers and cabin campers have access 24 hours. Visitor center open daily 9–5.

HOW TO GET THERE

32 miles south of Washington, DC, and 20 miles north of Fredericksburg, VA, via I–95 and Exit 150 (Rte. 619) west. Closest airports: Reagan, Dulles.

CONTACT

Prince William Forest Park (18100 Park Headquarters Rd., Triangle, VA 22172, tel. 703/221–7181, www.nps.gov/prwi).

Richmond National Battlefield Park

In southeastern Virginia, in Richmond

Between 1861 and 1865, Union armies repeatedly tried to capture Richmond, capital of the Confederacy, to end the Civil War. Three of those campaigns came within a few miles of the city. The 2,000-acre park commemorates 13 different sites associated with those campaigns, including the battlefields at Gaines' Mill, Malvern Hill, and Cold Harbor. The park was authorized on March 2, 1936.

WHAT TO SEE & DO

Picnicking at Fort Harrison, touring battlefield sites. **Facilities:** Visitor center with audiovisual programs and film (5th and Tredegar Sts.); 4 contact stations: Chimborazo Medical Museum, Cold Harbor, Glendale Cemetery, and Fort Harrison; interpretive walking trails at Gaines' Mill, Cold Harbor, Malvern Hill, Fort Harrison, and Drewry's Bluff; tour roads at Cold Harbor and Fort Harrison; audio stations. Bookstores. **Programs & Events:** Self-guided driving tours (CD available); ranger-led walking tours, talks, living history (June–Aug.). Battle anniversary commemorations: Drewry's Bluff (May 15), Cold Harbor (June 3), Seven Days' Battle (June 26–July 1), and Fort Harrison (Sept. 29). **Tips & Hints:** Plan to spend at least a day visiting all 13 sites. Busiest June and July, least crowded Jan. and Feb.

FEES & HOURS

Free. Parking fee at Tredegar St. visitor center $3 per hour or free with admission to American Civil War Center. Battlefield sites open daily dawn–dusk. Chimborazo Medical Museum, Tredegar Iron Works, Cold Harbor open daily 9–5. Glendale and Fort Harrison contact stations open June–Aug., daily 9–5; Sept.–May, hours vary.

HOW TO GET THERE

The Tredegar visitor center (5th and Tredegar Sts.) is accessed via I–95. Southbound use Exit 75, northbound use Exit 74C west and then follow signs. From I–64 westbound, Exit 5th St. Closest airport: Richmond (7 miles).

CONTACT

Richmond National Battlefield Park (3215 E. Broad St., Richmond, VA 23223, tel. 804/226–1981, fax 804/771–8522, www.nps.gov/rich).

Shenandoah National Park

In northwestern Virginia, near Luray

Skyline Drive, which winds along the crest of the Blue Ridge Mountains between Front Royal and Waynesboro, is the central feature of the park. Along the 105-mile drive are 75 pullouts that overlook mountain peaks, gorges, and hollows. The heavily forested park also has 500 miles of trails, including a section of the Appalachian Trail, along which are streams, waterfalls, black bear, and deer. The 197,411-acre park was authorized in 1926 and established in 1935.

WHAT TO SEE & DO

Bird-watching, fishing, hiking, horseback riding (guided rides, Skyland), picnicking, scenic drives. **Facilities:** 2 visitor centers: Dickey Ridge (mile 4.6), Harry F. Byrd (mile 51). Overlooks, wayside exhibits, amphitheaters, 500 miles of hiking trails. Book and map sales areas, fire pits and grates, picnic tables, gas, gift shops, laundries, showers. **Programs & Events:** Ranger-led nature and night walks, talks, evening programs (mostly late May–Oct.). **Tips & Hints:** Plan to spend at least two days for visit. Go in spring for wildflowers, migratory birds, and full streams leading to waterfalls; summer for more deer and bear sightings; fall for foliage; and winter for clearest views. Stay off rocks above waterfalls. Avoid fall weekends when the park is crowded with leaf-peepers. Park is usually 10 degrees cooler than valley below. Busiest July and Oct., least crowded Jan. and Feb.

FOOD, LODGING & SUPPLIES

Camping: 4 campgrounds in the park: Big Meadow (mile 51.3, tel. 877/444–6777; 217 sites; $20; flush toilets, showers; reservations required; closed Dec.–Apr.), Lewis Mountain (mile 57.5; 32 sites; $15; flush toilets, showers; closed Nov.–Apr.), Loft Mountain (mile 79.5; 219 sites; $15; flush toilets, showers; closed Nov.–May), Mathews Arm (mile 22.1; 179 sites; $15; flush toilets; closed Nov.–May). Potomac Appalachian Trail Club (tel. 703/242–0693, www.patc.net; 25 cabins; $25–$60; pit toilets). Backcountry camping allowed with permit. **Hotels:** In the park: Big Meadows Lodge (mile 51.3, tel. 800/999–4714; 97 rooms; $115–$195; closed Nov.–mid-Apr.), Lewis Mountain (mile 57.5, tel. 866/875–8456; 10 cabins; $110–$130), Skyland (mile 41.7, tel. 800/999–4714; 179 rooms, 20 cabins, 6 suites; $115–$275; closed Dec.–Mar.). **Restaurants:** In the park: Big Meadows Lodge (mile 51.3; $6–$25), Big Meadows Wayside (mile 51.2; $4–$8; closed Nov.–Mar.), Elkwallow (mile 24.1; $4–$7; closed Nov.–Mar.), Loft Mountain Wayside (mile 79.5; $4–$7; closed Nov.–mid-Apr.), Skyland (mile 41.7; $6–$25; closed Dec.–Mar.). **Groceries & Gear:** Elkwallow (mile 24.1), Big Meadows (mile 51.3), Lewis Mountain (mile 57.5), and Loft Mountain (mile 79.5).

FEES, HOURS & REGULATIONS

Entrance fee: $5 per person, $10 per vehicle Dec.–Feb.; $8 per person, $15 per vehicle Mar.–Nov. Backcountry permit (free) required. Virginia fishing license required. Reservations required for horseback rides (tel. 540/999–2212). No hunting or feeding wild animals. Leashed pets only. No pets on some trails. No bicycles or motorized vehicles on trails. No open fires except in campgrounds and picnic areas. Park open daily. Park headquarters (on U.S. 211 east of Luray) open weekdays 8–4:30. Visitor centers typically open Apr.–Nov., daily 8:30–5. Skyline Dr. closes during bad weather and at night during hunting season.

HOW TO GET THERE

The park is between Front Royal and Waynesboro. The north entrance is on U.S. 340 in Front Royal. Enter the central district via U.S. 211 and U.S. 33. The south entrance is just east of Waynesboro on U.S. 250 and I–64. Closest airports: Charlottesville-Staunton (20 miles), Albemarle (45 miles), Dulles (80 miles).

CONTACTS

Shenandoah National Park (3655 U.S. 211 E, Luray, VA 22835-9036, tel. 540/999–3500, fax 540/999–3601, www.nps.gov/shen). ARA-MARK–Shenandoah National Park (Box 727, Luray, VA 22835, tel. 800/999–4714, www.visitshenandoah.com). Front Royal Chamber of Commerce (104 E. Main St., Front Royal, VA 22630, tel. 540/635–3185 or 800/338–2576, www.frontroyalchamber.com). Harrisonburg-Rockingham Chamber of Commerce (800 Country Club Rd., Harrisonburg, VA 22802, tel. 540/434-3862, www.hrchamber.org). Madison County Chamber of Commerce (110 N. Main St., Suite A, Madison, VA 22727, tel. 540/948–4455, www.madison-va.com). Shenandoah Valley Travel Association (277 W. Old Cross Rd., New Market, VA 22844, tel. 540/740-3132 or 800/847–4878, www.visitshenandoah.org). Waynesboro Chamber of Commerce (503 W. Main St., Waynesboro, VA 22980, tel. 540/942–6600).

Wolf Trap National Park for the Performing Arts

In northeastern Virginia, in Vienna

Wolf Trap is the only national park dedicated to the performing arts. Within the boundaries of the park are 130 acres of rolling hills and woods. The Filene Center is an open-air performing arts pavilion that accommodates 7,000 people, including 3,200 on the lawn, from May to September. Along with the Barns of Wolf Trap, a 352-seat indoor theater in a rebuilt 18th-century barn just outside the park boundary, it hosts performances ranging from opera to dance to rock. The park was authorized on October 15, 1966.

WHAT TO SEE & DO

Attending performances, picnicking. **Facilities:** Performing arts pavilion, outdoor amphitheater, restaurant. Picnic area. **Programs & Events:** Performances (the Barns, year-round). Filene Center performances (May–Sept.), Theatre-in-the Woods performances for children (tel.

703/255–1824, June–Aug.), backstage tour of the Filene Center (tel. 703/255–1827, Oct.–Apr.). **Tips & Hints:** Arrive early for best lawn seats. Filene Center gates open about 1½ hours before performance. Bring a picnic. Busiest July and Aug., least crowded Oct.–Apr.

FOOD & LODGING

⚠ **Camping:** None in park. In Fairfax Station: Burke Lake Park (Ox Rd. off Burke Lake Rd., tel. 703/323–6601; 200 sites; $28; flush toilets, showers; closed late Oct.–mid-Apr.). In Reston: Lake Fairfax Park (Lake Fairfax Dr. off Baron Cameron Ave., tel. 703/471–5415; 136 sites; $28–$45; flush toilets, showers, hookups). 🏨 **Hotels:** None in park. In Tysons Corner: Comfort Inn (1587 Spring Hill Rd., tel. 703/448–8020, www.comfortinn.com; 250 rooms; $90–$190), Tysons Corner Marriott (8028 Leesburg Pike, tel. 703/734–3200, www.marriott.com; 396 rooms, 3 suites; $99–$319). ✕ **Restaurants:** In the park: Ovations (tel. 703/255–4017; $4–$12). In Vienna: Café Renaissance (163 Glyndon St., tel. 703/938–3311; $20–$40; no lunch weekends), Clyde's (8332 Leesburg Pike, tel. 703/734–1901; $10–$20).

FEES & HOURS

Performance fees vary. Tickets available by phone (tel. 703/255–1868), online (www.wolftrap.org), or in person at the Filene Center (weekdays 10–6, weekends noon–5, performance nights until 9).

HOW TO GET THERE

Take Exit 67 off I–66 and Exit 12 off Capital Beltway to reach Rte. 267 west (Dulles Toll Rd.). Follow signs to local exits, pay toll, and exit at the Wolf Trap ramp. The Filene Center is on the right. From Rte. 7 west, turn left on Towlston Rd., go 1 mile to Filene Center on left. From West Falls Church Metro station (Orange line), take Wolf Trap Shuttle (tel. 202/637–7000). Closest airports: Dulles (14 miles), Reagan (14 miles).

CONTACTS

Wolf Trap National Park for the Performing Arts (1551 Trap Rd., Vienna, VA 22182, tel. 703/255–1800, www.nps.gov/wotr). Wolf Trap Foundation (1645 Trap Rd., Vienna, VA 22182, tel. 703/938–2404, www.wolftrap.org.

See Also

Appalachian National Scenic Trail, West Virginia. *Assateague Island National Seashore,* Maryland. *Blue Ridge Parkway,* North Carolina. *Cumberland Gap National Historical Park,* Kentucky. *Harpers Ferry National Historical Park,* West Virginia. *Potomac Heritage National Scenic Trail,* District of Columbia. *Green Springs National Historic Landmark District, Historic Jamestowne National Historic Site, Red Hill Patrick Henry National Memorial, and Shenandoah Valley Battlefields,* in Other National Parklands.

WASHINGTON

Ebey's Landing National Historical Reserve

On Whidbey Island

This rural historic district preserves an unbroken historical record of Puget Sound exploration and settlement from the 19th century to the present. Historic farms, still under cultivation in the prairies of Whidbey Island, reveal land-use patterns unchanged since settlers claimed the land in the 1850s under the Donation Land Claim Act. Two state parks and the Victorian seaport community of Coupeville are also in the reserve. The prairies, seaport, and dramatic coastal beaches and cliffs create a cultural landscape of national significance. The 19,000-acre reserve was authorized on November 10, 1978.

WHAT TO SEE & DO

Bird-watching, boating, hiking, picnicking, scuba diving, self-guided touring of Coupeville and surroundings on foot, by bike, or by car. **Facilities:** Island County Historical Museum (downtown Coupeville), scenic vistas and pullouts, wayside exhibits, historic homes and farmsteads, trails, boat launch area. **Programs & Events:** Self-guided tours; interpretive walks (June–Sept.). **Tips & Hints:** Stop at museum to pick up brochure for self-guided tours of Coupeville and surrounding reserve. Use caution on beach to avoid being caught on headlands during high tides. Busiest July and Aug., least crowded Dec. and Jan.

FOOD, LODGING & SUPPLIES

Camping: In the park: Fort Casey State Park (1280 Engle Rd., Coupeville, tel. 360/678–4519; 35 sites; $12–$36; flush toilets, showers, hookups), Fort Ebey State Park (400 Hill Valley Dr., Coupeville, tel. 360/678–4636; 50 sites; $12–$36; flush toilets, showers, hookups; reservations required). **Hotels:** In the park: Captain Whidbey Inn (2072 Captain Whidbey Inn Rd., Coupeville, tel. 360/678–4097; 32 rooms, 3 cottages; $103–$240). **Restaurants:** In the park: Christopher's (103 N.W. Coveland St., Coupeville, tel. 360/678–5480; $16–$22). **Groceries & Gear:** In the park: Prairie Center Red Apple Market (408 S. Main St., Coupeville, tel. 360/678–5611).

FEES, HOURS & REGULATIONS

Free. No beach fires. Respect property rights of landowners. Hike on designated trails only. Leashed pets only. No collecting driftwood, plants, rocks, or other natural features. State parks open 8–dusk. Island County Historical Museum open May–Sept., daily 10–5; Oct.–Apr., daily 10–4.

HOW TO GET THERE

The reserve, on central Whidbey Island, can be reached by car via Rte. 20 or by the Washington State Ferry system (tel. 206/464–6400; 888/808–7977 in Washington), which provides year-round car and passenger service from Port Townsend and Mukilteo. Closest airports: Oak Harbor (8 miles), Seattle–Tacoma (90 miles).

CONTACTS

Ebey's Landing National Historical Reserve (Box 774, Coupeville, WA 98239, tel. 360/678–6084, www.nps.gov/ebla). Oak Harbor Chamber of Commerce (32630 Rte. 20, Oak Harbor, WA 98277, tel. 360/675–3755, www.oakharborchamber.com).

Fort Vancouver National Historic Site

In southwestern Washington, in Vancouver

This Columbia River site displays rebuilt structures from the 19th-century fort that was a key fur-trading post in North America. More than 20 Hudson's Bay Company posts in the Northwest shipped their furs here between 1825 and 1860 for shipment overseas. The fort attracted American emigrants newly arrived in the Oregon country and played a significant role in the settlement of the Northwest. The fort was established as a Park Service unit in 1947.

WHAT TO SEE & DO

Picnicking, touring fort and blacksmith shop. **Facilities:** Visitor center (Evergreen Blvd.), reconstructed fort, blacksmith shop, carpenter shop, Kaiser Shipyard. Gift shop, picnic shelter and tables. **Programs & Events:** Guided tours or costumed interpreters in buildings (late June–Labor Day), special presentations (June–Sept., weekends). Soldier's Bivouac (late May), Brigade Encampment (June), Campfires and Candlelight Tour (Sept.), Christmas at the Fort (early Dec.). **Tips & Hints:** Go during special events to see the fort at its most vibrant. Go May–Oct. for best weather. Winter is rainy season, spring is school-group season. Busiest May–July, least crowded Dec. and Jan.

FEES, HOURS & REGULATIONS

Entrance fee: $3 per person. No dogs. No smoking. No food or drink inside fort. Park and visitor center open Mon.–Sat. 9–5, Sun. noon–5 during daylight saving time, closes an hour earlier during standard time.

HOW TO GET THERE

From I–5, exit on Mill Plain Blvd. Go east. Turn right on Fort Vancouver Way and left on Evergreen Blvd. to reach visitor center. Closest airport: Portland, OR (6 miles).

CONTACTS

Fort Vancouver National Historic Site (612 E. Reserve St., Vancouver, WA 98661, tel. 360/816–6230 or 800/832–3599, www.nps.gov/fova).

Greater Vancouver Chamber of Commerce (404 E. 15th St., Suite 11, Vancouver, WA 98663, tel. 360/694–2588, www.vancouverusa.com).

Lake Chelan
National Recreation Area

In north-central Washington, near Stehekin

Lake Chelan rests in a trough carved by glaciers in the Cascade Range. The recreation area is part of North Cascades National Park. With a depth of 1,500 feet, it's the nation's third-deepest lake. Although the lake's average width is less than 2 miles, it extends almost 55 miles into the Cascade Mountains. At its deepest point, Lake Chelan drops to 400 feet below sea level. The Stehekin River drainage area and the upper 4 miles of the lake are protected by the recreation area. The 61,958-acre area was established on October 2, 1968.

WHAT TO SEE & DO

Bicycling (rentals), boating (rentals), cross-country skiing, fishing, hiking, horseback riding and pack trips (rentals), hunting, mountain climbing, picnicking, river rafting, snowshoeing (rentals). **Facilities:** Golden West Visitor Center (Stehekin Landing), art gallery, wayside exhibits, self-guided interpretive trails. Book and map sales areas, post office. **Programs & Events:** Interpretive talks, guided walks, campfire programs, Junior Ranger programs. **Tips & Hints:** Be prepared for rapid weather changes. The area is primarily a wilderness park with few activities. Hang all food out of the reach of bears in backcountry. Beware of hazardous stream crossings. Check conditions before starting trips. Busiest July and Aug., least crowded Jan. and Feb.

FOOD, LODGING & SUPPLIES

Camping: 5 campgrounds in the recreation area: Bullion (along the Stehekin River, 10 miles north of the Golden West Visitor Center; 2 walk-in sites; free; pit toilets), Harlequin (on the western bank of the Stehekin River, 5 miles north of the Golden West Visitor Center; 6 walk-in sites; free; pit toilets), High Bridge (on Stehekin River Rd., 11 miles north of the Golden West Visitor Center; 2 walk-in sites; free; pit toilets), Purple Point (near Stehekin Landing; 7 walk-in sites; free; flush toilets), Tumwater (along the Stehekin River, 12 miles north of the Golden West Visitor Center; 2 walk-in sites; free; pit toilets). Camping permits are required for all sites and can be obtained at Lake Chelan or Stehekin. Backcountry and boat-in sites available along Stehekin Valley Road and along Lake Chelan. See also North Cascades National Park and Ross Lake National Recreation Area. **Hotels:** In the park: North Cascades Stehekin Lodge (tel. 509/682–4494; 28 rooms; $118–$194; hike, seaplane, or boat in only). In Stehekin: Stehekin Valley Ranch (Stehekin Valley Rd., tel. 509/682–4677 or 800/536–0745, www.stehekinvalleyranch.com; 14 cabins; $90–$150; closed Oct.–May), Silver Bay Inn & Cabins (Silver Bay Rd., tel. 509/682–2212; 4 units; $145–$375). **Restaurants:** None in park. In Stehekin:

Stehekin Valley Ranch (Stehekin Valley Rd., tel. 509/682–4677 or 800/536–0745, www.stehekinvalleyranch.com; $8–$20; closed Oct.–mid-June). ⚲ **Groceries & Gear:** None in park. In Chelan: Safeway (106 W. Manson Rd., tel. 509/682–2615), Lake Chelan Sports (132 E. Woodin Ave., tel. 509/682–2629).

FEES, HOURS & REGULATIONS

Free. Shuttle bus fee: $6 per zone each way on bus in the Stehekin Valley. Backcountry permit (free) required for all backcountry camping, issued in person at visitor centers. Use of federal docks on lake requires Forest Service dock permit ($5 per day or $40 annual). Washington state fishing and hunting licenses required. Hunting permitted in recreation area only. Leashed pets only. Recreation area open daily. Heavy winter snows restrict travel and close roads. Golden West Visitor Center open seasonally.

HOW TO GET THERE

The main access to Stehekin is by boat (tel. 509/682–2224) or float-plane (tel. 509/682–5555) from the town of Chelan on U.S. 97. Area can be reached by hiking trail in summer. Closest airport: Seattle–Tacoma (177 miles).

CONTACTS

North Cascades National Park Service Complex (810 Rte. 20, Sedro-Woolley, WA 98284, tel. 360/854–7200, 360/854–7365, fax 360/856–1934, www.nps.gov/noca). Lake Chelan Tourist Information (102 E. Johnson St., Lake Chelan, WA 98816, tel. 509/682–3503 or 800/424–3526, www.lakechelan.com).

Lake Roosevelt National Recreation Area

In northeastern Washington, near Grand Coulee

The 1941 damming of the Columbia River, which was part of the Columbia River Basin project, created a 150-mile lake. Named for President Franklin D. Roosevelt, the lake is the largest recreation feature in the recreation area. Boating, fishing, swimming, camping, and hiking are all available, as are tours of Fort Spokane and the dam. Coulee Dam Recreation Area was administered under a cooperative agreement signed in 1946 with the Bureau of Reclamation, Bureau of Indian Affairs, and the U.S. Department of Interior; revised and renegotiated in 1990 by the Bureau of Reclamation, Bureau of Indian Affairs, National Park Service, Colville Confederated Tribes, and the Spokane Tribe of Indians; and renamed in 1997.

WHAT TO SEE & DO

Bird-watching, boating (rentals in Keller Ferry, Fort Spokane, Seven Bays, and Kettle Falls), fishing, hiking, hunting, picnicking, swimming, touring Fort Spokane and Grand Coulee Dam, waterskiing. **Facilities:** Two visitor centers: Fort Spokane Visitor Center and Museum (Miles

Creston Rd., in the southeast portion of the park), Kettle Falls Information Center (U.S. Hwy. 395 and State Hwy. 25, in the central portion of the park); bathhouse, boat dump stations, boat ramps. Picnic areas. **Programs & Events:** Guided canoe trips (mid-June–Labor Day), campfire programs, children's programs, interpretive talks, guided hikes. **Tips & Hints:** Check fluctuating water levels Apr.–June. Wear life preserver while boating. Busiest July and Aug., least crowded Dec. and Jan.

FOOD, LODGING & SUPPLIES

Camping: 27 campgrounds in the park (640 sites and some group sites; $10; some flush toilets, some vault toilets). **Hotels:** None in park. In Grand Coulee: Columbia River Inn (10 Lincoln Ave., tel. 509/633–2100 or 800/633–6421; 35 rooms; $80–$120), Coulee House (110 Roosevelt Way, tel. 509/633–1101 or 800/715–7767, www.columbiariverinn.com; 61 rooms; $99–$169). **Restaurants:** None in park. In Coulee Dam: Melody Restaurant (512 River Dr., tel. 509/633–1151; $8–$15). In Grand Coulee: Flo's Café (316 Spokane Way, tel. 509/633–3216; $4–$7). **Groceries & Gear:** In the park: Coulee Dam Harvest (304 Mead Way, tel. 509/633–2202. In Grand Coulee: Safeway (320 Midway Ave., at Hwy. 155, tel. 509/633–2411).

FEES, HOURS & REGULATIONS

Free. Boat launch permit ($6) required. Washington fishing and hunting permits required. No off-road vehicle use. Recreation area open daily. Fort Spokane Visitor Center open Memorial Day–Labor Day, daily 9–5. Kettle Falls Visitor Information center open daily 9-5.

HOW TO GET THERE

From I–90, the recreation area headquarters in Coulee Dam can be reached via Exit 179, then north on Rte. 17 east, and Rte. 155 north to Coulee Dam. From Spokane, take U.S. 2 west to Rte. 174, then Rte. 155 north to Coulee Dam. Closest airport: Spokane (80 miles).

CONTACTS

Lake Roosevelt National Recreation Area (1008 Crest Dr., Coulee Dam, WA 99116, tel. 509/633–9441, www.nps.gov/laro). Grand Coulee Dam Area Chamber of Commerce (Box 760, 306 Midway, Grand Coulee, WA 99133-0760, tel. 800/268–5332 or 509/633–3074, www.grandcouleedam.org).

Mount Rainier National Park

In the west-central part of the state, near Ashford

This majestic 14,410-foot volcanic mountain, now glacier capped, sports rain forests with 1,000-year-old trees at its base, waterfalls, and subalpine flowering meadows. Native Americans called it "Tahoma," the snowy mountain. The 235,613-acre park is 97% wilderness. It was established on March 2, 1899.

WHAT TO SEE & DO

Backpacking, bird-watching, cross-country skiing (rentals, Longmire), fishing, hiking, horseback riding, mountain climbing, picnicking, snowshoeing, wildflower and wildlife viewing. **Facilities:** 4 visitor centers and museums: Henry M. Jackson Memorial Visitor Center (at Paradise), Ohanapecosh (State Hwy. 123, in the park's southeastern corner), Sunrise (in the park's northeastern corner), Longmire Museum (on the park's southeastern border); White River wilderness information center (on the park's eastern edge), trails. Gift shops, picnic areas. **Programs & Events:** Ranger-led interpretive programs and walks, campfire programs, movies and slide programs (late June–Labor Day), guided snowshoe walks (Paradise, late Dec.–Mar., weekends). **Tips & Hints:** Bring rain gear. Get gas before entering park. Go on weekdays Sept.–early Oct. to avoid crowds, late June–late Aug. for wildflowers in subalpine meadows, Sept.–early Oct. for elk-mating season, Dec.–Apr. for cross-country ski season. Busiest July and Aug., least crowded Dec.–Feb.

FOOD, LODGING & SUPPLIES

⚠ **Camping:** 4 campgrounds in the park: Cougar Rock (State Rte. 706, 14 miles east of Ashford; 173 sites; $12–$15; flush toilets; closed mid-Oct.–May), Mowich Lake (State Hwy. 165, 6 miles from the Mowich entrance; tent camping area; free; vault toilets; closed mid-Oct.–mid-June), Ohanapecosh (State Rte. 123, 4 miles north of State Rte. 12; 188 sites; $12–15; flush toilets; closed mid-Oct.–late May), White River (on the northeast side of the park, 5 miles west of the White River entrance; 112 sites; $12; flush toilets; closed mid-Oct.–late May). Backcountry camping allowed. 🏨 **Hotels:** In the park: National Park Inn (Rte. 706, 10 miles east of Nisqually entrance, tel. 360/569–2275; 25 rooms; $114–$196) ✗ **Restaurants:** In the park: National Park Inn (Rte. 706, tel. 360/569–2411; $11–$24). In Ashford: Alexander's Country Inn (37515 Rte. 706 E., tel. 360/569–2300; $12–$27; closed Mon.–Thurs. Oct.–Apr.). ⛽ **Groceries & Gear:** In the park: General Store at National Park Inn (Rte. 706, Longmire Visitor Complex, tel. 360/569–2411).

FEES, HOURS & REGULATIONS

Entrance fee: $5 per person on foot, bicycle, motorcycle, or bus; $15 per vehicle. Backcountry permit (free) required. Climbers must register with park and pay $30 fee. No bikes on trails. Longmire Museum open daily 9–5. Henry Jackson Visitor Center open Sept.–mid-June, daily 10-6; mid-June–Aug., daily 10–7. Ohanapecosh Visitor Center open late May–Oct., daily 10–5. Sunrise Visitor Center open July–late Sept., daily 9–5. White River Wilderness Information Center open late June-late Sept., daily 9–5.

HOW TO GET THERE

The park can be reached from I–5, U.S. 12, and Rtes. 7, 706, 123, 410, and 165. The park's southwest Nisqually entrance, on Rte. 706, is open daily. Closest airport: Seattle-Tacoma (70 miles).

CONTACT

Mount Rainier National Park (55210 238th Ave. E, Star Route, Ashford, WA 98304-9751, tel. 360/569–2211, www.nps.gov/mora).

North Cascades National Park

In northwestern Washington, near Marblemount

Nearly all wilderness, the 505,000-acre North Cascades National Park contains some of America's most breathtakingly beautiful scenery. Attractions include more than 300 glaciers, as well as waterfalls, rivers, lakes, lush forests, and diverse flora and fauna. The park was established on October 2, 1968.

WHAT TO SEE & DO

Bird and wildlife viewing, backpacking, fishing, hiking, horseback riding (rentals at Stehekin Valley Ranch), mountain climbing (rentals in Stehekin), river running (rentals at Stehekin Valley Ranch). **Facilities:** Visitor center (North Cascades, mile 120 on Rte. 20 near Newhalem), Wilderness Information Center (Marblemount, mile 105 on Rte. 20), Glacier Public Service Center (Glacier, Rte. 542), Headquarters Information Center (Sedro-Woolley on Rte. 20), Golden West Visitor Center (Stehekin Valley Rd., Stehekin). Ranger-led interpretive walks, evening talks, expedition walks, boat tours (late June-Sept.). **Tips & Hints:** Visit mid-June–late Sept. for best weather. Heavy snow and rain, depending on elevation, characterize the North Cascades from fall into spring. Snow is usually off all but the highest trails by late July. Summer storms are common. Be prepared for rain and wind. Take good, light rain gear and tent if you are going into high and remote areas. Warm, waterproof clothing and a tent are virtually mandatory for spring, fall, and winter trips into the backcountry. Hang food and other items with fragrance at least 15 feet up and 5 feet out from tree trunk, away from animals, in backcountry, or check out a bear-proof canister at park facilities. Be cautious crossing streams. Crossing snowfields and glaciers may require special equipment. Fragile vegetation, such as heather, particularly in subalpine areas, is easily damaged by foot traffic. Practice "Leave No Trace" hiking and camping techniques to minimize your impact on wilderness. Busiest July and Aug., least crowded Nov.–Apr.

FOOD, LODGING & SUPPLIES

🏕 **Camping:** See Lake Chelan and Ross Lake national recreation areas. Backcountry camping allowed. 🏨 **Hotels:** In the park: See Lake Chelan and Ross Lake national recreation areas. In Winthrop: Chewuch Inn (223 White Ave., tel. 509/996–3107 or 800/747–3107; 11 rooms, 6 cabins; $95–$200). In Mazama: Freestone Inn (31 Early Winters Dr., tel. 509/996–3906 or 800/639–3809, www.freestoneinn.com; 12 rooms, 5 condos, 15 cabins; $170–$275). ✗ **Restaurants:** In the park: See Lake Chelan National Recreation Area. In Marblemount: Buffalo Run Restaurant (60084 Rte. 20, tel. 360/873–2461; $9–$32). In Winthrop: Arrowleaf Bistro (253 Riverside Ave., tel. 509/996–3919; $20–$32). ⛽ **Groceries & Gear:** None in park. In Newhalem: Skagit General Store (Rte. 20, ½ mile east of turnoff to the North Cascades Visitor Center, tel. 206/386–4489).

FEES, HOURS & REGULATIONS

Free. Permit required (free) for backcountry camping, available at Wilderness Information Center (Marblemount; closed mid-Oct.–May) and National Park Headquarters. Permits issued in person only, up to one day before trip. Shuttle buses operate in Stehekin Valley and serve the south end of the park. No pets on shuttle. Leashed dogs only on Pacific Crest Trail and recreation areas. No pets wilderness national park. No wood fires except in forested, low-elevation areas with iron fire grates. No grazing of horses; bring feed. Washington state fishing license required. No hunting. No mountain or trail bikes or mechanized or motorized equipment on trails. Park open daily. Access limited by snow in winter.

HOW TO GET THERE

The park is divided by North Cascades Highway (Rte. 20), which runs from Burlington (I–5) on the west side to Okanogan on the east side, with branch routes to Baker Lake (at Concrete) and the Cascade River (at Marblemount). Hiking access and roadside views of the northwest corner of the park are available from Rte. 542, east from Bellingham. Two gravel roads enter the park: the Cascade River Rd. from Marblemount and the Stehekin Valley Rd. from Lake Chelan National Recreation Area. The latter does not connect to any roads outside the Stehekin Valley. Closest airport: Seattle–Tacoma (140 miles).

CONTACTS

North Cascades National Park Service Complex (810 Rte. 20, Sedro-Woolley, WA 98284, tel. 360/854–7200, fax 360/856–1934, www.nps.gov/noca). Chelan Chamber of Commerce (Box 216, Chelan, WA 98816, tel. 509/682–2022 or 800/424–3526, www.lakechelan.com). Concrete Chamber of Commerce. Methow Valley Central Reservations (Box 505, Winthrop, WA 98862, tel. 509/996–2148 or 800/422–3048, www.centralreservations.net). Mount Vernon Chamber of Commerce (105 E. Kincaid St., Suite 101, Mount Vernon, WA 98273, tel. 360/428–8547, www.mountvernonchamber.com). Wenatchee Valley Chamber of Commerce (2 S. Mission St., Wenatchee, WA 98801, tel. 509/662–2116 or 800/572–7753, www.wenatchee.org). Winthrop Chamber of Commerce (202 Riverside St., Winthrop, WA 98862, tel. 509/996–2125, www.winthropwashington.com). Also see Lake Chelan and Ross Lake national recreation areas.

Olympic National Park

In northwestern Washington, near Port Angeles

Olympic encompasses three distinctly different ecosystems—rugged glacier-capped mountains, more than 73 miles of wild Pacific coast, and magnificent stands of old-growth and temperate rain forest. About 95% of the park is designated wilderness, so these diverse ecosystems are largely pristine in character. Isolated for eons by glacial ice, the waters of Puget Sound, and the Strait of Juan de Fuca, the Olympic

Peninsula has developed its own distinct array of plants and animals. Eight kinds of plants and 15 kinds of animals are found on the peninsula that live nowhere else in the world. Mount Olympus National Monument was proclaimed in 1909, transferred to the Park Service in 1933, renamed and redesignated in 1938, and designated a Biosphere Reserve in 1976 and a World Heritage Site in 1981.

WHAT TO SEE & DO

Backpacking, bird and wildlife viewing, fishing, hiking, mountain climbing, picnicking, scenic drives, skiing, snowshoeing, swimming. **Facilities:** 3 visitor centers: Port Angeles, Hurricane Ridge, and Hoh Rain Forest. 7 ranger stations, 168 miles of roads, 600 miles of trails. **Programs & Events:** Ranger-led programs and activities (late June–Sept.); ranger-led snowshoe walks (Dec.–Mar., weekends); one- to three-day field seminars on natural history; nature photography; kayak, canoe, and backpacking outings (Apr.–Oct., tel. 360/928–3720, www.naturebridge.org). **Tips & Hints:** Drive to Hurricane Ridge for high country and mountain vistas; Hoh Rain Forest, where 12 feet of rain a year creates huge trees and greenery; and Rialto, Kalaloch, or Ruby Beach for view of Pacific beaches. Come prepared for a variety of weather. Bring rain gear and layered clothing. Buy topographic maps for most hikes (tel. 360/565–2195). Busiest Aug. and Sept., least crowded Jan. and Feb.

FOOD, LODGING & SUPPLIES

🐾 **Camping:** 16 campgrounds in the park (tel. 360/565–3130; about 925 sites; $10–$18; some flush toilets, some pit toilets). Backcountry camping allowed. 🏨 **Hotels:** In the park: Kalaloch Lodge (157151 Hwy. 101, tel. 360/962–2271; 15 rooms, 44 cabins; $200–$348), Lake Crescent Lodge (416 Lake Crescent Rd., tel. 360/928–3211; 52 rooms, 18 cabins; $108–$220; closed Nov.–Apr.). In Quinault: Lake Quinault Lodge (South Shore Rd., tel. 360/288–2900 or 800/562–6672; 92 rooms, 1 suite; $90–$230). ✕ **Restaurants:** In the park: Kalaloch Lodge (U.S. 101, tel. 360/962–2271; $8–$22), Lake Crescent Lodge (416 Lake Crescent Rd., tel. 360/928–3211; $9–$16). In Sequim: Three Crabs (11 Three Crabs Rd., tel. 360/683–4264, www.the3crabs.com; $12–$39). ⛁ **Groceries & Gear:** In Sequim: Safeway (680 W. Washington St., tel. 360/681–2905).

FEES, HOURS & REGULATIONS

Entrance fee: $5 per person on bicycle or bus; $15 per vehicle. RV sewage dump station fee: $5 per use. Ozette parking fee: $1 per day. Backcountry permit ($5–$7, tel. 360/565–3100) required. Stay on trails and use existing wilderness campsites. Park open daily. Hours vary at visitor center in Port Angeles; may be closed Tues. and Wed. in winter. Hours vary at Hurricane Ridge and Hoh River Rain Forest visitor centers.

HOW TO GET THERE

The park, which occupies the center of the Olympic Peninsula and a 73-mile strip along the Pacific Coast, can be reached from the Seattle–Tacoma area via U.S. 101 or by ferry (www.wsdot.wa.gov/ferries). For car and passenger ferry service between Victoria, British Columbia, and Port Angeles, call 360/457–4491. For passenger ferry service in summer between Victoria and Port Angeles, call 360/452–8088. Closest airport: Fairchild International in Port Angeles (20 miles).

CONTACTS

Olympic National Park (600 E. Park Ave., Port Angeles, WA 98362-6798, tel. 360/565–3130, www.nps.gov/olym). North Olympic Peninsula Visitor & Convention Bureau (Box 670, Port Angeles, WA 98362, tel. 360/452–8552 or 800/942–4042, www.olympicpeninsula.org).

Ross Lake National Recreation Area

In northwestern Washington, near Marblemount

The 118,000-acre recreation area provides the corridor for the popular North Cascades Highway (Rte. 20). It contains three lakes—12,000-acre Ross Lake, 910-acre Diablo Lake, and 210-acre Gorge Lake. The area was established on October 2, 1968, as part of North Cascades National Park Complex.

WHAT TO SEE & DO

Bird and wildlife viewing, boating (rentals, Ross Lake Resort), canoeing, fishing, hiking, hunting, picnicking, river rafting, rock climbing, scenic drives. **Facilities:** North Cascades Visitor Center (Rte. 20 near Newhalem), North Cascades Environmental Learning Center (Diablo Lake, tel. 206/526–2560), amphitheaters, trails, wayside exhibits, boat launching ramps. Book and map sales area. **Programs & Events:** Interpretive talks, guided walks, campfire programs, Junior Ranger programs. **Tips & Hints:** Be prepared for rapid changes in weather. The surrounding area is primarily a wilderness park with few activities. Hang all food out of the reach of bears. Check stream conditions before starting trips. Crossing snowfields may require special equipment. Go July–Oct. for best weather. Visit in Dec. and Jan. for eagle viewing in the upper Skagit Valley. Busiest July and Aug., least crowded Dec. and Jan.

FOOD, LODGING & SUPPLIES

Camping: 4 campgrounds in the park: Colonial Creek (Rte. 20 at Diablo Lake; 130 sites; $12; flush toilets; closed Oct.–mid-May), Goodell Creek (Rte. 20, ½ mile west of Newhalem; 21 tent sites; $10), Hozomeen (access from the north; 152 walk-in tent sites; free; vault toilets; closed Nov.–May), Newhalem Creek (Rte. 20 near Newhalem; 111 sites; $12; flush toilets; closed mid-Oct.–mid-May). Backcountry camping allowed. **Hotels:** In the park: Ross Lake Resort (tel. 206/386–4437, www.rosslakeresort.com; 15 cabins; $122–$261; walk in or boat in only; open mid-June–Sept.). **Restaurants:** None in park. See Lake Chelan National Recreation Area and North Cascades National Park. **Groceries & Gear:** None in park. See Lake Chelan National Recreation Area and North Cascades National Park.

FEES, HOURS & REGULATIONS

Free. Permits required (free) for all backcountry and boat-in camping available at Wilderness Information Center (tel. 360/854–7245, May–Oct.) and National Park Headquarters (tel. 360/854–7200, Nov.–Apr.). Permits issued in person only, up to one day before trip. Washington state fishing and hunting licenses required. Leashed pets only on trails. Recreation area open daily. North Cascades Visitor Center open May–Oct., daily 9–5. Wilderness Information Center (Marblemount) open Sun.–Thurs. 8–4:30, Fri. and Sat. 7–6. Part of Rte. 20 closes in winter. Exact opening and closing dates of highway depend on snow and avalanche conditions.

HOW TO GET THERE

Access to the area is via Rte. 20 from Burlington to the west and Winthrop to the east. The north end of Ross Lake is reached by a 39-mile gravel road exiting from Trans-Canada Rte. 1 near Hope, BC, following the Silver-Skagit Rd. There is no road access from Rte. 20 to the south end of Ross Lake. Closest airport: Seattle–Tacoma (140 miles).

CONTACTS

North Cascades National Park Service Complex (810 Rte. 20, Sedro Woolley, WA 98284, tel. 360/854–7200, fax 360/856–1934, www.nps.gov/noca). Concrete Chamber of Commerce (45770 Main St., Concrete, WA 98237, tel. 360/853-8784, www.concrete-wa.com). Sedro-Woolley Chamber of Commerce (714 Metcalf St., Sedro-Woolley, WA 98284, tel. 360/855–1841, www.sedro-woolley.com).

San Juan Island National Historical Park

On San Juan Island

Commemorated in this park are the 1853–72 events relating to the settlement of the Oregon boundary dispute between the United States and Great Britain. In 1859, military forces from both countries confronted each other in a crisis precipitated by the nations' dual claims to the island and the death of a Hudson's Bay Company pig at the hands of an American farmer. On view are remains of American and British camps. The island is also home to glacial landscapes with grasslands, forests, beaches, tide pools, and lagoons. The park was authorized in 1966.

WHAT TO SEE & DO

Beachcombing, hiking, picnicking, walking. **Facilities:** 2 contact stations with interpretive exhibits (American Camp, 6 miles from Friday Harbor; and English Camp, off West Valley Rd., between Yachthaven and Roche Harbor roads), beaches, trails. Sales outlets, picnic areas with tables, fire pits and grates. **Programs & Events:** Guided walks (June–Aug.), historical reenactments (June–Aug., Sat.), cultural and natural-history programs (June–Aug., Fri.–Sun.). **Tips & Hints:** Go in late spring for wildflowers, summer for whale-watching and good weather, winter for migrating birds. Busiest July and Aug., least crowded Nov. and Dec.

FOOD, LODGING & SUPPLIES

Camping: None in park. In Friday Harbor: San Juan County Park (50 San Juan Park Dr., tel. 360/378–8420, www.sanjuanco.com/parks; 34 sites; $32–$45; flush toilets), Snug Harbor Resort (1997 Mitchell Bay Rd., tel. 360/378–4762, www.snugresort.com; 10 sites; $20–$30; flush toilets). **Hotels:** None in park. In Friday Harbor: Friday Harbor House (130 West St., tel. 360/378–8455, www.fridayharborhouse. com; 23 rooms; $225–$325), Birdrock Hotel (35 First St., tel. 360/378–5848 or 800/352–2632, www.birdrockhotel.com; 15 rooms; $127–$297). **Restaurants:** None in park. In Friday Harbor: Duck Soup Inn (50 Duck Soup La., tel. 360/378–4878, www.ducksoupinn.com; $19–$38), Friday Harbor House Restaurant (130 West St., tel. 360/378–8453, www.fridayharborhouse.com; $22–$34). **Groceries & Gear:** None in park. In Friday Harbor: King's Market (100 Spring St. W., tel. 360/378–4505).

FEES, HOURS & REGULATIONS

Free. Permits required (free) for horseback riding. Washington state fishing license required. Shellfish–seaweed license required for clamming. No hunting or collecting. Leashed pets only. Bikes permitted on Mitchell Hill trail network; otherwise bikes and motorized vehicles restricted to roads and parking areas. Park grounds open daily dawn–11 PM. American Camp contact station open Memorial Day–Labor Day, daily 8:30–5; Labor Day–Memorial Day, Thurs.–Sun. 8:30–4:30. English Camp contact station open Memorial Day–Labor Day, daily 8:30–5.

HOW TO GET THERE

The island is accessible by Washington State Ferries from Anacortes (83 miles north of Seattle) or from Sidney, BC (15 miles north of Victoria). Closest airports: Friday Harbor (3½ miles), Seattle–Tacoma (121 miles).

CONTACTS

San Juan Island National Historical Park (Box 429, Friday Harbor, WA 98250, tel. 360/378–2240, ext. 2233, www.nps.gov/sajh). San Juan Island Chamber of Commerce (Box 98, Friday Harbor, WA 98250–0098, tel. 360/378–5240, www.sanjuanisland.org).

Whitman Mission National Historic Site

In southeastern Washington, near Walla Walla

Marcus and Narcissa Whitman founded a Protestant mission here in 1836 to convert the Cayuse people to Christianity and provide a way station for Oregon Trail pioneers. In 1847, a measles epidemic killed half the Cayuse. The survivors blamed Marcus Whitman for his inability to cure the measles and killed him, his wife, and 11 others on November 29, 1847. Another 50 hostages were ransomed a month later by agents from the Hudson's Bay Company. The site was authorized in 1936 and renamed in 1963.

WHAT TO SEE & DO

Picnicking, touring original building sites, walking a section of the Oregon Trail, visiting mass grave of Whitman and others. **Facilities:** Visitor center with 24-minute film, trails, wayside exhibits. Book sales area, picnic area with tables. **Programs & Events:** Cultural demonstrations (June–Aug., weekends), ranger walks and talks (mid-June-Aug.). **Tips & Hints:** Wear walking shoes. The best times to visit are mid-summer and fall. Busiest May and June, least crowded Dec. and Jan.

FOOD, LODGING & SUPPLIES

Camping: None in park. In College Place: Country Estate (938 Scenic View Dr., tel. 509/529–5442; 4 sites; $25; showers, toilets, hookups). Near Touchet: Pierce's Green Valley RV Park (24676 W. U.S. 12, tel. 509/394–2387, www.piercesgreenvalley.com; 40 sites; $10–$30; vault toilets, hookups). **Hotels:** None in park. In Walla Walla: La Quinta Inn & Suites (520 N. Second Ave., tel. 509/525–2522, www.lq.com; 61 rooms, 5 suites; $79–$139), Marcus Whitman Hotel (6 W. Rose St., tel. 509/525–2200, www.marcuswhitmanhotel.com; 127 rooms, 22 suites; $159–$275). **✕ Restaurants:** None in park. In Walla Walla: Backstage Bistro (230 E. Main St., tel. 509/526–0690; $15–$25), South Fork Grill (1129 S. Second Ave., tel. 509/522–4777; $19–$32; closed Mon.). **Groceries & Gear:** None in park. In College Place: Walmart Superstore (1700 S.E. Meadowbrook Blvd., tel. 509/525–3468).

FEES, HOURS & REGULATIONS

Free. No hunting. Leashed pets only. Walk bicycles on trails. Park open daily dawn–dusk. Visitor center open June–Aug., daily 8–6; Sept.-May, daily 8–4:30, hours may vary.

HOW TO GET THERE

7 miles west of Walla Walla, off U.S. 12. Closest airport: Walla Walla.

CONTACTS

Whitman Mission National Historic Site (328 Whitman Mission Rd., Walla Walla, WA 99362, tel. 509/522–6360, fax 509/522–6355, www.nps.gov/whmi). Walla Walla Area Chamber of Commerce (Box 644, Walla Walla, WA 99362, tel. 509/525–0850, www.wwchamber.com).

See Also

Klondike Gold Rush National Historical Park, Alaska. *Nez Perce National Historical Park,* Idaho. *Lewis & Clark National Historic Trail, Oregon National Scenic Trail, and Pacific Crest National Scenic Trail,* in Other National Parklands.

WEST VIRGINIA

Appalachian
National Scenic Trail   🦆🦆

In the Appalachian Mountains, from Katahdin, ME, to Springer Mountain, GA

The 2,176-mile trail was the nation's first designated national scenic trail. The federally protected trail corridor protects the habitats of hundreds of rare, threatened, and endangered species and preserves some of the East Coast's finest remaining wildlands. Topography along the trail ranges from the rugged White Mountains in New Hampshire to the rolling farmlands of Pennsylvania's Cumberland Valley to the high-elevation grassy balds of Roan Mountain, Tennessee. The trail was built by volunteers and completed in 1937. It's maintained and managed primarily by volunteers, whose efforts are coordinated by the nonprofit Appalachian Trail Conservancy. It became a national scenic trail in 1968.

WHAT TO SEE & DO

Backpacking, hiking. **Facilities:** Two visitor centers: Harpers Ferry Appalachian Trail Visitor Center (799 Washington St., Harpers Ferry, WV, open weekdays 9–5, weekends and holidays 9–4), Boiling Springs Appalachian Trail Information Center (4 E. First St., Boiling Springs, PA, open weekdays 9–4). Trail facilities are primitive: 3-sided overnight shelters, tent pads, pit toilets. Map/guidebook sales areas. **Tips & Hints:** Carry map, compass, whistle (3 blasts are an international call for help), flashlight (with extra batteries), sharp knife, fire starter (a candle, for instance), waterproof matches, first-aid kit, extra food, water (and some means to treat naturally occurring water), warm clothing and rain gear, and a heavy-duty garbage bag (to serve as an emergency shelter). Busiest June–Aug., least crowded Nov.–Apr.

LODGING

⛺ **Camping:** In the park: 260 three-sided shelters (first come, first served) available about a day's hike apart along the trail; backcountry camping allowed. 🏨 **Hotels:** In the park: Appalachian Mountain Club Cabins (Gorham, NH, between Franconia Notch and Wildcat Ridge, tel. 603/466–2727; 8 huts; $40 self-service, $100 full service; full-service cabins closed Nov.–Feb.). ✗ **Restaurants:** None in park. ⛲ **Groceries & Gear:** None in park.

FEES, HOURS & REGULATIONS

Free. Overnight camping permits or user registration required at Great Smoky Mountains and Shenandoah national parks (see separate entries) and parts of the White Mountain National Forest in New Hampshire and Baxter State Park in Maine. No motor vehicles, bicycles, or mountain bikes on off-road sections. No horses or pack animals except in part of Great Smoky Mountains National Park. Leashed dogs only. Hunting is allowed on many of the lands through which the trail passes. No restrooms. Trail open year-round.

HOW TO GET THERE

The trail has more than 500 access points along its 2,181-mile length from Katahdin, Maine, to Springer Mountain, Georgia. It passes through Maine, New Hampshire, Vermont, Massachusetts, Connecticut, New York, New Jersey, Pennsylvania, Maryland, West Virginia, Virginia, Tennessee, North Carolina, and Georgia.

CONTACTS

Appalachian Trail Conservancy (799 Washington St., Harpers Ferry, WV 25425, tel. 304/535–6331, fax 304/535–2667, www.appalachiantrail. org).

Bluestone
National Scenic River

In southern West Virginia, between Hinton and Princeton

This scenic river preserves relatively unspoiled land in southern West Virginia, contains natural and historic features of the Appalachian plateau, and offers excellent warm-water fishing, hiking, boating, and scenery in its lower 11 miles. The river was authorized on October 26, 1988.

WHAT TO SEE & DO

Bicycling, canoeing, fishing, hiking, horseback riding, hunting, white-water boating. **Facilities:** Bluestone Trail, 8 miles. **Programs & Events:** Guided hikes, interpretive programs (June–Nov.). **Tips & Hints:** Intermediate white-water boating skill required. The Bluestone is frequently too high or too low for boating. Busiest July and Aug., least crowded Jan. and Feb.

FOOD, LODGING & SUPPLIES

Camping: None in park. In Bluestone State Park: Meador Campground (off Rte. 20, at mouth of Bluestone River, tel. 304/466–2805; 122 sites; $9–$23; flush toilets, showers, hookups). In Pipestem Resort State Park: Pipestem Resort Campground (off Rte. 20, 12 miles south of Hinton, tel. 304/466–1800; 82 sites; $21–$27; flush toilets, showers, hookups). **Hotels:** None in park. In Pipestem Resort State Park: McKeever Lodge (off Rte. 20, tel. 304/466–1800; 113 rooms; $77–$172), Mountain Creek Lodge (off Rte. 20, tel. 304/466–1800; 30 rooms; $68–$87; accessible by tramway only). **X Restaurants:** None in park. In Pipestem Resort State Park: Bluestone Dining Room (McKeever Lodge, tel. 304/466–1800 Ext. 368; $7–$27), Mountain Creek Dining Room (Mountain Creek Lodge, tel. 304/466–1800 Ext. 387; $12–$34). **Groceries & Gear:** None in park. In Hinton: Kroger's (308 Stokes Dr., tel. 304/466–4888). In Fayetteville: Ultimate Rafting (Gateway Rd., tel. 800/470–7238).

FEES, HOURS & REGULATIONS

Free. No hunting or trapping in state park, but allowed in National River during state hunting seasons. Open 24 hours.

HOW TO GET THERE

The scenic river is south of Hinton and northeast of Princeton. Access is through the Bluestone and Pipestem Resort state parks on Rte. 20 (May–Oct.). A tram that can transport boats provides access to the river from Pipestem Resort State Park. Closest airport: Charleston (95 miles).

CONTACTS

Bluestone National Scenic River (Box 246, Glen Jean, WV 25846, tel. 304/465–0508, www.nps.gov/blue). West Virginia State Chamber of Commerce (90 McCorkle Ave. SW, South Charleston, WV 25303, tel. 800/225–5982, www.callwva.com).

Gauley River
National Recreation Area

In southern West Virginia, near Summersville

About 25 miles of free-flowing Gauley River and 6 miles of the Meadow River have Class V+ rapids and are some of the most challenging white-water boating sites in the East. The area was authorized on October 26, 1988.

WHAT TO SEE & DO

Fishing, hunting, kayaking, trapping, white-water boating. **Facilities:** Visitor information available at Canyon Rim Visitor Center; see New River Gorge National River. U.S. Army Corps of Engineers visitor center at Summerville Dam. **Programs & Events:** Ranger-led hikes (Sept. and Oct.), Civil War battle reenactments (every other Sept., at Carnifex Ferry Battlefield State Park). **Tips & Hints:** Most land along the Gauley River is privately owned. Go to Carnifex Ferry Battlefield State Park for scenic overlook and to access hiking trails. Go weekends mid-Sept.–mid-Oct. for rafting season, which depends on releases from Summerville Dam. Gauley River has Class V+ rapids and requires expert boating skills or travel with licensed white-water outfitter. Busiest Sept. and Oct., least crowded Dec. and Jan.

FOOD, LODGING & SUPPLIES

🏕 **Camping:** In the park: Gauley Tailwaters (18 sites; free; vault toilets, no water). In Clifftop: Babcock State Park (Rte. 41, tel. 304/438–3004; 52 sites; $20–$23; flush toilets, showers, hookups). In Mount Nebo: Battle Run Campground (Rte. 129 off U.S. 19, tel. 304/872–3459; 117 sites; $16–$24; flush toilets, showers, hookups; closed mid-Oct.–Apr.). 🏨 **Hotels:** None in park. In Clifftop: Babcock State Park (Rte. 41, tel. 304/438–3004; 28 cabins; $54–$123). In Ansted: Hawk's Nest (177 E. Main St., tel. 304/658–5212; 31 rooms; $77–$110). ✖ **Restaurants:** None in park. In Ansted: Hawk's Nest (177 E. Main St., tel. 304/658–

5212; $10–$20). In Canvas: Feed Box Saloon (Grove's Rd./Rte. 39, tel. 304/872–1603; $14–$23). ⚮ **Groceries & Gear:** None in park. In Oak Hill: Kroger's (411 Mall Rd., tel. 304/469–2921).

FEES, HOURS & REGULATIONS
Free. West Virginia state license required for fishing and hunting. Open 24 hours.

HOW TO GET THERE
The recreation area is between Summersville Dam and the town of Swiss. Access is via Rte. 129 at the Summersville Dam, off U.S. 19. Other access points include Carnifex Ferry Battlefield State Park, off Rte. 129, and Swiss Rd., off Rte. 39. Closest airport: Charleston (75 miles).

CONTACTS
Gauley River National Recreation Area (Box 246, Glen Jean, WV 25846, tel. 304/465–0508, www.nps.gov/gari). West Virginia State Chamber of Commerce (90 McCorkle Ave. SW, South Charleston, WV 25303, tel. 800/225–5982, www.callwva.com).

Harpers Ferry National Historical Park

In eastern West Virginia, in Harpers Ferry

John Brown's raid on Harpers Ferry in 1859 thrust this small West Virginia town into national prominence. Located at the scenic confluence of the Shenandoah and Potomac Rivers, the park includes 3,647 acres in the states of West Virginia, Virginia, and Maryland. A variety of museums, exhibits, and trails illustrate the six nationally significant themes interpreted here—natural environment, industry, the Brown raid, the Civil War, African American history, and transportation—and how they are connected. Harpers Ferry was designated as a national monument in 1944 and changed to a national historical park in 1968.

WHAT TO SEE & DO
Fishing, hiking, picnicking, rock climbing, visiting museums and exhibits. **Facilities:** Visitor center (Cavalier Heights District) and visitor information center (Lower Town District); museums, exhibits, trails with wayside exhibits. Bookstore, picnic area. **Programs & Events:** Ranger-guided tours (June 15–Aug. 15), concerts (June–Sept.), living-history programs. Independence Celebration, Christmas Celebration. **Tips & Hints:** Stay on trails. Go in fall for foliage. Busiest Aug. and Oct., least crowded Jan. and Feb.

FOOD, LODGING & SUPPLIES
⚮ **Camping:** None in park. In Harpers Ferry: KOA (near park entrance, U.S. 340, tel. 304/535–6895, www.koa.com; 270 sites, 36 cabins, 4 lodges; $30–$42, $50–$135 cabins, $159 lodges; flush toilets, showers, hookups). 🛏 **Hotels:** None in park. In Harpers Ferry: Quality

425

Hotel Conference Center (4328 William L. Wilson Freeway, tel. 304/535–6302, www.qualityinn.com; 100 rooms; $98–$189). ✖ **Restaurants:** None in park. In Harpers Ferry: Anvil (1290 W. Washington St., tel. 304/535–2582; $15–$25). ⚲ **Groceries & Gear:** None in park. In Charles Town: Walmart (96 Patrick Henry Way, tel. 304/728–2720).

FEES, HOURS & REGULATIONS

Entrance fee: $5 per person for on foot or bicycle, $10 per vehicle. Rock-climbing registration required at ranger station. West Virginia, Maryland, or Virginia state fishing license required. No hunting. No bikes or motorized or mechanized equipment on trails. Leashed pets only. Park open daily. Visitor center open daily 8–5.

HOW TO GET THERE

In the eastern panhandle of West Virginia, 65 miles northwest of Washington, DC, and 20 miles southwest of Frederick, MD, via U.S. 340. Closest airport: Dulles (50 miles).

CONTACTS

Harpers Ferry National Historical Park (Box 65, Harpers Ferry, WV 25425, tel. 304/535–6223, fax 304/535–6244, www.nps.gov/hafe). Jefferson County Chamber of Commerce (29 Keyes Ferry Rd., Suite 200, Charles Town, WV 25414, tel. 304/725–2055, www.jeffersoncountywvchamber.org).

New River Gorge National River

In southern West Virginia, from Hinton to Hawks Nest

New River protects 53 miles of free-flowing waterway. The 73,000-acre park and surroundings are rich in cultural and natural history and contain an abundance of scenic and recreational opportunities. The New River is one of the most renowned fishing streams in the state and offers premier white-water boating. The river, one of the oldest on the continent, has cut a deep gorge that exposes rocks 330 million years old and harbors rare plants. The site was authorized on November 10, 1978.

WHAT TO SEE & DO

Fishing, hiking, horseback riding, hunting, mountain biking (rentals in Fayetteville), picnicking, recreational climbing, white-water boating. **Facilities:** 4 visitor centers: Canyon Rim (U.S. 19, 2 miles north of Fayetteville), Thurmond Depot (Rte. 25, 7 miles from the Glen Jean exit of U.S. 19), Grandview (Rte. 9, 6 miles north of I–64 Exit 129B), Sandstone (at I–64 Exit 139); amphitheater, boardwalk, hiking trails. Bookstores, picnic shelters, tables, fire grates. **Programs & Events:** Ranger-led walks, hikes, videos. Guided walks, hikes, and mountain bike trips (all May–Oct.). New River Train (Oct., tel. 304/453–1451 or 866/639–7487), New River Gorge Bridge Pedestrian Day (3rd Sat. in Oct.). **Tips & Hints:** The park is very long and narrow, with several access points into the gorge. Book white-water rafting trips on Sundays or weekdays to get discounts and avoid Saturday crowds. Narrow, winding, one-lane roads require driving with passenger-side wheels on the shoulder when meeting oncoming traffic. Some park roads are unsuitable for large recreational vehicles. Stay off CSX railroad property that runs through park. Go Apr., May, Sept., and Oct. for cool, crisp weather; mid-May for Grandview rhododendron blooms; late June–early July for wild rhododendron blooms; Apr.–Sept. for peak bird migrations; mid-Oct. for peak fall foliage. Busiest July and Aug., least crowded Jan. and Feb.

FOOD, LODGING & SUPPLIES

🐾 **Camping:** 8 campgrounds in the park: Army Camp (in the middle of the park; 11 sites; free; pit toilets, no water), Brooklyn (northern end of the park near Babcock State Park; 3 sites; free; no water, pit toilets), Gauley Tailwaters (in Gauley River National Recreation Area below the dam; 18 drive-in sites for tents and RVs; free; no water, pit toilets), Glade Creek (northwest of the Sandstone Visitor Center; 6 sites; free; pit toilets, no water), Grandview Sandbar (east of Army Camp; 16 sites; free; pit toilets, no water), Stone Cliff (south of the Thurmond Historic District; 7 sites; free; pit toilets, no water, alcohol prohibited), Thayer (near Silo Rapids; 4 sites; free; pit toilets, no water), War Ridge (8 sites; free; pit toilets, no water), Brooklyn (north end of the park, near Babcock State Park; 3 sites; free; pit toilets, no water). Backcountry camping allowed. See Bluestone National Scenic River. ⛺ **Hotels:** None in park. See Bluestone National Scenic River. ✖ **Restaurants:** None in park. See Bluestone National Scenic River. 🛒 **Groceries & Gear:** None in park. See Bluestone National Scenic River.

FEES, HOURS & REGULATIONS

Free. Picnic shelter and group camping area require reservation and fees (tel. 304/465–0508 Burnwood and Dunglen; tel. 304/465–6555 Grandview). West Virginia state fishing and hunting license required. Contact park about no-hunting zones. No trapping. No recreational climbing at Grandview. Leashed pets only. Swimming and wading not recommended because of strong currents and rocks. No alcohol at park headquarters, Dunglen, Grandview, and Stonecliff. Bikes on designated trails only. Park open daily. Canyon Rim Visitor Center open daily 9–5. Thurmond Depot Visitor Center open Memorial Day–Labor Day, daily 10–5; intermittent weekend hours in spring and fall. Grandview Visitor Center open Memorial Day–Labor Day, daily noon–5. Sandstone Visitor Center open daily 9–5.

HOW TO GET THERE

The river is one hour (65 miles) east of Charleston and 20 minutes (30 miles) from Beckley. It's accessible from the West Virginia Tpke., I–64 and 77, and U.S. 19 and 60. Closest airports: Beckley (30 miles), Charleston (65 miles).

CONTACTS

New River Gorge National River (Box 246, Glen Jean, WV 25846, tel. 304/465–0508, fax 304/465–0591, www.nps.gov/neri). Fayette County

Chamber of Commerce (310 W. Oyler Ave., Oak Hill, WV 25901, tel. 304/465–5617 or 800/927–0263, www.fayettecounty.com). Southern West Virginia Convention & Visitor Bureau, (1406 Harper Rd., Beckley, WV 25801, tel. 800/847–4898, fax 304/252–2252, www.visitwv.com or www.visitwv.org). West Virginia State Chamber of Commerce (90 McCorkle Ave. SW, South Charleston, WV 25303, tel. 800/225–5982, www.callwva.com). West Virginia Travel Council (Box 50312, 2101 Washington St. E, Charleston, WV 25305-0317, tel. 800/225–5982, www.visitwv.com).

See Also

Chesapeake & Ohio Canal National Historical Park, Maryland. *National Coal Heritage Area,* in Other National Parklands.

WISCONSIN

Apostle Islands
National Lakeshore

On the south shore of Lake Superior, 90 miles east of Duluth, MN

Twenty-one islands in the world's largest freshwater lake, plus 12 miles of mainland shoreline, make up this park. There are pristine beaches, sandstone cliffs, sea caves, wetlands, and dense forests to explore. Native Americans, loggers, quarrymen, farmers, and commercial fishermen left their marks on the islands—today you can see their old quarries and a few old cabins. Six historic light stations host exhibits about the region's maritime history. Waterside campsites throughout the islands, some accessible only by kayak, make for a true back-to-nature experience. The park was established on September 26, 1970.

WHAT TO SEE & DO

Beachcombing, boating, camping, cross-country skiing on frozen Lake Superior, fishing, hiking, hunting, kayaking (rentals in Bayfield), picnicking, sailing (rentals in Bayfield), scuba diving, swimming, touring lighthouses. **Facilities:** 2 visitor centers: Bayfield Visitor Center (415 Washington Ave., Bayfield) and Little Sand Bay Visitor Center (13 miles north of Bayfield); interpretive exhibits, movies, guided and self-guided tours, hiking trails, docks. Book and map sales. **Programs & Events:** Daily lighthouse lens talks (on request) at Bayfield Visitor Center, guided lighthouse tours (mid-June–mid-Sept.), guided hikes, campfire programs (mid-June–Labor Day). **Tips & Hints:** Monitor marine forecasts; weather can change dramatically on short notice. Water is available from wells on two islands. Go May and June for best flowers, July and Aug. for moderate waves, May and Sept. for bird migrations, Feb. and Mar. for over-ice travel to islands. Take insect repellent, especially June–Aug. Busiest July and Aug., no access to the islands in Dec. and Jan.

FOOD, LODGING & SUPPLIES

🔺 **Camping:** In the park: 64 backcountry and group sites are available on 19 of the 21 islands. On Madeline Island: Big Bay State Park (tel. 888/947–2757; 60 sites; $15–$17; flush toilets, showers). 🏨 **Hotels:** None in Park. In Bayfield: Bayfield Inn (20 Rittenhouse Ave., tel. 800/382–0995, www.bayfieldinn.com; 21 rooms; $125–$215). ✗ **Restaurants:** None in park. In Bayfield: Maggie's Restaurant (257 Manypenny Ave., tel. 715/779–5641; $7–$12), Old Rittenhouse Inn (301 Rittenhouse Ave., tel. 715/779–5111; $5–$55; no lunch Nov.–May). ⛪ **Groceries & Gear:** None in park. In Bayfield: Andy's IGA (213 Rittenhouse Ave., tel. 715/779–5415), Wild by Nature (200 Rittenhouse Ave., tel. 715/779–5075).

FEES, HOURS & REGULATIONS

Free. Parking fee at Meyers Beach ($3). Lighthouse tours at Raspberry Island ($3 per person or $8 for family). Camping permits ($10; tel. 715/779–3397) required. Overnight docking fee ($10–$20). Wisconsin state hunting license and fishing license with Great Lakes trout stamp required. Scuba permit (free) required. Leashed pets only. No bikes on trails. No motorized vehicles on islands. No metal detectors. No personal watercraft or floatplanes. No snowmobiles, except for use for fishing, hunting, trapping, and other specific purposes, on Lake Superior. No hunting Memorial Day–Labor Day. Park open daily. Bayfield Visitor Center open Memorial Day–Labor Day, daily 8–5; Labor Day–Memorial Day, weekdays 8–4:30. Little Sand Bay Visitor Center open mid-June–Labor Day, daily 9–5.

HOW TO GET THERE

The visitor center is one block from Rte. 13 in Bayfield, WI; 23 miles north of Ashland, WI; and 90 miles east of Duluth, MN. Closest airport: Duluth.

CONTACTS

Apostle Islands National Lakeshore (415 Washington Ave., Bayfield, WI 54814, tel. 715/779–3397, fax 715/779–3049, www.nps.gov/apis). Bayfield Chamber of Commerce (42 S. Broad St., Bayfield, WI 54814, tel. 800/447–4094, fax 715/779–5080, www.bayfield.org).

St. Croix National Scenic Riverway

On the Minnesota–Wisconsin border, northeast of St. Paul, MN

Free-flowing and unpolluted, the beautiful St. Croix River and its Namekagon tributary flow through some of the most scenic and least developed country in the upper Midwest. The 252-mile stretch of protected river is lined with forestland and is gentle enough for canoeing. The park was authorized on October 2, 1968.

WHAT TO SEE & DO

Bird and wildlife viewing, boating, canoeing (rentals in St. Croix Falls), cross-country skiing, fishing, hiking, hunting, kayaking, snowshoeing, swimming, tubing. **Facilities:** 2 visitor centers: St. Croix River (St. Croix Falls, WI), Namekagon (Trego, WI); self-guided tours, hiking trails. Bookstores, covered picnic tables. **Programs & Events:** Campfire programs at state parks (June–Aug.). **Tips & Hints:** Watch for deer ticks. Wear life preservers. Bring extra paddle, insect repellent, small gas stove, and drinking water if canoeing. Expect challenging canoeing for beginners. Go Apr.–Oct. for ice-free river, in May for migrating birds, May and June for wildflowers, late Sept.–early Oct. for fall colors, Oct. for waterfowl. Busiest July and Aug., least crowded Jan. and Feb.

FOOD, LODGING & SUPPLIES

⚠️ **Camping:** In the park: backcountry sites along river. In St. Croix Falls: Wisconsin Interstate State Park (Rte. 35 near U.S. 8, tel. 715/483–3747; 85 sites; $8–$12). 🏨 **Hotels:** None in park. In St. Croix Falls: Dalles House Motel (726 Vincent St. S, tel. 715/483–3206 or 888/725–6913, www.dalleshousemotel.com; 47 rooms; $66–$149). ✕ **Restaurants:** None in park. In St. Croix Falls: Loggers Bar & Grill (2071 Glacier Dr., tel. 715/483–2504, www.loggersgrill.com; $8–$18. ⛽ **Groceries & Gear:** In St. Croix Falls: St. Croix Outdoors (1298 198th St., tel. 715/483–9515), Walmart (2179 U.S. 8, tel. 715/483–5200).

FEES, HOURS & REGULATIONS

Free. Make picnic shelter reservations at Osceola Landing. Minnesota or Wisconsin state fishing and hunting regulations apply. Leashed pets only. No bicycles or motorized vehicles on trails. Obey slow speed and no-wake zones on river. No trapping. Park open daily. St. Croix Visitor Center open mid-Apr.–mid-Oct., 8–4:30; mid-Oct.-mid-Apr., weekdays 9–4. Namekagon Visitor Center open May and Sept., weekends 9–4:30; Memorial Day–Labor Day, daily 9–4:30.

HOW TO GET THERE

Entrance in St. Croix Falls, at corner of Massachusetts and Hamilton Sts. There are more than 60 other access points along riverway. Closest airport: Minneapolis–St. Paul (55 miles).

CONTACTS

St. Croix National Scenic Riverway (401 N. Hamilton St., St. Croix Falls, WI 54024, tel. 715/483–2274, fax 715/483–3288, www.nps.gov/sacn). Minnesota Department of Natural Resources Information Center (500 Lafayette Rd., St. Paul, MN 55101, tel. 651/296–6157, www.dnr.state.mn.us). Wisconsin Department of Natural Resources Bureau of Parks and Recreation (Dept. of Natural Resources, Box 7921, Madison, WI 53707-7921, tel. 608/266–2181, www.dnr.wi.gov). Minnesota Office of Tourism (121 7th Pl. E, 100 Metro Sq., St. Paul, MN 55101-2112, tel. 800/657–3700, www.exploreminnesota.com). Polk County Information Center (710 Rte. 35 S, St. Croix Falls, WI 54024, tel. 715/483–1410). Wisconsin Division of Tourism (201 W. Washington Ave., Madison, WI 53703, tel. 800/372–2737, www.travelwisconsin.com).

See Also

Ice Age National Scenic Trail, Ice Age National Scientific Reserve, Lewis & Clark National Historic Trail, and North Country National Scenic Trail, in Other National Parklands.

WYOMING

Devils Tower National Monument

In northeastern Wyoming, near Devils Tower

Devils Tower was the nation's first national monument. An igneous intrusion exposed by erosion, Devils Tower rises 867 feet from its base and is a magnet for rock climbers. Today it's surrounded by pine forests of the Black Hills and the grasslands of the rolling plains. A healthy prairie-dog town thrives on the property. The tower remains sacred to numerous Plains Indian tribes. The monument was proclaimed in 1906.

WHAT TO SEE & DO

Hiking, picnicking, rock climbing. **Facilities:** Visitor center, wayside exhibits, trails. Bookstore, picnic area with pavilion and fire grates. **Programs & Events:** Guided walking tours, special cultural programs, and evening campfire programs (Memorial Day–Labor Day). Western Cultural Festival and Cowboy Poetry Festival (Labor Day weekend). **Tips & Hints:** Plan to spend at least two hours visiting the monument. Prepare for summer heat of 95°F or higher. A voluntary climbing closure, instituted to respect Native American traditions, takes place during June. Busiest July and Aug., least crowded Dec.–Feb.

FOOD, LODGING & SUPPLIES

Camping: In the park: Belle Fourche Campground (50 sites; $12; flush toilets). Nearby: Devils Tower KOA (Rtes. 110 and 24, tel. 307/467–5395 or 800/562–5785, www.koa.com; 156 sites, 11 cabins; $17–$116; flush toilets, showers, hookups; closed Oct.–Apr.). **Hotels:** None in park. In Sundance: Bear Lodge Motel (218 Cleveland St., tel. 307/283–1611, www.rangeweb.net/~bearlodge; 33 rooms; $52–$120), Rodeway Inn Sundance (26 Rte. 585, tel. 307/283–3737, www.rodewayinn.com; 42 rooms; $60–$100). **Restaurants:** None in park. In Sundance: Aro Restaurant & Lounge (203 Cleveland St., tel. 307/283–2000; $6–$15), Higbee's Café (101 N. 3rd St., 307/283–2165; $6–$12). **Groceries:** In Sundance: Decker's Market (7th and Cleveland St., tel. 307/283–3155).

FEES, HOURS & REGULATIONS

Entrance fee: $5 per person on foot, bicycle, or motorcycle; $10 per vehicle. Climbers must register with park. No backcountry camping. No hunting or collecting park resource materials. No pets on tower or on trails. Leashed pets elsewhere. No vehicles, including bicycles, off maintained roadways. Park open daily. Visitor center open Memorial Day–Labor Day, daily 8–8; Mar.–Memorial Day and Labor Day–Oct., daily 8:30–5, hours vary.

HOW TO GET THERE

From I–90, the monument can be reached via U.S. 14 north and Rte. 24. Closest airport: Gillette (60 miles).

CONTACTS

Devils Tower National Monument (Box 10, Devils Tower, WY 82714, tel. 307/467–5283, fax 307/467–5350, www.nps.gov/deto). Sundance Chamber of Commerce (Box 1004, Sundance, WY 82729, tel. 307/ 283–1000, www.sundancewyoming.com).

Fort Laramie National Historic Site

In southeastern Wyoming, near Fort Laramie

The 12 restored historic buildings on the site interpret life at this "Queen Outpost of the Frontier Army." During the 1800s the Wyoming wilderness fort on the Laramie River, near the river's confluence with the Platte, played a crucial role in the West's transformation. First serving as a fur-trading center, the fort later became a military garrison along the Oregon Trail. The military post played an essential role in western army operations during the Indian wars. After 41 years of service, the post closed in 1890. The site was proclaimed a national monument in 1938 and redesignated a national historic site in 1960.

WHAT TO SEE & DO

Touring the fort. **Facilities:** Visitor center with interpretive exhibits, fort. Bookstore. **Programs & Events:** Self-guided and audio tours. Interpretive programs, guided tours, living-history demonstrations (June–Aug.). **Tips & Hints:** Busiest July and Aug., least crowded Dec. and Jan.

FOOD, LODGING & SUPPLIES

Camping: None in park. In Lingle: Pony Soldier RV Park (2302A U.S. 26, tel. 307/837–3078, www.ponysoldierrvpark.com; 65 sites; $20–$30; flush toilets, showers, hookups). **Hotels:** None in park. In Torrington: Motel 6 (1555 S. Main St., tel. 307/532–4011, www.motel6. com; 52 rooms; $69–$79), Grandma's Inn (U.S. 78 W, tel. 307/532–4064; 10 rooms, 3 suites; $42–$108). **Restaurants:** None in park. In Torrington: Little Moon Lake Supper Club (316 E. U.S. 26, Torrington, tel. 307/532–5750; $10–$20; closed Sun.). **Groceries & Gear:** None in park. In Guernsey: Thrifty Foods (452 W. Whalen St., tel. 307/ 836–2266).

FEES & HOURS

Entrance fee: $3 adults, free ages 16 and under. Fort grounds open daily 8–dusk. Visitor center open mid-May–Labor Day, daily 8–dusk; Labor Day–mid-May, daily 8–4:30.

HOW TO GET THERE

3 miles southwest of the town of Fort Laramie, on Rte. 160. Closest airport: Torrington (20 miles).

CONTACTS

Fort Laramie National Historic Site (965 Gray Rocks Rd., Fort Laramie, WY 82212, tel. 307/837–2221, fax 307/837-2120, www.nps.gov/fola).

Fossil Butte
National Monument

In southwestern Wyoming, near Kemmerer

The 8,198-acre site contains one of the world's best-preserved and most complete paleoecosystems of fossilized plants, fish, insects, mammals, birds, and reptiles. The fossilized remnants of this freshwater lake date to a period of warmer climate that existed 50 million years ago. The monument was established in 1972.

WHAT TO SEE & DO

Hiking, picnicking, scenic driving. **Facilities:** Visitor center, trails, horseback riding routes. Bookstore, picnic area. **Programs & Events:** Exhibit tours, quarry programs, fossil preparation demonstrations (June–Aug.). **Tips & Hints:** Hiking trails are 6,600 feet to 7,500 feet above sea level and considered moderately strenuous. Go in late summer for best weather. Go in June for wildflowers. Busiest July and Aug., least crowded Dec. and Jan.

FOOD, LODGING & SUPPLIES

Camping: None in park. In Kemmerer: Foothills RV Park (U.S. 189 N, Kemmerer, tel. 307/877–6634; 72 sites; $30; flush toilets, showers, hookups), Kemmerer Community Campground (Rte. 233, near city hall; 5 tent sites; $5; pit toilet). **Hotels:** None in park. In Diamondville: Energy Inn (3 U.S. 30, tel. 307/877–6901; 42 rooms; $55). In Kemmerer: Fairview Motel (61 U.S. 30, tel. 307/877–3938 or 800/247–3938; 61 rooms; $49–$59). **Restaurants:** None in park. In Kemmerer: Bootleggers (817 S. Main St., tel. 307/828-3067; $8–$21. **Groceries & Gear:** None in park. In Kemmerer: Ridley's Pharmacy (620 Pine Ave., tel. 307/877–4209).

FEES, HOURS & REGULATIONS

Free. No hunting. Leashed pets only. Park open daily. Visitor center open May–Sept., daily 9–5:30; Oct.-Apr., daily 8–4:30.

HOW TO GET THERE

13 miles west of Kemmerer, on U.S. 30. Closest airports: Rock Springs, WY (100 miles), Salt Lake City, UT (145 miles).

CONTACTS

Fossil Butte National Monument (864 Chicken Creek Rd., Box 592, Kemmerer, WY 83101, tel. 307/877–4455, fax 307/877–4457, www.nps.gov/fobu). Kemmerer Chamber of Commerce (800 Pine Ave., Kemmerer, WY 83101-2907, tel. 307/877–9761, www.kemmerer.org).

Grand Teton National Park

In northwestern Wyoming, near Jackson

Towering more than a mile above the valley known as Jackson Hole, the Grand Teton rises 13,770 feet above sea level. Twelve Teton peaks reach above 12,000 feet, high enough to support a dozen mountain glaciers. The park offers ribbons of green riparian plants bordering the Snake River and other streams, sagebrush flats, lodgepole pine and spruce forests, subalpine meadows, and alpine stone fields. Adjacent to the park is the National Elk Refuge, a winter feeding ground for the largest migrating elk herd in North America. Moose, buffalo, pronghorn antelope, bears, eagles, and trumpeter swans also inhabit the park. The park was initially established on February 26, 1929. Through the 1930s, John D. Rockefeller Jr. purchased 35,000 acres of valley land from local ranchers and donated 33,000 acres to the National Park Service in 1949. In 1950 the current boundaries of the park were established with the inclusion of the valley land.

WHAT TO SEE & DO

Backpacking, bicycling (rentals, Dornan's and in Jackson), boating, canoeing, fishing (rentals, in park and in Jackson), floating (rentals, in park and in Jackson), hiking, horseback riding (rentals, Colter Bay and Jackson Lake Lodge), mountaineering, scenic drives, skiing, snowmobiling (rentals, Flagg Ranch), snowshoeing, swimming, wildlife viewing. **Facilities:** 3 visitor centers: Moose (12 miles north of Jackson on U.S. 89/191/26), Jenny Lake (20 miles north of Jackson on Teton Park Rd.), and Colter Bay (42 miles north of Jackson on U.S. 89/191/26), Flagg Ranch Information Station (16 miles north of Colter Bay on U.S. 89/191/26). Auditorium, Indian Arts Museum, amphitheater at Colter Bay; 100 miles of scenic roads; 200 miles of trails. Bookstores, gas, gift shops, marina. **Programs & Events:** Ranger-led walks, talks, museum tours, evening audiovisual presentations, campfire programs (early June–late Sept.). **Tips & Hints:** Make reservations in summer for lodging and dining. Summer highs are near 85°F, lows near 45°F; winters are long and cold, with heavy snows Dec.–Feb. and daytime temperatures at or below freezing. Bring rain gear spring and fall. Busiest July and Aug., least crowded Oct., Nov., Jan., and Apr.

FOOD, LODGING & SUPPLIES

Camping: 7 campgrounds in the park: Colter Bay (25 miles north of Moose; 350 sites; $17; flush toilets, showers), Colter Bay RV Park (25 miles north of Moose; tel. 307/543–2811; 112 sites; $39; flush toilets, showers, hookups), Flagg Ranch (John D. Rockefeller Jr. Memorial Parkway, 5 miles north of Grand Teton National Park; 175 sites; $22–$40; flush toilets, showers, hookups), Gros Ventre (12 miles southeast of Moose; 360 sites; $17; flush toilets), Jenny Lake (8 miles north of Moose; 49 tent sites; $19; flush toilets), Lizard Creek (at the north end of the park, 32 miles north of Moose; 60 sites; $17; flush toilets), Signal Mountain (9 miles north of Jenny Lake; 86 sites; $17; flush toilets).

Backcountry camping allowed (permit required; see below). 🏨 **Hotels:** In the park: American Alpine Club Climber's Ranch dormitory (tel. 307/733–7271; 60 beds; $14 per night with membership; closed Oct.–May), Colter Bay Village (tel. 307/543–3100 or 800/628–9988; 166 cabins; $149–$229; closed late Sept.–May), Dornan's Spur Ranch Cabins (tel. 307/733–2522; 12 cabins; $175–$250), Flagg Ranch (tel. 800/443–2311; 92 cabins; $180–$250; closed Oct.–mid-May), Jackson Lake Lodge (tel. 307/543–3100 or 800/628–9988; 385 rooms; $239–$800; closed late Oct.–mid-May), Jenny Lake Lodge (tel. 307/733–4647 or 800/628–9988; 37 cabins; $620; closed mid-Oct.–late May), Moulton Ranch Cabins (tel. 307/733–3749 or 208/529–2354; 5 cabins; $95–$249; closed Sept.–Memorial Day), Signal Mountain Lodge (tel. 800/672–6012; 47 rooms, 32 cabins; $156–$285; closed mid-Oct.–mid-May), Triangle X Ranch (tel. 307/733–2183; 22 cabins; $1,680–$2,380 per person per week; closed Nov.–Dec. 26 and Mar.–late May). ✗ **Restaurants:** In the park: Dornan's (tel. 307/733–2415; $9–$16), Flagg Ranch (tel. 800/443–2311; $12–$29), Jackson Lake Lodge (tel. 307/543–3100; $23–$37), Jenny Lake Lodge Dining Room (tel. 307/733–4647 or 800/628–9988; $81 prix-fixe; closed Oct.–May), Signal Mountain Lodge (tel. 800/672–6012; $14–$29). ⛁ **Groceries & Gear:** Colter Bay Village, Dornan's, South Jenny Lake, Signal Mountain, Colter Bay, and Flagg Ranch.

FEES, HOURS & REGULATIONS

Entrance fee: $25 per car, good for seven days in Yellowstone and Grand Teton national parks. Backcountry permit required (free). Backcountry campsite reservations ($25) available Jan.–May 15 and up to 24 hours before first night's stay. Permit required (fee varies depending on boat type) for all watercraft. Wyoming state fishing license required. Park open daily. Moose Visitor Center open Memorial Day–Labor Day, daily 8–7; Labor Day–Memorial Day, daily 8–5. Jenny Lake Visitor Center open June–Labor Day, daily 8-7, Labor Day-Memorial Day, daily 8-5. Colter Bay Visitor Center open mid-May–June and Labor Day-Oct. 8, daily 8–5; June–Labor Day, daily 8–7. Flagg Ranch Information Station open June–Labor Day, daily 9–3:30.

HOW TO GET THERE

The Craig Thomas Discovery Visitor Center is 12 miles north of Jackson on U.S. 26, 89, and 191. Closest airport: Jackson Hole (8 miles).

CONTACTS

Grand Teton National Park (Drawer 170, Moose, WY 83012, tel. 307/739–3300, fax 307/739–3438, www.nps.gov/grte). Jackson Chamber of Commerce (Box 550 or 114 Center St., Jackson, WY 83001, tel. 307/733–3316, www.jacksonholechamber.com).

John D. Rockefeller Jr. Memorial Parkway

In northwestern Wyoming, near Jackson

This scenic 82-mile corridor commemorates Rockefeller's role in aiding the establishment of many parks, including Grand Teton. The parkway connects West Thumb in Yellowstone with the south entrance of Grand Teton National Park. The 23,777-acre parkway was authorized on August 25, 1972.

WHAT TO SEE & DO

See Grand Teton National Park.

FOOD, LODGING & SUPPLIES

None in park. See Grand Teton National Park.

CONTACTS

John D. Rockefeller Jr. Memorial Parkway (c/o Grand Teton National Park, Drawer 170, Moose, WY 83012, tel. 307/733–2880, www.nps.gov/jodr).

Yellowstone National Park

In northwestern Wyoming

Yellowstone, the world's oldest national park, is a true wilderness, one of the few large natural areas (2.2 million acres) remaining in the lower 48 states. Led by the fabled Old Faithful, the park has approximately 10,000 hydrothermal features, the largest concentration of active geysers on the planet. Human history in the park is evidenced by cultural sites dating back at least 10,000 years. The park's more than 400 miles of roads and 1,000 miles of trails allow visitors to see bison, bighorn sheep, elk, grizzly bears, moose, wolves, pronghorn, and trumpeter swans. The park was established in 1872 and designated a Biosphere Reserve in 1976 and a World Heritage Site in 1978.

WHAT TO SEE & DO

Backpacking, bicycling, bird and wildlife viewing, boating, bus touring, canoeing, cross-country skiing, fishing, hiking, horseback riding, photography touring, picnicking, snow-coach touring, snowmobiling, wildlife and nature touring. **Facilities:** 5 visitor centers: Albright (Mammoth Hot Springs), Old Faithful, Canyon, Fishing Bridge, and Grant Village. Norris Geyser Basin Museum and Bookstore; Museum of the National Park Ranger (Norris); Madison and West Thumb information stations; scenic roads; overlooks; 13 self-guided nature trails; 1,000 miles of backcountry trails. Bookstores, gasoline, gift shops, marina, religious services. **Programs & Events:** Exhibits at Albright Visitor Center at Mammoth Hot Springs, Old Faithful Visitor Education Center, and Canyon Visitor Education Center. Ranger-led talks, demonstrations, walks, and hikes (mostly June–Aug.). **Tips & Hints:** Start your Yellowstone experience at the exceptional new $27 million Old Faithful Visitor Education Center and learn about the park's hydrothermal features, volcanic geology, and scientific investigations via engaging interactive exhibits. Make lodging and camping reservations as early as possible. Limit your travels to one or two areas if you have one day or less to spend in the park. Allow two days or more to see major park attractions. Expect slow traveling July and Aug. because of crowds. Busiest July and Aug., least crowded May and Oct.

FOOD, LODGING & SUPPLIES

⛺ **Camping:** More than 200 back-country camping sites are scattered throughout the park, but most visitors opt for Yellowstone's 12 front-country campgrounds (2,150 sites; $12–$45; some flush toilets, some vault toilets, some showers, some hookups). Reserve through Xanterra Parks & Resorts (tel. 307/344–7311 or 866/439–7375). 🏨 **Hotels:** In the park: Canyon Lodge Cabins (tel. 307/344-7311, www.yellowstonenationalparklodges.com; 532 cabins; $98–$183; closed mid-Sept.–May), Grant Village (tel. 307/344-7311; 300 rooms; $155; closed late Sept.–late May), Lake Lodge (tel. 307/344-7311; 36 rooms; $75–$183; closed mid-Sept.–mid-June), Lake Yellowstone Hotel & Cabins (tel. 307/344–7311; 158 rooms, 102 cabins; $135–$223; closed late Sept.–mid-May), Mammoth Hot Springs Hotel (tel. 307/344–7311; 97 rooms, 115 cabins; $87–$125; closed early Oct.–mid-Dec. and Mar.–Apr.), Old Faithful Inn (tel. 307/344–7311; 327 rooms, 6 suites; $96–$236; closed mid-Oct.–mid-May), Old Faithful Lodge Cabins (tel. 307/344–7311; 99 cabins; $67–$110; closed mid-Sept.–mid-May), Old Faithful Snow Lodge & Cabins (tel. 307/344–7311; 100 rooms; $98–$229; closed mid-Oct.–mid-Dec. and mid-Mar.–mid-Apr.), Roosevelt Lodge and Cabins (tel. 307/344–7311; 80 cabins; $65–$110; closed early Sept.–early June). ✕ **Restaurants:** In the park: snack bars, cafeterias ($5–$10), and/or full-service restaurants ($9–$15) at all park lodgings. ⛲ **Groceries & Gear:** In the park: general stores at Bridge Bay, Canyon, Fishing Bridge, Grant Village, Lake, Mammoth Hot Springs, Old Faithful, and Tower Fall.

FEES, HOURS & REGULATIONS

Entrance fee: $12 per bicyclist, walk-in, or skier 16 and up; $25 per vehicle; $20 per snowmobile or motorcycle. Fee valid for seven days in Yellowstone and Grand Teton national parks. An annual pass to the two parks costs $50. Lodging and activity reservations (tel. 866/439–7370). Backcountry permit required ($20, if more than 48 hours in advance, free otherwise; reservations available: Backcountry Office, Box 168, Yellowstone National Park, WY 82190). No commercial hauling or travel through park. Permit required for fishing and boating. Anglers 16 and older must purchase an $18 three-day permit, a $25 seven-day permit, or a $40 season permit; those 15 and younger need a free permit or must fish under the direct supervision of an adult with a permit. A state license is not needed to fish in Yellowstone National Park. Peak season is mid-Apr.–late Oct. All park roads close at 8 AM after first Sun. in Nov. except North Entrance road to Northeast entrance. Only over-snow vehicles are allowed on other park roads during winter season, which begins mid-Dec. and runs through mid-Mar. Only the road from the north entrance at Gardiner, MT, to northeast entrance at Cooke City, MT, is open to cars year-round. Over-snow vehicles only on other park roads. Albright Visitor Center open daily, hours vary. Old Faithful Visitor Education Center open mid-Apr.–early Nov., daily, hours vary; mid-Dec.–mid-Mar., daily, hours vary. Fishing Bridge, Grant Village, Madison Information Station, Norris Geyser Basin Museum, West Thumb Information Station, and Museum of the National Park Ranger open late May–mid-Sept., daily 9–5. Canyon Visitor Education Center, Madison Information Station, and Norris Geyser Basin Museum open late May–early Oct., daily, hours vary.

HOW TO GET THERE

There are five park entrances. To reach the north entrance, take U.S. 89 from I–90 at Livingston, MT; northeast entrance, take U.S. 212 from I–90 at Billings, MT, or Rte. 296 from Cody, WY; west entrance, take U.S. 191 from Bozeman, MT, or U.S. 20 from Idaho Falls, ID; east entrance, take U.S. 16 from Cody, WY; south entrance, take U.S. 89 from Jackson, WY. Closest airports: West Yellowstone (June–early Sept.; 5 miles), Cody (90 miles), Jackson, WY (115 miles), Bozeman, MT (105 miles), Idaho Falls, ID (135 miles), Billings, MT (195 miles).

CONTACTS

Yellowstone National Park (Box 168, Yellowstone National Park, WY 82190-0168, tel. 307/344–7381, 307/344–7311 lodging reservations, www.nps.gov/yell). Big Sky Chamber of Commerce (80 Snowy Mountain Circle, Big Sky, MT 59716, tel. 800/943–4111, www.bigskychamber.com), Billings Chamber of Commerce (Box 31177 or 815 S. 27th St., Billings, MT 59101, tel. 800/735–2635, www.billingschamber.com). Bozeman Chamber of Commerce (Box B, Bozeman, MT 59771 or 2000 Commerce Way, Bozeman, MT 59715, tel. 406/586–5421, www.bozemanchamber.com). Cody Chamber of Commerce (836 Sheridan Ave., Cody, WY 82414, tel. 307/587–2777, www.codychamber.org). Dubois Chamber of Commerce (616 W. Ramshorn St., Dubois, WY 82513, tel. 307/455–2556, www.duboiswyomingchamber.org). Cooke City–Silver Gate Chamber of Commerce (Box 1071 or 206 W. Main St., Cooke City, MT 59020, tel. 406/838–2495, www.cookecitychamber.org). Gardiner Chamber of Commerce (Box 81 or 222 Park St., Gardiner, MT 59030, tel. 406/848–7971, www.gardinerchamber.com). Greater Idaho Falls Chamber of Commerce and Eastern Idaho Visitor Information Center (630 W. Broadway St., Idaho Falls, ID 83405–0498, tel. 208/523–1010 or 866/365–6943, www.idahofallschamber.com). Jackson Chamber of Commerce (Box 550 or 112 Center St., Jackson, WY 83001, tel. 307/733–3316, www.jacksonholechamber.com). Livingston Chamber of Commerce (303 E. Park St., Livingston, MT 59047, tel. 406/222–0850, www.livingston-chamber.com). Red Lodge Chamber of Commerce (701 N. Broadway Ave., Red Lodge, MT 59068, tel. 406/446–1718, www.redlodgechamber.org). West Yellowstone Chamber of Commerce (30 Yellowstone Ave., West Yellowstone, WY 59758, tel. 406/646–7701, www.destinationyellowstone.com).

See Also

Bighorn Canyon National Recreation Area, Montana. *California National Historic Trail, Continental Divide National Scenic Trail, Mormon Pioneer National Historic Trail, Nez Perce National Historic Trail, Oregon National Scenic Trail,* and *Pony Express National Historic Trail,* in Other National Parklands.

AMERICAN SAMOA

National Park of American Samoa

In the South Pacific

An oceanic rain forest, the Indo-Pacific coral reef, and 3,000-year-old Samoan culture are protected in this park. It's on three tropical volcanic islands—the main island of Tutuila and the Manua Islands of Ofu and Tau—separated by 60 miles of water. The park, which also protects the habitat of two species of flying fox (fruit bats), was authorized in 1988 and established in 1993.

WHAT TO SEE & DO

Bat and bird-watching, hiking on shore, hiking to the summit of Mt. Alava (1,610 feet), scenic drives on Tutuila, snorkeling on Ofu. **Facilities:** National Park Visitor Center (Pago Pago), trails with interpretive signage. **Programs and Activities:** See website. **Tips & Hints:** Come prepared to experience Samoa on Samoan terms. Wear conservative clothing (no skimpy swimsuits) and remember that Sunday is a religious day there (most stores are closed). Be open to new cultural experiences, and don't expect the same standards for visitor services that can be found on the mainland. The weather is hot and humid all year. Bring binoculars and snorkel gear. Always hike and snorkel with a partner. Stay away from breaking waves and steep areas. Don't touch coral, especially fire coral, which produces a nasty sting. Don't swim near an "ava"—a crevice in the reef face where water drains out as the tide goes out. Carry plenty of water. Visit May–Sept. (winter in the Southern Hemisphere), when the temperature is about 80°F with southeast trade winds and less rain, but expect rain almost every day.

FOOD, LODGING & SUPPLIES

Hotels: None in park. In Pago Pago: Motu-o-Fiafiaga B&B (on the main road from the airport, tel. 684/633–7777; 12 rooms, 1 penthouse; $60–$100, $125 penthouse). **Restaurants:** None in park. In Pago Pago: Sadie's Hotels (on the main road from the airport, tel. 684/633–5900; $8–$17). Evalani's Cabaret Lounge (Motu-o-fiafiaga B&B, on the main road from the airport, tel. 684/633–7777; $8–$16). **Groceries & Gear:** None in park. In Tafuna: K-S Mart (airport road, tel. 684/699–5241).

FEES, HOURS & REGULATIONS

Free. No fishing. No restrooms in park. Park open daily. Visitor center open weekdays 8-4:30.

HOW TO GET THERE

Park headquarters and visitor center are in Pago Pago, American Samoa. Closest airport: Pago Pago International (10 miles).

CONTACTS

National Park of American Samoa (Pago Pago, American Samoa 96799, tel. 684/633–7082, fax 684/633–7083, www.nps.gov/npsa). Tourism Office (Dept. of Commerce, American Samoa Government, Pago Pago, American Samoa 96799, tel. 684/699–9805).

GUAM

War in the Pacific National Historical Park

In the Pacific Ocean, on Guam

This park has seven sites, including the summit of Mt. Tenjo (1,033 feet), underwater relics on the offshore coral reefs (132 feet), former battlegrounds, and aging gun emplacements and trenches. The sites commemorate the battles that were fought there in the last months of World War II. The park was authorized on August 18, 1978.

WHAT TO SEE & DO

Hiking, picnicking, scuba diving, touring historic battle sites. **Facilities:** T. Stell Newman Visitor Center (Sumay), trails. **Programs & Events:** Ranger-led walks and talks. **Tips & Hints:** A new $5 million visitor center opened in 2012. The park's trails and beaches have sustained severe erosion, but remain open. Live ordnance still can be found in the park. Report any ammunition or military explosives you find on- or offshore. Some open caves still may contain booby traps. Some areas of the park are privately owned; observe NO TRESPASSING signs. Busiest Feb. and Mar., least crowded Aug.–Oct.

FOOD, LODGING & SUPPLIES

Camping: None in park. In Yona: Tagachang Beach Park (tel. 671/475–6288; backcountry camping; $2; permit required). **Hotels:** None in park. In Tumon: Hotel Nikko Guam (245 Gun Beach Rd., Tumon, tel. 671/649–8815, www.jalhotels.com/guam; 492 rooms; $320–$880), Hyatt Regency Guam (1155 Pale San Vitores Rd., tel. 671/647–1234, www.guam.regency.hyatt.com; 455 rooms and suites; $325–$4,165). **Restaurants:** None in park. In Tamuning: Lone Star Steak House (615 S. Marine Dr., tel. 671/646–6061; $7–$40). **Groceries & Gear:** None in park. In Tamuning: Oka Pay-Less Super Market (291 Farenholt Ave., tel. 671/646–9301).

FEES, HOURS & REGULATIONS

Free. All park units are open daily 7–5. T. Stell Newman Visitor Center open daily 9–4:30. Overlook is limited to walk-in visits after 5.

HOW TO GET THERE

Guam, the southernmost island of the Mariana Islands, is in the West Pacific, 1,500 miles south of Tokyo and 6,100 miles west of San Francisco. Guam is 15 hours ahead of Eastern Standard Time and doesn't observe daylight saving time. The park consists of seven units, all on the Philippine Sea (west) side of the island.

CONTACTS

War in the Pacific National Historical Park (135 Murray Blvd., Ste. 100, Hagatna, Guam 96910, tel. 671/333–4050, fax 671/477–7781, www.nps.gov/wapa). Guam Department of Parks and Recreation (Box 2950, Hagatna, Guam 96932, tel. 671/472–2887 or 671/477–8280). Guam Hotel & Restaurant Association (Box 8565, Tamuning, Guam 96931, tel. 671/649–1447, fax 671/649–8565, www.ghra.org.

See Also

American Memorial Park, in Other National Parklands.

PUERTO RICO

San Juan
National Historic Site

In San Juan

The site preserves the Spanish colonial fortifications of San Felipe del Morro, San Cristóbal, El Cañuelo, and the city walls and the San Juan gate. These ancient stone fortifications built along the Atlantic Coast protected Spain's possessions and its trade monopoly in the New World. Begun by Spanish troops in the 16th century, the massive masonry defenses are the oldest European-style fortifications within the territory of the United States. The site was established in 1949 and designated a World Heritage Site in 1983.

WHAT TO SEE & DO

Jogging, picnicking, taking tunnel and lighthouse tours, touring fortifications. **Facilities:** Visitor center at San Cristóbal; wayside exhibits, furnished troop quarters exhibits (San Cristóbal and El Morro). Bookstores. **Programs & Events:** Orientation talks every hour on the hour, daily, at both fortifications. Interpretive programs on weekends. Ranger-guided tours (San Cristóbal: tunnel tour Sat. at 10:30 in English, Sun. at 10:30 in Spanish; El Morro: lighthouse tour Sat. at 10:30 in Spanish and 2:30 in English, Sun. at 10:30 in English and 2:30 in Spanish, video (daily, every 15 minutes, alternating English and Spanish). Storytelling sessions and cannon-firing demonstrations (3rd Sun. of each month). **Tips & Hints:** Surfaces are uneven in fortifications; wear appropriate walking shoes. Inside forts, surfaces are slippery during rain. Avoid metal sentry boxes during lightning. Busiest in Dec.–Mar., least crowded Aug. and Sept.

FEES, HOURS & REGULATIONS

Entrance fee: $3, free ages 15 and under. Fort El Cañuelo closed to public. Puerto Rico fishing permit required. No pets in forts, leashed pets only on Fort El Morro grounds. Shirts and shoes required in forts. No smoking in forts. No disturbing of plants and wildlife. No food or drinks in forts. Minors must be with adults. No climbing on walls. For campers in all Puerto Rico forests, permits must be obtained from the Department of Natural and Environmental Resources (Box 9066600, Pta. de Tierra, San Juan, Puerto Rico, 00906-6600, tel. 787/724–3647, fax 787/721–5984). The office is in San Juan next to Club Nautico marina by the bridges. Park open daily 9–6.

HOW TO GET THERE

Castillo Fort San Felipe del Morro and Castillo Fort San Cristóbal are on Norzagaray St. in Old San Juan. Closest airport: San Juan (5 miles).

CONTACTS

San Juan National Historic Site (501 Norzagaray St., San Juan, PR 00901-2094, tel. 787/729–6777, fax 787/289–7972, www.nps.gov/saju). Puerto Rico Tourism Co. (Box 902, La Pricesa Bldg., #2, Paseo La Princesa, Old San Juan Station, San Juan, PR 00902-3960, tel. 800/ 866–7827, fax 787/722-5208, www.topuertorico.org).

VIRGIN ISLANDS

Buck Island Reef National Monument

On St. Croix

A magnificent elkhorn coral barrier reef, shallow-water lagoon, and marine garden encircle this uninhabited 180-acre tropical dry-forest island that rises 328 feet above the Caribbean waters. The island is a habitat for the endangered brown pelican, hawksbill and leatherback turtles, and the threatened green turtle. Charter boats take visitors to the beach and for a snorkel tour of the underwater interpretive trail. The monument was established December 28, 1961.

WHAT TO SEE & DO

Boating, hiking, kayaking, picnicking, sailing, scuba diving, snorkeling, swimming. **Facilities:** Beaches, underwater interpretive trail, picnic areas, island trail, dock. Interpretive display boards. **Tips & Hints:** Don't touch the coral; it's easily damaged and can injure you. Go Dec. or Apr. for blooms. Take into account rainy seasons in Nov. and Mar. and hurricane season July–Sept. Busiest Dec.–Apr., least crowded Sept. and Oct.

FOOD, LODGING & SUPPLIES

None on island. See Christiansted National Historic Site.

FEES, HOURS & REGULATIONS

Free. Boat trips: $40 for a half day, $70 for a full day. Reservations recommended. Big Beard Adventures (tel. 340/773–4482); Charis (tel. 340/773–9027); Clyde, Inc. (tel. 340/773–8520); Diva (tel. 340/778–4675); Milemark Water Sports (tel. 340/773–2628); and Buck Island and Terero Charters (tel. 340/773–3161). No spearfishing or pets. No fishing or collecting. Island and underwater trail closed at night. Vessels can anchor up to two weeks off West Beach. Pit toilets only on island. Park is open daily sunrise–sunset. Information is available from Christiansted National Historic Site (see separate entry). Visitor Center in downtown Christiansted, St. Croix, Virgin Islands. Open daily 8:30–4:30.

HOW TO GET THERE

1½ miles off the northeast side of St. Croix, Virgin Islands. Closest airport: Henry Rohlsen Airport (8 miles west of Christiansted).

CONTACTS

Buck Island Reef National Monument (Danish Customs House, Kings Wharf 100, Christiansted, St. Croix, VI 00820-4611, tel. 340/773–1460, fax 340/773–5995, www.nps.gov/buis). Christiansted Visitors Bureau (Box 4538, Christiansted, St. Croix, VI 00822, tel. 340/773–0495). Virgin Islands Department of Tourism (Box 6400, St. Thomas, VI 00804, tel. 800/372–8784, www.visitusvi.com).

Christiansted National Historic Site

In Christiansted, St. Croix

The site protects 18th- and 19th-century buildings in the heart of the historic area of Christiansted, the capital of the former Danish West Indies. Attractions include museums at Fort Christiansvaern and the Steeple Building, and other historic buildings are being renovated. The site was designated Virgin Islands National Historic Site in 1952 and renamed in 1961.

WHAT TO SEE & DO

Self-guided walking tours of historic area, touring museums at fort and steeple. **Facilities:** Visitor contact station at Fort Christiansvaern, Steeple Building Museum. **Programs & Events:** Ranger-led tour daily at 10 and 1:30. **Tips & Hints:** Begin tour at fort. Busiest Feb. and Mar., least crowded Sept.–Dec.

FOOD & LODGING

Hotels: None in park. In Christiansted: Caravelle Hotel (44A Queen Cross St., tel. 340/773–0687, www.hotelcaravelle.com; 44 rooms; $145–$180), Company House (2 Company St., tel. 340/773–1377, www.companyhousehotel.com; 34 rooms; $97–$102), Holger Danske Hotel (1200 King Cross St., tel. 340/773–3600, www.holgerhotel. com; 40 rooms; $94–$156), Hotel on the Cay (Protestant Cay, tel. 340/ 773–2035 or 855/654–0301, www.hotelonthecay.com; 53 rooms; $109– $149). ✗ **Restaurants:** None in park. In Christiansted: Harbormaster Restaurant (Hotel on the Cay, tel. 340/773–2035, www.hotelonthecay. com; $11–$35), RumRunners Restaurant (Caravelle Hotel, 44A Queen Cross St., tel. 340/773–6585, www.hotelcaravelle.com; $8–$28).

FEES & HOURS

Park grounds are free. Entrance fee: $3 adults for Fort and Steeple Building Museum. Site, visitor center, and museum open daily 8:30– 4:30. Museum open weekdays 8–5, weekends 9–5.

HOW TO GET THERE

The site is in the heart of Christiansted, surrounded by the Christiansted Historic District. The visitor contact station is at Fort Christiansvaern. Park headquarters is in the Danish Customs House. Closest airport: Henry Rohlsen on St. Croix (8 miles west of Christiansted).

CONTACTS

Christiansted National Historic Site (2100 Church St., #100, Christiansted, VI 00820, tel. 340/773–1460, www.nps.gov/chri). Christiansted Visitors Bureau (Box 4538, Christiansted, St. Croix, VI 00822, tel. 340/773–0495). Virgin Islands Department of Tourism (Box 6400, St. Thomas, VI 00804, tel. 800/372–8784, www.visitusvi.com).

Salt River Bay National Historical Park & Ecological Preserve

On St. Croix

All major cultural periods in the history of the U.S. Virgin Islands are included in this park. It's the only known site where members of the Columbus expedition set foot on what is now U.S. territory. The park contains the only ceremonial prehistoric ball court ever discovered in the Lesser Antilles, village middens, and burial grounds. Various European groups, including the Spanish, French, Dutch, English, and Danish, attempted to colonize the area during the post-Columbian period. The site is marked by Fort Sale, an earthworks fortification remaining from the Dutch period of occupation. The site was authorized on February 24, 1992.

WHAT TO SEE & DO

Hiking, kayaking, scuba diving (rentals, Anchor Dive Center), snorkeling, swimming, touring historic and prehistoric sites. **Facilities:** Visitor contact station (above Columbus landing site on the west side of the Salt River), overviews. **Programs & Events:** Ranger talks (year-round, on request when visitor center is open), temporary exhibits.

FOOD & LODGING

None in park. See Christiansted National Historic Site.

FEES & HOURS

Free. Visitor center open Nov. 14–June 15, Tues.–Thurs. 9–4.

HOW TO GET THERE

Visitor center is on the wharf in downtown Christiansted. Closest airport: Henry Rohlsen on St. Croix (8 miles west of Christiansted).

CONTACTS

Salt River Bay National Historical Park & Ecological Preserve (c/o Christiansted National Historic Site, Danish Custom House, Kings Wharf, 2100 Church St., #100, Christiansted, VI 00820, tel. 340/773–1460, www.nps.gov/sari). Christiansted Visitors Bureau (Box 4538, Christiansted, St. Croix, VI 00822, tel. 340/773–0495). Virgin Islands Department of Tourism (Box 6400, St. Thomas, VI 00804, tel. 800/372–8784, www.visitusvi.com).

Virgin Islands Coral Reef National Monument

Submerged lands in the Atlantic ocean and Caribbean Sea off St. John

The park preserves 12,708 acres of submerged lands off St. John in the U.S. Virgin Islands and is part of an underwater platform that extends several miles from shore to the deepest part of the Atlantic. Many species, including migrating whales, dolphins, brown pelicans, terns, and sea turtles, live in a delicate balance here, interlinked through complex relationships developed over tens of thousands of years. The monument was created by presidential proclamation in 2001.

WHAT TO SEE & DO

Scuba diving, snorkeling. **Facilities:** See Virgin Islands National Park. **Tips & Hints:** Entire park is submerged. Diving and snorkeling is permitted from Hurricane Hole. No offshore moorings available for private boats. Monument is designated a "no-take zone," but hardnose fishing is allowed on the south side of the monument where new moorings have been constructed, and bait fishing is allowed at Hurricane Hole.

FEES, HOURS & REGULATIONS

Free. Permit required for fishing in Hurricane Hole; inquire at visitor center. Land access from Hurricane Hole only. Park open daily.

HOW TO GET THERE

A portion of the National Monument off St. John, Hurricane Hole, can be reached via Centerline Rd. Monument is approximately 3 miles east of Coral Bay. Hourly ferry service from Red Hook, St. Thomas, is available to St. John and operates 6 AM–midnight. Less frequent ferries make the trip from Charlotte Amalie. Closest airport: St. Thomas.

CONTACTS

Virgin Islands Coral Reef National Monument (1300 Cruz Bay Creek, St. John, VI 00830, tel. 340/776–6201, www.nps.gov/viis). Virgin Islands Department of Tourism (Box 6400, St. Thomas, VI 00804, tel. 800/372–8784, www.visitusvi.com).

Virgin Islands National Park

On St. John and on Hassel Island in Charlotte Amalie Harbor, St. Thomas

The park covers about half of St. John Island as well as Hassel Island in St. Thomas harbor and includes quiet coves, white-sand beaches, tropical forests, wildlife, wildflowers, breathtaking views, and offshore coral reefs. Also protected are early Carib Indian relics and the remains of Danish colonial sugar plantations. The park was authorized on August 2, 1956.

WHAT TO SEE & DO

Bird-watching, boating, fishing, hiking, picnicking, sailing, scenic drives, scuba diving, snorkeling (rentals), swimming, kayaking, windsurfing. **Facilities:** Visitor center (Cruz Bay, 5-minute walk from public ferry dock), information kiosk (Trunk Bay), bulletin boards, self-guided underwater trail, hiking trails. Book and map sales area (visitor center and Trunk Bay), picnic areas. **Programs & Events:** Guided island hikes, snorkeling trips, cultural history demonstrations, evening programs. Advance registration and transportation fees required in some cases. Black History Month Commemoration (Annaberg Sugar Plantation, late Feb.), St. John's Carnival (week ending July 4). **Tips & Hints:** Wear light cotton clothes and lightweight trousers to help protect against insect bites. Casual clothes are sufficient for most restaurants. Busiest Dec.-Mar., least crowded Sept. and Oct.

FOOD, LODGING & SUPPLIES

Camping: In the park: Cinnamon Bay Campground (North Shore Rd., Cruz Bay, tel. 800/539–9998 or 340/776–6330; 31 tent sites, 50 tent-cabins; $32–$105; flush toilets, showers). **Hotels:** In the park: Cinnamon Bay Cabins (North Shore Rd., Cruz Bay, tel. 800/539–9998; 40 cabins; $81–$105). **Restaurants:** In the park: T'ree Lizard Restaurant (Cinnamon Bay; $7–$19). Snack bars at Cruz Bay, Maho Bay, and Trunk Bay. **Groceries & Gear:** In the park: Camp store and water-sports shop at Cinnamon Bay (tel. 800/539–9998).

FEES, HOURS & REGULATIONS

Free except Trunk Bay ($4 adults, free ages 15 and under). Make campground reservations for winter four to six months in advance. Most popular park areas are easily accessed by taxi, otherwise known as safari buses. Rental vehicles are needed to travel to more remote parts of the island. Boat rentals and charters are necessary to visit some of the park bays that do not have road access. Park open daily. Visitor center open daily 8–4:30.

HOW TO GET THERE

The park on St. John is reached via North Shore or Centerline Rds. Hourly ferry service from Red Hook, St. Thomas, is available to St. John and operates 6 AM–midnight. Less frequent ferries make the trip from Charlotte Amalie. Closest airport: St. Thomas.

CONTACTS

Park Headquarters, Virgin Islands National Park (1300 Cruz Bay Creek, St. John, VI 00830, tel. 340/776–6201, www.nps.gov/viis). Virgin Islands Department of Tourism (Box 6400, St. Thomas, VI 00804, tel. 800/372–8784, www.visitusvi.com).

Other National Parklands

SPECIAL-INTEREST PARKS

The categories below are included to help you find the parks that relate to your interest in a specific aspect of our country's history and culture.

African American History Sites

African Burial Ground National Monument, New York.

Booker T. Washington National Monument, Virginia.

Boston African American National Historic Site, Massachusetts.

Brown v. Board of Education National Historic Site, Kansas.

Carter G. Woodson Home National Historic Site, District of Columbia.

Cumberland Island National Seashore, Georgia.

Dayton Aviation Heritage National Historical Park, Ohio.

Frederick Douglass National Historic Site, District of Columbia.

George Washington Carver National Monument, Missouri.

Harpers Ferry National Historic Park, West Virginia.

Jefferson National Expansion Memorial, Missouri.

Little Rock Central High School National Historic Site, Arkansas.

Maggie L. Walker National Historic Site, Virginia.

Martin Luther King Jr. Memorial, District of Columbia.

Martin Luther King Jr. National Historic Site, Georgia.

Mary McLeod Bethune Council House National Historic Site, District of Columbia.

Natchez National Historic Park, Mississippi.

New Orleans Jazz National Historical Park, Louisiana.

Nicodemus National Historic Site, Kansas.

Tuskegee Airmen National Historic Site, Alabama.

Tuskegee Institute National Historic Site, Alabama.

Archaeological & Paleontological Sites

Agate Fossil Beds National Monument, Nebraska.

Alibates Flint Quarries National Monument, Texas.

Aztec Ruins National Monument, New Mexico.

Badlands National Park, South Dakota.

Bandelier National Monument, New Mexico.

Canyon de Chelly National Monument, Arizona.

Casa Grande Ruins National Monument, Arizona.

Chaco Culture National Historical Park, New Mexico.

Dinosaur National Monument, Colorado.

Effigy Mounds National Monument, Iowa.
Florissant Fossil Beds National Monument, Colorado.
Fossil Butte National Monument, Wyoming.
Gila Cliff Dwellings National Monument, New Mexico.
Hagerman Fossil Beds National Monument, Idaho.
Hopewell Culture National Historical Park, Ohio.
Hovenweep National Monument, Colorado.
John Day Fossil Beds National Monument, Oregon.
Kaloko-Honokohau National Historical Park, Hawaii.
Mesa Verde National Park, Colorado.
Montezuma Castle National Monument, Arizona.
Navajo National Monument, Arizona.
Ocmulgee National Monument, Georgia.
Petroglyph National Monument, New Mexico.
Pipestone National Monument, Minnesota.
Poverty Point National Monument, Louisiana.
Pu'ukohola Heiau National Historic Site, Hawaii.
Theodore Roosevelt National Park, North Dakota.
Tonto National Monument, Arizona.
Tuzigoot National Monument, Arizona.
Walnut Canyon National Monument, Arizona.
Wupatki National Monument, Arizona.
Yucca House National Monument, Colorado.

Battlefields

Big Hole National Battlefield, Montana.
Colonial National Historical Park, Virginia.
Cowpens National Battlefield, South Carolina.
Fort Necessity National Battlefield, Pennsylvania.
Guilford Courthouse National Military Park, North Carolina.
Horseshoe Bend National Military Park, Alabama.
Jean Lafitte National Historical Park, Louisiana.
Kings Mountain National Military Park, South Carolina.
Little Bighorn Battlefield National Monument, Montana.
Minute Man National Historical Park, Massachusetts.
Moores Creek National Battlefield, North Carolina.
Palo Alto Battlefield National Historical Park, Texas.
River Raisin National Battlefield Park, Michigan.
Rock Creek Park, District of Columbia.
Sand Creek Massacre National Historic Site, Colorado.
Saratoga National Historical Park, New York.
War in the Pacific National Historical Park, Guam.
Washita Battlefield National Historic Site, Oklahoma.
World War II Valor in the Pacific National Monument, Hawaii.

Civil War Sites

Andersonville National Historic Site, Georgia.

Antietam National Battlefield, Maryland.

Appomattox Court House National Historical Park, Virginia.

Arkansas Post National Memorial, Arkansas.

Brices Cross Roads National Battlefield Site, Mississippi.

Cedar Creek & Belle Grove National Historical Park, Virginia.

Chickamauga & Chattanooga National Military Park, Georgia.

Fort Donelson National Battlefield, Tennessee.

Fort Monroe National Monument, Virginia.

Fort Pulaski National Monument, Georgia.

Fort Sumter National Monument, South Carolina.

Fredericksburg & Spotsylvania County Battlefields Memorial National Military Park, Virginia.

Gettysburg National Military Park, Pennsylvania.

Harpers Ferry National Historical Park, West Virginia.

Kennesaw Mountain National Battlefield Park, Georgia.

Manassas National Battlefield Park, Virginia.

Monocacy National Battlefield, Maryland.

Pea Ridge National Military Park, Arkansas.

Pecos National Historical Park, New Mexico.

Petersburg National Battlefield, Virginia.

Richmond National Battlefield Park, Virginia.

Shiloh National Military Park, Tennessee.

Stones River National Battlefield, Tennessee.

Tupelo National Battlefield, Mississippi.

Vicksburg National Military Park, Mississippi.

Wilson's Creek National Battlefield, Missouri.

Hispanic Heritage Sites & Sites that Relate to America's Discovery

Amistad National Recreation Area, Texas.

Arkansas Post National Memorial, Arkansas.

Big Bend National Park, Texas.

Biscayne National Park, Florida.

Cabrillo National Monument, California.

Canyon de Chelly National Monument, Arizona.

Castillo de San Marcos National Monument, Florida.

Chamizal National Memorial, Texas.

Channel Islands National Park, California.

Christiansted National Historic Site, Virgin Islands.

Coronado National Memorial, Arizona.

Cumberland Island National Seashore, Georgia.

De Soto National Memorial, Florida.

Dry Tortugas National Park, Florida.

El Morro National Monument, New Mexico.

Fort Caroline National Memorial, Florida.

Fort Clatsop National Memorial, Oregon.

Fort Frederica National Monument, Georgia

Fort Matanzas National Monument, Florida.

Fort Point National Historic Site, California.

Golden Gate National Recreation Area, California.

Grand Portage National Monument, Minnesota.

Gulf Islands National Seashore, Florida and Mississippi.

Knife River Indian Villages National Historic Site,
North Dakota.

Padre Island National Seashore, Texas.

Palo Alto Battlefield National Historical Park, Texas.

Pecos National Historical Park, New Mexico.

Point Reyes National Seashore, California.

Salinas Pueblo Missions National Monument, New Mexico.

Salt River Bay National Historical Park & Ecological
Preserve, Virgin Islands.

San Antonio Missions National Historical Park, Texas.

San Juan National Historic Site, Puerto Rico.

Santa Monica Mountains National Recreation Area,
California.

Timucuan Ecological & Historic Preserve, Florida.

Tumacacori National Monument, Arizona.

Wrangell–St. Elias National Park & Preserve, Alaska.

Presidential History Sites

Abraham Lincoln Birthplace National Historical Park,
Kentucky.

Adams National Historic Site, Massachusetts.

Andrew Johnson National Historic Site, Tennessee.

Eisenhower National Historic Site, Pennsylvania.

Eleanor Roosevelt National Historic Site, New York.

Ford's Theatre National Historic Site, District of Columbia.

Franklin Delano Roosevelt Memorial, District of Columbia.

General Grant National Memorial, New York.

George Washington Birthplace National Monument, Virginia.

Harry S Truman National Historic Site, Missouri.

Herbert Hoover National Historic Site, Iowa.

Home of Franklin D. Roosevelt National Historic Site,
New York.

James A. Garfield National Historic Site, Ohio.

Jefferson National Expansion Memorial, Missouri.

Jimmy Carter National Historic Site, Georgia.

John Fitzgerald Kennedy National Historic Site, Massachusetts.

Lincoln Boyhood Home National Monument, Indiana.

Lincoln Home National Historic Site, Illinois.

Lincoln Memorial, District of Columbia.

Longfellow House–Washington's Headquarters National Historic Site, Massachusetts.

Lyndon Baines Johnson Memorial Grove on the Potomac, District of Columbia.

Lyndon Baines Johnson National Historical Park, Texas.

Martin Van Buren National Historic Site, New York.

Mount Rushmore National Memorial, South Dakota.

President William Jefferson Clinton Birthplace National Historic Site, Arkansas.

Sagamore Hill National Historic Site, New York.

Shenandoah National Park, Virginia.

Theodore Roosevelt Birthplace National Historic Site, New York.

Theodore Roosevelt Inaugural National Historic Site, New York.

Theodore Roosevelt Island National Memorial, District of Columbia.

Theodore Roosevelt National Park, North Dakota.

Thomas Jefferson Memorial, District of Columbia.

Ulysses S. Grant National Historic Site, Missouri.

Washington Monument, District of Columbia.

White House, District of Columbia.

William Howard Taft National Historic Site, Ohio.

Volcanoes, Caves & Hot Springs

Capulin Volcano National Monument, New Mexico.

Carlsbad Caverns National Park, New Mexico.

Crater Lake National Park, Oregon.

Craters of the Moon National Monument & Preserve, Idaho.

Devils Postpile National Monument, California.

Devils Tower National Monument, Wyoming.

El Malpais National Monument, New Mexico.

Great Basin National Park, Nevada.

Haleakala National Park, Hawaii.

Hawaii Volcanoes National Park, Hawaii.

Hot Springs National Park, Arkansas

Jewel Cave National Monument, South Dakota.

Lassen Volcanic National Park, California.

Lava Beds National Monument, California.
Mammoth Cave National Park, Kentucky.
Oregon Caves National Monument, Oregon.
Pinnacles National Monument, California.
Russell Cave National Monument, Alabama.
Sequoia National Park, California.
Sunset Crater Volcano National Monument, Arizona.
Timpanogos Cave National Monument, Utah.
Wind Cave National Park, South Dakota.
Yellowstone National Park, Wyoming.

Women's History Sites

Clara Barton National Historic Site, Maryland.
Eleanor Roosevelt National Historic Site, New York.
Lowell National Historical Park, Massachusetts.
Maggie L. Walker National Historic Site, Virginia.
Mary McLeod Bethune Council House National Historic
Site, District of Columbia.
Sewall-Belmont House National Historic Site, District
of Columbia.
Whitman Mission National Historic Site, Washington.
Women's Rights National Historical Park, New York.

World Heritage Sites

Carlsbad Caverns National Park, New Mexico.
Chaco Culture National Historical Park, New Mexico.
Everglades National Park, Florida.
Glacier Bay National Park and Preserve, Alaska.
Glacier National Park, Montana.
Grand Canyon National Park, Arizona.
Great Smoky Mountains National Park, Tennessee.
Hawaii Volcanoes National Park, Hawaii.
Independence National Historical Park, Pennsylvania.
Mammoth Cave National Park, Kentucky.
Mesa Verde National Park, Colorado.
Olympic National Park, Washington.
Redwood National Park, California.
San Juan National Historic Site, Puerto Rico.
Statue of Liberty National Monument, New York.
Wrangell–St. Elias National Park & Preserve, Alaska.
Yellowstone National Park, Wyoming.
Yosemite National Park, California.

AFFILIATED AREAS

AIDS Memorial Grove National Memorial

This memorial in Golden Gate Park in San Francisco is dedicated to individuals who have died as a result of acquired immune deficiency syndrome (AIDS). It's also in support of those who are living with AIDS and their loved ones and caregivers. The memorial was authorized on November 12, 1996.

CONTACT

AIDS Memorial Grove National Memorial (Box 2270, San Francisco, CA 94126–2270, tel. 415/765–0497, www.aidsmemorial.org).

Aleutian World War II National Historic Area

Preserved here are lands owned by the Ounalaska Corporation on the island of Amaknak. The site interprets the history of the Aleut people and the role they and the Aleutian Islands played in the defense of the United States in World War II. It was authorized on November 12, 1996.

CONTACT

Aleutian World War II National Historic Area (Box 149, 400 Salmon Way, Unalaska, AK 99685, tel. 907/581–1276, www.ounalashka.com).

American Memorial Park

This site on the island of Saipan in the Northern Mariana Islands honors the sacrifices made during the Mariana Campaign of World War II. Recreational facilities, a World War II museum, and a flag monument keep alive the memory of more than 4,000 U.S. military personnel and local islanders who died in June 1944. The park was authorized on August 18, 1978.

CONTACT

American Memorial Park (Box 5189 CHRB, Saipan, MP 96950, tel. 670/234–7202 or 670/234–7607, fax 670/234–6698, www.nps.gov/amme).

Benjamin Franklin National Memorial

In the Rotunda of the Franklin Institute, a 20-foot, 30-ton seated statue of Franklin, sculpted by James Earle Fraser, honors the inventor-statesman. The memorial was designated on October 25, 1972, and is owned and administered by the Franklin Institute.

CONTACT
Benjamin Franklin National Memorial (Franklin Institute, 222 N. 20th
St., Philadelphia, PA 19103, tel. 215/448–1200, www2.fi.edu).

Chicago Portage National Historic Site

A portion of the portage between the Great Lakes and the Mississippi,
discovered by French explorers Jacques Marquette and Louis Joliet, is
preserved here. The site was designated on January 3, 1952, and is administered by the Forest Preserve District of Cook County.

CONTACT
Chicago Portage National Historic Site (c/o Forest Preserve District of
Cook County, 536 N. Harlem Ave., River Forest, IL 60305, tel. 800/
870–3666, www.chicagoportage.org).

Chimney Rock National Historic Site

Pioneers traveling west along the Oregon Trail often camped near this
famous landmark, which stands 500 feet above the Platte River. The
site was designated on August 2, 1956, is owned by Nebraska, and is
administered by the city of Bayard, the Nebraska State Historical Society, and the National Park Service under a cooperative agreement of
June 21, 1956.

CONTACT
Chimney Rock National Historic Site (Scotts Bluff National Monument, Box 27, Gering, NE 69341, tel. 308/436–9700, fax 308/436–7611,
www.nps.gov/scbl).

David A. Berger National Memorial

This monument serves as a reminder of the violence that took place in
Munich at the 1972 Olympic Games.

CONTACT
David A. Berger National Memorial (Mandel Jewish Community Center, 26001 S. Woodland Rd., Beachwood, OH 44122, tel. 216/831–
0700, www.nps.gov/dabe).

Delaware & Lehigh National Heritage Corridor

The corridor showcases the Delaware, Lehigh, and Wyoming Valleys
where anthracite coal was discovered, canals were built, and iron was
first poured. During the Industrial Revolution, these canals and their
associated early railroads gave access to the coalfields of eastern Pennsylvania. The corridor includes museums with displays about the region's cultural and industrial history and two state parks. It's
administered by a federal commission appointed by the secretary of the

interior and the governor of Pennsylvania working with a consortium of state, county, local, and private landowners. It was designated on November 18, 1988, and reauthorized in 1998.

CONTACT

Delaware & Lehigh National Heritage Corridor (2750 Hugh Moore Park Rd., Easton, PA 18042, 610/923–3548, fax 610/923–0537, www.delawareandlehigh.org).

Father Marquette National Memorial

The life and work of Father Jacques Marquette, French priest and explorer, is memorialized here. The site is in Michigan Straits State Park, near St. Ignace, Michigan, where he founded a Jesuit mission in 1671 and was buried in 1678. The memorial was authorized on December 20, 1975.

CONTACT

Father Marquette National Memorial (Parks Division, Dept. of Natural Resources, Box 30028, Lansing, MI 48900, tel. 800/827–7007).

Gloria Dei (Old Swedes') Church National Historic Site

This, the second-oldest Swedish church in the United States, was founded in 1677. The present structure, a splendid example of 17th-century Swedish church architecture, was erected about 1700. The site was designated on November 17, 1942, and is owned and administered by the Corporation of Gloria Dei (Old Swedes') Church.

CONTACT

Gloria Dei (Old Swedes') Church National Historic Site (Columbus Blvd. and Christian St., Philadelphia, PA 19147, tel. 215/389–1513, fax 215/861–4950, www.nps.gov/glde).

Green Springs National Historic Landmark District

This portion of Louisa County in Virginia's Piedmont has fine rural manor houses and related buildings (none of which are open to the public) in an unmarred landscape. In 1974 the district was declared a national historic landmark by the secretary of the interior.

CONTACT

Green Springs National Historic Landmark District (Fredericksburg and Spotsylvania National Military Park, 120 Catham La., Fredericksburg, VA 22405, tel. 540/371–1112, www.nps.gov/grsp).

Historic Camden

Camden was established in 1732 and at that time was known as Fredericksburg Township. In 1768 the village was named Camden in honor of Charles Pratt, Lord Camden, a British Parliamentary champion of colonial rights. The town was occupied by the British under Lord Cornwallis from June 1, 1780, until May 9, 1781. It was one of the few frontier settlements to have hosted two battles during the American Revolution: the first on August 16, 1780, and the second on April 25, 1781. The Historic Camden Revolutionary War Site was authorized on May 24, 1982.

CONTACT

Historic Camden (Box 710, Camden, SC 29020, tel. 803/432–9841, www.historic-camden.net).

Ice Age National Scientific Reserve

This country's first national scientific reserve is home to nationally significant features of continental glaciation. State parks in the area are open to the public. The reserve was authorized on October 13, 1964.

CONTACT

Ice Age National Scientific Reserve (Wisconsin Dept. of Natural Resources, 101 S. Webster St., Madison, WI 53707–7921, tel. 608/441–5610 or 608/266–2621).

Illinois & Michigan Canal National Heritage Corridor

This canal was built in the 1830s and 1840s along the portage between Lake Michigan and the Illinois River, which had long been used as a Native American trade route. The canal rapidly transformed Chicago from an isolated crossroads into a critical transportation hub between the East and the developing Midwest. A 61-mile recreational trail follows the canal towpath. The corridor was designated on August 24, 1984.

CONTACT

Illinois & Michigan Canal National Heritage Corridor (Canal Corridor Association (754 1st St., LaSalle, IL 61301, tel. 815/220–1848, www.canalcor.org).

International Peace Garden

This 2,300-acre park, with its exquisite garden, is on the North Dakota–Manitoba border. It serves as a unique tribute to the peace and friendship between the people of Canada and the United States.

CONTACT

International Peace Garden (10939 Hwy. 281, Dunseith, ND 58329, tel. 701/263–4390 or 888/432–6733, www.peacegarden.com).

Inupiat Heritage Center

This center is affiliated with New Bedford Whaling National Historical Park to commemorate more than 2,000 19th-century whaling trips from New Bedford to the western Arctic. The center collects, preserves, and exhibits historical material, art objects, and scientific displays. The center was designated February 3, 1999.

CONTACT

Inupiat Heritage Center (Box 69, Barrow, AK 99723, tel. 907/852–0422, www.nps.gov/inup).

Jamestown National Historic Site

Part of the site of the first permanent British settlement in North America (1607) is on the upper end of Jamestown Island, scene of the first representative legislative government on this continent, July 30, 1619. The site was designated on December 18, 1940, and is owned and administered by the Association for the Preservation of Virginia Antiquities. The remainder of Jamestown site and island is part of Colonial National Historical Park.

CONTACT

Jamestown National Historic Site (c/o Preservation Virginia, 204 W. Franklin St., Richmond, VA 23220-5012, tel. 804/648–1889, fax 804/775–0802, www.apva.org/jr).

John H. Chafee Blackstone River Valley National Heritage Corridor

The American Industrial Revolution began in the mills (including Slater Mill), villages, and associated transportation networks in the Blackstone Valley, which runs along some 46 miles of river and canals from Worcester, Massachusetts, to Providence, Rhode Island. The corridor was established on November 10, 1986.

CONTACT

John H. Chafee Blackstone River Valley National Heritage Corridor (1 Depot Sq., Woonsocket, RI 02895, tel. 401/762–0250, fax 401/762–0530, www.nps.gov/blac).

Lower East Side Tenement National Historic District

The heart of the Lower East Side Tenement Museum is its landmark tenement building, home to more than 7,000 people from 20 nations between 1863 and 1935. The museum promotes tolerance and historical perspective at this gateway to America. The district was designated on November 12, 1998.

CONTACT

Lower East Side Tenement Museum National Historic Site (108 Orchard St., New York, NY 10002, tel. 212/982–8420 or 212/431–0233, www.nps.gov/loea or www.tenement.org).

McLoughlin House National Historic Site

Dr. John McLoughlin, often called the "Father of Oregon," was prominent in the development of the Pacific Northwest as "chief factor" (superintendent) of Fort Vancouver. He lived in this house between 1847 and 1857. The site was designated a national historic site on June 27, 1945. It is owned and administered by the McLoughlin Memorial Association.

CONTACT

McLoughlin House National Historic Site (713 Center St., Oregon City, OR 97045, tel. 360/816–6230 or 503/656–5151, www.nps.gov/mcho or www.mcloughlinhouse.org).

New Jersey Coastal Heritage Trail

From the Raritan Bay near New York City south to Cape May and along the Delaware River and Bay, this scenic vehicular trail explores the diverse resources along New Jersey's coast through a series of interpretive themes. Lighthouses, boardwalks, historic communities, wildlife habitats, and migratory flyways are part of the trail. There are fees for some activities sponsored by private and public institutions. The trail was authorized on October 20, 1988.

CONTACT

New Jersey Coastal Heritage Trail Route (c/o New Jersey Pinelands National Reserve, 15 Springfield Rd., New Lisbon, NJ 08064, tel. 609/894–7300 or 856/447–0103, www.nps.gov/neje).

Oklahoma City National Memorial & Museum

On the site of the former Alfred P. Murrah Federal Building, this memorial pays tribute to the 168 people killed in the bombing on April 19, 1995. It was, at the time, the deadliest terrorist attack ever on American soil. One component of the memorial is composed of 168 bronze-and-glass chairs arranged in nine rows, representing the number of victims and the number of floors of the Murrah Building when the explosion occurred. The site includes the Outdoor Symbolic Memorial, the Memorial Museum, and the Oklahoma City National Memorial Institute for the Prevention of Terrorism. The memorial was authorized on October 9, 1997, and dedicated on April 19, 2000.

CONTACTS

Oklahoma City National Memorial (Box 676, Oklahoma City, OK 73101, tel. 405/609–8855, fax 405/609–8863, www.nps.gov/okci).

Pinelands National Reserve

The area is a sandy coastal plain of more than 1.1 million acres of low, dense pine and oak forests, streams, wetlands, cranberry bogs and blueberry fields, historic iron and glass factories, and small towns. Most facilities are provided within state forests, parks, and wildlife management areas. The reserve was authorized on November 10, 1978, and designated a Biosphere Reserve in 1983.

CONTACT

Pinelands National Reserve (New Jersey Pinelands Commission, 15 Springfield Rd., New Lisbon, NJ 08064, tel. 609/894–7300, www.nps. gov/pine).

Quinebaug & Shetucket Rivers Valley National Heritage Corridor

The Quinebaug and Shetucket Rivers Valley in Connecticut is one of the last unspoiled and undeveloped areas in the northeastern United States. It has remained largely intact, including important aboriginal archaeological sites, excellent water quality, beautiful rural landscapes, architecturally significant mill structures and mill villages, and a large acreage of parks and other permanent open space. The corridor encompasses 850 square miles and includes 25 towns. It was authorized on November 2, 1994.

CONTACT

Quinebaug & Shetucket Rivers Valley National Heritage Corridor (Quinebaug-Shetucket Heritage Corridor, Inc., 107 Providence St., Putnam, CT 06260, tel. 860/963–7226 or 866/363–7226, fax 860/928–2189, www.nps.gov/qush or www.thelastgreenvalley.org).

Red Hill Patrick Henry National Memorial

The law office and grave of the fiery Virginia legislator and orator are preserved at this small plantation along with a reconstruction of Patrick Henry's last home and a museum. The memorial was authorized on May 13, 1986.

CONTACT

Red Hill Patrick Henry National Memorial (Patrick Henry Memorial Foundation, 1250 Red Hill Rd., Brookneal, VA 24528–3302, tel. 434/376–2044 or 800/514–7463, www.redhill.org).

Roosevelt Campobello International Park

President Franklin D. Roosevelt spent many vacations at his 34-room summer home on Campobello Island in New Brunswick's Bay of Fundy. The house and grounds include a visitor center, flower gardens, and historic furnishings. The park was established on July 7, 1964, and is owned and administered by the United States–Canadian Commission.

CONTACT
Roosevelt Campobello International Park (Box 129, Lubec, ME 04652, tel. 506/752–2922, fax 506/752–6000, www.nps.gov/roca or www.fdr.net).

Sewall-Belmont House National Historic Site

Rebuilt after fire damage from the War of 1812, this redbrick house is one of the oldest on Capitol Hill. It has been the National Woman's Party Headquarters since 1929 and commemorates the party's founder and woman's suffrage leader, Alice Paul, and associates. It's open on a limited basis. The site was authorized on October 26, 1974.

CONTACT
Sewall-Belmont House National Historic Site (c/o Sewall-Belmont House and Museum, 144 Constitution Ave. NE, Washington, DC 20002-5608, tel. 202/546–1210, www.nps.gov/sebe or www.sewallbelmont.org).

Touro Synagogue National Historic Site

This is the oldest synagogue in the United States. Designed by colonial architect Peter Harrison and dedicated in 1763, it is a fine example of 18th-century Georgian architecture. It was designated on March 5, 1940.

CONTACT
Touro Synagogue National Historic Site (c/o The Touro Synagogue Foundation, 85 Touro St., Newport, RI 02840, tel. 401/847–4794, www.nps.gov/tosy or www.tourosynagogue.org).

Thomas Cole National Historic Site

This is the Hudson River home of the eminent British-American landscape painter Thomas Cole (1801–48). He is recognized as the founder of the Hudson River School, America's first indigenous school of landscape painting. Cole created some of his great paintings, including the *Voyage of Life* series, in the small studio on the property. He lived in the 1815 Federal-style house. The site is owned and operated by the Greene County Historical Society, and it was authorized on December 9, 1999.

CONTACT
Thomas Cole National Historic Site (218 Spring St., Box 426, Catskill, NY 12414, tel. 519/943–7465, fax 518/943–0652, www.nps.gov/thco or www.thomascole.org).

NATIONAL
HERITAGE AREAS

America's Agricultural Heritage Partnership

Sites in this 37-county region of northeastern Iowa illustrate the transformation that took place as mechanization paved the way for a distinctly American system of industrialized agriculture. Tractor design and manufacture, mechanized farming, corn-hog production, dairying, beef cattle feeding, and meatpacking continue to characterize this region. The cultural histories of family farming and agribusiness are equally well represented. Primary federal assistance is being provided by the U.S. Department of Agriculture. It was authorized on November 12, 1996.

CONTACT

America's Agricultural Heritage Partnership (Silos & Smokestacks National Heritage Area, Fowler Building, 604 Lafayette St., Suite 202, Box 2845, Waterloo, IA 50704-2845, tel. 319/234–4567, fax 319/234–8228, www.silosandsmokestacks.org).

Augusta Canal National Heritage Area

This 7-mile corridor follows the full length of the best-preserved canal of its kind remaining in the southern United States. The canal transformed Augusta into an important regional industrial area on the eve of the Civil War, and was instrumental in the post–Civil War relocation of much of the nation's textile industry to the South. The area was authorized on November 12, 1996.

CONTACT

Augusta Canal National Heritage Area (1450 Greene St., Suite 400, Augusta, GA 30901, tel. 706/823–0440, 800/659–8926, www.nps.gov/auca).

Cache La Poudre Corridor

The Cache La Poudre River Corridor is in north-central Colorado, beginning at the eastern end of the Arapahoe-Roosevelt National Forest and extending east through Fort Collins and Larimer County to Greeley and Weld County. The boundary of the 40-mile corridor is the river's 100-year floodplain. It commemorates the role of water development and management in the American West. The area was authorized on October 19, 2000.

CONTACTS

Cache La Poudre Corridor (www.nps.gov/cala). City of Greeley (1100 10th St., Suite 101, Greeley, CO 80631). Larimer County (Box 1190, Fort Collins, CO 80522, 970/350–9424, greeleygov.com).

Cane River National Heritage Area

Before becoming part of the United States, this area at the intersection of the Spanish and French realms in the New World gave rise to the unique Creole culture in a rural setting. The area supports the oldest community in the territory encompassed by the Louisiana Purchase. Historic plantations, Cane River Creole National Historical Park, and three state commemorative areas keep the region's Creole heritage alive. The area was authorized on November 2, 1994.

CONTACT
Cane River National Heritage Area (452 Jefferson St., Suite 150, Natchitoches, LA 71458, tel. 318/356–5555, fax 318/356–8222, www. nps.gov/crha or www.caneriverheritage.org).

Delaware & Lehigh National Heritage Corridor

See Affiliated Areas.

Erie Canalway National Heritage Corridor

The 524-mile canal system, opened in 1825, is an engineering marvel that knitted together New England, New York, and the west, spreading commerce and ideas. The area was authorized on December 21, 2000.

CONTACT
Erie Canalway National Heritage Corridor (Box 219, Waterford, NY 12188, tel. 518/237–7000, fax 518/237–7640, www.nps.gov/erie or www. eriecanalway.org).

Essex National Heritage Area

Essex County is a 500-square-mile area north of Boston along the Atlantic Coast and the Merrimack River. It includes thousands of historic sites that illuminate colonial settlement, the development of the shoe and textile industries, and the growth and decline of the maritime industries—including fishing, privateering, and the China trade. It was authorized on November 12, 1996.

CONTACT
Essex National Heritage Commission, Inc. (221 Essex St., Suite 41, Salem, MA 01970, tel. 978/740–0444, www.nps.gov/esse or www. essexheritage.org).

Hudson River Valley National Heritage Area

From Troy to New York City, the Hudson River Valley contains a rich assemblage of natural features and nationally significant cultural and historical sites. The valley has maintained the scenic, rural character that inspired the Hudson Valley School of landscape painting and the Knickerbocker writers. Recreational opportunities are found on the river, in the mountains and parklands, and on greenway trails. The area was authorized on November 12, 1996.

CONTACT

Hudson River Valley National Heritage Area (Hudson River Valley Greenway and Conservancy, Capitol Bldg., Capitol Station, Room 254, Albany, NY 12224, tel. 518/473–3835, www.nps.gov/hurv or www. hudsonrivervalley.com).

Illinois & Michigan Canal National Heritage Corridor

See Affiliated Areas.

John H. Chafee Blackstone River Valley National Heritage Corridor

See Affiliated Areas.

Lackawanna Valley National Heritage Area

The 40-mile-long Lackawanna Heritage Valley is at the center of what was once the world's most productive anthracite field. Located in Pennsylvania, the heritage area commemorates the history and culture of the anthracite coal mining industry, a cornerstone of the American industrial legacy. A combination of trails, museums, and other attractions help tell the story of anthracite. The area was authorized on October 6, 2000.

CONTACT

Lackawanna Heritage Valley Authority (Scranton Life Building, 538 Spruce St., Suite 516, Scranton, PA 18503, tel. 570/963–6730, fax 570/963–6732, www.nps.gov/lhva or www.lhva.org).

Motor Cities National Heritage Area

Southeast Michigan, which includes the "Motor Cities" of Detroit, Lansing, and Flint, is the region that put the world on wheels. The heritage area consists of six significant corridors. This collection of auto-related museums, attractions, activities, and events exists to preserve and interpret the story of the automobile and was authorized November 6, 1998.

CONTACT

Motor Cities National Heritage Area (200 Renaissance Ctr., Suite 3148, Detroit, MI 48243, tel. 313/259–3425, fax 313/259–5254, www. nps.gov/auto or www.motorcities.org).

National Coal Heritage Area

The cultural geography here has been profoundly influenced over the last 125 years by the pervasive role of the coal mines. The communities in these 11 counties in southern West Virginia reflect their origins as "company towns" formed by local traditions, waves of immigrant workers, and the dominance of the mining companies. Ethnic neighborhoods and the physical infrastructure of the mines are still clearly seen throughout the region. The area was authorized on November 12, 1996.

CONTACT

National Coal Heritage Area (Coal Heritage Highway Authority/ National Coal Heritage Area, 100 Kelly Ave., Box 15, Oak Hill, WV 25901, tel. 304/465–3720 or 855/982–2625, fax 304/465-3719, www. nps.gov/history/heritageareas or www.coalheritage.org).

Ohio & Erie Canal National Heritage Corridor

This area of northeast Ohio celebrates the canal that enabled shipping between Lake Erie and the Ohio River and vaulted Ohio into commercial prominence in the early 1830s. The canal and towpath trail pass through agricultural lands and rural villages into industrial communities such as Akron, Canton, and Cleveland that trace their prosperity to the coming of the canal. (See also Cuyahoga Valley National Recreation Area.) The area was authorized on November 12, 1996.

CONTACT

Ohio & Erie Canal National Heritage Corridor (Ohio & Erie Canalway Coalition, 47 W. Exchange St., Akron, OH 44308, tel. 330/374–5657, www.nps.gov/nr/travel/ohioeriecanal or www.ohioeriecanal.org).

Quinebaug & Shetucket Rivers Valley National Heritage Corridor

See Affiliated Areas.

Rivers of Steel National Heritage Area

Steel made a great imprint on the Pittsburgh region in the late 19th and early 20th century. The industry made possible railroads, skyscrapers, and shipbuilding while altering corporate practice and labor organization. There are remnants of numerous mills as well as communities founded by mill workers, many of which are linked by hiking trails and riverboat tours. The area was authorized on November 12, 1996.

CONTACT

Rivers of Steel National Heritage Area (The Bost Building, 623 E. 8th Ave., Homestead, PA 15120, tel. 412/464–4020, fax 412/464–4417, www.nps.gov/rist or www.riversofsteel.com).

Schuylkill River Valley National Heritage Area

Encompassing the 128-mile Schuylkill River Valley as it passes through five counties, the heritage area includes three national park areas, the city of Philadelphia, and many early communities and canal towns. The area has pre-Revolutionary mills, late-19th-century factories, and numerous historic districts and cultural attractions. The area was authorized on October 6, 2000.

CONTACT

Schuylkill River Heritage Area (140 College Dr., Pottstown, PA 19464, tel. 484/945–0200, fax 484/945–0204, www.nps.gov/scrv or www. schuylkillriver.org).

Shenandoah Valley Battlefields National Historic District

This fertile agricultural valley was of strategic value to both sides in the Civil War, with the result that it became the site for 15 battles in the conflict. It was authorized on November 12, 1996.

CONTACT

Shenandoah Valley Battlefields Foundation (298 W. Old Cross Rd., New Market, VA 22844, tel. 540/740-4545 or 888/689–4545, www. shenandoahatwar.org).

South Carolina Heritage Corridor

Two routes through 14 counties in western South Carolina begin in the mill villages, waterfalls, and mountains of the Up Country; run through historic courthouse towns and military sites and along the Savannah River; and follow the Edisto River and the South Carolina Railroad to the Low Country's wealth of African American and antebellum history, centered in and around historic Charleston. The area was authorized on November 12, 1996.

CONTACT

South Carolina Heritage Corridor (405 Main St., Edgefield, SC 29824, tel. 803/637–0877, fax 803/637–6237, www.nps.gov/soca or www. sc-heritagecorridor.org).

Southwestern Pennsylvania Industrial Heritage Route

This 500-mile route travels through nine counties of southwestern Pennsylvania and features hundreds of sites relating to the nation's industrial story. Included are the Altoona Railyards, the Johnstown Flood

National Memorial and Museum, the steel mills of Johnstown, and Horseshoe Curve, a 19th-century engineering marvel built by the Pennsylvania Railroad. It is also called the Path of Progress National Heritage Route. The site was authorized on November 19, 1988.

CONTACT

Southwestern Pennsylvania Industrial Heritage Route (Southwestern Pennsylvania Heritage Preservation Commission, Box 565, 105 Zee Plaza, Hollidaysburg, PA 16648, tel. 814/696–9380, fax 814/696–9569, www.cr.nps.gov/heritageareas).

Tennessee Civil War Heritage Area

A number of areas throughout Tennessee preserve and interpret the legacy of the Civil War there. Heritage resources are focused on important events, geographic factors, decisive battles, engagements, and strategic maneuvers of the war, and the effect of the war on Tennessee's residents. The area was authorized on November 12, 1996.

CONTACT

Tennessee Civil War Heritage Area (1417 E. Main St., Murfreesboro, TN 37132, tel. 615/494–8916, fax 615/898–5614, www.nps.gov/tecw).

Wheeling National Heritage Area

Once the capital of West Virginia, Wheeling marked the northernmost navigable port on the Ohio River. It became a thriving commercial, industrial, and cultural center, and by 1818 was the terminus of the National Road, our nation's first highway. The area was authorized on October 11, 2000.

CONTACT

Wheeling National Heritage Area Corporation (400 Main St., Wheeling, WV 26003, tel. 304/232–3087, fax 304/232–1812, www.nps.gov/whee or www.wheelingheritage.org).

Yuma Crossing National Heritage Area

This natural ford on the mighty Colorado River has been a gathering spot for people for more than 500 years. It was an important 19th-century landmark during the westward expansion of our nation. The area was authorized on October 19, 2000.

CONTACT

Riverfront Development Office (180 W. 1st St., Suite E, Yuma, AZ 85364, tel. 928/373–5198, fax 929/373–5191, www.nps.gov/yucr).

NATIONAL TRAILS SYSTEM

Appalachian National Scenic Trail

See the West Virginia section for a full description.

CONTACTS

Appalachian National Scenic Trail (Box 50, Harpers Ferry, WV 25425, 304/535–6278, www.nps.gov/appa). Appalachian Trail Conservancy (799 Washington St., Box 807, Harpers Ferry, WV 25425, tel. 304/535–6278 or 304/535–6331, fax 304/535–2667, www.appalachiantrail.org).

California National Historic Trail

The California Trail is a system of overland routes, starting at numerous points along the Missouri River and ending at many locations in California and Oregon. Over these trails passed one of America's great mass migrations, seeking the promise of gold and a new life in California in the late 1840s and 1850s. Traces of their struggles and triumphs are still evident at many trail sites. The trail was established on August 3, 1992.

CONTACT

California National Historic Trail (National Park Service, 324 S. State St., Suite 200, Box 30, Salt Lake City, UT 84111, tel. 801/741–1012, fax 801/741–1102, www.nps.gov/cali/).

Continental Divide National Scenic Trail

Running the length of the Rocky Mountains near the Continental Divide, this trail extends from Canada's Waterton Lake into Montana, along the Idaho border, and on to Wyoming, Colorado, and New Mexico, ending at the U.S.–Mexico border. It was established on November 10, 1978.

CONTACT

Continental Divide National Scenic Trail (Rocky Mountain National Park, 1000 Hwy. 36, Estes Park, CO 80517–8397, tel. 970/586–1206, www.nps.gov/romo).

El Camino Real de Tierra Adentro

From 1598 to 1882, the 1,600-mile Camino Real de Tierra Adentro provided an important link between Mexico City and Santa Fe. As such it aided exploration, colonization, economic development, and subsequent cultural interaction among Spanish, Anglo, and Native American people. Only the 404-mile portion of the trail in the United States is designated as a National Historic Trail. The trail was established on October 13, 2000.

CONTACTS

El Camino Real International Heritage Center (National Trails Intermountain Region, National Park Service, Box 728, Santa Fe, NM 87505, tel. 505/988–6098, fax 505/986–5214, www.nps.gov/elca). El Camino Real International Heritage Center (Box 175, Socorro, NM 87801, tel. 575/854–3600, www.caminorealheritage.org).

Florida National Scenic Trail

The trail runs the length of Florida from Big Cypress National Preserve near Miami to Gulf Islands National Seashore near Pensacola Beach. It's the only national scenic trail that explores tropical and subtropical regions. More than 600 miles have been developed for public use. The trail was established on March 28, 1983.

CONTACT

Florida National Scenic Trail (Florida Trail Association, 5415 S.W. 13th St., Gainesville, FL 32608, tel. 352/378–8823 or 877/445–3352, www. floridatrail.org).

Ice Age National Scenic Trail

Winding over Wisconsin's glacial moraines, the trail links six of the nine units of the Ice Age National Scientific Reserve. It traverses significant features of Wisconsin's glacial heritage. Approximately 500 miles are open to public use; additional miles are being developed. It was authorized on October 3, 1980.

CONTACT

Ice Age National Scenic Trail (National Park Service, 700 Rayovac Dr., Suite 100, Madison, WI 53711, tel. 608/441–5610, fax 608/441–5606, www.nps.gov/iatr).

Iditarod National Historic Trail

One of Alaska's preeminent Gold Rush Trails, the 2,350-mile Iditarod extends from Seward to Nome and is composed of a network of trails and side trails developed at the turn of the 20th century. It was established on November 20, 1978.

CONTACTS

Iditarod National Historic Trail (Bureau of Land Management, 6881 Abbott Loop Rd., Anchorage, AK 99507, www.blm.gov). Iditarod National Historic Trail, Inc. (Box 2323, Seward, AK 99664, 907/443–5226, www.iditarodnationalhistorictrail.org).

Juan Bautista de Anza National Historic Trail

This trail commemorates the route of a party of Spanish soldier-settlers and their families, led by Lieutenant-Colonel Juan Bautista de Anza, from Sonora, Mexico, to found a presidio and mission at the port of San Francisco. The trail includes an autoroute linking more than 100 sites and 150 miles of trails in Arizona and California for recreational hiking. The 1,200-mile trail was established on August 15, 1990.

CONTACT

Juan Bautista de Anza National Historic Trail (333 Bush St., Suite 500, San Francisco, CA 94104, tel. 415/623–2340, fax 415/623–2387, www.nps.gov/juba).

Lewis & Clark National Historic Trail

The route of the 1804–06 Lewis and Clark Expedition extends 3,700 miles, from the Mississippi River in Illinois to the Pacific Ocean at the mouth of the Columbia River in Oregon. Water routes, hiking trails, and marked highways follow the explorer's out-bound and return routes. The trail was established on November 10, 1978.

CONTACT

Lewis and Clark National Historic Trail (National Park Service, 601 Riverfront Dr., Omaha, NE 68102, tel. 402/661–1804, www.nps.gov/lecl).

Mormon Pioneer National Historic Trail

This 1,300-mile trail follows the route over which Brigham Young led the Mormons from Nauvoo, Illinois, to the site of modern Salt Lake City, Utah, in 1846–47. A driving-tour route has been marked near the trail corridor. It was established on November 10, 1978.

CONTACT

Mormon Pioneer National Historic Trail (National Park Service, 324 S. State St., Suite 200, Box 30, Salt Lake City, UT 84111, tel. 801/741–1012 Ext. 119, www.nps.gov/mopi).

Natchez Trace National Scenic Trail

See the Mississippi chapter for a full description.

CONTACT

Natchez Trace National Scenic Trail (2680 Natchez Trace Pkwy., Tupelo, MS 38804, tel. 800/305–7417, www.nps.gov/natt).

Nez Perce National Historic Trail

The 1,170-mile Nez Perce trail commemorates the flight of five bands of Nez Perce Indians in 1877. It begins in northeastern Oregon, extends across Idaho and western and central Montana, bisecting Yellowstone National Park in Wyoming and ending near the Bear Paw Mountains. It was established on October 6, 1986.

CONTACT

Nez Perce National Historic Trail (39063 Hwy. 95, Spaulding, ID 83540–9715, tel. 208/843–7001, fax 208/843–7003, www.nps.gov/nepe).

North Country National Scenic Trail

The trail connects seven northern-tier states extending from Crown Point, New York, to Lake Sakakawea in North Dakota, where it connects with the Lewis & Clark National Historic Trail. Approximately 1,650 miles are open to public use. Additional miles are being developed. The trail was established on March 5, 1980.

CONTACT

North Country National Scenic Trail (National Park Service, 700 Rayovac Dr., Suite 100, Madison, WI 53711, tel. 608/441–5610, fax 608/441–5606, www.nps.gov/noco).

Oregon National Historic Trail

Tens of thousands of pioneers followed this 2,170-mile trail west from Independence, Missouri, to Oregon City, Oregon, between 1841 and 1860. The trail was established on November 10, 1978.

CONTACT

Oregon National Historic Trail (National Park Service, 324 S. State St., Suite 200, Salt Lake City, UT 84111, tel. 801/741–1012 Ext. 119, www.nps.gov/oreg).

Overmountain Victory National Historic Trail

This 300-mile route follows the path of American Revolution patriots who mustered in western Virginia and eastern Tennessee and came across the mountains of North Carolina to Kings Mountain, South Carolina, where they defeated British-led Loyalist militia in 1780. The trail was established on September 8, 1980.

CONTACT

Overmountain Victory National Historic Trail (2635 Park Rd., Blacksburg, SC 29702, tel. 864/936–3477, www.nps.gov/ovvi).

Pacific Crest National Scenic Trail

Extending from the Mexican border northward along the Sierra and Cascade peaks of California, Oregon, and Washington, the 2,650-mile trail reaches the Canadian border near Ross Lake, Washington. The trail, which is one of the two initial components of the National Trails System, was established on October 2, 1968.

CONTACT

Pacific Crest National Trail Association (1331 Garden Hwy., Sacramento, CA 95833, tel. 916/285–1846, fax 916/285–1865, www.pcta.org).

Pony Express National Historic Trail

For 18 months, 1860–61, riders on horseback carried mail 1,800 miles between St. Joseph, Missouri, and Sacramento, California, in less than 10 days, proving that a regular communications link to the Pacific coast was possible. Most of the 150 relay stations no longer exist. The trail was established on August 3, 1992.

CONTACT

Pony Express National Historic Trail (National Park Service, 324 S. State St., Suite 200, Salt Lake City, UT 84111, tel. 801/741–1012 Ext. 119, www.nps.gov/poex).

Potomac Heritage National Scenic Trail

See the District of Columbia chapter for a full description.

CONTACT

Potomac Heritage National Scenic Trail (Box B, Harpers Ferry, WV 25425, tel. 304/535–4014, www.nps.gov/pohe).

Santa Fe National Historic Trail

This route of the Santa Fe Trail extends from a point near Arrow Rock, Missouri, through Kansas, Oklahoma, and Colorado to Santa Fe, New Mexico. To date, 20 certified sites and segments are open for public use.

CONTACT

Santa Fe National Historic Trail (Box 728, Santa Fe, NM 57504-0728, tel. 505/988–6888, fax 801/741–1102, www.nps.gov/safe).

Selma to Montgomery National Historic Trail

This trail commemorates a 1965 voting rights march led by Dr. Martin Luther King Jr. The marchers walked along U.S. 80 from Brown Chapel A.M.E. Church in Selma, Alabama, to the state capitol in Montgomery. The march helped inspire passage of voting-rights legislation signed by President Lyndon Johnson on August 6, 1965. The trail was established on November 12, 1965.

CONTACTS

Selma to Montgomery National Historic Trail (Lowndes Interpretive Center, 7002 Hwy. 80, Hayneville, AL 36040, tel. 334/877–1984, fax 334/877-1985. Selma Interpretive Center, 2 Broad St., Selma, AL 36701, tel. 334/872–0509, fax 334/872–2645, www.nps.gov/semo).

Trail of Tears National Historic Trail

The Trail of Tears commemorates two of the land and water routes used for the forced removal of more than 15,000 Cherokees from their ancestral lands in North Carolina, Tennessee, Georgia, and Alabama to the Indian Territories of Oklahoma and Arkansas. The journey lasted from June 1838 to March 1839. The trail was established on December 16, 1987.

CONTACTS

Trail of Tears National Historic Trail (National Park Service, Long Distance Trails Group, Box 728, Santa Fe, NM 87504-0728, tel. 505/988–6888, www.nps.gov/trte). Trail of Tears Association (1100 N. University, Suite 143, Little Rock, AR 72207, tel. 501/666–9032, fax 501/666–5875, www.nationaltota.org).

WILD & SCENIC RIVERS SYSTEM

Alagnak Wild River

See the Alaska chapter for a full description.

CONTACT

Alagnak Wild River (Alagnak Wild River, 1 King Salmon Mall, King Salmon, AK 99613, tel. 907/246–3305, www.nps.gov/alag).

Alatna Wild River

The stream lies wholly within Gates of the Arctic National Park & Preserve, Alaska, in the Central Brooks Range. Wildlife, scenery, and interesting geologic features abound in the river corridor. The river was authorized on December 2, 1980.

CONTACT

Alatna Wild River (Gates of the Arctic National Park & Preserve, Box 30, Bettles, AK 99726, tel. 907/692–5494, fax 907/692–5400, www.nps.gov/gaar).

Aniakchak Wild River

The river, which lies within Aniakchak National Monument & Preserve, Alaska, flows out of Surprise Lake and plunges spectacularly through "The Gates."

CONTACT

Aniakchak Wild River (Aniakchak National Monument & Preserve, 1 King Salmon Mall, Box 245, King Salmon, AK 99613, tel. 907/246–3305, www.nps.gov/ania).

Bluestone National Scenic River

See the West Virginia chapter for a full description.

CONTACT

Bluestone National Scenic River (c/o New River Gorge National River, Box 246, Glen Jean, WV 25846-0246, tel. 304/465–0508 or 304/466–0417, fax 304/465–0591, www.nps.gov/lue).

Charley Wild River

Lying within Yukon-Charley Rivers National Preserve, Alaska, this stream is known for the exceptional clarity of its water. For the experienced canoer or kayaker, it offers many miles of white-water challenges. The river was authorized on December 2, 1980.

CONTACT

Charley Wild River (Yukon-Charley Rivers National Preserve, Box 167, Eagle, AK 99738-0167, tel. 907/547–2234, www.nps.gov/yuch).

Chilikadrotna Wild River

The river lies within Lake Clark National Park & Preserve, Alaska. Long stretches of swift water and outstanding fishing are exceptional features. The river was authorized on December 2, 1980.

CONTACT

Chilikadrotna Wild River (Lake Clark National Park & Preserve, 240 W. 5th Ave., Suite 236, Anchorage, AK 99501, tel. 907/644–3626 or 907/781–2218, fax 907/644-3810, www.nps.gov/lacl).

Farmington River (West Branch)

The river is an important habitat for wildlife, and the Farmington River Valley is currently one of the few places in Connecticut with nesting bald eagles. Atlantic salmon may soon return to the river after an absence of decades. Recreational value, rare wildlife, outstanding fisheries, and a rich history are some of the features of the Farmington.

CONTACT

Farmington River (National Park Service, 15 State St., Boston, MA 02109, tel. 617/223–5225).

Flathead River

Branches of the Flathead River border the western and southern boundaries of Glacier National Park, Montana. These areas are popular for fishing, floating, and recreation.

CONTACT

Flathead River (Glacier National Park, Box 128, West Glacier, MT 59936-0128, tel. 406/888–7800, fax 406/888–7808, www.nps.gov/glac).

Great Egg Harbor Scenic & Recreational River

See the New Jersey chapter for a full description.

CONTACT

Great Egg Harbor Scenic & Recreational River (National Park Service, 200 Chestnut St., Philadelphia, PA 19106, tel. 215/597–5823, www.nps. gov/greg).

John Wild River

The river flows south through the Anaktuvuk Pass of Alaska's Brooks Range, and its valley is an important migration route for the Arctic Caribou herd. Gates of the Arctic National Park & Preserve contains the wild river. The river was authorized on December 2, 1980.

CONTACT

John Wild River (Gates of the Arctic National Park & Preserve, Box 30, Bettles, AK 99726, tel. 907/692–5494, fax 907/692–5400, www.nps.gov/gaar).

Kern River

This river includes both the North and South forks of the Kern. The South Fork is totally free-flowing. It descends through deep gorges with large granite outcroppings and domes interspersed with open meadows. The upper 48 miles of the North Fork flow through Sequoia National Park & Golden Trout Wilderness. The river was authorized on November 24, 1987.

CONTACT

Kern River (Sequoia & Kings Canyon National Parks, 47050 Generals Hwy., Three Rivers, CA 93271-9651, tel. 559/565–3341, www.nps.gov/seki).

Kings River

The river includes the entire Middle and South forks, which are largely in Kings Canyon National Park. Beginning in glacial lakes above timberline, the rivers flow through deep, steep-sided canyons, over falls and cataracts, eventually becoming an outstanding white-water rafting river in its lower reaches in Sequoia National Forest. Geology, scenery, recreation, fish, wildlife, and history are all significant aspects. It was authorized on November 3, 1987.

CONTACT

Kings River (Sequoia & Kings Canyon National Parks, 47050 Generals Hwy., Three Rivers, CA 93271-9651, tel. 559/565–3341, www.nps.gov/seki).

Kobuk Wild River

Kobuk Wild River is contained within Gates of the Arctic National Park & Preserve, Alaska. From its headwaters in the Endicott Mountains, the stream courses south through a wide valley and passes through two scenic canyons. It was authorized on December 2, 1980.

CONTACT

Kobuk Wild River (Kobuk Valley National Park, Box 1029, Kotzebue, AK 99752, tel. 907/442–3890, 907/442–3760, www.nps.gov/kova).

Lamprey Wild & Scenic River

This segment of the Lamprey River, extending from the Bunker Pond Dam in Epping downstream 24 miles to the confluence with the Picassic River in Newmarket, provides conservation opportunities for associated shorelands, floodplains, and wetlands. The Lamprey is considered the most important anadromous fish resource in New Hampshire. It was authorized on November 12, 1996.

CONTACT

Lamprey Wild & Scenic River (Boston System Support Office, Rivers and Trails Dept., 15 State St., Boston, MA 02109, tel. 617/223–5191, www.lampreyriver.org).

Lower Delaware Wild & Scenic River

The corridor contains the site of Washington's famous crossing of the Delaware River. Sheer cliffs that rise 400 feet above the river are home to rare flora and fauna in this region, including the prickly pear cactus. It was authorized on November 1, 2000.

CONTACT

Lower Delaware Wild & Scenic River (200 Chestnut St., Philadelphia, PA 19106-2818, tel. 215/597–6482, fax 215/597–5747, www.nps.gov/lode).

Maurice National Scenic & Recreational River

Portions of the Maurice River and three of its main tributaries, the Manumuskim River and the Menantico and Muskee Creeks, were designated to protect critical habitat on the Atlantic Flyway. It was authorized on December 1, 1993.

CONTACT

Maurice National Scenic & Recreational River (c/o Northeast Region, National Park Service, 200 Chestnut St., Philadelphia, PA 19106-2818, tel. 215/597–6482, fax 215/597–5747, www.nps.gov/nero/rivers/maurice.htm.

Merced River

Including the main stem and the South Fork, the Merced flows 81 miles in alternating pools, cascades, and waterfalls through Yosemite's superlative scenery—from glaciated peaks to lakes, alpine and subalpine meadows, glacially carved valleys, and gorges of spectacular proportions. It was authorized on November 2, 1987.

CONTACT

Merced River (Yosemite National Park, Box 577, Yosemite National Park, CA 95389-0577, tel. 209/372–0200, www.nps.gov/yose).

Middle Delaware River

See the Pennsylvania chapter for a full description.

CONTACT

Middle Delaware River (Delaware Water Gap National Recreation Area, River Rd., Bushkill, PA 18324, tel. 570/426–2452, fax 570/426–2402, www.nps.gov/dewa).

Missouri National Recreational River

See the Nebraska chapter for a full description.

CONTACT

Missouri National Recreational River (508 E. 2nd St., Yankton, SD 57078, tel. 605/665–0209, fax 605/665–4183, www.nps.gov/mnrr).

Mulchatna Wild River

Mulchatna Wild River, which lies within Lake Clark National Park & Preserve, Alaska, is exceptionally scenic as it flows out of Turquoise Lake with the glacier-clad Chigmit Mountains to the east. Moose and caribou inhabit the area. The river was authorized on December 2, 1980.

CONTACT

Mulchatna Wild River (Lake Clark National Park & Preserve, 240 W. 5th Ave., Suite 236, Anchorage, AK 99501, tel. 907/644–3626 or 907/781–2218, fax 907/644-3810, www.nps.gov/lacl).

Niobrara National Scenic Riverway

See the Nebraska chapter for a full description.

CONTACT

Niobrara National Scenic Riverway (214 W. Hwy. 20, Box 319, Valentine, NE 69201, tel. 402/376–1901, fax 402/376–1949, www.nps.gov/niob).

Noatak Wild River

Noatak Wild River is in Gates of the Arctic National Park & Preserve and Noatak National Preserve in Alaska. The Noatak drains the largest mountain-ringed river basin in America that is still virtually unaffected by human activities. It was authorized on December 2, 1980.

CONTACT

Noatak Wild River (Gates of the Arctic National Park & Preserve, Box 30, Bettles, AK 99726, tel. 907/692–5494, fax 907/692–5400, www.nps.gov/noat).

North Fork of the Koyukuk Wild River

The river flows from the south flank of the Arctic Divide through broad, glacially carved valleys beside the rugged Endicott Mountains in Alaska's Central Brooks Range. It was authorized on December 2, 1980.

CONTACT
North Fork of the Koyukuk Wild River (Gates of the Arctic National Park & Preserve, Box 30, Fairbanks, AK 99726, tel. 907/692–5494, fax 907/692–5400, www.nps.gov/gaar).

Obed Wild & Scenic River

See the Tennessee chapter for a full description.

CONTACT
Obed Wild & Scenic River (Box 429, Wartburg, TN 37887-0429, tel. 423/346–6294, www.nps.gov/obed).

Rio Grande Wild & Scenic River

See the Texas chapter for a full description.

CONTACT
Rio Grande Wild & Scenic River (Box 129, Big Bend National Park TX 79834-0129, tel. 432/477–2251, fax 432/477–1175, www.nps.gov/rigr).

St. Croix National Scenic Riverway

See the Wisconsin chapter for a full description.

CONTACT
St. Croix National Scenic Riverway (401 N. Hamilton St., Saint Croix Falls, WI 54024, tel. 715/483–2274 or 715/483-3284, fax 715/483–3288, www.nps.gov/sacn).

Salmon Wild River

Salmon Wild River, within Kobuk Valley National Park, Alaska, is small but exceptionally beautiful, with deep blue-green pools and many rock outcroppings. It was authorized on December 2, 1980.

CONTACT
Salmon Wild River (Kobuk Valley National Park, Box 1029, Kotzebue, AK 99752, tel. 907/442-3890 or 907/442–3760, www.nps.gov/kova).

Sudbury, Assabet & Concord Rivers

Located about 25 miles west of Boston, the rivers are remarkably undeveloped and provide recreational opportunities in a natural setting. Ten of the river miles lie within the boundary of the Great Meadows National Wildlife Refuge. Historic sites of national importance, including many in the Minute Man National Historical Park, are near the rivers in Concord.

CONTACT

Sudbury, Assabet & Concord Rivers (15 State St., Boston, MA 02109, tel. 617/223–5225, www.sudbury-assabet-concord.org).

Tinayguk Wild River

Alaska's 44-mile Tinayguk River is the largest tributary of the North Fork of the Koyukuk. Both lie entirely within the pristine environment of Gates of the Arctic National Park. It was authorized on December 2, 1980.

CONTACT

Tinayguk Wild River (Gates of the Arctic National Park & Preserve, Box 30, Fairbanks, AK 99726, tel. 907/692–5494, fax 907/692–5400, www.nps.gov/gaar).

Tlikakila Wild River

Located about 100 air miles west of Anchorage in Lake Clark National Park, Alaska, the 51-mile Tlikakila Wild River is closely flanked by glaciers, 10,000-foot-high rock-and-snow-capped mountains, and perpendicular cliffs. It was authorized on December 2, 1980.

CONTACTS

Tlikakila Wild River (Lake Clark National Park & Preserve: Administrative Headquarters, 240 W. 5th Ave., Suite 236, Anchorage, AK 99501, tel. 907/644–3626). Field Headquarters (1 Park Place, Port Alsworth, AK 99653, tel. 907/781–2218, www.nps.gov/lacl).

Tuolumne River

The Tuolumne originates from snowmelt off Mounts Dana and Lydell in Yosemite National Park and courses 54 miles before crossing into Stanislaus National Forest. The national forest segment contains some of the most noted white water in the high Sierras and is an extremely popular rafting stream. It was authorized on September 28, 1981.

CONTACT

Tuolumne River (Yosemite National Park, Box 577, Yosemite, CA 95389-0577, tel. 209/372–0200, www.nps.gov/yose).

Upper Delaware River

See the Pennsylvania chapter for a full description.

CONTACT

Upper Delaware River (274 River Rd., Beach Lake, PA 18405, tel. 570/685–4871 or 570/729–7134, 845/252–7100 for river conditions, fax 570/729–8565, www.nps.gov/upde).

White Clay Creek

CONTACT

White Clay Creek (National Park Service, 200 Chestnut St., Philadelphia, PA 19106, tel. 215/597-6482, fax 215/597-5747, www.nps.gov/nero/rivers/whiteclay.htm).

LODGING CONTACT INFORMATION

HOTELS

Adam's Mark	tel. 716/845–5100	www.adamsmark.com
Baymont Inns	tel. 877/229–6668	www.baymontinns.com
Best Western	tel. 800/528–1234	www.bestwestern.com
Choice	tel. 800/424–6423	www.choicehotels.com
Clarion	tel. 800/424–6423	www.choicehotels.com
Comfort Inn	tel. 800/424–6423	www.choicehotels.com
Days Inn	tel. 800/329–7466	www.daysinn.com
Doubletree	tel. 800/222–8733	www.doubletree.com
Embassy Suites	tel. 800/362–2779	www.embassysuites.com
Fairfield Inn	tel. 888/236–2427	www.fairfieldinn.com
Four Seasons	tel. 800/332–3442	www.fourseasons.com
Hilton	tel. 800/445–8667	www.hilton.com
Holiday Inn	tel. 800/465–4329	www.holidayinn.com
Howard Johnson	tel. 800/446–4656	www.hojo.com
Hyatt Hotels & Resorts	tel. 800/233–1234	www.hyatt.com
Inter-Continental	tel. 800/327–0200	www.intercontinental. com
La Quinta	tel. 800/531–5900	www.laquinta.com
Marriott	tel. 888 236–2427	www.marriott.com
Le Meridien	tel. 800/543–4300	www.lemeridien-hotels. com
Nikko Hotels International	tel. 800/645–5687	www.jalhotels.com
Omni	tel. 888/444–6664	www.omnihotels.com
Quality Inn	tel. 877/424–6423	www.qualityinn.com
Radisson	tel. 888/201–1718	www.radisson.com
Ramada	tel. 800/272–6232	www.ramada.com
Red Lion Hotels	tel. 800/733–5466	www.redlion.rdln.com
Renaissance Hotels & Resorts	tel. 888/236–2427	www.renaissancehotels. com
Ritz-Carlton	tel. 800/542–8680	www.ritzcarlton.com

Sheraton	tel. 800/325–3535	www.starwood.com/ sheraton
Sleep Inn	tel. 877/424–6423	www.sleepinn.com
Westin Hotels & Resorts	tel. 800/937–8461	www.starwood.com/ westin
Wyndham Hotels & Resorts	tel. 877/999–3223	www.wyndham.com

MOTELS

Budget Host Inns	tel. 800/283–4678	www.budgethost.com
Econo Lodge	tel. 877/424–6423	www.econolodge.com
Friendship Inns	tel. 800/453–4511	www.friendshipinn.com
Motel 6	tel. 800/466–8356	www.motel6.com
Rodeway	tel. 877/424–6423	www.rodewayinn.com
Super 8	tel. 800/800–8000	www.super8.com.

Index

INDEX

Abraham Lincoln Birthplace National Historic Site *171–172*
Acadia National Park *180–181*
Adams National Historical Park *196*
African Burial Ground National Monument *277–278*
Agate Fossil Beds National Monument *246–247*
AIDS Memorial Grove National Memorial *460*
Alagnak Wild River *8, 480*
Alatna Wild River *480*
Aleutian World War II National Historic Area *460*
Alibates Flint Quarries National Monument *365*
Allegheny Portage Railroad National Historic Site *326–327*
American Memorial Park *460*
America's Agricultural Heritage Partnership *468*
Amistad National Recreation Area *366–367*
Andersonville National Historic Site *133–134*
Andrew Johnson National Historic Site *356*
Aniakchak National Monument & Preserve *9, 480*
Aniakchak Wild River *480*
Antietam National Battlefield *183–184*
Apostle Islands National Lakeshore *429–430*
Appalachian National Scenic Trail *422–423, 474*
Appomattox Court House National Historical Park *392–393*
Arches National Park *379–380*
Arkansas Post National Memorial *50–51*
Arlington House, the Robert E. Lee Memorial *393*
Assateague Island National Seashore *184–186*
Augusta Canal National Heritage Area *468*
Aztec Ruins National Monument *262–263*

Badlands National Park *350–351*
Bandelier National Monument *263–264*
Benjamin Franklin National Memorial *460*
Bent's Old Fort National Historic Site *89–90*
Bering Land Bridge National Preserve *9–11*
Big Bend National Park *367–368*
Big Cypress National Preserve *120–121*
Big Hole National Battlefield *239–240*
Big South Fork National River & Recreation Area *357–358*
Big Thicket National Preserve *368–369*
Bighorn Canyon National Recreation Area *240–241*
Biscayne National Park *121–122*
Black Canyon of the Gunnison National Park *90–91*
Blue Ridge Parkway *297–298*
Bluestone National Scenic River *423–424, 480*
Booker T. Washington National Monument *394*

Boston African American National Historic Site. *197*
Boston Harbor Islands National Recreation Area. *198–199*
Boston National Historical Park. *199–200*
Brices Cross Roads National Battlefield Site *225–226*
Brown v. Board of Education National Historic Site *165*
Bryce Canyon National Park *380–381*
Buck Island Reef National Monument *447–448*
Buffalo National River *51–52*

Cabrillo National Monument. *59–60*
Cache la Poudre Corridor *468*
California National Historic Trail. *474*
Canaveral National Seashore *122–123*
Cane River Creole National Historical Park *175–176*
Cane River National Heritage Area. *469*
Canyon de Chelly National Monument. *27*
Canyonlands National Park *381–382*
Cape Cod National Seashore *200–201*
Cape Hatteras National Seashore *299–300*
Cape Krusenstern National Monument *11–12*
Cape Lookout National Seashore *300–301*
Capitol Reef National Park *382–383*
Capulin Volcano National Monument. *264–265*
Carl Sandburg Home National Historic Site. *301–302*
Carlsbad Caverns National Park *265–266*
Carter G. Woodson Home *105–106*
Casa Grande Ruins National Monument *28*
Castillo de San Marcos National Monument. *123–124*
Castle Clinton National Monument. *278*
Catoctin Mountain Park. *186–187*
Cedar Breaks National Monument *383–384*
Cedar Creek & Belle Grove National Historical Park *396–396*
Chaco Culture National Historical Park *267–268*
Chamizal National Memorial. *369–370*
Channel Islands National Park. *60–61*
Charles Pinckney National Historic Site *343*
Charley Wild River. *480–481*
Chattahoochee River National Recreation Area. *134*
Chesapeake & Ohio Canal National Historical Park. *187–188*
Chicago Portage National Historic Site. *461*
Chickamauga & Chattanooga National Military Park. *135–136*
Chickasaw National Recreation Area. *318–319*
Chilikadrotna Wild River *481*
Chimney Rock National Historic Site *461*
Chiricahua National Monument *29*
Christiansted National Historic Site *448–449*
City of Rocks National Reserve *151–152*
Clara Barton National Historic Site. *189*
Colonial National Historical Park *396–397*

Colorado National Monument *91–92*
Congaree National Park *343–344*
Constitution Gardens *106*
Continental Divide National Scenic Trail *474*
Coronado National Memorial *30*
Cowpens National Battlefield *345*
Crater Lake National Park *321–322*
Craters of the Moon National Monument & Preserve *152–153*
Cumberland Gap National Historical Park *172–173*
Cumberland Island National Seashore *136–137*
Curecanti National Recreation Area *92–93*
Cuyahoga Valley National Park *311–312*

David A. Berger National Memorial *461*
Dayton Aviation Heritage National Historical Park *312–313*
De Soto National Memorial *124*
Death Valley National Park *61–63*
Delaware & Lehigh National Heritage Corridor *461–462*
Delaware Water Gap National Recreation Area *327–328*
Denali National Park & Preserve *12–13*
Devils Postpile National Monument *63–64*
Devils Tower National Monument *432–433*
Dinosaur National Monument *93–94*
Dry Tortugas National Park *125*

Ebey's Landing National Historical Reserve *409–410*
Edgar Allan Poe National Historic Site *328–329*
Effigy Mounds National Monument *162–163*
Eisenhower National Historic Site *329–330*
El Camino Real de Tierra Adentro *474–475*
El Malpais National Monument *268–269*
El Morro National Monument *269–270*
Eleanor Roosevelt National Historic Site *279*
Erie Canalway National Heritage Corridor *469*
Essex National Heritage Area *469*
Eugene O'Neill National Historic Site *64–65*
Everglades National Park *125–127*

Farmington River (West Branch) *481*
Father Marquette National Memorial *462*
Federal Hall National Memorial *280*
Fire Island National Seashore *280–282*
First Ladies National Historic Site *313*
Flathead River *481*
Flight 93 National Memorial *330–331*
Florida National Scenic Trail *475*
Florissant Fossil Beds National Monument *94–95*
Ford's Theatre National Historic Site *106–107*
Fort Bowie National Historic Site *31*

Fort Caroline National Memorial *127–128*
Fort Davis National Historic Site. *370–371*
Fort Donelson National Battlefield *358–359*
Fort Frederica National Monument *137–138*
Fort Laramie National Historic Site *433–434*
Fort Larned National Historic Site *165–166*
Fort Matanzas National Monument *128–129*
Fort McHenry National Monument & Historic Shrine *189–190*
Fort Monroe National Monument. *397–398*
Fort Necessity National Battlefield *331–332*
Fort Point National Historic Site. *65–66*
Fort Pulaski National Monument *138–139*
Fort Raleigh National Historic Site *302–303*
Fort Scott National Historic Site *166–167*
Fort Smith National Historic Site *52–53*
Fort Stanwix National Monument. *282–283*
Fort Sumter National Monument *346*
Fort Union National Monument *270–271*
Fort Union Trading Post National Historic Site *307*
Fort Vancouver National Historic Site. *410–411*
Fort Washington Park. *190–191*
Fossil Butte National Monument *434*
Franklin Delano Roosevelt Memorial *107–108*
Frederick Douglass National Historic Site *108*
Frederick Law Olmsted National Historic Site. *202*
Fredericksburg & Spotsylvania County Battlefields
Memorial National Military Park. *398–399*
Friendship Hill National Historic Site. *332*

Gates of the Arctic National Park & Preserve. *14–15*
Gateway National Recreation Area *283–284*
Gauley River National Recreation Area *424–425*
General Grant National Memorial. *285*
George Rogers Clark National Historical Park *158*
George Washington Birthplace National Monument *399–400*
George Washington Carver National Monument *232–233*
George Washington Memorial Parkway *400–401*
Gettysburg National Military Park. *333–334*
Gila Cliff Dwellings National Monument *271–272*
Glacier Bay National Park & Preserve. *15–16*
Glacier National Park *241–243*
Glen Canyon National Recreation Area *32–33*
Gloria Dei (Old Swedes') Church National Historic Site. *462*
Golden Gate National Recreation Area. *66–67*
Golden Spike National Historic Site *384–385*
Governors Island National Monument *285–286*
Grand Canyon National Park. *33–36*
Grand Portage National Monument *219–220*
Grand Teton National Park *435–436*

Grant-Kohrs Ranch National Historic Site *243–244*
Great Basin National Park *253–254*
Great Egg Harbor National
Scenic & Recreational River *258–259, 481*
Great Sand Dunes National Park & Preserve *96–97*
Great Smoky Mountains National Park *359–360*
Green Springs National Historic Landmark District *462*
Greenbelt Park *191–192*
Guadalupe Mountains National Park *371–372*
Guilford Courthouse National Military Park *303–304*
Gulf Islands National Seashore *129–130*

Hagerman Fossil Beds National Monument *153–154*
Haleakala National Park *143–144*
Hamilton Grange National Memorial *286–287*
Hampton National Historic Site *192*
Harpers Ferry National Historical Park *425–426*
Harry S. Truman National Historic Site *233–234*
Hawaii Volcanoes National Park *144–145*
Herbert Hoover National Historic Site *163–164*
Historic Camden *463*
Hohokam Pima National Monument *36*
Home of Franklin D. Roosevelt National Historic Site *287–288*
Homestead National Monument of America *247–248*
Hopewell Culture National Historical Park *314*
Hopewell Furnace National Historic Site *334*
Horseshoe Bend National Military Park *3–4*
Hot Springs National Park *53–54*
Hovenweep National Monument *97–98*
Hubbell Trading Post National Historic Site *36–37*
Hudson River Valley National Heritage Area *469–470*

Ice Age National Scenic Trail *463, 475*
Ice Age National Scientific Reserve *463*
Iditarod National Historic Trail *475*
Illinois & Michigan Canal National Heritage Corridor *463*
Independence National Historical Park *335*
Indiana Dunes National Lakeshore *159–160*
International Peace Garden *463*
Inupiat Heritage Center *464*
Isle Royale National Park *211–212*

James A. Garfield National Historic Site *314–315*
Jamestown National Historic Site *464*
Jean Lafitte National Historical Park & Preserve *176–177*
Jefferson National Expansion Memorial *234–235*
Jewel Cave National Monument *351–352*
Jimmy Carter National Historic Site *139–140*
John D. Rockefeller Jr. Memorial Parkway *437*
John Day Fossil Beds National Monument *323–324*

John Fitzgerald Kennedy National Historic Site. *202–203*
John H. Chafee Blackstone River Valley
National Heritage Corridor *464*
John Muir National Historic Site. *67–68*
John Wild River *482*
Johnstown Flood National Memorial. *335–336*
Joshua Tree National Park *68–69*
Juan Bautista de Anza National Historic Trail. *476*

Kalaupapa National Historical Park. *145–146*
Kaloko-Honokohau National Historical Park *146–147*
Katmai National Park & Preserve *16–17*
Kenai Fjords National Park *17–18*
Kennesaw Mountain National Battlefield Park. *140*
Kern River. *482*
Keweenaw National Historical Park *212–214*
Kings Canyon National Park *83–85*
Kings Mountain National Military Park. *347*
Kings River *482*
Klondike Gold Rush National Historical Park *18–20*
Knife River Indian Villages National Historic Site *308*
Kobuk Valley National Park. *20–21*
Kobuk Wild River. *482*
Korean War Veterans Memorial. *109*

Lackawanna Valley National Heritage Area *470*
Lake Chelan National Recreation Area. *411–412*
Lake Clark National Park & Preserve *21–22*
Lake Mead National Recreation Area. *254–255*
Lake Meredith National Recreation Area. *372–373*
Lake Roosevelt National Recreation Area. *412–413*
Lamprey Wild & Scenic River *483*
Lassen Volcanic National Park. *70–71*
Lava Beds National Monument. *71–72*
Lewis and Clark National Historic Trail *476*
Lewis and Clark National Historical Park *322–223*
Lincoln Boyhood National Memorial *160–161*
Lincoln Home National Historic Site *157*
Lincoln Memorial. *109–110*
Little Bighorn Battlefield National Monument. *244–245*
Little River Canyon National Preserve *4–5*
Little Rock Central High School National Historic Site. *55*
Longfellow House-Washington's Headquarters
National Historic Site. *203–204*
Lowell National Historical Park. *204–205*
Lower Delaware Wild & Scenic River. *483*
Lower East Side Tenement National Historic District. *464–465*
Lyndon B. Johnson National Historical Park. *373–375*
Lyndon Baines Johnson Memorial Grove on the Potomac. *110*

Maggie L. Walker National Historic Site. *401–402*

Mammoth Cave National Park. *173–174*

Manassas National Battlefield Park *402–403*

Manzanar National Historic Site *72–73*

Marsh-Billings-Rockefeller National Historical Park *390–391*

Martin Luther King, Jr. Memorial *111*

Martin Luther King Jr. National Historic Site. *141*

Martin Van Buren National Historic Site *288–289*

Mary McLeod Bethune Council House
National Historic Site. *111–112*

Maurice National Scenic & Recreational River *483*

McLoughlin House National Historic Site *465*

Memorial Parks. *113*

Merced River *483*

Mesa Verde National Park *98–99*

Middle Delaware National Scenic River *336–337*

Middle Delaware River *484*

Minidoka National Historic Site *154–155*

Minute Man National Historical Park *205–206*

Minuteman Missile National Historic Site *352–353*

Mississippi National River & Recreation Area *220–221*

Missouri National Recreational River *248–249, 484*

Mojave National Preserve *73–75*

Monocacy National Battlefield. *192–193*

Montezuma Castle National Monument *37–38*

Moores Creek National Battlefield *304–305*

Mormon Pioneer National Historic Trail. *476*

Morristown National Historical Park. *259*

Motor Cities National Heritage Area. *470*

Mount Rainier National Park. *413–414*

Mount Rushmore National Memorial *353–354*

Muir Woods National Monument *75*

Mulchatna Wild River *484*

Natchez National Historical Park. *226–227*

Natchez Trace National Scenic Trail *227–228, 476*

Natchez Trace Parkway *228–229*

National Coal Heritage Area *471*

National Mall and Memorial Parks *112–113*

National Park of American Samoa. *441–442*

Natural Bridges National Monument *385–386*

Navajo National Monument. *38–39*

New Bedford Whaling National Historical Park. *206–207*

New Jersey Coastal Heritage Trail. *465*

New Orleans Jazz National Historical Park. *177–178*

New River Gorge National River. *426–428*

Nez Perce National Historic Trail *476–477*

Nez Perce National Historical Park. *155–156*

Nicodemus National Historic Site *168*

Ninety Six National Historic Site 348–349
Niobrara National Scenic River 249–250, 484
Noatak National Preserve 22–23
Noatak Wild River 484
North Cascades National Park 415–416
North Country National Scenic Trail 477
North Fork of the Koyukuk Wild River 485
Obed Wild & Scenic River 360–361, 485
Ocmulgee National Monument 141–142
Ohio & Erie Canal National Heritage Corridor 471
Oklahoma City National Memorial & Museum 465
Olympic National Park 416–418
Oregon Caves National Monument 324–325
Oregon National Historic Trail 477
Organ Pipe Cactus National Monument 39–40
Overmountain Victory National Historic Trail 477
Ozark National Scenic Riverways 235–236

Pacific Crest National Scenic Trail 477–478
Padre Island National Seashore 375–376
Paterson Great Falls National Historical Park 260
Pea Ridge National Military Park 57–57
Pecos National Historical Park 272–273
Pennsylvania Avenue National Historic Site 114–115
Perry's Victory & International Peace Memorial 315–316
Petersburg National Battlefield 403–404
Petrified Forest National Park 40–41
Petroglyph National Monument 273–274
Pictured Rocks National Lakeshore 214–215
Pinelands National Reserve 466
Pinnacles National Monument 76–77
Pipe Spring National Monument 41–42
Pipestone National Monument 222
Piscataway Park 193–194
Point Reyes National Seashore 77–78
Pony Express National Historic Trail 478
Port Chicago Naval Magazine Memorial 78–79
Potomac Heritage National Scenic Trail 114–115, 478
Poverty Point National Monument/State Historic Site 178–179
President William Jefferson Clinton Birthplace
National Historic Site 57–58
Prince William Forest Park 404–405
Pu'uhonua o Honaunau National Historical Park 147–148
Pu'ukohola Heiau National Historic Site 148–149

Quinebaug & Shetucket Rivers Valley
National Heritage Corridor 466

Rainbow Bridge National Monument 386–387
Red Hill Patrick Henry National Memorial 466

Redwood National and State Parks *79–80*
Richmond National Battlefield Park *405*
Rio Grande Wild & Scenic River. *377, 485*
River Raisin National Battlefield Park. *216–217*
Rivers of Steel National Heritage Area *471*
Rock Creek Park. *115–116*
Rocky Mountain National Park *99–101*
Roger Williams National Memorial *342*
Roosevelt Campobello International Park. *466–467*
Rosie the Riveter/World War II Home Front
National Historical Park. *80–81*
Ross Lake National Recreation Area. *418–419*
Russell Cave National Monument *5–6*

Sagamore Hill National Historical Site *289–290*
Saguaro National Park *42–43*
St. Croix Island International Historic Site *181–182*
Saint Croix National Scenic Riverway *430–431, 485*
Saint-Gaudens National Historic Site *256–257*
Saint Paul's Church National Historic Site *290–291*
Salem Maritime National Historic Site *208*
Salinas Pueblo Missions National Monument. *274–275*
Salmon Wild River *485*
Salt River Bay National Historical Park & Ecological Preserve *449*
San Antonio Missions National Historical Park. *377–378*
San Francisco Maritime National Historical Park. *81–82*
San Juan Island National Historical Park *419–420*
San Juan National Historic Site *445–446*
Sand Creek Massacre National Historic Site. *101–102*
Santa Fe National Historic Trail *478*
Santa Monica Mountains National Recreation Area. *82–83*
Saratoga National Historical Park *291–292*
Saugus Iron Works National Historic Site. *208–209*
Schuylkill River Valley National Heritage Area. *472*
Scotts Bluff National Monument. *251–252*
Selma to Montgomery National Historic Trail *478*
Sequoia & Kings Canyon National Parks. *83–85*
Sewall-Belmont House National Historic Site *467*
Shenandoah National Park. *406–407*
Shenandoah Valley Battlefields National Historic District. *472*
Shiloh National Military Park. *361–362*
Sitka National Historical Park *23–24*
Sleeping Bear Dunes National Lakeshore. *217–218*
South Carolina Heritage Corridor *472*
Southwestern Pennsylvania Industrial Heritage Route *472–473*
Springfield Armory National Historic Site *209–210*
Statue of Liberty National Monument *292–293*
Steamtown National Historic Site *337*
Stones River National Battlefield. *362–363*

Sudbury, Assabet & Concord Rivers *485–486*
Sunset Crater Volcano National Monument *44–45*

Tallgrass Prairie National Preserve *169–170*
Tennessee Civil War Heritage Area *473*
Thaddeus Kosciuszko National Memorial *338*
Theodore Roosevelt Birthplace National Historic Site *293–294*
Theodore Roosevelt Inaugural National Historic Site *294–295*
Theodore Roosevelt Island *116*
Theodore Roosevelt National Park *309–310*
Thomas Cole National Historic Site *467*
Thomas Edison National Historical Park *260–261*
Thomas Jefferson Memorial *117*
Thomas Stone National Historic Site *194–195*
Timpanogos Cave National Monument *387–388*
Timucuan Ecological & Historic Preserve *131–132*
Tinayguk Wild River *486*
Tlikakila Wild River *486*
Tonto National Monument *45–46*
Touro Synagogue National Historic Site *467*
Trail of Tears National Historic Trail *479*
Tumacácori National Historical Park *46–47*
Tuolomne River *486*
Tupelo National Battlefield *229–230*
Tuskegee Airmen National Historic Site *6*
Tuskegee Institute National Historic Site *7*
Tuzigoot National Monument *47*

Ulysses S. Grant National Historic Site *236–237*
Upper Delaware Scenic & Recreational River *338–339, 486–487*

Valley Forge National Historical Park *339–341*
Vanderbilt Mansion National Historic Site *295*
Vicksburg National Military Park *230–231*
Vietnam Veterans Memorial *117–118*
Virgin Islands Coral Reef National Monument *450*
Virgin Islands National Park *450–451*
Voyageurs National Park *223–224*

Walnut Canyon National Monument *48*
War in the Pacific National Historical Park *443–444*
Washington Monument *118*
Washita Battlefield National Historic Site *319–320*
Weir Farm National Historic Site *103–104*
Wheeling National Heritage Area *473*
Whiskeytown-Shasta-Trinity National Recreation Area *85–86*
White Clay Creek *487*
White House *118–119*
White Sands National Monument *275–276*
Whitman Mission National Historic Site *420–421*

William Howard Taft National Historic Site *316–317*

Wilson's Creek National Battlefield *237–238*

Wind Cave National Park *354–355*

Wolf Trap National Park for the Performing Arts *407–408*

Women's Rights National Historical Park *295–296*

World War II Home Front National Historical Park *81–82*

World War II Valor in the Pacific National Monument *149–150*

Wrangell-St. Elias National Park & Preserve *24–25*

Wright Brothers National Memorial *305–306*

Wupatki National Monument *49*

Yellowstone National Park *437–439*

Yosemite National Park *86–88*

Yucca House National Monument *102*

Yuma Crossing National Heritage Area *473*

Yukon-Charley Rivers National Preserve *25–26*

Zion National Park *388–389*

Photo Credits

ML

1-13